# GOING NOWHERE

# GOING NOWHERE

## A MEMOIR

### JOAN RUDDOCK

Biteback Publishing

First published in Great Britain in 2016 by
Biteback Publishing Ltd
Westminster Tower
3 Albert Embankment
London SE1 7SP
Copyright © Joan Ruddock 2016

ISBN 978-1-84954-997-4

10 9 8 7 6 5 4 3 2 1

A CIP catalogue record for this book is available from the British Library.

Set in Agmena Pro and Didot by Adrian McLaughlin

Printed and bound in Great Britain by
CPI Group (UK) Ltd, Croydon CR0 4YY

MIX
Paper from
responsible sources
FSC® C020471

*For my husband Frank and my mother Eileen,*
*and in memory of my late husband Keith and my father Ken.*

# CONTENTS

# PROLOGUE

*'Joan Ruddock, widely thought to have been on the fast-track to high office, is going nowhere'*

— *The Independent*, 10 May 1997

I froze. This was a briefing from Tony's office – just one of the many that would follow as colleagues were dispatched via the media. My fate was sealed, my parliamentary career over. After winning my third general election in Lewisham Deptford, I'd gone to the Southbank, catching the end of the national party's celebrations. A quick drink and a bear hug from a bleary-eyed Robin Cook and then outside for Tony's arrival. As they got onto the platform, Cherie tugged at Tony's sleeve – 'There's Joan' – and we all waved to each other. The sun rose in the glorious dawn sky behind us. A sense of euphoria was everywhere.

It had been a long journey.

Chapter One

# EARLY YEARS

I grew up in Pontypool in the eastern valley of Monmouthshire. A place uncertain of its identity as mines closed, factories rose on green-field sites and the new town of Cwmbran began to draw people and commerce further down the valley.

My father Ken's formative years were spent in Pontypool, while my mother grew up in the country near the village of Goytre. My father was born in 1914, the youngest of three brothers, and was soon deprived of a father, who went to fight in the Great War. Dad grew up to be bright and ambitious, winning a scholarship to the local 'West Mon' boys' grammar. He loved school, was good at maths and French and worked hard for his matriculation, the school exam system of the day.

But life at home was difficult. His father had been badly gassed in the trenches and came home disabled. He was given a grant to retrain as a cobbler making wooden clogs and he opened a small shop in Pontypool. After the initial struggle he appeared to be making a success of his new trade, but money was tight and the pain from his injuries relentless. The family struggled to find the shilling they needed to pay the doctor. When he came, the doctor prescribed a diet of two soft-boiled eggs a day, oblivious to the fact that the family could never afford to buy them.

One day my grandfather went away and never came back. Throughout his life my father maintained that he had died of war wounds; the truth was very different. He had taken his own life. He died leaving my grandmother five months pregnant. My father never knew that my mother told us the family secret and such was the stigma attached to suicide that I never raised it with him.

Everything changed for my father. His oldest brother had left home, having falsified his age and joined the army at fourteen. His middle brother, Phil, was working in the cobbler's shop but was addicted to gambling: family folklore has it he won and lost £1,000 in a single day. The business failed and Phil left for London. Dad had no choice. He went to work – a fifteen-year-old boy with a family to support. The mass unemployment of the 1930s brought further misery to the valley towns and a trek to the soup kitchens for food.

The boy grew to manhood working outdoors in all weathers, developing muscles of iron and dragging himself to evening classes to improve his prospects. He became a fitter with the local gas and water company. His work took him into the hovels of the sprawling slums in Trosnant and occasionally to the few grand houses of the better off. He often recalled how he had once gone to a smart house in Abersychan and made the mistake of knocking at the front door. Roy Jenkins's mother told him in no uncertain terms that workmen should call at the back!

Life improved for my father when he met my mother, Eileen.

My mother, too, had suffered a cruel twist of fate in her early years. Her parents and grandparents lived in the country, where her father started work at the age of twelve, employed as a gamekeeper's assistant at the local 'big house', Goytre Hall. He moved on to work as a gardener at another great house belonging to the Hanbury-Tenisons and lived in a bothy in the yard. There he developed a lifelong passion for growing plants and exotic flowers. Like many of his generation, he witnessed the extravagance of the rich. The family's extensive estates provided the opportunity for summer picnics. The squire would ride on horseback, his wife and children in a carriage, while my grandfather and other servants carried the great wicker baskets full of china, glass and silver up the mountainside. Though he was never envious and always careful with the family finances, my grandfather developed an eye for fine things and in later years loved to go to auctions and house sales. I still treasure a large mirror in an oak frame that he purchased at one such sale.

Inevitably the time came to volunteer for the army and Granddad went to Newport for his medical. His future wife, my grandmother, had extracted a promise: she would stand by the local railway line and he would wave as the train passed on its way to Hereford's recruitment centre. She waited but no wave came – my grandfather had failed the medical. Rheumatic fever in childhood had left him with a weak heart, so he returned to a life of manual labour and lived to be eighty.

They began married life in a tiny rented house, from which my grandfather ran a milk round, buying the milk from a local farmer. A few years and one daughter, Eileen (my mother), later he realised his ambition to own land. The farmer who supplied the milk gave him a loan sufficient to buy a cottage with several fields. Granddad ploughed and planted everything himself. He then added an orchard of plums, cherries, apples and pears. When two more daughters, Betty and Audrey, were born, he set about building an extension to the cottage.

My grandmother's life was equally hard and she was ever conscious of her husband's disappointment that they had no sons. They never made much money but they had control over their own lives, secure employment and always ate well when others went hungry.

When my gran's grandfather died, his unmarried daughter Elizabeth (Bess) was left living alone in a house in Goytre. My mother's great-aunt Bess was a formidable woman. She had been jilted at the altar and had no time for men. Instead, she made a career for herself in the refreshment rooms at Cardiff railway station. Making this daily journey was testament to her intrepid spirit. Few local people ever travelled as far as Cardiff.

This strongly independent woman was to be a major influence on my mother's life. At the age of four, Eileen was sent to live with Aunt Bess. As she grew up my mother acquired many of the tastes and passions of her aunt and probably also a little of her discontent. My mother remembers being terrified of going to bed in a four-poster with curtains, which she could reach only from a stool and in which she was plunged into darkness when the candle was blown out. Reading was my mother's main leisure pursuit. She devoured every one of the classics she found in the bookcase and secretly some of the ones on the top shelf! School itself was basic. The boys and girls were taught in three classes in a single room with a big coke stove in the middle. Mum remembers that a cup of hot cocoa could be bought for a ½d but that she never had the money to take to school.

Aunt Bess kept chickens and supplied local villagers who called at the door to make their purchases. One Friday, Aunt Bess, already a sick woman, called from her bedroom window to a couple who regularly bought from her and asked them to come in as she wanted to see them. It was pouring with rain so they excused themselves, hurrying on, saying they would come another day.

They were too late. Aunt Bess suffered a fatal stroke and her will was never witnessed.

The will bequeathed everything to my mother, but other relatives refused to honour it. My mother's life changed instantly. She had lost her favourite aunt, the life she had come to accept and the inheritance she might have had. It was clear she wouldn't be allowed to stay at school much longer. Back home with her parents, Eileen was now part of the labour force, essential to keeping the family business viable as the Depression of the 1930s began to take its toll.

Eileen's headmaster went to speak to her father and begged him to keep her in school so she could go on to the grammar. It was a lost cause. There was no money for a uniform or the bus fares that would be needed, and there was plenty of work to be done at home. My mother was heartbroken and even to this day she can remember the names of the three girls who passed the exam and went to grammar school.

Soon Eileen was getting up at 5 a.m. to pick fruit and vegetables for the market in Pontypool, where her mother had a stall. Winters were the worst, picking frost-covered sprouts without gloves and bunching up daffodils. After picking, it was on to the milk round with her father. On Saturdays she stayed home to clean the house and do the washing for the family of five. Her reward was 2s 6d a week – enough for the small pleasures of a bus ride into Pontypool and a visit to the cinema.

My grandfather expected a man's work from his daughters, but he was also a man who believed in getting some pleasure from life. He acquired one of the earliest cars in the valley, a 'sit up and beg' with canvas top and a brake outside the cab. My mother loved to ride in the car and the later acquisition of a van enabled the whole family to go for picnics in the Wye Valley in summer. At the earliest opportunity Eileen learned to drive and passed her test aged seventeen at the first attempt, becoming the first woman in the area to gain a licence.

Granddad's other passion was the village show. He would enter every conceivable competition along with all the women of the family, who were expert at baking and flower-arranging. The family's successes were recorded on the silver cups regularly displayed on top of the piano.

My parents met as war clouds were gathering over Europe. There was a brief period of the normal courting rituals of dances and cinema visits, culminating in an engagement. One exceptional weekend they went with another engaged couple to Jersey and took a day trip to St Malo on the French coast, where my father proudly demonstrated his schoolboy French.

They married in 1941, spending a brief honeymoon at Machen watching incendiary bombs falling all around them as the Germans attempted to hit Newport Docks. They rented a small house in Griffithstown and counted themselves lucky that my father was in a reserved occupation. Nonetheless, the war years were hard. Gas fitters sometimes received near-fatal doses of poisonous coal gas as they worked, the hours were long and fire watching at night was compulsory for those in reserved occupations. My mother was also eligible for the call-up. Most of the local women were sent to the munitions factory, but Mum's skills won her a job as a van driver, delivering bread until she became pregnant in 1943. I was born on 28 December.

The war over, my parents decided to embark on a new life. Dad envied my grandfather's independence and resolved to try to emulate it. Granddad loaned them the money to buy a cottage with grounds on the banks of the Monmouthshire Canal. My father continued his day job and they worked all hours to plant crops and a small orchard. It was a time of great promise and one Christmas Eve we went to my grandparents' home and stayed the night. My earliest memory is of that Christmas morning when I was given a huge spinning top with a plunger mechanism, decorated with bands of bright colours. It was the first mechanical toy I had ever seen and it was mesmerising. All the food for Christmas lunch was home-grown, reared or picked and cooked in the oven attached to the coal fire, which was kept roaring from early morning to provide heat. We always ate around the big circular wooden table that nearly filled the room. As the sky darkened, the large oil lamp that hung over the table was lit and the familiar smell of burning oil filled the room. It was time for my grandmother to go to the piano and play Christmas carols. It was a magical day for a toddler and probably one of well-being for the adults, all of whom had cause to be grateful that they had come through the war largely unscathed.

My sister Susan was born in April 1946, a baby as fair and blue-eyed as I was dark. My parents continued to build up their enterprise, adding a pig to the chickens they already reared. But, at the end of January 1947, tragedy struck. It started to snow and continued to do so until the end of March – one of the worst winters ever recorded. The weight of the snow crushed all the glass cloches nurturing precious lettuce plants and damaged the greenhouse. In the pig cot, the sow had given birth to a litter of piglets, all of them suffocated by the snow. The chickens were saved only when my mother dug a trench from the house to feed them. My father, meanwhile, was working day and night dealing with gas and water emergencies caused by the bad weather.

The final catastrophe was revealed in the thaw. All the fruit trees, their main stems damaged by rabbits, were dead. My parents' dream was at an end. All their money was gone and they had to sell up to repay their loan.

It was a time of deep despair. Dad's mother was diagnosed with terminal cancer and my mother had a miscarriage. My father would never forget his mother's agonising death. Although he became a Tory later on, he was a life-long supporter of the NHS.

My parents sold up and repaid their debt to my grandfather. They moved into a 1930s council house at 6 College Road in Penygarn, which they were to share with Joy, my father's orphaned nineteen-year-old sister. Auntie Joy found solace in caring for Susan, my mother by this time being at breaking point. For the rest of his life my father yearned to be self-employed and to own his own home. Towards the end of his life, he had saved enough to buy a bungalow, but he was forever a 'wage slave'.

In 1949, Dad applied to the newly opened British Nylon Spinners factory. The job had good prospects and benefits – a social club, sports teams and family outings. But behind the factory doors men were working without any of the protection of today's health and safety laws. Temperatures on the spinning floors reached over 100°F and were accompanied by incessant loud noise and strong chemical odours. The operatives were organised into shifts to ensure continuous running – three different patterns in succession, including one of nights, in seven-day rotations. My father, always a tense man, could never sleep properly and we grew up having to creep around the house during the weeks of night shifts. Frequently irritable, Dad escaped to find peace at his allotments, from which he supplied us all his life with vegetables, fruit and flowers.

Joy was now working as a nursery nurse, finding her way in the world and meeting men. Rows were frequent between the adults, not helped by the fact that Joy's work brought her into contact with infectious diseases that were not then under control. My poor mother had her hands full as one after another of us contracted measles, mumps, chicken pox and finally jaundice. The only upside for us children was having a fire lit in the small grate in our otherwise freezing bedroom and hearing the gas lights 'popping' on the wall. My mother never ceased to minister to us, even finding ways of baking cakes without fat, which was banned for jaundiced patients. Auntie Joy eventually left home and life became easier for my parents, but I realise now that Susan also lost her surrogate mother. The family's finances improved. We went on day trips to Barry Island with our cousins, John and Robert Miles, visited Mum's sister Audrey in Port Talbot and once my father's middle brother Phil (now settled down with a no-nonsense wife) in Sussex.

My parents were natural entrepreneurs. My father was not deterred by the tenancy rules. The house was spacious – three double bedrooms, a living room, sitting room and kitchen. Dad rewired the electricity downstairs and extended it to the bedrooms. He also made wooden furniture and an amazing doll's house and rocking horse for us children. My mother made all of our clothes and beautiful lampshades, soft furnishings and rugs. Against the front wall my father planted a peach tree and every summer we enjoyed the delicious fruits. At the back Susan and I had our own small gardens, ensuring that both of us developed a lifelong interest in gardening. We ate well but my parents could never afford luxuries. Across the road lived two children with whom we were friends. Their mothers were both cleaners but nonetheless they were the College Road 'snobs'. The husbands belonged to the local golf club and I distinctly remember one occasion when both wives came to show my mother the long evening gowns they had made. To this day I can remember them, one in green, white and black checked taffeta and the other in petrol blue. I also remember the acute disappointment I felt on behalf of my mother, who I knew had no such dresses.

Life at College Road was not without its dramas. When Dad became a foreman and later a supervisor he had crossed a line. Our neighbour, Aldo Davis, at the end of the road was in the union. During one particularly difficult strike, the neighbours stopped speaking to my parents, upsetting my mother. I was determined to find out what was going on so I took myself to the factory gates and questioned the men on the picket line! I don't think I became much the wiser and they no doubt thought I was exceedingly strange. On another occasion a neighbour and factory employee was travelling back to Pontypool in the executive jet, having been required to go to one of the other factory sites, when the plane crashed, killing all the occupants. He was probably the only person in the street who had ever flown. No one could believe what had happened.

My father began to concern himself with our education. Susan and I were attending the Penygarn primary school, which was pleasant and easy-going, but not likely to get anyone into a grammar school. We were swiftly transferred to a church school in Pontypool, forcing us to walk a mile each way up and down the steep hills of the valley.

School was an old Victorian building staffed by an eccentric group of people. In my first class, miscreants had to bend over to be spanked by our elderly female teacher with a leather slipper. In my final class, Mr Hughes regularly threw china ink pots or wooden board rubbers (lessons were taught on blackboards with chalk) at offending pupils. Classrooms were freezing in winter, heated by a single coal-burning stove on which we roasted chestnuts and tried to thaw the frozen milk in the quarter-pint glass bottles provided by the new welfare state. Playtimes were hard, with both girls and boys taking part in regular fights. I guess we never told our parents of the violence, or perhaps it was just considered the norm for the times.

There was great excitement in our house in early May 1953. My parents were going to buy a television. No one else had one on our street, but, as for so many others at the time, it was a prerequisite for our seeing the Queen's coronation. It was a big brown cabinet with a tiny, tiny screen. Resourceful as ever, my father bought a big magnifier and mounted it on a stand in front of the box. Neighbours came in and everyone was glued to the set. We children had to keep very quiet.

I was a good student but far too cautious. The 11 + exam was strictly timed. My father was advised that while I would certainly get things right, I'd take too long doing so. The remedy was test papers, which my father sent away for and put into immediate practice. I was forced to improve my speed in arithmetic and to practise the types of puzzles set for the intelligence papers.

Thus began a lifetime of fearing failure. Many nights I cried myself to sleep, certain that I was going to fail. I was ten years old. On the day of the results I went to school in a state of terror. Mr Hughes announced that the names of successful students would be called in alphabetical order and if called the person should stand on his or her seat. My surname was Anthony and I was trembling. My name was called, the first of five – two girls and three boys. That moment stayed with me for years and made me a passionate supporter of comprehensive education. I knew then that that day would determine my life chances. Thrilled as I was by my own success, I nonetheless remember looking around and seeing virtually the whole class still seated and wondering what would happen to them.

With confirmation that I'd been accepted at the Pontypool Grammar School for Girls came a long list of uniform requirements. There was only one supplier, Fowler's – the expensive clothes store in town. When some friends of my parents visited I was required to don the bottle-green gymslip, white blouse, blazer and school tie. Carrying the heavy leather, metal-buckled school satchel, I then mounted a stool and turned around slowly. I was on my way to a better life.

I loved my school. It was run entirely by women and was done so superbly, at least for those of us destined to do well academically. By some process, lost to me now, I became form captain in my first year, later a prefect and finally Head Girl. I was lucky to be an all-rounder, holding my own across the curriculum, in athletics and games, music and art. I had no outstanding talents but I was always focused, always keen to prove myself and confront the fear of failure. My parents had never thought beyond grammar school, but the parents of my best friends Roselle Hewlett and Wendy Jenkins were all teachers. Their daughters were expected to go to university and soon I began to think about it for myself. Then I met Keith.

On summer weekends I would often meet Wendy to play tennis in Pontypool Park. On one such occasion, we realised we were attracting the attention of the two young men on the court opposite. We knew Derek, a boy with a bad reputation, but not the other one. We accepted an invitation to coffee at Fulgoni's and were introduced. Keith was his cousin, home from his first year at London University. He walked me home. We talked about my upcoming exams and his physics course at Imperial. He was the ideal boyfriend – home in the holidays and serious about study. I was fourteen. We fell passionately in love and spent the next thirty years together.

When Keith came home, cinema was the main source of entertainment and our greatest adventure a meal in the Chinese restaurant that opened in Newport. It was the first restaurant in which I had ever eaten and chicken with pineapple and cashew nuts became my regular order.

Inevitably, passion grew. One warm summer day a year after we met we went for a walk. Keith steered us to a sun-dappled clearing in the wood and we made love for the first time. It was a moment of utter rapture. I wasn't yet sixteen. It never occurred to me that it was against the law or that it meant anything less than a lifetime's commitment.

At school we chose our subject options early on, which provided relief for me from some of the immensely boring arts subjects. History was the worst. We never got beyond the Tudors, leaving me with a deficiency for life. Once the teacher herself was so bored she fell asleep in her own lesson. Scripture, however, was more fun. Miss Davis was a breath of fresh air. She had a large bust and a nipped-in waist, wore tight dresses and very high heels, but best of all she had scientific explanations for all the miracles. Looking back, I wonder if she wasn't an atheist! I opted for science subjects plus Latin and French alongside the compulsory English literature, English grammar and maths. My friends and I all passed our O-levels with flying colours and went on to the segregated science and arts sixth forms.

Pontypool Girls' Grammar was one of the best. Miss Francis, our headmistress, was a formidable woman. She had a regal bearing, a beaked nose and grey hair swept up into a firm French pleat. She ran a civics class for both first years and sixth-formers. First years were set the task of writing and performing a medieval mystery play. It was a great leveller – a challenge and not exactly fun. She also quizzed us on which newspapers we had at home. I remember feeling there was something not quite right when I declared the *Daily Express*. Miss Francis read the *Manchester Guardian*, of which I had never heard.

At one end of the old building were the large bay windows of Miss Francis's study, looking out onto the lawn tennis court. A prolific and very old lilac wisteria grew over the windows, leaving me with an abiding memory of scented summer air while we played tennis after school. Strange how these memories should stick when the south Wales climate more usually delivered grey drizzle. Every day we walked ('no running, girls!') through long corridors lined with prints of the world's most famous art and every morning we heard classical music as we filed into assembly. As a result, I became familiar with most of the great classical works of music, but could never name a single one. When everyone was seated, Miss Francis would enter and we would scramble to our feet. She would then address us. On one memorable occasion, when I and several others were sporting beehive hairstyles (of the Amy Winehouse variety), Miss Francis gave us a lecture on the relationship between extravagant hair and the fall of the Roman Empire.

We were surrounded by culture. Library books supplemented coursework, we sang in choirs and availed ourselves of free instruments on which to take free music lessons. I chose the cello. Although I played in the school orchestra I never applied myself as well as I might have done and regret keeping up with neither the cello nor indeed the piano, which I'd played in earlier years. My sister Susan, who had followed me into the school, had much greater success, playing the double bass in both the Monmouthshire Youth Orchestra and the Welsh National Youth Orchestra. My friend Roselle also had real musical talent and became a wonderful cellist. She was the eldest of six children, all of whom dazzled in their different ways despite being born female. They were six for want of a son. There was also a drama and a debating society. Desna O'Sullivan was the star of the latter but it was not for me. I did want to take part in the drama classes, however, despite the fear of forgetting my lines. My one claim to fame was playing Prospero in *The Tempest*, my heavy disguise leading my father to ask my mother, halfway through a public performance, 'Where's Joan?'

Sixth form was a joy. Miss Powell was an inspiring teacher who treated us as adults and taught both botany and zoology. It was a time of great enquiry and interest. In 1961, Yuri Gagarin became the first man in space; in 1962, Crick and Watson were awarded the Nobel Prize for cracking the genetic code; and in 1969 Neil Armstrong would become the first man to set foot on the moon.

Botany was my favourite and already my chosen subject for university. Most universities had dropped Latin as an entry requirement, but I knew Imperial College valued German so I got permission to join a third-form class once a week and studied in my lunch hours. Having no particular skills in languages, I realised this was a tall order. I approached it scientifically: I would learn as many of the words in the glossary as possible. In the event, I got my O-level but spoke precious little German.

One of the high points of this time was my increasing interest in current affairs and a consequent invitation to a conference organised by the Council for Education in World Citizenship (CEWC).* Called 'Black and White', it focused on race relations, which was always an interest of mine. One of the lectures I attended was given by the woman General Secretary of the Fabian Society. She was none other than Shirley Williams,† who went on to have an illustrious career in politics. I was totally inspired. I had never heard a socialist and feminist speak. I resolved there and then to join the Labour Party.

Miss Francis thought I might enter for Oxford but I was adamant: Imperial College was my choice. While I had been told by Keith that it was second only to Cambridge for science, Miss Francis dismissed it as a 'technical college'. My greatest fear was that I wouldn't get in, so Keith found out only on the day of my interview that I had applied. Imperial offered me a place to do botany with two years of chemistry, conditional on an A and two Bs at A-level.

---

* The CEWC was established in 1939 to promote the importance of political and civic engagement across national boundaries. It merged with the Citizenship Foundation in 2008.
† Now Baroness Williams of Crosby (Lib Dem).

The exams went well but, just like the 11+, waiting for the results was agony. They would appear first in the local newspaper. I remember staying in bed on the appointed day until my mother brought it to me. I was awarded a state scholarship, which meant I didn't have to apply to the local authority for the free grant then available to cover both tuition and accommodation. I duly received a letter of congratulation from the local director of education: 'I have been informed by the Ministry of Education that you have been successful in winning a state scholarship...'

It was addressed to *Mr* J. M. Anthony.

waiting for the results...
...paper, I remember...
...ight it to me. I was awarde...
...apply to the local authori...
...uation and accommodation...
...local director of education...
...cation that you have be...

## Chapter Two

# UNIVERSITY

T he summer passed in a haze of sunshine and happiness. My parents' dearest wishes for their daughters' education were fulfilled. Susan got her O-levels and opted for the arts sixth form. Keith and I got engaged and planned to marry the following year. I was only eighteen but no one I knew had ever lived with someone outside marriage and I didn't want to spend my university years in a hostel.

At home, money was still tight. My mother worked on Saturdays at a cake stall in the market and continued to make most of the family's clothes. We prepared a university wardrobe of sensible skirts and blouses, matched with V-necked sweaters (thankfully bought as my mother was no knitter). It was little more than a school uniform but the Swinging Sixties were hardly underway and certainly invisible in south Wales.

I was already familiar with Imperial, having been allowed to visit Keith (despite parental trepidation). On the first occasion he met me at Paddington and took me straight to Covent Garden to queue up for that night's opera. I was without a coat and wearing an outfit specially purchased for the trip. After a while, a light drizzle began to fall, frizzing my hair and matting my lime-green mohair sweater. Our tickets were duly purchased. We were to stand for the whole of Wagner's *Götterdämmerung*. We must have looked a pair of freaks as we stood behind men in formal dress and aristocratic women in full-length evening gowns. In the interval we were first out of the door. I threw myself onto the red velvet sofa while Keith purchased our strawberry ice creams. Wagner was never a favourite but I was hugely impressed by the soaring voices, falling masonry and clouds of 'smoke' that accompanied the denouement as Brünnhilde threw herself into the flames.

I secured accommodation at Canterbury Hall, a hostel near King's Cross for women students run by London University. On either side of the corridors were pairs of basic rooms with a shared bathroom. I was to share with Veronica, a leggy blonde who was studying physics. She was middle class and convent-educated. Along the corridor we met Camille, a Bristol girl with a posh accent and a dramatic turn of phrase, together with Ivana, the daughter of a professional Czech refugee family. They went to the exotic-sounding School of Slavonic and East European Studies.

These were girls unlike any I had met in south Wales. This was immediately apparent from the underwear on the line in our shared bathroom. Mine was M&S white, which I'd attempted to dye turquoise to cover its worn appearance. Veronica had matching sets in heavy lace – one cream, the other navy. We were from a different class. Nonetheless, we had great fun, enduring the bad food and the strict rules. All visitors had to sign in and at curfew I'd often get a call on the intercom: 'Miss Anthony, you've got a man in your room – send him down immediately.'

Professor W. O. James, head of the botany department, gave the first lecture series. It was riveting stuff explaining the pathways of photosynthesis. We were just a dozen students, two of us girls. Janet and I were chalk and cheese and never became friends, which was a shame. We were just 123 women among 2,756 men. My engaged status gave me a great sense of freedom and an ability to make male friends easily. The bar, however, was men only, as were the various drinking clubs to which Keith belonged. Women were automatically enrolled as members of the Imperial College

Women's Association, headed up by Lady Anne Thorne, one of the very few women on the academic staff. Our only privilege was access to a lounge where occasional sherry parties were held in our honour. From time to time assaults on the bar were attempted by women students, but as I didn't like beer or vomiting men I wasn't too bothered. The ban on women remained throughout my years as a student.

I had always been interested in foreign affairs and also felt it was time to join the Labour Club. Imperial's three constituent colleges – the Royal School of Mines, the City and Guilds College (engineering) and the Royal College of Science – attracted outstanding students from all over Asia, Africa and the Middle East. As a member of the International Relations Club, I soon had friends from many continents.

Just when life was particularly happy and promising, a terrible international crisis occurred that threatened us all. In mid-October the news broke that Soviet nuclear weapons were being sited in Cuba, the Caribbean island on America's doorstep. President Kennedy immediately ordered a quarantine (amounting to a blockage) and demanded the withdrawal of the weapons. Two days later Soviet Premier Khrushchev wrote a letter to Kennedy accusing him of 'an act of aggression propelling humankind into the abyss of a world nuclear missile war'. Then a Soviet missile crew shot down a U2 spy plane. The world held its breath.

The missiles of the superpowers carried massive warheads that could deliver thousands of Hiroshimas with radioactive fallout over the whole of Europe. Everyone was glued to television and radio reports, terrified that Kennedy would react to the provocation. Behind the scenes, frantic negotiations eventually ended the standoff with assistance from U Thant, the UN Secretary General. Kennedy was hailed as a hero. The UN agreement meant the dismantling of the Soviet missiles and an agreement by the US never to invade Cuba. What we were not told was that the Soviet deployment was a direct response to the earlier deployment of US nuclear weapons, aimed at the USSR, in Turkey and Italy. It was this action, coupled with the failed US attempt to overthrow the Cuban regime the previous year, that had provoked Khrushchev into action. The European deployment of American missiles was never revealed, and their dismantling as part of the UN agreement was kept secret.

In college we kept up a hectic schedule. There were lectures every day followed by hours of laboratory work and experiments to write up. Once a month Keith and I went back to Wales to see our families where I indulged in wedding planning. Neither Keith nor I were believers but we opted for tradition. My mother would make all the dresses. I chose the most expensive material I could afford – an exquisite white satin embroidered with silky white flowers. For 'going away' I bought an A-line turquoise wool suit and a matching tulle hat. I spent more than the price of the suit on a pair of dark-brown suede stilettos, a matching bag and a pair of elbow-length suede gloves. We all dressed like our mothers in those days.

Our bridesmaids, sisters Susan and Ruth, had cream satin dresses and my cousin Gaye and Julie, a family friend, had blue. My five-year-old cousin Kym was a flower girl. The night before the wedding, Susan, Mum and I decorated the church with cream and blue flowers, grown by my father and grandfather. My mother made all the bouquets and button-holes. We tried to limit the expenses at the reception but at the last minute my father got carried away and ordered champagne all round.

It was a wonderful day and we left in a state of euphoria for our honeymoon in Sussex. Dad's brother Phil and his wife Jean had arranged to stay in Wales for a week so that we could have their house in Horsham. I was very much in awe of my Auntie Jean and knew we would have to take care of the house. In truth we spent most of our time in bed, except for a trip to Brighton where the pebble beach was a great disappointment after the smooth rolling sands of Barry Island. I dutifully swept the floors before my aunt's return inspection, only to be told that I obviously hadn't taken up the mats.

I had never been abroad. School trips to France were unaffordable but I'd never really felt deprived. Keith, however, had an insatiable desire to travel.

As a talented violin player, he had been a member of the Welsh National Youth Orchestra and was now playing in a number of orchestras in London. His playing and love of music had led to a couple of trips to the continent. Now we had an opportunity to supplement the honeymoon in Sussex.

Dr Freddie Whitehead was a larger-than-life character who taught taxonomy. He was married to a woman from Yugoslavia and had, we suspected, a flamboyant lifestyle. So it wasn't a great surprise to learn that my compulsory field trip at the end of year one was to Yugoslavia. My marriage was no secret, so it followed that I should ask if Keith could join us. Freddie readily agreed.

Keith was to more than earn his keep, but he also nearly derailed the whole trip. We arrived by train in Split where we unloaded our luggage and began walking to the exit. Keith, who was slightly ahead, was suddenly apprehended by two men and was marched off. Everybody was stunned. Freddie's wife ran after them, shouting in Serbo-Croat. Inside the office, as Keith recounted later, he saw a man nonchalantly leaning against the wall smoking and two uniformed officers seated at a desk. Keith is shown a packet of condoms and the police point to the other man. Apparently two plain-clothes officers had followed this man, who was a known pick-pocket. They were very anxious for Keith to press charges, which would, of course, have been disastrous for the trip. Somehow, Mrs Whitehead got him released and thankfully the 'evidence' was returned intact.

We had an amazing time. In between observing the Mediterranean flora and documenting habitats, we had plenty of time to enjoy ourselves. We journeyed south from Split to Montenegro. We were to stay in a hostel in the mountains that necessitated carrying not only the totality of our luggage but also a number of huge books which made up our Latin flora.

Our final stay was to be in Dubrovnik and we were making the journey by sea when a huge storm blew up unexpectedly. These were times before communication was possible with parents at home and they had no idea where we were. Little did we know that as we were rocked at sea a major earthquake had hit Skopje. We were to learn later that over 1,000 people were dead, many more injured and 200,000 people made homeless. At home, the local paper that had featured our wedding now ran a scare story about the honeymoon couple in an earthquake zone. Dubrovnik was our reward for all our hard work. A bit more observation and collecting of specimens, and then we were taken to a performance of Verdi's *Nabucco*. It was staged outdoors with spectacular effects, including straw bales set alight across ancient ramparts.

Back in London, I found a bedsitter with kitchen and bath in Earl's Court for eight guineas a week (£8.40) in a multi-occupied terraced house. A door had been placed at the top of the stairs with a plastic awning connecting it to the ceiling. In reality this meant anyone could climb over our 'front door', but we had no fears – it was simply thrilling to have our own place. Below us lived a couple of girls who were always coming and going and having a lot of male visitors. The man on the ground floor rarely appeared, though we once saw him smoking cocaine. No one bothered us except when I once answered the street door to two police officers who promptly kicked in the door to the ground-floor flat.

One day that November we were going to the lift in the physics department where Keith had his lab when we heard the shocking news of President Kennedy's assassination. We rushed to the Common Room and like so many millions sat glued to the television screen. Keith was no great fan of Kennedy and told dark tales about his father; but I was caught up in the whole glamour of his presidency and felt quite devastated.

Our landlord was an artist and soon after we moved into Kempsford Gardens he asked if I would sit for him as he hoped to enter a portrait into the Royal Academy Summer Exhibition. I duly arrived at his Chelsea studio. I had my hair in the French-style pleat then in vogue, and wore a plain navy sweater. Mark enquired whether I could let my hair down and wear something brighter, but with a singular lack of imagination I insisted on the status quo. Mark liked to listen to music as he painted and told me he anticipated we would have time to listen to every one of Shostakovich's symphonies. We did exactly that. A rather sombre portrait emerged and I'm not sure it was ever exhibited. Even though I didn't like it very much we decided to buy it and somehow managed to raise the £70. Fifty years on it looks much better and is a pleasant reminder of very happy times.

Keith's career was flourishing and he was set to take up a post-doctoral position once he had completed his thesis on macular degeneration. Although a physicist, working in the optics department meant that he had an opportunity to collaborate with medics and carry out experiments on patients who volunteered to spend hours in his darkroom. We were surrounded by fascinating people, all absorbed by their research but much given to partying and hard drinking. Drugs, however, were little in evidence. Keith was passionately opposed to cigarette smoking and having read of the links with lung cancer I soon gave up my occasional habit.

News from home was not so good. My mother had had lots of gynaecological problems for years but her GP (a Catholic) had told her that the only remedy was a hysterectomy, which couldn't be undertaken as she was 'still of childbearing years'. She continued to suffer, becoming anaemic from blood loss. After fainting one day she had had enough and a hysterectomy was arranged, which would mean a long convalescence and which would be hard on Susan, who was doing her A-levels.

There was also a huge scandal on College Road. The son of one of our neighbours had been arrested and charged with homosexual offences. He was the older brother of a girl I often played with and the last time I saw him was at her birthday party when I was about thirteen. I thought he was incredibly handsome and hoped he would become my boyfriend. Needless to say he never did and now it turned out he might go to prison.*

That summer was to be Keith's and my first great adventure. Yugoslavia had whetted my appetite for travel so we bought a European railway timetable and chose Istanbul. We would have a two-night stay on the train (sharing

---

* Homosexuality was only partly decriminalised three years later when it became lawful only in private between consenting adults aged over twenty-one.

with four strangers in couchettes), four nights in Istanbul and a two-night return journey. There were no cheap flights in those days and indeed few ordinary people ever flew anywhere. It was an incredible journey, the great clunking, lumbering train being pulled across Europe to constantly changing scenery, smells and language. We bought our food from the people who crowded onto the platform whenever the train stopped. On day three the heat rose sharply along with the terrible stench from the toilets, but we reached Istanbul without incident.

We had no experience of other cultures and looked around us in amazement. Istanbul fifty years ago was a very different place from the modern, Westernised city it is today. Poverty was everywhere and hard physical labour in evidence as men, bent double with heavy loads, struggled up the steep, cobbled streets of the old city. We walked and walked, occasionally using the communal taxis when we thought we understood where they were going. The crowds, the noise, the smells, the darkness at night – all were strange to us London visitors. We stayed in a cheap hotel and ate with pleasure the local dishes we found in the café below. Every table had a small statue of Ataturk, the great military leader who became the first President of Turkey and the founder of the Republic, separating religion from the secular state. For me he was a special hero, having taken the extraordinary step of giving equal rights to women in marriage and divorce and removing the obligation to wear the veil.

We were in awe of the architecture. The magnificent 400-year-old Süleymaniye Mosque was just breathtaking. An absolutely vast structure with huge domes and four tall minarets, built by the richest and most powerful Ottoman emperor, Süleyman the Magnificent, the natural light from the high windows in the interior is supplemented with hundreds of lamps hung in huge concentric circles.

Our next visit was to the 300-year-old Blue Mosque, named for the 20,000 handmade blue tiles and blue painted upper galleries. It was breathtakingly beautiful, with two stained-glass windows, supplemented by chandeliers.

The other dominating building in the old city was the Ayasofya. Originally a Greek Orthodox church built in 537, it was converted to a mosque after the Ottomans took Constantinople in 1453 and then secularised as a museum in 1931.

It was absolutely impossible to do justice to this place in such a brief stay. We were overwhelmed and snatched an all-too-brief visit to the Topkapi Palace. A vast storehouse of treasures, we were directed to their most precious exhibit – a colossal 86-carat pear-shaped diamond.

We returned exhilarated and determined to use whatever little money we had to travel at every opportunity.

Susan passed her A-levels and accepted a place at Holborn College of Law, Languages and Commerce to do modern languages and business studies, where she would do well. We also moved house. We were keen to get an unfurnished place and I found a first-floor balcony flat in Earl's Court Square that had magnificent great windows, high ceilings and a kitchen and bathroom created by dividing up what had been a vast drawing room. We bought a bed and my father constructed a large bookcase and room divider to separate it from the rest of the room, which now boasted a turquoise wool three-piece suite. I spent a fortune on yards of heavy wool fabric in complementary shades of blue and my mother made the curtains to enclose the great windows. We had, of course, never lived anywhere with central heating, so we failed to realise the significance of its absence. Our single, two-bar electric fire couldn't possibly heat this great Victorian room. Needless to say we froze, and were deeply embarrassed when Welsh family friends Edward and Chris Williams visited us on their honeymoon.

I was now in my final year and choices had to be made for my dissertation. I chose the ecology option, which meant living at the college field station. I thought I would get lots of revision done, but the field work occupied our days and there were far too many distractions as Keith came for weekends. Suddenly finals were upon us and I was desperately underprepared. I started working ten hours a day and kept it up for the two weeks prior to the exams.

Not the best of preparation and it cost me the First I was expected to get. Years later, one of my professors introduced me as one of his best students 'who got a First of course' – I didn't disabuse him.

But consolation was already planned for the summer break. A very unusual man had joined the physics department. His name was Leonti Planskoy. He was much older than Keith but they quickly became close friends, sharing a passion for both culture and research.

I was greatly in awe of Planskoy and we always called him by his surname. He introduced us to some friends of his who were of a similar age and who in turn invited Keith and me to dinner at the English Speaking Union. This was a grand occasion for us. As we passed a copy of the Declaration of Independence, I remember our host exclaiming, 'The greatest confidence trick ever perpetrated on mankind.' It was an unforgettable evening, not least because we chose roast beef for dinner, only to be presented with thin slices swimming in blood. I squirmed as I forced it down. The evening couldn't have been too disastrous, however, as we were subsequently offered assistance with our next adventure. We had spoken of our ambition to visit the Middle East and our host volunteered a friend in Beirut. We didn't hesitate – despite the stinking toilets we booked another return train journey to Istanbul and a flight from Istanbul to Beirut. This was a time of currency restriction and we could take only £120 each out of the country. Frankly we couldn't raise a penny more anyway, so off we went.

I had never flown before and neither had anyone in my family. I later rationalised the panic attack I suffered as triggered by the memory of the fear I had felt as a child when taken on the Big Dipper at Barry Island. But, whatever the reason, I was clearly terrified of flying. Mercifully it was a short flight. The 'friend in Beirut' turned out to be the Belgian ambassador. He lived in a penthouse overlooking the ocean. We had never seen such luxury. One of my abiding memories is of the pink marble bathroom with soft pink toilet tissue, never experienced by those of us who had seen newspaper replaced by crisp, non-absorbent Izal in the toilets of south Wales.

Beirut was spectacularly beautiful and hugely wealthy. Our immediate goal was to see Baalbeck. A place of settlement for around 9,000 years, its major interest for us was the magnificent Roman ruins. Six Corinthian columns towered above the site. The biggest of the three temples, dedicated to Jupiter, was built on a podium, which, 2,000 years later, is still used as a performance stage for the international music festival. The whole place was quite mesmerising.

We got the festival programme and hoped to book but the prices were way beyond our means. Most intriguing to our Western eyes was the discovery that an Egyptian singer was more expensive than the Berlin Philharmonic! Her name, Umm Kulthum, meant nothing to us, but we were later to learn that she was considered the greatest Middle Eastern female singer of her day and sheiks got into their private jets to fly to hear her in concert wherever she performed.

Our next stop was Damascus, but before leaving I told the ambassador that I'd heard of a place called Ma'loula – a village oasis in the desert where they still spoke Aramaic (purportedly the language of Jesus Christ). He was amazed that anyone in England would have heard of it, but immediately put it on our itinerary.

We loved Damascus, though the heat was overpowering. We were completely unaware of the risks and walked for hours in the midday sun. As we walked along the biblical street called Straight, I suddenly saw stars before my eyes and fainted from heat stroke. A kindly shopkeeper took me into the cool souk and gave me some water. The bazaar was magical, full of gold and silver and fabulous silks – so cheap I could afford to buy a brocade stole with silver thread.

We were met and lunched by a Syrian friend of the ambassador who took us to his home in the old city and arranged for us to visit the Umayyad Mosque, the Great Mosque of Damascus built in the eighth century. I was given a cotton sheet to put over my head and arms but there were no other restrictions on our visit. The Umayyad is one of the oldest and largest mosques in the world, retaining many of its original features. The vastness of its courtyard, surrounded by colonnades and topped with domes and minarets, was breathtaking. Inside we saw the gold mosaics and enamelled tiles and fountains, all so much finer for their lack of any portrayal of human form.

Ma'loula was everything I expected: a tiny green oasis rising from the desert, built into the mountainside more than 3,000 feet up and visible long before we reached it. There were two important monasteries to be visited. Mar Sarkis, built on the site of a pagan temple with elements dating back to the Byzantine era, is Greek Catholic. Mar Thecla is Greek Orthodox.

The village was home to both Christians and Muslims. Forty-seven years later, to my utter horror, I was to hear of Ma'loula again in the context of the civil war in Syria, where it became a battlefield between Al-Qaeda-linked fighters and the Syrian Army. We went on to see the vast ancient ruins of Palmyra rising from the desert sands and wondered how people 2,000 years ago could have built its colossal triumphal arch, spectacular colonnades, temples and viaduct. Great statues and reliefs added to its wonder and we were quite overwhelmed. Tragically, much of Palmyra's unique treasure would be destroyed by so-called Islamic State in 2015.

We left Syria for Jordan, again courtesy of the ambassador, and arrived in Amman, where for the first time we felt less than comfortable. It was, however, just our base for exploring. Our first visit was to Jerash.

Jerash was spectacular. An ancient site dating from 83 BC, it was rebuilt by the Romans in 64 AD, destroyed and then rebuilt twice more to become a flourishing city in the second and third centuries. Its desert setting provided a stunning backdrop to the long colonnaded street with more than 100 columns still standing. There was so much to explore – a great theatre and many temples – but the blazing sun and Keith's acute diarrhoea limited our stay.

In between sightseeing, we travelled about in communal taxis where we were taken aback by the number of young people who spoke English. Showing their ID cards, they impressed upon us that they were Palestinians, not Jordanians. Years later I realised that these were the children of Palestinian refugees forced to flee their lands in the 1948 Arab-Israeli War.

The highlight of our tour was the visit to Jerusalem (East Jerusalem was then in Jordan). None of the present-day security was in force and there was no threat to our safety. We were able to visit the seventh-century Muslim shrine, the Dome of the Rock, with its magnificent tiled exterior, great golden dome and glorious interior of red and gold mosaics. We walked throughout the old city, marvelling at the extraordinary history displayed at every turn. The Church of the Holy Sepulchre was our next visit. Originally the site of a pagan temple, it was built as two connected churches in the fourth century to cover the sites of the crucifixion of Christ and the resurrection. As non-believers, it held no special significance for us, but its age, history and architecture couldn't fail to thrill.

Our final visit was to the Dead Sea to experience the extraordinary phenomenon of floating in its dense waters. We were now totally intoxicated by our travels and greedy for more. We found a travel agent advertising trips to the ancient, rose-red city of Petra; we were desperate to go but, at £5 each, it was out of the question. Our last option was an offer by our return driver to take us into Iraq. We were definitely up for that but an outbreak of cholera closed the borders so it was back to Beirut and, for me, the terrifying return flight to Istanbul.

Keith had completed his post-doctoral work and was now a lecturer. He was still earning very little but I spotted an opportunity. The college owned two grand houses in Prince's Gate, newly refurbished for the maths department and with the top floor of each converted into flats. They were advertised for rent, unfurnished, to young members of staff. We secured a seven-year lease and promptly became neighbours of Mick Jagger and Marianne Faithfull, though in truth we never saw them. We went to the Danish Design Centre in Knightsbridge and bought a wonderful teak dining table and chairs, which were to last for over thirty years. It was a great party venue and we made full use of it. Five minutes' walk took us to our departments and we could eat twice a day in the refectory (chips with everything – I only weighed 8½ stone).

Our everyday pleasures were simple. We were at the heart of swinging London. The King's Road was one stop on the Tube, Hyde Park five minutes away and if I wanted to make a special meal I could shop in Harrods' food hall. Somehow the sun always seemed to be shining as we dressed in our best and paraded up and down the King's Road – a whole afternoon's pleasure for the price of a coffee. You never knew who you might see. One day the American rock star Jimi Hendrix nearly knocked me over as he leaped over the side of his open-top sports car.

Music of all kinds was a big part of our life. Keith kept up his violin playing and took every opportunity to buy tickets for the Albert Hall (on our doorstep) and Southbank concerts. Among the highlights of those years were sublime performances by the great Russian soloists David Oistrakh and Mstislav Rostropovich. We also 'discovered' the great Indian sitar player Ravi Shankar, whose fame in the West was later to spread rapidly following a collaboration with George Harrison (Keith mightily disapproved).

My intention had always been to be a teacher, but my ambition was thwarted. Following the degree results, I wrote to the Inner London Education Authority (ILEA) to ask about vacancies. I received a smudged cyclostyled letter in reply. The ILEA did not permit graduates to teach in its schools without a teaching qualification (quite right, but they were unique at the time). They recommended I enrol on a teacher-training course or find a post in a private school. I was outraged at the latter suggestion from a Labour authority and we couldn't afford to fund a further year of study. The solution was to apply for a demonstrator's job in the botany department. The genetics lecturer Richard Threlfall needed someone to assist him and I was duly appointed on the magnificent salary of £800 per annum.

Within a few months of my taking up the post, Richard became ill. One of the MSc courses had a genetics module and I was asked to teach it! So much for the ILEA. I loved my job, which combined lab teaching with a bit of basic research. After two years, I was advised to switch to full-time research and potentially a lectureship. But, just six months on, I would find myself thoroughly depressed. I realised that what I enjoyed was contact with people and the isolated, painstaking work of a researcher was not for me. I'd already done enough work – a final push and writing up were all that stood between me and my PhD.

Throughout my undergraduate years Keith and I were always politically active. International politics was our greatest interest and Imperial had so many overseas students that individual national societies flourished; I joined most of them. It was a time of great turbulence in Africa. In 1960, Kwame Nkrumah became the first President of the Republic of Ghana. Revolutionary struggles were taking place all over the continent and we followed them avidly. Our greatest hero was Nelson Mandela, sentenced to life imprisonment under apartheid in 1964, but there were others. Zambia gained independence in 1964 under another towering figure, Kenneth Kaunda. A year later, fearful of the tide of black resistance, Ian Smith, the white supremacist Prime Minister of Southern Rhodesia, made a declaration of unilateral independence from Britain. These struggles became our focus for activism and we demonstrated frequently outside the South African and Rhodesian embassies.

Even before I went to university I had been aware of the Anti-Apartheid Movement, established in 1960 following the Sharpeville massacre during which sixty-nine unarmed protestors were shot dead by the South African police. Now we joined the college branch, participated in their demonstrations and strictly observed the boycott of South African goods. My constant campaigning led to my being elected president of the International Relations Club (IRC).

That year our travels in the Middle East also led to greater involvement in the Arab Society, in which my IRC treasurer, Faiz Nadir, was active. It was mainly social, with lots of delicious Iraqi food and late-night listening to Umm Kulthum on Egyptian radio. But everything changed when tension between Israel and Egypt escalated in the summer of 1967. Nasser mobilised his forces along the Israeli border, leading to a pre-emptive strike by Israel that wiped out the Egyptian air force. Night after night we sat with our Arab friends listening to the reports of the Six Day War. Israel overwhelmed the Arab nations that joined the fight, taking the Gaza Strip and the Sinai Peninsula from Egypt, the West Bank and East Jerusalem from Jordan and the Golan Heights from Syria. In six days, Israel tripled the area under its control. We and our friends were absolutely devastated.

The following year, 1968, was a turning point in my life. The UN was gearing up for the twentieth anniversary of the Declaration of Human Rights, which begins 'All human beings are born free and equal in dignity and rights'. I decided that the IRC should make a contribution by staging an exhibition. It wasn't difficult; human rights were being violated on every continent. The exhibition illustrated each point of the Declaration in different countries with details of accompanying campaigns. Then I asked myself whether anything in the Declaration applied to Britain. Shelter, the national campaign for the homeless, was already hitting the headlines with shocking evidence of homelessness in Britain. Article 25 of the Declaration referred to the right to a standard of living adequate for the health and well-being of people, including housing, so I invited Des Wilson, the dynamic New Zealander leading Shelter, to speak at the exhibition's launch. I was inspired. My growing feeling that I should quit my science was reinforced. In the one seriously reckless act of my life, I left Imperial and gave myself three months in which to think and get a job. It was to be the first and last time in fifty years that I wasn't gainfully employed.

While active in the politics of race internationally, I was also very conscious of the degree of racial prejudice in Britain. Many people had emigrated to London from Commonwealth countries and when I was looking for flats in 1963–64 it was quite common to see notices saying 'No Blacks'. Keith, on his own arrival in London, even saw one saying 'No Chinese, No Welsh'!

In 1965, the Labour government delivered the Race Relations Act, which outlawed discrimination on the 'grounds of colour, race, or ethnic or national origins' in public places and led to the establishment of the Race Relations Board to consider complaints. In the United States the battle for civil rights was at its peak and in 1968 one of its most charismatic leaders, Martin Luther

King, was assassinated. In Britain, a second race relations Bill, outlawing discrimination in housing, was scheduled for debate on 23 April. On 20 April, Enoch Powell MP, shadow Secretary of State for Defence, addressed a meeting of the Conservative Political Centre. Earlier that week he had told a journalist, 'I'm going to make a speech at the weekend and it's going to go up "fizz" like a rocket but whereas all rockets fall to the Earth, this one is going to stay up.'

He was right. It became known as the 'Rivers of Blood' speech. In it he said: 'We must be mad, literally mad as a nation to be permitting the annual inflow of some 50,000 dependents ... It is like watching a nation busily engaged in heaping up its own funeral pyre.' He ended his peroration by quoting from *The Aeneid*: 'As I look ahead I am filled with foreboding. Like the Roman, I seem to see "the River Tiber flowing with much blood"!'

To his credit, Edward Heath, the Tory leader, sacked him.

There was clearly work to be done and I was unemployed. I applied for jobs with both the Race Relations Board and the United Nations Association. To my astonishment (there wasn't the competition for jobs there is today) I received no acknowledgement from the RRB. The UNA did respond and went into a long, drawn-out process with dates stretching far ahead. Impatient as always, I looked elsewhere and spotted an ad for a regional organiser for Shelter – a great opportunity.

Meanwhile, I'd been asked to represent UK UN students at a UN Human Rights Youth Conference in Geneva. Students came from all over the world and I was immediately drawn to a beautiful woman of my own age. Shala came from Persia (now Iran), which was a great surprise given the Shah's repressive politics. It was an amazing experience over the two weeks, with speakers from many continents and deep philosophical discussions. Shala returned to her studies in the US but we kept in touch. She was planning to return home to Tehran for the summer holidays and invited us to join her. We couldn't resist. Keith had an encyclopaedic knowledge of geography and ancient civilisations so he added Isfahan and Shiraz to our itinerary and proposed we fly on to Cairo to visit an Egyptian colleague. We began our visit in Tehran, staying with Shala's sister Shirin and brother-in-law Mehdi. They lived behind high walls in a house with a fine garden. The family was very hospitable, Westernised and living a comfortable life. We experienced for the first time the delicious perfumed spices of Persian cuisine, my favourite being stewed lamb with bitter cherries and golden rice.

A visit to the theatre was an amazing experience. We sat in good, soft seats a way back from the stage, but the area immediately in front of us was occupied entirely by men who could easily have been at a boxing match. The first belly dancer was an exquisite, slim young woman who drew little praise from the crowd. Subsequent dancers appeared in increasing sizes until the last one, grossly overweight to my eyes, proved the crowd's favourite, her unique talent being to rotate the tassels on her nipples in different directions. The men roared and threw empty beer bottles onto the stage in appreciation.

Shala was also keen to show us Tehran's oldest historic monument, the Golestan Palace. Built during the eighteenth and nineteenth centuries, it was a complex of palaces, halls and museums, offering beautiful artefacts, glorious tiled walls, domes and exquisite Persian mirror work.

We began our long journey to Isfahan through the desert on a local bus. We had very little money, no language and no means of communication if we did encounter any trouble. We planned to eat very sparingly and drink only the hot sweet tea that was on sale at the roadside.

The landscape was unrelenting, arid, with the occasional oasis where the bus would stop. On one such stop we saw a great golden dome of a mosque in the distance and expressed interest in it. An English-speaking traveller came up to warn us that we shouldn't even consider visiting the city of Qom. He told us a Western woman had been badly injured in an acid attack the previous year. Unknown to us, a certain Ayatollah Khomeini had led his opposition to the Shah from Qom a few years earlier, before his exile in France.

Toilets were a serious concern as we never knew when one might be available and inevitably it would be a stinking open pit. At one stop, however, we were shown to two rows of wooden huts, with stable doors. I thought the wooden bench inside with a hole was a great improvement. Once seated, I looked out only to see a row of bearded old men opposite, all looking directly at me over the doors of their huts – an unnerving experience.

By the time we reached Isfahan we were both suffering severe stomach problems, but fortunately we were able to find a comfortable hotel and live on boiled milk and digestive biscuits for the next forty-eight hours. The main purpose of our visit was to see the great Shah Mosque. We were stunned by the extraordinary intricacy of the tiles that covered both the exterior and interior of the building. Deep blues, sparkling turquoise and green radiated an intense light that was mesmerising. I cannot think of a more beautiful building – comparable perhaps with the Taj Mahal, which I was to see many years later. We also visited the Ali Qapu Palace and Imperial Bazaar, built at the same time, and bought some tiny turquoise thimble-sized glasses decorated with gold calligraphy.

We boarded a bus again to make our final journey to Shiraz. Shiraz was known for its poets, gardens and wine. It is said that the oldest sample of wine in the world was found in clay jars discovered from the Neolithic period. The poet Omar Khayyam (1048–1131) heaps praise on Shirazi wine in his famous Rubáiyát. Today, winemaking is banned by Iran's Islamist regime. Two famous Persian poets, Hafez and Saadi, came from Shiraz and while we didn't hear any poetry, we did visit the beautiful, cool gardens with fountains in which their work might have been read.

Our goal was to visit Persepolis, founded by Darius I in 518BC as the capital of the empire. A huge complex was erected on a vast terrace up to twenty metres high, partly built into the mountain. Accessed by a double flight of stairs, the terraces were covered with friezes of contemporary figures – soldiers, noblemen, lions and magnificent winged bulls. Fifteen colossal marble pillars still stand, along with a towering gateway and palace remains. UNESCO deems it to be one of the world's greatest archaeological sites, among those with no equivalent. We could only agree. It was awesome and much was made by our guide of the fact that in 330BC Persepolis was captured by Alexander the Great, whose army then set fire to the ancient palaces and looted its imperial treasury.

Back in Tehran, we said our goodbyes and left for Egypt. We were met in Cairo by Keith's colleague Professor Ishák, an intensely kind and jovial man. We were introduced to his family and then settled into our hotel. There were few Western tourists in Egypt in those days and we had unrestricted access to all the sites. Like everyone before and since we were amazed at the vast size of the pyramids and the Sphinx and taken aback by the fact that we just walked from the street, across a stretch of sand, weeds and rubble and there they were. Tehran had accustomed us to heat, noise and smells but the huge numbers of people thronging the streets at all times, constantly on the move and dressed in what looked like pyjamas, was a shock. We had our first experience of pitta bread, sampling the delicious falafel 'sandwiches' sold on the streets.

The bazaars were heaving with handmade goods, metal, glass, stone and exquisite jewellery. I hardly knew where to look but settled on a beautiful gold and turquoise ring. The colours of Ancient Egypt were everywhere. Our next visit was to the national museum. We found it heavily sandbagged, a legacy of the Six Day War with Israel. It was a sad place but its Ancient Egyptian treasures were marvellous.

Alexandria was recommended for a visit. We went to the railway station and found an amazing train. Modern, fast and with air conditioning, it was totally unlike the ancient British rail carriages we travelled in so frequently at home. I believe it was built in Hungary and must have been part of a push to increase tourism.

Alexandria was a joy. We spent the day on the beach, in and out of the water, taking only occasional shelter under the palm-leaf umbrellas. As soon as I got back onto the train I became freezing cold and couldn't stop shaking. Nausea swept over me as I suffered another case of heat stress. The bonus was an instant, all-over deep tan, which didn't leave me for some months. We knew we would have to return to Egypt.

Fifteen years later we realised our dream when we took a boat down the Nile to visit Luxor and Abu Simbel. Luxor was the stopping-off point for the Valley of the Kings, where we visited the great tombs of Ancient Egypt, some of which are no longer open to visitors. I was apprehensive going into the very narrow tunnels with only the guide's torch to follow and walking down for what seemed like ages until suddenly, to my relief, we came into the great high burial chamber. We were awestruck by the spectacular paintings of mythical figures, human with animal heads, and hieroglyphs decorating corridors and chambers and a roof painted dark blue with stars, built over 3,000 years ago.

We went on to Abu Simbel where we saw the colossal statues of the Temple of Ramesses. The Great Temple was completed around 1265BC with four twenty-metre statues of the pharaoh decorating its façade and carved directly from the rock face. These were sights never to be forgotten.

Back home, we reflected on the extreme contrast of rich and poor in Persia – surely a place ripe for revolution. But with a police state, no trade unions or political parties, we couldn't imagine how it could get started. We never thought of the mosques and neither did the CIA.

Before leaving for Tehran, I'd had an interview with Shelter and explained I would be going away. Once home, I couldn't wait to get in the door where, to my delight, was a letter telling me I'd got the job – starting straight away.

## Chapter Three

# SHELTER

S helter was a hive of activity, very different from my quiet laboratory at Imperial. Des Wilson was an autocratic but inspiring boss. He had adopted an aggressive marketing approach, entirely different from other charities. As one of the regional organisers, my job was to set up Shelter groups wherever we had donor contacts. This involved approaching people direct or occasionally responding to requests. Groups would be helped with fundraising activities they could do locally, supported with materials to distribute and kept in touch with HQ through regular Shelter Groups newsletters. This was not as easy as it sounds. It meant travelling on public transport to anywhere in the Home Counties and getting home again after evening meetings; these were the days before computers, emails and mobile phones. Despite all my political activities at Imperial I was not a confident speaker. Des, however, was, and we took our messages from him. I wrote a speech by hand and then read it out at my very first Shelter engagement. Even as I did so I realised the deadening effect it was having on my audience. But I learned my lesson. I took advice and practised in advance and made it more personal. I got better and the year flew by with lots of new experiences, setting up a number of new groups and learning the geography of southern England.

Des was hugely ambitious and always restless. If things didn't go his way he would don dark glasses, his face like thunder. We used to tiptoe around him until the mood passed. After a year in the job, I was promoted to head the Groups Department when my boss Liz moved to PR. I learned all my managerial skills in that job as we embarked on a major expansion (assisted by showings of the iconic film *Cathy Come Home*), with the aim of raising £1 million a year.

I recruited new regional organisers to a total of twelve, covering all of England and Wales (Scotland had its own campaign led by Ron Dick). I opened regional offices in Birmingham, Cardiff, Bristol and Manchester and hired a fleet of cars to enable the regional organisers to cover more ground. I had a budget of £40,000 and a target to raise £250,000. I was twenty-six years old and a woman! Nowhere else would I have been given such responsibility, but Des surrounded himself with young women. Cindy Barlow ran our administration, Eileen Ware the youth department and Liz Wills press and publicity. Pat Spiers was a roving regional organiser, Liz Doyle ran special events and even Helene Middleweek* joined us for a short period.

I was spoiled as groups director by the support of Juliet Cairns. I became very fond of Juliet, who was a brilliant shorthand typist and organiser and whose skills ensured that I never learned how to do any admin myself. My regional organisers were also young and keen to take initiatives. They were a talented bunch. Notably, one of them, Mike Daube, went on to run the anti-smoking campaign ASH and ended up as a professor of public health in Australia, leading the campaign for plain-packaging of cigarettes.

The late 1960s were wonderful years to be young in London. Everything was changing and we felt a glorious sense of freedom to do anything we wanted. In the summer of 1969, the Rolling Stones gave a free concert in Hyde Park. I dressed in a mini-skirted fine mohair lilac dress with pearl buttons and purple suede flats. It was a fabulous day of music and sunshine.

---

* Later Baroness Hayman and Lord Speaker of the House of Lords.

Butterflies were released in vast numbers from the stage, and we were having the time of our lives.

September 1970: My grandfather had a heart attack. Although he was eighty years old he had always seemed quite fit and not long before I had seen him on a ladder up a cherry tree. We hastened to south Wales to visit him in hospital. It felt like a farewell and back in London when I call for an update he is dead. A sad family funeral but a good life lived. Saddest of all was the certainty that my grandmother would have to leave their country cottage and the fields and orchards that had sustained them all their lives.

Then I received a most unusual invitation. Roselle, my friend from school, invited me and Wendy to her wedding. I hadn't heard from Roselle in years. We met once after we both went to university in London. She subsequently went to South Africa where she worked with Christiaan Barnard (who performed the world's first heart transplant). The wedding was a lovely event, with Ruth, one of her many talented sisters, singing.

A year later we received terrible news. Roselle was dead. She was only twenty-eight. The cause was unclear but it may have been an accidental overdose of prescription drugs and overwork. Her husband brought her body back for the family funeral, which Wendy and I attended. Ruth sang again and our hearts broke.

Shelter was the most brilliant training ground for campaigners and although for many of us it ended badly, no one regretted their time there. Liz Wills moved on to begin a successful new career in the arts in Newcastle in mid-1970 and new people joined. The following year, both Des and Cindy left. Our housing director, John Willis, who had a much more traditional managerial style, took over from Des. Ron Dick, our Scottish director, came to London to be John's deputy, and one of my regional organisers, Doug Smith, was promoted to be his assistant in charge of overall fundraising.

After two years as Shelter groups director I was appointed director of research and publications in 1972. This was a welcome new challenge. Shelter

had expanded its range of activities to supporting regeneration projects in Liverpool and Bradford. These became my responsibility. The Shelter Neighbourhood
Action Project (SNAP) was led by a mercurial Irish man with radical views, Des
McConaghy. Working in an area of extreme deprivation, Liverpool 8, the project
was always a rollercoaster and punch-ups with some of our collaborators never
far from our door. Nonetheless, we were able to demonstrate urban regeneration
led by the voluntary sector and the potential for renovation over slum clearance.

Keith had been awarded a Royal Society Exchange Scholarship to work
with a remarkable Swedish scientist, Gunnar Svaetichin. Gunnar was living
and working in Caracas and pioneering single-cell electrophysiological recording, which Keith wanted to learn. We'd previously met him at a conference
in Italy. He was good looking, utterly charming and very good company.
Keith liked him very much, sharing his passion for both science and politics.

The lease on our college flat was coming to an end and it was obvious
to me that a house purchase was necessary. But, just when we should have
focused on our domestic future, Keith was off for an extended stay in Caracas.
We had lived and worked in South Kensington for more than eight years. The
only other places I knew were Richmond, Barnes and Islington – all homes
of friends. Only Islington was affordable but in the brief conversation we had
before he left, Keith dismissed the whole borough as a concrete jungle. I was
left to figure out what to do next. It was to be a fateful decision. Life would
have been very different if we'd gone to live in Islington.

Keith's father had died in 1966 and his mother was now in her seventies.
My parents were still very active and my grandmother, aunts and uncles were
all living in south Wales. Keith and I visited frequently so I turned my attention to Reading, on the Great Western rail route. Pat Spiers, now in charge
of London and events at Shelter, had moved to Tilehurst, close to Reading, and commuted to London daily, so I saw it as a practical proposition.
Pat, who was to become a lifelong friend, had an interesting background.
She was probably the only person on the team who had experienced Shelter-
type housing conditions, having lived with her parents and sister in a single

room in post-war London until the age of ten. Her much older father had been gassed in the First World War and died on her thirteenth birthday, leaving her with a huge sense of insecurity.

After a search of the surrounding areas, I found a modern semi in a village called Burghfield Common. There was a regular bus service a few minutes' walk away to Reading railway station. Communications with Venezuela by landline were difficult and hugely expensive. I hardly got informed consent from Keith, but I ploughed on, ensuring everything would be in place for him to sign on his return. When he came back he dined out for months on the story that he had returned from South America to find he was now living forty-five miles away from the place he had left.

I was also Shelter's liaison with the squatter movement. As homelessness grew in the '60s Jim Radford and Ron Bailey led a group in south London. With Shelter support they obtained licences from local authorities to use rundown properties the councils couldn't use themselves. Homeless families were housed while they waited on long lists for council tenancies and ultimate security.

We decided to use our combined knowledge to argue the case for a legal framework to tackle homelessness. Ron Bailey did the research, leaving me with the immense task of checking and editing his vast handwritten script. The Grief Report was a seminal work, but it would be five years and a huge campaign before the British government finally legislated. The Housing (Homeless Persons) Act 1977 provided the first statutory definition of homelessness and placed clear duties on councils to assist local families.

John Willis decided to move on and the trustees advertised for a new director. I applied. I had the distinct impression that I was not being seriously considered and when the trustees appointed a Geoffrey Martin from Northern Ireland we were all shocked. He appeared to have no relevant experience and none of us had any involvement in his appointment. We'd always been such a close-knit team – we'd built the organisation together and somehow expected to have a say in its future. The trustees arranged for him to address a full staff meeting. He came and our worst fears were realised. When asked about his ambitions, he replied, 'to get into British politics', which was 'difficult for an Ulsterman'. Clearly Shelter was a great opportunity for him, but not his appointment for us. Of course he wasn't to blame. Our trustees, made up of various vicars and priests, knew very little about the day-to-day functioning of the organisation.

I decided it was time to move on, as did Pat. I was asked to stay on to teach Geoff 'everything he needs to know'. Nothing could have made me more angry. For the first time in my life I thought I had been discriminated against.

Keith's career was flourishing but academic salaries were pitifully low. A prolific writer of research papers, he was being invited to speak all over Europe but we knew the only monetary advancement would come through the slow rise from lecturer to reader to professor and that could take a lifetime. Then we had a stroke of luck. A publisher of a series of books for young people invited me and Eileen Ware (who had left just before Geoffrey Martin arrived) to write a volume on housing. We were paid handsomely and I rewarded myself with a 'fun fur' – high fashion at the time. It consisted of bands of genuine red fox fur interspaced with matching suede. Teamed with my beige suede high boots, it was the perfect outfit for weekends in the West End. Years later, I put it back into its huge cloth bag and stuffed it into a textile recycling bin to hide my shame.

I knew it would take time to find a permanent job, so I applied for a short contract with the charity Young Volunteer Force, set up and run by Anthony Steen. He was another charismatic leader who went on to become a Tory MP. It was a great place to work and I spent much of my time on a renovation project in the West Country, repointing stone walls. Meanwhile, my friend Pat was also temporarily employed and looking for a new career. So, with her husband and his friend Chris they decided to set up an art gallery in Henley. Very enterprising but a huge risk I thought. Five years later, when the gallery was still a fledgling business, Ross would leave Pat, much to the concern of all their friends.

Shelter had pioneered the concept of housing aid centres, building on the work of the Catholic Housing Aid Society (CHAS) headed by yet another charismatic man, Father Eamon Casey. Eamon was an ebullient personality, passionate about the poor and the homeless and always up for a laugh. Shelter opened its first housing aid centre, SHAC, in London.

Inspired by SHAC, the Oxford branch of CHAS decided to set up a housing aid centre in 1973 and advertised for a director. My application for the job succeeded and I was soon in Oxford planning the centre with chair of the board, Molly Walsh. The city council had provided a plot of land where a prefabricated building would be sited. It was just the challenge I needed. I would have a deputy and a receptionist and recruit and train volunteers. We employed Barbara Gatehouse as our receptionist, who, like many of us, later made the transition into Labour politics, becoming a city councillor in 1979.

Barbara did the straightforward, one-off advice at the front desk with in-depth advice and follow-ups being done by the rest of us. To assist us in cases of harassment, illegal eviction and housing issues related to marital breakdown, we recruited a group of volunteer lawyers. We began to see a side of life few would have thought existed in the 'city of dreaming spires'. I never forgot the day a desperate woman sought our advice on escaping a violent husband. After some hours we found a place for her in a refuge (the Women's Aid movement had just started). She left us to return to collect her belongings. Her husband, anticipating her movements, was waiting and murdered her.

I also experienced a direct personal trauma when I closed the interview room door, allowing a distressed client to sit between me and it. The man had a superficial wound around his neck that was gently oozing blood. He immediately produced the knife that he had used on himself and began to make threats, trapping me for some hours. Talking people down is an essential skill for those working in frontline agencies and my experience then stood me in good stead in later life.

That year we had another opportunity to travel. Vinod, a friend from Imperial, had gone to Brazil to design dams. Our summer holiday was spent with Keith doing a stint in Caracas and then an exciting stay in Rio. The city was spectacular, the beaches glorious and we had a fabulous time. But never without drama. I nearly put my bare foot on a rattlesnake and, more importantly, my favourite lilac crepe trouser suit, which I bought in Biba, was ruined when Vinod's maid decided to wash and shrink it.

Imperial was still providing us with lots of social activities. One evening on our way to a dinner at the college, a charming young man took my coat in the cloakroom. He was one of Keith's newest PhD students, a Turkish Cypriot named Mustapha Djamgoz. He and his talented wife Sabire were to become lifelong friends.

We actively campaigned for a Labour victory at both the 1974 general elections. Our candidate in Newbury was fighting a hopeless battle and as she lived far away she understandably put in very little time. Keith and I worked in Reading North, our local marginal seat, in the October election but sadly we didn't manage to help Harold Wilson with his meagre three-seat majority.

In November I was delegated to attend the Labour Party's national conference. A year earlier General Pinochet had overthrown the democratically elected President of Chile, the socialist Salvador Allende. Always a follower of international politics, I was in my seat for the debate on Chile. A young man with a mane of red hair made an electrifying speech calling for support for the Chile Solidarity Campaign. He was Neil Kinnock.

Chile was unusual in South America, having enjoyed over forty years of democratic rule when Allende was elected President in November 1970. An ardent socialist, he adopted policies of nationalisation that quickly drew opposition from the right wing. Three years on, the Christian Democrats withdrew their support and called for his overthrow and the CIA backed a coup led by General Augusto Pinochet. Allende died at the presidential palace and Pinochet took control of the country on 11 September. He was to run Chile as a military dictatorship until 1990.

Inspired by Neil Kinnock, I became a member of the Chile Solidarity Campaign run by Diane Dixon, and subsequently an active member of its executive committee.

Pinochet soon began a ruthless persecution of known socialists and any-one suspected of opposing the coup. More than 27,000 were tortured and 50,000 arrested and interrogated. Between 1973 and 1990 more than 3,000 people were killed by state agents or 'disappeared'. One of the first to be taken, within hours of the death of Allende, was Víctor Jara. He was a folk singer and theatre director. Five days later, his British-born wife, Joan, was summoned to the morgue to collect his tortured, bullet-ridden body. The release of the body was conditional on a private burial and soon afterwards Joan and her daughters fled to Britain.

Joan Jara and Víctor's haunting music played a seminal role in Chile Soli-darity. I met her then and again decades later when she visited Britain from Santiago, where she had returned in 1983. In 2009, Victor's body would be exhumed on a judge's orders. When he was reburied thousands turned out for the funeral.

My political activities were increasing and Keith's career was going from strength to strength. He acquired more and more PhD students and gave immensely popular lectures to undergraduates. Invitations to international conferences multiplied and whenever I could I went with him. Over the years we travelled to most European capitals and to the US. Our lives were happy and stimulating and we were settled in Burghfield. We made local friends, went frequently to private views at Pat's gallery and concerts when we could. Keith made a couple more visits to Venezuela to further his collaboration with Gunnar. I further developed my interests in housing, giving a short course of lectures at the FE college in Oxford.

By 1997 I was chair of the local Labour Party and we were two years away from the next general election. Our very good friends Eleni and James Cubitt argued for a local candidate who could raise visibility and work hard. I was asked to step up to the plate.

Attributing an importance to the local general election contest that it didn't warrant, I decided to look for a job in Newbury. I applied for a post advertised with the Manpower Services Commission programme, helping unemployed young people. It was based at Berkshire County Council's local careers office. It proved to be the only boring job of my life. After running my own show at OXHAC, I found the constraints of a local authority stifling. The staff were perfectly nice but the young people were lacking in spirit and work was hard to find in rural Berkshire. We did our best and probably did some good, but it was politics that sustained me.

Around the same time, I realised my biological clock was ticking and we began to think that my failure to become pregnant needed investigation. We went through the usual tests and discussions and found the whole process deeply disturbing. I began to doubt whether we wanted a child enough to cope with the medicalised sex we were being asked to undertake. One day I went to the Royal Berkshire Hospital to collect the results of some routine tests and was seen by a woman doctor, probably ten years my junior. She looked at the results and told me they had an abnormally high reading. I asked what this might mean, to which she replied, nonchalantly, 'a brain tumour'. I managed to remain calm and asked her what would happen next. She gave me a form and said I would need an X-ray, which could be done later in the day. And after that? I asked. 'If necessary you will be referred to the John Radcliffe in Oxford,' she responded. 'We don't do brain surgery here.'

I needed to find a phone box to ring the office and explain why I wouldn't be in work. I crossed a busy road, realising, as I reached the other side, that it was a miracle I hadn't been run over. The results were to come through in a week. We lived in torment and, although mightily relieved when the results proved negative, we were angry. There had been no explanation or discussion and we certainly didn't ever want to go back to the clinic.

In 1978 my sister Susan decided to give up her job in the Education Department in Bristol as she wanted to have children. She had previously had a rather exciting job working for the First Boston Corporation when they lived in London carrying Bearer Bonds to various European cities. She was now talking of doing an Open University arts degree, which would give her more choice in employment and fit in with bringing up kids.

Three years previously the IRA had resumed their bombing campaign in London targeting stores, the tube and train stations. Lives were lost and then the most shocking event occurred at the House of Commons. Airey Neave, the Tory shadow Northern Ireland Secretary, was killed by the INLA, who planted a bomb under his car in the Commons car park. No one seemed to have the slightest idea how to bring an end to this conflict.

I was now Labour's candidate for the Newbury constituency, and my campaign received a great boost when the national party made a recruitment poster using a photograph of me speaking at conference. My election address listed the Labour government's achievements – control of prices, bringing inflation down from 26 per cent to 10 per cent, supporting programmes for the unemployed, increasing pensions, introducing child benefit and new benefits for disabled people. I also included improvements in working conditions introduced through the Health and Safety at Work Act 1974 and the setting up of the British National Oil company to secure the profits from North Sea oil.

The Tories then (as now) were fighting on a platform of huge reductions in public expenditure to fund tax cuts and higher charges for dental work and prescriptions. Being the naive idealists that we were, we paid no attention to the poll results for the '74 elections. The incumbent Tory MP, Michael McNair-Wilson, had beaten the Liberal candidate by just 1,000 votes at both elections. Now, five years later, this was a Liberal target seat with the squeeze on us.

The Liberals were determined to win the seat and dirty tricks abounded. One leaflet was circulated stating that I had secretly agreed to advise Labour voters to vote Liberal. Reports came back that I was being impersonated in phone calls with the message that I wanted my supporters to vote Liberal. We reported the matter to the authorities and the atmosphere soured. At the count, the Tory vote had risen significantly while the Liberals' was reduced. Tony Richards, the Liberal candidate, threw an insulting remark in my direction and nearly provoked a fist fight with Keith. I lost my deposit but I'd got the bug. I knew I would want to stand again.

Much more serious than my defeat was the defeat of the Callaghan government and the election of Margaret Thatcher. Her success was mirrored in the US a year later when Republican Ronald Reagan defeated Jimmy Carter. The '80s thus ushered in a new era of right-wing politics, new economic ideologies and a deepening of the Cold War.

My campaign over, I was job hunting again, looking for a new challenge. It came in the form of the Citizens Advice Bureau. The Reading branch needed a new manager. I applied and got an interview. My political activities were discussed and I was able to give an undertaking of my professionalism and ability to be impartial in the job. I got it. The CAB nationally recognised the need to improve the quality of advice given, to ensure its objectivity and accuracy. I could see this was necessary in Reading but I proceeded with care.

When I became the parliamentary candidate for Newbury I decided I ought to investigate policy areas of which I had no prior knowledge. An obvious one was defence. Ever since the Cuban Missile Crisis of 1962 there had been an on/off dialogue between the two superpowers and attempts to place limits on strategic nuclear weaponry. I decided to contact the Campaign for Nuclear Disarmament (CND) in order to learn more. The received wisdom of the time (and still held by many today) was that mutually assured destruction (MAD) acted as a deterrent and guaranteed peace. Having read CND's literature, however, I was inclined to believe that MAD was just that and a terrible threat to our real security. Defence was not, however, an issue in the election and I thought little more about it.

In December, Keith made another visit to Venezuela to further his collaboration with Gunnar and suggested I joined him for a short holiday. I really wanted to go but I'd never flown alone before. I made an appointment with my GP and explained the problem. He was sympathetic and gave me a small supply of Valium. Sabire and Mustapha lived near Heathrow and so I asked Mustapha to take me to the airport to ensure I got on the flight.

The journey was a nightmare and I had to change planes in Miami. I went to the ladies' room and saw myself in the mirror. My eyes were bright red. The maximum dose of Valium with an excess of alcohol was probably not a good thing and I had to do the rest of the journey without props.

IVIC (Instituto Venezolano de Investigaciones Científicas) was a stunning place set on the top of a mountain. There was little of interest in Caracas itself but driving through the heavily forested slopes was magical. Of all the many interesting and unusual people with whom Keith was working, one researcher was particularly engaging – a Venezuelan agronomist called Rafael Herrera, who spent much of his time making dangerous trips to the Amazon and told us of a lucky escape from death by coral snake. His lovely wife Gunn-Marie was Dutch and they had three small children. I liked them very much and when they later came to the UK for a year's sabbatical they found a rented house near us in Burghfield where their fourth child was born.

Another colleague offered to take us to his family's holiday home, which was set in forest next to the seashore. We accepted with alacrity, little knowing how tortuous the car journey would be as we climbed for hours up roads that never stopped turning until I was completely dizzy. When finally we descended and reached the other side we could see the incredible blue of the ocean and it was all worth it. The house was made of brick with ventilation holes just above floor level. It was serenely cool compared to the fierce temperatures outside but there was a very strong smell of kerosene. Our hosts apologised for this but told us it was necessary to coat the floor to keep out the many deadly snakes that inhabited the jungle! As I have an absolute horror of snakes, this was not great news.

We spent a wonderful afternoon on the silver sands picking up coconuts that had fallen from the palm trees and swimming in the gloriously warm turquoise water. We went indoors for a fine supper and commented on the unusual metal disks hanging from the ceiling, thinking they must be an art installation, though they looked rather rough. We were told that they were there to interfere with the radar of the vampire bats that could enter the house at night. Only a large quantity of red wine offered me any chance of being able to sleep and I was so glad it was only one night.

After a few more days we were off for another adventure, from Caracas to Lima with a stopover in Quito airport. The latter was an extraordinary experience. We walked straight off the plane into a marketplace where every stall was displaying emeralds. It was quite unbelievable, a veritable Aladdin's cave, but unfortunately beyond our means. We found Lima a fine city with a great historical centre made up of the Plaza Mayor and colonial architectural gems including the cathedral, the Monastery of San Francisco and the Convent of Santo Domingo.

The many museums focused on pre-Columbian art, which was what we were most interested in. Keith also had to see the national university as he was photographing ancient universities all over the world, hoping one day to produce a book of colour plates together with the histories of the buildings. The University of San Marcos was founded in 1551 and is the oldest continuously functioning university in the Americas. It was a beautiful building. There was obviously a lot of poverty and migrants in the city. Local potters were selling their wares on the street and I bought a small dish with a simple design, which I guess was a pre-Columbian copy. We left Lima and flew on to Cusco, which was the site of the historic capital of the Inca Empire. It was built in the Urubamba valley, which meant a terrifying descent between the mountains of the high Andes.

There was just too much to see in this small city, beginning with the magnificent Plaza de Armas. There were Inca remains everywhere but mainly foundations and walls built upon by the Spanish conquerors of four centuries ago. We felt affronted by the underlying destruction and less inclined to visit the great cathedral and churches that were obviously fine architecture in their own right. There were lots of artisans working in the Barrio de San Blas and I was particularly taken by the silver work. Everything was very cheap and I bought a slim smoke-coloured glass vase with Inca designs etched in silver.

On our first night we were exhausted and looked forward to dinner in our hotel. We ordered a bottle of wine, which appeared to be an unusual request. After a long search a bottle covered in thick dust was produced. It was a strong delicious red and we consumed the lot. Later I woke with an extreme headache and remembered that we were 11,000 feet up and I probably had altitude sickness exacerbated by the wine. Luckily I recovered the next day and after more sightseeing we took the train to Machu Picchu.

Machu Picchu's unique location in a saddle between two mountains 7,000 feet up created a spectacular vista. We had read up on its fabulous history and its rediscovery in 1911 by Hiram Bingham. A lot of restoration work had taken place since then and the site was just breathtakingly beautiful. I was so thrilled as we climbed to the highest point that I ran up the last few steps, only to pass out momentarily because of the altitude. The buildings dated from around 1450 and although later abandoned and ruined, the dry stone walls were remarkably well preserved, giving the clearest outlines of what the whole settlement would have looked like. There were around 200 dwellings, a massive tower, religious and royal buildings, vast terraces for agriculture, channelled water and the so called Inca trail, which still allowed tourists to walk the several days journey from Cusco. Ours was a truly magical day and one of the most memorable visits of our lives.

While nothing could ever compare with Machu Picchu we were not finished. We spent a day in the splendid city of Arequipa with its unique blend of European and native architecture. The historic centre was a feast for the eyes, being built largely of the local volcanic stone, which was pink or pearly in colour, and we visited the chapels and convent of Santa Domingo. Our final visit was to Puno in the far south of Peru, situated between the shores of Lake Titicaca and the surrounding mountains. It is cooled by its high altitude and the sunlight is intense. For the first time we were seeing an agricultural community with native Indian women in traditional dress and bowler hats tending their herds on the mountainsides. Alpaca, lamas and sheep provided the yarn of the very colourful textiles on sale in the markets. We couldn't resist some souvenirs but our aim was to sail on the lake.

Lake Titicaca is the highest navigable lake in the world and it was a thrilling sight. Fortunately, Keith knew a little Spanish so he was able to negotiate a trip for us in a coracle-type boat oared by a local. The sky was a deep azure blue and we were thrilled to set off across the lake with hardly a sound or breeze in the air. Just as we were thoroughly relaxed and enchanted by the scenery we saw water seeping up from the wooden base of the craft. Our boat man got a metal scoop and casually started to throw water overboard while still taking us away from the shore. We began to feel distinctly uneasy. Keith didn't swim and we feared the lake might be full of piranhas. Our beautiful relaxing afternoon at an end, we insisted on being taken back and with a seriously water-logged boat we made it to the shore not a moment too soon. Time to end our South American adventure and return home for a family Christmas.

Chapter Four

# CND

*'War does not determine who is right – only who is left.'*

– BERTRAND RUSSELL

While we were away, NATO announced that 572 US Pershing II missiles and ground-launched Cruise missiles would be deployed in Europe in retaliation for the Soviet deployment of SS-20s. One hundred and sixty US missiles would be based in Britain. Then the Soviet Union invaded Afghanistan to prop up its Marxist regime. Tension grew and people began to speculate where in Britain US missiles would be based. By the New Year people were beginning to mobilise in East Anglia and in Oxford where US bases had remained since the Second World War. When Parliament returned after the Christmas recess there was further shocking news. The Labour government, elected on a commitment to run down Britain's own nuclear fleet, had secretly spent £1 billion on its modernisation. The result of these revelations was a sharp increase in CND's membership and a planned Labour Party march in June.

West Germany (Germany was divided into East and West until 1990), the Netherlands, Belgium and Italy were also destined to receive US weapons, prompting the noted academic Edward Thompson, Mary Kaldor and others to set up European Nuclear Disarmament (END) in February 1980. END did not seek to become a mass movement but rather to appeal to people east and west to reject nuclear weapons.

Further deadly secrets were emerging. *Panorama* exposed the existence of a government film entitled *Protect and Survive*, which was to be transmitted in the event of a nuclear war. Journalists such as Duncan Campbell gave further exposure to government civil defence plans. These included internment for activists if nuclear war seemed likely and executions if necessary for the maintenance of law and order after a nuclear exchange.

My life had settled into a much more relaxed routine centred around work, the Labour Party and visits to friends and family. At CAB, my deputy Jackie Griffiths and I were making changes and working closely with the regional staff and the National Association of Citizens Advice Bureaux (NACAB). On 17 June 1980, after attending one of the regular area meetings, I got to the station in time to buy a local newspaper for my return journey. The headline jumped off the front page: 'US missiles for Greenham Common'.

My heart sank – I wasn't ready for another campaign. But by the time I reached Reading I knew there was no option. As soon as I got home I rang Geoff Peppiatt, our Labour Party secretary. We announced we were setting up the 'Newbury Campaign Against Cruise Missiles'. We acknowledged we were Labour activists, but stressed it would be non-partisan and open to anyone. We got front-page stories in the local press but nothing else happened, so we decided to write to *The Guardian*, explaining our case against the missiles. There was a huge response from all over the country; our campaign was truly launched. Thatcher's government had not only announced the sites for the American weapons but also the government's intention to buy the Trident nuclear missile system. CND was resurgent and our local campaign, although not unilateralist, agreed to work with them.

The MoD made an extraordinary decision. They would come to Newbury to explain to stakeholders the reasons for siting the weapons at Greenham

Common. The hapless Francis Pym, Secretary of State for Defence, was dispatched to the meeting at the Newbury Racecourse. It was a ticket-only affair but my status as past parliamentary candidate guaranteed me a place. It was surreal. We were given a glossy brochure, all blue skies and white fluffy clouds with pictures of the missile launchers. The text contained the chilling sentence: 'The aim of using them would be to persuade the Russian leadership, even at the eleventh hour, to draw back.' Thus Cruise missiles were firmly established as first-strike, war-fighting weapons and the nuclear war would be in Europe.

It's hard for people who didn't live through that era to imagine how real the threat was. For decades, the Soviet Union had made huge efforts to match every advance in nuclear weaponry made by the US and they then had over 50,000 nuclear weapons between them. The 1962 Cuban Missile Crisis had not faded from memory and the 1968 Soviet invasion of Czechoslovakia had proved the ruthlessness of the regime. Tension between the superpowers mounted as more and more bellicose statements emanated from the Reagan camp.

Those of us who set out to oppose the missiles made it our business to learn the detailed facts about the warheads, their payloads, their delivery systems and the consequences of their use. Eminent scientists and medics were quick to join in, providing invaluable briefings and subsequently setting up their own campaigns, Scientists Against Nuclear Arms (SANA) and the Medical Campaign Against Nuclear Weapons (MCANW). Very soon many campaigners knew more about nuclear strategy than those who defended it. The year of 1980 saw the thirty-fifth anniversary of the US atomic bombing of the Japanese cities of Hiroshima and Nagasaki in 1945. It was marked all over Britain, exposing the myth that nuclear weapons would never be used.

CND called its first demonstration in years for 26 October. I had already been co-opted onto the CND National Council because of my activities in Newbury, and now I was asked to address the rally. The content was not difficult – I had only to refer to the MOD brochure – but I was terrified. As I advanced towards the microphone at the edge of the plinth in Trafalgar Square, I felt physically sick. For a moment I thought I might topple over the edge into the 80,000-strong crowd. It was my first significant rally speech. I made it. The day was a triumph for CND and as Edward Thompson urged 'feel your strength', so we did.

The local campaign in Newbury was attracting a lot of attention, particularly from overseas broadcasters who wanted to film the base and interview me. Fortunately, our home in Burghfield Common was halfway between Newbury and Reading so I could get up very early, drive to the base and still be back in time for the day's work at Reading. I was scrupulous about my time but it required precision management as I would complete a day's work, jump on a train for London CND's HQ and get back home by 11 p.m.

Ours was not the only campaign attracting media attention. Roger and Sue Spiller were prime movers in setting up East Anglia CND. With RAF Molesworth in their area they had a ready focus. Roger was a trade union organiser and long-time CND member who had worked at both Aldermaston and Harwell. Sue was a teacher and they had two small children, but for years they worked selflessly for the movement.

Our CAB was going from strength to strength. As the 1980s recession began to hit Reading (the Silicon Valley of its day) more and more people turned to the CAB. Jackie Griffiths brought a wealth of counselling experience with her and put it to good use in our training for volunteers. In those days many women stayed at home longer with young children and we decided to target this group. We reckoned they might welcome an outside challenge and see volunteering as a preparation for a return to work. We were right. Women came forward in large numbers. We organised group interviewing sessions, testing out people's values and attitudes. It was vital to find people who would not be judgemental, who would be prepared to learn and who had the stomach for some of the less pleasant encounters with individual clients in a small interview room. We recruited an amazing group of women, all of whom gave their all – compassion, intellect and unfailing commitment to cover their shifts.

Keith and I continued to visit our families as often as we could. I was now well used to driving to Pontypool (I tried repeatedly but failed to persuade Keith to learn). The M4 motorway, only ten years old, was close to the house and traffic was free-flowing. My parents had moved from our council house to a bungalow further down Penygarn Hill. Most importantly, Dad still had ownership of two allotments, which were five minutes' walk away. These were his pride and joy and sustained him in his retirement (retirement at sixty-two was compulsory).

Just as the rewards for a lifetime of hard work were on offer, however, my father's health gave cause for concern. He suffered a series of small strokes, none of which fortunately left him with permanent impairment. He'd been resolute in giving up smoking the moment his arterial sclerosis was diagnosed, but now he required hospital treatment. I left my mother and Keith at his bedside and went to see the consultant. He explained they could do nothing to reverse the damage to his arteries and a pattern of small strokes and possible heart attacks was to be expected.

My grandmother, who was now ninety and nearly blind, was also ailing. Since my grandfather died eleven years before, she had been living with her daughter Bette and her husband Ray in Barry. I could see she was slipping away and made a last visit. She died peacefully at home in 1981. Her death was keenly felt by my mother who was devoted to her. Her funeral was held at the Croesyceiliog crematorium where my grandfather was previously cremated. She was to be much missed.

Some months later, Keith was invited to a conference in Mexico to be held at a beach resort in Cancun, a place we'd never heard of. The attraction was not the beach but the opportunity to explore the culture of the ancient Mesoamerican civilisations. It was a joke in our house that I did all the basic jobs like buying houses, cars and running the household, while Keith took charge of the really important ones, like choosing music and arranging holidays. This one was no exception. We flew to Mexico City and were stunned by the massive highways, clogged with traffic, and the cacophony of noise and exuberance in this hugely populated city.

Our first goal was to visit the site of the ancient city of Teotihuacan, founded around 200BC. It was a spectacular place, having a long, central roadway called the Street of the Dead, with the Great Pyramid of the Moon at one end and the even larger Pyramid of the Sun to one side. These were colossal structures and the huge scale of the place was overwhelming. Other buildings and platforms indicate a great market, apartments for thousands of residents, a palace and the Pyramid of the Feathered Serpent. The latter is six stories high with extraordinary great sculptures of the heads of feathered serpents at each level. Having never realised that great pyramids were to be found outside of Egypt, I was stunned by what we were seeing.

Our stay in Mexico City was short but we got to sample the food in one of its famous restaurants. Keith ordered the speciality – chicken in chocolate sauce – while I settled for a 'safe' steak and chips. I took my first bite and felt a piercing pain in my palate. As I recovered, a warm feeling of well-being spread from my brain to my body. The steak was garnished with tiny chillies that were definitely a drug of choice. I didn't take to the chocolate sauce, so for our next few nights we happily repeated our individual experiences.

We travelled south from Mexico City into the jungle where the temperature was in the eighties with humidity to match. I'd never experienced such conditions and soon found myself in saturated clothes. Our stay was to be brief so we took an organised tour to the ruins of Palenque. A much smaller site but with some of the very best Mayan carving, it made for another memorable visit. Our tour completed, we were taken to an outdoor restaurant in the jungle where we were served a highly spiced, moist dish of chicken and fruit cooked in banana leaves. Utterly delicious, but we paid for it the next day.

We travelled on to our final destination, the remains of the great Mayan city of Chichen Itza, in existence from 600–1200AD. The site was organised into giant platforms supporting many buildings, all connected by paved roadways. There were two outstanding features, the Great Ball Court and the colossal step pyramid, El Castillo. Most archaeological evidence points to a game between two teams using a heavy rubber ball and possibly some kind of stick or racquet. Chichen Itza has the largest known ball court, 168 by 70 metres, with walls standing eight metres high. Set high up at right angles in each of the walls was a huge stone ring carved with serpents. It had sinister associations: the Great Ball Court panels depicted the decapitation of players. At one end of the court we saw a typical Mayan statue of a Chac Mool – a figure on its back with knees drawn up and supporting itself on raised elbows. We were told this was a place of human sacrifice. There was also the suggestion that, rather than a rubber ball, a severed head was used in the games. Gruesome but fascinating.

El Castillo, or the Temple of Kukulkan, again displaying carved winged serpent heads, was equally unforgettable. At nearly thirty metres high the climb was a challenge, but infinitely worth the effort. The pyramid also held a very special treasure that it was possible to visit. Keith, intrepid as ever, went. I stayed. Even he came back shaken. The narrow stair plummeted at a steep angle but at the bottom was the most extraordinary sight – a Chac Mool statue and a throne in the shape of a jaguar, painted red with spots made of inlaid jade. Needless to say it's not possible to make that visit today.

Our great adventure over, we attended the scientific conference of which I remember nothing except for an ambulance in the middle of the night carrying away another victim of Montezuma's revenge.

Some time before we left for Mexico I'd been contacted by a woman called Ann Pettit. She told me she was going to organise a walk from Cardiff to Greenham Common to protest against Cruise missiles and wanted support from the local group. I was delighted to be able to promise whatever was needed but regretted that I was unlikely to be around when they arrived. On my return, I found the women (and a few men) hadn't left. Arriving on 5 September, they had been infuriated by the refusal of government ministers to debate with them and disappointed with their lack of media coverage. So they chained themselves to the perimeter fence and vowed not to leave.

Thus 'Women for Life on Earth' began what was to become the Greenham Common Women's Peace Camp, which would remain in one form or another for the next nineteen years. Having decided to stay, the women's first request to me was for a Portakabin. I found one, and it was duly driven onto the land outside the perimeter fence. Crucially, the women agreed that the men who had been on the march should be asked to leave and no men be allowed to stay overnight in future. Greenham was to become the greatest feminist movement of the latter part of the twentieth century.

It was a lovely autumn and my parents made a rare visit to Burghfield Common. We had a happy time and I presented my father with a straw hat I'd bought for him in Mexico. When it was time for them to leave I hugged him, conscious of his strong, bony body and the slightly salty tang of his suntanned face. It was to be our last goodbye.

Despite the trip to Mexico I'd managed to save some holiday days to enable me to go to the Labour Party conference in Brighton and do some CND fringe meetings. I left very early to return on the Friday morning. As I drove into the CAB car park someone shouted to me to come in quickly. My sister was on the phone: my father was dead. It was a terrible shock. I'd expected further ill health but not sudden death. How would my mother cope? She was only sixty and just beginning to enjoy my father's freedom from the stresses of factory life. I went directly to Paddington, not trusting myself to drive, and got picked up by Susan and David at Bristol Parkway.

The funeral directors were in the house when I arrived. After embracing and talking with my mother I stepped out into the hallway and saw the shocking sight of my father's body being carried away in a rolled-up old carpet. The days passed in a haze of arrangements with many tears and broken nights. I went to the funeral parlour to pay my last respects. Through my tears I smiled as I saw my father's hands, laid formally across his body. There was thick soil under his long, hard fingernails. He had died on returning home from his precious allotment. Somehow I thought it fitting that he took a bit of it to the grave. He was cremated at Croesyceiliog in a simple ceremony with all the family present, followed by a funeral tea at home. I was given time off to stay with my mother a bit longer, to help with the transition to life in an empty house. It was an important grieving time for all of us.

Later that month, CND held its biggest ever demonstration to date. I now came under pressure to stand for the chair of CND, but with a full-time job and a widowed mother it really wasn't the time. The only declared candidate was Dr John Cox, for years a central figure in CND and a man who had kept the faith when the movement was in decline. But he was a member of the Communist Party and felt it essential that he fought a contested election, so he persuaded me to stand, expecting that I would subsequently become a vice-chair. Cathy Ashton* (later to be replaced by Mick Elliot) was treasurer and a supporter of John, so I thought becoming one of a strong team of officers would be manageable.

I was readily identified with the Greenham women, both because of my physical proximity in Newbury and my own feminist credentials. I knew this wouldn't be popular in some parts of the movement as many of the activists were political and trade union men who found the concept of women-only spaces alien. To my utter surprise, however, I was elected chair at the November AGM and Roger Spiller was elected vice-chair. I was warmly embraced by our General Secretary, Monsignor Bruce Kent, a Catholic priest. Suddenly I had a huge responsibility to fulfil.

The winter of 1981 was the first big test for the peace camp. Outside the perimeter fence the collection of caravans and Portakabins grew and a large communal space was developed for meetings and visitors. I visited frequently and made friends with Helen John, Fran De'Ath, Lynne Jones and Rebecca Johnson. I found the cold unbearable. I was often ashamed of my overwhelming desire to get back into my car and a warm home. But, like the growing army of supporters, I was utterly inspired by the women who lived there.

At CND, we had constant policy decisions to make, fundraising campaigns to arrange, literature to write and endless speaking engagements to fulfil as groups organised in all parts of the country.

Nuclear physicist Professor Tom Kibble from Imperial College and Professor Mike Pentz of the Open University provided vital scientific briefings through SANA and Mike soon joined us on the National Council. They gave

---

* Later Baroness Ashton and EU Foreign Minister.

us chapter and verse on not only the weaponry and the catastrophic consequences of its use, but also the ineffectiveness of civil defence. It was the latter
that drew many local authorities into the ambit of the peace movement. The
Tory government had persisted in its policy of encouraging local authorities
to build nuclear bunkers. One such authority was Mid Glamorgan, where
protestors showed enormous courage as they lay on the high walls of the
bunker while workmen continued to pour concrete. The site was 'blacked'
by trade unions and eventually the bunker building was abandoned. Other
local authorities then decided to open their bunkers for public inspection.
Civil nuclear defence became a subject of derision, not least at the hands of
the popular comedian Jasper Carrott. Oblivious to the success of the nuclear-
free movement, the government planned a nationwide civil defence exercise
for 1982, codenamed 'Hard Rock'. In the event, so many local authorities
refused to take part that the government was forced to abandon it.

By 1982, CND had enormous calls on its resources and demands for
assistance and support. It was essential to develop clear principles and guidelines through motions at annual conference. One of the most contentious
was direct action, i.e. law breaking. We made the brave decision to commit
the whole movement to supporting non-violent direct action in the pursuit
of opposition to nuclear weapons. We also made it clear that we opposed all
nuclear weapons, East and West. Despite this, the right-wing press constantly
accused us of bias, of taking Kremlin gold and in effect being traitors to our
country. They hounded Bruce Kent, who fought back tenaciously – always
casting an eye over his shoulder at the hierarchy of the Catholic Church.
As my tasks became clearer, I decided to ask my CAB chair Jill Pitkeathley
(later Baroness Pitkeathley) whether I could work a four-day week. Jackie
was happy to do an extra day and it would enable me to eke out my holiday
entitlement to cover necessary overseas visits.

I put my new flexibility to good use by joining a CND delegation to Moscow
that was led by former minister Hugh Jenkins. I could stay for only a couple of
days but Bruce, Roger and Sue would stay on. Before we left we had a meeting

with Zhores Medvedev, a biochemist whose challenge to the Soviet authorities over nuclear waste had led to his passport being cancelled while at a conference in the UK. Now unable to return home, he asked us to see his brother Roy and take a gift for him. We stayed at the Ukraina Hotel, which Russians were not normally allowed to enter, so we had to alert the staff and send our interpreter to meet Roy. Just before our visitor was due we got a knock on the door – an electrician had come to change the lightbulb! Our meeting went well and we all laughed at the fact that we knew they were listening.

Mass demonstrations took months to organise in the days before mobile phones, emails and social media. Letters had to be sent and leaflets and posters distributed for display. Our next demonstration was planned for 6 June 1982. The timing was fixed as part of the international preparations for a UN Special Session on Disarmament. Little did we know that by then Britain would be at war with Argentina over the Falkland Islands.

A quarter of a million people turned out in London and only five people withdrew their membership because of CND's opposition to the Falklands War. Six days later, Bruce addressed a rally of nearly 1 million in the US. Even in the Soviet Union they demonstrated, mostly in opposition to NATO, but a few banners said (in Russian) 'For a nuclear-free Europe', implicitly criticising the Soviet deployment of SS-20s.

At this time the BBC had a TV series called *Man Alive*, in which they threw someone into the proverbial lion's den and they suggested they fly me to Chicago to debate with the American Legion. I accepted with trepidation. Brigadier Michael Harbottle, who had joined the campaign, agreed to be my seconder. No sooner had I accepted than CND got an invitation to address the UN General Assembly. This would mean my going to the States two weeks running, each time flying out one day, performing the next and then returning the day after.

In Chicago, Hugh Purcell, the producer, explained the format, to be chaired by a youthful presenter called Nick Ross. We would put our case for nuclear disarmament and then enter into discussion. Our audience was, predictably, convinced that deterrence had 'kept the peace' despite the many proxy wars fought by the superpowers. They also asserted that the US was behind the Soviet Union in weaponry while all independent analysis said the opposite. Our strongest suit was that Cruise and Pershing were first-strike weapons and as such fundamentally undermining of deterrence, which is based on a threat to retaliate. If deterrence failed, the nuclear holocaust would be on our soil, not in the US.

It was a thrilling event, housed in a kind of hut at American Legion Post 134. I melted under the lights and my bare legs were eaten alive by mosquitoes. Outwardly we keep our cool, even when a big burly guy got up from the front row in anger and took off his jacket. We expected him to throw a punch at Michael but he resumed his seat. It's assumed I am a disgraceful pacifist. We were coming to the end of the programme when one of the very senior men made a much quieter contribution – one of those more in sorrow than anger. He talked of appeasement in the 1930s and how Britain became pacifist and how it's clear we were doing the same again with the arguments we had put forward. Michael was outraged at this and started to reply but Nick Ross interjected and asked for my opinion. I said if Britain were invaded I would be in the resistance and would fight, but what I could not do was accept that millions of Britons should die in a nuclear exchange. That was not pacifism. When the programme was broadcast it ended very effectively with this passionate statement, but of course there was no meeting of minds. The *Radio Times* carried a really fun cartoon depicting Michael and me climbing to a summit with a flag captioned 'Peace Through Disarmament' and a troop of Legionnaires on the other side with a flag captioned 'Arm for Peace'. Hugh Purcell gave me the original and it still hangs in the bathroom today.

Back in London I was preparing my speech for the UN when news came through of yet another IRA bombing. This time an army barracks was hit and eleven people were killed. Nowhere in London felt safe. My speech had to be timed to exactly nine minutes and I felt overawed at the thought of delivering it. CND's resources didn't allow for a minder so Keith offered to come with me. We joined the line at immigration (not the first time for either of us). I went up and answered the usual questions. When I said the purpose of my visit the official called to a colleague 'she's going to that conference'. After a short discussion I was led away with Keith following. I was then grilled about my job and other personal details. The officer left and I wondered if CAB was on the list of subversive organisations. A puzzled officer returned so I volunteer that CND might be of interest. Then he demanded to know what I was going to say in my speech. I was incensed. This was the UN I was going to, but I had to stay calm. We'd heard that delegates from certain organisations had already been turned back. I said I would speak about peace. Then it was Keith's turn – 'open your briefcase'. My heart sank. Keith always carried his work around. His briefcase opened to pages and pages of mathematical calculations. After examining the lot, the official snapped the briefcase shut and said 'have a nice day' as he waved us on.

We were met by Cora Weiss, a peace activist and major movement donor who was very welcoming and whisked us off to a dinner party. I was struggling to stay awake and worried about my speech. That day's session had been addressed by both Ronald Reagan and Margaret Thatcher. The following day was the turn of NGOs including CND.

I was trembling and overawed to be looking out into the great hall of the General Assembly. I delivered the speech well and to time and was warmly applauded by representatives of non-aligned states. Delegates rushed up afterwards demanding copies. We hadn't brought any but Keith – pre-warned – went out to a photocopy shop and produced seventy copies. Demand outstripped supply – I was on a high.

Back in the UK we had a critical decision to make. Greenham Women were planning a mass demonstration at the base for December. They wanted CND support but insisted that it be women only. Some men objected, wanting to join in and arguing that they would not be staying, only demonstrating. I had no doubt about what we should do and the decision was taken to give support on the women's terms. This was high stakes. The plan was to embrace the base first and then blockade it the next day. It was estimated that around 30,000 women would be needed to go right round the perimeter fence. The women came. All day they hung mementoes of family – photographs of children, pieces of cloth, toys, flowers – on the fence and then completed the circle. As dusk fell, women at the main gate sat down en masse. There was a moment of silence. No soldiers or police advanced on the crowds. Then there was singing and candles and a few tears. No woman who was there has ever forgotten that day. In the hours of darkness, I drove around the base delivering supplies, exchanging greetings and marvelling at the extraordinary sense of empowerment gained in that peaceful act of defiance.

By now I was frequently appearing on TV and as a consequence I was asked to appear on that most prestigious of programmes, BBC's *Question Time*. I was petrified at the thought. Robin Day was a formidable chairman and the panel were required to have dinner with him before the show. Just before we went on air he picked a fight with me and left me trembling as I went on stage. Unlike today's politicians, I had no one to brief me. During the show, Tory Julian Critchley dismissed me as of no consequence in matters of defence and I ended the evening determined never to go on again. Within days the producer was writing to me to say how many angry letters they had had about Critchley and that I must come back soon.

Going home for Christmas was a sad occasion. A year after my father's death, my mother sold the bungalow perched on the side of Penygarn Hill with its big, west-facing bay windows and beautiful sunsets. She bought a maisonette in Yate, close to my sister Susan and her family. I felt deeply the loss of my father and the separation from the town we had always known as home. I also feared for my mother in her new environment, without any friends or the activities that had previously shaped her life.

'Embrace the Base' had been designed as a mass participation exercise, but many of the Greenham Women were committed to non-violent direct action of a more risky kind. As the sun rose at dawn on New Year's Day 1983, women joined hands and danced on the half-built nuclear silos inside the base, having scaled the razor-wire fences in the dead of night. Forty-four women were charged with breach of the peace but the picture went around the world.

1983 was general election year and attacks on CND escalated dramatically. We repeatedly asked to debate with ministers but to no avail. On one occasion I was invited onto the *Jimmy Young Show*, a popular radio programme at the time, ostensibly for a debate. Then I was told I'd be interviewed first and Michael Heseltine (Secretary of State for Defence) would follow. On leaving the studio I asked to use a phone. As I dialled out an assistant rushed up and begged me to leave. The Secretary of State, who had been listening to the radio in his car, was refusing to enter the building until I had left! Years later I got a report from my friend Pat of a talk he'd given in Henley-on-Thames when he paid tribute to me as an opponent.

At CND we were planning our next big event, a fourteen-mile human chain that would link the nuclear warhead factory at Burghfield to the nuclear research station at Aldermaston and on to Greenham Common (where the link would be all female). It was a tough call, requiring a lot of negotiation with Thames Valley Police. We were all set for Good Friday.

Hysterical media coverage preceded the demonstration, with one tabloid headlined 'Village in CND Siege'. We estimated that 100,000 people would be needed to cover the fourteen-mile route when arms were linked. People of all ages came, from babies in buggies to grandparents on sticks, holding aloft balloons and flowers in an entirely peaceful and good-humoured demonstration. A critical piece in the *Sunday Telegraph* followed, however, prompting a Burghfield grocer living next to the road to write to the editor:

> As a grocer living in Burghfield Common fronting onto the road lined by CND last Good Friday, I feel compelled to state your article last Sunday commenting on the rubbish left is totally untrue.
>
> In actual fact, Burghfield Common has not been as clean and tidy in the eleven months I have lived here as it was the morning after the demonstration.

Customers coming into the shop on Saturday morning, a great many of whom were very anti and hostile earlier in the week, said that in all fairness to CND, they had to be congratulated, first on the behaviour of their people and secondly for the tremendous effort that had obviously been put in to cleaning up the route.

A Thames Valley police officer epitomised the spirit of the day, when late on Friday afternoon, wearing a daffodil given to him by CND, he came into the shop, his face wreathed in a smile, and said what a good day it had been and he would have CND anytime rather than a football crowd, 'You know they're for peace – they won't throw things at you...'

Bruce and I were now in constant demand for speaking engagements abroad as well as at home. Another request fell to me in the form of a speaking tour of the US – nine cities in ten days. For someone who hated flying this was quite an ask. Nevertheless, I would fly to New York, where Cora Weiss had arranged a big event at the Riverside Church, then on to the Midwest, California and back to the east coast. It was an amazing experience. I would be picked up at each airport, taken on a round of media interviews, speak at public meetings, stay with complete strangers before getting on to the next flight. Many of my hosts were active church members but there were also people from little-known left-wing groups and the professions. One night in the Midwest I stayed with a Trotskyist family who fed me on hippy food and put me to sleep in a bed of multi-coloured quilts – the insanitary condition of which I fortunately didn't notice until the morning.

I flew on to Los Angeles where I found the gate for my connection to Santa Barbara. To my utter horror, I saw the plane was a tiny turboprop. Panic. There were two seats on the right-hand side with a man seated at the window. I took the empty seat, hysteria rising. Realising I couldn't deal with this alone, I explained to my neighbour how badly I was feeling and how I hoped I wouldn't disturb him. He was immediately reassuring and offered to hold my hand for take-off. I didn't refuse. Then he told me he worked for NASA. If he had only known he was holding the hand of an 'enemy of the state'. But I had never been more grateful.

Having survived the ordeal, I did my usual round of media and meetings at the university. At the end of the evening I was handed over to a thirty-something man who was to take me home for the night and to the airport in the morning. When we arrived at his apartment it was clear there was no welcoming wife and family. We were alone and I felt distinctly uncomfortable. I managed some desultory conversation over a coffee and then went to my room. There was of course no lock on the door and although there was a landline I realised I had no idea where I was. Being dog tired, I fell asleep despite my unease, only to wake suddenly in the early hours to find my host standing over me. I experienced a moment of terror and gave him a long, hard stare. He mumbled and retreated. Heart pounding, I dressed quickly and went downstairs. With no ability to get out and call a cab I stuck to the agreement and later got in his car. Never was I so relieved to arrive at an airport.

My mammoth tour over, I was waiting for a plane home when my name was called over the public address system. It could only be bad news. I was being warned of a front-page story in the *Sunday Times* entitled 'CND's leading lady in clash over cash cut'. It began: 'The government is cutting back its grant to Citizens Advice Bureaux, partly because of displeasure at the political activities of the chairman of the Campaign for Nuclear Disarmament, Joan Ruddock, who is a bureau employee at Reading.' I couldn't believe what I was hearing. My own conscience was clear but the idea that I was putting the whole CAB service in jeopardy was too horrible to contemplate.

Back in Britain, I went immediately to meet with Lady Ricketts, the chair of NACAB, and Elizabeth Filkin,* the new CEO. They couldn't have been more supportive, as were my own bureau workers and my chair Jill Pitkeath-

---

* Elizabeth went on to an illustrious, though controversial, career that included time spent as Parliamentary Commissioner for Standards.

ley. Apparently the previous summer Dr Gerard Vaughan, the Tory consumer affairs minister, had told NACAB he was unhappy with the quality of some CABs and some people's 'inappropriate political activity'. When pressed to give examples, he had named me. NACAB had asked for details, but none were forthcoming. Unknown to me, they had carried out an internal inquiry and found no case to answer. Nonetheless, in a letter dated 23 March, the minister had informed Lady Ricketts that the grant for the current financial year would be £3 million compared to £6 million the previous year, with further consideration in September. If ever there was a case of political interference at CAB, this was it.

A John Kent cartoon appeared in *The Guardian*, providing a moment of light relief at a very dark time. It depicted Dr Vaughan sitting across the desk from me at the bureau saying, 'I'd like advice on how to sack you.' Another original still hanging on my bathroom wall!

I could do nothing, but Dr Vaughan had stirred a hornets' nest and my virtue was about to be defended in the House of Commons. On 11 April, David Ennals, the Labour MP for Norwich North, raised a point of order in an attempt to get a debate on the NACAB funding. He quoted Elizabeth Filkin, saying that I had been scrupulous in devoting none of my time at the Bureau to political activities. Speaker Thomas refused the debate request.

The next day Dr Vaughan was forced to make a statement to the House. He began by saying that the government had the fullest confidence in the Citizens Advice Bureau movement as a whole (he'd obviously been made aware that thousands of CAB volunteer workers voted Tory). He went on to say that he felt it was proper to enquire whether NACAB 'was being used effectively'. He referred to allegations of 'campaigns that some people have seen as going outside the scope of the service'. Tory MPs piled in to defend the CAB service and Labour MPs pressed him again on the specific references to me. He waffled on, praising CABs and asserting that his actions re NACAB 'have absolutely nothing to do with Mrs Ruddock and the CND movement'.

But then came the Exocet. His Tory neighbour Michael McNair-Wilson, the MP for Newbury who I opposed in the 1979 general election, asked his Honourable Friend to 'accept my delight at his reassurance that there is no suspicion in his mind of any link between CAB and CND ... She is my constituent and I should wish him to know that in my opinion she would never let her zeal for CND affect her work for the Bureau in any way.' To which Vaughan replied: 'I have never implied there was any connection between the CAB movement and the CND movement.' What?!

Labour MPs kept up the pressure at Department of Trade questions on the 25th and Prime Minister's Questions (PMQs) on the 28th. Dr Vaughan was forced to withdraw his 'implied' criticism and after the June general election he lost his job in the reshuffle and NACAB's grant was doubled. How different things would have been for me but for the courage and integrity of NACAB's chief personnel.

Demonstrations grew all over the country while government attacks continued unabated. Michael Heseltine wrote to all Tory candidates giving details of leading CND personalities and painting us all as agents of a left-wing conspiracy. Bruce Kent, our General Secretary, could not be labelled as a political activist so he was portrayed as a naive idealist who had been duped by the Russians. Cruel cartoons appeared and accusations of accepting 'Russian gold' were frequent. Public opinion polls consistently showed majority opposition to Cruise missiles but CND's voice wasn't heard in the mainstream debate. Margaret Thatcher was returned to office with an increased majority.

Some good news. Susan completed her OU course and got a BA. I was amazed at her commitment – I really don't think I would have had the discipline to work from home. She was to follow it up with a PGCE so she could become a primary school teacher. Ten years on she would take an MA – I really admired her effort.

On 22 October, CND held its biggest ever demonstration in Hyde Park, recorded as 1 million people by the BBC when I did an anniversary interview thirty years later. On the morning of the demonstration, *The Guardian* published a leaked document giving the date for the arrival of Cruise missiles at Greenham as 1 November, despite the fact that disarmament negotiations were underway in Geneva. The government planned to keep the missiles' arrival secret until Michael Heseltine made a statement to the House.

Despite the huge surge in support for the peace movement, the next day the *Sunday Times* headlined the demonstration 'Sunset for CND' and predicted that its 'outer fringes could now turn to increasingly desperate activities'. It was, however, the media that turned increasingly to desperate tactics. One day I got a call from a tabloid reporter who told me she had some really important information that she couldn't give me over the phone. This I understood as we all suspected that CND was under surveillance and possibly phone-tapped. I agreed to meet her after work one evening in a café of her choosing. She leaned across the table and told me, 'confidentially', that stories were circulating of an affair between Bruce Kent and myself. She held my astonished gaze and said she would guarantee sympathetic treatment if I told her my story. I wanted to laugh out loud but I realised how serious it was. I was happily married and Bruce was a Catholic priest. How would we prove a negative? I gathered my wits, told her there was absolutely no truth in the stories, she would find no proof and that CND would definitely sue if her paper printed any such lies. In the event they didn't, but the *Daily Mail* printed a tiny diary item noting that Bruce and I were 'enjoying candle-lit dinners'. It certainly was true that we had gone to discuss some confidential business in a convenient café after a CND meeting and they did indeed have tea lights on the tables!

In the country our popularity grew, such that we were both nominated for the BBC annual poll of the Man and Woman of the Year. Margaret Thatcher won but rumour had it that actually I did! I was certainly the runner-up and apparently some nominations were disqualified because they were said to have been organised on a bus full of Greenham women! Who knows?!

On 17 December, the IRA bombed Harrods. Six people were killed and ninety injured.

With the imminent arrival of Cruise missiles at Greenham, Michael Heseltine warned that armed guards might shoot protestors who entered secure areas.

When the missiles did arrive, women at Greenham wept in anger and frustration. Press hysteria reached a climax with the notable headlines 'CND plan shooting of a "peace martyr"' and 'CND holding hands with IRA'. The former claimed that we had volunteers who had agreed to be shot and wounded by colleagues to create an incident at the base. The latter was more serious. It referred to two small spontaneous and non-violent demos organised by London CND groups on 20 December to mark the first mobilisation of US missiles on British roads. While Londoners were understandably nervous, there could be no justification for linking these peaceful demonstrations with lethal bombings. Four months later, the Press Council ruled in favour of CND and called the headline 'irresponsible in the extreme'.

The MoD had claimed that Cruise missiles, when deployed, would melt into the countryside,* but we were determined they would not. An elaborate communications network was devised between women at the base and local activists to sound the alarm every time the missiles went on manoeuvres. Meanwhile, the authorities took every possible measure to remove the Greenham peace camps. Through a series of court actions, all of the caravans were removed from the site. The result was that the women built themselves igloo-shaped benders – tree branches covered with polythene. No one could quite believe they would continue to sleep in these exposed conditions throughout the winter, but they did.

Direct action and evictions at Greenham and elsewhere over these years led to hundreds of people being arrested and numerous Greenham women were repeatedly incarcerated in Holloway prison. CND tactics switched in 1984 to highlighting the extent of American bases and facilities in the UK. With 135 of them, there was scope for every CND group in the country to participate. There was increasing focus, too, on Molesworth in rural Cambridgeshire, which had been designated the second Cruise missile base in England.

---

\* The launchers on which they were mounted were fifty-four feet long and eight feet wide and travelled in convoys.

Ever since its resurgence following the NATO decision to deploy US nuclear weapons in Europe, CND had cooperated with sister movements in Western Europe. In Germany, the charismatic founder of Die Grünen (the Green Party), Petra Kelly, had shot to international fame supported by her partner, the former general Gert Bastian. Petra was a human dynamo. She spoke at an incredible rate and addressed rallies with unbridled passion. I greatly admired her intellect and her energy. She repeatedly drove herself to the point of exhaustion and illness and was to die in tragic circumstances some years later.

CND always made it clear that we opposed Russian SS-20s deployed in Eastern Europe as much as US Cruise and Pershing. Nonetheless, we believed it important to talk and so we accepted an invitation from the Soviet Peace Council, which we knew was an arm of the state. We were treated as important guests and I was given a huge suite in the Ukraina Hotel, one of the great Stalinist 'wedding cake' constructions. The food was terrible, breakfast in particular offering sauerkraut and very underdone cold boiled eggs. We could sympathise with the Russian view that the US had led the nuclear arms race and they simply followed, but we challenged the escalation brought about by the SS-20s. We pointed to the overwhelming forces on both sides and the pernicious war-fighting nature of the intermediate weapons. They said the Soviet Union would not strike first but beyond that there was little meeting of minds.

Outside the official peace council, we found much more openness. At the Institute for US and Canadian Studies we met men and women interested in how citizens like us could challenge their governments so defiantly. They were also developing public opinion polling and it was clear these were possible future leaders who might take their country in a different direction.

One night our hosts, the official Peace Committee, provided us with tickets for the Bolshoi. We gratefully accepted, planning to escape after the first act and rendezvous with some dissidents at their home. We managed to make the complicated journey in the snow to the block of flats in the suburbs, only to find guards at the door preventing us from making contact with the residents. We decided to insist and sat down outside. Rather foolhardy for someone who felt the cold badly, but we were determined to make a stand. After some time a van drove up and the KGB ordered us to get in. We refused, daring them to manhandle us. The standoff continued until eventually the van left and we realised nothing more could come of our visit. By now all public transport had ceased and we were absolutely frozen and forced to walk back to our hotel. After some time, with rigid faces and stinging ears, we saw a bus. It had no lights or passengers but was clearly going in our direction. We flagged it down and miraculously the driver opened his doors to us.

Many requests for international visits continued to arrive at CND HQ. One was from the Japanese peace movement, inviting me to visit Hiroshima for an international peace gathering on the anniversary of the American bombing of the city on 6 August 1945. We had also been under pressure to send someone to Australia, so it was agreed that I would do both. Still benefiting from my four-day week and dipping into my annual leave at CAB, I was able to buy a round-the-world ticket stopping off in Tokyo, then Auckland, Melbourne and Singapore, from where I would take a private week off in Bangkok to holiday with Keith.

The frantic schedule began with my arrival in Tokyo after a seventeen-hour flight. I was going directly to a 100th birthday celebration for a monk who had spent all his life working in the peace movement. I struggled to stay awake as I was driven through Tokyo's rush hour traffic. When we reached the glittering ballroom where the event was being staged everyone was seated for dinner. My hosts explained that I must begin my speech with greetings in Japanese! After a few moments of panic, I forced my brain into gear, learned the words and got up and made the speech.

In Japan we had a round of meetings, all arranged by the Japanese Peace Committee. Most harrowing was meeting survivors of the atomic bombing and hearing their histories, and talking to doctors about the horrific birth defects that followed in the next generation and the cancer deaths among adults. There was also much evidence of a cover-up as all the recovery and hospital programmes of the time were under the control of the American military, whose records were not available to the Japanese. Then there was the visit to the peace park with the bombed-out cathedral that still stands today. We came upon it suddenly – in the sunshine, with ice cream vans and the usual tourist paraphernalia, which felt very strange for a site of such awesome significance. It was very different when we returned for the anniversary ceremony. This was so moving – a huge, silent audience and an overwhelming sense of sorrow. I felt very emotional as I made my speech. In a remarkable coincidence, I returned from the platform to find myself standing with Doreen, a woman councillor from my hometown of Pontypool. We listened together to Lukas Beckmann, a German campaigner who was instrumental in the founding of Die Grünen. Lukas, like Petra Kelly, was a great speaker. Doreen was in tears – 'how wonderful to hear a young German speak of peace and reconciliation'. (Anti-German feeling was still strong in Britain decades after the Second World War.)

From Hiroshima we moved on to Nagasaki, where in 1945 the second American atomic bomb had been dropped three days later. Keith arrived to join me and we went to bed exhausted. A few hours later we woke to find the beds moving across the floor and people shouting in the corridor. We realised it was an earthquake, but after a few minutes' consideration and no alarm we decided to go back to sleep. In the morning we saw wide cracks in the street but no further obvious damage.

There was just one other ceremony and then we were done. Keith saw me off on my next journey to New Zealand while he began a series of meetings and collaborations with Japanese colleagues. I had had to pack two separate wardrobes, formal summer clothes for Japan and winter for Australia. As I checked in I was found to be overweight. The Japanese had given me an assortment of huge books and an extremely heavy temple bell. I couldn't abandon them so I paid up – just hoping my meagre funds would last for the rest of the trip. The New Zealand peace movement had heard of my visit to

Australia and had asked for a brief stopover. They were incredibly hospitable and were working hard to get New Zealand declared a nuclear-free zone. Although neither New Zealand nor Australia had nuclear weapons of their own, they were tied into treaties with the US, which meant they participated in nuclear exercises.

Melbourne was an eye-opener, much more cosmopolitan than I had imagined and a contrast to Auckland, which still had a 1950s feel. Most audiences just wanted to hear our story and were horrified to think that war-fighting nuclear weapons from both sides were being sited in Europe. They were passionate about keeping their part of the planet out of the sphere of any potential nuclear exchange. After a similar round of meetings in Adelaide, I returned to Melbourne for a very special trip to a sheep farm in the outback. We drove for hours on long straight roads with the horizon stretching as far as the eye could see on either side. Experiencing that vastness must be what everyone remembers about Australia. But more was to come. My hosts took me out to see the land around their house on a bitterly cold day with frost glinting on the wattle trees and kangaroos jumping out of our path. The sun was intense in a blue sky and I noticed the farmer's odd headgear – flaps of sacking hanging down around his face – a protection against repeated skin cancer. That evening I spoke at a meeting in their barn – people came from a 100-mile radius, driving through a pitch-black night illuminated by stars I had never seen before.

My reward was to fly back to Bangkok to join Keith for a few days of real holiday. We had a lovely hotel and spent our days visiting Buddhist temples and tranquil tropical gardens and enjoying great food in sumptuous surroundings.

We returned to our work routines and CND meetings for me. It was the party conference season, which we followed with interest as always, but then came the terrible news that the IRA had bombed the Grand Hotel in Brighton where the Prime Minister and Cabinet members were staying during the Tory Party conference. Mrs Thatcher survived the assassination attempt but five other leading Tories died and many were injured.

At CND we continued to receive requests to travel abroad and other officers and Bruce made numerous journeys. Then we received one for a CND delegation to China. As the fifth declared nuclear weapons state, China was a potential player in any multilateral disarmament talks and independent of the Soviet and US spheres of influence. We decided we had to accept and four people were chosen: Roger Spiller, Mick Elliot, Janet Bloomfield and myself. We also took our own interpreter, Richard. By taking off four working days I could carve out the ten days necessary for the trip. It was an amazing experience. The Chinese proved far less bound by protocols than the Japanese and were much given to making jokes about the Russians. Of course, our unilateralism was a mystery to them but they had an obvious economic interest in not being part of a nuclear arms race.

Our most important meetings were with the foreign ministry officials who 'explained' China's need for nuclear weapons. They were a counter to Soviet hegemony and would be used only in retaliation, never first strike. We were also given a high-level meeting with officials of the party and an introduction to one of the veterans of Mao's Long March. At Peking (now Beijing) University we were able to meet with students and to show the film *Nuclear Winter*. Although generally well informed on the issues, the students were surprised by the film. Officials argued that while Chinese nuclear weapons were sufficient for deterrence they would not cause a nuclear winter. We were also treated to a visit to the awesome Great Wall and to the Forbidden City. We took the overnight train to Shanghai for further meetings and on to Nanjing. As we prepared for our last evening in Nanjing we were told it would be polite to invite our hosts to a meal in a local restaurant. We readily agreed – never before having experienced the (very hot) Szechuan food. In order to get the food at Chinese, not foreign, prices, our hosts booked the meal. This caused immense confusion for the staff who had a strict protocol for the serving of food depending on who was the chief host and chief guest. Then I learned that after my speech each of us should raise a toast in the local spirit, mao-tai (made from sorghum). Although the glasses were tiny every mouthful of the foul-tasting liquid was torture – and there were twelve toasts. I stayed on my feet but was violently sick in my hotel room soon after retiring. Back in Peking we found on our last night we were to be honoured with a banquet in the Great Hall of the People. It was a magnificent occasion until we came to the dessert – ice cream floating in a bowl of mao-tai.

It was of course a strange experience to be treated to such extravagance but it was normal behaviour for communist regimes at that time. The lavish reception we received made no impact on our thinking or our arguments – we opposed all nuclear weapons and we had very well-rehearsed arguments ready to counter any justifications from governments East or West. And while the officials' positions were intransigent, there were always some people who were prepared to hear our arguments and concede that the nuclear arms race was a potential threat to everyone.

I had telephoned my mother every day since my father died in 1981 but doing so from China was a problem. I managed to put through a couple of calls on a poor line assuring her that all was well with me. Little did I know that that was not the case for her. I returned home to the awful news that my sister Susan had cancer. She was just thirty-eight and had two sons, Ben and Nick. I had no idea what the prognosis might be. Fortunately, it was a weekend and I went straight to see her. Everyone was in shock. She owed her life to an observant doctor who had noticed something on her upper arm when she was taking Nick for a routine visit. It was a deadly melanoma. A big piece of flesh had been gouged out of her arm and radiotherapy administered. My mother, now settled ten minutes' walk away, took charge of Susan's home and children. We had only to wait and hope there was no spread of the disease. It was a difficult time.

Back at the CAB, Jackie was more and more in demand for counselling courses as the number of marital breakdowns coming through the doors increased. She wanted to devote more time to additional training and to return in the New Year to her former hours. I couldn't object. I'd been so fortunate in the support I had received and so enjoyed my work that returning to a five-day week was the only option.

At Molesworth in East Anglia, around 100 peace campaigners were enduring a bitter winter in the open. On 5 February 1985, in the dead of night, 1,500
soldiers and hundreds of police arrived and hastily removed the campaigners
and erected a barbed-wire fence at an estimated cost of £1 million. Sue and
Roger Spiller had already been alerted by activists who saw the convoy leave
its barracks and Roger ensured the media covered the event and interviewed
him. Later in the day Michael Heseltine arrived in his flak jacket to personally congratulate the soldiers on site. In no time the fence was hung with
placards with pictures of Cruise missiles and the message 'return to sender'.

Devastating news appeared in *The Guardian* on 21 February. They reported
that the previous night Channel 4 had banned a documentary on MI5's Official
Secrets by 20/20 Vision. The newspaper printed a full account. It was spine-chill-
ing stuff. Of course we always suspected but to see it in print was just sickening.
An MI5 whistleblower, Cathy Massiter, revealed how she was responsible for surveillance on CND from 1981 until she resigned in 1983. She detailed MI5 phone
taps, agent infiltration and the use of MI5 material for party political purposes.

We had always assumed there was an agent volunteering at CND HQ and
that our phones might be tapped, but I for one had been reluctant to believe
that the state could have gone to such lengths. Cathy Massiter's testimony
demonstrated that they did indeed go to such lengths and they did so without justification. This was the crux of the matter. For state security agencies
to tap private phones they had to establish the threat of espionage, sabotage
or subversion. Cathy Massiter rightly argued that carrying out surveillance
on myself and others and tapping phones could not be justified.

CND was not the only target. Trade unions and civil liberties organisations were also in the frame. Leading Labour politicians were outraged and
Neil Kinnock, as Leader of the Opposition, demanded an inquiry. With very
limited terms of reference, Lord Bridges was tasked with an investigation into
the granting of warrants. Bruce Kent wrote to Home Secretary Leon Brittan
expressing his concern that files being kept on him by MI5 were inaccurate:
'I am not a communist, crypto or otherwise.'

The inquiry was swift and of course a complete whitewash. Margaret Thatcher sent a letter to Neil containing an extract from the otherwise secret findings. The short extract concluded that 'no warrant for interception has been issued in contravention of the appropriate criteria'. Strong protests were made by Neil Kinnock and David Steel, the leader of the Liberal Party. Gerald Kaufman, Labour's shadow Home Secretary, argued that the most serious allegations had not been answered, including falsely classifying individuals as subversives to give legitimacy to the issue of warrants and using material obtained by MI5 for party political purposes. Channel 4 was under huge pressure to show the documentary, which was screened the day after the Thatcher letter was published.

Significantly, no warrant was ever issued for Cathy Massiter's arrest under the Official Secrets Act. *The Times* reported that 'ministers have decided there must be no prosecution of those concerned in making the film', in sharp contrast to the Prime Minister's statement a month earlier when referring to the prosecution of Clive Ponting: 'Ministers have absolutely no role in deciding (in official secrets cases) whether to prosecute.'

Opinions were divided at CND. Some people expected nothing less and argued there was nothing we could do; others that it was such an outrage we must fight back. We decided to campaign and our excellent press officer Gill Reeve was commissioned to make contact with Cathy Massiter. We decided to take the issue to the next CND Council and take legal advice in the meantime. As it all sank in I reflected on my own experiences. The day when I pressed the bar on my landline handset to end one call and clear the line for the next, only to hear the conversation I had just had, played back as a recording. And the time when we were leaving for holiday and on turning back to close the door heard a strange beep emanating from a phone handset. Even more sinister was the time we were woken in the middle of the night by the crunch of footsteps on our gravel drive and saw two men on ladders working at the top of the telegraph pole that served our property. I knew now that all my movements had been monitored, which might explain the spooky postcards that regularly arrived at my home with detailed knowledge of my whereabouts and overseas trips. But worst of all I felt so invaded, particularly given it had all started at a time of family grief over the death of my father.

Bruce finally got a reply from Leon Brittan, who said he was fully satisfied that the Security Service was 'absolutely free of political bias or influence'. Referring to how the directive was defined (espionage, sabotage and subversion), Brittan said 'no member of CND need fear that he is the object of surveillance unless his own actions and intentions bring him within the strict criteria set out in the definition'. This, of course, was outrageous and Bruce responded, eliciting a brief reply that, in countering threats of terrorism, espionage and subversion, the security services must be allowed to operate in secrecy – 'this means that false and misleading allegations have to go unanswered'.

CND Council decided to give us the backing to take legal action and we engaged Bindmans as our solicitors. In July they made an application for a judicial review on behalf of myself, John Cox and Bruce Kent in 'the matter of a warrant signed by the Secretary of State for the Home Department in or about August 1983'. Cathy Massiter, an MI5 intelligence officer for twelve years, provided a sworn affidavit in preparation for the court case. In it she said:

> I had the task of conducting the service's investigation into Communist and other forms of subversive influence and activity in the peace movement, including the Campaign for Nuclear Disarmament ... I became concerned that the tasks which I, as an intelligence officer, was being called upon to perform and the uses to which information which I had gathered was being put were guided by considerations not solely related to defence of the Realm.
>
> [...] There was however a consciousness within the security service that we were not to be controlled by political objectives and considerations. However, it seemed to me that the scale and nature of the investigation that we were undertaking into the peace movement – and into CND in particular – were determined more by the latter's political importance than by the real security significance of subversive elements in it.

[...] Once CND began to grow in the late 1970s our study of it increased so the investigation of it became virtually my whole task by the time I left the service.

[...] It was suggested to the service that as CND had adopted policies which were also espoused by certain subversive organisations, that was itself evidence that the influence of subversives over CND was greater than the number of their members within the organisation might suggest.

[...] Similarly, it was felt within the service that we were likely to be questioned about the true political affiliations of Mrs Joan Ruddock ... It was fully recognised by the service that she had no subversive affiliations and therefore she could not be recorded under any of the usual subversive categories. She was in fact recorded as a 'contact of a hostile intelligence service' after giving an interview to a Soviet journalist based in London who was suspected of being a KGB intelligence officer. In her file, we recorded Special Branch references to her movements ... press cuttings, products of mail and telephone interceptions obtained through active investigation of other targets (for example the Communist Party and John Cox) and police reports, for example recording her appearance at demonstrations or public meetings. References to her in reports from agents working in, for example, the Communist Party would also appear on her file.

[...] As time went on we perceived it as more than ever necessary that we should be able to answer very precisely whatever questions were asked about CND and its subversive penetration. One of the means that was used was the introduction of an agent, Harry Newton, into CND headquarters. Mr Newton joined CND in 1982 and his first job for us was to attend CND annual conference.

[...] In March 1983 Mr Heseltine established a special unit within the Ministry for Defence called Defence Secretariat 19 (DS19) whose task it was to combat CND propaganda on unilateral nuclear disarmament

... I was instructed by my superiors to go through MI5's files and extract non-classified information from published sources on any extreme left-wing affiliations of CND's leaders. I prepared a report, which was passed to DS19.

[...] I received a message via my branch director that the deputy Director-General of MI5 was prepared to consider favourably an application from me for a telephone intercept on a member of the Communist Party within CND. John Cox, a Vice-President of CND, was selected since he was well known as a member of the Communist Party and had been involved in CND practically since its inception. Also, he lived in Wales and therefore would need to be in frequent telephone contact with CND headquarters. However, we had absolutely no evidence, as required by the guidelines, that he was concerned in any criminal activity or that he was engaged in a major subversive or espionage activity which was likely to injure the national interest. On the contrary, nothing from our coverage of the Communist Party and its Peace Committee gave us grounds to suspect that they were manipulating CND.

I saw the products of the intercept in the form of transcripts of recorded telephone conversations.

August 1985 marked the fortieth anniversary of the US atomic bombings of Hiroshima and Nagasaki. Earlier in the year Mikhail Gorbachev had come to power in the Soviet Union. He marked Hiroshima day by announcing a unilateral moratorium on Soviet testing of nuclear weapons together with an invitation to the United States to conclude a comprehensive test-ban treaty. This was a new kind of President. In December he would come to the UK and Margaret Thatcher would pronounce that he was a man she could do business with.

I had already given notice to CND that I wouldn't stand again for chair but would be happy to become a vice-chair for one year only to help with the transition. Not only did I have a lot of extra work to do for CAB but I was also contemplating a return to party politics. Having become a national figure as chair of CND, I'd received lots of invitations to contest Labour selections for parliamentary seats prior to the 1983 election. I turned them down. It was vital I remained non-party political for as long as I was chair of CND and CND was, I thought, a more important cause. But now Brian Revell, a local TGWU official with whom I'd worked closely during the miners' strike and who had set up the Berkshire Anti-Nuclear Campaign, began urging me to look for a seat.

Then I got an approach from the Labour Party in my home town of Pontypool. They anticipated that Leo Abse, the sitting MP, would be announcing his retirement. Leo had had an illustrious career in Parliament, bringing in Private Members' Bills to decriminalise homosexuality and liberalise divorce laws.

It was a thrilling possibility. Keith's career was proving hugely successful and there was no doubt that he would remain at Imperial. But we were still travelling home to see our families whenever we could and a work base and second home in the Torfaen constituency would enable us to maintain even closer contact. The odds were against me, however. Despite my family and upbringing I was still an outsider, having lived in London almost all my adult life. None of our family members were active in the Labour Party locally and – worst of all – I was a woman! Welsh society was notoriously misogynist and Ann Clwyd, the only woman out of thirty-eight Welsh MPs, was known to have had a very hard time. Nonetheless, I had to try.

Over the summer I met local supporters and a meeting was organised for me to speak about the peace movement. There was lots of press speculation but it was late September before Leo announced he was indeed stepping down. In October I declared my interest. The *Free Press of Monmouthshire*, under editor Don Touhig, took a keen interest, always stressing my outsider status.

My campaign to obtain the parliamentary seat in Torfaen did not go well. I was still inexperienced in the ways of the Labour movement. Both Paul Murphy, the local Constituency Labour Party (CLP) secretary and leading contender, and I were TGWU members, which presented the union with a problem of endorsement. I had very good relations with all the general secretaries of Labour-affiliated unions at the time because of my role in CND. I was also the holder of the Frank Cousins* peace medal, but this was a regional decision.

The regional secretary, Midlander George Wright, agreed to see me. After being kept waiting for half an hour I was ushered in to be greeted with 'Hello, Flower'. I didn't rate my chances. I was supported by a lovely group of people but Paul was the better candidate. At the final hustings, I was the runner-up. Paul became MP for Torfaen in 1987 and Secretary of State for Wales in 1999. Ann Clwyd (elected in 1984) remained the only Welsh woman MP until the Labour landslide of 1997, after the bitterly contested battle over all-women shortlists.

The year 1985 drew to an end with my being asked to do a programme called *Moments* for BBC TV South. It's a similar format to *Desert Island Discs*, the only programme I've ever wanted to be on. They assembled a wonderful collection of TV pictures representing key moments in my life, mostly political, from the first Labour government of my generation to Martin Luther King's 'I have a dream speech' and demonstrations against the Vietnam War and against nuclear weapons. But I got some music too. They showed film of the south Wales valleys where I grew up, with the Treorchy Male Choir singing my favourite 'Myfanwy' and Mick Jagger performing at the free Rolling Stones concert in Hyde Park. Quite the most enjoyable programme I've ever made. Jenni Murray† was a really sympathetic interviewer and frankly the whole thing was a great ego trip!

Paul Johns was elected as chair of CND at the 1985 annual conference and I drew breath for the first time in four years. The year ended with a summit between Reagan and Gorbachev in Geneva. In the New Year we prepared for the first anniversary of the construction of the perimeter fence

---

* Former General Secretary of the TGWU.

† Jenni would become the presenter of Radio 4's *Woman's Hour* in 1987, a role she still performs today.

at Molesworth. No missiles were due to arrive for some time but we decided on a national demonstration in support of a symbolic blockade of the base. Despite freezing conditions, 6,000 people sat in the snow and prevented all movements at the site.

The following year, 1986, was to prove a year of unexpected events, causing CND to organise impromptu demonstrations of civil disobedience. In the early hours of 15 April, US strike aircraft left British bases on a secret mission to bomb Libya. Today such actions have become commonplace with the use of drones, but in the midst of a Cold War, with vast nuclear armouries ever poised to obliterate the world, this was a frightening development. We organised one of the largest ever sit-downs in front of the US embassy and thousands of people crowded into Oxford Street, stopping all the traffic. People demonstrated at every US base in Britain, mindful of the fact that the American use of British bases brought real danger to our shores.

Then came Chernobyl. On 26 April, a nuclear power station at Chernobyl in the USSR suffered what was then the world's worst nuclear accident. With their usual secrecy, the Soviet authorities had fought the fierce reactor fire while keeping a news blackout. Only when radiation began to be registered in Western Europe were they forced to make an announcement. The radiation cloud spread across the whole of Britain, demonstrating in a small way the horror of nuclear explosions anywhere on the continent. The government imposed a 21-day ban on the movement and slaughter of sheep in north Wales, clearly failing to recognise the persistence of radiation. When the extent of the radioactive contamination was realised, nearly 10,000 farms were subjected to restrictions. Mandatory testing for radioactivity would not be lifted for twenty-six years. With thirty-eight nuclear reactors in the UK, much press comment followed.

Having failed in Torfaen, I'd little stomach for another contest but I got another invitation from a Lewisham Deptford branch that I'd turned down some months earlier. They still hadn't started their selection. Then I got a note from Harriet Harman: 'Joan, Deptford is wide open – go for it!' I didn't know Harriet then, but such action was typical of her – always looking out for other women. It worked. I entered the contest.

I had no idea what I was getting into. John Silkin, the sitting MP for over twenty years and former minister and Chief Whip in Harold Wilson's government, had been repeatedly challenged by a group of hard-left activists in the controlling general management committee of the party. John was an old-style patrician MP who had a grand house in Kent and a flat in Westminster. He was well respected by many and well known to the electorate but a hard core of members wanted a completely different form of representation. They used the local press against him, made his life a misery and flouted party rules. As a consequence, the constituency party was suspended for two years. With John announcing that he would stand down at the next general election, the National Executive Committee (NEC) decided to let the party proceed with a selection. Over twenty candidates came forward to begin the rounds of party branches. I had been friends with our leader, Neil Kinnock, and his wife Glenys for years and knew many of the trade union leaders who dominated the party conferences in the '80s, but this was going to be a very local battleground in a constituency riven by division. There was clearly a desire not to have a white man and there was no favoured son as in Torfaen. I had a good story to tell – my working-class upbringing, my anti-racist activism and my leadership of the peace movement (shortly to come to an end). I also had no difficulty promising to move into the constituency if selected and prioritising advice surgeries in this most deprived of areas. I received encouragement from a host of party members including Pauline Morrison, Jim Stevenson, Jimi and Sandra Adefiranye, Maggie Coulthard, Marita Sanders and Ivor Mason. I was also driven around on a familiarisation exercise by council leader Dave Sullivan. Endless meetings ensued and the months passed. Other candidates fell by the wayside and I knew I was in with a chance.

For a while it appeared the selection would progress to shortlisting but then the NEC discovered Deptford was operating a Black section giving voting rights to an ethnic minorities subgroup, which was then illegal under party rules. This was particularly significant as the hard-left faction had decided that backing a black candidate was the best way to stop my progress. They chose a local electrician – Clifton Graham. At party conference that September a member of the NEC took me aside and said they were intending to suspend Deptford CLP once again but I was not to worry – the NEC would impose me as the prospective Labour candidate. My reaction was instant. I wouldn't be imposed. They could take a chance on me or suspend, when I would withdraw. It was the best decision I ever made. I had to win on merit and I went straight back to the constituency to get stuck in.

It was now clear to me that I couldn't go on working at the CAB and put everything into the contest, so I decided to hand in my notice. It would be a wrench to leave but I had to do it.

Meanwhile, I received a very surprising invitation from the city of Vancouver. They were celebrating their centenary and were organising an official peace festival. I accepted an invitation to speak. It was a unique experience. The rally was held in a football stadium with giant TV screens at each end. The echo was off-putting when I spoke but thrilling all the same. My speech was subsequently included in the official book commemorating the centenary.

On my return I got a phone call from our friend Pat. She had been staying in Suffolk where she had met a man at a party whom she clearly liked very much. It was so sudden and their lives were so unconnected I was deeply anxious for her. Some months later Keith and I got the chance to meet David with her in Reading. He seemed very nice but he was about to take early retirement from teaching maths and he'd never lived in the south-east. It all seemed a bit of a risk, but the following year David moved to live with Pat and to begin a second career as a harpsichord maker – something he had previously done as a hobby.

In Deptford, three people were shortlisted. Late on in the process a black woman had been persuaded to enter the race as some of Clifton's supporters decided to abandon him. The selection conference was held in the Labour club in Lewisham – a dismal place where the questioning was tough, with key hard-left demands repeated. I had no problems with commitments on where to live and surgeries – I wouldn't have had anything else – but there was one demand too far: that I should be the CLP's delegate to Westminster, to be told what to do and how to vote. I refused. I would always be accountable, I would always advise if my view differed from that of the CLP and I would report back, but I had to be my own person, true to the values I'd espoused over the past eight months. After a gruelling five hours, I won. My supporters were euphoric but the secretary took me aside, pointed her finger between my eyes and said: 'You will never stand here again.'

Dazed, I made the short walk to the station where Keith was anxiously waiting. He was thrilled and we set off amid great excitement to join friends for a very late celebratory supper north of the river. We spent a very happy Christmas visiting both mothers, sisters, aunts and uncles, crossing back and forth on the Severn Bridge. There was so much to do. House-hunting was the first priority.

The year ended with the US breaching the SALT II treaty and the USSR declaring they would end their moratorium on nuclear testing if the US did not reciprocate. On 5 January, the US undertook another nuclear test, provoking a Soviet response a month later. Then, just as things looked particularly bad, Gorbachev proposed an agreement to remove all intermediate nuclear weapons from Europe – exactly what we had campaigned for for the past seven years. Later the Intermediate-Range Nuclear Forces Treaty 1987 was concluded, banning nuclear and conventional ground-launched ballistic and Cruise missiles with ranges of 300–3,400 miles. When US and Soviet intermediate-range weapons were withdrawn, the US argued it was as a result of their strength. We had no doubt that we had played our part. It was the Gorbachev initiative that began it and one of the young men around him at the time told me 'we learned from your example'.

Keith had been commuting from Reading for fourteen years so I thought he would be delighted to move back to London. On the contrary, I began to realise he wasn't interested in finding a Lewisham home. I decided to look on Telegraph Hill as houses were still affordable at that time and it offered very easy access to central London from New Cross Gate station. In no time I had sold one house and bought another. But then I made a big mistake. I decided the house needed gutting and it was best got on with before the election. The whole place was damp, needing a damp-proof course and central heating, a new kitchen and bathroom and the conversion of the smallest bedroom to a shower room. I cannot imagine how I organised it all but I can well remember my agent, Jim Stevenson, stepping over a gap in the exposed floorboards and saying to Keith, 'If I were you, mate, I'd move out.'

I put us through an incredible period of stress and then on 26 April I got a phone call from Labour HQ: John Silkin had just died of a heart attack. I was stunned. John had been very supportive and I'd accompanied him to a number of his surgeries. He had everything to look forward to – a seat in the Lords and a fulfilling retirement with his lovely wife Rosamund. Then I was told I might have to fight a by-election.

John's funeral was held in a packed St Paul's church in Deptford. It was an intensely moving occasion with Rosamund, a former actress, reciting Christina Rossetti's beautiful poem 'Remember'. Although he was Jewish, John had always been close to Father David Diamond, the Anglo-Catholic priest who ministered at St Paul's, and it was a testament to his love of Deptford that he wanted his funeral there. Early on John had told me the two most important people I should work with were Father Diamond and his former curate, now the vicar of All Saints in New Cross, Father Owen Beament. Sure enough, I became good friends with both, having made it clear that, as an evangelical atheist, I couldn't be expected to pray with them. For years they were kind enough to find me a non-religious text to read at the Christmas carol service. I also inherited a small charity called Deptford into the '80s, which had been set up by John, Owen, David and Roger Norman, then editor of the *Mercury* newspaper. The charity gave small sums to people in need who fell through the welfare net and also small grants to community organisations. We were to rename it Deptford into the '90s as we came to the end of the decade and then Deptford First as the millennium passed.

A general election didn't have to be held until 1988, but in the days before fixed parliaments, Prime Ministers tended to go much earlier. In the event, the election was called for 11 June 1987. We had a stand-pipe in the kitchen but my literature recorded that I was indeed living in the constituency. In common with all Labour candidates I stood on a manifesto for jobs, a minimum wage, pre-school places for three- and four-year-olds, increased pensions and against the poll tax proposed by the Tories. We also promised to cut hospital waiting lists, phase out prescription charges and invest in medical research, particularly research on Aids. It was a manifesto to be proud of.

Chapter Five

# PARLIAMENT

M y life was about to become dominated by my diary. I had never kept a record of daily events but now I needed to and I also resolved that, if elected, I would produce a detailed monthly report to the GMC (the management committee of the constituency Labour Party). The rest of this memoir is drawn from those records.

\* \* \*

Lewisham East was held by the Tory Colin Moynihan on a slim majority and our jointly owned Labour Club was situated in that constituency, so it made sense for Lewisham East to have a free run for the election. Jim Stevenson and I secured a run-down vacant property in Deptford High Street, cleaned it up and got a banner made for the shop front. With money from the TGWU and some local donations, we produced a simple series of leaflets and posters, all of which we designed ourselves. We were not required to conform to a party style so I chose a deep ruby red and had diamond-shaped posters with my name across the middle. With a loyal band of activists, we tramped the streets daily.

Election night was incredibly tense as we waited for the counting of Lewisham's two marginal seats. There was huge disappointment when Russell Profitt, a local teacher and the first black president of Goldsmiths students' union, failed to win Lewisham East from Colin Moynihan, who doubled his majority. Jim Dowd similarly failed to oust John Maples in Lewisham West. As a result I was hardly in a happy mood as we paced around the room willing the piles of pink ballot papers to grow in the counting agents' baskets. We needn't have worried. I won with a slightly increased majority on 1983 and over 49 per cent of the votes cast. The declaration was a thrill and I received two wonderful bouquets of red flowers, one from Keith and the other from my mother, who had kept house for us for the duration of the campaign.

My first report to the GMC gives a graphic account of the start of my parliamentary life:

> Everything seems designed to make life difficult. There is no induction programme, no comprehensive handbook and no training in how to be an effective backbencher. Protocol and language ensure that the newcomer gets lost, breaks rules, cannot work out the business of the day and is thus unlikely to disturb the establishment. No wonder one MP managed to haunt the corridors for twenty-one years before making his maiden speech. Some of us are trying to get these matters taken seriously by the Parliamentary Labour Party (PLP) as it clearly makes a nonsense of parliamentary democracy. Three-quarters of the new Labour intake of seventy MPs (one third of the PLP) have come from local government and are conscious of the much inferior working conditions and practices of Parliament. I am certainly experiencing the worst physical conditions and resource allocation of my working life.
>
> **Parliamentary Business**
> The Queen's Speech outlined the major pieces of legislation to be brought forward in this session of Parliament, including the reform

of local government finance (poll tax); a housing Bill; an education Bill allowing schools to opt out of local authority control and London local authorities to opt out of the Inner London Education Authority, ILEA; an immigration Bill, taking away the rights of people who came to this country prior to 1973 to bring in dependents still living overseas; and Bills to privatise the electricity and water industries.

I made my maiden speech during the four-day debate on the Queen's Speech, using the opportunity to highlight the needs of people in Deptford, the injustice of present immigration laws, the resourcefulness of the local community and the ability of local democracy to provide the necessary services and infrastructure had it not been starved of resources by Thatcher's policies.

### Parliamentary Role

There are numerous ways to try to make a contribution within Parliament. Backbenchers are apparently called, on average, four times a year to speak in debates and I have spoken five times already! Thus other opportunities have to be created by interrupting ministers while they speak and putting written and oral questions to ministers and the Prime Minister. All oral questions are drawn by ballot, I have put in hundreds of questions, ranging from defence through transport to immigration. I have been called in PMQs when I attacked the government's record on health, pointing out that to meet government guidelines Lewisham Hospital was drawing up plans to close one surgical ward and two of its four new operating theatres and accepting emergencies only, thus quadrupling the waiting list. I asked if the PM was prepared to allow people to die in Lewisham (amid Tory shouts of 'shame').

### Advice Sessions

Maggie Coulthard, my full-time PA, and I attend two advice sessions every fortnight, covering the south of the constituency in a Friday

evening session at Brockley School and the north in a Saturday morning session at the Albany. People also contact us by letter or telephone
at the office. Currently we are dealing with the ongoing problems of
200 constituents, 45 per cent of which are housing, 19 per cent immigration and 8 per cent benefits, with the remaining 28 per cent covering
an enormous range from pedestrian crossings to industrial relations.

18 November: An awful fire has happened at King's Cross underground
station, killing thirty-one people and injuring another 100. Terrible scenes
that put horror into the minds of all of us using the Tube. Smoking has been
banned on the underground for three years, but there's much speculation
about a dropped match or cigarette. Frank Dobson is the local MP.

I'm put on my first Bill committee. No one explains what is expected of
a back-bench Member and I'm utterly confused when our shadow ministers
table amendments that are the opposite of what I assume our position to be.
These are apparently 'probing' amendments that are used to extract information from ministers and then dropped. The Bill deals with authorising
inspections of American bases in the UK as part of the Intermediate Nuclear
Forces Treaty between the Soviet Union and the US.

We launch a campaign against David Alton's Private Member's Bill on
abortion. I'm still lucky in the ballot for oral questions, including another
to the PM, and keep up the pressure on the cuts to the health service. The
newly formed Labour Women's Caucus is working hard on the Alton Bill.
Our strategy is to achieve the maximum opposition at second reading, set
for 22 January. We don't want the Bill in committee, where Alton would be
pressing an eighteen-week limit. The London group nominate me for the
Council of Europe and the accompanying position in the Western European
Union. I am duly elected.

In January 1988 I interview sixteen of the ninety-six people who've applied
for my half-time researcher's job. I appoint Gill Keep, who makes a splendid
team with Maggie.

The Tories' housing, poll tax, immigration and education Bills are now in committee and colleagues are spending many sleepless nights trying to expose the monstrous nature of these attacks on the basic fabric of people's lives. The local government Bill was bad enough, forcing privatisation on local councils and restricting their ability to practise contract compliance, but now they've accepted an amendment to prohibit the 'promotion of homosexuality'.

My initial success in getting called in debates has come to an end. I've been told I have spoken more than average and as a result I couldn't get called in either the health debate or the Alton Bill. It's so frustrating. I'm also frustrated by the factions in the local party. With so much legislation to fight against there should be a lot to unite party members in campaigning but so many prefer to attack those (including me) with whom they don't agree.

I take up the case of Lewisham Council, which has been capped and has already had to make substantial cuts. Ridley's response is to attack Lewisham for giving money to 'gays'. I attack back, citing the need for counselling services in the age of Aids.

One of our few successes is to win a vote on the floor of the House in favour of bringing in television to record our proceedings, though 264 MPs vote against. My friend Joan Walley and I are so excited we start clapping, as do many others – possibly the first time that clapping (which is not allowed) has been heard in the Chamber – instead of the 'hear, hears' and stamping of male feet.

I've been appointed a member of the committee that will scrutinise the Alton Bill. I am finding life very hard, though not as hard as Joan Walley. She has two young sons and has opted to sell her London home and establish the family in Stoke-on-Trent. The boys miss their mum so much and it is clearly a torment for Joan to be away from them Monday to Friday. I'm fortunate to be going home each night but with 40 per cent of our sittings going to midnight or beyond it's pretty disruptive for Keith. I'm also under pressure in the constituency party. Those who threatened to get rid of me make my life hell at the monthly committee meetings and I often go home tearful.

As always I'm determined to do everything to perfection and though Keith gamely irons his shirts I'm finding myself doing domestic work virtually all day every Sunday. This can't go on. Despite Keith's total opposition, I hire a cleaner. It's the first sign that my priorities diverge from Keith's.

Increasingly I'm dealing with constituents' problems involving Lewisham Council, who are having to make cuts to libraries, lunch clubs and the voluntary sector. I've had such difficulties dealing with some of the officers that I've demanded a meeting with the leader and chief executive to discuss my role. I could go to the press every week attacking them and making my name but I'd much prefer to meet behind closed doors. We agree to a monthly meeting (an arrangement that is to continue for the rest of my parliamentary life).

A major problem is brought to me by the tenants on the Silwood Estate. Massive illegal fly-tipping is plaguing their lives. It's absolutely extraordinary. A whole area adjacent to hundreds of homes is being used to dump tons of builders' rubble. The heavy lorries thunder past houses with doors directly on the street, throwing up clouds of dust and small stones, turn the corner, dump their load and drive off at speed. The whole area is blighted by this activity and anyone who challenges it is roundly abused.

There are endless meetings about the abolition of ILEA and its consequences, problems at the hospitals and the local FE college SELTEC. A brighter spot is the possibility of the Docklands Light Railway being extended to Lewisham.

The committee stage of the Alton Bill begins on Wednesday 23 March, commencing with a sittings motion. David Alton wants open-ended sessions on three days a week. We spend the next two and a half hours debating this, with the Alton side accusing us of wanting to delay the Bill and the rest of us detailing our parliamentary commitments and the impossibility of clearing diaries without notice. New Tory MP Teresa Gorman, who famously put her age back ten years to get selected, makes a feisty contribution on our side. She attacks David Alton for holding a meeting in her constituency without notifying her (parliamentary convention) with the result she is bombarded with postcards saying 26,000 people in her constituency are praying for her to change her mind. Dr Lewis Moonie, a new Scottish Labour colleague, also objects to the 'praying and fasting' on his behalf and pronounces himself an atheist. This is going to be a very lively committee.

We end up with six sessions, usually running until 10 p.m. but going on to 12.32 a.m. on the penultimate day. I have a lot to say, particularly on the circumstances of women that can lead to an abortion request after eighteen weeks, because of hostile doctors who won't refer. The Alton team make much of the fact that caring homes can be found for unwanted babies but we point to 30,000 children awaiting adoption or fostering. Peter Turnham, a Tory who has adopted a disabled boy, proves a great ally. I say that as a woman who would have liked to have had children it would be immoral to seek to assuage my distress by making another woman carry an unwanted pregnancy and then suffer the guilt and distress of giving the child away.

Someone behind me is called to speak. I turn and see a rather crumpled looking man, unknown to me. He has a pleasant, open face, floppy brown hair and is softly spoken. His name is Frank Doran, the newly elected Member for Aberdeen South, who gives comparisons with other countries where the most liberal laws are matched by the lowest abortion rate.

Our strongest reason for not supporting the change in the law is that it is already illegal to abort a foetus at twenty-eight weeks and in practice the limit is now twenty-four weeks. No one has been able to show viability below twenty-four weeks but to outlaw any abortion beyond eighteen weeks will cause huge distress to those women who have been unable to access services prior to that time.

Amazingly, the Alton team then put forward an amendment to allow abortion beyond eighteen weeks for minors who have been raped or made pregnant through incest – as though these offences were less damaging to a nineteen- or twenty-year-old. We strongly oppose.

None of our amendments pass so the Bill leaves committee with the eighteen-week limit in place. The battle will now be taken to the floor of the House. Little do I know that my being on the committee with Frank Doran will have a profound effect on both our lives and those of our families.

I've been appointed to the select committee on televising the proceedings of the House. We receive huge amounts of paperwork and appoint experts to advise. There are two immediate challenges: some Tories who want to talk for ever in the hope the experiment will never start, and two committee members who want to see private companies take over the task.

4 April sees me demonstrating with CND at Aldermaston. I'm still a member of CND's National Council. I'm also chair of the parliamentary CND group and a member of Labour's back-bench committee on defence, trying to raise the profile of anti-nuclear work in the House. I spend two days in Brussels as a guest of the NATO Alerts network, women parliamentarians and researchers from all NATO countries. I'm also working with women campaigners from the island of Belau (Palau) who took the US to court for violating their nuclear-free status. We show their video at the House of Commons. At the end of the month I'm at the South-East London Anti-Apartheid Conference at Goldsmiths College and on May Day I address a huge rally organised by the south-east trade unions at Alexandra Palace. There's a move to get a higher profile for environmental issues within the party so I join the Socialist Environment and Resources Association (SERA).

In the constituency I organise a meeting between the council's chief executive and the CEO of the London Waste Regulation Authority to see what can be done for the Silwood residents. Both parties assure me they are doing what they can and warn me of the dangers of getting involved. Apparently it's well known that the perpetrators are hardened criminals who go around with 'sawn-off shotguns'.

Things are not going well on the select committee on TV. Our technical advisors are struggling to find a way of providing sufficient lighting to enable TV cameras to function. Because of English Heritage, they have to fit what is effectively strip lighting behind the top edges of the last tier of seats on both sides of the Chamber. After months of work we are to view demonstrations.

It's a farce. Long glass lighting panels have been propped in place. A ghostly green light appears. Even if they could do the job they look hideous and are extremely unlikely to persuade reluctant Members to vote for such change.

I have a flash of inspiration. At our next session I ask why we cannot propose central hanging lights such as those that grace the Lords Chamber. This has never been considered because of EH but now our advisors agree to investigate. Lo and behold they discover that before the Chamber was burned down in 1834 there were indeed central hanging lights. The problem is solved. Our specialist advisor quips that they should be called the Ruddock lights, but sadly it doesn't catch on. Our report is eventually approved by the House on 12 June.

6 May: Report stage of the Alton Bill. Frank Doran, who I've got to know over the past months, has the first amendment. He proceeds to speak for half an hour. Frank's background is interesting. He left school at sixteen to work for the Scottish Hydro Board and fortunately found a manager who took an interest in him. As a consequence, he went to university in his twenties when he was already married and the father of two boys. He then built up a success-ful legal practice before running first for a Euro seat and then for Westminster.

We are successful – the Bill is defeated after four hours. But other hopes are dashed in the Lords as the government round up enough peers to carry the poll tax and the abolition of ILEA. Rumour has it that one elderly aris-tocrat, entirely unfamiliar with the Lords Chamber, tried to order a G&T from a doorman (in their eighteenth-century dress they could, of course, be mistaken for the domestic staff of a stately home).

On the Council of Europe, I'm working on illegal drugs policy and spend a couple of days at a World Health Organization meeting in Copenhagen. It's the Whitsun recess and the following day I go to Washington for a 'Beyond Containment' conference organised by the coalition for a New Foreign Policy. I exchange a lot of information with people who are working on arms control in the State Department and also go to the Pentagon. I spend some

time with Jesse Jackson's campaign, which has the best foreign policy position of any Americans I've met.

Back at Westminster for an unusual event: a debate on women's health
with nearly equal numbers of women and men in the Chamber. The atmosphere is greatly changed. Teresa Gorman, the outspoken Tory MP, makes
a terrific speech. Her focus is on menopausal women, of which she is one,
and her advocacy of hormone replacement therapy. Never can the House
have heard such a speech, referencing all the awful symptoms that make life
a misery for about a third of women. I doubt if periods and tampons have
been spoken of in this Chamber before. Teresa does love to shock but she
is serious. I press the minister on several points, including delays in cancer
screening and radiological standards, which are currently based on the adult
male and do not accurately reflect the effects of radiation on women and girls.

It will be our twenty-fifth wedding anniversary on 3 July and I'm busy
planning a party for friends and family at Imperial's Ascot field station. The
grounds will be lovely at this time of the year and there's plenty of overnight
accommodation available for guests. My sister and mother will come to help
me with all the catering. I find a lovely blue-and-white silk dress and get
everything organised in good time as I'll be in Athens for a Council of Europe
meeting immediately before the event. It's a wonderful evening – the food is
great, lots of wine and dancing. Keith is happy too and makes a speech. Only
later do I recall that the speech was mostly about the past, perhaps a reflection of our being apart so much recently.

As the session draws to a close the Tories are using the guillotine to get
their legislation through the Commons, following several defeats in the Lords.
I visit nine primary schools one Friday to see the results of their 'Armada'
plates, made for the Deptford festival. I visit churches, drug centres, colleges
and youth clubs. I take part in two Mandela marches and speak at innumerable meetings. One treat – Keith and I attend the first night of the Proms
at the invitation of the BBC. But the most surprising invitation is from the
MoD. They want me to give a lecture as part of their officers' training course

at Greenwich Naval College. I accept with alacrity. Then I get approached by the Health Authority who are proposing to close Sydenham Children's Hospital. I'll have to make a visit so we postpone our holiday to mid-August.

Sydenham is an emotive issue. The hospital is Victorian but people love it and many children have been successfully treated there. My Labour colleague Jim Dowd is a member of the health authority and we make a visit together. The buildings are pretty primitive but it is the consultants who convince me. They say that they no longer feel they can operate safely and the premises cannot be adapted. I seek guarantees about the timing of the transition and finance if they relocate to temporary buildings at Lewisham Hospital.

Increasingly people are contacting us by phone and letter but surgeries are also well attended. Over half the constituents are presenting with housing problems. The vast council estates are grim environments with huge repair problems. Now that Thatcher has banned new council building, overcrowding is increasing dramatically as growing families can't move on and extended families pile in together. There has also been discrimination in letting policies with black families facing the worst of the conditions. Benefit problems and immigration issues make up another third of the caseload. MPs have the power to put a 'stop' on deportations, which creates a huge amount of work dealing with emergencies that are entirely unpredictable. The Tories will soon remove this power. Maggie and Gill work flat out and provide an excellent service for me and constituents alike.

6 July: There's been a terrible disaster in the North Sea. An oil production platform, the Piper Alpha, has blown up. Frank Doran has many constituents who are dead or bereft. Frank's involvement with this tragic event will continue throughout his career. Later in the year Neil Kinnock appoints him as Labour's spokesperson on oil and gas in Tony Blair's energy team.

28 September: Party conference, and I do my usual quota of speaking at fringe meetings and one special event – the launch of *Voices for One World*, a book

to which I've contributed. One World was the brainchild of Glenys Kinnock, who had a long-standing interest in development. She invited Joan Lestor, then spokesperson on international development, and myself to become founder members.

We three women frequently shared platforms around the country. My role was to argue the disarmament case and an end to the arms race, with its waste of resources and lives. One World, later One World Action, campaigned for peace, equality (with a strong emphasis on women), democracy and freedom. Heady stuff.

For twenty years OWA worked with development partners throughout Asia, Africa and Latin America with an annual income in the millions and a glittering following of stars among its supporters. Although a supporter throughout its existence I would sadly decide to withdraw from my active role when Neil changed party policy on nuclear disarmament.

Parliament resumes on 19 October with a two-day debate on defence. I'm called on the first day and highlight the government's isolation in Europe in their opposition to arms control and desire for nuclear modernisation. Earlier in the year George Younger, then Secretary of State for Defence, had let slip on *Panorama* that the government had taken the decision to buy a new nuclear weapons system without any debate or even a statement in Parliament. At a Tribune conference, I chair a workshop on defence and disarmament. Change is in the air. It's depressingly apparent that there is a willingness among delegates to dump Labour's existing policy of unilateral nuclear disarmament. Subsequently, I make a detailed submission to the party's defence review.

I've been given a week off to go to Chile. I've been campaigning with Chile Solidarity since it was set up in the wake of the assassination of President Allende in 1973. Fifteen years on, and after a huge international campaign and the immense courage of Chile's opposition, the dictator General Pinochet agreed to conduct a plebiscite to determine whether he should stay in power. Chile Solidarity and the TGWU decided to send a delegation of two

– Margaret Prosser, the union's women's officer, and myself – to Santiago if
the No vote won. On 5 October the No vote triumphs. We are jubilant, if a
little nervous about our impending trip. The rationale for the presence of
international delegations in the country now is to witness what happens in
the aftermath of the plebiscite. Another coup is a possibility. No one is certain that Pinochet and his henchmen will abide by the decision.

When we arrive in Chile we are aware of the very real tension and sense of
danger but also of triumph and relief. The challenge is how to move democracy forward. The opposition to Pinochet is a coalition ranging from the
revolutionary MIR through communists and socialists to Christian Democrats. We hear of the terrible suffering of those whose relatives are among
the 'disappeared' – people who were arrested, tortured and probably killed,
but whose bodies were never produced. They are mainly women who have
kept silent witness demonstrations for years. There is much gratitude for
the solidarity campaigns across the world and a plea for continuing support as the long transition to democracy begins. Margaret and I promise to
raise £1,000 to buy the material for a women's garment cooperative that has
already acquired machines and is training machinists. It is all a deeply moving experience. I return home haunted by the memories.

November proves to be a month of unprecedented travel. I do one weekend in Bristol for One World Action, a second in Hamburg for the peace
movement and a third at the CND national conference. Because sittings of
the House don't begin until 2.30 p.m. and votes at the start of a new session
are not until 10 p.m., I'm able to get out and back in a day for a SERA meeting on toxic waste and a health committee in Paris for the Council of Europe.

*The London Programme* has asked me to contribute to a piece they are
doing on one of my constituents, George Long, who is in prison for murder. George was one of a number of people who wrote to me protesting his
innocence following my election. It looked a hopeless case to me but then
I discovered Ludovic Kennedy (a well-known writer and broadcaster) was
supporting him and believed he was innocent.

In late 1978, fourteen-year-old Gary Wilson's body was found dumped in a back yard in Deptford High Street. He had been sexually assaulted, stabbed and strangled. In January 1979, the police arrested George Long. George, a former soldier with drink and drugs problems and severe depression, was a fantasist and had attempted suicide more than once. On the night after the murder, George showed his then girlfriend a knife that he said he'd taken off the man who had murdered Gary. Subsequently his sister was picked up in a random police check and she repeated the story. When George was later called for interview he arrived hours late after a lengthy drinking session and police soon found inconsistencies in his story. They asked him if he liked Elvis and he replied that he did. It transpired that the victim was strangled by an Elvis belt. The police pressed him, suggesting he had killed the boy by stabbing him. George says he didn't want to admit he'd made up his earlier story. He just wanted to get out of the police station. Under duress he confessed to the murder, somehow imagining that it would get sorted out later. It didn't. Without any forensic evidence or any witnesses, George Long was tried, convicted and sentenced to life imprisonment. He's already served eight years and because he insists on his innocence he will never get parole. *George Long: Was the Wrong Man Sent to Prison?* is transmitted on 25 November.

1 December: One amazing day. I have been drawn number five in the ballot for Private Members' Bills. This means I'm guaranteed time to bring in a Bill of my choosing. I'm besieged by people and campaigns pressing their causes but I remember my promise to the Silwood tenants. They have shown the most remarkable courage, noting down the registration numbers of the vehicles they see dumping and openly campaigning despite all the intimidation. I told them if ever I got a place in the ballot I would try to change the law. Now's my chance.

I have three weeks in which to work out what powers are needed and get a Bill drafted. The latter is no simple task: parliamentary and legal language is the preserve of experts and I have access to none. Joan Walley puts me in

touch with the Institute of Environmental Health. They are very helpful
and delighted at the prospect of new legislation. They arrange contact with
Jeff Cooper of the London Waste Regulatory Authority and the process is
underway. I also consult Frank Doran who, as a lawyer, has some idea about
how legislation is drafted. I ask him to be one of my sponsors.

The first goal is to get a long title. This title has to encompass everything
that might be needed in the body of the Bill. If it's too narrow, then scope for
drafting and amendments later will be limited. With the help of the parliamentary clerk who deals with Private Members' Bills I draft a title: 'To provide for
the registration of carriers of controlled waste and to make further provision
with respect to the powers exercisable in relation to vehicles, shown to have
been used in illegal waste disposal.' The Delphic second sentence is devised
by the clerk to give me cover for what I really want, a power to seize and hold
vehicles apprehended in fly-tipping. I've already been told that the government, while sympathetic to establishing a registration scheme, is absolutely
opposed to any powers to seize vehicles. With the innocence of inexperience,
I don't realise that Private Members' Bills only get through if governments allow.

I go back to tell the Silwood tenants the good news and the local press
cover the story. I'm conscious of being watched and possibly followed when
I go to the estate. My red Ford Sierra is easily spotted and I don't want to find
my tyres slashed. Carol and her neighbours are suffering more harassment
and reports are coming in of similar activities in neighbouring boroughs.
The extent of the Docklands redevelopment is such that this is clearly going
to escalate. One day the wife of a very active environmental health officer in
Southwark gets a warning from a man with a sawn-off shotgun. This is getting deadly serious and I take care never to go to Silwood after dark.

The rest of December settles into the routine of local meetings, visits and
Council of Europe. I'm now familiar with the Western European Union
and confident enough to make a major speech challenging its central plank
– the indefinite possession of nuclear weapons. In Paris we have a presentation on the Rights of Children, a new convention being considered at the UN

and in Europe. Not all visits and constituency events are onerous. Some are fun and uplifting, like the visit to Tidemill Primary School where they are collecting buttons for a charity in Mozambique. One of the delights of working in such a diverse community is the links that are forged with other countries which have meaning for the children. The office workload is, however, cause for concern and the Private Member's Bill will take all Gill's time. She agrees to work another half-day a week and I employ a local woman, Sandra Den Hertog, to help with typing. Staff and office costs are reimbursed but the total at the end of my first year reveals I've subsidised my office to the tune of £5,000 out of a salary of £21,000. I'll have to get a grip on that.

MPs who were elected in 1987 have already been offered places on Labour's front bench. I've not wanted to become a shadow minister so soon in my career as it limits activity in other fields. However, Neil asks me to join John Prescott's transport team and specifically to speak on transport in London. I'm not entirely sure it's what I want but I agree and take up the position in the New Year. It coincides with a major transport issue in my own constituency.

The government has proposed a rail link to the Channel Tunnel. I can never see the words 'Channel Tunnel' without thinking of my father. He always believed a tunnel would be built and pledged to buy shares in it the minute the company was launched. But, sadly, it didn't happen until four years after my father died. Every time I use these wonderful trains I imagine how utterly thrilled he would have been to make the journey.

The train link proposals are mad and involve tunnelling under a good chunk of my constituency. Residents are up in arms and this is going to be a major campaign.

January and February 1989 are dominated by my need to get up to speed on the transport brief and prepare for the second reading of my fly-tipping Bill, which is set for 24 February. Fifteen hundred people attend the public meeting in Brockley on the rail link, which is unprecedented.

Somehow I also manage to attend the Labour Party's women's conference and the local government conference and do workshops at both. I also speak at a peace conference in Swansea. But it is the Private Member's Bill that is to be the highlight of 1989.

I have a surprising ally at the London Waste Regulatory Authority. Their chair is none other than a Tory woman councillor, Joan Wykes, who proves an enthusiastic supporter of my Bill. The Road Haulage Association also pledges support, as do many professionals wrestling with the problem across the country. It's clear that making it compulsory to register as a carrier of waste won't be sufficient. Payment of fines won't be enough of a deterrent as there's big money at stake. Disposing legally of builders' waste costs around £200 a ton and 75 per cent of it has to be taken out of London. Seizing lorries is the only answer and I've got to go for it.

Tory grandees Sir George Young and Sir Hugh Rossi (chair of the Environment Select Committee) agree to be sponsors alongside close Labour friends Joan Walley, Harriet Harman and Frank Doran.

Frank and I are now seeing each other outside of work. He likes cooking at his flat and it suits us both to avoid the awful Commons food while we wait for the 10 o'clock vote. I'm conscious that this friendship has crossed a boundary when I'm upset to find he's going to Aberdeen as usual and won't be in the House for the second reading of my Bill.

24 February: The first debate of my Private Member's Bill (called the second reading). In my speech I explain the difficulties in taking prosecutions under the existing law as it is almost impossible to identify the offending party. I note that 90 per cent of fly-tipped waste in London is coming from construction sites, at least 1 million tons at any one time, imposing a huge cost on local authorities who are expected to clean it up. I end my opening speech by describing what has happened on the Silwood Estate, where 'roads have been blocked, a new industrial estate severely blighted and residents' lives made utterly miserable by airborne litter, dust, dirt and mud underfoot'.

The minister on duty is the Conservative Virginia Bottomley. Virginia comments on the composition of the House this Friday. The Bill's author (me), the shadow minister, Joan Walley, the minister and the deputy speaker (Betty Boothroyd) are all women! This is indeed remarkable as there are only forty-one of us out of 650 MPs. Her response to the debate is congratulatory and supportive until predictably she comes to Part II, dealing with the confiscation of vehicles. While expressing sympathy with the goal she says the government 'are not convinced this is the most effective way'. Nonetheless, she ends by hoping that the House will agree to the Bill going into committee.

The real battle begins as we prepare for the committee stage. Meetings are arranged with civil servants at the Department of the Environment, where officials have a real understanding of the Bill. Part II of the Bill, however, requires the support of the Home Office, which they believe is impossible. I'm told that a safe passage will be guaranteed if Part II is dropped. I refuse.

In between the meetings I'm having to do more and more on the transport front bench. I meet anti-roads campaigners at London's Archway and pro-roads lobbyists from the West Country. John Prescott and I are coordinating meetings with all the London anti-rail link protestors. I'm thoroughly enjoying the challenge, though the constant late nights and early mornings take their toll. One evening I have to attend the Millwall Football Club (in my constituency) annual dinner, only to leave to attend a transport debate starting at 10 p.m. The next day I go to Germany for a two-day foreign affairs meeting, then back to a day that begins with a meeting of TGWU officials about buses, followed by a coastguards' lobby, then a meeting with END on Labour's defence policy review. As if this were not bad enough, I then have two transport debates, one starting at 10.20 p.m., the other at 4.10 a.m. Peter Bottomley is the minister and so lightheaded are we both at four in the morning that we collapse in laughter at one point in the proceedings. I reflect ruefully on the fact that I'm doing a schools meeting in a few hours' time.

This tradition of all-night sittings is ludicrous. On one occasion I venture to say as much to an older male colleague as we order cocoa in the Members' tearoom at 3.30 a.m. He advises me not to become a whinger and tells me I'll get used to it. My response, more polite than I felt, was 'if I do I'll be as mad as the rest of you!' I resolved there and then to try to do something about the hours.

Last December there was a rail crash at Clapham Junction due to a signal failure. Thirty-five were killed and 100 injured. On 4 March there is another rail crash, this time at Purley. Six are dead and eighty injured. Just two days later two commuter trains crash at Glasgow Bellgrove, killing one passenger and one of the drivers. John Prescott is constantly on his feet in the Chamber dealing with these tragedies.

I work hard with the assistance of Michael Jack, the clerk on the Private Member's Bill, finally crafting an amendment to Part II that will make it easier for government to support but still creates the power of seizure and disposal. I have every hope of saving Part II of the Bill, despite a very late-night encounter with the Secretary of State, Nicholas Ridley, who pointed his finger between my eyes and said, 'We could blow you out of the water!'

7 April: I attend an address given by Mikhail Gorbachev at the Guildhall. I'm a great fan of Gorbachev. His policies of glasnost (openness) and perestroika (restructuring) have begun to fundamentally change the old order in the USSR. Last year he announced the withdrawal of Soviet troops from Afghanistan and freedom for the Eastern bloc countries to determine their own internal affairs. The latter decision was to lead to a rapid dismantling of pro-Soviet regimes in Eastern Europe. It's a great privilege to hear directly from a man shaping history in our time.

15 April: News is coming in of a horrific accident at the Hillsborough Stadium in Sheffield during a football match between Liverpool and Nottingham Forest. The TV pictures are awful and many people must be dead.

The Channel Tunnel rail link proposals seem to have reached their final stage. There will be ventilation shafts at St Norbert Road, Hilly Fields and Ladywell Fields in my constituency, with the largest construction site in Lewisham

East at Hither Green. People are extremely fearful about the noise and vibration from the tunnelling and even the threat of houses collapsing. For years we've been told it was impossible to extend Tube lines into south London as the ground was not suitable for tunnelling! I talk to BR about compensation plans.

I go out campaigning as often as possible for the Euro elections, including travelling to Oxford and Southampton to help their Labour candidates. The results are excellent. We have won forty-five seats, the Tories thirty-two; a complete reversal of the position in 1984.

With so many campaigns both nationally and locally I continue to get a lot of media coverage. I'm still terrified of going on *Any Questions?* and *Question Time* but as a frontbencher there's no way I can turn them down.

Before the committee stage of my Private Member's Bill I find myself having to take three transport debates on consecutive nights. Preparation for these debates is really hard as junior shadow ministers have no resources beyond the staff (part-time) we employ ourselves. My subjects in one week range from a European directive on driver licensing to the Fennel report on the King's Cross Fire and the Road Traffic Bill.

We spend a morning in committee on my fly-tipping Bill. Frank Doran, Simon Hughes (my Lib Dem neighbour in Bermondsey) and I do all the talking. My amendment to the Bill passes and we proceed to report and third reading two days later. I am jubilant. My Bill completes all its stages in the Lords and finally passes. I'm in the Chamber awaiting Royal Assent. Betty Boothroyd will call the names of the Bills. I hold my breath. If anyone says 'object' I'm done for! She says, 'The Control of Pollution (Amendment) Act 1989'. Silence. It passes. *The Guardian* carries a large photograph of me alongside an article describing the Private Member's Bill procedure. It notes: 'Ms Ruddock's achievement can be measured by the massacre tomorrow of nearly 50 other Private Members' Bills...' I'm absolutely thrilled.

Meanwhile, Keith's career goes from strength to strength. He has become a professor of biophysics and is recognised around the world. His PhD students are highly successful under his guidance and he is very popular with undergraduates. Until I entered Parliament I had taken the closest interest in his work, sharing in the disappointments and the triumphs of the roller-coaster academic life. Now the myriad of new influences on me, particularly Frank, is making me impatient with much that I have previously cherished. I am, without justification, becoming dissatisfied with my life.

I've been contacted by a prison visitor called Chris Palmer who has been visiting my constituent George Long in prison. My attention has also been drawn to a lecture given by Ludovic Kennedy to the Howard League for Penal Reform. It's a remarkable speech:

> Let me remind you of some of these cases. In that of Timothy Evans, hanged for a murder he did not commit, the police first brow beat a confession out of him in the middle of the night, and then persuaded some workmen to retract a statement ... that would have gone a long way to clearing him. In the Patrick Meehan case they rigged an identification parade and planted incriminating evidence. In the Luton Post Office murder they bribed one member of the gang ... to name three totally innocent men ... In the Confait case they bullied confessions out of three young men that resulted in the conviction for murder ... And today there languishes in Long Lartin at Evesham a young man called George Long who has been in prison now for ten years, convicted of a murder solely as a result of another so-called confession ... and which, having seen him and read the papers on his case, I am as certain as he is that he did not commit.

I will follow up with Chris Palmer to see what can be done.

Parliament goes into recess on 28 July after the traditional all-night adjournment debate and, after a couple more weeks of grappling with the backlog, I finally get to go on holiday. Keith and I have arranged to go to the Italian lakes, a place we both love, but I'm a poor companion. I know I'm causing the deterioration in our relationship but I just can't make myself behave better. I make us both unhappy, though at times we're also still so close. I don't know what I'm going to do and two weeks away isn't enough time to think anything through.

Back in London I've a full September diary that includes appearing on *Any Questions?* and an important meeting with British Rail. The route of the Channel Tunnel rail link has now been shelved for a year, which is absolutely hopeless for constituents along the route who need to sell their properties in order to move for work, or in one case retire back to the Caribbean. We had managed to get BR agreement to buy two of the homes but there's no guarantee the sales will go ahead now.

18 September: As a shadow minister for transport with special responsibility for London I'm invited to attend the memorial service for the victims of the *Marchioness* disaster. This terrible accident occurred while we were out of the country but I have since read the reports. In the early hours of 20 August the pleasure boat *Marchioness* was run down by the *Bowbelle*, a dredger many times its size. There were 131 people on board, including crew and catering staff and a large group of young people celebrating the birthday of one of their friends. Fifty-one people died, in a river familiar to Londoners and tourists alike as a place of leisure. It is a very poignant service and I am pressed to meet with relatives of the dead to discuss the subsequent inquiry.

Parliament opens on Tuesday 17 October, when I'm number five at PMQs. I've also drawn number one at Thursday's PMQs. In the event Geoffrey Howe is standing in for Mrs Thatcher. On Tuesday I ask him about the Health Education Authority report that people on income support have to spend 40–50 per cent of their income to eat properly. He gives me a meaningless answer about rising living standards for all. On Thursday I ask what advice he has for Londoners meeting mortgage repayments that have gone up by £161 per month when average joint income remains the same. He says (to gasps) that it's for householders and citizens to make up their own minds!

I'm meeting Alexei Pankin, one of the young researchers at the US and

Canada Institute in Moscow, who is visiting Britain. I'm really keen to hear from him about the progress of glasnost. I leave the Chamber and run down the back stairs. Near the bottom I lose my footing on the loose, worn carpet and fall down the last few steps, landing heavily on my left hand. I pick myself up and rush to Central Lobby to take Alexei for tea. In no time I can't stand the pain in my wrist and see it is swelling very rapidly. Regrettably I call an end to our brief meeting and go in search of Frank, who takes me to St Thomas'. After all the usual tests and X-rays I'm found to have broken my wrist, which will have to be plastered to my elbow.

This might have been an opportunity for Keith and I to get closer but it doesn't happen. Now I can't drive and everything is more fraught than ever. I'm impossible at home (where we now live separately) and it's terrible for Keith as he is preparing his inaugural lecture as Professor of Biophysics. It's so important and I don't know how we're going to get through this. In the event I'm thoroughly awkward at the reception, though I've got Joan Walley for company. Keith is absolutely brilliant. He's so articulate and funny while also demonstrating complete mastery of his subject. I could cry but hold myself together and leave early for a 10 o'clock vote. I know I've hurt him terribly.

The government rushes to complete its controversial Bills on privatisation and public service reform. The rift between Margaret Thatcher and Nigel Lawson, which results in his resignation, has given us all great satisfaction. Throughout this time I've had the additional anxiety of facing reselection. It is now the rule that approximately halfway through the expected parliamentary term all Labour candidates are subject to a reselection process by their local party members. Given the splits in my party when I was selected at the end of 1986 I've been facing this process with trepidation. Fortunately, the threats of my opponents fail to materialise and by the end of the year I've been reselected.

9 November: The Berlin Wall falls. What a triumph for the courageous people who sought democracy for East Germany. I never expected to see such rapid change.

At the State Opening of Parliament the experiment on televising the Chamber begins. Strict rules are in place regarding what the cameras can and cannot record. All very exciting but some apprehension as to whether MPs will play to the gallery.

My fractured wrist leads to a serious backlog in our paperwork, but I keep up with engagements. On a single Friday in November I visit the Deptford Skills Centre, the ambulance station, Hyde Housing HQ, hold meetings with the leader of the council and the local Turkish community about the allocation of local resources, get a briefing on the combined heat and power plant and end with a Deptford into the '90s fundraising dinner.

I have been approached by Thalia Campbell. She has access to parts of the huge peace banner that went around the Pentagon in one of the most spectacular demonstrations in the US on 4 August 1985. The idea of displaying this in the House of Commons is really exciting but as always there will be obstacles to be overcome. First, you only get a place in the Upper Waiting Hall exhibition space by ballot so I have to win a place. Then the exhibition content has to be agreed by the relevant department of government. Clearly there is no way this could be supported by the MoD!

I put in for the ballot and get a place. Now the challenge. I decide to ask for sponsorship from the Minister for the Arts and refer to the fine needlework that will be displayed. To my utter amazement I get permission. The banners are really beautiful and their content quite moving. We set about organising their hanging for a summer exhibition and I will launch it with an appropriate speech!

21 December and I'm giving a reading at the launch of the Bernt Carlsson Memorial Trust. Bernt was Assistant Secretary General at the UN and UN Commissioner for Namibia. We had worked with him at One World. Exactly one year ago to the day Bernt was flying to New York on Pan Am flight 103 when it exploded over Lockerbie, killing all 243 passengers, sixteen crew members and eleven people on the ground.

My activities end on a more cheerful note when we send off a number of dustcarts donated by Lewisham Council as part of Nicaraguan Solidarity, another organisation I support.

Keith and I have never missed a Christmas with our families and resolve not to break with tradition. We do, however, spend the shortest possible time there and I take my mother into my confidence about our situation, warning her not to say anything to Keith or his family.

In January 1990 I convene a walkabout on the Silwood Estate with council officers and the police. This is the beginning of a long process to clean up the area and effect redevelopment of the fly-tipped land. I address a number of transport conferences and a rally of ambulance workers protesting about the government's attitude to their dispute. The government's unpopularity grows with the privatisation programmes for electricity and water and the poll tax. Maggie Coulthard, who has done a terrific job for me for the past three years, has accepted a new post in Cardiff as a European officer. I'm not only sad to see her going but wonder how I will get anyone to take on our onerous caseload.

A constant round of meetings with representatives of transport providers, users and trade unions representing the workers, from roads to rail, to aviation and shipping. I'm also still receiving lots of media requests and suffer the ordeal of *Question Time* and other high-profile programmes. But there are occasional highlights, such as the reception at the ICA for Václav Havel, the charismatic playwright elected this year as the first democratic President of Czechoslovakia in forty-one years.

11 February: This is a sight I never thought I would see. Nelson Mandela is walking out of prison, holding Winnie Mandela's hand. Tears run down my face, no doubt in company with millions of others, as the event is broadcast live across the world. He looks astonishingly fit and entirely recognisable, even though he's been behind bars for twenty-seven years.

The end of his incarceration has been signalled for some months, ever since the new state president, F. W. de Klerk, released all other ANC prisoners.

But to see him walking free is just incredible. This is a man of seventy-one years of age, whose last appearance in public was at his trial in 1964 when he was sentenced to life imprisonment.

Within hours of his release he is speaking of peace and reconciliation and within days to a crowd of 100,000 people. But the struggle is not over. There will be four years of violent upheaval before the general election in 1994 when all black South Africans at last secure the right to vote.

I am number three at PMQs and it's a great opportunity to ask about the government's failure to join continuing sanctions against South Africa following Mandela's release. I begin my question: 'If the Prime Minister had just spent twenty-seven years in prison...' when I am interrupted by a shout from Gerald Kaufman 'as she should'. The House erupts in laughter and I can't continue. As is customary I resume my seat. The Speaker struggles to gain order. I stand again and repeat: 'If the Prime Minister...' Members are convulsed again and the Speaker is shouting to be heard, eventually saying, 'I have never heard the House behave in this way at Prime Minister's Question Time'. I stand for the third time and manage to deliver my question with dignity. Thatcher of course replies that she is against sanctions, saying this is not the way to keep South Africa as the most prosperous economy in Africa.

Years later one of my colleagues who was then running media training courses for MPs told me he always used clips of those exchanges to demonstrate how to keep your cool in the Chamber and not be intimidated. Needless to say I was flattered.

15 February: I've been tipped off by Ken Livingstone that the Comic Strip team have made a programme on the abolition of the GLC and I am portrayed in it. I watch with great apprehension when it appears on TV but it's absolutely hilarious. I'm in the role of CND leader but also a single mother and lover of Ken. My character is played by Dawn French playing Cher. I'm seriously thrilled. It ends with Ken having to put a stake through

Thatcher's heart as she rises up from the grave in which she was buried after the revolution. There is an equally hilarious sequel when one of my mother's Tory friends tells her she was shocked to find that I was 'married' to that Ken Livingstone!

We get excellent results in the May local elections and at last the party is pulling together more effectively. The street surgeries give us lots of cover and mean more party members get used to leafleting.

In Parliament we have a number of successes, including the cancellation of the roads assessment schemes, which have been a running sore for months. Another great success is the seminar on women and transport co-hosted by Jo Richardson and myself. But government cuts continue to take their toll in the constituency, most recently in employment training and childcare allowances, ending much-needed programmes for women.

I have been asked to assist the *Marchioness* families as they strive to get answers to what happened. The media coverage of the events has portrayed the victims as a group of pleasure-seeking rich kids, as though they somehow contributed to their own demise. The parents are naturally distraught. We go to see the Secretary of State for Transport, Cecil Parkinson, to make the case for a public inquiry.

Later in May I attend the National Union of Seamen's conference in Aberdeen for two days. Frank's also invited as the local MP so I get to see him on home turf.

A few days later I get flown to Brussels on BA's new 767 to discuss aviation policy. Not my favourite mode of transport and I can't bring myself to accompany John Prescott when we're invited to fly Concorde!

The June recess is devoted to finding Maggie's replacement – a wonderful woman called Katerina Pasternak – and we say goodbye to Maggie with a party at the end of the month.

My personal life is in meltdown. I really want to move out and get my head together. I could stay with Joan but Keith refuses to cooperate and I don't want things to escalate into a public drama.

Cecil Parkinson makes a statement to the House on the Channel Tunnel rail link giving us the worst of all worlds. No decision on the route is taken and for now existing routes will be used. He takes a lot of flak from both sides of the House. John Prescott's solution is to promise a commission to be set up when we get into government to find a new route and report in six months. It will provide a dedicated track running from the coast with King's Cross as the major interchange. We will also keep open options to use Stratford and continue with Waterloo.

One of the joys of my constituency is the huge variety of cultural events to which I get invited. The latest is put on by Vani Fine Arts, operating at the Ackroyd Centre. Lots of children sitting on the floor playing baby sitars and making a lovely sound. Another pleasant event is turning the first sod at Deptford Wharf for a major new housing estate to be built by the council and housing association partners. Another raft of Bills gets pushed through including the NHS and Community Care Act allowing the Secretary of State to designate some NHS hospitals as self-governing trusts. If Guy's Hospital opts out, the links with Lewisham and North Southwark Health Authority will be severed. Lewisham people will definitely be the losers. Guy's will be able to increase its income from private patients, drop any services it wishes and give preference to patients from other health authorities in order to win contracts. Labour's shadow Health Minister Harriet Harman is launching a major campaign against the opt-outs.

Opposition to the poll tax in England is gathering momentum, with campaigns of non-compliance mirroring those in Scotland where the tax was introduced by the Tories a year earlier. In March there's a major poll tax riot following a rally in central London. One hundred and thirteen people are hurt and more than 400 arrested, but the PM refuses to back down.

I am responsible for a number of transport measures, the most impor- tant of which is the extension of the Jubilee Line Bill. It is debated for five and a half hours, mostly because of concerns about the impact on Parliament Square! The main thrust of my speech is a critique of the government's policy, pressure to keep the Bermondsey and Southwark stations in the Bill and a plea to make the new line fully accessible to wheelchair-bound passengers.

Nelson and Winnie Mandela are visiting London and we are privileged to have them address a separate meeting of the PLP, which Frank and I attend. Afterwards I am thrilled to chat with Winnie. I never thought I'd see the day when they were free, let alone meet them in person.

20 July: The IRA have resumed their bombing campaign. The London Stock Exchange has been massively damaged but fortunately the area had already been evacuated before the bomb went off.

2 August: Iraqi troops invade Kuwait leading to international condemnation and the immediate imposition of economic sanctions against Iraq by the UN Security Council. US President George Bush acts unilaterally, sending troops into Saudi Arabia and seeking support (granted) from other countries, including Britain. For me personally it is a small crisis. I believe passionately that the UN should be the authority in such cases and that existing sanctions should be given a chance to bite. I freely express my views and find them reflected in Neil Kinnock's speech when Parliament is recalled in September. I vote with the government as requested by the party but in all the subsequent debates I cannot do this and consistently abstain.

My crowded constituency programme runs right into August when the whole transport team goes on a fact-finding visit to the continent. We've all got the next general election in mind and the possibility that we will be in government and be able to tackle the massive under-investment in infrastructure. We visit projects in Germany, the Netherlands, France and Belgium over a five-day period. In the Netherlands we learn that they have a twenty-year plan to double the number of people using public transport and visit one bus company where they tell us they raise only 30 per cent of their revenue from fares, the rest is subsidy! Front-bench activity continues into the September recess with visits to Rotterdam and to Brussels to attend the transport committee of the EC and a briefing from the European Commission. September ends as usual with the party conference.

This year has been a total nightmare. The background to every waking hour has been the never-ending trauma in my private life. I have pleaded with Keith to agree to a trial separation to let me try to sort myself out. He has tried but he can't. I've offered to go together for counselling but he refuses. I know it's my fault and I know I could end this but I won't. My friendship with Frank slowly slipped into a love affair. We didn't deceive our partners and at one level we both wanted it not to happen. We all descend into the abyss and ultimately everyone behaves badly. I want to get away from both of them but there is no way for me to easily disappear.

Keith can't bear the thought of other people knowing and thus my obvious solution of going to stay with Joan Walley, who would keep our secret, is vetoed. I am afraid to look for a private rental as it would mean dealing with a local landlord, so instead I decide to find a new-build property and buy it. I do everything in secret, right up until the day I move out with a single suitcase. I hate myself for what I'm doing but I can't stop. Keith and I had been married for twenty-seven years and I love him still but not enough to stay. I live in constant torment while having to maintain my public face and meet my political commitments.

As soon as I move I decide to turn down every media invitation that isn't directly connected to my transport brief. Keith begs me not to tell anyone and it is the least I can do, but in the event it is a bad decision. I will lead this secret life amid continuing desperate misery for the next six months. At the new-build I know no one and I can come and go without the need to explain myself. No one in the party is any the wiser. Frank has also moved out of his home and now stays with a friend in Aberdeen. Occasionally he stays with me but no one is ever happy.

Labour now has a fourteen-point lead in the opinion polls and Mrs Thatcher looks increasingly autocratic and unpopular. Then turmoil erupts as Geoffrey Howe, her deputy Prime Minister, resigns. Thatcher looks doomed. Nonetheless, the following week the Queen's Speech goes ahead. There are two transport Bills that I will be leading on for Labour. In the Road Traffic Bill, I press the government to introduce random breath-testing. We get one concession on safety – the government promises to bring in the compulsory wearing of rear seatbelts.

There is mounting speculation about a challenge to the PM. Howe's devastating critique of her leadership in his resignation speech on 13 November is the trigger. The next day she is challenged by Michael Heseltine. She fails to win the first ballot by four votes and defiantly declares she will fight on and fight to win. But after consultations she withdraws. Before the month is out Mrs Thatcher has gone and John Major is Prime Minister.

I have continued to receive representations about George Long. His case so troubles me that I've decided to go and visit him in prison. He's in Long Lartin and I've asked Frank to accompany me. This is my first visit to a prison and a chilling experience. I don't take to George Long. He seems a cold, distant figure who I feel might have been capable of violence. However, as our conversation progresses I become convinced that he is indeed innocent. The question is, what can be done?

I appear on *Any Questions?* and have to answer a question on the Gulf crisis. I argue that under international law intervention requires a UN decision and we have to find a new way of conducting international affairs in times of conflict. I'm ridiculed by other panel members and Jonathan Dimbleby tries to make trouble for me by saying Neil Kinnock takes a different view. I stick to my position but I know colleagues in the PLP will be complaining about it. I'm not the only one urging the party to stay with the UN and for the moment Neil tolerates our expressing our views.

On 29 November the Security Council passes a resolution giving Iraq until 15 January to withdraw from Kuwait and empowering member states to use all necessary means to force Iraq out. Iraq responds with a proposal to withdraw from Kuwait provided all foreign troops leave the region and that an agreement is reached regarding the Palestinian problem and the dismantling of both Israel and Iraq's weapons of mass destruction.

17 December: There's to be a vote on the reintroduction of the death penalty. Polls still show a majority of the public in favour, even after the huge publicity given to cases where a miscarriage of justice occurred. Alongside the abomination of the state paying one individual to kill another, the fact that the wrong person might be executed seems to me to be an overwhelming argument against. The majority of MPs agree. The amendment is defeated.

The year ends with a pleasurable duty. British Rail is removing the vast fly-tips from the Silwood Arches and I'm asked to turn the first sod in their redevelopment of the arches as small business units.

I'm absolutely dreading Christmas. Keith is adamant his mother cannot be told of our separation. I arrange for us to meet up and go together to his family's Christmas meal. My heart is breaking. I don't know how I could be inflicting such pain on a man I have loved so much and with whom I've spent all my adult life. Somehow we survive.

28 December: My birthday. I'm forty-seven years old but most of the time I feel as unhinged as a hysterical teenager. In fact, I was more stable at seventeen than I am now.

We return to Westminster for another Gulf debate. On 17 January, lying in bed, I hear the announcement that aerial bombardment has begun. My heart sinks. I can't believe we are at war again. When accepting a shadow minister's job you take on some collective responsibility for the party so I have to consider whether I should resign. I don't feel any need to stay on the front bench but a resignation now would be portrayed as a quarrel with our party leader rather than a protest over government policy, for which I'm not voting.

An extensive discussion takes place at a very well-attended meeting of the Supper Club.* At least a dozen of us frontbenchers, including shadow

---

* A group set up by Ian McCartney and Allan Roberts, two Labour MPs who were dissatisfied with the Tribune Group obsession with shadow Cabinet slates and saw the need for progressive people to discuss policy.

Cabinet members, are anxious about the direction Neil might take on the war. UN resolution 678 seeks the restoration of 'peace and security', which could give cover for regime change. Three days later and a piece appears in the *The Independent*. It begins: 'The Labour Party was split from top to bottom over the Gulf war … as it emerged that members of Neil Kinnock's front-bench team had privately broken ranks…' Clare Short, John Prescott, Chris Smith, Jo Richardson and myself are named in the article.

Despite the ongoing crisis, normal parliamentary business has to continue. I have sole opposition responsibility for the first time for a government Bill. This takes an enormous amount of time and effort. It covers major provisions on road safety, changes to the law regarding driving offences, red routes, bus lanes and various kinds of parking in London. Actual committee sessions for the debates run from 10.30 a.m. to 1 p.m. and 4.30 p.m. to 7 p.m. on both Tuesdays and Thursdays.

7 February: The IRA has launched a mortar attack on 10 Downing Street in broad daylight. John Major and his war Cabinet were apparently meeting at the time, discussing the Gulf War. Two shells overshot the building, failing to explode. One shell exploded in the rear garden and four people were injured. The US military has bombed a civilian air raid shelter in Baghdad using laser-guided 'smart bombs'. Over 300 people are dead. Next day I do interviews on the way the Gulf War is being conducted. The bombing has reached such a stage that I call into question the coalition's war aims. I call on the Labour leadership and the government to review their strategy. This is a sacking offence. Neil calls me in and reminds me of the rules. I accept I could now be sacked at any time but I'm not going to resign. Clare Short takes the opposite view and resigns at the next debate, when I again abstain. I still manage to make my views clear with more interviews discussing the war aims and argue the need for a post-war settlement that will include action on that Middle East running sore, Palestine. After five days of ground assault, beginning on 24 February, the coalition declares a ceasefire in the Gulf. Formal terms will

be set by UN resolution in April, but officially Operation Desert Storm (as it's been called) won't end for another four years.

Another meeting of the Supper Club has been organised. We've hardly assembled in our upstairs pub room when a tabloid journalist and photographer burst in. People dive for cover and the meeting is abandoned, never to be reconvened.

18 February: A bomb explodes at Paddington station, damaging the building but causing no casualties. Three hours later another bomb explodes at Victoria station, killing one man and injuring thirty-eight others. For years the government has failed to invest in British Rail and London Underground. Both are now in crisis and the renewed IRA bombing campaign in London has added to people's concerns about the safety of public transport.

In the constituency I'm doing lots of work with our two agencies supporting people addicted to drugs. Their work is remarkable, though so challenging. I'm amazed to find young heroin addicts who are able to hold down jobs and somehow cope with life with the aid of methadone. The needle exchange is highly controversial but, with Aids the greatest threat, it has to be justified. But it's not all doom and gloom. I go to Lewisham Theatre for an absolutely splendid programme of dancing and singing to celebrate Chinese New Year, put on by Mr Truong of the Lewisham Indo-Chinese Community Association.

March opens with a transport conference in Stafford, followed by a series of events celebrating International Women's Day.

The Transport Select Committee has issued a report critical of London Transport's management of their £93 million deficit. This is another opportunity for us and I lead for Labour, pointing out the effects of the current round of cuts on service delivery and the extent of those to come. As if this wasn't bad enough, the government publishes, on the same day, a consultation on privatising London buses! Transport is now very high on the political agenda.

14 March: Front-page news: the Birmingham Six have been released.* I'm alone at home getting ready to leave when the phone rings. It's Frank. The *Today* newspaper has a huge picture of me on their front page under the headline 'We are in love say MPs'. They carry a story and name both Keith and Frank's wife, Pat. I can't believe it. Neither of us has ever spoken to any journalist and only my immediate family know where I live. I am utterly horrified. I must ring Keith, who, apart from Christmas, has refused any contact with me since I left. This is totally beyond my control but I can't apologise enough to Keith and I know Frank is doing the same with Pat. Neither of them will talk to journalists but they'll undoubtedly be harassed.

I close all the curtains and lock the doors. We've tried so hard not to hurt people further and not to bring the party into disrepute. Journalists start banging on my door and calling through the letterbox. I'm embarrassed for my neighbours, but it appears one of them has spoken to the newspaper. How could we end up being a front-page scandal after all this time? I'm desperately worried about Keith and his mother, who still knows nothing.

Before long the house is surrounded. I take advice from Labour HQ. They warn me to speak quietly and keep away from the walls, against which microphones are likely to be held. We expect it to be over quickly if no one gives interviews; Pat and Keith are solid on that. But then the bombshell drops. The *Daily Mail* has gone to Keith's mother's house in south Wales, where she still lives alone. She's ninety years old and quite frail. They force her to let them in, tell her about our separation and photograph our wedding picture that sits on her mantelpiece.

I am devastated and furious at the same time. Vi is utterly devoted to Keith and has no idea I have left him. As for Keith, this is the very worst he could have imagined. I know we have to get help. Geoffrey Bindman is the obvious person. He takes my call immediately and promises to take action

---

* The Birmingham Six were six men sentenced to life imprisonment in 1975 for the Birmingham pub bombings. Labour MP and author Chris Mullin was pivotal in exposing this miscarriage of justice and securing their release after a lengthy campaign.

to stop publication of the wedding photograph, which had been obtained without permission.

I also ring Father Owen, who knows the situation. I explain what has happened and the fact I can't get out. He arranges to come as soon as it gets dark. He will back his car into the space in front of the house and I'll jump in to be driven off immediately. It works, but as we drive off in the dark a photographer jumps in front of us, flashing away and just avoiding a collision with the car.

Geoffrey Bindman succeeds and the *Mail* don't publish the photograph. All four of us are pursued but no one says a word. Dignity is maintained but everyone is badly hurt. My constituency party's policy during the selection process was not to ask any questions about people's personal lives, so I know I won't have a problem, but the coverage is deeply embarrassing.

Friday evening, I have a meeting of the Deptford First committee but thankfully no surgery. The following week I have an endless round of meetings culminating in a weekend planning meeting with the whole transport team in Oxford. We've all been working on our plans for government and I'm planning a document on an integrated transport policy for London. I'm also looking at greening our policy to meet the growing challenge of air pollution. I've been getting technical advice on road pricing and believe this could work in London with beacons that would automatically read number plates and charge drivers. Representatives of all the transport unions are present at our meeting. The whole team has good relations with the TU researchers and leadership and our proposals are well received – even mine, to my great surprise.

Huge job cuts have been announced for Guy's and Lewisham hospitals, as the first stage of the opt-out proposals runs into difficulties. I raise the issues in the House.

There's also a proposal to remove a fire engine from New Cross fire station and Lewisham Council wants to close a failing school. It's a depressing situation, brightened only by invitations from amazing voluntary organisations, such as the Marsha Phoenix Trust and lively social groups such as the Turkish Cypriots' event at Goldsmiths College.

Tory panic on the poll tax produces emergency legislation rushed through in a single day.

I'm known for my campaigning on women's issues but I'm still surprised to receive a request from the Foreign Office to have lunch with the visiting Australian Minister for Women's Affairs. We must establish a women's ministry as Jo Richardson has proposed when we get into government.

Legislation on dangerous dogs is rushed through in twenty-four hours with the Commons sitting until 3 a.m. Panic measures once again.

I'm now seeing more of Frank, who often stays at my tiny house. I've also got to know my very nice immediate neighbours – a solitary young man who is clearly ill and Vee, a very elegant black woman living with her son. One day I'm obliged to accompany the Archbishop of Canterbury on a visit to the newly opened Wavelengths – a state-of-the-art leisure centre in Deptford, followed by a service in St Paul's Church. Frank, who's not familiar with Deptford itself, is to meet me after the service. Apparently he arrives early and decides to find a pub. Seeing one with a Belhaven sign (a well-known Scottish brewer) Frank enters the gloomy interior, where he finds two other customers and no Belhaven beer. Nonetheless, he settles down in a corner seat with his newspaper and half a pint. Within minutes he is joined by a woman who first greets and then propositions him. This is Frank's memorable introduction to Deptford.

Another train crash, this time near Glasgow, where four people are killed and twenty-two injured.

Frank and I are getting away for a couple of weeks. One of my active GC* members, Helen, has a house in the Dordogne that she rents cheaply to friends. This is a wonderful opportunity for us to escape and we grasp it gratefully.

Frank and I also attend Pat and David's wedding. (Pat will now be known as Pat Jordan Evans.) A truly happy occasion. Theirs is a great relationship and the gallery and harpsichord-making are both flourishing.

---

* As the GMC had been renamed.

Another important event is the launch of Labour's commitment to 'A New Sex Equality Bill'. This is an issue very close to my heart, along with my commitment to racial equality and work with black organisations in the constituency.

Frank, meanwhile, has worrying news of his dad, who is suspected of having lung cancer. He has obviously been ill for some time. Frank goes to Edinburgh to take his father for tests. When he speaks to the consultant afterwards he is told his father's condition is terminal.

Speculation is growing about a possible autumn general election. The Tories have overtaken us in the polls and John Major is having a field day on the international stage. We have around 1,000 members and I decide to mail everyone with a general election alert and a pro-forma asking for commitments to help with canvassing, leaflet deliveries and mailings. We think the campaign will cost around £6,000 so I also ask for donations.

I do five fringe meetings on transport at the party conference, another round of constituency and transport meetings, then back to Westminster for a mere seven days before the session ends officially with no election called.

Keith has been appointed head of the biophysics group at Imperial. This is so well deserved and I feel terrible that I've undermined all his joy at this recognition of his talent.

The centrepiece of the Queen's Speech at the end of October is the legislation to replace the poll tax with a council tax. Rarely can a government have had to introduce a Bill to remedy a major Act introduced within the same parliament. It's going to be rushed through in an effort to save the Tories at the coming general election. My brief continues to throw up key issues, not least the constant breakdowns on the London Underground of lifts and escalators, which are falling apart due to lack of investment. I press the minister for ring-fenced funds. The government has also announced it will hive off the Docklands Light Railway to the London Docklands Development Corporation who, by their own admission, know nothing about running a railway. December is dominated by debates on Maastricht, with the debate on the outcome of the conference providing the occasion for one of Neil's best performances.

Big issues have been dominating the constituency postbag. British Rail have decided to close a road bridge linking two parts of Honor Oak. This is absolutely vital to local residents and 1,000 signatures are raised on a petition in a very short time. I'm in negotiations with both BR and the council pressing for a solution to keep it open. I've also been trying to mediate between Goldsmiths' management and students after an injunction was taken out to end student occupation, and with tenants and residents associations and the police about plans to end community policing. There is never a dull moment in Deptford!

One very pleasant duty is my attendance at the Mayor's carol service at St Paul's Deptford. This is the wonderful church where Father David Diamond is the priest and where John Silkin's funeral was held. It was designed by Thomas Archer, the architect of the more famous St John's in Smith Square, close to the House of Commons. John Betjeman described the church as 'a pearl at the heart of Deptford'. Like many atheists I love the architecture of the best religious buildings, their serenity and church music. Being brought up in south Wales, singing is second nature and I know all the Christmas carols. I have to do a reading but with respect to my preferences I'm given a poem as usual. A lovely evening.

20 December: I've just returned to the office after doing some Christmas shopping when I get a frantic phone call from Katerina. Keith has been trying to get hold of me. His mother is dead. I know he will be devastated so I ring and arrange to see him immediately and drive him to his sister's home in Bray. Keith is torn between needing my comfort and hating me for what I've done. He insists I attend the funeral, which is what I want to do, but feel I am bound to cause offence. It's an entirely private affair held in the front room of his mother's tiny house. I am overwhelmed with emotion but relieved to be able to be close to Keith and supporting him, even for a short time. Susan and my mother are the only non-family members attending.

I spend a pleasant evening before Parliament resumes at a concert given by the Docklands Sinfonietta, performing in Deptford. They've asked me to be a patron and I'm delighted to accept. Loads more meetings as usual but good news too. Lewisham Council has agreed to rebuild the Honor Oak footbridge with a contribution from BR, the reorganisation of the police has been postponed to allow for further consultation and Deptford will get extra officers to meet our special needs. Most importantly I have obtained a meeting with Home Office minister Peter Lloyd to discuss the George Long case, which, thanks to the dogged campaigning of Chris Palmer, now George's girlfriend, has definitely advanced.

Katerina and Gill are working brilliantly but we end up with very considerable backlogs as we get to each recess. Last summer we hardly got up to date before the session resumed and now we know we will have to clear the decks before the general election. Katerina has again analysed our casework, which changes very little, but she's picked out examples where our interventions have been successful. This is important as caseworkers can all too easily be overwhelmed by the misery and despair that comes to an MP in a deprived area such as ours. We write up some positive examples for my report to the CLP AGM in February:

- Persuading the immigration authorities to allow an eighteen-month-old child to enter the country. Her mother, a British citizen, had given birth overseas but had not realised that she should have obtained a certificate of entitlement to British citizenship for her child – the child was refused entry because of this error.
- Helping to get a young single mother rehoused (she had been in B&B accommodation in Lewisham for over eighteen months before my complaint to Southwark Council's Homeless Persons Unit).
- Helping to get a mother who was threatened with violence by her ex-partner rehoused.
- Securing settlement of a compensation claim against the council

by tenants whose home had been repeatedly flooded due to blocked drains (they were awarded £1,750).

- Securing settlement of a long dispute over claims for Sickness Benefit and Invalidity Benefit. The constituent received over £3,000 in backdated benefits.

- Securing settlement of a long dispute over a claim for Invalid Care Allowance (the constituent received over £1,700 in backdated benefits).

- Getting an operation date for a young woman who had a fibroid (she had already had two operations cancelled and by the time she was operated on, the fibroid was the size of a 22-week-old foetus).

- Getting the council to repaint double-yellow lines in front of a doctor's garage.

Some issues brought to us by individuals are repeated so often that I have to try to find a community-wide solution. Repeatedly – at surgeries, in letters and telephone calls – constituents complain about cockroaches in their homes. By writing to all the tenants and residents associations in Deptford I eventually manage to build up an idea of how widespread the problem is and discuss the issue with the council's new housing solicitor. The council must be persuaded to seek warrants to gain entry to flats where residents will not consent to the treatment of their homes. Clearly this is a very sensitive issue but, given that cockroaches cause considerable distress to those plagued by them, I cannot see any alternative. Complaints about noise pollution are also increasing.

28 February: London Bridge station has been bombed by the IRA. Twenty-eight people are injured.

We find a temporary letting in Deptford High Street as a general election HQ. Once we get the contract we go in to clean and disinfect and give it a lick of paint. Jim Stevenson is able to get BT to fast-track a couple of phone lines and we organise a print of introductory leaflets. As a seat with a 'safe' majority we have to do everything ourselves so I'm adding drafting leaflets to the rest of my busy workload.

The House is now a farce as legislation is guillotined and the Tories use their position to promote themselves for the election, which Major will call on 11 March. We debate the extension of the DLR to Lewisham and Deptford, which is hugely important to us, and I pledge from the front bench that Labour will return the DLR to London Transport when we win the general election. The election is a daunting prospect. Labour has a small lead in the polls and we're all more determined than ever to rid Britain of a government that has ruined public services and devastated communities such as mine.

Frank is in a very different position. Employment in the North Sea delivers high wages and the standard of living in Aberdeen is in sharp contrast to Lewisham and most Labour areas. John Smith, shadow Chancellor, has outlined tax increases that Frank fears will have a major impact on oil workers in Aberdeen. At one meeting on an offshore platform Frank starts to expound the virtues of Labour's approach to health and safety in the industry. But nobody wants to listen – all they want to talk about is the proposed tax increases. Every one of them is earning above John Smith's new threshold. When Frank relates this to John, he is told 'what may be bad for Aberdeen is good for the rest of the country'.

Frank didn't expect to win the seat last time so this will be an uphill task. He's had an incredibly high profile and worked extremely hard but it may not be enough. We don't really discuss it. MPs have to fight to win no matter what the odds. It'll be a hard time for both of us without support at home and with painful memories always bursting through. As always the momentum of the campaign carries me along. I have to do various visits as a transport frontbencher but most of the time I'm pounding the streets of the constituency, knocking on doors, organising party members and going home exhausted every day. John Smith issues a detailed shadow Budget on 17 March in advance of the manifesto. Unknown to me, Frank considers this to be the final nail in the coffin for him.

The right-wing media keeps up a vicious assault on Neil Kinnock, and the Tories have massive posters backing their negative campaigning. I begin to think the best we can hope for is a hung parliament.

Jim Dowd is the candidate again in Lewisham West and a new candidate, Bridget Prentice, is standing in Lewisham East. We have to win both seats if Labour has any chance of forming a government. It's a thrilling prospect but all my enthusiasm is tempered by my concerns for Frank and also for Keith, who I know must be feeling particularly hurt at this time of my very public local presence.

On the Saturday before the election Frank spends most of the day at his father's bedside and then travels back to Aberdeen. Next morning, he calls me to say his father is dead. I want to fly up to be with him but he tells me the campaign is more important. We are both very emotional. Frank's mother puts huge pressure on the funeral director to give her the earliest possible date for the funeral. She is determined it must be held before the election to give Frank the best chance of holding onto his seat. His father is cremated on Wednesday.

9 April: The ominous front page of *The Sun*. Neil's face is superimposed on a lightbulb, urging 'the last person to leave Britain' to 'please turn out the lights' if Labour wins. After being driven around all day by Jim and constantly addressing whole neighbourhoods from the loudspeaker I go home and change, put on a lovely red linen suit with a fresh red rose supplied by my mum. As usual the two marginals will be counted first.

We win them. Bridget has a majority of 1,095 and Jim of 1,809. But then I take a phone call from Frank. He's lost. I stand riveted to the ground, not knowing where to look, desperately trying to compose my face. I go to the ladies' toilets and call him back but it's a perfunctory call; the Aberdeen declaration is about to begin. I tell those closest to me but I have to keep up appearances for the next three hours while my own count is completed. Even as we celebrate Jim and Bridget's success we can see from the TV commentary that we're not doing well enough. My own majority nearly doubles to over 12,000. I make my acceptance speech but my mind is in turmoil and I can't wait to speak to Frank. We go back to HQ to thank all those who've worked and waited for us. We've had a great campaign in Lewisham but we've lost the country and I feel gutted for Neil and Glenys.

My priority is to see Frank, who can't wait to get out of Aberdeen and fly to London. Coming after so much recent trauma, the death of his father and loss of the seat are devastating. He wants to go away somewhere so we fly back to Aberdeen, pick up the car and drive to Kyleakin where we get the ferry to Skye. This is my first visit to a Scottish island and its bleak and misty emptiness soothes our despair. We spend three days talking and consoling each other. The future is too difficult to contemplate.

Parliament meets at the beginning of May for the taking of oaths and the Queen's Speech. I limit myself to the former as I'm far too depressed to stomach a House full of gloating Tories. Frank is one of only five Labour MPs to have lost his seat. I don't know how we're going to cope. He gets a winding-up allowance so there's no immediate financial panic but he doesn't feel he can go back to law in Scotland and he can't practise in England.

The government introduces paving measures for the privatisation of British Rail and British Coal. Network SouthEast announces huge operating losses and I continue to battle with ministers over red routes and the widening of the M25. Frank, meanwhile, is winding up his office in Aberdeen and contemplating his future.

With Neil's resignation the party is gearing up for a special conference in July to elect his successor and deputy. Margaret Beckett is seeking nomination for the deputy leadership, along with John Prescott and Bryan Gould. I feel compelled to support Margaret as I believe the leadership must be shared between the genders. This puts me on a collision course with John's backers, who threaten me as a consequence. I'm really sick at making this decision as John has been a good friend and has every right to expect my loyalty.

The House rises early on 16 July and the special conference is held on 18 July. I vote for John Smith and Margaret Beckett, both of whom are elected.

New leadership means reshuffles. While I was really keen to have responsibility for transport in government there seems little point now in continuing with the brief in opposition. Frankly, with my private life in meltdown I'm interested in very little. Parliament is in recess but I'm spending time catching up. The shadow Cabinet posts are being distributed and as I'm leaving one afternoon Tony Blair (who I don't know at all) calls over and asks for my phone number.

I knew someone would want to talk to me about future portfolios so I let people know I'm staying with Joan Walley in Stoke. No sooner are we there than I get a call – it's John Smith telling me that Tony Blair would like me to join his Home Office team. This is not what I expected. I know nothing about Home Office policies and certainly have no interest in them. I ask John if I could have time to consider the offer. I wasn't sure I wanted to work with someone I didn't know on a brief I didn't want. I ring Frank in Scotland. He'd worked as a shadow minister in Tony's energy team. Frank's advice is to go for it. 'Tony's good to work with and full of ideas.' He thinks a new challenge is just what I need. Without enthusiasm I accept and make arrangements to meet up with Tony. Other members of the team are Alun Michael, a Welsh MP, and Graham Allen from Nottingham. I'm to be shadow Prisons Minister and responsible for crime and policing in London and race relations.

Frank has to look for employment and doesn't want to lose contact with Aberdeen. He goes round the oil companies with a proposition. Using his knowledge and contacts, built up as Labour's oil and gas spokesperson, he is able to offer insights into trade union positions that will be helpful to the oil companies. Surprisingly they are up for it as apparently many realise they don't have a good understanding of the unions and the unions are keen to cooperate with Frank.

16 September: Britain crashes out of the ERM. John Major took Britain into the European Exchange Rate Mechanism only two years ago and desperate attempts have been made to stay in. Norman Lamont, the Chancellor,

has raised interest rates from 10 per cent to 12 per cent (with a promise to raise them to 15 per cent) but all has failed. I'm on *Any Questions?* two days later.

Parliament is recalled on 24 September for a statement on the ERM crisis. Major's speech is poor and John Smith's excellent.

Frank has managed to set up a small consultancy providing services to a few local authorities as well as the oil industry. This is just enough to enable him to keep his flat in Aberdeen and go up for his Labour Party monthly meetings. It's crucial he keeps in touch and makes himself available if he is ever to contest the seat again.

At party conference I'm now doing fringe meetings on prison reform, on young offenders and attending the Police Federation reception. The November Queen's Speech contains a commitment to changing the Sunday trading laws, which will fall to the Home Office. No one in our shadow team wants to take it on and Alun Michael in particular can't do it as he's a committed supporter of the 'Keep Sunday Special' campaign.

I use my first Home Office question time to attack the government's plans to privatise the prison service and call for the full implementation of the Woolf report into prison reform. My first debate is on crime and policing in London where I raise the issue of the rise in racist attacks and the need to take action.

Every so often someone comes to my surgery with a desperate story that shocks even the case-hardened MP. A lovely young woman tells of the horrific violent rape she endured in Greece. She very nearly lost her life as the perpetrator attempted to strangle her. She was on a very small island and her assailant was quickly arrested and held in custody. She insisted on charges being pressed and asked a friend in the UK to contact the British embassy in Athens. They said she would have to reach Athens first. She was forced to travel on the same boat as her attacker and once in Athens she was made to stand in line for hours and then shout the details of her case through a glass screen. She was treated rudely and unsympathetically. She is not asking me for any help, but simply to protest. I am horrified. After satisfying myself there is nothing more I can do, I promise to write to the Foreign Secretary. In due course I get a good response – new and specific training is to be given to all consular staff.

19 October: The saddest news. Petra Kelly, founder of the German Green Party, and her partner Gert Bastian have been found shot dead. I'm really shocked and upset. I never had the chance to get to know Petra properly but we met a few times during the CND years. No one lived her life with greater intensity. She exuded passion and it's impossible to imagine she could be dead.

A furore over Lewisham Council's plans to sell off the Carnegie-endowed library on Lewisham Way. I'm completely opposed and am supporting a group of artists whose licence to occupy a decommissioned school at Hilly Fields has been terminated by the council. They want to move into the library but clearly have no hope of buying it. I'm negotiating hard. We have to struggle to keep such buildings in public ownership. Not only are they part of the precious local heritage but they are vital to the sustainability of our local arts community. After a long battle, we are successful and the artists move into the library, which becomes known as the Art House.

Concern is growing over the London Ambulance service and we are hastily arranging meetings. I raise a local case with the minister. An eighteen-year-old woman has tragically died of an asthma attack at home. The ambulance took half an hour to reach her at 4 o'clock in the morning.

I've started getting to grips with the Sunday trading laws. Personally I'd much prefer there was no trading on Sundays but the supermarkets have defied the law and started opening. Tony is in favour of change and the shadow Cabinet will support him, although there will be a free vote. Ray Powell, a senior whip known for trading favours for blank ballot papers in shadow Cabinet elections, is leading the opposition to Tony via the Keep Sunday Special group.

The key to my approach will be the views of the unions as my greatest concern is for the people who will have to work (mainly women). I meet with the minister Peter Lloyd to explore the government's approach and set out how we might respond. Many Labour MPs are opposed, including many of my friends. It's a poisoned chalice and I'm not going to do it unless I can satisfy my own conscience.

The unions' bottom line is no coercion on existing workers to do Sunday shifts and double pay for all. Tesco is already paying double on Sundays but there's no guarantee this would happen if the law were to be changed. My first test is to visit the local Tesco store and ask to discuss the experiences (in private) of those who are currently working on Sundays. I'm surprised by the answers. Some are young people working one day for pocket money. They tell me it's much better than having nothing to do and nowhere to go. Then I speak to women with families at home. They tell me it's a relief to be out, forces Dad to do childcare and gives them money they need. They all present as volunteers and no one has any complaints. Quite hard for me to maintain my position!

Prison is awful. It was the one thing I dreaded as a CND activist. Just the thought of being enclosed in a cell made me suffer claustrophobia. Now I'm seeing the reality at Holloway. I talk to lots of the women about why they are there and their attitudes to both prison and to life in general. Most are in for less serious offences such as shoplifting and failure to pay fines. They are clearly not dangerous and ought to be punished in the community. The worst problem is separation from children and the worry about their care, especially for the single mothers. Babies are allowed in Holloway but only up to the age of six months. The prison staff and governor appear to have reasonable attitudes to their charges and efforts are made to engage the women in activities. There is one particular group of women that clearly ought not to be incarcerated. They are mainly from South America. Their stories are similar – desperate poverty, children to support and offers of quick money if they act as drug mules. They are as much victims of the drug dealers as those who end up as addicts. Many have poor English and no means of making contact with their children on another continent, let alone sending them money. Sentences are often long – a burden to the British taxpayer without any benefit in deterrence as the women are entirely expendable to the drug overlords. They should be deported on conviction.

I've been invited to a conference in Greenwich, organised by the Anti-Racist Alliance. I'm stunned to learn just how bad the situation is. Within the Greenwich area alone there have been three violent deaths of young black men: Roland Adams, Orville Blair and Rohit Duggal, at the hands of white youths. Speaker after speaker accuses the police of not doing enough to bring the perpetrators to justice. A young lawyer, Imran Khan, is particularly impressive.

November ends with the long-awaited statement on Sunday trading with Kenneth Clarke setting out the timetable. We make it clear we will only support the measure if it includes statutory and comprehensive employment protection. This is my bottom line and I'm satisfied I can see it through, though Ray Powell is going to be a problem. I leave directly for another appearance on *Question Time*.

Some good constituency news. My Parliamentary Questions (PQs) on delays faced by claimants for disability living allowance have paid off – literally. Fifteen of the twenty claims are successful and eleven constituents received over £14,000 in backdated benefits, but I'm still battling with the council over the old Deptford Library.

It's been a rollercoaster politically. The government has often been in disarray over the economy, the pit closure plan and Maastricht in particular. Events in Yugoslavia and Somalia have also been a continuing subject of debate. Unemployment continues to rise as do levels of crime in London. There is little to be cheerful about. Constant turmoil in my private life has left me unable to interest myself in anything outside the constituency and front-bench brief and my interest in foreign affairs wanes. The siege of Sarajevo has continued since April. Serb atrocities in eastern Bosnia are mounting; whole villages are being ransacked and all the Muslim men killed and the majority of the women raped. The UN Protection Force has had its mandate extended but it makes little difference.

It's been hard for the parliamentary party to recover from the devastating general election defeat, and overall there is still an air of despondency.

The start of the New Year is dominated by Maastricht debates and everyone is quickly exhausted by the late nights. In March 1993, Mark Fisher introduces a Private Member's Bill on freedom of information, which also gets a second reading. Serb forces have killed the deputy Prime Minister of Bosnia-Herzegovina and Croats are now also at war with Bosnian Muslims.

This month I'm visiting Wolds prison in Humberside and Pentonville here in London and beginning to get a clear view of the very necessary reforms needed, not least to discourage reoffending. Tony is making a name for himself with his effective debating style and his forensic examination of the government's case, no matter what the issue. This month in both the crime debate and the renewal of the Prevention of Terrorism Act he regularly out-manoeuvred Ken Clarke.

Easter recess and I make a disastrous visit to Aberdeen, where I have an accident that results in an emergency operation to remove a torn cartilage in my knee. It's too bad for keyhole surgery so I end up in great pain, bandaged, plastered and on crutches. I'm amazed at how quickly I adapt to the crutches but it's a very good lesson in understanding the extra burdens faced in daily living by people with impaired mobility. I cancel loads of engagements and only go in for my front-bench duties and voting.

22 April. There's been another murder of a young black man in neighbour-ing Eltham. Apparently eighteen-year-old Stephen Lawrence was waiting at a bus stop in the evening with a friend when they were set upon by five white youths. Stephen was stabbed and left to die.

Back on my feet with the usual twenty-plus engagements in May. There's a major reshuffle in government and Michael Howard is appointed Home Secretary.

The parents of Stephen Lawrence hold a press conference to complain that not enough is being done to catch his killers. Two days later they have a symbolic meeting with Nelson Mandela.

My research into racially motivated crimes has been given added momentum by the Stephen Lawrence killing and I'm preparing a report for publication in July. I arrange a meeting with the Greenwich Council leadership and the local police chief to discuss racial attacks in south London.

3 July: Keith and I were married thirty years ago today. I'm so sad.

The month is truly hectic. The launch of my paper on racial attacks attracts a lot of attention and results in lots of meetings with interested parties, such as the Commission for Racial Equality and the Chief Commissioner of the Metropolitan Police. I publish the statistics from all the police forces in England and Wales. Racial incidents have risen dramatically in the past four years to 7,793 in 1992. I argue that the actual level could be as high as 70,000 as the British Crime Survey notes only one in ten such incidents are reported. While familiar with events in south London, I am shocked to find that in Blaenavon, so close to my childhood home, a shop owned by a black family has been burned to the ground in an arson attack. I record fatalities from London, Birmingham and Manchester and quote a Preston survey that found the majority of non-white people admitted some member of the family had suffered racial harassment.

Britain is not alone – the rising tide of racism appears to be Europe-wide. Racial violence is being fed and inflamed by the activities of the far right and neo-Nazi groups. Although the connection cannot be proved, many people think the opening of the British National Party's HQ in Bexley in 1990 has been a factor in the dramatic increase in the number of racial incidents in south-east London.

My report analyses the way that reported incidents are dealt with and finds evidence that racially motivated physical attacks tend to be classed as 'common assault'. Common assault is a non-arrestable offence and victims are directed towards civil action – hardly an appropriate response. I also note that only 1 per cent of police officers in England and Wales are from ethnic minorities; only 5 per cent of the magistrates appointed in 1991; 30 per cent of main grade probation officers; three out of 451 circuit judges and only 173 out of 24,135 prison officers. These figures paint a stark picture of the racial divides in our society more than a quarter of a century after race discrimination legislation was first introduced by Labour.

Frank has been asked by Bill Morris, General Secretary of the TGWU, to run the unions' political fund ballot. He will have to organise campaigns for over 6 million union members in over thirty unions throughout the UK. This is the second time ballots have been required following the Conservative government's imposition of a ten-year cycle of ballots for unions that wished to operate a political fund. Frank will be based at the TUC and the job will last for three years, taking us probably to the next election. This is a great relief as Frank can now earn just enough to live in London, travel to Aberdeen, keep the flat and have a political profile.

It's summer and I've lots of events to attend that emphasise what is positive: the Women in Politics exhibition in the House, the Bangladeshi Women's annual cultural event, delightful end-of-term exhibitions at primary schools, the Deptford Festival, an exhibition at the now flourishing Art House in the old library and the Fordham Park Festival.

Parliament ends in spectacular fashion. In the 22 July debate on the Social Chapter the government manages to defeat Labour's amendment by only a single vote and then loses its own vote immediately afterwards. As a consequence, there's a vote of confidence in John Major on Friday, which the government win easily, but damage has been done.

This is my third year in my rabbit-hutch home. All the rooms are so small that I'm finding it quite oppressive. It brings home to me how utterly awful it is for the thousands of overcrowded families who live in similar spaces, albeit in flats, not even a terraced house. I'm a bit ashamed to feel this way. Every week I see exhausted mothers with fractious, sickly children in my surgeries explaining how they all sleep in one room, with no privacy, nowhere to do homework and nowhere to keep possessions, which are often moulded by damp conditions and condensation. But I also have a financial imperative:

like so many other people I'm in negative equity. My fear is if I wait any longer I'll never be able to move.

Months of painful negotiations with Keith ensue. I don't want him to have to sell up but I do want him to raise some money for me on the house we own together, which is now almost mortgage free. I lose £20,000 on the sale but manage to secure a mortgage and buy an Edwardian semi in Ladywell. Finances are very strained but it will be a new start when Frank and I move in in October.

My last meeting before the recess is held at the request of the Stephen Lawrence family. Charges have been dropped against those accused of Stephen's murder. Despite the fact that the names of the suspects were provided to the police from various sources within three days of the crime, no arrests were made for a further two weeks. There is something badly wrong with their investigation and together with their lawyers we go to see Peter Lloyd at the Home Office to demand action.

The recess is disrupted by my researcher Gill deciding to move on after six years' invaluable work. Nearly 500 people apply for the job, a real headache. I appoint Antonia Bunnin.

Millwall's new stadium is to be opened by John Smith and Frank and I are invited. The New Den is the first new all-seater stadium to be completed after the Taylor report on the Hillsborough disaster. Sporting Lisbon, a top European team then managed by Bobby Robson, has come to play a friendly. None of this is of great interest to me but Frank is in his element.

Pressure mounts in September as I'm trying to sort out the house move, provide supervision for Antonia and cover a host of previously arranged meetings and events. There's a press conference organised by the Stephen Lawrence family at the House of Commons and a march and vigil that I attend a few days later.

In Lewisham, we are extremely fortunate in having some excellent black community leaders. Foremost among them is Sybil Phoenix. Sybil came aged thirty to the UK from Guyana in 1957, already a trained youth worker and assistant minister in the Methodist church. When her ten-year-old daughter

Marsha was killed in an accident Sybil turned from her personal tragedy to found the Marsha Phoenix Trust to provide housing for homeless girls. She was also one of the first people at the scene of the appalling New Cross fire of 1981 when fourteen young black people died. Ever since, Sybil's role in the community has been appreciated and now Goldsmiths College is to make her an Honorary Fellow. I'm delighted to attend the ceremony and the Warden's dinner to honour her and others at the end of September.

Sadly, the very next day I'm speaking at the London memorial service for Petra Kelly. Theories about her death have abounded since last October but I think it's probably true that Gert shot her and them himself, most likely a murder rather than a double suicide. What isn't contested is that they loved each other and had an intense mutual dependency that may have been the motivation for Gert's actions. A Nazi tank commander and member of a right-wing party, Gert Bastian was the least likely ally of the left-wing Kelly. He was also married and twenty-four years her senior. But, having re-joined the army after the war and become a general, Bastian couldn't accept the planned deployment of war-fighting nuclear weapons on German soil. He resigned from the army and signed, with Petra Kelly, the founding document of the peace movement, the Krefeld Appeal. They were soon inseparable, but perhaps Gert's declining health and advancing years led him to believe they couldn't go on. Petra was just forty-four when she died. At her memorial I quote 'I am a dangerous woman' by Joan Cavanagh, which I'd heard Petra herself use. Its ends:

> *I am dangerous because*
> *I won't give up or shut up*
> *Or put up with your version of reality.*
> *You have conspired to sell my life quite cheaply*
> *And I am especially dangerous*
> *Because I will never forgive nor forget*
> *Or ever conspire*
> *To sell your life in return.*

Before the recess Tony Blair pressed me to stand for the shadow Cabinet. At first I was reluctant but then decided I'd better oblige. Knowing that most such elections were fixed by the whips or, I suspected, the leader's office, I didn't exert myself. In the event I got a respectable first timer's forty-seven votes, but realised no effort had been made by Tony.

Michael Howard declares 'prison works' at his party's conference, giving me the chance to table a huge raft of questions on prisons and prisoners on our return to Westminster. I've already published a paper on the effects of the privatisation and contracting-out process in our prisons. Many prisons are overcrowded, with sometimes three prisoners in a single cell and there are also wings where prisoners are locked up for twenty-three hours a day. Rehabilitation this isn't.

I attend a wonderful performance by Beverley Glean's dance company IRIE! at the newly reopened Albany. Such a joy. I've also received an unusual invitation. The National Theatre has invited me to join a panel discussion following a production of David Hare's trilogy of plays about British institutions. It's the final one, *The Absence of War*, which is a thinly disguised portrayal of Neil Kinnock. The performance is excellent, with John Thaw in the lead role, but to me it's not a fair representation and I have a lot to say on the panel.

Another meeting with Home Office minister Peter Lloyd to discuss the Sunday Trading Bill, which is due to be published in a couple of weeks' time. A round of intense discussions and media interviews follows its publication. Tony opens the debate on 29 November, arguing that while we all agree change is required to the outdated 1950s act it is the nature of that change which has to be settled. In my closing speech I argue that an extra financial reward for Sunday working would give proper recognition to the continuing special nature of Sunday. I indicate that we will seek amendments to ensure choice about working and double pay for doing so.

30 November: The Budget is designed to hold the Tory Party together but will continue to inflict blows on people's living standards. One positive

announcement is that the extension of the Docklands Light Railway to Lewisham can go ahead, if private funding can be found. I immediately table PQs to get more information. The lack of underground lines in Lewisham has always been a limitation on travel to work and this link will bring new hope to the unemployed.

Options are to be presented on Sunday trading. The partial deregulation option passes on a free vote. The Bill will now go into committee and I have to give our whips the names of MPs willing to serve on it. As I will be putting forward the shadow Cabinet's agreed line from the front bench, it's important I have a majority of members on my side of the committee to support me. I include the most vociferous advocate, Janet Anderson.

Days later, I am furious. The list has now been published by the Committee of Selection and Janet is not on it. Five supporters of the Keep Sunday Special Campaign, including Ray Powell himself, are. This is intolerable. I am doing what the leadership wants and being thoroughly undermined. Tony has got to sort this. He has been reluctant to confront the whips but I insist, saying I can't be expected to take the Bill forward unless we have guarantees of no sabotage. He agrees to a meeting with Don Dixon, the deputy chief, where I'm obliged to do most of the talking.

The final week has last votes Monday to Thursday at 11.37 p.m., 12.10 a.m. (House adjourned 6.19 a.m.), 2.45 a.m. and 11.24 p.m. respectively, ensuring that everyone goes home exhausted with only days to plan for Christmas.

I'm no exception. In the past two months I've been trying to get the house organised. Damp was apparent as soon as we moved in so I arranged to get a damp-proof course installed. This has been done but I didn't realise how long it would take to dry out and the impossibility of repainting the rooms until it had. This is a bit of a disaster as I've invited my family to visit Frank and me in London for the first time.

# 1994

We go into committee for the Sunday Trading Bill beginning with a day of spoiling tactics led by David Alton, another Keep Sunday Special fanatic. Six of my ten Labour members support Alton's first motion, making for a less than satisfactory first day. We devote the next five sittings of the committee to losing amendments or withdrawing them after debate so that we can bring them back at report stage. Labour members are now voting en bloc and our position is focused on ensuring safeguards for workers and limiting to six hours the opening times of major stores.

In February we debate the employment clauses of the Sunday Trading Bill. I table dozens of amendments and secure a number of small concessions, but the government refuse to budge on double-time payments. The high profile debate did, however, enable USDAW (the shop workers' union) to secure voluntary commitments from all the major companies.

1 February: Jo Richardson is dead. This is such a sad end. Jo was our shadow Minister for Women and a truly dynamic woman until she had to have an extremely serious operation that resulted in her neck and head being held in a brace. Finally, she needed a wheelchair and the House of Commons authorities failed to make any provision for her to return to the Commons. She nonetheless represented her Barking constituents right up to the end. As always there is immediate speculation about the by-election that will follow. I attend her sad funeral.

Two weeks later we have debates on two important issues of principle: capital punishment and the age of consent for gay men. For the second time the return of capital punishment is resoundingly rejected. The age of consent is a more fraught affair. This is the first debate on the issue since homosexual acts between men over twenty-one were decriminalised by the Labour government in 1967. The outspoken former Tory minister Edwina Currie has tabled an amendment to lower the age of consent to sixteen. This is Labour policy and although it is a free vote, the majority of Labour MPs (including me) support the amendment. We lose by just twenty-seven votes. A subsequent amendment in favour of age eighteen passes easily. This is a huge disappointment in my constituency with its large gay community but I'm sure equality with heterosexuals will be achieved before too long.

We are overwhelmed with benefits issues, Child Support Agency incompetence, failure to pay from the Social Fund that is hundreds of thousands of pounds in surplus and sick people unable to get NHS treatment. To cap it all, London Electricity announce they are closing their Deptford High Street Customer Service Centre on which they have made the poorest constituents dependent for charging their electricity keys.

By the end of February, we have completed the Commons stages of the Sunday Trading Bill. The government tables amendments to meet various demands of ours and Home Office minister Peter Lloyd and I lead our supporters into the yes lobby where we win by 311 votes to 218. This has been an experience like no other, negotiating for half a year to achieve a consensus with a Tory minister and a shop workers' union! I've made real enemies in the Whips' Office but the leadership has been well served.

17 March: I launch my second report, 'Racial Attacks – the rising tide', and visit Tower Hamlets with Tony Blair. This leads to lots more meetings, a conference in Manchester organised by the Anti-Racist Alliance and a meeting with leader John Smith and the CRE prior to the launch of an all-party anti-racist compact for the forthcoming elections.

We are receiving a great number of petition forms as part of the Save Guy's campaign that Bridget, Jim and I launched in Lewisham. People from all over London are supporting and once 1 million have signed up the petition will be presented to the Secretary of State. Lewisham Hospital is also being affected by government cuts. Seventy compulsory redundancies have been announced without warning, neither the unions nor MPs being told in advance. We organise urgent meetings with the staff, management and commissioning authorities and I speak in a Commons debate on the health service in London.

27 April: The first democratic elections on a universal franchise are held in South Africa. The remarkable scene of millions of black people standing in line for hours as they wait to vote brings tears to my eyes. The ANC takes 62 per cent of the vote and Nelson Mandela is elected President.

I've had a confidential letter signed by Home Secretary Michael Howard leaked to me. It makes clear that the government only intend to introduce minimal concessions on racial violence because of their embarrassment in the face of increasing pressure from Labour and some Tory backbenchers. When Parliament returns after the Easter recess our amendments to the Criminal Justice Bill are duly defeated and only the publication of racially inflammatory material becomes an arrestable offence. I do my bit for the 5 May local elections and the Lewisham results are excellent. Particularly rewarding is the defeat of the National Front candidate in Marlowe ward, who only polls 203 votes.

I've prepared a paper on women and justice covering women as victims of crime, perpetrators of crime, women in prison and women working in the criminal justice system. The differences with men are very striking, with the result that women suffer detriment and discrimination. Forty-five per cent of women victims of homicide are killed by current or former partners compared with 8 per cent of men. I argue for a range of changes to the treatment and protection of women. Over 90 per cent of women in prison have committed non-violent offences, but because the population is so small there are only twelve women's prisons in the whole of England and Wales. One of the consequences is that while *nine* out of ten relationships survive when men are in prison, only *one* in ten survive for women. Not only are women often imprisoned far from home and partners but also from their children (47 per cent have dependent children, 12 per cent of whom go into care). I argue for more community sentences for women and the possibility of weekend prisons such as they have on the continent.

12 May: Frank leaves early for a trade union meeting and I'm listening to Radio 4 as I prepare for work. I am stopped in my tracks. News is coming in that John Smith has had another heart attack. I get dressed quickly, fearing the worst. Then the news comes: John Smith is dead.

I cannot believe it. He was so full of vigour and so full of hope for the next election. I make haste to the Commons, which is transformed from the usual hustle and bustle. People are standing around speaking in low voices, all commiserating with one another. The business of the Commons is rearranged so that tributes can be paid. The whole House is genuinely in mourning. Prime Minister John Major makes a superb tribute to John, very perceptive in all its parts. Margaret Beckett, who now becomes our leader, speaks with equal passion, painting a picture of John with which we can all identify. When she ends with the words of the speech he made only last night – 'The opportunity to serve our country – that is all we ask' – the tears are flowing down my cheeks. I am not alone.

Tony is in Scotland and rushing back. There are huge implications for Gordon Brown and him. I go to see Anji [Hunter, Tony's PA] and ask if someone shouldn't go to Heathrow to meet him. Anji tells me Cherie will be doing that.

We go to Edinburgh for John's funeral. It is an immensely moving and sombre occasion. Afterwards we go to Parliament House. I'm wearing an elegant black hat, which I decide to take off for the reception and place on the cloakroom rack in the entrance hall. We are just about to leave when there is a great crash and shards of heavy glass fall down from the skylight. My hat is sliced in half. I shudder to think what would have happened if I'd gone to collect it moments earlier.

For the first time I visit Frank's mother and sisters who all live in Edinburgh.

I get on with the day job but everything is in turmoil. Tony is going for the leadership. Like many others, I'd assumed it would be Gordon and that I'd support him. The suspense lasts for days until Gordon announces he won't run. I'm keen to help but there's no invitation to join the campaign committee. Tony himself is on a high and happy for me to get on with my portfolio uninterrupted. He does, however, give me just one assignment: he wants to get Clare Short into his camp to influence the left. I can't help but be disappointed. I've deputised a lot for him and would have expected him to value my contribution and my own left-wing credentials a bit more.

The Euro election campaign is now in full swing and I'm campaigning all over the country. There will also be parliamentary by-elections on the same day and Margaret Hodge has been selected in Barking, following Jo's death. I go to help Margaret, who needs all the assistance she can get. The leader of the Labour group boasts that he has been a councillor for forty years but has never needed to knock on a single door! I also do some campaigning for Gisela Gschaider who is our German-born Euro candidate for the Worcester and South Warwickshire seat. I'm impressed and not surprised when she confides she would like to contest a Westminster seat. However, though married to a Brit and settled here for twenty years, she still has German citizenship, which makes her ineligible. She asks if I could help after the Euro election, which she doesn't expect to win. I promise to do so. To my surprise, my request to the Tory minister to get her citizenship application fast-tracked succeeds. Gisela takes her married name, Stuart, and gets selected for Birmingham Edgbaston, a seat held by the formidable Tory MP Jill Knight.

9 June: Labour is overwhelmingly successful in the Euro elections. I'm really pleased when Glenys Kinnock is elected. When we return to the Commons on the 14th we are able to welcome four new Labour MPs, including Margaret Hodge. It's a good time to be doing *Any Questions?*, which I do in Somerset three days later.

Four days on and I'm in the Commons for the final stage of the Sunday Trading Bill. A significant amendment has come back from the Lords giving an exemption for garden centres and DIY stores from the six-hour limit for trading on Sundays. I vigorously oppose it and we win on a free vote

293 to 160. The next day, the Home Affairs Select Committee publish their long-awaited report into racial violence and harassment. Vindication of everything I've been saying and further isolation for Michael Howard.

21 July: I remain true to my feminist credentials by voting for Margaret for deputy. Tony is easily elected but John Prescott becomes his deputy. Afterwards we go to Church House for a celebration. When Tony, Cherie and Neil are led onto the balcony for photographs, Anji pushes me forward to join them. The next day a lovely photograph of four very happy people graces the front cover of *The Times*.

Frank and I decide it's time for a real holiday, which we take in France in August.

With no parliamentary sittings in September I'm able to arrange daytime meetings with the various authorities that are giving my constituents grief. Railtrack is top of the list – dragging their feet over the Mantle Road footbridge and cutting down swathes of vegetation along the track from New Cross to Honor Oak. SELCHP (South East London Combined Heat and Power) continues to cause concern and complaints and we're fighting another battle with London Underground. Visits to Strangeways and Gartree prisons are also on my list, as is the completion of a paper on the government's prison privatisation programme. This couldn't be more apposite as one security scandal after another breaks over the next few weeks. I end up doing more media in September than during the whole of the rest of the year combined.

The October Labour Party conference in Blackpool is an event to look forward to. I'm doing fringe events on racial harassment with the CRE, on prison privatisation with the Prison Officers Association and on policing in London with the Association of London Authorities. Frank is doing lots of union meetings. Tony's first speech as leader is superb and we are all extremely optimistic about the future. I wonder, though, at the point in rewriting Clause IV, which means nothing to most people and which will be hard-fought in the party.

People have started canvassing for the shadow Cabinet elections. I'm expected to stand again but I'm approached by Clare Short's researcher who asks me not to stand in order to help get Clare elected. In a real misjudgement I step aside and support a 'sister'. Tony as leader will make all the appointments, beginning with those who are successful in the shadow Cabinet elections. Jack Straw, who was Tony's campaign manager, is to take over his Home Affairs brief. Tony rings and, with no prior discussion, says, 'I want you to go to Gordon.' I immediately protest that I don't know anything about Treasury matters and I can't believe I could do a good job in that post. It is a fateful decision for which I will pay dearly. He asks me what I want. Frankly, I expected a discussion, still thinking of us as part of a team rather than him as the all-powerful leader.

After seven years in Parliament I was still hopelessly naive. I suggested shadow minister for London but it was already allocated. Then I asked for time and rang Robin Cook. Robin was the one person I could approach for a job as I had always taken a keen interest in foreign affairs and was a member of the party's Foreign Policy Commission. He is sorry, he'd already made promises, but offers to help if he can. I asked about the shadow women's portfolio but he told me it was going to Clare. Then he said what about the green job? Tony was thinking of offering it to Dawn Primarolo. I get straight back to Tony – it is the ideal job for me with my science background. He agrees immediately and Dawn joins Gordon's Treasury team, where she will have one of the longest ministerial careers in the Labour government.

I'm delighted to have the shadow environmental protection brief. It's in Frank Dobson's local government team but Tony has designated it a self-standing post.

Within a day of my taking the brief the Royal Commission publishes its report into transport and the environment. We are to use one of our opposition days to debate the issue in a week's time. The following day there's a Lib Dem-initiated debate on energy conservation, which sees me leading for Labour. It is one of the extraordinary features of parliamentary life that shadow and government ministers can lead debates on issues they may have only picked up the day or week before. Fortunately, the House goes into a thirteen-day recess prior to the Queen's Speech and I'm able to rapidly get up to speed.

The government is struggling. The Queen's Speech contains few surprises and an expected flagship, the privatisation of the Post Office, is left out. The debate on the European Communities (Finance) Bill is a fiasco and Major is forced to make the issue a vote of confidence. The Tory Party is hopelessly divided and the government weak.

30 November: I take part in my first environment oral questions. I highlight the ridiculous situation whereby power stations that invest in technology to reduce pollution have found that the National Grid is being forced to buy electricity from cheaper, dirtier power stations instead.

The government publishes its Environment Bill in the Lords. I will be leading on this in the Commons so I have a massive amount of work to get through. Despite attempts to buy off their back-bench rebels, the government is resoundingly defeated in the vote on VAT on fuel. The Tories' cynical policy of raising indirect taxes to pay for income tax cuts is exposed. We are jubilant.

I receive a special invitation from Goldsmiths. Michael Caine wasn't able to attend the public degree ceremony where he was due to be honoured. As a result, there is a very select private event and I'm invited. I am thrilled to meet him and his wife, Shakira, who is just as beautiful and charming as I'd always imagined.

Good news on Guy's. In response to our campaign proposals, commissioned from management consultants, the Secretary of State has begun a consultation process. The petition has passed the 1 million mark and will be presented to Parliament.

What a year. At least I've been reselected to fight the next election, with nominations from all eight branches.

## 1995

The extent of my brief is enormous. In January alone I have meetings with the Royal Institute of Chartered Surveyors, fishing associations to discuss angling policy, the clean air campaign, the water companies' association, the Council for the Protection of Rural England and the officers of the National Rivers Authority, plus I am to address a biofuels conference in Lincolnshire. Next month I've got a range of meetings from Boots to the London Waste Regulation Authority on aspects of packaging.

I'm heading for a showdown with the CLP. The divisive forces that drove out John Silkin are still active. I am frequently criticised, not least for supporting Tony Blair for leader. I point out that 51 per cent of our members supported him. I put up with so much mean behaviour in the early years and frankly I'm fed up with it.

There is also now evidence of serious irregularities. Halfway through last year the secretary stopped mailing my GC reports to delegates and stopped sending meeting notices to me. All this was done in the lead-up to the reselection process. Key members of Drake ward still wanted to see me deselected. They didn't succeed but interestingly when the ward did vote in favour of my reselection the secretary failed to notify me. I write an open letter to the CLP detailing the problems and appealing for a more open and inclusive party that starts campaigning and participating in wider community activities. Then I find the secretary is sitting on the ballot papers sent from HQ for distribution to all members for the Clause IV vote. I warn them that a formal complaint will be made if they do not comply. I'm having to make a concerted effort to confront those responsible and shore up the support of those (the majority) who are on my side.

21 April: In the Chamber to support Malcolm Wicks's Carers (Recognition and Services) Private Member's Bill. For the first time local authorities will have to assess the needs of carers in their area. Malcolm has worked really hard to get his Bill through and I'm delighted to see it succeed.

I'm devoting a huge amount of time to the Environment Bill. It is massive. There are 107 clauses and twenty schedules. I will have to work incredibly hard to get myself briefed and to organise amendments. Fortunately, the green groups and local government organisations are champing at the bit. I organise weekly briefing meetings and table the amendments on time for each committee session. Luckily, I have a good team of backbenchers who will join me on the committee. Many of them are keen environmentalists so we will have no trouble advancing our case.

The White Paper which preceded the Bill was mainly concerned with the setting up of the Environment Agency for England and Wales (EA) and the Scottish Environment Protection Agency (SEPA) but, during consultations, many other issues were added. As the government will have a majority of votes we can't expect to win concessions in the committee but we will scrutinise every clause, sometimes calling a vote but often withdrawing the amendment so that we can make another attempt at report stage. We begin on 27 April with a raft of amendments. On our first vote we have ten votes in favour of our amendment and the Tories twelve against. This will be the pattern, but often a minister may find some merit in an amendment and then the government itself will bring one forward at report stage. We will sit on Tuesdays and Thursdays, usually twice a day finishing at 7 p.m., when of course we are still required to stay for votes in the main Chamber.

30 April: Greenpeace activists have occupied the Brent Spar, an oil storage and tanker-loading buoy in the Brent oilfield, in protest at the government's support for Shell's proposal to dump the structure (147m high and 29m in diameter) in deep waters off the west coast of Scotland. With PCBs, crude oil, heavy metals and low-level radioactive waste on board this is outrageous.* I'm immediately asked for comment by the media and wholeheartedly

---

* Greenpeace estimates of the amount of oil left on board were subsequently found to have been exaggerated and they apologised to Shell.

condemn Shell, without consulting. Fortunately Frank Dobson agrees otherwise we might have had a problem with the team at the Department of Trade and Industry (DTI) who have to deal with these multinationals all the time.

Greenpeace mounts a vigorous campaign and people all over northern Europe begin boycotting Shell products. I've only just started to buy from Shell garages, having kept up a personal boycott throughout all the years of Shell's activities in apartheid South Africa. So it's no hardship for me. The German government issues a formal objection to the British government about the dumping plan. A week later I use my slot in environment questions to tackle John Gummer on the issue. Then Shell evicts the Greenpeace activists from the Brent Spar, causing another surge in support. By the end of June, Shell's resistance crumbles and they issue a statement acknowledging that their 'position as a major European enterprise has become untenable'.

This is a triumph for the environmental movement and I am thrilled to be on the right side of the argument. During the next four years various decommissioning plans will be explored until it is finally disposed of on shore and used to provide the foundations for a new ferry terminal.

A major planning application at New Cross is really troubling me. Sainsbury's want to build a big store, which is welcome, but there are lots of issues with their plans and particularly with the proposal to site a huge bingo hall alongside it accompanied by fast-food outlets. I know the council desperately wants regeneration but they need to be tougher in their approach.

My mother is seventy-five on 10 May. It's hard to believe it's fourteen years since my father died. Mum is remarkable, having made a life for herself, supported my sister and her grandchildren and kept herself fit and active. We have a party at Susan's house with lots of family members attending including my Danish cousin, Sandra. My father's elder brother married a Danish woman and had no contact with the family for many years. I've met Sandra about three times over as many decades but she is now married to a Scot so it will be nice to see her more often.

My time is now dominated by the twice-weekly meetings of the committee on the Environment Bill. This is a huge commitment and entails a Monday pre-meet with the local authority associations and with the Labour MPs on the committee. Between 2 and 18 May we have nine sessions covering the nature of the agencies, their accountability and waste regulation and transfer. On 23 May we start on national parks and go through from morning until nine minutes to midnight. The Bill has not lived up to our expectations but we strongly support the creation of the EA and SEPA. These agencies will be vital to a Labour government's environment programmes.

Parliament breaks up for the Whitsun recess on 25 May but is quickly recalled. There's been a huge escalation in the long and bloody Bosnian War. I'm ashamed to say I've found it impossible to keep myself briefed on this issue over the past three years due to both political and personal pressures. Serbs have launched new artillery attacks against civilians in Srebrenica and Goražde, followed by a massacre at Tuzla. Soldiers from the UN Protection Force are being attacked by both sides and three days ago thirty-three members of the Royal Watch Fusiliers were taken hostage. The PM makes a careful statement and is supported by Tony. Not much can be done in Westminster.

We resume our work in the Environment Bill committee on 6 June with amendments on a national waste strategy and go on until midnight. We've still got access to environmental information, Sites of Special Scientific Interest and the major topic of air quality to cover. To everyone's enormous relief, we finish on 15 June.

Things are improving in the constituency with Keir Simmons and Kumar Jacob producing a constituency newsletter and another new members' meeting at the Commons. I've also got two street surgeries planned involving the local councillors in Marlowe and Evelyn. We let 600 households know we are coming. Around half a dozen leaflets appear in windows, enabling us to give people a decent amount of time in their own homes to tell us what they need.

I'm turning my attention to finance. Most people don't realise that constituency parties have to raise all the money they need to finance their own local general election campaign. I'm lucky enough to be sponsored by the TGWU, which means we can expect a £3,000 donation that will cover half our costs. Contrary to general belief, we are not expected to give anything in return – just get the candidate re-elected. A fundraising lunch, a dinner and a barbecue are organised during the summer and swell the funds. We are becoming overwhelmed with casework. My last surgery at the Albany lasted five hours and many MPs in London are finding their caseworkers under severe strain and managing serious backlogs. We've lost advice and support services at the CAB, the Women's Centre and elsewhere due to government cuts imposed on Lewisham Council. More and more people are turning to us.

Report and third reading of the Environment Bill are scheduled for 27 and 28 June. The Bill has ended up 365 pages long and now has 123 clauses and twenty-four schedules. A decision has to be taken as to whether we vote with the government at third reading. It's now clear that while pressure from us and the conservation and green groups has led to some improvements in the Bill on air quality, contaminated land, old mineral planning permissions and hedgerows, our concerns about the cost benefit duties on the agencies have not been addressed.

My third reading speech begins after midnight. I argue that a fundamental conflict has been built in and that commercial interests have been put ahead of the interests of the environment – a particular example of which is the removal of quiet enjoyment from one of the purposes of the national parks. I announce that we have considered voting against but will not do so, as we support, and had ourselves advocated, setting up environment agencies and national park authorities, so we will abstain. I end by saying confidently that our consolation will be that when the agencies come into operation we can expect to be in government.

July brings more terrible news from the Balkans. Following the Tuzla massacre, there has been a genocidal killing of more than 8,000 Bosniaks near Srebrenica. Refugees sought safety in the Dutch compound but Dutch forces expelled most, despite knowing that the few hundred men of military age who were within the group would be killed.*

Released from the Environment Bill, I'm now doing a bit of travelling. Frank and I go to the Littleborough and Saddleworth by-election. I then take part in the Rolling Rose campaign in Wales and finally present Labour's environment policy at a conference in Oxford. Having worked through the Easter and Whitsun recesses I'm determined to have a proper holiday and we go to France at the end of July. I also spend some time in Aberdeen where Frank is now actively pursuing reselection. After a boundary review, an extra seat has been created. Half of his old seat of Aberdeen South has been merged with half of Bob Hughes's Aberdeen North seat to form Aberdeen Central. It's clear that Labour would expect to win both North and Central. Frank hoped Bob would stand in the new North seat but he has decided he wants to compete for Central. This was the last thing Frank wanted – to compete with a friend. Nonetheless, he has no choice because all his work has been in the South and Central areas. This is now a tremendous worry. I can't bear the thought of Frank being out of Parliament for good.

I've got another headache awaiting me when I return as I have to get cover for Katerina, my wonderful caseworker, who is pregnant. I've received 200 applications from the advertisement for her six months' maternity leave. I appoint Fiona Roberts, who proves herself up for the job (she is still doing casework, albeit remotely from Wales, for a succession of MPs twenty years later). One of the great pleasures of my life has been recruiting and training able young people, particularly women, who have gone on to successful careers elsewhere.

We are encouraged to visit sister socialist parties to look at relevant policies, so I spend a couple of days in Hungary at the end of the summer recess. Hungary is bankrupt, with even basic services such as mains drainage being

---

* Later it will become clear that these events signified the bloody climax of the 1992–95 Bosnian War. In July 2014, a civil court in the Hague will order the Netherlands to compensate the families of the more than 300 men who were turned over to the Bosnian Serb forces and killed.

woefully inadequate. It certainly puts into context our own privileged position and potential for much more environmental action. Despite their problems, the Hungarian Socialist party has made a priority of passing enabling legislation on the environment.

Other front-bench visits take in Shropshire and Staffordshire to support local campaigners opposed to open-cast mining. Open-cast coal now accounts for one third of national coal output, compared with one-tenth in 1979. In Yorkshire I go to meet the company that owns one of the largest tracts of peatland in Europe. There are serious issues about sustainability and I can see this will soon become a hot issue. Probably my most important initiative is with the CBI. I've asked the head of environment to set up a series of meetings for me with relevant senior industrialists to discuss sustainable development and Labour's programme. We manage to fit in two long meetings in September. They are extremely useful and it's gratifying to know the CBI is seriously contemplating working with us in government.

To Brighton for the Labour Party conference. It's a very busy and important conference for me. The whole environment team makes a presentation and I also get the opportunity to address the conference during the environment debate. I haven't done this since my CND days. Importantly I also address a seminar for invited business guests, where there appears to be genuine interest in Labour's policies and no concerted resistance. Alan Howarth, a respected Tory MP with a strong social conscience, defects to Labour on the eve of the Tory Party conference, giving us a further boost.

Frank has gone to Aberdeen for the parliamentary selection contest. He has worked tremendously hard, contacting everyone who might be a supporter. The contest is hard fought. I have to stay in London and am on tenterhooks all day. When at last I get the phone call, Frank has won by a single vote. Selection contests are a tremendous strain on candidates in any circumstance and inevitably cost a great deal of money, but this one is an immense relief to us. Frank is very concerned about Bob. Fortunately, Tony offers him a place in the Lords for after the election.

I've received an odd letter from a Dr Marion North, Principal of Laban. This is apparently a contemporary dance school located next to Goldsmiths College but I've never heard of it or noticed the building. When we do meet it's a revelation. For years Laban has existed as an essentially private college without the benefit of public money. The students have a great record of success and Dr North is clearly an exceptional woman. They have outgrown their ill-assorted buildings and want to relocate. We are soon on first-name terms and Marion tells me her real ambition is to find a plot of land for a new build. My heart sinks: finding land in the inner city is a very tall order. She says she wants to build either in Greenwich or Lewisham. Already much taken with the idea, I tell her it has to be in Lewisham.

I'm now seriously planning for government. Our previous shadow Environment Secretary, Chris Smith, led on the production of our major policy document 'In Trust for Tomorrow'. This will be our blueprint, but all the policies need work to ensure they can be introduced and are practicable. My priorities for the coming year will be consolidating our work with environmental organisations, including pressure groups, and working with our DTI team and business leaders.

I have several important meetings before the session ends, lunch with Sir Crispin Tickell, chair of the government Panel on Sustainable Development (a significant ally), and another lunch at the Danish embassy with the EU Environment Commissioner. I also meet the impressive Fiona Reynolds, who chairs the Council for the Protection of Rural England. I spend three more days in Brussels, this time for a meeting of GLOBE. GLOBE was founded in 1989 by legislators from the US Congress including John Kerry,* the European Parliament, Japanese Diet and the Russian Duma. Its mission is to respond to urgent environmental challenges through the development and advancement of legislation. I don't think it carries much weight and is rather bureaucratic, but there is potential there and we certainly need pressure in Parliaments to bolster progressive governments.

---

* US Secretary of State from February 2013 to time of writing.

I'm developing a keen interest in renewable energy and attend a seminar on solar PV. I'm really excited by the potential for change in the way we use and produce energy. This has to be one of the priorities for us in government.

In the short break before the Queen's Speech I attend the Labour Women's Conference. I've always emphasised that I'm not just an MP, but a *woman* MP. We've got to get more women into Westminster and the women's organisation in the party is crucial to that aim. I chair an afternoon workshop and give as much encouragement as I can to other women.

The Tory government is in disarray and the country is suffering from its lurch to the right. Over 1 million people – and rising – are in negative equity on their mortgages and there are more than 1 million fewer jobs than when Major took office. The NHS is in crisis and the government refuses to recognise the disaster of rail privatisation, despite the fact that one of the first privatisations, the London-Tilbury-Southend line, has had to be halted due to suspected fraud. The Queen's Speech shows how few ideas and what little energy the government has left. John Major is a captive of the right of his party and the Asylum and Immigration Bill will enable them to play the race card right up to the general election. The month ends with the Budget, where despite the pretence of tax cuts we are able to show that the average family will be paying £670 a year more than in 1992.

21 November: The Bosnian War is brought to an end with the Dayton Peace Accords. It is now believed that more than 100,000 people were killed and an estimated 20,000–50,000 women, mainly Muslims, were raped. More than 1.5 million people were displaced. I soon see asylum seekers in my surgery and hear harrowing stories from women who are too afraid to tell their stories because of the shame it brings to their families.

I'm really concerned about the East London line. It has been closed for works for eight months and there is a real fear it may never reopen. I write to the Secretary of State and finally get a reply expressing the pious hope that London Underground will not have to seek its permanent closure.

Needless to say I've written back telling him it's his responsibility to ensure it does reopen and to say when.

1 December is World Aids Day and of particular significance in my constituency, which has a large gay community with whom I work, and serious HIV health problems. It's just a decade since the HIV virus was isolated and since the first high-profile casualty, film star Rock Hudson, announced he had Aids and subsequently died. Four years ago the rock star Freddie Mercury also died having announced he had Aids the previous day. It's still a greatly feared disease, attracting a considerable stigma. We hold an event in Deptford, letting off red balloons at Goldsmiths College.

More meetings on the brief. Importantly, I meet the chair and chief executive of the newly established Environment Agency. Then there's the Environment Industries Commission, the Energy Saving Trust, Waste Watch and Surfers Against Sewage! The latter have first-hand knowledge of our polluted seas and I'm certainly sympathetic to their cause and more than aware of the government's lax attitudes to implementing European legislation on water.

## 1996

In the New Year I'm being consulted about the content of an environment speech for Tony. This will be his first and is somewhat overdue. His researcher is extremely cautious and asks me if I'm absolutely sure about climate change. I'm astonished that anyone in her position can have any doubts, but I guess powerful industry interests will always be in their minds. I give a robust response and express my view that this will be the most important issue of the future. A scientific consensus on climate change emerged a decade ago when the Intergovernmental Panel on Climate Change (IPCC) (established by the World Meteorological Organization) produced its first assessment report. A second assessment report was published just last year.

A major blow to Labour's flagship policy of designating certain constituency selections as all-women shortlists. A Leeds industrial tribunal has found in favour of two Labour men who argued they had been discriminated against by not being able to apply for parliamentary seats because they were all-women shortlists. This has to be wrong. There is no employer of MPs and the tribunal appears to have treated selection as though it were a job interview. Labour HQ immediately suspends the policy to take legal advice. An appeal is obviously needed but this close to an election it is decided against. At least no self-respecting constituency is going to select either of the men involved.

Yet another disaster hits the government on 15 February when an oil tanker leaks millions of gallons of oil at Milford Haven, affecting one of Britain's most beautiful and important wildlife areas. The government's failure to implement the earlier Donaldson report undoubtedly led to delays in bringing the disaster under control.

13 March: Sixteen children and their teacher have been killed at a primary school in Dunblane. MPs are naturally shocked and party politics set aside as tributes are made in the House. The following week Tony proposes examining the issue of handguns kept in the home, on an all-party basis. Clearly something must be done to try to prevent such a tragedy happening again.

The EU has banned exports of our beef on account of the prevalence of BSE ('mad cow disease'). The first known case in British cattle was recorded in 1986 and since then various measures have been in place to try to stem the disease. Six years ago, John Gummer, then Agriculture Minister, famously fed a hamburger to his four-year-old daughter in an attempt to convince the public that British beef was safe. Its transmission to humans in the form of a variant of the fatal disease CJD has just been reported. There has been an immediate collapse in sales in Britain but the government seems paralysed to act. Labour is arguing for a selective slaughter of cattle, but Stephen Dorrell shows remarkable arrogance and contempt for people's fears, saying, 'It is the public who are mad, not the cows.'*

---

* The EU ban was to last for ten years. 180,000 British cattle were found to be affected and 4.4 million were eventually slaughtered as part of an eradication programme.

Numerous battles in the constituency have come to a head. There's been a partial reprieve on the fire stations where I've been actively supporting the firefighters, and the proposed sale of the old Kitto Road library has been put on hold. I've argued strongly that the council should keep such buildings for community use when they can no longer run services themselves. A major embarrassment is the old army and navy site in Lewisham town centre. It's completely derelict and after we all reluctantly agreed it should become a police station the Met has done nothing. I meet with Sir Paul Condon, the commissioner, to urge him to get the site cleaned up and to find a temporary use pending their own development decisions (lack of money, of course). I mark International Women's Day by speaking at a splendid rally in south Wales and then go on to visit the site of the *Sea Empress* disaster at Milford Haven. I also meet up with our candidate Julie Morgan at a key seat visit to her constituency of Cardiff North. We are beginning to pull together our policies in readiness for a possible autumn general election. Policies will be ready for the National Policy Forum in May and then a comprehensive policy document will be presented to annual conference. This will be our pre-manifesto programme. The process is to be called 'Road to the Manifesto'. I'll need to get my own priorities thought through.

My only front-bench duty in the House is a debate on the role of particulates in air pollution. This is a fairly new area of concern. These tiny particles are thought to be responsible for 10,000 premature deaths per annum in the UK. Their production in vehicle exhausts is a major threat as the number of vehicles continues to increase.

11 April: Labour's Brian Jenkins wins the South-East Staffordshire by-election and John Major's grip on his party looks ever more shaky. Another threatened rebellion on the Housing Bill brings the government within two votes of defeat.

My caseworker, Katerina, returns from maternity leave and Fiona has left her the smallest backlog ever. Pity I can't keep them both.

Twice in the past I've been in hospital for minor procedures to deal with fibroids in my uterus. Recently the symptoms have been much worse and my GP refers me to St Thomas' Hospital, which is conveniently located across Westminster Bridge. I'm sitting on the edge of the bed, half-naked, when the consultant returns to give me the results of his examinations. With no preamble he says, 'We'll do the works.' I elicit an explanation – a complete hysterectomy and removal of my ovaries. It's clear that I'm shocked, which provokes a response: 'I can promise you I'll make the cut so you'll be able to wear a bikini again'! I ask if I could get dressed before we discuss things any further.

In his office he takes down a calendar and asks if I can come in any time from two weeks hence. Another shock. I know from constituents that the average waiting time is eight months. I enquire if I have cancer. He says unlikely but you can never tell until you operate. Seeing my hesitation, he gives me his card and tells me to call when I'm ready. How on earth am I going to take six weeks off (the predicted recovery time)? The apparent urgency is a worry but I suspect I may be getting special treatment because I'm an MP. Frank and I work out the best time. I won't be able to do my surgeries, which is my greatest worry, but Frank nobly agrees to take them on.

I'm apprehensive about the surgery. I've recently been dealing with the family of a constituent who had the same operation at the same hospital and died. Rationally I know our circumstances are not the same but it makes me think about that remote possibility.

I want to tell Keith, just in case something goes wrong and he would be left with unresolved grief. I haven't seen him for a very long time and his phone goes unanswered. The day before the operation I drop a note through his door, which he gets on his return from a visit to the US, immediately ringing Mum to ask to see me but it's too late. When I come round from the operation I'm amazed to find I can't sit up and I lie for many hours in agony. Next morning I'm introduced to the excellent little squeezy gadget that allows me to introduce measured doses of morphine into my bloodstream, which eases the pain considerably. Frank comes to see me immediately, and later my family bring Keith and leave us alone for the final few minutes. It's a precious time of deep communication, of love and of sorrow. We embrace and I hope so much that I will now be able to see him again. I never will.

In the two weeks before going into hospital I'd addressed two national conferences, met with industry bosses of the Sand and Gravel Association, chaired an excellent Institute for Public Policy Research (IPPR) seminar exploring Labour's policy on access to the countryside, appeared on *Any Questions?*, been on the front bench for two debates on the water industry and attended a wonderful performance at the Albany given by IRIE!. I also reorganised all the outstanding business at the office in the final twenty-four hours.

Now, I'm amazingly weak with reminders to do nothing – not even to lift a kettle. Frank is a saint, looking after me around the clock. The weather is lovely and I find myself happy to do nothing as I recline on a lounger and read. Glenda Jackson sends me a crate of little bottles of champagne – what a lovely surprise – and Margaret Hodge pays me a visit. I need to get fit in case there's an autumn election.

I start doing paperwork again and Frank drives me to the Commons for important votes. Parliament is now dominated by the BSE crisis. In an effort to get the EU ban lifted, John Major agrees to the slaughter of another 67,000 cattle but he gets no agreed timetable and no agreed guarantee on lifting the ban.

Bad news on the East London line – the reopening has been postponed again until next summer. I'm pressing for a better replacement bus service. I get news of more problems with the plans to demolish the old Deptford Library and build an Indo-Chinese Community Centre. This is one issue that can't be dealt with on paper so I go to my first constituency meeting a month after the operation. A lot of negotiation and a solution is found but many are unhappy about demolishing old buildings, though the cost of adapting them is prohibitive. The franchise for South Eastern (which includes Deptford) has been awarded to Connex Rail, a subsidiary of a French water company. What is the world coming to?

10 July: I return to work full-time just in time for a vote on MPs' pay. This is an invidious system. Our pay should be linked to a civil service grade and we should have nothing to do with it. A large increase is proposed and frankly I'm all for it as I certainly don't feel I'm paid an appropriate rate for the job. Frank tells me he recalls voting on our salaries in 1987 and remarked to Edward Heath that in all the years he campaigned against Heath's government, he never imagined that he would find himself shoulder to shoulder with him in the voting lobby. Heath replied, 'Young man, this will happen twice in every parliament – once on pay and once on hanging!'

Next day, Nelson Mandela's historic address to MPs and Lords in West-minster Hall. A splendid occasion – one of those days when it's possible to rise above all other cares and be touched by a vision of a better world.

I've been invited to accept an honorary fellowship at Goldsmiths. This is a great surprise and I'm thrilled.

Frank's job with the political fund ballots has ended. All of the ballots have been won with increased turnouts and majorities. Before the final wind-up, Bill Morris, who chaired the oversight committee, offered Frank another part-time job organising a series of industry conferences for the TGWU. A reward for a good job done and another means of keeping our finances afloat until the election.

Tory woes continue. The Home Affairs Select Committee has issued its report on handgun ownership. The committee has split, with Tory MPs caving in to pressure and rejecting the idea of a ban on keeping handguns at home, despite the fact that no evidence was produced as to the need to keep them at home. It emerges that the special advisor to the committee was himself a member of the gun lobby. Labour members produce a report calling for a ban on keeping handguns at home and our front bench adopts the policy.

It is well known that Tony doesn't want either Michael Meacher or Gavin Strang in his Cabinet, but they both get re-elected to the shadow Cabinet at the end of July. Party policy dictates that the shadow Cabinet becomes the Cabinet following a successful general election. Each team is now organising an away day. I'm already at ours in Oxford with shadow Environment Secretary Frank Dobson when I'm called away to take a phone call from Tony. He tells me he wants to give environmental protection a higher profile and so it will occupy a separate shadow ministry. Michael Meacher will be the shadow secretary and I will be his deputy. He hopes I will be happy to work with Michael. Naturally I'm relieved to keep my job but surprised at the development, as there's been no discussion with Frank as far as I'm aware.

I'm off on holiday for three weeks following the conference but I make plans to meet Michael on my return. I give him an extensive brief on the portfolio and of course the many documents that I've written over the past few years. He is gracious and grateful and I'll have no difficulty working with him.

The highlight of my agenda when I return will be the Goldsmiths' Fellowship. Several people become fellows at the same ceremony and one is asked to make a speech in reply. I'm to do the speech. I regard this as extremely onerous. It's an academic institution where so many people's careers depend on good writing and even better ideas. After a huge effort I think I've crafted a speech that might just make the grade. My proposer, Professor Sally Tomlinson, heaps such praise on me that I feel quite emotional. My mother and Frank are in the audience. Fortunately, my speech is well received and I get to return to my seat for a short respite before the champagne reception and the photographs on the back lawn under a blue sky. A very happy day.

I'm back doing my constituency advice surgeries, much to Frank's relief. Occasionally we get a little light relief from the weight of housing problems as a constituent raises something completely different. One such case is a juror who gets in touch to say that while car and motorcycle users get a mileage allowance for their journeys to court, she, as a cyclist, does not. We take this up with the chief executive of the Court Service and she is 'exceptionally' awarded 5.6p per mile and the Treasury will be asked in January to add allowances for cyclists to the jurors' regulations!

My report to the GC at the beginning of October expresses my concern at the lack of election planning in the branches. It's virtually impossible to get them to set their own canvassing schedules. Taking out the Christmas and New Year holidays we now have a mere thirty weeks to contact around 30,000 households. I've asked for a discussion, only to find voting prevents my attending the Wednesday meeting.

I do a record eleven fringe meetings at party conference and attend lots of other events. This is the last one before the general election and there is a fantastic atmosphere and a great sense of being on course for government.

Time for the Tories' final Queen's Speech. The backdrop is dire. Since 1979 the UK has fallen from thirteenth to eighteenth in the world prosperity league. Britain's national debt has doubled since John Major came to office in 1990 and since the last election the Tories have imposed the highest tax rises in history. Crime has doubled with recording of violent crime up 10 per cent in the past year alone. The Queen's Speech contains nothing that will tackle these issues. Most surprisingly it doesn't contain specific measures, such as combatting stalking and setting up a register of paedophiles, which the government had specifically promised. Home Secretary Michael Howard announces these are best left to Private Members' Bills! Under intense pressure from us, the PM does a spectacular U-turn later in the day and announces they will legislate after all.

I ask to see Tony to discuss the environment brief. He's concerned I might have a problem with Michael – on the contrary, we get on fine. No, my issue is the proposed separate ministry. I tell him I doubt he will want to make reorganising the Department of the Environment, which includes local government, a priority and there is the risk a separate environmental protection department will be too small and not sufficiently resourced to do the job we need. He's non-committal – so I cut to the chase. I tell him I'm concerned about my own position. I'm so committed to my job and know I can make a real contribution. I'm worried about my future. He is fulsome in his reassurance: 'Joan, you have a very bright future.'

5 November: A fun event. Frank and I are invited to the American embassy for the election-night party. Clinton wins his second term and it's a good augury for us.

The rest of the month is occupied by the usual round of front-bench and constituency events, but now I'm making a concerted effort to press branches into election campaign mode. The only way I can do this is to attend each branch meeting in turn. As they all meet on weekday evenings this means driving down to the meetings and then back for votes starting at 10 p.m. I manage to do all eight within the month but we still need to massively up our game. This is the trouble with seats perceived as safe. Local parties still don't feel the need to get onto the streets and meet the electorate. Personally, frequent appearances on TV mean I've a very high profile and I've fought so many local battles for people that I have no fears for my own re-election, but it's the principle. Local councillors especially need to be more accountable. One bright spot: an energetic young man called Matt Briggs wants to volunteer in our office. He can give us two days a week, which will be a great asset at this time.

November draws to a close with the Tories' last-gasp Budget. They have brought in twenty-two tax rises since 1992 and done nothing to strengthen the economy or equip the country for the future. With yet another crisis over European policy, John Major is left reeling from the onslaught of his right wing.

1 December: Tony Blair visits the Deptford campus at Lewisham College and gets a rapturous reception. I also get a further honour when I become an Honorary Fellow of Laban. One big crisis that has been brewing all year has come to a head. The local NHS funding body is over £18 million in deficit and all the pleas we've made to ministers have fallen on deaf ears. Now they've instructed Lewisham Hospital to cancel all non-urgent operations from January to March next year.

My very last commitment is the annual reception given by environment correspondents. I went last year and thoroughly enjoyed myself so I'm going again on 19 December – a proper opening of the festive season. I send my last Christmas cards. Like all MPs, I send hundreds to local stakeholders and party activists in mid-December and predictably the family are last minute. I always send to Keith. He never returns the favour but always sends a card for my birthday on the 28th, which I cherish.

A good evening out and I'm getting to bed around midnight. Frank has gone to Aberdeen to visit his family. There is a loud and persistent ring at the front door. I put on a dressing gown and go to the window – two police officers are on the doorstep. It must be the trouble at a neighbour's house opposite, I think. I've been dealing with it for some time and I'm annoyed they are troubling me now. I open the window to ask what the problem is. They ask me to come down.

They say they believe that I'm the wife of Keith Ruddock of Reservoir Road and that I would want to know that he has been badly injured in a road accident. It's very recent and he is in Lewisham Hospital. I'm utterly stunned. I go immediately to dress and gather up what I might need, including the address book – I know this is very serious. The officers are from the road traffic division. They don't know me but explain the local police made the connection. I'm incredibly grateful.

I arrive at A&E to a terrible scene. Keith is lying on a trolley in a treatment room. He is unconscious, blood is seeping from the back of his head, and rough stitches hold together the deep gash in his forehead. A large syringe is stuck into his groin and a doctor is using a kind of bellows to ventilate him. My sense of horror is overtaken by an overwhelming feeling of relief and gratitude that they got me here. Whatever happens I will take care of him, if only he can live. The doctor tells me I'm very brave but he has no idea what it means to be here and able to touch Keith's arm or his foot and just commune through the unconscious space. Time stands still.

Eventually they tell me they need to move him back to theatre but will keep me informed. I'm taken to a room and given Keith's possessions. His large soft leather bag has wine dripping through it – a Christmas gift that has been smashed. He had obviously packed up for the holiday before leaving college that night.

My first priority has to be to contact Keith's sister. I know she has moved house and I don't have her new address. I search Keith's bag. It's more than likely he will have his own contact book with him at this time of year. Sure enough it's there, but only contains the old address.

I ring my sister Susan and her husband David in the early hours. They share my shock and grief when I tell them I don't think Keith will recover. We promise to keep in touch and agree there is no point waking my mother at this time. They don't have Ruth's new address. I try directory enquiries: they have an ex-directory number and will not release it under any circumstances. My mind is in turmoil and I'm so afraid Keith isn't getting the best treatment for such a terrible injury. In recent years Keith collaborated with an eminent brain specialist called Chris Kennard. I decide I must contact him. I can only find a work number but I ring anyway. Somehow I manage to convince the woman who answers the phone. She says she hopes Prof. Kennard won't kill her over this and gives me his home number. Miraculously he wakes and answers.

I ring Frank who promises to come as soon as he can get a flight.

I continue to try to contact Keith's sister. The police call back to see me so I enlist their help. After some time, they tell me contact has been made and I get the phone number. All my calls are being made on a payphone, which adds to the desperation I feel. I'm constantly suppressing a feeling of rising panic. Frank is a great comfort on the phone. He'll get the first flight in the morning.

Chris arrives and the doctors take him to see Keith. He is able to view the scans and they decide to move Keith to the specialist brain injury unit, Atkinson Morley at St George's.

They say they need to stabilise him before attempting the move. Eventually we go to the loading bay. Once again the police offer to take me. We follow the ambulance with its silently flashing blue lights for what seems like hours. I wait again until eventually I'm called in. Keith is obviously in a deeper coma but attached to a ventilator and breathing soundlessly. His sister is on her way, having been alerted to the change of hospital. It's now early morning. I ring Keith's best friend Raad to give him the chance to say goodbye.

Eight hours after it all began I am asked to consent to switching off the life support. His beautiful brain is dead.

The staff are very kind and gently explain there will have to be a post-mortem. There is nothing to do but to go home and make more phone calls. I feel as though I am in a trance but I keep making the decisions and doing what has to be done. My mother is terribly upset. She always loved Keith and visited him in London even after we separated. It was a very special treat they shared when he took her for dinner at Rules and to a favourite opera at Covent Garden.

The local media already have the story which means we need to think about the empty house as burglary is rife. Keith's sister wants to remove all the valuables but says she needs to go home first. Keith's house keys are in his bag so I give everything to her and ask her to call me when they return to Reservoir Road.

People begin to arrive at home. Owen Beament, who has heard the news on local radio, then my sister Susan and her husband David and eventually Frank.

Hours pass. I cry. I make phone calls. I relate what I know: that Keith had been hit on a pedestrian crossing on the New Cross Road when walking home around midnight. The driver called the ambulance and police. I guess it was probably end-of-term drinks with his research team that led to him taking the last train.

I haven't heard from Keith's sister so I ring his home phone – she answers. Frank drives me to the house. I'm shocked to see their large car with boot open, filled with lots of our treasures. I'm in such a state of shock I don't assert myself and let the process continue. There's little conversation and I take some of our things myself. Weeks later I discover they had removed all our papers as they searched for a will.

The days pass in a blur. Nothing can happen until after the post-mortem.

It's Christmas. I buy a bunch of white lilies to take to Reservoir Road. I've always had a set of keys but never used them since I left. I get to the front door but I'm so traumatised I'm afraid I'll make a mistake with the alarm. The curtains remain closed and I put the lilies on the doorstep.

Frank drives us to my mum for the Christmas holiday. Keith's colleagues start to get in touch, expecting to be able to circulate details of the funeral arrangements. I've nothing to tell them except that it will be in south Wales.

Neither Keith nor I had wanted a divorce and I had never wanted to force him to sell the house so that I could take my share. I know he hasn't made a will and I am going to have to do all the administration. As the shock begins to pass, great waves of emotion engulf me. I have this overwhelming desire to go to a mountain top and howl. For the first time in my life I understand why women wail publicly in other cultures. This is a grief and a guilt that will never go away.

All the administration is based around St George's Hospital where the post-mortem takes place. Susan wants to say goodbye so we go together. It's snowing. Hardly able to keep back the tears I ask for the chapel, imagining that's where he will be. He isn't. We have to go to the mortuary. It's a harrowing experience but important to us both.

Ruth is arranging the funeral. When I contact her about the invitations she says it's private and will be held in the family home they used to live in and which is now occupied by Keith's nonagenarian uncles. I'm just numb. Keith was such a gregarious person. He has so many friends and music was at the very heart of his existence. He was also a committed atheist. This isn't right, but I feel I've surrendered all rights and I cannot argue. I do ask for the organ to be played in the church where the burial will take place.

Ten of us cram into the tiny front room, which is dominated by the large, ornate coffin. The local vicar mouths meaningless words and we get into the funeral cars and drive in slow procession to the churchyard. I wish I could descend into the grave. We go to the local pub for lunch where Janet,

Keith's favourite cousin, is particularly kind to me. I realise I've missed seeing her and her husband Adrian over the past few years. And the uncles, too. I always enjoyed their eccentric company and their outspoken views on the events of the day.

We return to Mum's home where Frank is waiting for us.

The post-mortem complete I begin the technicalities, register Keith's death and apply for probate. Somehow the world is still turning and the recess is at an end.

## 1997

First day back and I'm driving myself to work along New Cross Road. As I approach the pedestrian crossing I'm overcome by fear and almost stop the car. The impact of the car hitting Keith flashes before my eyes. I feel physically sick.

I park the car in the Commons car park. I'm just at the Members' Entrance when Tory MP Quentin Davies falls into step with me. 'Cheer up,' he says. 'You look like you've been to a funeral.' I realise colleagues have all been on Christmas holidays and news hasn't travelled far. I gently explain what has happened and he is mortified by his jocular remark, for which I forgive him instantly.

Letters of condolence are pouring in. Some are a great comfort and I reply to them all. They include a typed, meaningless one-liner from the chair of the PLP, an adequate one from Tony and a lovely, handwritten, very thoughtful one from John Major.

My diary has the usual mix of front-bench policy meetings with stakeholders, conferences, key seat visits and local constituency events. I do the lot. Particularly poignant is the visit to Kew Gardens to discuss their biodiversity work. Keith and I went there so often throughout our life together.

A few weeks later, I attend a service at St Paul's Church marking the anniversary of the 1981 New Cross fire in which fourteen young black people died.

I remember reading of the event in the newspaper at the time and it stuck, particularly because the family who held the party at which the fire happened were called Ruddock. George Francis, who chairs the New Cross Fire Committee, approaches me afterwards to ask if I can get the Met to reopen the inquest. My heart sinks. It's sixteen years since the fire and I cannot imagine what could be done at such a distance. I'm feeling pretty emotional too and though I promise to enquire I am weary at the thought of another campaign. The next day I write to our local police Chief Superintendent asking about the possibility of revisiting the evidence. Ten days later he writes back saying he can 'offer no hope of solving the case with what is already known … it will take someone to come forward and tell their story if the case is ever to be solved'.

I write to the Commissioner of the Met. He sets up a meeting for me with Commander Bill Griffiths and I present my case. I feel very passionately about this but at the same time I think there's hardly a chance that they will agree. My best hope is to get him to meet the families. To my surprise, the Commissioner agrees to Commander Griffiths meeting the families. They suggest Scotland Yard but I insist it must be local and so we arrange to meet at George and Tina Francis's home on 20 March. I am apprehensive. Most of the people who will be attending the meeting have no faith in the police and many are hostile. It is crucial that they're given their place and are respected. In the event, the long meeting, although tense, goes well and the families are properly heard. I feel they've made an impression on Commander Griffiths but there's still a long way to go. Two months later the Met will agree to reopen the case and announce a new inquiry led by DCI Newman. Quite a triumph.

There's been some media coverage of my involvement in trying to get a new inquiry, which results in hostile letters from strangers. I'm shocked to receive one that reads 'The killing by petrol bomb of fourteen nigger youth was excellent … there were 7,000 coloureds in 1937 now more like 7 million all <u>unwanted</u>'. Undoubtedly a reflection of the type of sentiment that was around at the time of the fire, when the National Front were very active in south-east London.

I'm also battling with the government on the crisis of cancelled operations at Lewisham Hospital (they'll do nothing). The East London line farce continues unabated as the minister tells me it will reopen in September this year, then nine days later the *Evening Standard* predicts it will be closed until the millennium. Jim Dowd and I table an Early Day Motion and get refused a ministerial meeting.

Tony launches our election strategy: 'Leading Britain in the Future'. It's designed to foster hope and optimism. Education is our priority – enabling people to achieve their full potential and to play their part in the dynamic high-skills economy we intend to create.

The Tories, by contrast, are scraping the barrel for ideas. The latest include splurging £60 million of public money on a new royal yacht. Opinion polls show I'm not the only one who thinks they are completely out of touch.

Demands for meetings on my front-bench portfolio continue to flood in. Everyone wants to press their priorities for change and, of course, for government money. At the end of the month I have an important meeting with senior civil servants in preparation for government. When asked for my three priorities for our manifesto I gave 20 per cent reduction in $CO_2$ emissions by 2010, 10 per cent renewable energy by the same date and setting up an Environmental Audit Committee to audit environmental performance across government, in a similar way to the Public Accounts Committee. I'm now taking advice on these policies from the civil servants. These meetings are crucial. Labour has been out of government for eighteen years and hardly anyone in the shadow Cabinet has any experience of governing.

The Tories reveal the privatisation of London Underground is to be a key manifesto promise! The whole country knows what chaos rail privatisation has caused. Even Tories are worried and a leaked letter reveals the return on the sale might be a little as £600 million despite the Tube being valued at up to £13 billion. As if to underline the farce, London Transport announces that the East London line will reopen 'early next year'. We shall see.

Former Tory Prime Minister Edward Heath has backed Labour plans for devolution, a minimum wage and the European Social Chapter. John Major's final humiliation comes on 27 February when Ben Chapman takes more than 50 per cent of the vote to make his 'safe Tory seat' Labour. The Tory government has lost its majority.

Jim Stevenson (my agent), Matt Briggs and Anne Shewring (deputy agents) and Kumar Jacob (our treasurer) are now bypassing the GC to work directly with the branches where there are many willing hands and competent campaigners. Once again I'm actively looking for a shop front on Deptford High Street where we can set up a visible campaign HQ.

Frank is spending as much time as possible in Aberdeen, raising his profile in the new constituency. I am so traumatised I'm no company anyway and can't draw any comfort from Frank's presence. In the months since Keith's death I have worked as hard as ever. There is nothing else I can do but I cry a lot at night. Sometimes I realise I've been crying in my sleep. I dream constantly and Keith is always my first thought in the morning. It's hard on Frank.

12 March: Keith would have been fifty-eight today.

The trauma of my personal life continues behind the public presence. I have further meetings with the transport police, who show me the location and explain what happened. Keith must have missed the last New Cross Gate train and taken one to New Cross, from where he had a longer walk. It's always been a dangerous crossing with dim Belisha beacons. The road divides in two directions and the driver was apparently lost on his way to play double bass in a late licensed pub. He was neither drunk nor speeding; he just didn't see Keith on the crossing. His car was an old Volvo with lots of metal and Keith was thrown into the air, splitting his skull on the central reservation. The driver has been charged. Arrangements are being made for the inquest, which of course I'll be attending.

Meanwhile Keith's sister and I are clearing the house. She gives me a paper to sign over the property on the basis that I had undertaken not to ask for anything more three years ago. At her request the college has searched Keith's office at Imperial and found some old notepaper with a list of wishes.

The college sends me a copy. It's not a will and it's dated the day he paid over the money for my house deposit. It has no validity and was written in anger but some of it I accept and will honour.

I refuse to sign over the house. Much though I'm consumed by guilt, we would never have had a house if it were not for my efforts. I couldn't live there with Frank but I'm not ready to give it up.

I get a letter threatening to drag me through the gutter press if I don't sign over the house. I've no option but to take it to the solicitor handling the probate. I cannot bear to think of Keith's memory being besmirched. Neither can I bear to lose all the lovely things we bought together over a lifetime of travelling the world. I know I would win in court but it is too awful to contemplate. Eventually I will settle for the return of my precious memorabilia and give the house away.

At the inquest I give the necessary evidence and answer a few questions. The man who killed Keith is clearly traumatised and nothing would be gained by a severe punishment. He will have to live with what he has done and he needs to be able to drive for his livelihood. I'm just glad it's over.

Imperial is planning a memorial and I'm asked to agree the programme and the guest list. Keith had a close relationship with a woman who had been his PhD student. Her daughter is a violinist who is to have his violin and she will play. I wish I could speak at the memorial but Keith is the only one who would have wanted that.

It takes place on 19 March. It's a harrowing experience for me but I am deeply touched by the kind words of his colleagues, especially those who have travelled long distances – including from the States – to pay their last respects. For so many people this is the end of an era and I know I'll never be able to set foot in the physics department again.

1 April: With just a month to go to the election Frank is now permanently in Aberdeen and I am pounding the streets every day. My weight is already down to nine stone so I've plenty of room for all the takeaways that are

sustaining me. Jim, Matt, Anne and Kumar are incredibly supportive. Each branch takes responsibility for leafleting, canvassing and preparing the rotas of people who will sit and take numbers at the polling stations. The central group prepares all the printed material, writes and organises the direct mail and the 40,000 election addresses for the freepost. HQ is a constant hive of activity as people offer to help, ask for posters and try to register to vote – only to be shocked to find it's too late. Ram Jatan, who lives locally, comes each day to unlock and ensure security for Katerina, who is having to do her casework in the makeshift office now that Parliament is closed.

We keep a list of volunteers and I write to each one in the last week thanking them for their efforts and inviting them to the election night party. My financial appeal to members has brought an excellent return. Together with money from my union we have enough to cover all our costs.

The mood on the streets is fantastic and despite my inner sorrows I am happy to be out campaigning. Frank returns for a short weekend in the middle of the month and we share our optimism for the future.

1 May: Election day and I'm up really early to start my day-long tour of all parts of the constituency, taking in all the polling stations and branch committee rooms. It's a beautiful, sunny day and Jim picks me up in his car covered in Labour posters, trailing balloons, and with loudspeakers strategically placed. I've got a well-practised routine whereby I can play a bit of music, then do a bit of sloganising, followed by more music. I'm also confident enough now to adjust my message to the local neighbourhood and even refer to people on the street. We are jubilant as the day wears on and the excitement increases. Everyone knows our theme tune: 'Things Can Only Get Better'. There is just one poignant moment when we drive past Reservoir Road. How could Keith not be alive to see this Labour government elected?

It's one amazing night. Frank has a great result in Aberdeen Central. This is the best news of all – now hopefully we can get some stability into our lives. My majority goes up to 18,878, with 56.1 per cent of the vote.

Bridget and Jim's results are terrific, both going from a slim 1,000-plus majority to over 12,000 and 14,000 respectively. We go to Ladywell Leisure Centre where, standing in the foyer watching the giant TV screen, I see Stephen Twigg's spectacular defeat of Michael Portillo. A great cheer goes up. They're doing reruns in the gaps between the results and I see the first declaration – it was Gisela Stuart winning Edgbaston. I can't help smiling at that.

## Chapter Six

# GOVERNMENT

*'With a few women in politics, women change; with many women in politics, politics change.'*

— MICHELLE BACHELET, President of Chile

It's a landslide. Tony and Cherie leave Sedgefield for London and I go back to greet those who have stayed the course at the Deptford High Street HQ. We are all jumping for joy.

Those who were around at the time will remember the sense of euphoria on the streets, the cheering crowds and enormous optimism for the future. My parliamentary life had been a long preparation for this moment: a Labour government in which I would be a minister. Lots of congratulations from friends and relatives and lots of catching up with Frank, who flew down from Aberdeen after his own count and celebrations.

We begin to see TV pictures of people being called into Downing Street and details of the Cabinet emerge. By Sunday, junior posts are being announced. I'm now frantic with worry. I just can't believe that Tony has dropped me after I've worked so closely with him.

Now I know I am not a minister. Tony, as I predicted, has not created a separate ministry. He has made Michael Meacher Minister of State for the Environment, thus avoiding giving him a Cabinet position. Towards the end of the day, when I'm in a deep depression, I get a call from the Chief Whip, Nick Brown, to tell me how sorry Tony is that he couldn't find a place for me. I am blazing and tell Nick to tell Tony he should have called me himself.

I'm at my absolute lowest. I've had a terrible twelve months and just when Frank and I should be celebrating I am plunged into deep despair once more. Everyone who knows me is embarrassed, not least my friends who have positions. Two members of the Cabinet say how sorry they are and make, with profound apologies, the only offer they can – for me to be their PPS. I appreciate their kindness but a bag carrier I won't be.

Within days Gordon, our new Chancellor, is throwing a party for back-benchers. Frank and I are invited. It seems churlish not to go but I'm in no mood for it. I make a great effort to look good and it is a fine party at No. 11. Charlie Whelan, Gordon's PR, greets me but asks what I'm doing there – surely I'm a minister? – his smile dies and he apologises.

People are genuinely puzzled. Most believe Tony and I must have had a falling out. No one has an explanation. I've insisted on seeing Tony. It's an extraordinary encounter. He tells me he likes me so much but he couldn't get me into the Cabinet. What does he mean? I've no wish to be liked, just respected and given the job I prepared for for three years. I never, ever expected or tried to get myself into the Cabinet. Then he compounds it by asking if I really wanted to be a minister and what about a select committee? It's a pointless interview and I feel crushed.

Harriet is as supportive as ever. She is to be Minister for Women in the Cabinet, alongside her major portfolio as Secretary of State for Social Security. We realise that this is an impossible task if there is to be a proper equalities programme and she suggests I could be her junior minister. This would be perfect and working with Harriet would be a great pleasure. Miracu-lously Tony agrees but there's one problem: the ministerial salaries budget is exhausted and I will have to take the post unpaid. I will get everything else –

the departmental office, civil servants, a car and driver. I know that all governments create extra posts, where salaries are not available, so there's no point in standing on principle.

11 June: I'm appointed the first ever full-time Minister for Women in a UK government. I'm absolutely thrilled but quickly deflated by adverse comment on the fact that I'm not being paid. Why was this announced? There's been no announcement accompanying the other unsalaried ministers. They are of course men and mostly with their own money. I'm pretty sure that I have been deliberately undermined. There are many around government and possibly in the No. 10 office who don't want any radical action that might challenge the carefully prepared safe image of a Blair government. But my joy at having an historic task before me knows no bounds. I get a phone call making arrangements for me to meet my civil servants at the Department of Social Security. I agree the arrangements and get the classic response: 'Yes, Minister'. I admit to a small thrill at the words. Harriet and I immediately set about scoping our agenda and making an assessment of how we can proceed. Because there's been no prior preparation, unlike in all existing departments, we are going to have to work from scratch. My private office is staffed by bright and pleasant young women who I guess are rather inexperienced. The office itself is grand and has been newly painted a light primrose yellow, with toning soft furnishings – rather feminine!

Ian McCartney, Minister of State at the DTI with the employment brief, has asked Frank to be his PPS. This is a really good opportunity because of Frank's involvement with trade unions. He will be able to contribute a lot and is especially thrilled at the prospect of the introduction of the Minimum Wage Bill.

Parliament is transformed, especially visually, with 120 women Members, double the number a month ago. All-women shortlists have enabled Labour to make the biggest ever change in women's representation. There are 101 of us, compared with twenty-one when I was first elected a decade ago. But the forces of darkness still prevail. A photo call of Tony with Labour's women MPs produces, instead of admiration, the soubriquet 'Blair's Babes'. This derogative term will be used again and again in an attempt to undermine women elected on all-women shortlists and any other woman politician the media choose to pick on.

The Conservatives, by contrast, have just thirteen women, the Lib Dems three and the SNP two. Finally, there is Betty Boothroyd, the Speaker, who by tradition forgoes party allegiance.

In the constituency we appear to have saved another community asset. The Carr Gomm charity were given use of the old library building on Kitto Road, pending further deliberations by the council. The project has been a success and I'm now supporting them to get the council's agreement to a permanent lease. Less helpful is the permanent status now accorded to the Greenwich lorry ban. Excellent for their residents of course but less so for everyone in the flats along Deptford Church Street, now plagued by HGVs. I'm arguing for air quality monitors on Crossfield flats and in the children's playground. Piecemeal solutions just create new hot spots elsewhere. We need a London-wide solution to the worst polluting vehicles and a limit on the size and weight of lorries going through the inner city.

Tony is going to the Earth Summit+5 in New York. This is really significant and I'm thrilled that he's championing an environmental cause so early in his premiership. It's only fourteen years since the UN set up the World Commission on Environment and Development and leaders began to appreciate just how much of our environment had been destroyed by industrialisation. Led by the remarkable Gro Harlem Brundtland, former Prime Minister of Norway, the Commission put forward the concept of sustainable development as an alternative to unfettered economic growth. It was described as development that 'meets the needs of the present without compromising the ability of future generations to meet their own needs'.

After the Commission published its report in 1987, the UN General Assembly called for a UN Conference on Environment and Development to be held in Rio in 1992. Some 108 governments adopted three major agreements, which were matched by two legally binding conventions – the United Nations Framework Convention on Climate Change and the Convention on Biological Diversity. These outcomes in Rio were the most significant agreements on the environment ever reached by the world community. The two conventions were opened for signatures and the conference became popularly known as the 'Earth Summit'. The UK signed both, ratifying the first in 1993 and the second in 1994. More than 160 countries have now ratified both conventions.

The outcome of Rio+5 is very disappointing. Observers note that little progress has been made in the past five years and the gap between north and south has widened. No agreement can be reached on a political statement. We in the UK will have to set an example and NGOs and grassroots activists are being encouraged to put maximum pressure on their governments – I think we can depend on that!

I have meetings with my Private Secretary Helen, her deputy Nicole and Diary Secretary Brinda. Harriet already has her team in place with special advisor Liz Kendall dealing with the women's agenda. My driver is a really nice guy called Karl who will be picking me up at 7.45 a.m. for 9 a.m. meetings or 8.45 a.m. when I don't have anything at 9 a.m.

There is a huge clamour from women's organisations to be involved in developing our agenda. Our work will revolve around three priority areas: childcare, action on violence against women and family-friendly working. In support of these three policy areas we will develop three processes, namely, mainstreaming the interests of women throughout all government departments, opening up a dialogue between women and government and improving the representation of women in public life. This is nothing short of a revolution and we have the fewest resources of any ministers to achieve it. I make some assessment of our potential political backing. We have twenty-one women ministers in government, five of whom are heading their departments. Several are definitely antipathetic but the majority are probably on side. Among the back-bench women MPs there are some very good sisters, including

Margaret Hodge, Julie Morgan, Barbara Follett, Oona King and Neil Kin-nock's former special advisor, Patricia Hewitt. Lorna Fitzsimons, the sparky, newly elected MP for Rochdale, is chair of the PLP Women's Committee and Meg Russell an equally enterprising National Women's Officer at Labour HQ. As civil servants cannot be involved in party meetings, I will get my researcher to invite backbenchers to meetings where I can share our agenda.

I have one very pleasant duty before the onslaught of formal meetings. I'm going to the government art collection to choose pictures for the bare walls of my pristine office. I signal ahead to the curator that I only want to see paintings by women artists. Predictably they haven't many and this is a unique request. Nonetheless, I manage to secure two Mary Feddens, a Bridget Riley and an Olwen Jones as part of my haul.

Devolution is an absolute priority for the new government and referenda will be held in September in Scotland and Wales to test further public sup-port for our proposals. If the votes are won then legislation will proceed to set up the new institutions. This will provide a major opportunity for women and I will need to work with women colleagues on the selection of candidates and organise appropriate visits. There are nine Labour women MPs holding Scottish seats and just four in Wales.

It's quite clear that the Women's National Commission hasn't made much impact on government for many years and we are going to have to make changes. One thing they do know about is the UK government's obligations to women as a result of the UN conventions we have signed. Not something that I recall ever being mentioned in the House.

It's not only women's NGOs that want to meet. There are also indus-try forums such as the one at BT, Women in Film and Television, providers such as Anne Longfield at the Kids' Club Network* and Jill Pitkeathley, my old CAB chair, representing the Carers National Association.† Refuge and

---

* Now 4Children.
† Now Carers UK.

Women's Aid are obvious priority contacts for our work on violence and many women are soon trooping through the doors of Whitehall to meet the first ever Ministers for Women.

It's thrilling stuff but we know we need to work fast to deliver and also to be seen to be accountable. This means we need debates and questions on the floor of the House. There is no provision for this and we will not have any legislation of our own. I prepare a paper for Harriet on parliamentary procedure. We have to be able to answer written questions and to have a slot for orals. All attempts by Labour MPs to table questions to us as Ministers for Women have been ruled out by the Table Office. They can only be addressed to Harriet as Secretary of State for Social Security. Civil servants always make their own enquiries of opposite numbers behind the scenes before any formal approaches are made and the feedback isn't good. Harriet and I will have to go to see Ann Taylor, who is the Leader of the House and not an obvious 'sister'. One important structure we do have is a Cabinet subcommittee, HS(W), where we control the agenda. Members of the committee are drawn from fourteen government departments. For the very first meeting all ministers are asked to report on their involvement/actions on equalities, in areas relevant to their own department.

Prior to my arrival, Harriet had commissioned a paper from IPPR on how to develop a public involvement strategy to enable government to understand women's priorities. We need to reach beyond those who are already organised into stakeholder groups. She has also engaged Anna Coote as a part-time special advisor.

Previous surveys have shown us that women feel less connected to politics and government than men and don't believe that politics/government is for them or is concerned about their issues. Women's chief concerns are very similar to men's but expressed differently. Post-election surveys are showing us that women are excited and optimistic about the prospect of change under Labour. Significantly, at the general election, for the first time since 1945, women and men voted in equal numbers for the Labour Party.

Indeed, there was a bigger swing (11 per cent) among women than men (8 per cent). Our challenge is how to reach beyond the small, elite minority in the stakeholder groups to the ordinary women of the silent majority. IPPR proposes a panel of 5,000 women, recruited by telephone and stratified by age, social class, region and ethnic background. They would be called upon up to four times a year to take part in quantitative survey work and qualitative group discussions or citizens' juries/workshops. I've been doing some work on these ideas with Anna. It's obviously the way forward and an informal approach to the WI produces an enthusiastic response.

Harriet and I are off to the Labour Party's Women's Conference in Bournemouth. Women's Conference is always very rewarding and we can expect a lot of support for our women's agenda. Harriet, however, will face opposition to the cut in lone parent benefit that Gordon insisted on. Attitudes to this benefit vary. Lone parents don't come to me asking for more benefit, they come asking for assistance to get into work. There is a strong work ethic among Caribbean and African women (the majority single parents locally) and what they want is opportunity and work that pays. Harriet will be promoting the New Deal for Lone Parents announced in Gordon's first Budget. Every lone parent on benefits will be invited to the job centre when her youngest child starts school. At this point an average woman could have been on benefits for up to ten years. She would then get a personal advisor to help with her job search, training and childcare. There will be no compunction to get into work and we have lots of promises to make on childcare, after-school clubs and nursery places. Our promise to legislate to establish a minimum wage is hugely popular – of the 1 million people earning less than £2.50 per hour, the majority are women. We won't neglect the elderly either. Women inevitably are the poorest pensioners.

A very long interview with Frances Hardy is published in the *Daily Mail*. It begins: 'She isn't a wife and she isn't a mother. So what makes Joan Ruddock think she is equipped for her new job…?' Despite the title, the piece goes on to give a favourable account of my life and times.

Issues of violence against women belong in the Home Office. In July, I meet with the relevant ministers: Alun Michael (crime), Joyce Quin (prisons) and Mike O'Brien (immigration). The discussions are useful and we look for ways we can work together. Officials will produce a position paper in September and ministers will meet again in October. There are major contributions to be sought from the Department for Environment, Transport and the Regions (DETR) and the Department of Health (DoH) as well as ourselves. I'm not sure Alun is so keen on our involvement but Joyce certainly is.

Transport is something I really do know about, especially in London, so I'm keen to meet Glenda Jackson at DETR. There's a lot going on – proposed regulation on London's mini-cabs; a consultation paper on an integrated transport policy; and the DETR initiative 'Secure Stations' to improve safety at railway stations. Glenda is very supportive.

Health is my final goal before I take a holiday in August. I have a meeting with the Women's Health and Screening Delegation and also with Tessa Jowell, the minister. I ask for Ministers for Women to be closely involved in the Review of Inequalities and Health and also flag up the advantages of joint campaigns, e.g. trying to prevent young girls taking up smoking. I also raise two issues referred to me by NGOs. My meeting with the Family Planning Association has provided disturbing evidence of severe reductions in the resources going to family planning, resulting in a much increased rate of unwanted pregnancies among older women. There is also evidence of continuing reluctance among GPs to refer women for abortions. I ask Tessa to look at self-referral to abortion facilities via the NHS. This would clearly cut the number of late abortions.

The New Deal for Lone Parents is ready for rollout – pretty impressive after less than three months in office. It's being launched in several test areas and I'm heading the one in Cardiff. There's a great turnout of lone parents and employers. I make a speech on the theme of the best welfare being work and the way government will provide support. It's well received. It's great to be part of a positive change programme.

Antonia is ready to move on and has got a job offer from the RCN to be their parliamentary officer. This is a very good opportunity and I'm delighted for her as now I'm a minister I won't have nearly as much work for a parliamentary researcher and most of the interesting work will be done by the civil servants. My solution is to ask around for someone who could fit this changed situation. Alicia Chater has worked for the party and is familiar with what I will need. She has ambitions to get a more senior job at Labour HQ so it is likely to be short term and suit us both.

24 July: The government publishes the White Paper on devolution. Donald Dewar, Secretary of State for Scotland, commits Labour to selecting equal numbers of women and men candidates for the elections and family-friendly working practices for the parliament. What a breakthrough!

It's time to take a holiday. I can't believe I've survived this year, with the inquest, the memorial, the general election and then the desperate initial rejection from government. Home life is still very difficult. I think about Keith every single day and grief is never far away. Frank has his own demons and is working flat-out in Aberdeen to re-establish himself. We are both exhausted. We find a cheap but large manor house near Sarlat. On arrival we observe that it's definitely seen better days. An elderly aristocratic woman greets us and explains she lives in the annexe. We are shown into what was obviously her family home, stuffed full of antiques including many large fine pictures on the walls. On holiday we never admit to being MPs if we can avoid it so Frank says he is a lawyer. This sets up an immediate bond with the Lady of the Manor as she tells us her late husband was a Scottish judge and a member of the House of Lords! We explore the bedrooms, which we can choose from, and settle for the one with the least damp sheets. It could have been a disaster but the whole place is fascinating and we are amazed to find huge carved wooden cupboards and chests, one dated in the 1500s. After two days our host announces she is leaving for a holiday and Frank takes her to the railway station. We really feel we have been left in charge of something quite special and make much use of the secluded tree-ringed swimming pool where no swim garments are required.

After two weeks of indulgence we return to give my mother a break in Aberdeen. This is Mum's first visit. She is very uncertain about our future together and Frank's flat is not the most comfortable, but the week is going well enough when we hear the extraordinary news that Princess Diana is dead. Whatever we thought of the circus surrounding her life, this is shocking news.

Frank is working hard in Scotland for the referendum on whether Scotland should have devolution. It's held on 11 September and I take the day off from the ministry for a day's political campaigning in Wales. I take the train to Newport – home territory – then on to Blackwood for a photo call and blitzing in Islwyn for the rest of the day. The referendum on establishing a Welsh Assembly is just a week away and it looks like a close result. Scotland is overwhelmingly in favour of a Scottish Parliament, but having been brought up in Monmouthshire (later Torfaen) I know that there's far less interest in a Cardiff assembly. It proves to be the case, with the overall result showing just 50.3 per cent in favour and 49.7 per cent against.

The next day I'm back in my own constituency. Today I have my regular meeting with the council leadership and Jim and Bridget. At midday I'm opening another branch of the 999 Club – a very successful local drop-in centre. I manage to squeeze in a visit to the Deptford Under-5s day at Deptford Park School and then on to my surgery at Honor Oak Community Centre. Before we finish, Karl arrives to drop off my weekend red box. The contents are exaggerated in their formality – every small invitation is accompanied by reasons why I should or should not be accepting. Civil servants work to very set patterns that slow everything down and seem to assume very little intelligence on the part of the minister. The private office provides the channel of communication between me and the civil servants developing our policy. It's clear I have to place my trust in Helen to get things done. We will have to speed up.

Amazing – some new women's toilets in the Commons. There have always been men's toilets in both division lobbies, discreetly placed behind unmarked wooden doors. Naturally I've not seen behind those doors in ten years of going through the lobbies but now I'm told there is a ladies' loo in each. Even more symbolic is the removal of the gentleman's barber in favour of a unisex salon. Taking early retirement, the barber protested that he was a victim of 'political correctness' and a 'change of morals'! He admitted he had been trained to do perms and colourings but didn't want to – a lucky escape for us women I've no doubt.

The highlight of the month is a trip to Belfast where the extraordinary Mo Mowlam has the historic task of trying to end the turmoil that is Northern Ireland. She has taken a deliberate decision to harness the power of women in the search for a new political settlement. I meet some remarkable women, notably from the Northern Ireland Women's Coalition. This party was set up last year by the Catholic academic Monica McWilliams and the Protestant social worker Pearl Sagar. It's a remarkable organisation, unashamedly feminist and non-sectarian. In the 1996 elections to the Northern Ireland Forum the coalition candidates didn't win any constituencies (not surprising) but under the top-up mechanism for representation of minor parties both Monica and Pearl got seats. They are women of great courage and will be key allies for Mo in the peace process. The position of women in Northern Ireland is dire and we will need to make a big effort if we are to improve it. I'm hugely impressed by Mo – she's absolutely the best person for this job.

The weeks fly by as we work across our various policy areas and meet numerous stakeholders, including Indira Patel – a member of the Women's National Commission (WNC) – who organises a visit to the Swaminarayan Hindu Temple in Neasden. This is a first for me and an amazing experience.

I have my first meeting with our press officers. This is going to be a tricky area as we know we're dealing with a hostile media. If we're to reach the average woman we are going to need proactive civil servants finding ways to communicate through women's magazines and women's pages in the broadsheets. We have appointed Pauline Barret as head of the Women's Unit. She worked at the ILO (International Labour Organisation) so she should understand our agenda.

Harriet calls a top-level meeting for us, Hilary Armstrong, Patricia Hewitt, Barbara Follett, Sally Morgan from No. 10 and special advisors Liz Kendall and Anna Coote. Meg Russell has prepared a paper on the state of women's representation at all levels of the party. When the party dropped all-women shortlists following the Leeds industrial tribunal ruling, an NEC working party was set up to consider women's future representation. The immediate challenge is the party itself, where only 40 per cent of members are women, and local government, where women councillors make up only 25 per cent of the total. There are no quotas operating for either. The 1995 conference decided that women should make up 40 per cent of councillors and 50 per cent of local government panel members and that group officers should be female in the same proportion as in the group as a whole. But these decisions have been reduced to the status of guidance only. Our progressive General Secretary, Tom Sawyer, has risen to the challenge and written to all local government committees stressing the need to have women on the panel, and to all party branches, asking them to draw up 50:50 shortlists. Selections are underway for next year's local elections.

Despite the unprecedented selections under all-women shortlists, women MPs make up less than a quarter of Labour's strength at Westminster. There are currently no mechanisms in place for future selections and given our majority we are unlikely to gain further seats. If we are not to go backwards we will need to focus on the seats of retiring members and unpredictable by-elections. New selection procedures are to be agreed in two years' time so we need to be on the case. But the biggest task is ensuring women's representation in the Scottish Parliament, Welsh Assembly and potentially a London-wide authority. On the latter we have no information.

The very best prospects for women are in the Scottish Parliament and Welsh Assembly. The Scottish Executive and NEC have agreed in principle that constituencies will be twinned in their selection process on the basis of winability and geography. Every pair of constituencies will have to select one woman and one man. This is an ingenious solution but only applicable in the case of new institutions. Elections are not expected until 1999 but that still means selections early next year, so no time to waste. Each body will also have a 'top-up' list where members do not have a constituency. This can easily be dealt with using the system of zipping adopted in other European countries, where men and women alternate on the party list. My task is to keep abreast of all these developments, intervening where necessary. We can't advocate equality in all other walks of life if we don't practise it in the party we control.

21 September and it's our first annual conference with Labour in power for eighteen years. There is massive security and long queues but the sun is shining and the mood is celebratory. We start with a reception for women delegates and visitors. The event is transformed by the attendance of so many newly elected women MPs. Harriet and I have always been active on this front but it's good to be here as ministers and we get a great reception. Harriet is so good at these meetings – enthusing everyone and generous in her references to me – but lone parents are still an issue and some women are bitterly critical of her.

I've got fringe meetings every day, beginning with the Labour Women's Network. This is a grassroots organisation of Labour women run by the formidable Val Price. It's been going for nearly a decade and is at the forefront of campaigning for women, supporting, encouraging and more recently training women candidates. They are very much a part of our success. I tell them this and promise that we are witnessing the beginning of the end of male supremacy in the House of Commons, the beginning of the end of a low pay economy with women trapped on poverty wages and the beginning of the end of government's failure to understand the reality of women's lives. Such optimism!

The next day it's a Zero Tolerance meeting. I outline our approach based on the findings of a consultation exercise completed a year before and the many consultations now underway. I flag up the new law on harassment that deals with stalking and our intention to change the law on questioning of witnesses by those accused of date rape along with commissioning research into the low conviction rate for rape. I pay tribute to the refuge movement and their care of more than 63,000 women during the previous year. We want to support and spread best practice. I end by saying we want to achieve a new national consensus that violence against women has no part in our society.

My next fringe meeting is organised by the trade union Unison, which has a majority of women members. As working women, these trade unionists have a vested interest in everything we are doing, from the £200 million we've invested in the lone parent programme to the £100 disregard in the new Family Credit towards childcare. Of most interest are our plans for a minimum wage benefiting the 600,000 women earning less than £2.50 an hour. Our fundamental review of pensions is also focusing on the needs of women. I tell them that the government will support the EU Working Time Directive and the Parental Leave Directive, which will give all employees the basic right to three months' unpaid leave following birth or the adoption of a child. In short we want to get women into work, get better pay for women in work and make sure women are able to get on in work.

Tony's conference speech is in his now familiar staccato delivery, punching out lines that uplift and inspire. It's extraordinary how much change we've made in less than five months. We've allocated an extra £2 billion for schools; signed the EU Social Chapter; set up the Low Pay Commission; delivered the Scottish and Welsh referenda; cut VAT on fuel; banned handguns; banned landmines; given councils the right to use money from selling council homes to help the homeless; and in Northern Ireland the ceasefire has been renewed and Republicans and Unionists are talking for the first time in decades. I'm on my feet with everyone else for the standing ovation with a lump in my throat, my sense of euphoria just slighted dented by the fact I don't think he mentioned women once.

There's a long conference resolution on the representation of women that congratulates the party on the historic change in the parliamentary party, reiterates the 1990 target that 50 per cent of the PLP should be female and calls for the NEC to find ways of further increasing women's representation.

This would be an ideal debate for a contribution from me but it's no longer enough to raise a hand from the floor. Conference is strictly controlled by the leadership and I'll only be called if they decide. I approach Anji, who runs Tony's office, as I know she was always a good friend when I was in Tony's team and I suspect she would not have approved of my being dumped. Amazingly I do get called. I'm quite good at rally speak after my many years in CND so I get it right and pick up on Tony's conference theme as I end: 'A government that is modern, fair and strong is one that draws on the talents of all its people. That is New Labour today. *This must be our promise to women.*'

I'm exhausted. There's been loads of socialising as well as all the tension around making speeches, asking questions and getting photographed. The latter is always a hazard of these occasions, dictating a great deal of time and attention be devoted to hair, make-up and clothes. A bit of light relief arrives in my ministerial box. *Woman* magazine has an article by Jane Simon suggesting additions to the Minister for Women agenda. Her hilarious list includes: fashion design licences only to be issued to those who have breasts and hips; supermodels to be banned; advertisements for anti-ageing products to specify the age of the model; haircare products to include credits for the entire team that created the model's 'easy to manage' hairdo; and Page 3 girls to be replaced by pictures of the newspaper editor in the shower! Since we get two mentions and a list of our own priorities this can do us no harm. There's also a copy of a full-page and flattering profile of me in the *South Wales Echo*. The only downside is the emphasis on my CND past, which never goes down well with No. 10.

I've started to review the UN Platform for Action agreed at the Beijing conference in 1995. This was the fourth UN conference on the rights of women, emphasising the gap between rights secured and the ability of women to exercise those rights. After a ten-year gap, delegates organised for Beijing by drawing up in advance a Declaration and Platform for Action aimed at achieving greater equality and opportunities for women. A remarkable document, it analyses the position of women under twelve different headings including economics, education, health, violence, armed conflict, decision-making and environment. Under each heading there is a list of strategic objectives. Most of the objectives are already embodied in promises and programmes being worked up across government.

One of the action points that I'm pretty certain no one has addressed in the UK is the production and dissemination of gender-disaggregated data across government. It's obvious if we don't have facts we can't make relevant decisions. I ask the Women's Unit to start investigating. We're also gathering our own statistics about how women fare within each government department's jurisdiction. Interesting areas for improvement include the Foreign Office – 65 per cent of staff are men; only nine out of 154 main embassies are run by women (and it's only twenty-five years since they stopped sacking women who got married). Robin Cook is up for change and has already organised an open day designed to attract more women and people from ethnic minorities. Within the judiciary less than 10 per cent of judges are women, only seven out of ninety-three High Court judges are women and there is only one woman Appeal Court Judge and there are no female Law Lords.

With several weeks of recess left, I'm off to Venice on Sunday afternoon for a meeting with women ministers from Italy and France. A full day of talks on Monday and back on the first flight Tuesday morning. It's great to share ideas with other ministers and find, not unexpectedly, that we share the same challenges.

The next day Frank leaves at 6 a.m. for a trip offshore. I hate him doing this as I've no faith in North Sea helicopters. I'm now in back-to-back meetings most days and having to attend several ad hoc ministerial groups. We're also working hard with Margaret Hodge on input into the childcare strategy. The policy is owned by the Department of Education, headed by David Blunkett, but our dialogue with women gives us the very best handle on how this policy should be developed. It's also interesting how many employers' organisations want to meet with us.

I spend a rare overnight with my mum, then it's up early in the morning and off to Bristol. I'm speaking at the South and West Labour Party Regional Women's Conference. I point out that in 1987 I was elected alongside the region's then only woman MP, Dawn Primarolo – now a Treasury minister. Today we have ten women MPs and it's the only region with an equal number of women and men. I review our women's agenda but add our commitments on education: computers in every one of our 32,000 schools, £2 billion building programme including fifteen new hospitals, one of which will be built in Swindon, the first minister for public health and £10 million to cut waiting times for breast cancer treatment. These are the policies that women voted for and I can demonstrate we're delivering. I get back on the train for Paddington and meet up with Frank who has returned home for supper, safe from the North Sea.

Until Parliament returns we can do a straight twelve hours on ministry business every day. Tuesday begins with Harriet and me meeting Foreign and Commonwealth Office (FCO) Minister Liz Symons to discuss the many international dimensions of our work. This is followed by my meeting with the National Women's Aid Federation, led by Nicola Harwin. While delighted to work with us they are impatient for change and there's no doubt they know what they're talking about. Next up is a meeting with Ann Taylor, the first woman leader of the Commons. We are pressing her on the modernisation of the House and over our own demand for parity with other ministers in having a slot for oral questions. It's extraordinary that we should have to fight these battles with our own side.

24 October: In Edinburgh, where the Women's National Commission and the British Council are holding a meeting on Women and Decision-Making to coincide with the Commonwealth Heads of Government meeting. Liz Symons opens the conference, pointing out that this is the first NGO gathering at a Commonwealth summit. She is followed by Henry McLeish, our Minister of State for Scotland, who also holds the brief for the women's agenda. He declares that the new Scottish Parliament, when built, will be

'women-friendly'. A day nursery will be included in the design and special consideration given to other facilities that women might need. He wants to see a Parliament that is less confrontational, more inclusive, more partici- pative and with more normal working hours – 'a more attractive prospect than Westminster'. He reiterates the commitment to the selection of equal numbers of women and men. An impressive woman, Dr Joan Stringer, EOC Commissioner for Scotland, follows up with statistics – a single woman judge out of twenty-six, no Sheriff Principals, only seven women out of 102 Sher- iffs and three out of twenty advocates. Clearly there's much more to do, as is borne out in the lively open session that follows. In my speech I am able to give the equivalent statistics for England and Wales and describe the machin- ery of government that we have put in place to bring about change. I also talk about our women's dialogue whereby we can respond to the priorities of ordinary women. The greatest of these is childcare, which the government is addressing with alacrity, and building on our programme for getting lone parents into work. Finally, I refer to the failure of mainstreaming to date and our determination to ensure it is made to work across government. During the rest of the day we hear from speakers from India and South Africa and conclude yet again how universal is the condition of women.

The next day, another WNC session and then on to meet Scottish women campaigners against violence, Zero Tolerance and Scottish Women's Aid, Engender and Rape Crisis. Then it's lunch at the Royal Society to discuss women in science and back to the airport for the flight to Heathrow.

It's vital that our dialogue involves women from other parts of the UK and not just London, so I'm in Birmingham, visiting a police domestic vio- lence unit in the city. We are committed to rolling out these specialist units across the country and I need to make some evaluation of their worth. I've no doubt that involving specially trained officers is a great improvement on the age-old attitude 'it's just a domestic'.

My diary card reminds me to wear a pink ribbon for breast cancer today. Lucky it did as I'm not at my best in the morning. Next day I'm at the

Home Office to discuss progress on domestic violence and my findings from all the recent meetings and visits I've made. I go on to support the launch of Women in Engineering at the DTI and to a photo call for Breakthrough Breast Cancer. Then it's PMQs and a short team meeting with my researcher Alicia before a pre-meeting on the Beijing Action Partnership. Friday I'm in Scotland for a Scottish Women's Conference. I congratulate Labour women including Rhona Brankin, who's chairing the conference, and Rosemary McKenna and Anne Maguire, two newly elected Scottish MPs, on their long struggle for equality in Scotland. It's sixty-eight years since Labour's first woman MP, Jennie Lee, was elected in North Lanarkshire. I tell them that the prospect of a Parliament in Scotland with equal numbers of women and men is raised by every women's organisation I meet. I quote George Lyttleton's advice to a lady, 'Seek to be good, but aim not to be great. A woman's noblest station is to retreat.' I declare that we women have no intention of retreating despite the growing murmurings that surely 101 Labour women MPs is enough! I also report the experience of one of those MPs at a recent engineers' dinner. A man asks, 'Who did you come with?' 'No one,' she replies. 'Then why are you here?' he responds. To his astonishment, she replies, 'Because I'm the local Member of Parliament.'

Since the Labour Party failed to challenge the tribunal case that found against all-women shortlists we've been in limbo. It's obvious to me that we should legislate, but Tony's not up for it so we've had to look elsewhere. Now we are faced with the suggestion that twinning might be illegal under the Sex Discrimination Act, which applies to the whole of the UK. Ever-cautious civil servants from the DfEE (who have responsibility for this) tell us the Amsterdam Treaty, which could be interpreted as exempting political parties from the equal treatment directive, cannot be applied retrospectively and will not be ratified until 1999; too late for Scotland. This is a battle we have to win.

I'm having lunch with Gaby Hinsliff of the *Daily Mail*. I'm never keen on lunching with journalists. Those working for the nationals never genuinely want to know about what you're doing. They're always after some information about the leadership, preferably something bad. To my surprise, the feature turns out well – a first for favourable coverage in the *Mail*.

Next day I leave home at 6.30 a.m. to fly to Frankfurt and then on to Ankara. I end the evening having dinner with our ambassador, Sir David Logan, at his residence. Sir David is keen to have a minister visit projects that the UK government is supporting, particularly the women's shelter, which as a man he can't enter. I'm told the places I will visit are not particularly safe so I will travel with Helen, my PS, in the ambassador's armour-plated car. It's a full day – visiting a refuge, an employment project and a childcare facility for poor mothers. I hear some horrific stories of violence and attempts by men to get to the shelter and the lack of enthusiasm by the local police for any action against their own gender. It's a really fulfilling day and I'm pleased that the Foreign Office is embracing the needs of women and recognising sensitivities in working with local NGOs.

Later I fly to Istanbul for a two-day conference on women's rights. At the end of the first evening the Turkish government puts on a reception for all the participants, which provides the opportunity for informal chats with a lot of women who luckily for us speak good English.

The days pass in an endless succession of meetings at the department. Fitting in constituency work is really hard. I'm trying to get round my Labour Party branches, which means finishing at the department, going back to the constituency and returning again for the late votes. I used to get car sick in my youth but now I have an iron focus on doing box work as I travel. I also have to squeeze in meetings with my staff. Frank hardly gets a look in.

Ethnic minority women suffer a double disadvantage in Britain today and I'm beginning a series of meetings to see how we can address this. I begin by meeting the Commission for Racial Equality, followed by an afternoon roundtable with organisations representing Chinese women, Asian women, International Black Women and the Southall Black Sisters. The latter are very impressive. They specialise in violence cases and came to national attention a few years ago with their campaign for the release of Kiranjit Ahluwalia, who had been imprisoned for life for the murder of her husband. Kiranjit suffered abuse and brutality for ten years before one day setting fire to her sleeping husband. Her lawyers told her there was no possible appeal against her sentence but the Southall Black Sisters set about trying to reopen the case. After two years of preparation her appeal was based on provocation and diminished responsibility.

The grounds of provocation had long been accepted in cases where men murdered their wives – the 'crime passionnel'. In law provocation embodied the requirement of a 'sudden and temporary loss of self-control'. Although the Court of Appeal rejected Kiranjit's defence of provocation they nonetheless made important statements, acknowledging that the current interpretation of the law excluded the experiences of battered women. For the first time cumulative provocation was recognised. Kiranjit won the right to a retrial on the grounds of diminished responsibility. She pleaded guilty to manslaughter and was sentenced to precisely the time she had already served – three years and four months – leading to her immediate release.

The case raised a fundamental question as to whether a woman should have to declare herself mentally unsound to get a fair trial. Other high-profile cases that attracted similar campaigns include those of Emma Humphreys in 1995 and Sara Thornton in 1996. Now the Southall Black Sisters are pressing us to get the defence of provocation abolished and the law changed to recognise the impact of years of abuse leading to 'slow burn rage'. Harriet and I will definitely need to take these issues on board.*

Nick Raynsford has launched the Greater London (Referendum) Bill. This will test public support for our proposals for an elected mayor and assembly. The referendum will be held on the same day as next year's local government elections.

---

* It took until 2003 to get a review of the law on homicide (instituted by the Home Office and strongly backed by Harriet Harman in her capacity as Solicitor General) and a further seven years for the law on provocation to be abolished and new partial defences – that were not biased towards men – to be introduced.

My ministerial workload constantly increases with the result that the constituency activity is squeezed into Fridays. Today is no exception. I do my box overnight and it's collected from my home before I leave at 9 a.m. It's my regular meeting with the council leadership. At midday I'm visiting the Positive Place, an advice and support centre for people with HIV. They are doing magnificent work and I hear many moving stories of cruel discrimination, ill-health, joblessness and homelessness. But it really is a positive place where people give their best. I cut a ribbon and then go on to a millennium tree planting at a local primary school. At 3.30 p.m. it's Ladywell Leisure Centre where I see about thirty people and the weekend red box is delivered. At 7.30 p.m. I'm attending a local meeting of the World Development Movement. Needless to say I get home too tired to eat, but I always open the box to see how much work I've got to get through over the weekend.

In the morning I'm off to Cardiff to address a Welsh Labour Women's Conference. Glenys Kinnock is speaking first. She is able to say that the Kalinka case, which was important in the outlawing of Labour's all-women shortlists, has been superseded. A new ruling has conceded that the positive action laws in North Rhine Westphalia are acceptable. Nonetheless, she doesn't underestimate the challenges we will face in devising the rules for selection for the Welsh Assembly. I follow with an acknowledgement that as a woman from the Valleys myself I am only too aware of the hostile territory in which women are working. But I say women are responding to the challenge – ninety women have answered Julie Morgan MP's call for women who might be interested in becoming members of the Assembly. I tell them we have to modernise our party as well as change the culture if the Labour Party is to become more attractive to women. I relate my own experiences. I confess it took me years and years to get myself into the sad culture of the composite* and express the wish that there are people here today who don't know what I'm talking about.

---

* Motions to Labour Party conference had to be composited in all-day meetings in smoke-filled rooms prior to conference using only words found in the individual motions submitted.

24 November: Karl picks me up at 8.30 a.m. for a day-long series of meetings at the department, beginning with a briefing for a speech at Islington Council. Speech writing at my level of civil service support is a real pain. Everything comes by way of standard paragraphs of dry facts. I'm constantly aware that I could write better myself but that's true of lots of things and clearly time doesn't allow me to do it. Thursday begins with a meeting with Tom Clarke, Minister for Film and Tourism at the Department for Culture, Media and Sport (DCMS), as part of my work across government to engage other departments in the women's agenda. I need him on side as there are many grievances expressed by women in film and television.

At the end of the month I'm back in Scotland (at least I get to see Frank) for a Saturday conference of Scottish Labour Women. My themes are similar to those I used in Wales just a week ago. Motivating women in the party is crucial to our role. They can spread the message, work for equality in their own communities, participate in women's NGOs and encourage more women to come forward to take up political positions. I urge them to strive for a world first – an elected parliament with equal numbers of women and men. This is a unique opportunity to transform political life and we mustn't let it pass.

Frank is worried about his mother, who has had a strange twitching and pain in her arm. She is going for tests.

1 December and picked up by Karl as usual. My first appointment is marked 'personal' in the diary. It should be the last with my solicitor, dealing with the final details of Keith's estate. The huge emotional trauma of losing Keith and now the house would totally take over my life if I were not working so hard. Back to the office and hours of meetings. At 3.30 p.m. I'm in the Chamber for a debate called by the opposition on our welfare plans, including lone parents' benefits. Harriet makes an excellent speech exposing the Tory record and detailing our new initiatives. Then it's to No. 10 where Tony is meeting all London Labour MPs and finally to an Arts for Labour reception in the Jubilee Room.

The next day I'm in Northern Ireland. The UK will hold the presidency of the EU for the first half of 1998 and we are exploring the possibility of a bid to hold one of the presidency meetings on women's rights here in Belfast. More meetings with leading women activists – always inspiring. Back to Heathrow and a meeting of the Labour Women's Parliamentary Committee, which I try not to miss. Then I drop into a reception given by the Pre-School Learning Alliance, attend a stocktaking meeting with Harriet and catch up with Katerina. Keeping abreast of all the constituency work gets harder and harder. I am particularly conscious of the heavy casework load and the fact that she has so little chance to offload onto me.

The following day I have a fascinating discussion with representatives of the British Diplomatic Spouses' Association. They have a significant equalities issue. Many of the women they represent have spent decades following their husbands around the world, being unpaid hostesses for embassy events. Then, with the children being educated back in Britain and off their hands, they have found themselves replaced by the proverbial 'younger woman'. These women are greatly disadvantaged, having no home to come back to, no income, few skills and often very little pension when they reach sixty. Clearly the FCO has benefited enormously from their service and must take some responsibility. We are already taking steps on pension sharing at divorce but more needs to be done for this largely invisible group.

Harriet has written a four-page letter to the Prime Minister formally setting out the value of our work in maintaining the women's vote, which came to us so spectacularly in May. She is right to point out the expectations women have of us and the fact that women tend to be less trustful of politicians and more disconnected from politics than men. There is also a danger that staying within spending limits across government may impact disproportionately on women. She goes on to illustrate how our work serves to connect women to government and stimulate ministers' interest in delivering for women through the Cabinet subcommittee. This committee is coordinating work on national childcare and action on violence across government and is already demonstrating its value. She also underlines the importance of opening up a new dialogue with women and indicates that this will include 'women's juries' to draw women into informed, deliberative discussions on our main policy commitments.

There's still much nervousness about the selection process for Scotland. The DfEE has legal responsibilities for the Sex Discrimination Act and David Blunkett is not willing to seek its amendment to clarify the position on positive action for political parties. We have obtained lots of information on the European experience that should be used to stiffen resolve across government. A Belgian statute of 1994 required 25 per cent of all party lists to be female, rising to 33 per cent in 1999. A Finnish statute of 1994 required a minimum of 40 per cent female and 40 per cent male appointments to all ad hoc public bodies. Quotas for political parties have been adopted by seven EU states including France and Germany. None has been challenged to date under the Equal Treatment Directive. Henry could put the issue beyond doubt with an amendment to the Scottish Parliament Bill but he's reluctant and frankly we don't want Scotland to be an exception. I decide to do some work of my own, drawing on party projections of how many seats we might expect to win in both new institutions.

I manage to get to my GC and find that hostile motions have been tabled by Drake ward, complaining of the selection procedures for candidates for next year's local elections, and from Crofton Park, on lone parent benefit. The latter is serious for me as it calls on the government to withdraw policy and on me to support the motion. Clearly I won't be doing that but I need to tackle the arguments head-on and explain why I'm supporting the government. This is the first big test for me and the constituency in facing the responsibilities of a party of government. I hold my own.

Locally a mix of good and bad news. I've made a written submission to the public inquiry on the Greenwich lorry ban. There's been an appalling increase in traffic along Deptford Church Street since the ban started. There's also been a lot of street violence around the Honor Oak Park shops so

I'm supporting their request for CCTV. Trouble too in Deptford Market between stallholders. I've made representations to the council for better enforcement of the rules by the Street Trading Officers. The good news is the local health authority has received a cash boost from the government of £442 million and both IRIE! Dance Theatre and Heart n Soul, based at the Albany, have received £200,000 each from the Arts Council.

Awful news for Frank: his mother has a brain tumour.

At last an agreement on oral questions. It's only taken six months to get to this but it's not our fault. Caroline Flint has tabled a question on the UK presidency of the EU, which gives me an opportunity to explain that the theme of our presidency will be employability where a major barrier is lack of childcare. This gives her the opportunity to give unfavourable comparisons of the UK with other EU countries and ask if we can learn from them. I am able to reply in the affirmative and announce that we will have a women ministers meeting in Belfast in May. So far so good; but then Cheryl Gillan is called. She is my opposite number and was an employment minister in the last government. She opens with the traditional welcome for a first appearance, but adds that 'Conservative members are particularly pleased that she has finally come out of the closet'. Guffaws all round. She challenges me to give a direct answer to her question, which is whether I support the 'proposals now sitting in the Treasury to abolish direct taxation for women'. I graciously thank her for her welcome, remind her that she was entirely invisible on women's issues in her ministerial role, sketch out our mission and end: 'As for her direct question, I give her this direct answer – there are no such proposals sitting in the Treasury.' Then it's over until the next orals in the New Year.

I've got a very troubling constituency case and can't make any progress with immigration officials. My only recourse is a direct meeting with the minister – not something I would normally request. The constituent is an asylum seeker from Algeria. He lives with a woman who has five children. After losing her husband she suffered great depression and has now become very dependent on the Algerian man. There is plenty of testimony that without him she would probably have a complete breakdown, with her children going into care. His asylum application has been outstanding for years and all attempts to regularise his status have failed. Algerians, in my experience, always present difficulties, no doubt because of the country's history of terrorism. I'm convinced it's in everyone's interests that he should stay and continue to support the family. I have a meeting with Mike O'Brien, who is accompanied by officials who are hostile and say they believe he has a wife in Algeria. This is not the line I expected them to take and I judge that it's not the real reason. However, I think my case is powerful and clearly Mike can see that after taking years to consider his case the Home Office must come up with real evidence against him. Mike will overrule his officials.

We're now hurtling towards the recess and it's time to make an end-of-term report. There are more than twenty achievements across government that are in the interests of women, in addition to the national delivery strategies we have prioritised on childcare, family-friendly working and action on violence against women. Changes underway range from the rather more obvious health and education to transport, immigration and the surprising agreement by the MoD to raise the number of posts available to women from 47 per cent to 70 per cent.

16 December: Our flagship Minimum Wage Bill has its second reading. Frank is very involved as PPS in the DTI. The Lib Dems vote with us but 145 Tories vote against. This shows their true colours – they are content to see people working hard for £1 an hour in twentieth-century Britain.

Harriet organises Christmas drinks, giving us the chance to thank the many women's organisations that have been working with us. The next day I meet with Jennifer Page, who is in charge of the Millennium Experience. I'm keen to know how women will be involved and represented in her plans. I also ask about women in the workforce. People are always surprised by these questions because no one really thinks much about their equalities policies, even when they have them. Then there's another round of Christmas drinks, this time with the politicians. I'm desperate to get home. Tonight is the first anniversary of Keith's fatal accident. A great well of grief has been with me all week. I need to cry. Sleep escapes me as I relive every moment of that Thursday night one year ago.

Frank is spending time with his family in Edinburgh, where everyone is bereft at his mother's illness. Then to my mother's for what will be another sad Christmas.

## 1998

New Year and Frank and I make a rare visit to the theatre. Frank loves theatre and it's impossible to go when we are in session. We go to the Old Vic to see *Slava's Snowshow*. He's an utterly extraordinary Russian clown and the show is both funny and incredibly moving. It's also pretty amazing to sit in a theatre and get covered in gently falling snow.

12 January: I'm back at the department getting some computer training. I also have a meeting with Harriet about maternity rights. As a mother of three who has worked throughout her life, Harriet has strong views on this subject. With Labour signing the Social Chapter, it's timely to look at provision in the UK, which lags behind many other European countries.

I've decided to write a formal letter to Harriet. This is one of those odd aspects of ministerial life. Even though we meet up every week and I can discuss anything with her, there are times when the more formal mechanism of the ministerial letter is deemed appropriate. I'm the recipient of quite a lot of the backlash against the removal of the single parent premium benefit and I'm keen to find some solutions. I argue that our aim to lift the poorest children out of poverty will only work if all single parents are able to get into work. Given there are no guarantees, we could still see persistent levels of child poverty. There's also the value of caring for children in the very early years and the necessity of this for some lone parents. Recognition of this will help those who could be stigmatised for not working. An early years premium could be the answer, paid for by taxing child benefit in line with our overall welfare to work strategy.

I'm also concerned that the New Deal for Lone Parents will prohibit women going into further and higher education. I know from constituency experience that many lone mothers on benefits are using their time to get qualifications that will benefit their future job search. I believe we need to look carefully at this issue under the new student loan arrangements. There's also the question of access to the New Deal for the unemployed. As lone parents are not required to register for work, they cannot access these programmes, even if they can do full-time work. They should be accepted as voluntary participants.

Maximising all potential sources of income is crucial to lone parents and we need to look at creating new and simple disregards, for example on maintenance payments. I also raise the matter of independent taxation as feelings are running very high in the NGOs with whom we have our dialogue. Of course I've made clear that we would not countenance the return of the man, as breadwinner, filing tax returns. But the problem is that the suggestion of joint disclosure and signature is not finding much support either. I can see why the state should take an interest in how finance is accrued within a household but if we are to win that argument we need to adopt a strategy soon.

Finally, I raise the issue of women's fertility. Feedback from women is telling me that our great emphasis on reducing teenage pregnancy is reducing older women's access to services, with abortion rates continuing to rise. Any charge for the pill, as discussed by the DoH, will exacerbate this. I've drafted a letter for Harriet to send to Frank Dobson.

19 January: Picked up at 7 a.m. for a breakfast visit to the Kids' Club Network with Alan Howarth, my opposite number at the DfEE. Then, six hours at our national childcare strategy conference, where everyone has their say on how to provide this crucial service. There is so much to do – finding providers,

training childcare staff, safeguarding children, organising the tax regime, working with local authorities and private sector companies. Never before has government thrown itself into this arena with so much effort. Back in the department for more briefings and then to a pleasurable reception for Natasha Walter, who has written a new book on feminism and is supportive of our mission.

Things are really hotting up over the legality of the twinning selection for the Scottish Parliament and Welsh Assembly. Maria Fyfe in Scotland and Julie Morgan in Wales have been looking at amendments to the Sex Discrimination Act that would remove any doubts and barrister Tess Gill has drafted appropriate clauses. There is also worrying news that the UK Men's Movement has received a legacy of £100,000 to mount challenges to our agenda.

20 January: The Wales Labour Party Executive announce that they have agreed a twinning procedure for the selection of candidates to the Welsh Assembly, which will ensure that 50 per cent of the candidates will be women. It has to be ratified by the National Executive of the Labour Party meeting next week. Harriet and I meet with David Blunkett, Donald Dewar and Jack Straw. We are determined that these mechanisms should be put in place.

Next day it's prep for orals and then an interview with Daisy Sampson of *The House* magazine, followed by a meeting to discuss women's juries. I'm very keen on using these techniques as an aid to policy development but I know they'll be controversial. There's such a strong case for recognising that women's patterns of behaviour differ from men's and these techniques will undoubtedly be more effective. Early evening I'm addressing my most unusual group yet, which just goes to prove a point. It's the Women's Aquatic Network! Then back for some late box work while waiting to vote on the Government of Wales Bill.

Major events this spring include our involvement in the EU presidency and the follow-up conference on the UN Programme for Action at the UN. I've taken an interest in the UN since I was a student so I'm much better placed than Harriet to deal with this. It's agreed I'll go to New York. I see this as a great opportunity to raise the profile of our work. It also means a great deal of careful preparation. I'm trying not to neglect the local party as we have really important elections and a referendum on the horizon, so occasionally I get off the whip, which this month means I do Drake ward and Ladywell branch meetings on a Thursday night with no return for voting.

More visits to childcare operators, a photo call with David Blunkett and a speech to Kids' Club Network. There's no doubt we can deliver on childcare, but family-friendly working is more difficult. Some aspects will come through legislation as a result of joining the Social Chapter, but much else depends on working with selected companies who are trailblazers, having already realised that recruitment and retention of women is in their interests. Apparently research indicates that large companies reckon it costs £10,000 to recruit and induct new employees and the loss of women as a result of having children is significant. Part-time working on return after maternity leave, job-sharing and an acceptance that women with childcare responsibilities should not be asked to work late are all policies that a few companies have found workable and to their benefit. This is heartening news.

I manage to get a full Friday in the constituency, beginning with our regular meeting with the council leadership. This is especially valuable now we've three Labour MPs in Lewisham, albeit Jim, Bridget and I don't always agree on everything. At lunchtime I visit the Laban Centre and then go on to my surgery at Honor Oak Community Centre. Later in the month I'm released to attend the CLP AGM and agree to attend the Marlowe Ward Valentine's evening fundraiser on Saturday. It's an interesting experience attending events where I'm virtually the only white person in the room. I'm so used to it and of course have a role, but it gives me an insight into what it must have been like when sometimes a black person would be the only person of colour in a workplace or social setting.

On Monday we have oral questions. Siobhain McDonagh helpfully asks about the Status of Women meeting in New York and takes up the issue of

domestic violence and the start of a week of awareness-raising in her constituency. This gives me the opportunity to announce that I will attend the
New York meeting and that we've given £30,000 to the Women's Aid helpline
in England. A few more packed days follow, including a meeting with the
Chancellor, another one-day visit to Brussels to address the Women's Rights
Committee as part of the presidency programme and a couple of one-on-one
ministerial meetings.

We've persuaded Ann Taylor that we should have a debate to mark International Women's Day. This means commissioning speech outlines a month
before as everything takes so long to turn around. We're also preparing for
my attendance at the UN conference, which means briefings with the FCO
as they are the lead for the presidency and they will prepare the speech!
A meeting is also scheduled with a new person from the No. 10 communications unit. It's strange: they come along full of expressions about how good
involving women is for the government but never end up promoting us or
our message to the media.

The weekend is spent in Scarborough at the Labour Party's local government conference. We are launching a women's taskforce booklet and making
a big push to get women into local government. Women are the major consumers of local government services but vastly underrepresented politically.

Halfway through February and I realise my hair needs some serious
attention. I'm so often 'on show' now but the overfull days and weekend
engagements mean I never find the time to go to my regular hairdresser.
I consult with other women ministers and find Michaeljohn in Albemarle
Street much favoured. So one Tuesday a discreet private engagement appears
in my diary. I start with a 9 a.m. Employment Action Plan meeting, go on to
a briefing for the WNC plenary I'll be attending and then break for the big
event. I'm back at 2 p.m. for a series of meetings followed by interviews for a
new deputy Private Secretary as Nicole is moving on – a constant feature of
the civil service. I settle for a really nice young woman called Anna-Maria.
Then I have a private half-hour meeting with Rakesh Mohan, who was in

the International Relations Club with me at Imperial. He saw news of my appointment and is now looking me up as he passes through London. He works for the World Bank – so interesting to find out what happens to people. Then to No. 11 for a reception for Emily's List. Founded by Barbara Follett and launched in 1993 on the seventy-fifth anniversary of votes for women, Emily's List raises money to help Labour women with the cost of seeking parliamentary selection. Prior to the general election, seventy women were helped with grants, twenty-six of them secured nomination and fourteen are now MPs. This is brilliant work and Barbara is a huge asset to the party.

The *Independent* newspaper, edited by Rosie Boycott, has been running a campaign on childcare and now wants to do a feature on our strategy. It's a joy to talk to a serious journalist about a serious agenda. I get almost half a page and a very nice photograph of me with the new haircut. I've also had a very surprising request. The British Tourist Board wants to do a feature for a magazine that is distributed through our embassies around the world. They want me to look to the future and predict who might succeed me as the local MP. Given the ethnic mix of my constituency I say I hope it will be a black woman. They then suggest I should be photographed with a suitable candidate. This is an odd suggestion but they obviously think it's good promotion for the UK! The photograph will be taken by Lord Lichfield so I can hardly refuse. Kumar, my CLP treasurer, has a nine-year-old daughter who fits the bill admirably and both parents and Sadhana agree. It's a somewhat daunting occasion at Lord Lichfield's large, cold and dark studio. The result is OK but not to my mind a particularly interesting photo. However, I later see it on the front cover of one of the magazines, which is rather pleasing.

For the past few weeks, Frank has been on the Minimum Wage Bill committee. After the first four sittings and constant filibustering by the Tories, including new boys John Bercow and Andrew Lansley, the committee was still on clause 1. Frank and Ian McCartney then decided to put forward an open-ended sittings motion in order to make progress on the Bill. Next morning (Tuesday) the committee met at 10.30 a.m., went on all day and through the night, eventually finishing at 1 p.m. Wednesday lunchtime. Exhausted though they were, Labour members were then forced to remain in the Commons for Wednesday night's 10 p.m. vote. Next day they started again at 10.30 a.m. and went through until 7 a.m. on Friday morning, allowing Frank to get his flight to Aberdeen. He later admitted, embarrassingly, to falling asleep at a university meeting in his constituency that afternoon!

Harriet is under terrible pressure on the welfare front. There's been a tremendous backlash against the lone parent cut, yet the Budget will demonstrate that the bigger child supplement within income support more than makes up for what was lost. Pauline (Barret) is also being less than helpful to Harriet.

A cracking oral questions session on 23 February. Solid questions from Labour colleagues, which enable me to give more information on what we are doing. Two Tory men and Cheryl Gillan, my Tory shadow, snipe and sneer. Julian Lewis pathetically asks if I have plans to improve the employability of Greenham women. It just shows what the Tories think about women. I'm able to handle anything thrown at me but sadly I think there are too many men on our side who think our mission is not serious. Three days later there are orchestrated attacks on Harriet across the media focusing on 'splits' between her and Frank Field. Most pernicious is Kevin Maguire in *The Mirror* under the headline 'Why Harriet must go'. This is so appalling. No. 10, who want these welfare policies, have done nothing to support her.

I'm particularly interested in the UN agenda and what successive governments have signed up to and done little about. There is a reporting regime and I discover we haven't fulfilled that obligation either. I set about rectifying this. It will be a considerable undertaking as all government departments will be asked to contribute and FCO, the Cabinet Office and No. 10 will all want control. One of the other aspects of presidency preparation is ministerial visits from other EU countries and requests for bilaterals. These fall to me and provide interesting insights into what other countries are doing. This week it's a visit from the Italian minister and her officials. There's also media interest and I do interviews for Swedish and Danish morning papers (both countries of course far ahead of us in terms of equality and childcare).

It takes weeks to knock my UN speech into shape and cover all the issues in briefings from different bits of the civil service. With the UK holding the presidency I will be speaking for the EU rather than just the UK. While the FCO people know the international conventions that trigger the UN meetings they have little feel for the new agenda Harriet and I are following. The result is I get briefings from my civil servants, then tell them what I want and then they meet their counterparts at the FCO to negotiate the next paragraph. Having run organisations myself and so many campaigns requiring instant decision-making, all this is so frustrating. We definitely need to up our unit's performance.

Katerina sends me a note saying Bea Campbell (feminist author) wants to meet me next week. She was told I would be in New York so left a message: 'The gal's done good this week – congratulations!' Spirits duly lifted. Bea is a great character whom I admire, though she can also be a very harsh critic.

We've decided to use Friday 27 February for our annual International Women's Day debate. Harriet opens saying this is an important moment for the government and for women. We are determined to achieve a real alignment between what women want and government intends. The focus of her speech is childcare and the opportunities for women to work. She deals easily with Tory interventions on minor points and announces that we are to pilot women's juries to reach out to those women who don't join organisations and therefore do not take part in the consultative exercises routinely carried out by all governments. Predictably the Tory shadow ministers, Gillian Shephard and Cheryl Gillan, attack the lone parent strategy, my unpaid status and lack of parliamentary appearances.

As the junior minister I get to make the closing speech. First of all I pay tribute to those who've spoken with particular praise for supportive contributions on our side. Our new women MPs are very vocal and offer a wide range of contributions, as does Malcolm Chisholm (Scotland). Lorna Fitzsimons,

Debra Shipley, Ann Cryer, Laura Moffatt, Bev Hughes, Caroline Flint and Julie Morgan all get honorary mentions on specific points, but I'm grateful too for interventions from Barbara Follett, Rosemary McKenna, Sandra Osborne and Julia Drown, all of whom will stick with the women's agenda throughout their years in Parliament. After the courtesies I get on to some substance and relate our work on the European agenda and our signing up to the Social Chapter. I also reference my attendance at the UN Commission on the Status of Women meeting next week. I ignore the taunts over my lack of pay. The Tories know the score perfectly well, but I round on them for criticising my lack of visibility. I'm able to say that I have answered more questions on women's issues in nine months than they answered in eighteen years. For good measure I also point out that the shadow secretary hasn't tabled a single question for answer to either Harriet or me. Then I'm off to New York.

My Private Secretary asked if we could fly Virgin Atlantic. I thought since BA was privatised there was no reason not to. We get to the airport with hours to kill. This is completely different from all the years when I travelled about campaigning. Then I arrived at the last possible moment and never looked at duty-free; now we have nothing to do but tour the designer shops. I spot a beautiful velour scarf in shades of purple and brown – a perfect complement to the suit I'll be wearing for meetings. It's Jaeger and horrendously expensive but with great feelings of guilt I buy it. I tell myself I may not be getting a salary but I should look the part. It's an overnight flight, first class. Helen hopes we can get the free manicure or massage advertised but somehow we miss out and it seems sensible to get a few hours' sleep after we've reviewed the briefings and had a good dinner.

On arrival we are met by members of the UK mission to the UN and taken directly to an initial briefing. My opening statement to the UN session will have four themes: violence against women; armed conflict and women; the human rights of women; and the girl child. Discussions have been going on for some time with the other EU member states but there is still further negotiation to be had and the draft speech needs finalising. I will also have bilateral meetings with other EU ministers, UN personnel and other individuals as the FCO deems appropriate. In addition, there will be a day for non-UN activity.

The UK Mission organises daily meetings throughout the session, constantly negotiating within the EU and with other key nations. I attend one of the sessions and discover that there is a ten-minute limit on the speech I'll be making but it's twenty minutes long. I am really angry. I've already had to change so much of the language to make it accessible. The high-ranking civil servant in charge tells me this is normal; the EU statement is one of the most important and we are expected to run over time (shades of empire). I'm not having that, I tell them; they can just go back and edit the speech to no more than twelve minutes (I tell them I expect to speak 120 words per minute, knowing I can speed up a bit if appropriate). I get a real thrill as I walk into the UN building for the session and recall that sixteen years ago I came here and addressed the UN General Assembly.

2 March: Finally, I get to deliver a statement I'm proud of. On violence against women we call for national plans such as those being developed in the UK. On armed conflict we propose the creation of an international criminal court that would integrate a gender perspective in its statute. On human rights we argue for an end to customary and traditional practices that are harmful to women, such as female genital mutilation, and on the girl child we propose the provision of information and counselling services to be carried out on a confidential basis, for both adolescent girls and boys, especially on the subject of personal relationships. Delegates from 134 countries including all the EU states are present, as well as 1,500 NGOs, including twenty-two from the UK. My speech is very warmly received and many congratulations follow. Am I perhaps the first UK *feminist* minister to address a UN Status of Women? This is the forty-second session!

Our ambassador to the UN, Sir John Weston, is very pleasant and puts on a reception that we co-host. More than 200 people attend and it's a great success. The British Council shows its new exhibition 'Women, Men, Democracy and Governance', which attracts wide interest. Good for them.

Altogether I undertake fourteen bilateral meetings in the next few days and I discuss mainstreaming within the UN with Angela King, the Secretary General's special advisor on gender. I discover on this trip that the UK is the only EU state not to have complied with the obligation to produce an action plan for the UN Commission on the Status of Women. This will have to be put right very quickly. The US Ambassador to the CSW tells me about work in the US on women's juries and mainstreaming but admits the latter is unlikely to get the support of Congress. Bill Clinton has set up a violence against women office in the Department of Justice. Bonnie Campbell, who heads it, tells me only eight states have a specific office of domestic violence. Theirs is an even greater challenge than ours but we share useful information on campaigning and public awareness-raising.

I'm particularly interested to meet the Chilean minister, Josefina Bilbao. The government adopted an equal opportunities plan in 1993 and every ministry is obliged to implement it. A year later they adopted a domestic violence law and the number of reported incidents has risen ever since. But enforcement is a problem as the judicial system in Chile is in a state of collapse. To my surprise I learn that divorce is not permitted, which clearly has a further impact on domestic violence. A divorce law has been passed in the lower chamber but the minister doesn't know how it will fare in the Senate.

An important meeting is scheduled with Barbara Prammer, the Austrian minister, as Austria will take over the presidency of the EU from us. We discuss the desirability of gender mainstreaming being brought into all four pillars of the EU employment guidelines, together with a strengthening of the fourth pillar on equal opportunities. Interestingly, Austria has good maternity and paternity leave and mothers and fathers can change leave around between them over a three-year period. My most useful meetings are with the Scandinavians. Norway has state-subsidised childcare from age one and most women work full time. A general equality act has been introduced and the government plans to compare wages across different areas. Positive action laws apply to political parties and the representation of women. Consequently, if a woman and man of equal qualifications apply for the same job, the job must be given to the woman if there is a gender deficit – imagine proposing that in Britain! Norway has also banned FGM.

The Swedish parliament is currently debating a new law on the issue of violence against women. Swedish police are now required to develop action plans and make annual reports to central government on their progress. But it is mainstreaming that is the greatest eye-opener. Every minister is required to be a minister for equality in his or her own area. In order to facilitate this there is a five-hour obligatory training course that even the Prime Minister is required to undertake.

Most enjoyably I have tea with Mary Robinson, UN High Commissioner for Human Rights. As the first woman President of the Republic of Ireland, she became one of my great heroines and I am thrilled to have the chance of such a special meeting. My non-UN day includes a roundtable made up of directors and presidents of major US women's organisations. Interestingly, lone parents are only required to work if childcare is provided. This has had a surprising consequence as existing working women have found themselves losing daycare slots to women on welfare going back to work. As a result, women in corporations are pressing employers to provide daycare and there is some recognition that business is losing some of its best employees because of the problem. The panel conclude that enormous progress has been made in terms of public careers and that virtually no job is closed to women via appointed office. However, elected office is proving much more difficult with only 20–25 per cent in state legislatures, nine women in the Senate and fifty in the House of Representatives out of 435 members. There are three women governors out of fifty states and two women in the Supreme Court. The latter is a major breakthrough but overall the picture is very disappointing. Some interesting parallels emerge with the UK. The number of women voting has increased to overtake men and they are voting disproportionately Democrat. However, it is becoming increasingly difficult to persuade women to stand for election due to the enormous media intrusion into candidates' personal and financial affairs. Needless to say I have plenty to contribute to this discussion.

On Thursday we leave for our overnight return flight completely exhausted, only to hear after a long wait that the aircraft has a technical problem. We are delayed three hours and I make a mental note to fly BA next time. Back at Heathrow we rush off the flight as I've got a programme to fulfil. Then I realise I've left my incredibly expensive scarf in the cabin storage above my seat. At the first opportunity we ring Virgin. They say there is little chance of recovering it as the aircraft has been completely cleaned. I enquire if they expect their cleaners to steal from them and ask what's happened to the aircraft. Interestingly they tell me it's been taken out of service, so they can, in fact, check. Later in the day when I've stopped telling myself it is divine retribution for such an extravagance, they call to say it's been found (I still wear it).

In my box is a briefing from Meg Russell, the Labour Party women's officer, in response to stories about Lord Chancellor Derry Irvine saying twinning might not be legal. It's an excellent document and we are very fortunate in having Meg working for us. She states again categorically that the party's decision to adopt the process was never dependent on a change in the law. In Scotland the chosen process is due to be endorsed at the Scottish conference and selections in paired constituencies will then get underway. In Wales there is to be a short period of consultation about pairing, with constituencies invited to either accept the system or propose an alternative that will deliver gender balance.

While I'm away, Frank is in Edinburgh with his mother who is now very sick. She went into a hospice but after a couple of days called to say she wanted to leave as 'everyone here seems to be dying'! She's now at home but there is no hope of recovery.

Saturday I get some rest and then on Sunday, International Women's Day, I go to watch my first women's football match. It's a World Cup qualifying match between England and Germany and conveniently held at my local club, Millwall. I fear a little jetlag sets in, or perhaps it's just my antipathy towards football. Monday and I'm off to a Girls Into Science event, followed by attendance at, and a report to, the Women's National Executive Committee. I do a Brussels follow-up meeting with two of our MEPs then the Met Commissioner, Paul Condon, and on to the British Council's International Women's Day reception in the Jubilee Room. I'm keen to support the British Council as I think they've moved beyond the stuffy image of old and are very much engaging with women. Another half-hour stint and I'm speaking at the IPPF (International Planned Parenthood Federation) reception. I'll get an hour on the red box before voting at 10 p.m.

It's the report stage of the Minimum Wage Bill and Frank has come back to participate in it. He is exhausted and desperately concerned about his mother. The debate goes on all night. In the early hours of the morning Frank's sister rings – his mother is dead. We can do nothing. Frank stays to vote, knowing that is what his mother would have wanted. When the debate is over he goes straight to Heathrow to fly to Edinburgh and his sisters.

11 March: A political strategy meeting involving SPADS and key campaigners. Not for the first time we discuss all-night sittings, pointing out the direct conflict between this and our government's policy on family-friendly working. We agree to raise the issue of the modernisation of the House with the chair of the PLP, Clive Soley. A delegation of women will also go to see Ann Taylor, the Leader of the House. Derry Irvine's very unwelcome intervention on twinning is condemned by all. Julie Morgan, representing Wales, and Maria Fyfe, Scotland, are seeing Derry tomorrow. Lorna will write to Tony and of course Harriet and I are on the case. I'm able to report back from the women's NEC where the party policy on twinning was restated with no change in the law required. We agree that the Welsh position is in need of support and that Harriet and I need to meet Welsh women MPs as soon as possible.

Good media coverage is still hard to get and it's clear that reliance on departmental press people will not achieve the kind of communications we would like. Women's magazines are obvious targets but the press office has no experience in this field. One rare request comes from *You* magazine where I'm interviewed by Melissa Benn.

My box contains a paper on the possible conclusions of the Presidency meeting we will have for European ministers for women in Belfast in May. This is the extraordinary way things work. The possible outcomes have to be agreed before the conference starts and it takes many months of negotiation to reach that point. As Presidency we produce the paper, get it endorsed by the European Commission and then circulate it, after translation, to all member states ahead of the meeting to identify the issues on which we seek a consensus. Some member states (pre-targeted) will then bring out the issues and the Presidency (me) will sum up. Clearly getting the initial paper right is crucial. Our aim must be to ensure women's employability is underpinned by good-quality childcare and family-friendly working. I give my steer. We need our conference to influence the revision of the EU employment guidelines due from the Commission this autumn.

12 March: Keith's birthday. I think about him every day but, as everyone who grieves knows, the anniversaries are particularly hard. I'd really like to take the day off and go to south Wales, but I'm out on a ministerial visit. At least I'm not at the Commons, which sits until 3 a.m. as the result of a Tory filibuster.

Two really tricky problems that are not in my brief but impact on all our work. One is the CSA (Child Support Agency) – which is such a good idea in principle but bad in practice – and the other is the EOC, which suffers from poor leadership and about which I received a damning indictment from a very respected former Commissioner. The DfEE has control of the latter and it looks like its civil servants are just too close to the organisation. We bring in a few experts, including Valerie Amos from the Lords who previously headed the EOC. We need our own coherent position to put to the DfEE. After a long day of political strategy meetings there's another reception to attend in the Lord Chancellor's apartment. I go reluctantly but end up being very impressed by the organisers, Womankind Worldwide. They have an excellent programme for supporting women in the developing world and I'll end up working with them for many years to come.

17 March: Budget day and Harriet gets credit for having persuaded Gordon to recognise the needs of working women with regards to childcare. Surprisingly, *The Sun* hails Harriet's great victory, only to ruin it by saying it will be her last. Polly Toynbee has a very useful post-Budget article in *The Guardian* headed 'How poor single parents will get their money back'. She accurately reflects our intentions to make work pay, even low pay, and to boost the incomes of both working and unemployed poor families whether there are one or two parents. In a simple question and answer she explains how the new Working Families Tax Credit will lift parents and children out of poverty. If only the government had been able to explain all this at the outset. The damage has been done. Few people affected will be reading this article but let's hope they'll realise the benefit when they get the money.

Frank and I go to Edinburgh for his mother's funeral. There's so much grief in our lives.

I've been developing our policy on public appointments and meeting ministers across government who have patronage, but we also need to encourage women directly to put themselves forward. I'm producing papers on each policy area for distribution through whatever networks we can access.

At our regular women ministers' group we take stock of where we are in our strategy. The work on the new dialogue is going well. There has been a positive response to the recruitment of women and the agenda will be with us in days. We're thinking of inviting a sympathetic journalist to attend as an observer.

I express my dissatisfaction with the correspondence unit. Replies take far too long. There would be outrage if MPs dealt with constituents' mail in this way. I give Pauline two days to get a draft standard letter to the recent postcard campaign and three to get copies of all the correspondence with the public in the past week on my desk. In future I want a monthly report on numbers and subjects of all correspondence dealt with by civil servants.

We've seen and commented on the first draft of the childcare green paper and note that as drafted it's not clear enough that women have a choice and are not being forced into work. A further draft is on its way.

I've discovered that officials have run into difficulties with their colleagues in the transport department on the integrated transport policy. Civil servants are very reluctant to admit failure. I insist ministers must be alerted sooner rather than later as ultimately this will be our failure. Similarly, I insist on an up-to-date analysis of where we are on the issue of violence against women. Again DfT appear to be dragging their feet. I'm sure they think it's none of our business but of course it's women whose travel patterns are most influenced by fear of violence. While we are making progress with the Home Office and DETR on domestic violence we have to cover the whole territory. Today I've got a meeting with South Essex Rape and Incest Crisis Centre who want to explain their work and the difficulties they face in getting funding when most Home Office money goes to Victim Support. They subsequently write a letter of thanks, saying, 'We are still in shock about the existence of a Women's Unit, we can't quite get used to having a voice and being heard after all this time in the political wilderness.'

I'm invited to a reception at South Africa House to meet the new High Commissioner, Cheryl Carolus. So often liberation movements in which women have played their part fail to appoint women to office once in government. Not so the ANC. It's a delight to meet Cheryl and poignant to hear her say that when she went to vote just four years ago, it was for the first time in her life. How proud I am to have been part of the anti-apartheid movement.

The controversy over twinning in Wales is hotting up. A 'Twin to Win' campaign and petition has been launched backed by, among others, MPs Ann Clwyd and Julie Morgan and MEPs Glenys Kinnock and Eluned Morgan. Their document is excellent, dispelling myths and setting out the constitutional basis and recording a commitment made by Tony when he addressed the Scottish Labour Party conference. Meg Russell tells me it's been sent to all Labour Party organisations in Wales and all 250 women who have expressed an interest in standing for the forty-seat Assembly (who says there's a shortage of women applicants!).

My box contains the draft conclusions for the Belfast conference. The paper in no way reflects the thrust of the presidency theme we want to achieve. It's based on employment rather than employability, which is very different. Throughout the whole document there are references that reflect the standard labour market approach from which we are seeking to move away. The language is also inappropriate at simple levels with references to husbands not partners and work rather than paid work (a sore point with women who stay at home to look after children) plus the assumption that all women are mothers. Some major revision required and fast.

7 April: I make the closing speech at a TUC conference, focusing on women's employment and flexible labour markets. Early April offers the welcome prospect of the Easter weekend break, but respite will be short-lived as there's plenty of constituency work to fit in and regular ministerial meetings. I've commissioned individual fact sheets on our six areas of work, which will be made into a pack for distribution around government and to stakeholders. It's taken months. The fact-files will come back and back. In the end I'm doing a rewrite myself. I know this is exactly what a minister shouldn't do but we have to get the tone right and time has run out. Our problem is the small number of staff in the unit and their need to respond to so many demands on issues of which they have little experience.

I make a visit to Berkshire Women's Aid in Reading to see the wonderful work they do in providing a sanctuary for women fleeing domestic violence. There's nothing to compare with hearing first-hand accounts from the women concerned. Inevitably they need more resources but are supportive of what we're trying to do.

*The Times* reports that the Lord Chancellor has told a group of Welsh MPs that the twinning arrangements for selecting candidates for the Scottish Parliament and Welsh Assembly are, in his opinion, 'unlawful'. In two days' time I'm speaking at the Wales Assembly of Women. We have got to hold the line, and I will definitely be saying no change in policy on twinning.

The army's efforts to recruit more women gets underway as the first women undergo the new 'gender-free' assessment process for recruits. Sometimes we find allies in the least likely places and I have a positive meeting with John Reid, the Secretary of State for Defence, on his department's plans for more family-friendly working. But we're not having such an easy ride with the DfEE, which is the lead on the family-friendly working strategy. The Women's Unit is struggling and I have to intervene. I'm also seeking support from DTI on family policy, particularly changes to parental leave and maternity rights.

Ron Davies, our Secretary of State for Wales, has dropped a bombshell. The *Western Mail* reports that a letter from Ron was read out at a meeting of the Welsh Executive, urging them to recognise that twinning would present the party with major difficulties and the party centrally would not fight a challenge to it. The chairman of the Campaign Against Twinning is quoted as saying this is an open door to making a legal challenge and they will do it. The executive decision will be made on 7 May. Harriet and I have got to ensure there's no backsliding in No. 10.

This is high politics but I think statistics might be our best bet. This is not a job for civil servants as it's a party matter so I do it myself. I take all the figures from the '97 general election and break them down to show the different percentages of women elected. In the eighty-six key seats where all women shortlists were applied, Labour delivered 50 per cent women MPs. In the non-key seats where we had surprise wins, the percentage of women MPs was 17 per cent. The percentage was also 17 per cent in the South-East Region, where there were no all-women shortlists. Furthermore, women make up 16 per cent of Scottish MPs at Westminster and 11 per cent of Welsh MPs.

By using party predictions of likely Labour wins in the Scottish Parliament and the Welsh Assembly, I can show that between ten and fifteen women would be elected in Scotland and three to seven women in Wales if there were *no* twinning. These figures are in marked contrast to the 50:50 position assured by twinning, which, using the same electoral predictions, would deliver thirty-one women Members of the Scottish Parliament and seventeen women Members of the Welsh Assembly. I'm confident I have a killer argument, but then I'm still a scientist at heart and this is politics.

I prepare a paper covering the political risks and the legal position as we see it and reference the recent Marschall decision of the European Court of Justice. This said where women were poorly represented in particular types of employment, a female candidate could be selected instead of an equally qualified male candidate. I end by pointing out that there has never been a challenge under the Equal Treatment Directive to any party's selection process, despite there being many forms of positive action in the EU.

The furore over twinning in Wales is never out of the newspapers. The electrical and engineering union (AEEU) has apparently been asked to consider a legal challenge as well as the anti-twinning pressure group and it's suggested they have the support of twenty CLPs. The deputy leader of Caerphilly County Council has also said he will mount a challenge in the courts. It is an extraordinary state of affairs. All we're proposing is an equal number of men and women to be selected. I up the ante by giving an interview to the *Western Mail*. I'm public enemy number one now but they've got their chance – if they can find another way to achieve equality in selection they can have it. But I know they can't – no one has spent more time looking into this than I have. This intervention doesn't endear me to No. 10. At a subsequent function, Sally Morgan, political secretary, tells me, 'Tony's not going to have it.' I'm not quite sure what she is threatening but I tell her as Minister for Women I have to do what I'm doing.

Our civil servants have been working hard on women and public appointments and dragging statistics from all departments. A draft strategy on increasing the number of women in public appointments has been commissioned in readiness for the Cabinet subcommittee in May. No doubt, we'll have a battle to get the Cabinet Secretary to sign up to it. The Strategic Communications Unit at No. 10 is working on a draft government annual report and we've managed to get agreement for the Women's Unit to contribute to all chapters in an attempt to mainstream the women's perspective. We're also working on our own report and record of achievement. There's no doubt we've done an enormous amount of work, but so much, inevitably, is process and policy making that won't be directly visible.

We've had a complete revision of the National Strategy on Violence Against Women following our intensive consultations. We're now requesting all departments make contributions to a national plan of action.

Now that our international obligations are being taken seriously, we're working simultaneously on both our report to the UN on progress on implementing the platform for action and initial preparations for the fourth UK report on the UN Convention on the Elimination of All Forms of Discrimination Against Women (CEDAW).

26 April: An interesting piece in the *Sunday Times*. Oona King is featured complaining about the long hours culture. She's dead right. Apparently almost everyone she talked to on returning from the Easter recess said they spent their break sleeping. Oona wants to see change but typically the piece ends: 'What would the 317 men on the Labour benches do with more freedom? Not all of them want to go back to their digs or home to their wives – whatever the babes say.' We will hear similar sentiments for years to come.

1 May: The papers are full of articles on Blair's first year in office. The *Telegraph* observes that he's broken all records. No newly elected Prime Minister and ruling party since the war has been as popular as he and Labour are today. Astonishingly, according to a Gallup poll, there has been an 8 per cent swing from the Conservatives to Labour in the past year. In an otherwise positive piece,

there is bad news for us: Harriet Harman, 'widely expected to be demoted, is the lowest ranking of the frontline Cabinet ministers'. The *Financial Times* adds to the misery, speculating that she is likely to be moved to a less prominent job, 'though it remains to be seen whether Mr Blair will sack her'.

Derry Irvine has slightly redeemed himself by appointing a record number of women QCs.

Over the next few days conflicting articles appear in the press. One suggests Tony wants to hang on to Harriet and will make a new women's ministry and I'll be her deputy. Another has her locked in battle with Peter Mandelson for the Cabinet Office job, currently held by David Clark (expected to be sacked). There's a bit of a fight back by Harriet's SPADS who get some positive stories in over the weekend on her proposals for the right of parents to take time off work to care for a sick child and her attempt to give maternity rights to the one in five low-paid workers who don't currently qualify for paid leave. I don't know how Harriet can stand it.

Monday afternoon and we're in Belfast for our final briefings at the hotel where we're staying. The next day is a full twelve-hour programme of bilateral discussions, a lunch including the EU Commissioner for Employment and Social Affairs, visits to local projects, a seminar organised by the NI EOC and a dinner hosted by Mo Mowlam. The visits to two women's centres are very instructive. I think few Westminster MPs, including myself, know much about NI beyond the violence and our attempts to forge a new peace process. The Windsor Women's Centre is in an area of traditional working-class terraced housing, at least 15 per cent of which have only outside toilets. Unemployment is running at 21 per cent and 71 per cent of women have no formal qualifications. Raising aspirations and providing training facilities with onsite childcare are priorities for the centre. Over 200 women are using it and it's clear this is the one chance they have of finding a route to a better life. Being Belfast, our next visit has to be to a women's centre in a Catholic area. The Footprints Centre also provides wrap-around childcare and training opportunities and both centres benefit from EU funding.

It's less than a month since the Good Friday Agreement between the British and Irish governments and just over two weeks to the simultaneous referenda, in NI and the Irish Republic, required to ratify the agreement. If they pass there should be elections to the new Northern Ireland Assembly this summer.

There is a desperate need for more women's political leadership in NI. Mo has worked closely with women wherever she can, ably assisted by her PPS, Helen Jackson MP. There are no Northern Irish women MPs at Westminster, no women MEPs and only 14 per cent of local councillors are women. We do everything we can to encourage women to put themselves forward for elected office and to bolster existing women's organisations. Our final day begins with an hour of presentations on aspects of women's employability – from a Dutch MEP who chairs the Women's Rights Committee, from the Swedish Employers' Confederation and from the ETUC. The conference then goes into closed session to hear from Commissioner Flynn and women ministers from several European countries. There's so much more happening elsewhere, particularly, of course, in Scandinavia. The Swedish minister has provided her own example of family-friendly working by bringing her ten-week-old son to the conference. It's her first official engagement since his birth but she explains that she and her partner can take a year's leave between them to care for a newborn. She's back at work because she has a general election to fight in the autumn, but in the meantime she works from home with state-of-the-art technology, including a camera for video conferencing that is supplied by the Parliament. The Lord Mayor of Belfast hosts a lunch and then it's back for the UK presentation followed by Austria and France before a discussion around the communiqué. Harriet sums up and the communiqué is agreed. Producing a communiqué from an international meeting of this kind takes months of pre-negotiation by officials who know their ministers' attitudes and government policies and negotiate accordingly. Although often both bland and written in formal language (they have to be translatable into all the languages of the member states), the art is to get in a few action points that the EU Commission is then obliged to consider. Ours reinforces many of the points that are on the UK agenda, but its importance lies in the European consensus achieved as much national employment and equalities legislation is derived from the EU. The communiqué stresses that affordable, accessible and high-quality childcare, parental and other leave schemes and family-friendly working policies are essential for women and men to combine their work and family responsibilities. It goes on to state that equality must be mainstreamed in all employment policies and urges the EU Commission to ensure that women's rights and needs are fully integrated into the 1999 Employment Guidelines. Harriet promises to ensure that the outcomes of our conference are fed into the preparation for the upcoming EU Summit in Cardiff.

As is the custom, all the visiting ministers receive a gift – my responsibility. Having rejected all the usual rubbish produced for such occasions, I secured elegant boxes of fine Irish linen napkins. My only disappointment is that I don't get one for myself!

The communiqué is presented to the press by Harriet and Commissioner Flynn and then it's over.

12 May: We're not voting on the Scotland Bill until 11 p.m. so I can go to my GC and get back again. My report is upbeat. I begin with the local elections – where we did extremely well – and note that no governing party has ever received such a strong endorsement twelve months after a general election victory. There was also a massive endorsement of our proposal for an elected mayor and assembly for London. Lewisham has been chosen, along with Southwark and Lambeth, to form one of the new Health Action Zones. This means more money, partnership working and finding new ways to tackle inequality. I record the Good Friday Agreement as a significant turning point in history and look forward to the 22 May referendum. I also report on progress on our five key election pledges – all of which are on track – and the new benefits being delivered to workers under the EU Working Time Directive. Long-term interest rates have fallen to their lowest level for thirty years.

Even though I'm unable to attend as many constituency events, I'm still intervening all over the place on issues. The Telegraph Hill Generation Club was threatened with closure, but the council has agreed to provide ongoing assistance and a charitable grant is to provide an all-weather play area. I've also successfully intervened with English Partnerships on behalf of the Lady Florence Trust to save and regenerate their historic building. Hatcham Wood School has gone into special measures and parents are coming to me anxious to avoid their children being enrolled there. This will be a self-defeating ordinance and the council needs to get its act together to ensure an improvement plan can succeed.

Casework continues apace bringing the occasional surprise, most recently an elderly man who didn't realise he had been living illegally in the UK for over twenty years and who had never previously come to the attention of the authorities. Fortunately, we've been able to secure a right to remain as there was no way he could have coped with deportation.

An update on our violence against women strategy for my report to the Cabinet subcommittee. We've contacted all local authorities to find out what they are doing and to identify best practice. Together with DETR and DoH we've commissioned research that will establish a comprehensive database on the provision of accommodation and support services for women fleeing domestic violence. We've also made progress with the Home Office, with Ministers for Women writing to all chief constables in England and Wales seeking information on the effectiveness of current police policy. The Home Office Police Research Group is complementing this by looking at effective organisational structures for policing domestic violence. We should get a draft report soon.

Our plan is to bring all of our work together and launch a comprehensive strategy in the autumn. I'm also pressing for work to improve the recording and consistency of domestic violence statistics. Without this we will not be able to evaluate and monitor the outcomes of our strategy. Ministers will have to make this happen as civil servants have not been able to agree. Other items for discussion include the abuse of contact arrangements by non-resident fathers, the question of whether there should be a single national helpline and how it might be funded and the use and effectiveness of personal alarms. We are certainly making progress but everyone is learning how time-consuming it is to bring major innovation to government and how much care is needed if policies are to be effective and sustainable.

We table our public appointments paper at the Cabinet subcommittee. The government is responsible for around 38,000 public appointments, with around 10,000 coming up each year. Half of the annual appointments are reappointments. Currently 32 per cent of appointments go to women. Fewer women than men apply, fewer women meet the selection criteria and fewer women are selected. The little research there is suggests applications depend to a large extent on word of mouth and personal contacts, enabling men to perpetuate the status quo. Women are less likely to meet the criteria as many appointments are drawn from people in senior positions and certain professions where there are fewer women. The actual selection of women varies from 34 per cent in NHS bodies to 19 per cent in public corporations. There has been a mere 2 per cent increase between 1994 and 1997. In Finland, where there is a statutory requirement for at least 40 per cent of each sex in public appointments, women's representation has increased from 25 per cent in 1980 to 48 per cent in 1996.

The Public Appointments Unit don't want us to have a role in this and there are sensitivities about the Commissioner's independence. However, given that the majority of appointments are for ministers to make, we have the power to make demands of all departments.

The solutions I'm putting to the Cabinet subcommittee are targets of 50:50 and the development of Action Plans through which to achieve them. We will need to establish a baseline, track women's applications, undertake proactive recruitment drives and subject reappointments to full recruitment procedures. This is an important element of the government's commitment to increasing the openness and accountability of quangos. This month we are also making a major push to develop the national action plan implementing the UN Platform for Action on Women. There are twelve areas of critical concern and we aim to involve ministers from all relevant departments. Our UN Ambassador has sent a very complimentary account of my visit to New York and the FCO has circulated the reporting telegram on progress. I'm now sending letters to my opposite numbers. This is a hugely important exercise obliging civil servants in eleven different departments, plus Wales, Scotland and Northern Ireland, to examine their policies with respect to women and report upon them. The UN Platform ranges from women and poverty through violence against women to women's health and education to institutional mechanisms for the advancement of women.

The other major work on mainstreaming is ready for launch. We know how vital this is if policy is to work for women, but it's a hard road and not the sort of thing that thrills No. 10. We launch on 18 May at the QEII Conference Centre. Over 100 people are signed up, all the significant NGOs, the WNC, EOC and lots of civil servants from the different departments who will take part in a workshop led by the Civil Service College. In addition to Harriet and me there will be presentations from Diana Lamplugh, who has done much excellent work on women's safety since the murder of her daughter Suzy, and Shelagh Diplock, who runs the excellent Fawcett Society. My task is to explain how each government department will have to analyse whether different groups (i.e. women and men) will suffer a differential impact from any policy they develop. If that impact cannot be justified in law then the policy or programme must be amended. Sounds simple but it's not easy to do and has taken months to negotiate around government. We are proposing a training and reporting regime with annual returns to the Women's Unit. Everyone gets a pack with our fact sheets on different topics, well-written and presented at long last and giving a serious account of our work and the amount of change underway. Good coverage in *The Guardian* and *The Times* the next day.

Harriet, David Blunkett and Chris Smith launch our green paper on the £300 million national childcare strategy. One million families are expected to benefit from the childcare tax credit announced in the March Budget. It's not just the poorest who will get help. After-school clubs will be expanded from the current 3,000 to 30,000, with arts, drama and sport all crucial components. Excellent coverage in *The Independent*, but our spirits are dampened by yet another reshuffle story on the same day in *The Guardian* and another the following day in the *Financial Times*. The latter is particularly pernicious, citing Alistair Darling as a possible replacement for Harriet and saying the possible creation of a full-time Cabinet post for Harriet on women's issues is opposed by Tony. Not to be outdone, *The Guardian* has another large piece with further fevered speculation and poll ratings for all the Cabinet. It's quite sickening.

Harriet has written a lengthy formal letter to Gordon about family-friendly employment, setting out the need to raise the priority of this policy. It is of course one of the best ways of reducing the welfare budget, enabling women to get into and to stay in work and for parents to balance work and family. Women now make up 45 per cent of the workforce and many have family responsibilities to children, elderly relatives or both. Fathers are also recognising the need to play their part in caring for their children. She also argues the business case for competitiveness and enabling companies to make the best use of the talents of as many people as possible. In addition, she advocates one week's paid paternity leave (at a cost of £20 million) as all the evidence indicates that fathers will not take leave at the birth of a child unless it's paid.

We continue to work flat-out with a last meeting on our women's dialogue work before the Whitsun recess. The reshuffle doesn't happen. No one from No. 10 ever speaks to me about my position and I believe that goes for everyone else as well. What a way to run an administration.

A large piece in the *Sunday Telegraph* headed 'they all need a holiday'. It's so true. Everyone is exhausted. Tony, as the paper points out, has visibly aged in this past year. We'd all like to delegate much more but many of the civil servants are not on top of our agendas so ministers end up micro-managing.

Six weeks ago we held our first women's jury in Nottingham with independent observers, including the Daycare Trust and expert witnesses enabling the women to deliberate on the development of a childcare strategy. The women were recruited at random by researchers outside shopping centres etc. They came from a wide range of backgrounds but had to be non-joiners. The second jury is now underway, deliberating on the question, 'What should be done to improve the quality of life for working mothers?' The women have had the opportunity to collect evidence and interview expert witnesses. They come up with a raft of recommendations, including good-quality, affordable childcare, a registration system for nannies and spot checks by parents on nurseries. They want encouragement rather than legislation for employers to be more family-friendly, including receiving tax relief on childcare vouchers and setting up crèches. They also believe employers should give a week's paid paternity leave and two weeks' unpaid leave to look after sick children. A fairly predictable set of outcomes in line with our own views, but what is important here is that these are not the views of women's organisations who lobby government and are primarily run by middle-class professionals. These are the views of individual women.

Joy Copley, who was one of the journalists invited to follow the jury, does us proud in the *Daily Telegraph*. A truly positive piece on our work. She not only explains the process and outcomes but also quotes some of the women, including Corinne, a single mother who said, 'It's been brilliant, one of the best things a government can do is listen to people. This is a chance to make a difference and have your say.' Should be good enough for No. 10 but I fear the financial cost of such deliberations will limit any further rollout.

1 June: Harriet continues to drive the department and the arrival of Fiona Reynolds is a major boost. She was the highly successful head of the Council for the Protection of Rural England. Fiona will replace Pauline as head of the Women's Unit, after Harriet won the battle to raise the salary and recruit from outside the civil service. She has great lobbying skills and will be much more effective negotiating around government.

I am struggling with our UN Action Plan. The material coming from the different departments varies widely in content, style and relevance.

International development is strongest and DCMS weakest. Once again I'm into detailed drafting territory and it's going to be hugely difficult to comply with our international obligations and present an objective assessment of our government's work. I think Harriet realises No. 10 will want a PR document, while I think we should have something more studied. There's also the constant tension about whether we're even going to be allowed to finish the tasks in hand. There's just nothing for it but to work even harder – the alternative would be to stop and paralyse the whole department from now to the summer recess.

An unusual request: I have lunch with the Royal College of Obstetricians and Gynaecologists' president, Sir Naran Patel. He wants to discuss with me the findings of the Royal College, namely that domestic violence increases during pregnancy. Then back to the department for speech preparation – there seem to be loads of speeches and interviews this month. In the next few days I visit Newham Action Against Domestic Violence and meet with the LGA Equal Opportunities panel. Then it's first meetings with Martin Sixsmith, Harriet's new press officer, and Fiona Reynolds, the new head of the Women's Unit.

Reform of both the EOC and WNC continues to drag on. In late June we have the WNC plenary when we get our proposals adopted. The EOC is a tougher nut to crack but we continue to have input.

Whatever the media comment on women ministers, there are plenty of organisations that want to hear from us. Within the month I've spoken to a number of organisations and conferences including Agenda 21, Family Service Units, the Women in Business Group of the London Chamber of Commerce, Rape Crisis Federation, the Family Planning Association and Women Into Business. There is a great sense that this is a government that could deliver for women and they want to talk to us.

We have our regular political dialogue meeting. This is a useful strategy group. Meg Russell and Lorna Fitzsimons are incredibly helpful. It is, however, disappointing that this is the third meeting to which Sally Morgan from

No. 10 has given her apologies. Obviously not a fan of our project. None-theless, we've won the argument on twinning and interviews for the panel are about to begin in Wales. In Scotland, sixty women have already been approved for the panel.

22 June: Ann Keen, the Labour MP for Brentford and Isleworth, has tabled an amendment to the Crime and Disorder Bill to create an equal age of con-sent for heterosexual and gay young people.* Ann was inspired to work for gay equality when she rediscovered the son she had given up for adoption thirty years ago. They were reunited in 1995 when he traced her, having discovered by accident at the age of twenty-eight that he was adopted. On finding that he was gay, Ann became active in the campaign and is now lead-ing the charge at Westminster.

On Friday after a hectic day of engagements, speaking at lunchtime and an afternoon surgery, I get the 9.30 p.m. sleeper to Aberdeen to spend a welcome weekend with Frank. Back in London on Monday and at 7.30 a.m. I'm doing a down-the-line interview for BBC Radio Bristol before get-ting the 9.15 a.m. train from Paddington. My speech is part of our launch of the childcare green paper, with ministers covering different parts of the country to address invited audiences of interested professionals and NGOs. Then it's back to Temple Meads and off to Taunton for a few hours' campaigning, reaching home again at a quarter to eleven. Needless to say the benefits of my two days in Scotland have been well and truly dissipated!

To Nottingham for an evening meeting of the party's women's task force followed by a weekend national women's conference. There's a parade of women ministers with good stories to tell. I'm really pleased with my own speech, which I've been able to draft myself, albeit it includes lots of

---

* Ann's amendment was carried by the Commons but went on to be removed by the House of Lords. The government allowed the issue to be dropped so that it would not lose the entire Bill. The age of consent was later equalised by the Sexual Offences (Amendment) Act 2000.

departmental material. Harriet and I are very well received throughout the weekend and it's hard to imagine our jobs are on the line.

I have a meeting with the Royal College of Midwives who want to brief us on a variety of women's issues from their own experience. In the evening a very special constituency engagement: Goldsmiths has refurbished the old Deptford Town Hall and I am to officiate at the reopening ceremony and unveil a plaque in my name. Ken Gregory, the excellent warden, has taken on board my plea for community organisations to be able to hire rooms and this will be mentioned in both our speeches. There's a dinner to celebrate afterwards and it's a thoroughly enjoyable evening.

3 July: Today is my thirty-fifth wedding anniversary and just eighteen months since Keith's death. I still feel devastated and never stop thinking of him for a single day.

8 July: My diary card announces it's Karl, my driver's, birthday. It is typical of the civil service to make me aware. I'm not big on birthdays (mine being 28 December) but it's a nice touch. Karl, a young man with a family, has been infinitely kind to me throughout the past year and a soothing influence during many exhausting days. The day begins with a meeting about our website – part of our efforts to further our dialogue with women. At lunchtime I do a TV interview for an old Labour colleague, Mike Walsh.

A follow-up on a much earlier meeting on women's employment that I had with Jennifer Page, CEO of the Millennium Experience. I'm onsite to meet women engineers working on the construction. A hugely rewarding visit. Two of the women have played a leading role in the planning of the construction and all are superb role models for women in engineering. Obviously I ask about discrimination and their stories are varied, but one – a black woman – has a very scary tale of working on the Channel Tunnel rail link and eventually having to leave for her own safety. They are all proud of the work they are doing and the structure looks magnificent. We line up for a great hard-hat photo.

In the evening Tony Blair is giving a reception for ministers, which I happily attend. I heard much later from a whip that this was his way of saying farewell to those who would be sacked – obvious really – but at the time he was as charming as ever.

A few more days of regular meetings and obligatory summer receptions and I'm off to Newcastle as guest speaker at the Women of the North lunch. I dash back to Bristol for my nephew Nick's eighteenth birthday party. On Monday another party. Meg Russell is leaving the Labour Party to become a researcher at UCL. She is extremely able and will no doubt make her mark there. On Thursday it's Cardiff for a meeting with lone parents but the highlight of the week is to be a huge and glittering reception at the Foreign Office, co-hosted by Liz Symons and myself, in honour of the Global Summit for Women. This is a US-based organisation regarded as the premier business and economic forum for women. They are having a London launch and are already working across many countries and in dialogue with women ministers. I go along, fortunately having prepared and rehearsed a short speech with a few good jokes. Liz Symons cancels. My speech is well received and Liz's absence means I am the one to get presented with their badge of honour. It's a gold brooch in the shape of an eagle, which has what looks like a ruby for an eye and is perched on a large pearl. They tell me only a few women have them, including Hillary Clinton. I might have taken this with a pinch of salt were it not for the fact that some time later I see a newspaper photograph of her on a state visit wearing said brooch! It was a splendid occasion and I couldn't help but feel a bit grand hosting a reception for our government in the famous Durbar Court.

Frank has made an offer on an amazing house just on the edge of his constituency. It's an old steading (converted stone barn) on the banks of the River Don. It's utterly idyllic and costs less than a flat in my constituency. It also has a large garden – currently just a lawn and rose beds, but I'm going to transform it.

We're in our last days before summer recess and there's so much to complete. The major task is the report to the UN on our progress against the UN

Platform for Action. Fiona Reynolds has knocked this into shape and it's ready for publication. But we've been halted in our tracks by one Alun Evans at the Strategic Communications Unit at No. 10. As I feared, our international commitments mean nothing to him. He even suggests that 'at worst it might lay the government open to ridicule'. It's a phenomenal body of work and has forced every department of government to examine how its policies match up to the highest international aspirations for equality between women and men. It's a major blow. Mr Evans suggests that if it 'really is unavoidable' then the document should be redrafted (by them) and sent to the UN without publication. What a dreadful waste.

The reshuffle is now inevitable and dreaded by so many of us. For the first time my civil servants voice their opinions. They have no doubt that Harriet will go but they say they think I'll be kept in post. Sure enough, Harriet, Gavin Strang and David Clark all lose their jobs. I am so sorry for Harriet. She has done more than anybody ever in Parliament for equalities and much of her perceived failures in Social Security stem from differences in Gordon and Tony's economic agendas and the constant undermining of her by Frank Field.

I get asked to go to see Tony in his Westminster office. He's sitting there with the Cabinet Office Secretary. He smiles and says simply, 'I'm sorry I have to let you go.' I blurt out: 'No, you don't!' and ask to know why. There is, of course, no explanation, so I ask what is going to happen to our commitments to women and the Women's Unit. He says Margaret Jay (Leader of the Lords) will take on the women's brief. Margaret is a very talented woman but hardly suited to the post. A natural aristocrat with the task of removing hereditary peers, I don't believe she will be able to take our work forward. I tell Tony she absolutely must have a deputy in the Commons if all our efforts are not to be wasted. It's clear I have no hope of persuading him to keep me but the point goes home (he subsequently appoints Tessa Jowell as part-time Minister for Women in the Commons).

I leave heartbroken for the second time. I maintain my dignity and as I close the door Anji Hunter rushes out from a side room and takes me in.

She's very kind, saying, oddly, that it wasn't her decision. I've always liked Anji and I think she respected me from the time I was in Tony's team. It's a small comfort. By now the tears are welling up and I need to ring Frank and then return to the department to say goodbye. It is hard to take leave of Helen, Anna-Maria and Brinda. Karl takes me home for the last time.

Being sacked is a horrible experience for anyone but a second rejection from someone I had previously worked with so closely and served so loyally is devastating. I feel completely worthless. I go over and over in my mind as to the reasons, but with hindsight there was none of substance. I just wasn't valued and I didn't fit the New Labour project. In my naivety I didn't appreciate that being dependent only on patronage from the Prime Minister made me very vulnerable. John Prescott was utterly loyal to his former team members but I had sacrificed his support when backing Margaret Beckett for deputy. Margaret was no sister and would never repay my support. I'd rejected a shadow post with Gordon, who was also fiercely loyal to his team members. Really, I had only myself to blame. But it didn't help. In two years I'd lost my womb, my husband, my house and now my ministerial job. I couldn't feel much worse.

Lovely letters arrive, colleagues express their sympathy and enquire after the reason. The only saving grace is the recess – time to lick wounds.

Chapter Seven

# BACK BENCHES

*'Activism is the price I pay for living on the planet.'*

— ALICE WALKER

Everyone knows it's a thankless task being a backbencher when your party is in government. After running things myself, standing up simply to make supportive speeches or ask patsy questions is hardly stimulating. I have to find new things to do and I'm not ready to commit to a select committee covering a portfolio where I've been a shadow minister. Harriet's got the right idea: she's set up a Childcare Commission and is determined to get back into government. My first task is to recruit a new researcher. I choose Heidi Alexander, whose only paid job has been on the ski slopes, but she is very bright, engaging and enthusiastic and shares my values even though she is not a member of the party. She will prove to be a brilliant choice.

Occasionally someone says something encouraging and I begin to think perhaps life's still worth living. One day Paul Boateng – one of our rising stars who I don't really know – stops me to say it's all so unjust and I should get on TV instead. Such an unlikely prospect but I'm sure it was genuinely meant and if I'm honest I've had a lot of media experience.

Then the most surprising thing happens. Mike Walsh, who interviewed me recently and produces a show for a cable TV company, asks me if I'd like to be considered for a role as a presenter! Of course I've never heard of the channel and I'd have to go for an audition but I've got to accept. They are going to run a six-part series on 'women's issues'. It's not easy to learn to stand, move around the studio audience, speak to autocue and cut to interviewing on the sofa, but I do it and watch the videos afterwards. To my amazement they hire me. What an experience.

We manage the time because all the shows are pre-recorded. It's hugely challenging but thrilling – scripted parts off autocue, ad-libbing for the sofa interviews. I can't believe I can actually do this but, yes, here I am hosting a chat show transmitted on the *Living* channel for real. At the end of the series I do a one-to-one interview with Mo Mowlam. An amazing woman and sad revelations about her childhood. This is the best thing I've done. By the end of the series my confidence has had a great boost and I'm truly grateful. I guess Paul would have told me to get an agent and try for something else but as a woman I think my age is against me and I'd probably need to lose a stone as well. It's enough to have had the experience and although I'd have loved to do more I know I need to find my way again as an MP.

My interest has been sparked by coverage of the commercial production of genetically modified foods. Apparently they are being introduced into the UK without any scrutiny or announcement. While we were recovering from our traumas in France in August, a huge controversy broke around a scientist called Árpád Pusztai who for over thirty years worked at the Rowett in Aberdeen, the UK's leading food safety institute. He prematurely revealed the results of his experiments on feeding GM potatoes to pigs. A world-renowned expert on proteins who was a supporter of GM, he spoke out because he was alarmed by the changes he found in the linings of the pigs' guts. He's now been vilified and his contract terminated. The stakes are high. Huge US food corporations have invested billions in this technology over the past decade and there are no controls operating over their production.

This is definitely something I can get my teeth into. Having done genetic research myself I understand the science.

The EU has put in place a Novel Foods Regulation, which applies to any food that has no significant consumption history prior to May 1997. No long-term scientific monitoring of consumption is being undertaken. There's also a simplified procedure based on substantial equivalence where a novel food is simply considered 'substantially equivalent' to one already on the market.

GM tomato puree has made it to the shelves of Sainsbury's and Safeway. Selling more cheaply than the non-GM equivalent, it has proved popular with customers. A few years ago, the *Daily Mail*, reporting on a range of US GM research and products including potential transfers of animal genes to plants, coined the term 'Frankenstein foods'. Public concern is rising and we need some parliamentary scrutiny – I'm on the case.

## 1999

The House of Lords Select Committee on the European Community has published a report on GM crops. Totally uncritical, it appears to have adopted wholesale the advertising campaign of Monsanto, a US-based multinational agrochemical company, concluding that GM offers 'higher crop yields, better nutritional content, fewer herbicides and pesticides and cheaper food for consumers'. They even support the use of the 'terminator' gene, designed to ensure that seed is sterile, thus ensuring farmers have to buy the GM seed every year rather than harvesting their own.

27 January: I've got a slot for a Ten-Minute Rule Bill. Like most women I get breast cancer screening and talking to my consultant, Professor Ian Fentiman, I've discovered that there is no register of women undergoing prophylactic mastectomy. This process of removing healthy breasts is being increasingly undertaken by women who have a strong family history of gene-induced breast cancer. He has been pressing for this with no success so I've drafted a Bill to

set up a national registry and present it with the support of the Royal College of Nursing, Imperial Cancer Research and the UK Breast Cancer Coalition.

Joan Walley initiates a debate on GMOs and I take the opportunity to make my first speech on the subject. I argue that food is not just another commodity but the sustenance of life, and public hostility to GM is entirely rational. Risks have to be weighed against benefits. When the manufacturers' proudest boast is that there is no intrinsic difference between GM and non-GM, where is the nutritional benefit? I criticise the House of Lords report for saying 'Once the regulatory process has ensured safety...' There can be no absolute safety and the precautionary principle should apply.

Finally, I point to the fact that transfer of genes from one species to another does not occur in nature, which is what makes genetic engineering unpredictable and uncontrollable and could change our environment irreversibly. Since genes from viruses and bacteria are used in the process and have never been part of the human diet, they could prove a risk to human health.

My activities have already attracted attention and the *Independent on Sunday* has asked for an article. I quickly commission expert briefings. Under the heading 'Monsanto's claim that GM crops will end world hunger is spurious', I argue that enough food is produced in developing countries but other factors prevent its consumption. People starve because they are too poor to buy food, because they are denied access to land, or because their lives are disrupted by civil war. Significantly, the two main GM crops being grown commercially in the US are soya beans and maize, the bulk of which are used for animal feed, providing meat for the well-fed, while more than two-thirds of people globally are vegetarian. Nonetheless I point out there is interest in getting developing countries to grow GM crops for Western markets. But genetically modified seeds with 'technology protection systems' (the 'terminator' genes) are designed to be sterile, thus offering no benefit to local people whose tradition is to harvest their seed for replanting.

I further argue that herbicide-resistant crops, while superficially more attractive to developing countries, also make poor farmers dependent on expensive chemicals, undermining more sustainable farming methods. I end by referring to the international biosafety protocol, currently being negotiated, which must give every country the right to exercise the precautionary principle in respect of GMOs and which must establish an international liability regime.

14 February: John Prescott announces he has ordered a judicial inquiry into the 'collision between the *Marchioness* and the *Bowbelle*, and the search and rescue operations that followed the collision'. This is a follow-on to the inquiry begun last August into safety and the circumstances of the disaster. It's taken ten years of campaigning to get this result but I'm pleased John has kept the promise he gave us in opposition. A separate inquiry will examine why the hands of twenty-seven victims were cut off to allow fingerprint identification. I just hope the outcomes will bring some comfort to the families.

The *Independent on Sunday* has published a huge article on the New Cross fire headlined it 'was not a race attack'. This has been common currency among the families from the start of my involvement but there are still powerful voices in the black community who believe otherwise. I get an update from DCI Peter Newman. They've assembled a lot of new information and done a lot of computer modelling, based on new interviews, that can pinpoint who was where and when in relation to the start of the blaze. When the Macpherson Report into Stephen Lawrence's murder is published later in the month, the Met is labelled institutionally racist. Many of us have suspected this for years but to hear it from a senior judge is shocking. Vindication for Doreen and Neville Lawrence who are in the Public Gallery for Jack Straw's statement. I ask for the New Cross fire case to be looked at in the follow-up action announced by Jack.

I attend the launch of the Five Year Freeze campaign and discuss strategies with a lot of activists I haven't worked with before. GeneWatch, run by Sue Mayer, is particularly impressive. The Freeze is an alliance of twenty-nine national organisations covering a very wide spectrum of interests. The case is robust – a five-year freeze on growing genetically engineered crops for any commercial purpose and on importing genetically modified foods and patenting of genetic resources for food and farm crops.

The government reacts by sending every MP a letter from five Cabinet ministers, headed by John Prescott, setting out their reasons for opposing such a ban. Within days the Freeze campaign points to major discrepancies in the government's claims, which are substantial. Even more serious, it's been revealed that the British Retail Consortium warned ministers that shops could lose billions of pounds unless the government convinces the public GM is safe. Apparently, GM soya and maize are found, unlabelled, in most ready meals and a boycott could lead to a collapse in the market.

Twenty world-renowned scientists, led by Professor Vyvyan Howard, have come out in support of Árpád Pusztai, supporting his findings.* Supermarket switchboards are jammed as a result and company bosses react swiftly. M&S has banned all GM from its products; Sainsbury's will label forty own-label products that contain GM soya; Tesco announces that 150 GM products are already labelled but they will label 800 more; and Iceland bans all GM in its own-label foods.

We're just halfway through February and I haven't stopped. Then I get a letter from the National Federation of WIs telling me they will put a motion urging the government to adopt the Five Year Freeze to their annual conference in June. They are definitely a force to be reckoned with.

There is absolutely no doubt that whatever is done on labelling and food regulation, it won't be enough. Any assessment of GM crops has to include agricultural and biodiversity effects and that's what we need to campaign on. This field is moving so rapidly most MPs haven't a clue what's going on.

The first British court case for flouting the rules at a GM test site is brought against Monsanto, who plead guilty. They are further humiliated when the Advertising Standards Agency condemns their £1 million advertising campaign for making 'wrong, unproven, misleading and confusing' claims. Great!

---

* Published in *The Lancet* in November 1999.

I've been collecting my till receipts from both Tesco and Sainsbury's and now have hundreds of pounds' worth of purchases recorded from both. I send them to the CEOs asking if they can tell me whether any of the products contain GM. I get a very speedy reply from Tesco telling me they can't.

The government is under increasing pressure with Environment Minister Michael Meacher contradicting Jeff Rooker, and Jack Cunningham regularly making things worse in his enforcer role. *The Guardian* reveals that millions of pounds in inducements to expand operations in Britain have gone to GM companies, including Monsanto, and eighty-one meetings have been held with ministers and civil servants since the election. Lord Sainsbury has also been shown to have further involvement with the industry and David Hill, Labour's chief spin doctor until recently, has become a Monsanto advisor. It's even rumoured that No. 10 has telephoned Prince Charles to ask him to remove his anti-GM statements from his website!

*The Guardian* is to stage a GM debate at Westminster Central Hall (capacity 2,000) and I have been asked to be on the panel with Professor Steve Jones and George Monbiot. Turmoil in the government has forced the PM to intervene. He asserts the safety of GM foods and attacks 'scaremongering' by MPs, pressure groups and the media. He also rejects the three-year ban on commercial growing demanded by English Nature, official government advisors. The *Guardian* debate goes well and I feel I'm really making a contribution.

I'm still bruised by the lack of a ministerial job and it hurts me to see so many colleagues busy with their briefs but I guess if I were a minister I'd be expected to toe the line on GMOs and I would have discovered I couldn't. At least I'm really engaged in the campaign and working with lots of knowledgeable and stimulating people.

March opens with another blow to the GM industry and from an impeccable source. The National Pollen Research Unit has demonstrated that pollen can be carried up to nine miles by bees and more than 100 miles on the wind. This makes a complete nonsense of the 200-metre distance between GM and non-GM crops recommended by ACRE, the government's Advisory

Committee on Releases to the Environment. With commercial crop grow-ing due to start in the UK next year, the government is really under pressure.

Asda has announced it will instruct all its suppliers to remove all GM ingredients from its 900 own-label products. A week later, Sainsbury's spectacularly follows suit. But, in an extraordinary reply to a letter from a customer, Somerfield's quality assurance director writes, by 'avoiding eating any genetically modified ingredients or foods I regret to say in the near future you will starve'!

One of the aspects of genetic engineering that has had much less coverage is the use of antibiotic-resistant marker genes. These are used as a tool in the genetic engineering process not as an end product, but given their importance in medicine they deserve more attention. I decide to ask the Trade Minister about the testing of cosmetic products containing GM where antibiotics could be significant. He admits no assessment has been made but the government will support the development of guidelines for such products being brought forward by the European Commission. The exchange gets picked up by the media and the Cosmetic Toiletry and Perfumery Association confirm that GM ingredients are indeed being used.

12 March: Keith's birthday – he would have been sixty. I still think of him every single day and the pain never goes away. I realise I haven't once been able to listen to music at home since he died.

I get a reply from Sainsbury's. I haven't bought any GM foods but they can't be sure about the use of GM sources as carriers for certain ingredients. They also give me further details of their policy. If a GM-free source or a GM-free substitute cannot be found for an own-brand product they will discontinue the line. Proof positive of consumer power like we've never seen before.

A Canadian farmer is being pursued by Monsanto for damages and for the profits from his fields. They say he has used their GM canola (rape) without a licence. He maintains he has no wish to grow GM and his fields have been contaminated by seeds blown from the cut crops of his neighbours. Private

detectives are crawling over the land. Other farmers are reporting intimidation and threats from Monsanto agents. A real horror story is unfolding.

Another example of uncontrolled contamination is discovered by Trading Standards officers in Worcester. Tests by scientists show GM soya in sixty
out of 200 samples tested, only one of which was labelled.

It's May and after quite a lot of media exposure I get an invitation to
write for the glossy magazine *Country Living* and to speak at the Bath and
West Show. I feel I'm returning to my country roots and sometimes reflect
that I'm actually an inner-city MP. Fortunately, there's plenty of support in
the constituency for my stance and I think it's important MPs with a science
background make a contribution where they can.

A stroke of luck arrives in an approach by a BBC journalist, Boni Sones,
who's going freelance and offers her services for a day or so each week. This is
an excellent arrangement that will take the strain off the office. Fortunately,
Katerina's huge experience as my caseworker means she can work most of
the time unsupervised.

A year ago those of us who were members of the GLOBE international
parliamentary network set up an autonomous GLOBEUK. Sir Crispin Tickell
addresses our first AGM, laying out the five great challenges to the environment: human population increase; land degradation and decrease in soil
fertility; water problems (both freshwater and ocean pollution); destruction
of natural systems and services; and climate change. I and other GLOBE
members will continue to work on these issues throughout our time in Parliament. In our first campaign, we will take on the Export Credits Department,
which appears not to support any green technologies.

I greatly enjoy my day at the Bath and West Show and get an excellent
reception for my speech. Media reports are headlined 'Former/Ex-Minister
in Appeal for GM Freeze'! The most quoted passage is when I rhetorically
ask of the biotech companies 'why did they lobby the world's governments
to introduce new patent laws for seeds? Why did they fight regulation and
labelling? Why in the US did they deliberately and irresponsibly mix GM and

non-GM foods? Why? Because unlike most of the governments with which they were dealing, they recognised the awesome implications of this science and didn't want any questions asked.'

I assert that even if our instincts about what we eat are primeval, BSE taught us they are entirely rational. Finally, calling for the freeze to allow time to evaluate the facts, I say, 'It is our right to exercise choice over what we eat and to expect our government to regulate for quality and safety.'

Prince Charles had earlier accused the supporters of GM foods of using 'emotional blackmail' to argue their case, so for good measure we send him a copy of the speech and receive a personal reply. Meanwhile, Tony Blair has vowed not to bow to the 'tyranny' of pressure groups and Michael Meacher lets it be known that no one can be certain of the long-term consequences of the new technology.

GeneWatch has discovered that AgrEvo, the company developing GM herbicide-resistant oilseed rape, has applied to vary its UK consents to enable it to grow on over 12,000 acres. Clearly this is commercial growing not scientific experiment. We repeat our calls for a moratorium to get these matters under control.

Heidi tells me I've now tabled eighty-six PQs on GM since we started to get involved. My latest have at last secured official confirmation of an experiment with salmon in Scotland. Ten thousand salmon eggs were subject to genetic engineering to introduce a growth hormone and fifty fish grew to four times their normal size. The project was ended a year later.

News of the New Cross Fire investigation. DCI Newman has just returned from the US and Jamaica where he and DC Peter Burns have interviewed all the remaining family members and survivors who were at the party, plus one man who always denies being there despite others saying he definitely attended. All are willing to return to the UK if required.

August: The House is in recess and I'm in the usual frantic rush to finish everything I can before going on holiday. We've booked three weeks. I can't wait. I'm really looking forward to some quality time with Frank. At the last minute I get a really important request from the Soil Association. They want to launch a new initiative in October and are asking me to front it, alongside food writer Lynda Brown. It is to be called 'Women Say No to GMOs'. I'm already making the point at women's meetings that the opposition to GMOs is the most significant exercise of women's power in a long time, so this is right up my street.

August: Last year when we had no holiday plans Glenys Kinnock introduced us to Gabriella and Franco, who let property on their estate in Tuscany to friends. They were the most amazing hosts and the surrounding villages and countryside an absolute joy so now we are going again.

September: Everything is coming together for 'Women Say No to GMOs'. Organics Direct will host the website, Planet Organic and Iceland will take petitions and Paul McCartney (honouring his late wife Linda) will provide the opening endorsement. We have nine demands ranging from the right for all consumers and farmers to remain GM-free if they wish, to international action to prevent monopoly of the world's staple foods by global agrochemical companies. Lynda has got Anita Roddick, Jancis Robinson, Liz Earle, Caroline Conran and Trudie Styler on board and has good media and website contacts. My front -page quote ends: 'This is our chance to become more visible, more vocal and more powerful.' More names get added including Jerry Hall and Glenys Kinnock – and Boni adds some poetry!

I'm interviewed for the *Independent on Sunday*. Its subsequent article is headlined 'Saint Joan launches GM crusade – the former queen of grass roots activism has found a new target reports Geoffrey Lean'. A big boost.

I also do an interview for *The Guardian* and get nice letters in response. One woman offers a campaign slogan: 'If you think you're too small to make a difference – try sleeping with a mosquito.' Really makes me smile. The article itself is unusual, analysing my campaigning, heaping praise and observing that in contrast to CND I'm now 'leading a campaign the popular press does not despise'.

Worries about GM have resulted in a big increase in demand for organic food but production is low in the UK, which is resulting in supermarkets sucking in imports. Over the past year there's been a 40 per cent increase in sales. I get a slot for a Ten-Minute Rule Bill to take up the campaign. I present the Organic Food and Farming Targets Bill on 26 October. Within a day Sainsbury's contact me to sign up in support, followed the next day by Waitrose. Three months on, the Prime Minister will make a speech to the National Farmers' Union (NFU) in which he promises to treble the amount of organic produce by 2006.

So much excitement is building for the millennium celebrations. We're not trying to get seats for the official Millennium Dome events but my mother and Susan and David will come to stay for New Year's Eve. After the many difficulties of recent years it's good to have a marker to a new chapter.

## 2000

1 January: Glad we didn't go to the Dome. It proved a bit of a disaster – long queues, poor transport (the new Jubilee line), no food and very cold. We had a lovely evening – good dinner and wine and a celebration with fireworks and champagne at the top of Hilly Fields with lots of locals.

Frank and I go to Aberdeen for five days where, despite the wintry weather, I get a lot done in the garden.

After two years it's obvious that the New Cross fire inquiry needs more resources and so I appeal again to the Commissioner. I get a positive response. They will increase the size of the team investigating the New Cross fire and there are some new lines of enquiry. I write to the CPS asking them to ensure a speedy consideration of the evidence being sent and offer to meet with them.

The House returns and it's the usual round of debates and meetings. The most important event of the week is the debate on GMOs and biotechnology.

I'm really on top of this complex issue and it's rewarding to be able to challenge the complacency and assumptions that have allowed the government to go so far. They are definitely taking it all much more seriously now. I end with a passionate appeal on the biosafety protocol and am rewarded when Michael Meacher promises to oppose the US-led attempt to subordinate the biosafety protocol to the World Trade Organization.

Friday is packed. An early-morning meeting with Lewisham College, lunch at the Royal Naval College, an advice surgery and an evening concert by Sinfonia 21. I've become the secretary of the All-Party Parliamentary Group (APPG) on Breast Cancer, so a lot more additional meetings. One is with Delyth Morgan, who is the very impressive CEO of Breakthrough Breast Cancer, a new charity focused on research.

I am going to introduce a Ten-Minute Rule Bill to change the law to make it explicitly legal for political parties to adopt positive action where gender representation is unbalanced. We've done a thorough search of the European law and I have no doubt it's already legal but this will be for the avoidance of doubt.

The library has been able to tell me that since women were eligible to stand for Parliament, 4,432 MPs have been elected, of which just 239 (5 per cent) have been women.* At the rate of increase based on 1983 to 1997, parity would be reached in 2030 but if the rate slowed to previous levels then parity could be another seventy years away! An interesting but depressing piece in *The Independent* strengthens my hand. The approved list of Labour candidates for the next general election numbers 495 men and only 194 women. Pointing to those expected to find winnable seats (special advisors, officials at Millbank and friends of Blair), the article names nineteen people, only one of whom is a woman. New Labour MPs next year will be overwhelmingly white, male and middle-class.

---

* After the 2015 election there were still more men sitting in Parliament than the total number of women ever elected.

Heidi is mailing all our contacts, assembling the eleven all-party sponsors for the Bill and tabling an Early Day Motion (EDM). Lots of support is coming in and the Scottish and Welsh selections/elections are much referenced. Rhodri Morgan has done a great job in promoting women since he became First Minister and is now reporting that the Welsh Cabinet is the first executive body in the world to have an equal number of women and men members. Some people at Labour HQ are beginning to grasp the significance of losing the women's vote. Both Deborah Mattinson at Opinion Leader Research and the Fawcett Society have published important analyses of the women's vote and women's identification with women candidates. We get lots of media coverage throughout January and February and everything is ready for the Bill's second reading on 7 March. Harriet is also on the case and pressing the NEC for a comprehensive strategy towards women in the forthcoming general election campaign. At second reading, I explain the legal history and the fact that this simple, one-clause Bill is for the avoidance of doubt that positive action can be taken. I argue that men cannot bring a woman's perspective to the whole range of political concerns and that most women contribute to the House through different life experiences Also, research shows that women think that women politicians are more in touch with their lives than men. I also challenge the Tory men, asking how many of them felt patronised or that they are second-rate because they were shielded from female competition on *all-male* shortlists. Tory MP Anne McIntosh opposes the Bill but doesn't press a vote.

Ten-Minute Rule Bills go no further in legislation but they are an important way of raising an issue and initiating a campaign. They can often then be used as the basis for a Private Member's Bill or, in my case, I hope, adoption by government. Our aim is to get a commitment to legislate into the manifesto.

There's big news about GM rice engineered to add vitamin A. Vitamin A deficiency causes blindness in millions of children in the poorest countries. The project has had public funding and it is proposed to give free seeds to farmers. Difficult to argue against the sentiments but the arguments for safety testing and environmental impact are just as acute as with any GM crops. I also see this is a Western solution when what these children need is access to vegetables and fruit, not just a doctored mono diet of rice. The news breaks that the Rockefeller Foundation, which has been funding the development of genetically engineered rice, has made a startling admission. Claims have been exaggerated, they say. Apparently the average daily consumption of GM rice in Asia would only supply 8 per cent of the daily dose of the vitamin needed to prevent eye disease. The Foundation says the PR campaign on the rice has 'gone too far'.

'Women Say No to GMOs' petition forms are coming in all the time. Many of the women I worked with as Minister for Women have joined in. Boni has moved on and Lynda is busy writing a book so Heidi is picking up a lot of the slack, but whatever we do there is huge momentum on GM carrying all of us forward.

Interesting developments in the constituency. Two remarkable constituents have bought the early eighteenth-century Shipwright's Palace on Convoys Wharf, which I now know was the site of Henry VIII's naval shipyard. The property is listed and in a ruinous condition but they have set about restoring it. A really exciting project that will take many years.

Frank and I have accepted an invitation to go to India with the Labour Friends group. India is everything I imagined. We leave the airport in a whirl of heat, dust and a cacophony of sound. As we are official guests we're staying in a very lovely hotel that is cool and elegant with plants and flowers everywhere. The current government of India is a coalition led by the Hindu nationalist party, the BJP. Of course we'd much prefer our sister socialist party, Congress, to be in power but nonetheless Prime Minister Vajpayee promises to be an interesting man. He has quite an arresting presence – he is reputedly a poet and writer as well as a politician. We are aware of his attempts at a new peace process and last year's historic inauguration of the Delhi–Lahore bus service. He explains his vision for India. It's one of modernisation, pro-business, and encouraging private sector and foreign investment. There's a national highway development plan and a specific programme to connect highways to roads to unconnected villages. All in all, I come away quite impressed.

Frank, Ashok Kumar and I to go to Chandigarh. We are met by two soldiers at the railway station who sit with us for the three-hour journey and appear again when we return. Our first meeting is with the Chief Minister who tells us that 2 per cent of India's population live in the Punjab but it produces 60 per cent of India's grain. I have an interesting conversation with the Vice-Chancellor of the Punjab Agricultural University. They are finding heavy metals in the crops grown with added sewage sludge. Many farmers, however, grow without chemicals and he is interested in whether they could grow organically for Western markets. I undertake to make contacts for him with the Soil Association.

The Chief Minister assures us that there is no longer any violence in the Punjab (Sikh/non-Sikh violence having been endemic in the '80s and early '90s). Despite agriculture being their primary industry, they are successfully attracting foreign IT investment. Microsoft is establishing a centre at the engineering college and he would like more UK teachers on exchange programmes. A stimulating visit.

We arrive back in Delhi exhausted but find an invitation to a private home from one of the ministers. Thankfully it's not too onerous but like stepping back into the Raj – we are served tea and the thinnest, crustless cucumber sandwiches I've ever seen.

Next day I'm really ill – for sure the cucumber sandwiches – so I can't go on the day trip to Mumbai.

One of our ten days is reserved for sightseeing and we have the great privilege of going to the Taj Mahal. It is breathtakingly beautiful. Frank and I are able to break away from the rest and have a romantic few moments as we pose for our photograph.

Travelling to Kashmir presents me with a nightmare scenario. Although I've forced myself to suppress my fear of flying over the years, I cannot contemplate small planes. Now I discover for our safety we are to be flown in an eight-seater ministerial jet. I'm not at all sure I can do it. Fortunately, I took the precaution of getting a few tranquillisers from my GP before leaving. I feel extremely claustrophobic but off we go and I know there's no turning back. I can't look out despite my fellow passengers' exclamations of the wonders of flying over the Himalayas. We land amid great security and for the next few days we are surrounded by armed guards and our cars are preceded by police with a truckload of soldiers behind. Of course we know it's a very dangerous place but this level of militarism comes as quite a shock. On one of our journeys the armed guard from the front passenger seat has to get out to do some paperwork at a checkpoint. Our taxi driver immediately tells us how bad things are and how only independence will bring peace to Kashmir. We are astonished by his boldness and wonder if the man with the gun is there as much to protect us from drivers as from any external threat.

We receive endless briefings on the wars with Pakistan, the uprisings and the need for Indian administration. It's difficult not to wonder if the taxi driver isn't right, given the violent situation that pertains. We know that there are many political prisoners in the jail and ask if we can make a visit. We are told enquiries will be made but no visit is forthcoming. We keep up the pressure and on the last day we are told that there isn't time. We insist that we have the time and as we are flying in the private jet we cannot see the problem. Amazingly the authorities give in (can't imagine the UK government doing so). Conditions are predictably grim but having seen inside many British prisons I can see that compared to local conditions this jail is probably unexceptional. We quickly realise that prisoners are unlikely to benefit from talking to us, although a few do. We can draw no concrete conclusions but feel it was important to demonstrate our interest. Overall I conclude that Kashmir remains a tragedy and reflect on Britain's role in the partition of India. We arrive back at 5 a.m. on Sunday. That evening I fly to Edinburgh for a two-day conference on GMOs.

8 April: Bernie Grant is dead. He was such an ebullient character and one of our first black MPs. What a tragedy.

There's an important meeting in New Cross to plan work for the New Deal for Communities. This is a government programme to regenerate deprived communities, with a new emphasis on community development. With Greater London Authority (GLA) and mayoral elections coming up, I'm doing canvassing, street stalls and leafleting at railway stations. It's a big problem having Frank Dobson as our candidate and Ken Livingstone as an Independent. Ken is hugely popular in the constituency and I know lots of Labour voters are going to vote for him. Tony Blair has put us in a really stupid situation. After delivering our promise of a strategic authority and an elected mayor for London we are now handing political control to the Tories. So many Labour activists are fed up and it's really difficult to get people to campaign. It's the first time I've met real hostility on Lewisham streets.

Predictably, the Tories take control of the Assembly and Ken is elected as an independent mayor. What a political disaster for a PM with a huge majority in government and record personal ratings.

10 May: My mother's eightieth birthday. Six months ago I made arrangements for a big family party in an historic house in Wales. Then, six weeks ago, she had a stroke. Amazingly, she has made a wonderful recovery and the party is a great success.

We go to the official opening of the wonderful Tate Modern in the Turbine Hall, followed by Jenni Murray's birthday party that evening and Helena Kennedy's the next (both women I greatly admire). Then, a very special evening. Ravi Shankar is giving an eightieth birthday concert at the Barbican. I just have to go even though it will bring back so many memories of my life with Keith. At eighty he may not come again and I would never forgive myself if I missed the opportunity.

Michael Meacher makes an announcement on farm-scale trials. Given they were inevitable, at least there is more environmental and biodiversity evaluation than was originally expected. Also there is a commitment to no commercial growing of GM crops until the government is satisfied that there will be no unacceptable effects on the environment. But, a few weeks later Nick Brown has to make a statement explaining how GM-contaminated seed came to be planted in the UK. Apparently Advanta Seeds has told the government that one of its conventional seed crops grown in Canada came into contact with a GM crop nearby, which contaminated the 1998 seed. About 900 hectares were sown with this seed last year and around 4,700 this spring. Exactly the sort of thing we have been predicting. Advanta is offering to pay compensation. This only goes to illustrate why the Biosafety Protocol should have contained an international liability clause and why the US and other GM enthusiasts blocked it.

Pressure is mounting on the government over the selection of women and with Labour women's conference this month I'm determined to add to it. Heidi does a canvass of all those women who haven't yet signed my EDM, calling for support from all political parties for positive measures to address gender inequality and for my Sex Discrimination (Amendment) Bill. I'm doing another press release and Meg Russell, now at the Constitution Unit, has organised a seminar. She's also written an excellent paper covering the law and the experience of other European states. We're going to win this one!

For some time I've been a member of the Development Council for the new Laban and now we are launching the design of the new building. Some £5 million more needs to be raised but we are confident we can do it and the architects, Herzog and de Meuron, are such enthusiasts. On the weekend I've got the DAGE summer party – always a hazard with Harry Hayward who runs the organisation and who can be very challenging at times. This time he excels himself. Having invited me to the dance floor he literally sweeps me off my feet and the local newspaper photographer gets the picture. A deeply embarrassing front page follows!

I've decided to give evidence to the Intelligence and Security Committee who are doing a report. I know it's pointless but they need to hear what it's like to have been the subject of illegal surveillance.

July, and a great idea. We're to have a giant organic picnic in Greenwich Park and I've been asked to speak. I try to capture everything I believe in the fewest possible words:

Modern genetic engineering is the product of extraordinary human endeavour. It is exciting – it has been a power for good in the fight against human disease. But there is a world of a difference between the closed pharmaceutical system and putting GMOs at the heart of the human food chain and the natural environment. If things go wrong we can stop taking the pills – we may not be able to stop eating the food – especially if we can't identify it.

Genetic scientists have been ill-served by their masters in the biotech industry.

Every day there is a new claim – crops with higher yields, salt tolerant, cold tolerant, vitamin producing – everyone a winner in the race to feed the developing world.

Companies like Monsanto should stop giving scientists a bad name.

Your concern about the quality of the food you eat and the health of our environment is neither ignorant nor hysterical. It is not anti-science.

Indeed, organic farming and production depend on sound science, depend on rigorous testing, control and labelling.

It is sound science to question the transfer of herbicide resistance from GM crops to weeds in the countryside.

It is sound science to question the impact of insect tolerant crops on wildlife.

*It is sound science* to question claims that herbicide resistance means less chemical treatment.

I conclude by asking for a moment's reflection. Human life has been on this planet for 3 million years; farming for around 10,000 years; genetic modification for a mere 10,000 days. What's the hurry? Ours is a democratic society. It is our right to determine what we eat and how it is produced. This event sends that message to government.

As always at this time of year Frank and I are exhausted and many busy weeks lie ahead. Nonetheless, we've decided to go to the Globe Theatre on Sunday.

Neither of us has ever been before and Frank is constantly bemoaning the fact that we never go to the theatre, which he loves. A great experience – good seats, no rain, *Hamlet*.

8 July: A surprise event – a reunion at my old grammar school in Pontypool. It's now a mixed comprehensive but they are contacting all the old girls with an invitation to a reception and exhibition of past people and events. Sadly, all but one of my former teachers is dead. I meet up with a few contemporaries and it's all enjoyable, though the fabric of the school is much neglected. On Monday it's Harriet's birthday party at her home. Such a lovely event – she has so many good friends and she and Jack are great hosts.

After ten wonderful years of service, Katerina, my caseworker, is moving to be closer to her new family. This is a real wrench for me and I am so sorry to lose her. Most young people only stay for two or three years so I guess I'm in for a succession of caseworkers from now on. In the event I appoint Ruth Bransom, who will give me good service.

Summer recess and a meeting on Convoys Wharf. It's such an extraordinary site – vast acres of concrete that have below them some of the most important industrial history in the country. I'm really uneasy at the prospect of a modern development. John Miller, Lewisham's chief planning officer, and I meet with the architects and tour the site. The numerous warehouses will go but there is one building that is listed. From the outside, the Olympia is quite ugly but inside it is like a vast cathedral of soaring vaulted ironwork. This has to have huge potential as a public space.

I've received a petition with nearly 300 names from residents near the Water Tower in Dressington Avenue. The tower has been converted into flats and the developer has applied to have a power plant and mobile phone mast on the top. I'm very sympathetic to their case. I'm going to get expert advice on the risks but meanwhile I'll support them and contact the council about the planning issues.

A thoroughly enjoyable weekend in Aberdeen, with Sunday spent at

Sarah and Gordon's house to celebrate their wedding on 3 August. All informal and very relaxing; Gordon at his best.

September offers an exciting prospect. Frank and I are to move our offices to Portcullis House. This is the first contemporary building built by Parliament and specifically designed for the twenty-first century. Internally it is excellent. We each have an office with a shared staff space between (maximum of two staff each). It has all the necessary IT connections and, best of all, it's ecologically sound, with a ducted fresh-air system much cheaper and healthier than air conditioning. Little do we know that like many new buildings there will be loads of snags! The air-exchange system malfunctions causing a flood, fire alarms keep going off and the wonderful trees in the atrium that are part of the healthy environment become the subject of ridicule and criticism for their cost (they proved their worth and remained healthy and oxygenating for the rest of my parliamentary life!).

Mo Mowlam has announced she's leaving the Cabinet and standing down at the general election. This is really bad news. I'm so fond of Mo and she did an amazing job in Northern Ireland before being replaced by Peter Mandelson. We always knew that getting a standing ovation at the mere mention of her name in Tony Blair's speech last conference would see the knives out for her. After all she has endured in recovering from her brain tumour this is a real blow. Lots of media coverage and I'm asked to comment. She's such a role model for women and our most popular Cabinet minister with poll ratings well ahead of Tony. So sad.

With Parliament not sitting in September I've got four hectic weeks of constituency meetings at schools, the hospital, voluntary organisations, conferences and party meetings in preparation for a general election next year. Frank stays in London for a few days. Marion North has invited us to a performance of *The Car Man* at the Old Vic. It's Matthew Bourne's take on *Carmen* and a terrific show. Matthew is an alumnus of Laban and we are privileged to have supper with him and Marion afterwards. Frank has always followed contemporary dance and the contact with Laban will enrich our lives for many years to come.

And so to Brighton for the Labour Party conference. I've up to a dozen events to attend each day, including a few at which I'm performing. Sainsbury's are really taking organics seriously and I chair their 'Organics: the future of farming' meeting, which goes well with lots of excellent questions. The week ends, with a convivial dinner with my CLP delegates who are all buoyed up by the conference speeches.

Construction of the new Laban building is beginning on Creekside – a real triumph for Marion and all of us who are on course to raise the £24 million it will cost. On Wednesday I'm a guest at the Women of the Year lunch and assembly at the Café Royal. It's such a boost to still be thought of as a woman of some influence, even without the ministerial badge.

3 October: An extraordinary comment piece, covering half a page of *The Observer*, by Nick Cohen. He writes extensively about me, criticising my 'adulation' of Blair (!) and my 'complete character transformation' in the job of 'first and probably last full-time Minister for Women'. I can't make out where this has come from until halfway in when he reveals Tony will be at the launch next week of Tessa's report on 'Listening to Women'. He is scathing about Tony's hypocrisy and describes me as 'one of the most talented politicians in the Commons' and praises the policies I introduced!

One interesting comment on my sacking: 'The Downing Street Policy Unit made it clear that feminism had perpetrated the worst of modern crimes by growing up and becoming old'! Poisonous it may be but at least the debate is still alive, and I'm certainly not giving up.

The captain of the *Bowbelle*, the dredger that collided with the *Marchioness*, is giving evidence at Justice Clark's inquiry. Mr Henderson admits drinking six pints and sleeping only three hours before going out to work. The inquiry also heard the ship's cook was so drunk he had gone to sleep and the ship's helmsman wore thick glasses and a hearing aid. Under cross-examination the captain defended his decision not to release the dredger's lifebuoys when he knew his ship had struck another vessel, saying, 'At the time it was not a matter that was one of my top priorities.' What a dreadful testimony for the families to hear. Mr Henderson has been tried twice for failing to keep a proper lookout, but the first jury failed to reach a verdict and the second acquitted him. I find that extraordinary. Selections are well underway for parliamentary seats where MPs have announced they are standing down and it's not looking good for women. Tess Kingham and Jenny Jones have announced they are leaving Westminster after only one term. They and others criticise the hours, the attitudes and the huge difficulties of maintaining any sense of a work/life balance. Predictably this produces a chorus of 'if you can't stand the heat...' etc. rather than any analysis of the way Parliament is organised. The worst thing we can do is go backwards in numbers as only a critical mass of women will ever change this place.

11 October: Tragic news. Donald Dewar has died of a brain haemorrhage.

The following Wednesday I fly up to Glasgow for his funeral. This is an immensely sad occasion. It is a consolation that he did indeed see his dream of a devolved assembly realised and become First Minister, but how tragic that he should be dead just eighteen months later. Frank and I go on to Aberdeen for the weekend and reflect on life and politics.

The House returns. Betty Boothroyd is stepping down from the Speaker's chair and there has been much manoeuvring for her replacement. The favourite is Michael Martin and colleagues are chuffed at the prospect of a former steel welder assuming such high office. My problem with Michael is he hasn't the slightest notion of how to modernise the Commons, which is my passion. I am supporting David Clark and he has asked me to second his nomination. This is quite a responsibility but I've prepared thoroughly and hope I do a good job. Sadly, however, David is not successful, which is an opportunity lost, I'm certain.

Weekends are much taken up with canvassing for a local by-election but on Sunday afternoon I'm going to a private view at Advanced Graphics. They are an excellent company and one of their artists, Albert Irvin, does amazing abstracts with local themes (many years later I'm able to purchase one called 'Deptford' from Pat's Gallery and meet Albert again at his ninetieth birthday).

8 November: I'm on *Woman's Hour* for a discussion on modernisation. Eric Forth is also on. Since Eric speaks forever on Fridays to block Private Members' Bills and is thoroughly reactionary I don't have much competition for a female audience.

Two weeks later I take part in a modernisation debate in Westminster Hall. The government is putting through technical motions to ensure the Westminster Hall (second Chamber) 'experiment' and the Thursday 7 p.m. voting time continue after the election. I support but indicate the need for more changes. Predictably I get attacked by Eric Forth and John Bercow, the arch Tory right-winger.

December begins with a very busy weekend in the constituency. The degree ceremony at Laban is always an enjoyable event, which I'm pleased to attend. In the evening it's the Caribbean Cake event, which is a fundraiser for YouthAID, a project that gives much needed support primarily to black young people. Attending ethic minority events is one of the joys of being the MP for Lewisham Deptford. On one hand it's a duty that takes up my weekends but they're also rewarding. There are regular events put on by the separate Vietnamese groups (the Chinese-speaking and Vietnamese-speaking), Turkish, Tamil, Bangladeshi and Somali groups plus the civic events marking Black History Month. I often reflect that I wouldn't have had this variety if I'd become MP for Torfaen! I've also decided to organise a hearing for the New Cross fire families and survivors for 15 January next year, close to the twentieth anniversary. To do it properly I'm going to need quite a bit of money for transcribers and technicians – hopefully Lewisham Council will help.

6 December: I table another EDM supporting the Food and Farming Targets Bill. This time we get 267 signatures from ten different parties. The government just has to take notice of the groundswell of back-bench opinion. In

between it's SERA, GLOBE, Breast Cancer, the FPA and the launch of a
new campaign called Mast Action. Mobile phone operators are putting up
masts everywhere, often on public buildings and causing outrage among
residents who fear the effects of the radio waves. The science is unclear but
the companies are only concerned with expanding their networks and making money. My instincts are that the precautionary principle should apply.
Sensible proposals are to avoid siting near schools and not to put them on
public housing blocks without consulting local residents.

After much prevarication by No. 10 and lots of pressure from Labour backbenchers, the second reading of the Hunting Bill arrives on 18 December. I am
wholeheartedly in favour and this is the only occasion on which I'm in agreement
with the redoubtable Tory MP Ann Widdecombe, who votes with us. The next
day we have a vote on stem cell research, which I support. We have our staff
party on the 20th and the House rises the next day for the Christmas recess.

## 2001

Back on 8 January and my focus is on the New Cross fire. I've booked the Attlee
Suite and invited a panel of experts. Mike O'Brien (Home Office minister),
Barry Quirk (CEO of Lewisham Council) and Trevor Phillips (chair of the
London Assembly), have all accepted and those survivors and relatives of
the dead who want to speak are all lined up. It's going to be a harrowing occasion and I've needed to emphasise that this is to give public recognition to the
families' accounts and feelings, then and since, not an attempt to solve a crime.

Sunday: The twentieth anniversary service for the New Cross fire families at St Paul's. Father Peter Fellowes is as wonderful as ever.

15 January: I open the hearing, saying:

> Today most of us are convinced that the fire was not the result of a
> white racist attack but I believe there was another type of white crime

committed – the failure of the establishment and wider society to
acknowledge the pain and loss of the black families.

It is unthinkable today that such an event would not have been
immediately recorded in Parliament and condolences sent by the
Prime Minister – yet then nothing was said. For the families, I know
that, second only to the hurt of the loss of their loved ones, was the
hurt of being treated as second-class citizens.

George Francis, as chair of the families group, argues that if the Met cannot
bring prosecutions there has to be a new inquest and if that is not possible
then a public inquiry in which 'witnesses could be called to account for their
actions on the day our children died'. He describes his seventeen-year-old
son Gerry, a musician, and the events of the night of 18 January 1981. It's the
start of a harrowing three hours. Sandra Ruddock, whose 21-year-old husband died that night and who was five months pregnant at the time, gives a
particularly moving testimony and Wayne Haynes, a badly injured survivor,
gives voice to his anger and despair. Mike O'Brien speaks movingly at the
end, promising that their case has been heard and that they will be listened
to when they receive the results of the police inquiry. We are all drained by
the end but I think it has been worthwhile. The young Hansard writers we
employed are shocked by what they have heard.

12 January: Scientists in Oregon report that they have successfully created
the first GM monkey. They boast that they have inserted a jellyfish gene for
fluorescence into the monkey's DNA. Frankly this is sick. Furthermore, they
report that the monkey is not glowing because 'the gene has – for unknown
reasons – not been activated'.

The Freeze was launched two years ago and I do a piece for their
anniversary update. There are now 200 organisations in membership, representing 4 million people. We record that although a moratorium hasn't
been achieved there is very little genetically engineered food openly on sale.

The issue of GM animal feed is being addressed with announcements from Asda, Tesco and M&S that they will phase out GM animal feed from their own-brand products.

I also record that since 1997 back-bench MPs have led twenty-two GM debates, asked 1,600 questions and tabled twenty-five EDMs (I've just done the latest on GM animal feed). This has been an exemplary campaign linking parliamentary and extra-parliamentary activity.

Twenty-eight test sites for GM maize are announced. Together with oil-seed rape and beet sites already designated, there are now seventy-one across Britain. With the assistance of the pressure groups I table increasingly complex questions on the details of the trials.

26 February: Nick Brown comes to the House to report on the first case of foot and mouth disease in the UK for twenty years. Looks as though it might be serious. By the end of the month there's a mass slaughter of pigs and cattle across farms in England. A week later, the PM announces the general election will be postponed because of foot and mouth disease.

Some time ago Mike O'Brien told me the Home Office had a fund for memorials so I consulted the New Cross families and they were keen to apply. We've been successful; £5,000 awarded. The proposal is for a stained-glass window to be erected as part of the renovation at St Andrew's Church where many of the victims were youth club members. This is a real boost. A competition is arranged and a design by Isobel Hopwood is chosen.

I'm finding time for old friends, despite the hectic work schedule. I meet Leila, an Iraqi woman from Imperial. She and her husband now run a successful pharmacy business. Days later I accompany Sabire and Mustapha to a concert at Imperial College. I have great difficulty approaching the building and feel very emotional at the flood of memories of Keith. It was a challenge I had to meet but I won't want to do it again.

We've stepped up campaigning and there's no let-up in the constituency demands, including meetings at Lewisham College and Goldsmiths, opening a 'Girl Talk' exhibition at Lewisham Art House, attending the Women's Day events in Lewisham, followed by a Marsha Phoenix charity dinner. And that's just the first week of March. Also I'm frequently asked to appear on minor political programmes as a result of my many activities – rather more than when I was a minister!

I use the week after Easter for more campaigning and attend a meeting with the Brookmill Action Group who have objections to the Seagar development. After tramping the streets for days I'm glad to get back to Westminster until I get handed a letter from Derek Turner, the head of the new London-wide authority Transport for London. Without any consultation or prior notice, severe restrictions are to be placed on the New Cross Gate road bridge over the railway, a key part of the main A2. This is extraordinary. Heidi contacts Lewisham's council leader, Dave Sullivan, and GLA member Len Duvall, but neither had prior knowledge.

Apparently major weaknesses have been identified within the bridge and Railtrack is to undertake major works to strengthen it. Since my day started with a local arts launch, then DETR questions, a meeting with a group of Indian farmers, then a meeting with an Australian senator regarding breast cancer and finally a London Group meeting, I am not best pleased. We're on running whips until 10 p.m. every night so I sit down later to draft a response. I demand to know when they were first informed by Railtrack and why they didn't consult stakeholders, why the preparatory work started before anyone could respond to the press notice, when the contracts will be let by Railtrack and why they have taken the decision not to signal alternative routes. This is a recipe for chaos. The TfL letter indicates that it is forty-tonne lorries that pose the greatest risk so I ask why the lorries can't be banned from using the bridge until the work is completed.

I'm getting word that we will definitely have fewer women after the next election. Women standing down have been replaced by men so it's crucial retiring men are replaced by women. I ask for the figures. They confirm my worst fears. Where men are standing down in Labour-held seats, only 10 per cent have gone to women candidates. In non-Labour seats that we clearly have no chance of winning, 23 per cent of candidates are women. In Wales, every one of the seats where a Labour MP is standing down has gone to a man. Without all-women shortlists, Labour has reverted to type. So much for our aim of 50:50 selections. Lots of media coverage helped by Angela Browning the Tory shadow Leader of the House. There's been a row in the Tory Party over their abysmal failure to select women and Angela is quoted as saying, 'The overriding perception of what an MP looks like is usually male, with a nice wife doing a bit of work in the background and two dear photogenic children.' She accuses those selecting these candidates of often being 'prejudiced' and 'unprofessional'. Good for her! But, one positive result of our efforts, the government agree to legislate to amend the Sex Discrimination Act.

When TfL reply to my letter, it's obvious they did have time to consult but chose not to. Apparently this is the only route from the coast to central London that is sensible for forty-tonne lorries, which begs the question why they are allowed at all. By far the worst news is the difficulty of obtaining track possessions to demolish the old bridge and erect a new one. Only four weekend closures of the railway are required (services to and from Brighton) but despite Railtrack's ownership of the track they have to get permission from train operating company, Connex, who in theory can refuse for up to two years – a direct consequence of privatising the railways. This is terrible news. I was involved in the negotiation between Railtrack and Connex over the spending of an insubstantial amount from the Sainsbury's 106 agreement and it took three years! I write immediately to both Railtrack and Connex. Matters are further complicated by the fact that Connex has lost the franchise and Govia will take it over in eight weeks' time. My mailbag swells with constituents' complaints and suggestions. In no time I'm told that Sainsbury's have lost 6 per cent of their trade and one of the worst rat runs on Telegraph Hill, Drakefell Road, is gridlocked in rush hour and plagued by thundering lorries throughout the night. Unbelievably we are now being told the ownership of the New Cross Gate bridge is under dispute!

Dave Sullivan and I are meeting Ken Livingstone on 6 June – the day before polling day.

May Day and I'm opening the DAGE shop on Deptford High Street. This is Harry's pride and joy. He never ceases to tell me of his past career as a bank robber but he's definitely made good and with his development officer Tim they have managed to raise a lot of money to provide this drop-in centre for Deptford's elderly.

Next day we do the launch of the New Cross Gate New Deal for Communities (NXNDC). The application from the shadow board to government has been successful, with £45 million awarded for the ten-year programme. This is an extraordinary experiment to be based on local decision-making with local people in control.

*The Sun* has a feature on Tony Blair's telethon when he answered calls direct from the public – the first PM ever to do so. The accompanying photograph is superimposed on a shot taken of other people fielding calls and it's yours truly in the background!

7 June: General election day. This election campaign has gone like clockwork for me. It's my fourth and I know how to organise, how to plan a strategy, write the material and keep up the pressure on members to be active. The only innovation this time is a specific green leaflet detailing my many activities. Having been voted one of the greenest MPs in Westminster, I'm proud to put my record anyway, but Darren Johnson, a credible green activist, is standing for the first time. In the 1997 landslide over 70 per cent of my electorate voted Labour. There's no beating that, so we are bound to lose votes and percentage this time. In the event, my majority is over 15,000 and 65 per cent of the vote, so a happy outcome. Frank also easily retains his seat; though, having lost once, he's been nervous throughout.

The biggest upset in the Cabinet reshuffle is Robin Cook's demotion from the Foreign Office to Leader of the House. I feel really sorry for Robin, who was a real moderniser at the FCO. The small consolation is that he can now be a moderniser of the House. I shall apply for a place on the Modernisation Select Committee.

The House returns on Wednesday when we'll miss some Members and get to know new ones. I've got two urgent tasks. First, to write to David Blunkett, now Home Secretary in place of Jack Straw. The local coroner had written to Jack to ask if he would consider a public inquiry into the New Cross fire. The police have put out a statement today saying they support a new inquest but the coroner says privately she hasn't got the resources required. I write urgently to David.

My second task is to write to Stephen Byers, Patricia Hewitt and Robin Cook about our manifesto commitment to amend the law to permit positive action in the selection of candidates. I've got to press the case for including this in the Queen's Speech. I also send them copies of my Bill.

A prompt reply from John Denham, now the responsible Home Office minister, giving reasons why the department will not set up a public inquiry into the New Cross fire and why a second inquest is the appropriate course. He also offers to look at the issue of resources.

A commitment to legislate for positive action appears in the Queen's Speech. Lots of good media coverage referencing my efforts and a very complimentary letter from the Fawcett Society. A wholehearted welcome too from the EOC – what a change CEO Julie Mellor has made to that institution – followed by a nice letter from Stephen Byers thanking me for all my efforts! But Iain Duncan Smith, a candidate for the Tory leadership, attacks all-women shortlists, saying those elected are not of 'high quality'. I write a letter to *The Guardian* in response to their piece on IDS, which is published. Despite the jibe, he said he wanted more women MPs, so I point out that in the twenty-five Tory-held seats of retirees prior to the general election they failed to select a single woman. Furthermore, until recently, virtually all Tory MPs were selected from men-only shortlists!

11 July: Jean Corston is elected chair of the PLP – the first woman.

Frank and I decide we can miss the week of the Queen's Speech debates, which are always on one-line whips, and go to Aberdeen for a short break at Frank's house in the country. All too quickly I'm back to do a surgery. The caseload always rockets as a result of the election activity but the issues remain largely the same. One by one our major council estates are being renovated and the repairs backlog from the Tory years tackled. The programme brings its own problems of decants and issues of moving back or moving away and a decrease in the number of lettings while the work continues. The Labour government hasn't reversed the ban on council house building and although housing associations are being strongly encouraged, there's a very real shortage of decent property to rent and thousands of families are overcrowded.

Great news for the Stephen Lawrence Trust. The Millennium Commission has awarded them £4.4 million for their planned centre in memory of Stephen. Having had to intervene and bring the two sides together after local people raised objections, I'm so pleased that it will now go ahead.

Ken Livingstone is to introduce a congestion charging scheme in 2003 – first proposed by me in my transport plan for London a decade ago. Excellent.

August is an easier month with just a few meetings and surgeries. One important letter I must get off contains the latest round of complaints from constituents about Deptford station. All Connex's promises came to nothing. After every clean-up there's a slide back into graffiti, litter, urine and general filth. It's an unpleasant place not only for the public but also for the poor clerk who sits in a cold cupboard and who cannot be expected to tackle the multiple offenders. I write again to the MD who only two months ago made a speech about turning the company around.

Six months since the outbreak of foot and mouth, nearly 3.7 million animals have been slaughtered.

One of my party members has loaned us his holiday home in South Africa. We arrive in Cape Town in buoyant mood at the end of August and pick up our hire car. Then we realise it's seriously chilly and we are dressed for the sun. Ivor has given us directions to the local supermarket, so we drive to Fish Hoek where we'll be staying. By now the sky is darkening but the lush vegetation and flowers remind us that we are in a beautiful place and we drive on enthusiastically. The house is delightful but very cold. We read all the instructions left for us but there's no mention of central heating. Of course they wouldn't have expected it to be so cold. Then we spot the fire-place. Frank returns to the mall and finds wood for the fire while I unpack. Frank sets the fire and we look forward to getting warm at last. Suddenly the kitchen fills with choking smoke. We rush to the front room and see black smoke pouring from the fire-grate. It's clear the chimney is blocked off and we may be about to set the house on fire. All doors and windows are now flung open to the freezing weather and a major clean-up is underway. Our first holiday adventure in years has got off to a very bad start.

We survive a couple of miserable days of storms and then make contact with some friends of Ivor who have a wonderful house in what has become known as the Cape's pink quarter. They are so helpful; they say the storms are the worst anyone can remember and a ship has been wrecked in the har-bour. They recommend we go to the arid Little Karoo through the Swartberg Pass, which is not only a wonderful sight but will be warm. They ring ahead and book us a place to stay.

Our holiday begins. The road through the pass is spectacular though scary and all the hillsides are covered with protea in bloom. It's a wonderful sight and we are incredibly cheerful. We thoroughly enjoy our stay with hos-pitable people in interesting properties with excellent food. Eventually, we're told the weather is clearing in Cape Town so we look forward to our return.

As we drive back towards the city we test the car radio for a signal. It comes on and we hear 'They're flying into the second tower.' For a moment we can't understand what we're hearing but the voice is so doom-laden that we know it is a catastrophe. It's 9/11.

We go straight home and put on the television. The feed is coming from the BBC. Like millions of people everywhere we cannot leave our seats. Even-tually we have to get food, but there's no adjusting to this news and no thought that we are here for a holiday. We realise Parliament will be recalled and we will have to return.

Parliament is indeed recalled but airspace is closed for days and there is no prospect of getting a flight. It's unnerving to be so far from home when such a tragedy occurs. Everyone feels unsafe in some way. After several days of obsessively watching TV we decide we have to try to make the best of the week we have left. We drive to Cape Point and explore the rugged scenery and spectacular flora. We indulge ourselves, getting a photograph taken that can be mailed anywhere in the world. We don't know if it will get to my mother but we pay anyway. Mum is one of the few people who would recognise me in the photograph. My head is covered in my natural mass of curls, the exact opposite of the straightened style I usually wear. The battle to keep it straight on holiday in high humidity is too great and, anyway, it's a small gesture towards relaxation, which is so rare for us.

We had let the High Commission know that we were visiting and have a very pleasant introduction to Ann Grant, the delightful High Commissioner. She gives us contacts who arrange for us to visit Parliament (not in session) and a black township, Khayelitsha. We are really keen to see how black people are living as it's quite clear that there is little mixing of black and white in the area where we are staying. I was instantly struck by the separation in the mall. For someone living in Lewisham it was particularly striking – hardly a black shopper in sight, but lots of black workers.

Khayelitsha is of course a different world. Overcrowded, noisy, life on the street. We worry that locals might resent white tourists visiting but we are assured that it's one way to bring some money into the poverty-stricken community. Sure enough we are taken to several shops selling local handicrafts. We talk to the producers. What they really need is a means of marketing outside the township. They certainly have the creative skills and we are happy to buy something from every shop. We are then taken to meet a woman who has pioneered a bed and breakfast scheme and proudly tells us that Peter Hain stayed a night when he was Africa Minister.

We go to the airport knowing that nothing will ever be the same again. For someone with an innate fear of flying it's all too easy to imagine the utter horror of being on one of those planes. Security is tight.

My first day back and I'm off to the Lib Dem conference in Bournemouth to do a Fawcett Society fringe meeting about positive action. The Lib Dems have a really bad record on women's representation and despite their being overlooked there is a strong group of Lib Dem women vehemently opposed to all-women shortlists. They say they only want to be selected on merit – can't they see that's not happening?

A packed few days of fringe meetings at the Labour conference, on women and on environmental issues. All very worthwhile but my heart's not really in it now that Frank and I are not part of the inner circle as we used to be. We plan to leave early but then the conference is curtailed for a second recall of Parliament to debate Afghanistan.

4 October: The PM is presenting the case for supporting the US in military action in Afghanistan. He makes a good one. His statement is followed by a general debate. This is not a debate on which a vote will be taken, though no one doubts that this is the prelude to military action. After six and a half hours I am called by the Speaker.

I say that many of my constituents, while condemning the atrocities, have urged me to speak out against military action. They are right to regard me as a peace-maker, though never a pacifist, but this is not a choice between war and peace; it is a matter of justice. I accept that it's impossible to arrest and try bin Laden and that targeted military action is justified. I quote Tony Blair at party conference calling for a 'reordered world'. I point out that this will be self-defeating if it does not embrace a wider justice. Justice for the Palestinians must be one of its priorities, not only because it is right but because continuing injustices at the heart of the Arab world inevitably produce a recruiting ground for fanatics. I point to the many international treaties that would make our world a safer place that the US has not ratified, including the ABM (Anti-Ballistic Missile) treaty, the International Criminal Court, the Convention on Anti-personnel Mines and the Kyoto protocol on climate change. Too often powerful nations have fuelled regional conflicts to preserve their own economic interests and turned a blind eye to terrible human suffering in countries where they have no similar economic interests.

I warn that though we might need to work with the Northern Alliance now, we must ensure that we do not help them to impose another terrible regime on the people – particularly women – of Afghanistan. I say we must commit ourselves not just to massive humanitarian relief, but also to UN protection and future rebuilding. I end with: 'As ever, the greatest task ahead of the coalition will not be waging the war but winning the lasting peace in the reordered world of which the Prime Minister so eloquently spoke.' Two hours later we are on our way home with heavy hearts. By Sunday, US and UK forces have begun military action. Kabul, Jalalabad and Kandahar are under attack, and Parliament is recalled for the third time.

A bombshell from the coroner. She says she cannot conduct a new inquest into the New Cross fire. While acknowledging that the fresh evidence is significant she does not think it is likely to change the original verdict. She says there is neither the staffing nor the funds within the service to conduct such a complex inquest and ends: 'I can see that it may be necessary or desirable for this case to be the subject of judicial investigation of some sort. However, in my view, the case is quite unique and totally unsuited to the present inquest system.' Where do we go from here?

The pressures in the constituency are quite excessive. I'm at the Laban Development Council one day, the New Deal for Communities the next, then a visit to Deptford station with Connex staff and an important meeting with the chairman of News International about Convoys Wharf. They have agreed to scrap the plans drawn up by their architects that drew so much criticism and have engaged Richard Rogers to produce a master plan. This is good news.

I get a letter from Connex re. Deptford station, dated 10 October, replying to my letter of 3 August – from a 'Communications Officer'. She says, 'Oliver has asked me to reply but if after reading my letter you still wish for a reply from him, please let me know.' Where do these people come from? (Actually the answer is France!) I'm told they are trying to recruit platform staff and that they will be making improvements including repainting, improved CCTV and improved lighting, to be completed by April next year. What a farce. Whatever people said about British Rail they were never as bad as this lot.

Now, Railtrack has gone into administration – another disgraceful episode following privatisation. The Tories set up this extraordinary group of companies to own the tracks post-British Rail. Earlier this year, when they were making a loss, partly due to compensation paid out for the Hatfield rail crash, they went to government for a bailout and promptly paid £137 million in dividends to their shareholders. Ours is obviously just a small matter but my immediate concern is just what is going to happen to the New Cross Gate bridge works. It's only a matter of weeks since I heard that TFL has got an agreement with them to start work in December.

A very unusual appointment on Friday. The Museum of Garden History has arranged for a number of well-known people to have their portraits taken in their gardening clothes. I'm really flattered to be asked. There's nothing special about my gardening clothes but I've taken to wearing Marigolds (yellow rubber household gloves) rather than gardening gloves. This is because I like to keep my hands dry as my limited time for my favourite hobby means I have to go out in all weathers. The result is a very pleasing, rather humorous portrait giving prominence to the Marigolds. Thrilling to see it exhibited at the museum on a subsequent visit.

15 October: The House returns, fortunately not until the afternoon as I'm off to the Women of the Year luncheon again. I don't know how long I can expect such invitations but I do enjoy going and invariably sit with really interesting women. We're also back to meetings of the Modernisation Select Committee. Robin is great. He's full of ideas and enthusiasm and all of us Labour Members are keen to push the agenda. I get a long article on women's equality in the October edition of *The House* magazine.

The weeks pass with the routine of oral questions, select committee meetings and debates, most importantly the second reading of the Equal Representation Bill. I make a substantial speech and get put onto the standing committee of the Bill. I also host a lunch for Laban at the House of Commons addressed by the director of the Guggenheim Museum in Bilbao. Great to hear how the arts can aid regeneration.

But, despite all the ongoing commitments, I'm turning my attention to Afghanistan. The post-conflict activities of the international community will be critical and I am certain women will be bypassed. For years I've supported international campaigns in support of Afghan women, terrorised and abused by the Taliban regime. Lakhdar Brahimi has been appointed UN Special Representative for Afghanistan and he will be key to any talks involving interested parties to a post-Taliban government. I start asking the FCO and DfID what steps will be taken to involve women. I get a positive answer from Clare Short.

I get drawn for PMQs, which is a great chance to ask the PM about Afghan women. There is much interest in the formation of a post-Taliban government but undoubtedly the focus is on suitable men. I ask him to acknowledge that there are many courageous and able Afghan women in Afghanistan and in exile and ask him to examine the models of female participation that paved the way for women's involvement in the transitions in South Africa and Northern Ireland. Sniggers from some Tory men but those processes were crucial in ensuring women broke through the barriers to political participation.

Tony begins uncomfortably by saying that female participation would indeed be an innovation in Afghanistan … like most other people he is ignorant of the history of Afghan women in Parliament and as doctors and teachers and sees them only as victims of the Taliban. I keep up a barrage of written questions to the FCO and DFID, all aimed at making ministers aware that Afghan women want their rights.

Simon Carr in *The Independent* takes a pot shot at me for my PMQ, prompting me to write a letter to the editor, pointing out that Afghan women had the vote in 1965, electing five women then and seven again in 1988.

Nearer to home, the women's movement in Northern Ireland, helped by Mo Mowlam, successfully forced their way into the political process when all the elected representatives were men.

I write a similar letter to *The Guardian*, which had also commented some-what inaccurately on my question. In this I add that in the case on Northern Ireland, fourteen women were subsequently elected to the Northern Ireland Assembly and this year three women from Northern Ireland were elected to Westminster – the first in thirty years.

November: We've managed to track down an active Afghan community organisation in Harrow where the organiser, Sami Aziz, has agreed to Heidi and me visiting. Sami has invited a lot of women. I ask him if he would mind not joining us and after a momentary hesitation he agrees. It is one of the most extraordinary meetings I have ever held. The women are all different, of all ages, some with head scarves, some soberly dressed, others very fashion-ably. They pour out their stories and pass around photographs. The oldest woman could remember the reign of the last Afghan king who introduced a liberal constitution and an experiment with democracy in 1964. When he was overthrown in 1973 a succession of leaders of pro-Marxist regimes instituted numerous reforms. The chador was banned, forced marriage was banned and by 1978 women were accorded equal rights to education, jobs, health services and political participation. Constant struggles for leadership and coups meant the country was never at peace and tens of thousands of people were killed. Despite this I was meeting women with professional qualifica-tions who were showing me pictures of themselves enjoying city life in Kabul sporting miniskirts and looking very much as I did at their age. Many of these women had come to Britain as refugees, decades ago. Then there were the most recent arrivals, women who had survived the brutal Taliban regime that followed the fall of the communist regime in 1992 and its replacements by warring factions of US-backed mujahideen. I know about the Taliban and how they had effectively imprisoned women in their own homes. But to hear from these articulate women how they were not allowed to leave their homes unless in the company of a male – even a young son would do – how they were banned from working and their daughters banned from school was very moving. Some of the youngest women, most recently arrived, had been university students whose classes closed and who then risked their lives running underground schools to educate female children.

I am often close to tears listening to their testimonies. Their greatest concern now is for families left behind and for Afghanistan. They know that their country is in ruins. They all want to do something and for our government to understand Afghanistan and its peoples. I promise to do what I can and explain that I am already in touch with ministers and with the EU, trying to find out what provision will be made for women's participation in post-conflict negotiations.

I decide to set up an organisation to support my parliamentary work on Afghanistan. With everything else I do this will be a struggle but I can't think of anything more important. Ten days later Heidi and I have an organisation ready to launch. We call it the UK Women's Link with Afghan Women (UKWLAW).

9 November: Mazar-i-Sharif has fallen. The Taliban have withdrawn. Crucially, the aid organisations will now be able to distribute food to the 6 million people thought to be facing starvation. There is mounting criticism of the US use of cluster bombs and Pakistan's call to halt the bombing sends Bush to the UN.

13 November: Kabul has fallen. Last night the Taliban fled under cover of darkness and today Northern Alliance forces have arrived in the city. Most other Taliban strongholds will fall within days to a variety of warlords and their private armies, but tens of thousands of Taliban soldiers have disappeared. Around 2,000 Al-Qaeda and Taliban fighters are holed up in caves in the Tora Bora mountains, but repeated air strikes by the US fail to find their chief target, Osama bin Laden.

Despite my focus on Afghanistan, I have to sit on the first meeting of the committee stage of the Sex Discrimination (Election Candidates) Bill. We'll have two sessions a day, two days a week. It will be fun seeing the Tories and Lib Dems speaking against it.

I've got a number of prominent women to form an advisory board for the Link, including Jenni Murray, Glenys Kinnock, Annette Lawson of the Women's National Commission, Lesley Abdela of Project Parity, the writer Jean Stead and the Conservative MP Angela Watkinson. I'm also in touch with Afghan support organisations from many other countries and share websites and contacts with our members. We also encourage Members to support Afghan Aid, a charity specifically working with Afghan women.

We tip off various journalists and prepare to launch the Link on 13 November. I do *Woman's Hour* in the morning and invite my new Afghan women contacts to come and meet MPs. The women's stories are a surprise to many. These are not only refugees from the Taliban but from the mujahideen who took control after the defeat of the Russian-backed government and who imposed brutal conditions including rapes, sacking women teachers, removing all women from higher education and forcing parents to give their daughters to soldiers. Women are particularly concerned that the Northern Alliance, the current 'liberators' of Kabul, are many of the same men from those times.

Natasha Walter writes an excellent article in which she tells some of the women's stories and their concerns for the post-Taliban settlement. She gives details of the Link. The *Evening Standard* has an article headed 'Burqua Liberation is a Con', which gives me an opportunity to point out yet again that the oppression of women predates the Taliban and that's why Western women are pressing the international community to include women in the talks as it can't be left to those Afghans now in control.

My EDM on Afghanistan is going well, with increasing numbers of MPs signing. I send copies to ministers and get a good response. Other Labour women are also asking PQs, all of which elicit cautious responses. We are joined by Jenny Tonge from the Lib Dems. I can just imagine the civil servants sighing over those annoying feminists who are always going on about women when there is the important business of sorting out which men get what in the post-war settlement.

My attention has been drawn to UN Security Council resolution 1325. Adopted a year ago, it contains eighteen action clauses all relevant to the situation in Afghanistan. This should be the driver of the international community's behaviour but I doubt if many of the men negotiators have heard of it. Clause 8 'calls on all actors involved, when negotiating and implementing peace agreements, to adopt a gender perspective' and, in subclause (b), to 'involve women in all of the implementation mechanisms of the peace agreements'.

Lots of media interest over the next few days. Our aims are to raise awareness of Afghan women, to work towards their inclusion in any future government of Afghanistan and for the full restoration of their human rights. The first target is to get Afghan women included in the UN-sponsored talks that will take place in Bonn next month. These talks are for Afghan politicians to elect an interim president. We contact women parliamentarians in the Commons, House of Lords, Scottish Parliament and Welsh Assembly as well as our MEPs. Altogether we get 153 women parliamentarians signed up in support and send off our letter to Brahimi.

Women in Brussels are ahead of the game. They have decided to organise a conference of women alongside the official conference and I get invited. Fortunately, Maggie Coulthard, my former staff member, who is now working in the Parliament, is on hand to help with all the logistics.

4 & 5 December: The programme for the women's summit is really exciting. Fifty Afghan women are attending, many from exile in Pakistan. Pressure from women around the world has led to three Afghan women being included in the official talks and they will also join us. There are twenty-five women activists including me who are coming from the USA and Europe. The summit is being held in collaboration with the Gender Advisor to the UN Special

Envoy to Afghanistan, an excellent woman called Fatiha Serour, and UNI-FEM. Guest speakers include Mary Robinson, UN High Commissioner for Human Rights, and Eve Ensler, the American playwright whose V-Day performances have been funding Afghan women's projects for years.

Such an inspiring couple of days and the three women who have attended the official talks are optimistic. They expect to secure a Ministry for Women and to get some women appointed to other posts in the interim administration. They know they will have to be pushing all the time and preparing for the loya jirga (traditional Afghan meeting) that will follow and the commission that will work on the constitution. Sima Wali acknowledges the importance of the great pressure being exerted by women internationally and urges us to continue our support. She is particularly concerned that the Ministry of Reconstruction and Rehabilitation should involve women and is properly resourced. She urges Afghan women in exile to return. In Pakistan alone there is a fifty-strong group of Afghan women lawyers and she places particular emphasis on Afghan- and women-led NGOs and urges women not to emulate men's political leadership.

At the end of the summit we adopt the Brussels Proclamation. The key demands are:

- the right for women to vote and to be entitled to equal pay and equal access to healthcare, education and employment;
- an emergency plan for the reopening of schools by March 2002 for both girls and boys, a new curriculum and training for teachers;
- the inclusion of Afghan women lawyers in the development of a new constitution, which would include the principles of non-discrimination;
- the rebuilding of hospitals and provision of vital medicines, treatments and services, including psychological counselling and childcare;
- central inclusion of women in the loya jirga; and

Four generations at my Aunty Audrey's wedding in February 1950 (*left to right*): My mother, me, my great-grandmother and grandmother

Keith and me at the May Ball, Imperial College, 1961

Marrying Keith, St James's Church, Pontypool, 1963

1978 Labour Party poster of me speaking at a party conference

CND demonstration against US Cruise missiles, Trafalgar Square, 1980

ABOVE LEFT Controversy at the CAB, 1983

ABOVE RIGHT TUCND rally at Barrow shipyards, 1984

Election 1987, with agent Jim Stevenson and Maggie Coulthard

All the family (*left to right*): My father Ken, husband Keith, sister Susan, me with nephew Nick, brother-in-law David, mother Eileen with grandson Ben and Keith's mother, Vi

LEFT  Our silver wedding anniversary, 1988

RIGHT  Goldsmiths Honorary Fellowship with Hon. Fellows Andy Hawkins and Sybil Phoenix, 1996

At the National Portrait Gallery exhibition of photographs from their book *Faces of the Century*, including this one of Glenys Kinnock and me chosen by Helena Kennedy, 1999

ABOVE With women engineers on site at the Millennium Dome, 1998 © PRESS ASSOCIATION

RIGHT My mother at her eightieth birthday party with her sisters, Audrey and Bette, and their husbands, Ted and Ray, 2000

Meeting with Soraya
Perlika and colleagues
in the grounds of
the British embassy,
Kabul, 2002

Children imprisoned
with their mother in
Kabul, 2002

Afghan children in the
ruins of Kabul, 2002

ABOVE British Council Exchange visit to Zambia with Rose Banda MP, 2003

LEFT At the illegal Israeli wall in Palestine with John Bercow and Shirley Williams, 2004

With Chancellor Gordon Brown, minister Phil Hope and Principal Ruth Silver (*far right*) and students at Lewisham College, 2006

With Mary Robinson at the House of Commons, 2006

Launch of Harriet Harman's deputy leadership campaign, 2007

IDC visit to Ethiopia with a
local health worker, 2007

Minister for Biodiversity
with a golden eagle, 2007

Minister for Energy and
Climate Change in the
Arctic, 2009

Frank and me at our wedding reception, 2010

Tea with Aung San Suu Kyi at the Speaker's
House, 2012

LEFT The start of the Lewisham NHS protests with Heidi Alexander MP (later shadow Secretary for Health) and Jos Bell at Lewisham Clocktower, 2012

LEFT With the ICAN team at the conference on the humanitarian consequences of nuclear weapons, 2014

BELOW At Lewisham Town Hall to receive the Freedom of the Borough 2016 (*l to r*): Baroness Doreen Lawrence, Mayor of Lewisham Sir Steve Bullock, me, husband Frank, Heidi Alexander MP, former MP Bridget Prentice, Vicky Foxcroft MP and Rt Hon. Harriet Harman MP QC

- the protection of women from forced underage marriages and sexual harassment.

Our parallel meeting of women's rights activists produces a statement aimed at our own governments and the UN. The two declarations give us the clearest possible basis for all our future work. Little do I realise that I will indeed continue this work until the five-year programme outlined in Bonn comes to an end.

I return even more inspired and ready for the conference Heidi and I have organised for next Monday – UN Human Rights Day. We prepare a proposal in advance that we will put to the meeting at the end and also circulate the Brussels Proclamation.

Our conference is a great success. The London Afghan women tell their stories, which are heart-rending. They are all professional women or students who had to flee their country but have a deep feeling for it no matter how long they have been away. The main thrust of the afternoon is to look at the role of women post-conflict. Dorothy Mogotsi from the South Africa High Commission gives her account of the African experience and Lesley Abdela her experience of Kosovo.

We hear from Afghan Aid about women's projects in Afghanistan and from the head of the UN Information Centre in London on their view of the future.

Our proposal focusing on the international funds for Afghanistan is adopted unanimously. We urge the UK government and the UN to make the funds conditional on:

- the participation by women in decision-making over the granting of funds;
- the inclusion of women non-governmental organisations among recipients of the funds; and
- the use of the funds for implementation of the priorities outlined in the Brussels proclamation.

Two Afghan women are appointed to head ministries. Dr Suhaila Seddiqi is a medical doctor who apparently had a position in the military that enabled her to continue to practise when others were banned. She is to head the Health Ministry, and Dr Sima Samar, who I think is a lawyer, will be Minister for Women. I write to congratulate them both.

The Bonn conference concludes by agreeing to set up an Interim Authority and an International Security Assistance Force (ISAF). It also proposes an Afghan Constitution Commission, a loya jirga and the use of the 1964 constitution as the basis for a new constitution to be adopted by 4 January 2004. Hamid Karzai is chosen to be the chairman of the Interim Authority.

12 December: I take a delegation of Afghan women to meet Clare Short to discuss her department's support. She is launching a DfID project to fund girls' education in Afghanistan. Now No. 10 want in on the act and have asked me to find some Afghan women for a meeting where Cherie Blair will speak. Wahida Zalmai and Alia Zemaryalai agree to go.

The next day I have an adjournment debate on women's involvement in a post-Taliban government. This is my chance to lay down some markers as to what Afghan women expect and how the international community should support them. Knowing the battles we have, as women MPs, I've no confidence in our (largely male) diplomats' commitment to women's equality. One of the especially interesting contacts that has come up as a result of this work is V-Day, established by the American writer and activist Eve Ensler, who visited Afghanistan while the Taliban were in control. I've been asked to work with the committee who put on her iconic play *The Vagina Monologues*.

The chair of the New Cross Gate New Deal for Communities has resigned. I'm asked to take it on. This is the last thing I need, but they are desperate, and so I agree.

A rush of final meetings, a flurry of PQs on GMOs and Afghan women, the annual carol service and I'm off for a pre-Christmas few days in Aberdeen before we go to my mother's as usual.

## 2002

The Afghan work is now taking a huge amount of time as we are determined to keep abreast of everything that is developing in the international community and use the two Brussels statements and UN resolution 1325 to determine our programme.

I've called a meeting of our advisory group as there are some fundamental issues to sort out. We need money to finance our activities and already 300 women have signed up. We agree to set a minimum membership fee of £5. Many people contacting us want to raise money for Afghanistan but we decide we don't want to fundraise ourselves but will direct all efforts to Afghan Aid. Support is coming in from all over the country with women asking for advice on local activities and requesting Afghan women speakers. Fortunately, Wahida and Alia are very willing to do this.

14 January: Britain declares itself free of foot and mouth disease.

The EOC has published a damning report on discrimination in the selection of parliamentary candidates by all political parties. Eighty-one per cent of Conservative women and 60 per cent of Labour women candidates interviewed agreed that their party's selection process displayed a pro-male bias. The report makes a series of recommendations and refers to the scope for positive action that will be open to all parties as a result of new legislation. Vindication!

Managed to get through to speak to Sima Samar, the new Afghan Minister for Women's Affairs, in Kabul. She told me she was operating out of her front room with a satellite phone and a PC but no staff and no office. I immediately sent a letter to Clare Short who was attending the donor conference in Tokyo alerting her to this and tabled a question for Clare's orals next week.

I get a good response from Clare. She says she spoke with the President of the World Bank, and the UK and others will provide direct funding for the Ministry of Women's Affairs. This is a real breakthrough. I'm at the hairdresser's at 9 a.m. as I'll be on show all day and need to look my best. Back at the office two hours later to meet the Afghan women and take them to No. 10. Early evening I'm meeting Shukria, who wants to become an MP in Afghanistan, if ever such a thing becomes possible again. In the afternoon a brief introduction to Hamid Karzai, the interim President of Afghanistan, and to my great pleasure Sima Samar. The day ends with my attending a dinner at the FCO – a pleasant recognition of the huge amount of work I'm doing on Afghanistan. I sit next to the Defence Minister who spears his meat with his own knife and speaks little.

Constituency casework never stops. Much is routine but I've just received an extraordinary letter from a woman who writes that in 1958 she was expecting twins. Several times during clinic visits at Lambeth Hospital she was asked if she thought she could manage two babies, to which she gave assurances. When the babies were born, she says a boy and a girl were given to her and subsequently she and a nurse took them into a lift to travel to the ward. When the doors opened, another nurse was waiting with a pram and took both babies away. Later, just the boy baby was brought to the ward and thereafter, whenever she asked where her daughter was, she was told they didn't know and hadn't been on duty. It's the most extraordinary story, but it seems very unlikely someone would make this up after forty-four years. We will search records and track down her gynaecologist and follow every lead for the next four years to no avail. In desperation the constituent goes to the press and weeks later a woman comes forward. She lives locally and was adopted as a baby by a nurse now dead. Everything seems to fit and my constituent accepts her as her long-lost daughter.

We succeed in helping hundreds of people but it's the tragedies that you fail with that stick in the mind. We've had to give up on a Nigerian man whose children have been abandoned by their mother back home. The authorities here won't accept that he is their sole surviving relative and all our representations have come to nothing. I have more hope for a woman from Sierra Leone who thought her husband and children had been killed in the civil war. She has now been told her children are alive. We've already spent a year trying to get them into the UK. These lengthy, ongoing cases require a great deal of commitment from caseworkers, though of course we do get a lot of satisfaction if the outcome is positive.

This week I have an important meeting with the CEO of the NDC, a school visit, the funeral of a local activist, a meeting with the council leader about the Somali community's needs, a walkabout on Convoys and a Friday advice surgery. Chair of the shadow board of the NDC is a daunting task. The board is unlike any other, being composed of ten elected local residents and ten representatives from various sectors, some of whom have very little commitment to the project. We have a possible spend of £6 million in the current year and many conflicting priorities in the wish list of the residents.

Friday morning I'm at a meeting at Midi Music, one of Deptford's gems, which is led by the amazing entrepreneur Wozzy Brewster, a statuesque black woman. It's an academy of jazz and popular music, nurturing talent and enabling them to get employment in the music industry. A real dose of inspiration, followed by a rush to Paddington and a weekend women's conference in Cardiff to which I'm taking Sabah, a young Afghan woman only recently in the UK. We're both speaking.

February sees the usual round of daily meetings, debates and questions on all my current issues, ending with my mum arriving in London and all of us going to Chinese New Year celebrations followed by the half-term recess and a weekend in Scotland. A welcome pause and then back to London and new priorities. I need to do more work on GLOBE and on the Laban Development Council. These are major responsibilities and I devote the next few weeks to them.

26 February: The Sex Discrimination (Election Candidates) Bill is passed into law.

There is continuing turmoil over secondary education in Lewisham. We have so many different kinds of schools. Two current battles are underway – to halt personal interviews in the voluntary-aided schools and to secure a new, non-selective secondary school in north Lewisham. A local GP in my constituency has started a campaign for a new school in New Cross. She has a lot of backing in Telegraph Hill and the council really needs to respond. I arrange to meet her and other campaigners as I've been pressing the case myself for some time.

Demolition has begun on the Silwood Estate. This is one of Lewisham's successful bids to central government. One by one our depressing council estates are being completely refurbished or rebuilt. Silwood has been one of the least pleasant places to live but it will now be transformed at a cost of around £70 million. This is one of the best things the government is doing, alongside huge investment in schools and hospitals after decades of Tory neglect. The only quarrel I have with them is the failure to invest in new builds. We have so many overcrowded families and while whole estates are renewed it doesn't increase the number of properties available.

I am able to maintain contact with Sima Samar and Fatiha Serour in Kabul so we get first-hand information, which I use in a constant stream of letters, PQs, EDMs and the occasional speech. We have a clear list of demands from the Afghan Women's Ministry, which we disseminate in our monthly newsletter as well. Priorities include legal processes and transparent mechanisms for the loya jirga, a minimum 25 per cent representation of women at the loya jirga and full women's representations in elections.

Heidi and I organise a successful roundtable on women's political participation in the reconstruction process in Afghanistan, attended by government officials, academics, NGOs and members of UKWLAW. Our opening speakers are three women who are visiting the UK, sponsored by the FCO. The latter are immensely grateful to us for facilitating the contacts and enabling officials to access women's opinions. These courageous women give first-hand accounts of the huge difficulties faced by Afghan women trying to get their voices heard in Kabul. As a result, I co-author a paper, which we circulate to 100 women's organisations worldwide. I also meet Dr Abdullah Abdullah, the Afghan Foreign Minister.

In between all these activities we're getting a new website up and running and also doing lots of campaigning for the local government elections on 2 May.

31 March: The crucial emergency loya jirga in Afghanistan is to take place in June in Kabul. Only 160 of the 1,450 seats have been allocated to women. I send urgent emails to President Karzai and to Brahimi pointing out that the Ministry of Women's Affairs (after a consultation with women all over the country) has called for a quota of 25 per cent and 30 per cent is the UN norm for post-conflict situations. We also launch a petition detailing the Afghan women's demands, including requiring everyone appointed to the Transitional Authority (which will happen as a result of the loya jirga) to sign a personal declaration that includes respect for women's rights.

Unusually, I've got two foreign trips planned. My interest in green energy has got me a place on the PRASEG (Parliamentary Renewable and Sustainable Energy Group) delegation to Germany, ably led by Alan Whitehead. In three days we get briefings from ministers, officials and the European Wind Association. It is extraordinary what they are doing on both wind and solar. Driving down a motorway we see miles and miles of turbines lining the route. Officials tell us that the state undertook and won a referendum proposing 1 per cent of land be devoted to alternative energy. Instead of opposition they then found that tourism increased as people perceived their environment to be clean as well as beautiful. What a difference between UK and German attitudes – or is it just our failure to plan appropriately and choose the right narrative?

My second trip is also environmental – to the GLOBE Europe conference in Stockholm. There we concentrate on sustainable development issues in preparation for this summer's Johannesburg summit. A Westminster Hall debate on renewable energy enables me to focus on the developing world. I express concern at the financing of fossil fuel projects abroad and argue, in line with GLOBE's campaign, that 10 per cent of the UK Export Credit

Guarantee's budget should go to renewable energy projects. I'm delighted when later in the year it is announced that £50 million a year will be allocated for such projects.

The Met are in the High Court arguing for a new inquest into the New Cross fire. It's twenty-one years since the event and five years since I first approached the police for a new investigation.

The Modernisation Select Committee is making great progress under Robin's leadership and I never miss a meeting if I can avoid it. Select committee memberships are negotiated by the whips, who exercise immense patronage and hand out places as rewards to those who do their bidding. We are proposing a package of reforms, the most radical of which is an independent committee to appoint select committee members. I speak in the debate and Robin is excellent as always but we get defeated – the work of our own whips! It's taught us a lesson – we will have to organise if we want to win future modernisation proposals. The package we are working on is hugely exciting: changes to the parliamentary year, the hours of sitting, greater scrutiny of legislation and making question times more topical. Poor Robin – he's getting lots of stick in Cabinet!

At last we are getting some tangible results for the New Deal. We've got an outline design for the refurbishment of a local park – a priority identified by residents – and we have set up a series of consultations. There is also a desire to get neighbourhood wardens into the area. There's a pilot already operating on Honor Oak estate and they would be an asset in this area with its high prevalence of antisocial behaviour. All projects have to be tested against the agreed objectives of the community plan drawn up by the board. It's a hugely complicated matter for the appraisal panel who can easily be subject to undue pressure by individuals.

I've also set up a roundtable for stakeholders in New Cross Road. I've had to keep up constant representations to Railtrack, Connex and TfL but I think there's a wider agenda to be pursued about future plans for the station and its environs, involving Sainsbury's and Goldsmiths College.

11 June: The loya jirga is being convened in Kabul to elect the transitional government. Though women's numbers are small, they are determined to make an impact. Dr Massouda Jalal – a paediatrician and elected delegate from Kabul – has secured enough support to be a candidate for the presidency. This is extraordinary and though she has no chance against Karzai her courage is hugely symbolic. After decades of bitter civil war, 2 million women are thought to be heading fatherless households and they are the poorest of the poor. Dr Massouda should know – she works for the UN food programme.

On the second day, sixty or seventy delegates walk out of the loya jirga angry at the back-room deals and the presence of warlords (backed by gunmen) at the great meeting. Sima Samar, the current Women's Minister, adds to the drama and is quoted as saying, 'This is not democracy: it's a rubber stamp.' This is a very dangerous thing to say. She has already been the subject of vicious verbal attacks and police intimidation for speaking out against the burqa and violence. Within days and on the eve of ministerial appointments, Sima is accused of being 'Afghanistan's Salman Rushdie'. This is very frightening and we all fear for her safety. A week later the Supreme Court throws out a blasphemy charge against her but the damage is done. The religious establishment openly accuse her, and Karzai swears in a new Cabinet without a Minister for Women's Affairs.

The international community has got to focus on helping to build institutions and the rule of law, and I must keep up the pressure on the UK government. Fortunately, Mike O'Brien is very responsive, as is Sir Jeremy Greenstock, our permanent representative at the UN. I write to them both raising the issues of violence and the need for an extension of ISAF (the international security force set up last year and initially led by the UK).

July is proving to be an impossible month. One day I'm at the reopening of our Broadway Theatre by the Queen, another the topping-out ceremony of the new (giant) Lewisham police station and yet another at Lewisham People's Day. In between, there's *The Soul of Black Music* at the Albany and the opening night of the Greenwich Festival as well as numerous routine visits.

Now council officials, the Mayor of Lewisham and I are getting a briefing at the Richard Rogers partnership on the Convoys Wharf proposals. They are keen to get ahead and submit an outline planning application as soon as possible. The plans are clearly better than the previous ones and provide better integration with the local area and a proper mix of employment and housing, but there is so much more that remains to be done and I know there will be objections to the three very high towers proposed. I will be involved in this site for years to come.

Predictably, the New Cross Gate NDC board is mired in controversy and our CEO and Lewisham's director of regeneration are also at loggerheads. Getting all the processes in place to handle £45 million over ten years responsibly and meet local aspirations is a very tall order. There was lots of training, workshop provision and handing out of computers to be undertaken even before we could really start functioning. My position is also being challenged by a few and it would be easier to quit than stay but I know it's too important to put my own interests first.

I call an emergency meeting and the post of independent unpaid chair is confirmed. I agree to stay until someone is appointed. We also have to start the onerous process of advertising and interviewing for the permanent CEO. I expect that Ann, the interim CEO, will apply and stay, but it's not to be. By mid-August I'm taking phone calls and dictating letters from my holiday in Italy as we agree Ann will leave at the end of the month, leaving us without a CEO until October.

In the Commons, John Prescott makes a statement on sustainable communities, enabling me to make a plea for more affordable housing. I've been doing this all year and was part of an earlier women's delegation to Tony Blair on the same issue. In Lewisham we now have 1,800 homeless families in temporary accommodation. Annual lettings run at around the same level, making it impossible for people on the normal waiting list to get a home. Thousands of properties have been sold under right to buy – a policy we ought to stop until a new building programme is underway. John announces a £1.6 billion spend over the next three years but I fear it's too little too late.

August: Back from holiday I immediately leave for Johannesburg. In April GLOBE Europe drew up a set of demands for the summit and I'm now going to attend the GLOBE International meeting, which will run alongside the main conference. We've got IPU (Inter-Parliamentary Union) sponsorship, which means a business class flight and a comfortable hotel. At the airport we are met by amazing young people in colourful dress in ANC colours, all greeting us and assisting with directions. Large numbers of such young volunteers will be present throughout the summit and provide the model for the UK Olympics in 2012. The GLOBE demands are detailed and specific about halving poverty by 2015; combatting climate change, beginning with ratification of the Kyoto protocol (UK did in May) and support for renewables; promoting reform of the WTO and fair and sustainable trade; halving by 2015 the proportion of people denied safe drinking water; and securing transparency and accountability in decision-making. The UK government has a progressive agenda and invites us to frequent briefings. They are trying very hard to negotiate a commitment on renewable energy.

On the plane back to Heathrow I put it all out of my mind as anxiety overtakes me. I'm going to Afghanistan in less than a week's time. At the suggestion of Fatiha Serour, gender advisor to the UN Special Representative, I am spending a week in Kabul. I am keen to go but equally very apprehensive. I don't know of any other politician who's been there except the PM, who spent three hours at Bagram airbase in January. I have agreed to pay for my flight to and from Dubai from where I will travel on a UN plane to Kabul and stay at the embassy.

I travel comfortably to Dubai but then spend a few anxious hours finding and waiting for a UN flight. As these flights are not publically available there is some uncertainty about everything and no tickets or seat allocation. It's also a rather small and old-looking plane. Everything is basic and one cabin attendant is available to serve us juice. I try to calm myself and make conversation with the woman who is alongside me in the front seat. As we reach the high mountains surrounding Kabul, she (thankfully) warns me the plane will make a steep descent to avoid rocket attack. We land and I am bundled into an armoured jeep on the tarmac. I'm ordered to stay inside while British soldiers point their weapons at the luggage handlers and get them to retrieve my case from the cage into which it's just been thrown. Quick introductions, then I go to fasten my seatbelt. 'Don't do it,' I'm told – I have to be ready to get to the floor if there's an incident. As we travel I get a security briefing. This is serious stuff. Everyone is on alert; checkpoints and devastation are everywhere. It's fiercely hot for me but Afghans on the streets are wearing heavy coats. We approach the embassy – great concrete fortifications scattered everywhere as we zigzag in. This is no ordinary embassy. There's one intact stone building, a few tumbledown outhouses and Portakabins. The ambassador greets me warmly and tells me I will be able to do a really useful job engaging with Afghan women. I get another security briefing and am shown to the Portakabin that will be my home for the next week. I'm told that in the event of shots being fired or bombs dropped I'm to stay where I am and await rescue – 'we will get you out safely'! Food is also very basic but I'm so glad to get a solid meal and then fall into an exhausted sleep. I will have a very full programme every day and be accompanied by two bodyguards – I won't be walking anywhere!

At breakfast I learn of the fate of our embassy. Apparently we used to have a very fine one but withdrew after the Russian invasion, leaving it in the hands of the Pakistani government, so the present 'residence' is this tumbledown complex that was previously a hospital. Everyone has a tale to tell. Our cook was the last person in the original embassy and removed all the silver, keeping it hidden until he could return it last year (he would subsequently get an MBE). Ron Nash, the ambassador, is also a character and a risk-taker for sure. He's not allowed to have any of his family accompany him or even visit.

As we drive to my various appointments I see the devastation of war. Everywhere there is rubble, bombed-out buildings and makeshift homes. Shipping containers are beautifully painted with abstract and floral designs in bright colours offering shade and a place to sell poor products or possibly sleep. Plastic sheeting is everywhere and there are buckets at standpipes. The streets are swarming with people on the move on foot amid all the dust and filth. Broken-down taxis ply for trade. There are hardly any private cars, just army vehicles or UN white 4x4s. Everywhere noise and smells of sweet spices, bad (non-existent) drains and heat. I struggle to stay awake, even with all the stimulus of my first day. I'm also covered from head to foot in my special wardrobe. Most women are still wearing the blue burkas, which must be utterly suffocating.

The statistics on Afghanistan are staggering. Two million people in the north could run out of food by the end of the year. Seventy-five per cent have no access to toilet facilities, 25 per cent of Afghan children die before their fifth birthday and the country has the world's highest rate of maternal mortality. Despite the ongoing lack of infrastructure, 1 million refugees are returning from the camps in Pakistan and Iran. But progress in some areas is acknowledged. There's been a major landmine clearance (though many have lost limbs), fresh water supplies are being restored, schools rebuilt and nearly 3 million children enrolled – 40 per cent are girls in Kabul but only 10 per cent in Kandahar. Everyone I speak to raises the question of Iraq. It's been clear for some months that George Bush is considering an invasion and bombing intensity increased dramatically as part of the no-fly zone in August. Afghans are fearful that the international community's focus will move to the Middle East and they will be abandoned. There is still no trained police force in the country and no army with loyalty to central government. Every-one argues for the extension of ISAF.

I visit a couple of schools, one government-run in a derelict building, totally lacking facilities. The head teacher is a middle-aged woman who had taught secretly under the Taliban and is now happy to work openly, though distressed by the battle just to get pens and paper. The second school is run by an international NGO in better buildings and is girls only. They are so bright and enthusiastic and when I ask what they want to be when they grow up I'm told teacher, doctor and then – amazingly – pilot. Only a year ago they were banned from education for being female.

My next visit is to police HQ where I meet a sinister fellow who runs the Kabul force. He tells me he's recruited some women and I get to meet two of them. Their job is to deal with women offenders, which includes those who run away from violent husbands. It appears the female officers' job is to negotiate their return to their families! In the middle of the discussion there's a flurry of activity and we learn a bomb has been found outside, but is being defused!

On my third night I wake up with the most vicious stomach pains imaginable. I spend the night in my toilet closet in great distress. I'm used to travel bugs but this is very extreme. Fortunately, I have lots of pills but I'm still staggering at breakfast time. I have to confess my condition as I'm determined to keep to schedule. This prompts tales of everybody's sickness, including the fact that one embassy staff member had gone home at death's door after he was found to have a severe kidney infection arising from the water drunk in the embassy (I'm assured it's now being filtered). Salads are washed in a chemical solution!

9 September: Today is the first anniversary of the assassination of Ahmad Shah Massoud, the leader of the Northern Alliance. Security is very tight and there are fears of attacks. In two days' time I am due to visit the new Minister for Women, Habiba Sarabi, on the first anniversary of the bombing of the Twin Towers. I guess this wasn't the smartest time to make such a visit but like so many people before me I'm already absorbing the intangible magic that is Afghanistan and it's definitely worth coming.

Habiba Sarabi is a much less flamboyant character than Sima Samar, but quietly determined nonetheless. She wants international support for more resources and describes the efforts she and her team are making to encourage and support women. She's working with lots of women-led NGOs and points to the number of girls in school, the reopening of the family-planning service after ten years (Afghans have huge numbers of children) and the fact that women are working again. Nonetheless it is clear that she is walking a tightrope. She tells me of the universal concern among women, that a Department of Vice and Virtue has been opened within the Ministry of Religious Affairs. The very same department under the Taliban reinforced the most repressive subjugation of women in the name of Islam.

Next day the embassy has arranged for me to go to one of the neighbour- hoods to meet a local Afghan women's organisation led by professional women who were politically active during the period of communist control. In the afternoon I'm told security have said I can't go. I protest – I'm very keen to have this opportunity to meet a grassroots organisation. I question the secu- rity patrol who tell me there are armed men all over the housing complex and they cannot guarantee my safety. A compromise is reached – they will send a vehicle to collect the leaders and bring them to the embassy. We have a terrific meeting – there's such a sense of solidarity – these women just want what we all want. They've all worked as secret teachers under the Taliban and taken enormous risks. They are anxious that their previous associations with the Najibullah Marxist regime will prevent their getting funding from the international community. This would be an outrage given the US handed billions of dollars to the mujahideen and now openly fund warlords. I prom- ise to take up their requests.

My final day is a visit to the women's prison and then a lunch in a restau- rant with embassy officials and NGOs. I guess I'm one of the few MPs who is familiar with women's prisons, having been shadow Prisons Minister, so I'm expecting things to be grim. I'm not disappointed – cold, damp, gloomy, stone buildings house the women. The regime is brutal. They depend on rela- tives coming to the prison to bring them food and of course there is nothing for them to do. Most shocking is the children. Their presence is testimony to their mothers' crimes. The women who agree to speak to me were impris- oned for 'moral' offences. Men can simply tell their wives that they want a divorce and it's done. Women have no such rights. One of the prisoners was divorced in this way and subsequently had another marriage arranged for her (no choice) by her uncle. Then the first husband accused her of adul- tery, for which she was imprisoned. One woman, abandoned by her family, has all three of her children living with her in her cell. I think long and hard and then ask if I might photograph her children to publicise their plight. She readily agrees, declining to be photographed herself. The three children, in brightly coloured traditional dress, line up against the wall of the cell and look directly at the camera. It is the most poignant picture I will ever take and I will never forget them.

It's interesting to see the restaurant. Again security have gone ahead to check for any unusual activity and decided it's ok. This is one of the places foreigners are thought to be safe but the very fact they go there regularly creates a potential target. It's a pretty gloomy place but the food is good and it's a real farewell. I ask if I can go to the shops (there are a few still standing) before I leave. Great reluctance. My bodyguards surround me as my feet touch the pavement – automatics at the ready. They think I want to buy a carpet but of course that's impossible so I get taken to a stall with lovely silver and lapis lazuli. I've very little money but I manage to buy a tiny silver box, a pair of earrings and a carved wooden printer's block and traditional metal and wood flask for Frank.

I board my flight with trepidation – this is more scary for me than the whole week in Kabul. I am euphoric when I land safely in Dubai. I go straight to a glamorous food bar and order myself a plate of smoked salmon and a large glass of deliciously cold white wine. It's obvious I'm not the stoic adventurer I was in my youth!


16 September: Iraq agrees to the return of the weapons inspectors.

Back in London for just five days before I'm off to Cairo. This is the benefit of the long summer recess – it's possible to do a lot of international work. I've been invited to participate in an international conference on 'Women and Peace' hosted by Suzanne Mubarak, the President's wife. I was unsure about accepting given the nature of the regime but there is no democracy in the Middle East so if I want to meet progressive women there's not much choice. In Cairo a group of women are transferred to a small private plane for the flight to Sharm el-Sheikh, a place I've never visited. Once on the flight we find armed guards standing in the aisles, laughing and joking during take-off and landing – I am seriously unnerved. We are housed in a five-star hotel where the meetings are held. Sharm is a strange place – so totally artificial, as befits a resort in the desert. Not my kind of place at all but the meetings are fascinating: women from all over the Middle East who demonstrate again the universal demands of educated women everywhere and the essential role of women in peace-building. Everyone is fearful of a Western strike on Iraq.

24 September: Parliament has been recalled. I arrive back just in time for the debate. It's a very tense House. The government has published a fifty-page dossier detailing the history of Iraq's programme of weapons of mass destruction and the involvement of UN weapons inspectors until they were forced to withdraw four years ago. In his statement to the House, Tony asserts that 'the policy of containment is not working. The weapons of mass destruction programme ... is up and running now.' He also reports that Saddam has sought 'significant quantities of uranium from Africa'. But the most startling claim is that he has 'existing and active military plans for the use of chemical and biological weapons, which could be activated within forty-five minutes'.

After eight hours I get my chance to speak. I say I believe that President Bush has sought to use international support for the war against terrorism to justify regime change in Iraq. I argue that we do not have the justification of self-defence under international law that we had in the case of Afghanistan. I point out that, after a year of action waged by 10,000 combat and support troops, few Al-Qaeda militia have been captured and their leadership remains largely intact. Nothing, I suggest, could provide Al-Qaeda with more ready recruits than Saudi support for a US strike on Baghdad. I say I believe that such a war risks huge loss of life, massive environmental damage and the possible destabilisation of the very states in the Middle East that the US says it seeks to protect. I refer to the opinions of the women I met in Egypt just days ago and particularly the UN workers who told me they were quietly preparing the camps, transport and food supplies for the anticipated humanitarian crisis. I refer too to my visit to Afghanistan and the fear of people there that the US will walk away. I urge the government to secure the peaceful re-entry of the UN weapons inspectors and to reinvigorate the Middle East peace process.

The next day *The Sun* will carry the headline 'Brits 45 minutes from doom' and the *Daily Star* 'Mad Saddam ready to attack'. Of course, this is complete nonsense. There is no evidence that he has delivery systems capable of delivering WMD to Britain and the forty-five minutes is entirely spurious. But the government gets what it wants – justification for a claim of self-defence against Saddam.*

We return to recess and I've really got my hands full now. Apart from the international work, we are about to recruit a CEO for the New Deal and a whole host of constituency issues continue to press for attention. Mobile phone masts have attracted nationwide campaigns. The government is paying attention at last and we get some small changes but of course most will go ahead. I'm also still trying to keep abreast of the GM debate and put in PQs when stimulated by information from the Soil Association, FOE (Friends of the Earth) and Greenpeace. The Soil Association has just launched a review of the US experience, which is extremely telling. They demonstrate that GM has resulted in lower prices and income to farmers, higher government subsidies, lower soya yields, greater reliance on herbicides and widespread contamination of seed resources, conventional crops, organic crops and bulk commodities. In the UK, the farm-scale trials are coming to an end with this autumn's planting sites (the last) soon to be announced. The US is fighting back with complaints to the WTO about EU regulation. We've now had an effective moratorium in Europe on any new GM crop or food proposals for four years and our campaigns are as robust as ever. Legislation to be introduced next month will ensure that GM food and crops undergo a series of risk assessment tests before

---

* In June 2011, *The Observer* reveals a memo from Blair's foreign affairs advisor pointing to: 'The benefit of obscuring the fact that in terms of WMD Iraq is not exceptional.'

they are authorised for sale, marketing or planting anywhere in the EU. This will signal the end of the moratorium but it's likely many other EU countries will still not proceed with GM and we will make it as difficult as possible for the UK to respond, especially when our own trials have not been evaluated.

15 October: The House returns. My first priority is to sort out the modernisation canvassing. Martin Salter and Ann Coffey are leading on this and I've got Karen Buck to split London with me. The proposals are modest – moving the hours of business forward by three hours on Tuesdays and Wednesdays so that normally we'll start voting at 7 p.m. rather than 10 p.m. – yet they are attracting huge controversy. We also propose returning in September rather than October from the summer recess. We not only have to collect information on each proposal but also ask if people will actually come on the day as it will be a free vote. We know senior whips are opposed and are mounting a big campaign behind the scenes to get people to vote against. Robin has written an extremely persuasive letter to all MPs and YouGov has done a poll showing overwhelming public support for the proposals. The PM is completely disinterested as he isn't usually in the House at night.

I'm spending the weekend at a Wilton Park conference on Afghanistan to which I am invited because of my back-bench work. I have a lot to say. Mike O'Brien, Foreign Office Minister, is present throughout and takes on board much of what I say about women, police, security etc. It's so stimulating and a real privilege to spend a whole weekend in serious debate. I'm also able to talk to the Afghans who are attending. I've already sent my written report on my visit to both Mike and Jack Straw and eventually get detailed, constructive responses from both.

Over the next two weeks I manage to speak to everyone about the proposed change in sitting hours at least three times. Hopefully they are all telling the truth and our supporters will turn up. Tuesday sittings are the problem – a lot of people who are happy with earlier Wednesdays are opposed to the Tuesday changes.

It's an incredibly tense day. We start voting on the Tuesday hours at twenty past eleven at night! We win by just seven votes – a triumph for Robin and our team who did the work. I am thrilled. Tommy McAvoy, an important whip, is absolutely furious and lets it be known that we haven't heard the end of it.

The next day I'm in Westminster Hall debating a report by the Foreign Affairs Committee on international terrorism. I speak again of my Afghan experience and the paramount need for new security arrangements. I point out that the people in Kabul spoke well of ISAF despite their constant sense of insecurity, but they also said outside of the capital security was worse than before September 11th. I raise the dire state of the police and continuing intimidation of women. Not only are the men untrained, many are thought to be Taliban and they haven't been paid for three months. Likewise, the Afghan army recruits who, while getting housed and fed themselves, need money to send home to their families and none is forthcoming. Again I stress the vulnerability of women and refer to the fact that in the past few days four girls' schools in Wardak province, near Kabul, have been burned down.

The drive towards war is mounting. A report from Washington says the US is stockpiling landmines on US bases ringing Iraq. This is an outrage. US official policy is to stop using landmines anywhere in the world (except Korea) by next year. Mines are one of the worst legacies of war. Fifteen to twenty thousand people are killed or injured by mines every year, 80 per cent of whom are civilians and a third children.

8 November: The UN Security Council adopts resolution 1441, which contains a strengthened inspection regime. A week later Iraq confirms that it will implement the resolution and the advance inspection team arrives.

I spend the week visiting schools, Sure Start schemes and working on the NDC with our new CEO Clive Wilson. Most importantly, I'm hosting a roundtable on Deptford station. I'm absolutely fed up with the constant problems there and I've got all the stakeholders to agree to sit together and hear what I have to say. They agree to an ongoing series of meetings and Lewisham Council appoints a town centre manager. Little do I know that I will stay with this project for a decade.

Good news for the New Cross fire families. The High Court has ordered a new inquest and the local coroner will have to comply. The bad news is it will take up to a year before it can start.

As soon as the Queen's Speech is over we have the ballot for Private Members' Bills. I've got so much on but can't resist putting in for a place. Amazingly, I win again – I'm number five, which means I'm guaranteed parliamentary time. Unlike the first occasion I haven't made any promises to constituents so I'm free to choose. Friends of the Earth approach me with an outline of a Bill to increase recycling levels. This is a passion of mine. I receive over 1,000 letters, mostly from FOE supporters. The idea is to put a duty on local authorities to make collections at the doorstep. This should dramatically increase recycling rates. I pay a local cooperative to collect paper, cardboard, glass, plastic and aluminium foil from my own doorstep, so I know it can be done. How exciting.

I'm definitely going to do it. I don't agree with everything FOE have drafted but we can work on that. I quickly make appointments to see Michael Meacher, the minister, and his officials at DEFRA. Lots of good publicity. All my campaigning this year has meant my media profile has shot up again and although I don't get asked to do *Question Time* any more, I certainly get more coverage than when I was a minister.

The British Council has approached me as a result of my Afghan work. They are setting up pairing exchanges with women MPs from developing countries in Africa. They ask if I will take part and at the end of the month I spend three days with Rose Banda from Zambia. She is a delightful woman – full of enthusiasm and drive. The women get a programme from the British Council and talks from officials in Parliament as well as my programme in the constituency. How I'll find the time to go to Zambia I don't know but I'm committed now.

December and it's the usual rush to get things done before the recess. Loads to do in the constituency but one notable event is the opening of a new arts centre in one of the old industrial buildings on Creekside. Cockpit Arts offers small studios and rents affordable to self-employed artists starting out in business. It's a great project and wonderful to see investment coming to Deptford. There is already a thriving arts community, largely thanks to Goldsmiths, whose graduates tend to stay local. Finally, I tell the national party and my local constituency that I would like to stand again as the Labour candidate at the next general election. I can't believe they're thinking about it so soon, but that's the rule. Roll on Christmas.

## 2003

Back to the Commons and an evening reception at the FCO for British Heads of Mission. A surprising introduction to a woman called Dr Rosalind Marsden. She is to take over from Ron as our ambassador in Kabul. What a job! She will certainly be an asset in accessing women.

Our new hours start this week meaning that the House will convene at 11.30 a.m. on Tuesdays and Wednesdays and voting will start at 7 p.m. rather than 10 p.m. MPs will be expected to be in their constituencies on Fridays so there will be no government business, just Private Members' Bills. Hurrah!

I'll be taking every opportunity to raise Iraq at FCO, Defence and DfID questions from now on, but everyone is going to want to speak so getting opportunities will be difficult. I am, however, in great demand by the media so plenty of chances to get my views across.

10 January: Lots of heart-warming emails following my appearance on *Newsnight* last night. Typical is 'having endured the hordes of hypocritical pole-climbers wheeled out to defend the indefensible, your contribution was a beacon of hope'. If only we could win the argument with government – there's no doubt where public opinion is going.

The EU, under the Greek presidency, is on a peace mission in the Middle East, while Jack Straw is in Indonesia and Malaysia trying to get support for military action. Geoff Hoon, the Defence Secretary, is trying to whip up support from Turkey and secure use of its bases. Opinion in the PLP is hardening. The whips have been told that people will not support military action without a new UN mandate and proof from the UN weapons inspectors. I've read the reports of the amounts of munitions and delivery systems destroyed by the inspectors after the Gulf War. At the end of 1988 the International Atomic Energy Agency (IAEA) concluded 'on the basis of its findings, the Agency is able to state that there is no indication that Iraq possesses nuclear weapons or any meaningful amounts of weapons usable nuclear material or that Iraq has retained any practical capability (facilities or hardware) for the production of such material'.

I think it's extremely unlikely that in the past few years Saddam has been able to obtain nuclear material and restart the programmes. I guess he has stocks of ageing chemical shells but definitely no nuclear weapons. I just hope the inspectors will be given cooperation and the time to do their job. Even so there is no guarantee Bush and Blair will listen. Despite all the evidence to the contrary, George Bush managed to convince himself that Iraq and Al-Qaeda were one and the same.

20 January: Geoff Hoon makes a statement saying 26,000 troops are to be deployed in the Gulf along with 120 Challenger tanks and 150 armoured personnel carriers. He's determined to start a war. Next day there's an FCO statement and I ask Mike O'Brien, if the weapons inspectors discover WMD will they be given the opportunity to destroy them, in compliance with Resolution 1441, and if they do not, what then will be the justification for military action? He avoids the question saying destruction of the weapons would depend, to some extent, on the Iraqis.

Two days later a defence debate. I ask if pre-emption is now part of the UK's defence policy. I'm told it's 'simply part of self-defence' and that is the basis on which it would be justifiable in international law.

Geoff Hoon is back in the Commons. I tackle him on the Pentagon's weekend statement referring to 'an aerial bombardment so intense that the Iraqi forces will be disabled and demoralised'. I ask if he plans to commit British troops to such an assault and if he has made any estimate of the humanitarian cost? He evades the question. I feel physically sick. This is *my* government and *my* colleagues and they are set on war.

Hans Blix and Mohamed ElBaradei report to the UN. They have inspected 230 sites. They explain their methods and give details of possible chemical and biological supplies and rockets. The IAEA says there is no evidence that Iraq has restarted its nuclear programme. ElBaradei concludes, 'With our verification system now in place, barring exceptional circumstances and provided there is a sustained proactive cooperation by Iraq, we should be able, within the next few months, to provide credible assurance that Iraq has no nuclear weapons programme.'

Everything now depends on giving the inspectors time.

Iraq looms over everything. Both Heidi and I are also under pressure because I decided to mount an exhibition of recyclates in Portcullis to mark the second reading of my Private Member's Bill. Fortunately, we have a lot of keen manufacturers.

Then Margaret Beckett announces the government has decided to launch a public debate on GM. None of us trusts them to do this objectively but I tackle her on the clearly obvious flaw – the fact that the debate will end before the crop trial results are known!

The opposition call a debate on Iraq. I begin by pointing to the West's double standards and hypocrisy in previously arming and supporting the brutal dictatorship of Saddam. The question is whether the war would be just and proportionate and we must weigh in the balance the threat, the degree of force proposed and the humanitarian consequences. I remind the House of what happened in the Gulf War (which I believed to be legitimate and for which I voted):

> The UN estimates between 140,000 and 200,000 Iraqis died as a direct consequence of the war. More than two dozen factories and stores

containing chemical, biological and possibly nuclear material were hit
and toxins dispersed. Carcinogens from blazing oil wells were spread
across thousands of miles. The systematic bombing of electricity generating facilities and of water storage ... left survivors without drinking
water. Iraqi health services were overwhelmed. By April 1991 an estimated 1.5 million refugees had fled ... By May, between 15,000 and
20,000 of them were dead.

In response to those who say we can't do nothing I say we are not doing nothing. Iraq's military might has been reined in and the weapons inspectors have
authority to destroy weapons of mass destruction and their delivery systems.
I conclude with the record of the international community in Afghanistan:
'So little progress in reconstruction and just £5 billion in aid promised over
five years while Britain alone would spend $8 billion going to war in Iraq.'

EDMs are circulated calling for Parliament to be given a vote. I sign and
the number of signatures grows rapidly. I also get a letter from Lord Richard
Rogers, who is organising an advertisement for *The Guardian*. I sign and pay
my £100. He gets a great list of names supporting the simple message: 'Why
Iraq? Why now? The facts do not justify war. Join us by saying "no"'. A huge
campaign is also under way to get people to a demonstration the day after
the advert will appear.

The February recess enables me to catch up. The Stop the War march is
incredible. From the platform I can see that it's bigger than the biggest CND
demo and reports suggest 1 million people are on the streets. It's part of a
global coordination in 600 cities around the world. We learn later that the
protest in Rome involved around 3 million people and in Madrid 1.5 million.
It is such a moving sight; so many young people, such diversity, such emotion. Surely the government cannot ignore the strength of public opinion.

Recess over, and I'm off to a meeting with the London region of English
Heritage to discuss Convoys Wharf. Subsequently they send a formal letter to the developers outlining the history of the site as Henry VIII's naval

shipyard beginning in 1513. They list the historic connections – Sir Francis Drake and the *Golden Hind*, Tsar Peter the Great who studied shipbuilding there, the diarist John Evelyn whose house and garden were within the master plan area and Captain Cook whose vessels were equipped at the docks. They cite the national importance of the one major listed building, the Olympia, and draw attention to the extensive surviving archaeological remains beneath the site. They add, 'We believe a fresh approach is needed that makes better use of the qualities of the site in order to create a distinctive sense of place, informed by the character and history of the area, and a major destination in its own right.' I'm delighted.

The second reading of my Private Member's Bill is coming up next month and I am in intense negotiations with government officials and FOE. Although Michael Meacher is sympathetic there are real reservations and FOE's initial suggestion of half a dozen recycling streams is going nowhere. Finally, the government agrees to support the second reading, so we just need to ensure we get enough MPs to attend (it's a Friday). I also have the daunting task of tackling Eric Forth. The MP for Bromley and Chislehurst takes pride in the fact that he's never done a surgery and is always in the Commons on Friday to talk out Private Members' Bills. I ask for a meeting. He is courteous and leaves me with the feeling he won't be up to his usual tricks.


7 March: Blix and ElBaradei are back at the UN reporting on the weapons inspection. Blix acknowledges that three to four months into Resolution 1441 Iraqi cooperation could not constitute 'immediate'. However, he says that whatever the timing of cooperation, 'disarmament and its verification could not be instant'. The process would take months and he will submit a draft work programme to the Security Council. ElBaradei reports that after three months of intrusive inspections, the agency has found no evidence or plausible indication of the revival of a nuclear weapons programme in Iraq. France, Russia and China accept the spirit of these reports but Jack Straw takes a harder line.

There can be no justification for war. Every night I lie awake thinking about it. I feel a sense of profound powerlessness. How can intelligent men with a knowledge of the world behave so irrationally? But then I reflect on George Bush's ignorance and Tony Blair's lack of experience in foreign affairs before becoming Prime Minister. It seems bizarre that I should believe I know better than they do, but how can I think otherwise?

A delightful lunch at Shepherds to celebrate the end of the Laban Development Council and our success in achieving the new building on Creekside. My recyclates exhibition opens in Portcullis. I'm absolutely delighted with the results. Twenty companies are exhibiting and Heidi and Ruth have ensured everything is running like clockwork. No one has ever done anything like this before and it's a great boost for the companies and for my Bill. The range of products is extraordinary. My favourites include wholly compostable plant pots that feel exactly like plastic and luxurious soft fleeces that are made from recycled plastic bottles. I'm thrilled by the potential for whole new industries.

14 March: Up early and off to Westminster for my Private Member's Bill. I'm going to enjoy making my speech. I know this field backwards and have no worries about interventions or questions I can't answer. In the event, nineteen MPs make interventions resulting in my being on my feet for nearly an hour. They are all supportive and there's no hostility on either side – what a pleasant change.

I argue that as the law requires our household waste to be collected at or near our doorsteps, it is logical that material for recycling should be collected there as well. I acknowledge the role of supermarket sites but point out that many people do not shop there and 28 per cent of the population do not own cars. Currently 80 per cent of municipal waste goes to landfill – enough to fill the Albert Hall every hour of every day. I ask people to visualise that quantity spilling out hour after hour. Furthermore, waste production is expected to have doubled by 2020. I point to the ill effects of landfill, including on human health, climate change and adjacent property values. I answer numerous questions as I go along and then get to the description of the clauses. Clause 1 places a duty on the Secretary of State to produce an overarching framework for UK recycling or composting by 2010. The rest of the clauses ensure that local authorities provide the doorstep service, collecting at least two recyclable materials.

At half past twelve the DEFRA minister, Michael Meacher, sets out the government's support. He is fulsome in his praise for me and I know he shares my passion for recycling. Nonetheless, he has reservations and I know there are battles ahead. But, for now, second reading passes with unanimous support and no vote is needed.

My euphoria lasts an afternoon. More and more ominous news regarding Iraq. I cannot support the government. I lie awake at night checking and rechecking my own arguments, asking myself if am I sure or whether I am failing to grasp some aspect of this debate. Last week my Iraqi friend Leila invited us to lunch with a large group of Iraqi friends. We talked endlessly about the possibility of military intervention. They were all professional people, successful in the UK and all with reason to hate Saddam. But only one of them had any enthusiasm for war; the rest were apprehensive or opposed. One said, ominously, 'If Saddam goes there will be civil war.' Several still have family members in Iraq – what a terrible prospect for them.

Frank is home on Sunday. We are glued to the news. Blair is in the Azores meeting Bush and the Spanish and Portuguese Prime Ministers. They issue a call for a new Security Council resolution to challenge Saddam Hussein to take a strategic decision to destroy his weapons of mass destruction. This is a cynical ploy. On Monday, Chirac announces France would veto any second resolution, so they know they can't get one.

After a tense day in the Commons, Jack Straw arrives at the Dispatch Box at half-past eight in the evening to make a statement. There is an atmosphere of foreboding.

Jack outlines the efforts to get a second resolution but tells the House that there won't be one. He spells out why the UK will not support an alternative, proposed by France, Germany and Russia, to give the inspectors more time. Instead, the government will ask the House tomorrow to support 'participation in military operations'. He still maintains the pretence, adding 'should they be necessary'. He says a number of documents have been prepared to inform the debate. I feel utterly sick. I can hardly bring myself to stand up to indicate I want to ask a question. There must be a hundred people on their feet. Michael Ancram, Jack's Tory opposite number, puts it bluntly: 'The talking is over, diplomacy is at an end and tonight we face the grim prospect of war.'

I signal that I will not support the government tomorrow and then refer to Jack's reassurance that civilian casualties will be kept to a minimum. I say, 'The test of that policy will be no cluster bombs, no depleted uranium weapons and no targeting of food and water supplies.' Jack responds that the 'targeting will be very careful, proportionate and designed to attack military and legitimate targets'. I wish I could believe him.*

At 9.44 p.m. the Speaker calls Robin Cook to make a personal statement (he resigned from the Cabinet earlier). The House is silent. Typically, Robin begins with a joke to break the tension. He confesses he had forgotten how much better the view is from the back benches. With his usual forensic abilities, he takes apart the government's case: 'The reality is that Britain is being asked to embark on a war without agreement in any of the international bodies of which we are a leading partner – not NATO, not the European Union and, now, not the Security Council.' As a former Foreign Secretary he is well placed to point out that over the past decade the policy of containment has 'destroyed more weapons than in the Gulf War, dismantled Iraq's nuclear weapons programme and halted Saddam's medium- and long-range missiles programmes'. He acknowledges that Iraq may have some 'biological toxins and some battlefield chemical munitions' and reminds the House that in the 1980s it was the US that sold Saddam the anthrax agents and the

---

* Estimates will later suggest at least 100,000, but up to 200,500 Iraqi civilians died as a result of the conflict.

British government that approved the chemical and munitions factories. He ends by saying, 'I intend to join those tomorrow night who will vote against military action now. It is for that reason, and that reason alone, and with a heavy heart, that I resign from the government.' I'm fighting back the tears but jump to my feet and applaud. I doubt I will ever hear a more significant or moving speech.

Lots of discussion in the Commons and then Frank and I make our way to Bellamy's in 1 Parliament Street where Robin has invited us for a farewell drink. We arrive late, tired and sad for all of us. While the tragedy of Iraq is uppermost in our minds, I'm also aware this will be the end of our modernisation programme. Robin asks if we have a car, which we do. He doesn't want to take a government car or walk into a bunch of journalists so we drive him home.

18 March: A sleepless night and back to the Commons for the debate and vote. It's an historic occasion but I haven't put in to speak. There are no arguments to be made that Robin, I and many others have not already voiced. The government is not listening and I am deeply depressed.

I hear the Prime Minister's opening speech with increasing despair – I cannot now believe a word he says. How can this be the same man who led us into a government of such hope just six years ago? Peter Kilfoyle moves the amendment, which begins: 'The case for war against Iraq has not yet been established.' It is on this amendment that we will vote first and which those of us who oppose the government will support.

After nearly nine hours of debate, we vote. Many of us hoped Clare Short would have joined Robin in resigning but she doesn't. The die is cast.

We vote on the amended text opposing the government position. The result is 217 in favour, 396 against. To our credit a quarter of the Parliamentary Labour Party has voted against the government. I am exhausted, angry and emotional. I haven't the stomach to go back in and take part in a second pointless vote. Nothing will ever be the same again. Frank and I go home.

A day later the British military campaign begins and I'm back in the Commons for the statement on Iraq and humanitarian aid. All I can do now is question the prosecution of the war. My greatest concern is that cluster bombs and depleted uranium shells will be used. The legacy of the Gulf War is well documented and I raise this with Mike O'Brien, but of course no information is forthcoming.

I write a letter to my hundreds of party members explaining my vote. At the next PMQs, Tony Blair answers a question from Charles Kennedy on Iraqi-led post-conflict reconstruction. This gives me the opportunity to get up and ask if he thinks we can win hearts and minds when the US has announced post-war Iraq will be run by a former general who is president of an arms company and a declared supporter of Israel. The question is swatted away.

Three weeks later, Geoff Hoon makes an upbeat assessment of the progress in the Iraq War. Relatively few British lives have been lost, the RAF has flown 1,500 sorties and British ground troops have advanced on Basra. Baghdad is under attack. Neil Gerrard asks if any weapons of mass destruction have been found and suggests there may be none. Kate Hoey, Glenda Jackson and I all tackle him on the use of cluster bombs and their long-term legacy for civilians.

My work with the Afghan Women's Link continues uninterrupted and I keep asking questions to do my bit to keep Afghanistan on the agenda. Habiba Sarabi [Minister for Women], whom I met in Kabul last year, comes to London and we have a supportive private meeting and subsequently take part in an FCO seminar together.

A meeting of my Deptford Round Table at which we see an options study for the land around the station undertaken by the Richard Rogers partnership for the council. Redevelopment is essential to the improvements we all want. Really exciting and visionary. The listed carriage ramp could be a significant feature but very expensive to restore.

The NXNDC takes a lot of time: chairing board meetings, dealing with board members' ideas and differences and meeting the CEO to push forward the programme delivery. Health, education and skills training are the absolute priorities and we both need to fund new initiatives and make sure we maximise the delivery of council services to the New Deal area. It's a really difficult task and there's a lot of bureaucracy involved with both London region and central government having oversight.

Tremendous relief – the House goes into recess on 10 April and we can take a break.

The Iraqi government is no more but Saddam and his sons have escaped capture. All talk is of a new administration and I have no doubt the same mistakes as were made in Afghanistan will be made again. My focus now will be on the composition of the Interim Authority, the position of women (equal citizens under Saddam), the clean-up of cluster bombs and depleted uranium, and humanitarian relief. In no time my questions reveal that the leaders chosen by the US are all Shia, thus excluding all the Sunnis who have run previous administrations, and no women.

I'm involved in intense discussions with DEFRA over my Bill. They are seeking a major redraft and I'm rapidly losing patience. After many weeks Michael Meacher and I have an agreement whereby the government will table some amendments when we get into committee and I will support them. The major purpose of the Bill remains intact – relief all round. I've asked good friends and colleagues David Drew, Joan Walley, Glenda Jackson, Julie Morgan, John Austin, Clive Efford, Julie Drown and David Kidney to be committee members. On the Tory side there's one enthusiast, Greg Barker, who many years later will become my opposite number at the Department of Energy and Climate Change (DECC.)

1 May: Under a banner saying 'Mission Accomplished' George Bush on the deck of aircraft carrier USS *Abraham Lincoln* declares the Iraq War over.*

---

* The US will officially withdraw from Iraq eight years later.

A major conference in Baghdad on the future government of Iraq. My worst fears are realised when I learn of its composition. It's even an embarrassment for the UK government as the Americans exclude the sole woman delegate, Dr Besarani, put forward by the FCO. I raise the matter at business questions three days later to the embarrassment of John Reid, who actually gives a positive response. Paul Marsden gets an answer to the question many of us have been pursuing: Geoff Hoon admits the UK has used sixty-six air-delivered cluster bombs and about 8,000 shells. When the US figures were released the US Physicians for Human Rights estimated that their 1,500 cluster bombs translated into a minimum of 15,000 bomblets due to the known failure rate in detonation. This will be a terrible legacy.

Next day and I'm on a long flight to Lusaka. I'm doing the return visit to Rose Banda, the Zambian MP, as part of the British Council exchange scheme. I land in glorious sunshine but make the mistake of getting off the plane in the long comfortable t-shirt dress I've been wearing for the flight. I'm met by a formal welcoming party with my host in glamorous traditional dress and a brass band. Embarrassment over, I'm whisked away to my hotel. I've a busy schedule: meetings in Parliament and with women's organisations in the capital for three days, followed by four days in the constituency. This is a very poor country but people are very friendly and where I'm staying there are broad, calm streets lined with beautiful flowering and scented trees. The pavements are broken and there are obvious signs of poverty but the capital seems to function. Parliamentarians have the same system as the UK, representing individual constituencies. Many of these, including Rose's, are far away, so the Parliament sits for blocks of time during which MPs don't return home. All the issues faced by the professional women I meet are the same as ours but more intense and with additional burdens from their families and a critical lack of resources (absolutely no allowances from public funds to do the job).

We're off to Rose's constituency of Milanzi in eastern Zambia. We travel for seven hours in a 4x4. This is the real Africa – intense heat, insects and definitely no motorway service stations! I've taken large supplies of Wet Ones, a trick long learned from my travels, and I'm soon sharing them with the women travelling with me. The landscape is unrelenting scrub with a few flowering trees. We have to go into the bush to pee. I stamp hard on the ground and look around anxiously before squatting – undoubtedly this is snake-infested terrain.

After a long day we leave the tarmac roads for tracks through the bush. The ground is hard and dry and we frequently plummet into great dips. If it weren't for the constant lively conversation, I'd be sick at the constant bumping and banging of the vehicle but somehow I remain upbeat. Eventually we arrive at our 'hotel'. It's a simple building with primitive facilities. My small sparse room is dark and cool but I immediately note the rent in the mosquito net over my bed (at least I'm taking the pills and had numerous vaccinations before I left). At supper most people eat great piles of white, gelatinous maize, nshima, but it tastes of nothing and I'm relieved to find the house speciality is fried potatoes. Chips and a fried egg are perfect. I'll eat it every day. Rose explains that this place is on the border of the constituency and is the last place with electricity and running water.

Next morning, we set off on the track roads to Milanzi. We encounter groups of small round mud houses with thatched roofs surrounded by small cultivated plots and flowering plants. We meet no other vehicles, just people walking. The air is still and the scenery picturesque.

All the villagers have come out to greet us and are singing a song of welcome. I'm suddenly conscious that most of these people may not have seen a white woman in the flesh before.

My first duty is to greet the village chief. We sit formally on large wooden chairs for a conversation, drinks and photographs. At the end a live goat is brought in and presented to me. I accept graciously and am relieved to be told by Rose that we don't have to take it with us. It will be barbequed in my honour this evening for the benefit of the villagers.

I meet Rose's husband, a large avuncular man she calls 'the General'.

I presume he's an army man but now he's running a farm and experimenting with different crops. Maize monoculture and chopping trees for firewood have together reduced the forest and degraded the soil. Life is extremely hard for the thousands of small farmers trying to subsist, but grinding poverty and lack of government resources are almost insurmountable barriers to progress. Rose's house has a latrine for which I'm extremely grateful.

I talk to some of the villagers and see inside their homes. Having a wood fire in the centre of the hut on which to cook and heat the home in winter is a major hazard to health. The women tell me they walk many miles every day to collect water from the polluted river. All the supply for the family – for washing, drinking and cooking – must be brought every day by the women. They have large heavy plastic containers that they carry on their heads. I can't imagine carrying that weight of water every single day while walking in flip-flops through the bush in intense heat. Despite the appalling levels of hardship, people appear resilient and determined on self-help. Their priorities are boreholes for fresh water, school rooms and clinics.

Disease is a major factor. Aids is rampant, as is malaria, but the only clinic in the area has no hot water supply. I visit a school where the constant problem is storm damage – the tin roof blows off or leaks, and there is no glass for the windows. Then a visit to the court house – a tiny building in danger of collapse as termites have devoured the wooden beams.

I am treated to an open-air theatre performance attended by young and old. It's participants are local women, some of whom are teachers. The story revolves around Aids and the dangers for young people. It's as good as any fringe theatre in the UK. Back in Lusaka I ask our High Commissioner to seek DfID funding for Milanzi and Eastern Province where there is currently none, and few NGOs. The debt issue is also fundamental. Repayments to the international financial institutions are more than the annual education budget of the country with the result that there are 9,000 unemployed teachers.

Rose and her constituents' needs are fundamental: clean water, electricity, schools, anti-malaria programmes, clinics, roads and improved agriculture, plus the means of marketing and distributing produce. What a challenge.

15 May: Back in Westminster and a new issue – I and many other colleagues are very concerned about the possibility that a two-tier health system will result from the introduction of foundation hospitals. Guy's and St Thomas' will certainly qualify but this could leave Lewisham at a disadvantage. We're also in the remaining stages of the Criminal Justice Bill, which limits the right to trial by jury in complicated fraud cases, which is highly controversial. One good thing is the scrapping of 'double jeopardy', which currently prevents defendants from being tried twice for the same crime. This could be significant in the case of Stephen Lawrence's murder.

General Garner, the US administrator, has organised a conference on preparations for an interim Iraqi administration. Only one woman is included. I write to him, the Prime Minister and Kofi Annan reminding them of Iraqi women's history and the unanimous adoption of the UN Security Council Resolution 1325, which commits all member states to 'increased representation of women at all levels in institutions and mechanisms for the prevention, management and resolution of conflict'. The US administration has ordered the de-Ba'athification of Iraqi society and the disbandment of the 450,000-strong army. This is insane. In order to get a government job in Iraq you had to be a member of the Ba'ath Party under Saddam Hussein, so everyone who knows how to run anything is now out of a job.

Michael Meacher has tipped me off that Margaret Beckett has drafted a letter to Cabinet colleagues to say that DEFRA cannot support my Private Member's Bill. I'm shocked. I'm told the Treasury is to blame as they believe local authorities will ask central government to fund new facilities for them. My only chance will be to get to Gordon Brown. To my relief he agrees to a meeting. My arguments must be hard economics. I ask one of my contact companies to loan me one of their beautiful red fleeces. I also have a biodegradable garden pot, indistinguishable in appearance from plastic. I take my props and go in trepidation. I put them on Gordon's desk. While I can't see him in a scarlet fleece I know he'll be surprised to learn it's made by recycling plastic bottles. I have a good pitch – new state-of-the-art industries and jobs. And just as important is the fact that the UK will be facing huge fines if we don't comply with the European Landfill Directive and we certainly can't meet its targets unless we recycle more.

Things are going badly in Iraq. General Garner's role as administrator has been a total failure and he's been replaced by Paul Bremer. On 2 June, Sérgio Vieira de Mello, the UN Secretary General's representative, arrives in Baghdad and it appears the two men will work together.

We discuss the UN's role in a Westminster Hall debate. I argue that if the UN had been in charge we might have a smoother transition. The coalition forces have failed to restore vital water and electricity supplies and hospital services. None of the lessons of the Balkans, or indeed Afghanistan, have been learned. There is grave disorder and a huge degree of violence and the ludicrous situation where the US administrators have said every Iraqi has the right to carry a gun, including the freely available AK47s.

I criticise the efforts to appoint an Interim Authority – people with no credibility have been appointed, then sacked, then another conference convened with more people with no experience or expertise. The key to reconstruction must be international humanitarian law and human rights. Only the UN can conceivably provide the basis for reconstruction and relief. Iraq had an educated population and a modern infrastructure, which should have made it possible to construct a meaningful political process to Iraqi self-determination. I refer particularly to the status of women. Despite the brutal dictatorship they still made up 34 per cent of university and polytechnic teachers and 38 per cent of doctors. They had equal pay and no dress code. Now female students have been banned from Basra University unless they wear the hijab. A new kind of repression is emerging. Yarmouk hospital in Baghdad has recently reported 300 women rape victims.

Already the proposal to create a UN trust fund for the oil revenues has been dismissed. Instead, the coalition will control the flow of funds. I urge a greater role for the UN, concluding that only they have the impartiality, transparency and respect to play the central role that is required for reconstruction and rehabilitation.

The security position in Afghanistan has also been deteriorating in the past six months, greatly hindering the work of humanitarian organisations. Eighty organisations have signed a statement highlighting the need to expand ISAF beyond Kabul. Mine-clearing teams have been ambushed and world food programme deliveries are limited. I draft a letter to the NATO General Secretary and get it signed by MPs and peers.

Back on track with DEFRA. To my huge relief the government is now negotiating positively, thanks to Gordon's intervention. After three hours of relatively harmonious discussion and amendments voted through without divisions, the committee stage of my Bill is over. The report stage will take place on the floor of the House on 11 July.

The NDC is still taking up lots of time but we've made another breakthrough. We are funding neighbourhood wardens for New Cross Gate. They are a terrific group – black, white, male and female – and we get Yvette Cooper, the new minister in John Prescott's office, to come on a visit.

A pre-admission check at St Thomas'. After two years of physiotherapy for intense shoulder pain I've now got a diagnosis of carpal tunnel in my wrist! Four days later and the operation and an overnight stay. Miraculously the shoulder pain has gone. Two days off then my advice surgery on Friday.

The summer months bring some pleasant respite from the turmoil in Westminster. Brockley summer fayre, the Open Studios, the Deptford X festival, my Deptford First tea party and Lewisham People's Day – all annual rituals now but nonetheless enjoyable.

The Prime Minister has undertaken his usual summer reshuffle. He's sacked Michael Meacher and given his job to Elliot Morley, the junior Fisheries Minister. In no time Michael is speaking out, describing some of the tests carried out on GM as 'scientifically vacuous' and noting that government-sponsored research that proved negative was 'widely rubbished in government circles'. Michael also joins our little group of activists and we issue an all-party EDM calling for an extension of the GM public debate beyond its closing date of 18 July.

11 July: Report stage of my Private Member's Bill. Tory Sir Paul Beresford, who is concerned about green waste and rural authorities, has tabled a series of amendments. It's 12.30 p.m. and we are still debating them. Surely he's not going to try to wreck the Bill at this late stage. Eventually he says he is pleased with the answers to his probing questions and he can see 'the Honourable Member for Lewisham Deptford is looking anxiously at the clock'. Too right she is! He then withdraws his amendments.

At a minute to one I'm called to move the third reading of the Bill. This is largely a matter of thanking people. Numerous MPs add congratulations in short speeches and by 1.15 p.m. it's all over and my Bill is on its way to the Lords, where Anita Gale has agreed to sponsor it.

One vital task before the recess is to get signatories from 'the great and the good' to a letter to the Legal Services Commission. Legal aid has been refused to the New Cross families for representation at the new inquest ordered by the High Court last October. Our task is to convince the LSC's public interest advisory panel that there is a wider public interest in the families being represented. We will be successful and, in November, the best news of all, the New Cross fire inquest has been given a date – 2 February 2004 – *seven years* after I started my campaign and *twenty-three years* since the actual fire.

The last debate before the summer recess is one in which MPs can raise any issue. I've put in to speak as so much has been happening on the GM front when we've all been focused on Iraq. Fortunately, I get called. I begin by saying that with the exception of Iraq I believe GM is the greatest issue the House faces. The public debate on GM closes tomorrow. Last week the strategy unit reported on costs and benefits, two weeks ago the European Parliament ruled on labelling, traceability and coexistence, ending the moratorium on growing GM crops in Europe. The science review is expected next week, yet we have not had a single debate on the floor of the House (debates in Westminster Hall are back bench-led and not votable).

I point out the accumulation of evidence from around the world where GM is grown commercially – gene flow, pollen movements, contamination and the growth of herbicide-tolerant weeds and, most recently, reports of gene-stacking due to the pollination of one herbicide-tolerant variety by another. As for potential health effects, there are only ten published studies and more than half of those were carried out in collaboration with GM companies. I urge the Deputy Leader of the House, who will reply to the debate, to ensure a full debate takes place in September to take account of the wealth of information now available. And then it's recess – catch-up time and finally holiday.

19 August: A suicide bomber has driven a cement mixer into the UN compound in Baghdad. Vieira de Mello and at least twenty others are dead.

In line with the Modernisation Committee reforms, the House returns on 8 September for a short session before the conference season. Bills come back for their final votes and my own Bill passes its Lords stage unopposed.

My difficult time of chairing the NDC board comes to an end. I think the Partnership Board is now working well and we have a good staff team so my extended 'temporary' stint is almost over. We've delivered the Eckington Gardens refurbishment and some lighting improvements, funded teaching assistants and community workers in three local primary schools, set up a pilot employment and enterprise agency and completed a detailed (and depressing) health impact assessment. Next year should see much more delivery and a greater spend but it'll still be hard going.

We've lost the Brent East by-election, sadly caused by the premature death of Paul Daisley. This election clearly demonstrated public reaction to the Iraq War: Labour's vote fell by nearly 30 per cent – almost all transferred to Sarah Teather of the Liberal Democrats, who opposed the war.

Better news about the Albany Theatre. After years of near financial collapse and recent rescue, a new chief executive, Gavin Barlow, has been appointed. I'm impressed and optimistic he can make a go of it if he stays long enough.

Excellent news too for the New Cross fire families. David Lammy, our Constitutional Affairs Minister, supports our case and legal aid is to be made available for the inquest.

13 October: An excellent day. The Laban building has won the Sterling prize for architecture.

After the conference season, the House returns with final votes on the Water Bill, the Waste and Emissions Trading Bill and the Sexual Offences Bill. The latter includes important proposals to equalise the law in relation to sexual offences, repealing existing offences of buggery and gross indecency.

There's no let-up in casework and the housing situation continues to be dire. Ken Livingstone plans to get 17,000 new housing units in London by 2016, half of which would be affordable, but even that would only house half of those on current waiting lists. More positive is the amnesty that is now having an effect on many of our families with immigration problems. Those who made an application prior to October 2003 and who have at least one child are eligible.

John Denham, who to his great credit resigned over Iraq, has been doing a sterling job on the government's proposals for higher education and tuition fees. A group of us are meeting regularly to draw up amendments and to lobby ministers. There will be a serious revolt on second reading in the New Year unless concessions are made. I'm very worried about the debt levels for London students if the fees go up to £3,000 per annum. We need grants for the poorest students, which include many in London. I'm meeting with students and staff at Goldsmiths and have launched an online consultation.

The government has published the results of the three-year farm scale trials of GM crops. 'The results reveal significant differences in the effect on biodiversity when managing genetically herbicide-tolerant crops as compared to conventional crops.' Furthermore, some types of GM crops require less herbicide than conventional crops but others require more. I believe these results are another nail in the coffin for GM and get quoted saying as much in the media.

I manage to get called in business questions immediately following the publication and ask Peter Hain if, given the fact that two GM crops and their treatments were found to be harmful to wildlife, the science review was inconclusive and a cost-benefit analysis found no economic case, it isn't time for the commercialisation of GM crops to be debated in government time.

I've decided to accept a place on the EFRA Select Committee. This means I need to give up something to make time so I resign as chair of GLOBE, a position I've held for the past three years. For good measure I put in for a Westminster Hall debate on the science review on GM.

I secure my debate and refer extensively to the GM science review and the multiple uncertainties it reveals. Few MPs will have read it for sure and it will be easy for the minister responding to ignore what I'm saying, so I begin by recording that I have given the minister my questions in advance. Elliot treats the debate seriously and gives many answers. I think the only conclusion we might all agree on is that more research is needed.

30 October: My Household Waste Recycling Bill receives Royal Assent. It now becomes law and I'm absolutely thrilled. DEFRA tells me many councils are already in touch with the department and they envisage quite rapid progress. I'm also being asked to meet with companies and chair conferences.

Lots happening in the constituency with a new front opening up at Brockley Cross where a powerful local action group is challenging the council on its regeneration plans for the area. I am asked to address the AGM and it's quite clear they want me to champion their cause. My heart sinks at the thought of yet more work.

A day of action, planned in secret, is now underway at the arches at Deptford station. The police, planning enforcement, London Energy, Immigration Service, fire services and DSS make a combined raid. Tenants were using electricity supplies illegally, health and safety, planning and fire regulation breaches were identified and nine people are arrested for a variety of offences. At our next meeting, there's a sense of momentum among all the stakeholders, except Spacia. I remind them they have all the evidence they need to get rid of their head lessee, who has sublet to a bunch of criminals. Meanwhile, the council has a promise of £2.5 million from government and are forging ahead with the urban design plans.

13 December: Saddam Hussein is arrested crouching in a dirty hole at an isolated farm in Tikrit.

My final appearances in the Chamber in December are all in connection with Afghanistan where the security situation has deteriorated further. Fifteen aid workers have been targeted and killed, together with attacks on the UN that now mean one third of the country is out of bounds to both. I take up the issue of support for the UN electoral registration office, which in these treacherous conditions has been given eight months to complete a process it took eight years to achieve in Cambodia. Adam Ingram replies that he will get more details and write to me. It's good to be able to prompt ministers into making enquiries.

We've arranged a very special treat for my special birthday this year. We are going to spend five days in Marrakesh, covering the birthday and New Year. It's a magical time. The hotel is excellent, the weather mild and the birthday dinner in a restaurant with the floor strewn with rose petals. I've been before but everything is new to Frank and that adds to the enjoyment. We do all the usual sightseeing but wonder if New Year's Eve will be a disappointment. We've paid in advance for the event at the hotel where, despite being delicious, the meals have been a bit repetitive – couscous and couscous.

We step into the grand ballroom with its round tables, beautiful decorations and soft lighting. Dinner is a seven-course banquet of the very best French food and wine. What a joy. And then traditional dancers and fire eaters for entertainment. A truly memorable New Year. We are both very happy.

## 2004

First day back and Jack Straw comes to the House to make a statement on Libya. The UK has been working in secret with the Libyan authorities for nine months to document their nuclear and chemical weapons programmes with a view to their being ended under international supervision. This is quite a coup for the FCO and follows on from the Lockerbie trial and compensation being paid by the Libyans to the victims' families.

I ask Jack if he would agree that if the progress being made in Libya, and indeed in Iran, is to be continued and sustained, Israel too must surely be brought within the ambit of international disarmament agreements? Jack responds positively with the important statement that the 'UK government has long had a policy of seeking a nuclear-free area in the whole of the Middle East' (Israel is known to have nuclear weapons but never admits to it).

The Afghan loya jirga has concluded with agreement on a new constitution for an Islamic state. Meanwhile, Amnesty publish an article I've written for their magazine debating how promises to Afghan women are being broken.

> Women's rights are not a priority ... the lead countries in charge of justice reform and rebuilding the police force, Italy and Germany respectively, have taken few steps to ensure women's rights are part of their work. In my experience there is no shortage of women prepared to work in NGOs, to stand for office and to risk their lives as role models. Habiba Sarabi, the Minister for Women's Affairs, and Dr Sima Samar, head of the Human Rights Commission, are passionate advocates of the universality of women's rights. But only the international community can provide the security in which civil society can flourish and women's individual freedoms can be guaranteed. Only the international community can provide the training and infrastructure to support a legitimate constitutional process leading to democratic elections. Crucially, the international security force ISAF must be

extended outside Kabul. Without that all we will see is a continuation
of the back-sliding which is denying Afghan women their basic rights.

Some weeks later the government initiates a debate in Westminster Hall on
the development challenge in Afghanistan. I argue that women are central
to peace making, the economy and the building of democracy. Many women
are widows and must be enabled to work if their families are not to be forever dependent on food aid. I remind members that women once held half
the local government and civil service posts, 60 per cent of teaching posts
and 40 per cent of medical. It's these same women and their daughters who
were the backbone of the secret schools and health services that sustained
people during the Taliban regime. I point to the maternal deaths – still the
highest in the world – and to the fact that only 19 per cent of the electorate
registered for the forthcoming elections are women. More needs to be done.

The EFRA Select Committee is taking a lot of my time but it's fascinating work. The clerks do an excellent job, enabling us to digest vast amounts
of information and prepare ourselves to question expert witnesses. We are
now taking evidence on the marine environment. We've recently published
our report on the threat to dolphins and porpoises being caught in fishing
gear – thought to be the most significant threat to the species.

I'm up at DEFRA questions to ask the minister about Bayer's withdrawal
of GM seed applications from the UK national seed listing. I put it to the
minister that the motivation is the inability of the GM industry to sustain
its claims. The latest research shows that after initial reductions in the early
years, a massive increase in chemicals is now being applied to herbicide-
resistant GM crops as compared with non-GM. The increase for maize – the
only crop that received a slightly favourable result in the government's farm-
scale evaluations – was 29 per cent. Elliot says he expects this information
to be taken into account in the detailed evaluations. Good – it's a real effort to
keep abreast of all the developments, but if it weren't for our little group of
back-bench activists there would be no scrutiny.

After orals there's a statement from Charles Clarke informing us that the government is to introduce a Bill on higher education. This is the follow-up to the White Paper of a year ago on which a group of us have been vigorously lobbying. He's made a lot of concessions and the threshold for payback of student loans has been raised from £10,000 to £15,000. I challenge him on this as it's much too low for graduates starting employment in London and having to pay London living costs.

I'm still a member of the Modernisation Select Committee, though its work has become more tedious since Robin resigned. At least our current inquiry into connecting Parliament with the public is more stimulating and we get good evidence, particularly from the Hansard Society. One great concern is the pressure in some quarters for the new hours of the House to be reversed, which could happen when the vote is taken before the next general election. As a consequence, we set up an 'Hours Group' and we are now meeting to develop a strategy for the future. Ominously, the EDM seeking a review of the hours tabled by George Howarth at the end of last year has appeared again and now has 200 signatures. At the next orals I press the Leader of the House on moving modernisation forward by transferring Private Members' Bills from Friday to Tuesday evenings. Peter Hain acknowledges the proposition positively, but ends with 'there are counterbalancing arguments'. He knows the whips are absolutely opposed to such a move.

2 February: The reopened inquest into the New Cross fire. We are all tense and emotional as we file into the court talking and greeting each other. Then silence as we stand for the entry of the coroner. How traumatic for these families – a second inquest bringing back all the harsh memories of the first and the tragedy of the fire itself. This is going to be harrowing. The coroner, retired judge Gerald Butler, adds to his resume of events that 'those are the facts' but in 'themselves they do not begin to explain the terrible tragedy of these deaths or to demonstrate the grief and despair of the families. Nor do they show what is a remarkable story of persistence and

determination over the years on the part of many in order to achieve this new inquest.'

We stand for a minute's silence in memory of the dead. Then the coroner announces that he will begin with the formal identification. Each body is numbered in the order in which they were identified, where and when they died and their ages, addresses and occupations. It's chilling listening. Most died of suffocation at the scene. Two people could only be identified by dental records. Then he comes to body number eleven: Yvonne Ruddock, who died five days later of multiple injuries and a fractured skull. Then body number twelve: Glenton Powell, who died six days later of bronchopneumonia and severe burns, and finally body number thirteen: Paul Ruddock, who died three weeks later of bronchopneumonia and a fractured skull. I guess they all jumped from the bedroom windows. How terrible for the families reliving these events today.

Then legal submissions begin, starting with a plea for postponement as Mrs Armza Ruddock, in whose house the party was held, has not received legal aid. This is serious – she must be represented. The coroner says she will not need to be called at the outset so there is time. Next day I write urgently to David Lammy, the minister for legal aid.

Proceedings are expected to last for months and the families group will be there throughout. Next Wednesday I raise the matter at PMQs and receive an appropriate and sympathetic response.

The week ends with more pleasurable events. On Friday I visit the Kender redevelopment – another estate that's being completely transformed. On Saturday a celebration of the birth of Christopher Marlowe at St Nicholas's Church. Graham Corneck, the vicar, is a great history buff. Marlowe's bones are supposed to be buried in the churchyard. Dramatic readings by Antony Sher and Janet Suzman contribute to a most entertaining event. In the evening it's a Black History celebration at the 2000 Community Action Centre on the Pepys estate. Sunday – a much-needed rest.

A group of residents at Harding Place has had a terrible time with Telecom masts placed on the roof of their block by their freeholders. Now there are two more applications, one for a base station, which involves equipment at ground level as well as the roof. They are furious and demanding action. The council is sympathetic and refused permission but it's gone to appeal. I've been asked to convene a meeting between residents and the two mobile phone companies involved. Invitations are sent. When the meeting takes place a dozen residents and managers from O2 and Orange are present. The freeholders' management company hasn't turned up.

The residents have detailed and urgent objections. O2 are bullish, saying they expect to get the refusal overturned. Orange haven't yet submitted and are more conciliatory. The residents suggest the nearby trading estate where there is much greater freedom for the companies to work. Orange reveal that the freeholder will probably gain £4,000–£6,000 per operator for siting the masts. If the applications are to go ahead I will convene another meeting at which the freeholder must be represented. The companies agree to further discussion. Two weeks later I receive a letter from Orange thanking me for the meeting, saying they have listened to the views the residents – 'eloquently expressed' – and they have decided not to pursue their application. What a success – now it's just O2. I'll have to write to the Planning Inspectorate.

My recess ends with a flight to Warsaw with the EFRA Select Committee. We're doing a report on EU enlargement and this is a great opportunity to take evidence on the agricultural and environmental positions of Poland and Hungary. It's clear why Poland wants to join the EU. Really stimulating discussions, visits to farms and horticultural institutes and a few hours of sightseeing in Warsaw's old city. Bitterly cold but very picturesque in the snow.

With all that is happening I realise I have been mad to agree to take part in the celebrity performance of *The Vagina Monologues*. It's at the Old Vic, though we rehearse our parts individually in the Commons. I'm terrified I'll forget my lines and need more coaching to get my performance to the necessary standard. Of course no one's going to tell Glenda Jackson how to perform and Oona King is an absolute natural. A lot of giggling hides a lot of nerves for the rest of us.

Just as I'm arriving at the Old Vic for the rehearsal I see a woman ahead of me – faintly recognisable. I catch up with a make-up-free Jerry Hall. She will be the star of our show and is surprisingly approachable. In rehearsal I have a blank and have to be prompted. I'm wearing an incredibly tight-fitting Ben de Lisi evening dress covered in rhinestones – loaned for the performance. Can I possibly do justice to this? Frank and our friends Mustapha and Sabire will be in the audience – I struggle to hide my apprehension.

In the event we're all word-perfect and the whole show is the most exhilarating experience!

Another Deptford station meeting. Spacia are now seriously embarrassed as everyone makes it clear their failure to act decisively is holding up everyone else. Architects have been engaged to draw up some designs for a new station, which further underlines Spacia's isolation.

9 March: An important statement from Margaret Beckett on GM. The government has concluded, as a result of the trials, that commercial growing of GM beet and oilseed rape should be opposed throughout the EU but commercial growing of GM herbicide-tolerant maize should be supported. I jump up and down but the Speaker doesn't call me. Margaret does not anticipate any commercial growing before spring next year. She acknowledges the threat to organics and the need to look at separation distances and even the possibility of compensation to organic farmers.

I've accepted an invitation from Christian Aid to visit Palestine. This has long been an important cause for me and it's decades since I was there.

I'm travelling with John Bercow – the maverick right-wing Tory – and the Lib Dem Baroness Shirley Williams. We have to fly to Tel Aviv in order to get to our hotel in East Jerusalem. It's a modest guesthouse where we are made most welcome and given keys to our rooms. I'm just putting my small suitcase on the bed to unpack when there's an almighty bang. I rush downstairs, as do John and Shirley. It has to be a bomb. Shirley says to pull the curtains – that's what we did in the Blitz! The manager comes on the scene as sirens wail in nearby streets. We subsequently learn that it was an assassination by the Israelis using a guided missile. Welcome to Palestine.

Christian Aid has arranged an amazing schedule. We meet the UN, NGOs, human rights activists including the courageous Jewish organisation B'Tselem, former Israeli soldiers and many ordinary citizens. We see the absolute horror of the wall – running for miles upon miles and separating whole villages from their agricultural lands. The economy is completely destroyed. Palestinians are not allowed to fish in the sea and the once-thriving tourist industry is in collapse. Agricultural produce can't be exported and travel is severely restricted by the innumerable checkpoints manned by armed soldiers. The new roads built across Palestinian land are for illegal settlers only. It is deeply disturbing. Despite our different party allegiances we are all equally affected by what we see and the terrible injustice of it all.

Most shocking is the effect of the barrier wall around Qalqilya. Five villages have been completely cut off by the wall, separating Palestinians from Palestinians. People have to get permits to access their own agricultural land. Water and electricity are also in limited supply yet mains water and electricity pass through the villages to the illegal Israeli settlements. We hear pitiful stories of children taken ill and rushed to the barrier gates outside opening hours. All medical facilities are on the other side but soldiers refuse to allow them to pass. The wall is not always a wall, but often a razor-wire fence. In Jerusalem, the barrier, once completed, will put 200,000 Palestinians on the Israeli side, cut off from the rest of the West Bank. This is total madness and the daily humiliation of Palestinians is intolerable.

Our visit to Gaza is particularly affecting. We have been warned of the difficulties of getting through the single crossing point allowed open by the Israelis. We pass into a caged area with armed guards at each end. It's quite frightening and there's no indication of when we'll be allowed to pass. Everyone is tense and it's impossible to imagine what life must be like for the Palestinians who want to move in and out of Gaza for work, education, health or family reasons. It's little more than a prison camp. Indeed, the refugee camps still existing after so many years are grim. The UN seems equally besieged as it struggles to support the food programme and run local schools. One of the most poignant issues is the lack of water and the frequent disruption of water and electricity supplies. There are frequent attacks by the Israeli defence forces, particularly on Beit Hanoun, where villagers show us the bullet holes around their homes.

We travel to Gaza City and on to Khan Yunis and hope to go to the refugee camps in Rafah, but we are getting reports that it's too dangerous. In Khan Yunis we are taken to the UN and hear about the huge difficulties they face. As we walk to our car it is clear something is happening. People have transistor radios clamped to their ears and you can feel the tension. We get a message from the UN to get out of the town as quickly as possible. An Israeli attack is expected. Both Gaza City and Rafah are attacked, in retaliation for a double suicide bombing in Israel a few days earlier that killed ten people. Several Palestinians are dead – including two children – and more are injured. An unending cycle of violence.

I am deeply depressed by what we have seen yet we meet many wonderful people who have not given up. There is a huge desire for peace and development. How can the international community have let this situation endure for nearly forty years?

I'm back at the Commons when I'm asked to do *News 24*. The spiritual leader of Hamas, who was confined to a wheelchair and nearly blind aged sixty-seven, has just been assassinated by the Israelis. Both his bodyguards and nine bystanders were also killed. Peace can never be achieved this way. The new leader of Hamas declares war on the Israelis. Less than a month later he himself will be assassinated in the same way.

My first opportunity to ask a question on Palestine. Hilary Benn is answering. I tell him of my visit to Gaza.

> I saw farmers whose orchards had been ploughed up by Israeli tanks, fishermen deprived of fishing rights and a whole population trapped

in the equivalent of a prison lockdown. Following the announcement that food aid to Gaza is to be suspended, does my Rt Hon Friend agree that the present Israeli policy is leading to a humanitarian crisis? ... What contingency plans does he have for such a situation?

Hilary responds in kind, pointing out that 1.5 million Palestinians depend on food aid. He shares my concern and says the government is lobbying the Israeli government hard to ensure adequate humanitarian access.

19 April: The PM is making a statement on Iraq and the Middle East peace process. He refers to the ongoing difficulties and mounting Western casualties and pledges support for the transitional process from occupation to the handover of sovereignty from 30 June. The UN will have a central role and there will be elections in January next year. As for the Middle East peace process, he condemns the assassination of the Hamas leader and welcomes the planned Israeli withdrawal of settlements from Gaza. He argues this provides an opportunity for the Quartet to help the Palestinian Authority take the necessary measures so that a viable Palestinian state becomes not just a concept but a real possibility (the Quartet is made up of the UN, US, Russia and the EU, set up as a response to the election of Hamas).

This gives me my chance and I refer to my visit to Gaza and point out that withdrawal will not lead to peace if the perimeter areas continue to be bulldozed and there is no freedom of movement for Palestinians. The PM agrees but says while there are terrorist attacks within Israel there will always be retaliation. This of course is the crux of the problem – Israel retaliates with collective punishment and that only fuels more extreme individual acts by Palestinians.

At long last, a government-led debate on GM. I challenge the claims of pro-GM MPs. 'GM technology was not introduced to deal with problems in this country or the developing world. It was developed by companies seeking to control agricultural practices that would boost their profits.' I point out that 'the constructs that create genetically modified organisms are designed to cross species barriers. They introduce foreign DNA, bacteria and viruses and carry antibiotic-resistant markers. They are inherently unstable and are expressed in every part of the plant's natural genome.' Yet, the safety case is based on the companies' designation of substantial equivalence. This test was the basis of the government voting last week in favour of the Bt11 sweetcorn without having seen the complete scientific dossier. I refer to people falling ill with allergies in the US and the food company responsible having to recall $1 billion worth of food and another instance of a GM company paying a pro-GM German farmer for the death of twelve cows.

I go on to make a critique of the environmental issues and then directly the government:

> The science remains unproven, the economics unproven, and the public hostile, and the myth that GM will save the starving well on its way to being exploded, yet Members consistently vote for marketing consents for new GM foods to be sold in this country and were rescued from their desperate decision on the commercialisation of GM maize only by the company's decision to pull out of the UK.

The new inquest into the New Cross fire has lasted for three months. I have gone when I could and been impressed by the mass of evidence. I just don't know how to read the coroner. I have had a private discussion with him and it is clear he has been impressed by the way the families have conducted themselves and the compelling evidence that the police and forensic experts have presented. But will it be enough? I'm sick with worry for the families as I make my way to the court.

7 May: At 2 p.m. the coroner enters – my heart is thudding. He begins by setting out the events of 17/18 January 1981 and the first inquest into the thirteen deaths on 21 April 1981. He then explains his duties as coroner, including

'no verdict shall be framed in such a way as to appear to determine any question of: a) criminal liability on the part of the named person, or b) civil liability'. My heart sinks. He goes on to say:

> I have, however, adduced evidence and permitted evidence to be adduced which at first sight may have seemed to stretch beyond the permitted limits. It was I believe essential to do this in the particular circumstances of this inquest, where the Metropolitan Police have properly and pains-takingly sought to pursue every possible avenue, every possible lead in order to meet so far as possible the demands of justice.

My spirits soar. There follows a long presentation as he summarises all the evidence he has heard and points to the inconsistencies in many of the testimonies. In particular, he says, 'I have not I am sure always been told the truth and the question "where lies the truth?" can sometimes only be answered by determining who is the liar.'

He concludes that, despite denials, Mrs Gibbs and Norman Higgins *were* at the party. He concludes that Norman Higgins knows more about the origins of the fire than he has said. He refers to Mrs Ruddock's relationship with Norman's brother Maspan (Danny) and the fact that Danny often stayed with her at 439 New Cross Road. After a row between him and Mrs Ruddock, Danny Higgins left. He emigrated to the US in the summer of 1981 to be joined by Mrs Ruddock's daughter Dawn.

Eventually the coroner comes to the forensic evidence concerning the fire, which he repeats in some detail. Finally, his conclusions include the following:

1. There was no evidence whatsoever that a petrol bomb or other incendiary device had been introduced from outside the building and I consider it extremely unlikely this had occurred. However, at least two items, a photograph frame and a round coffee table, were removed from the front room at some point prior to or very early during the fire.

3. The fire originated on the armchair nearest the TV set. It spread from there to involve the curtains and subsequently the rest of the room.

5. The armchair was ignited by direct contact with a naked flame, such as that from a match or cigarette lighter. Although I cannot entirely rule out an accidentally dropped lit match, I consider it much more likely the flame was deliberately applied to the back rest.

He goes on to explain the relevant law of murder – not applicable – and manslaughter.

Then the bombshell:

> While I think it probable, that is to say more likely than not, that this fire was begun by a deliberate application of a flame to an armchair nearer to the television or perhaps the curtains in order to cause a fire, I cannot be sure as to this. Put another way, I am not satisfied beyond reasonable doubt that there was here an act of arson. It must follow I am unable to return a verdict of unlawful killing, but it must follow from what I have already said, namely that I think it probable there was here the deliberate application of a flame, I am unable to find a verdict of accident. The result is that in the case of each and every one of these deaths I must return an open verdict.

Gasps. I am totally stunned. It's wrong – it had to be unlawful. People shout, others sob, one woman collapses.

The coroner is continuing, paying tribute to the families, the police – everybody – but we don't want to know. I can hardly keep back my own tears as we stagger from the court.

We gather outside. Everyone is distressed. George Francis and I give interviews. I have no hesitation saying that I think there is enough evidence for unlawful killing. George and others are even more certain having sat through

all the evidence and seen the demeanour of those who gave it. There's immediate talk of a judicial review but I despair at the thought. Three weeks later,
the *Evening Standard* publishes an article speculating on the roles of Dawn
Ruddock and Danny Higgins, who both denied being at the house on the
night of the fire. At the time they were living together, Danny having ended
his relationship with Dawn's mother some months earlier. The *Standard* goes
further than anyone before in speculating that the fire could be related to
this 'love triangle'. They also indirectly criticise the coroner for cautioning
Dawn that she did not have to answer questions if there was a risk of incrimi-
nating herself. These are the issues that have haunted the families for years
and now there is no closure. I know the police are also bitterly disappointed
at the outcome.

Terrible news of torture of Iraqi prisoners in Abu Ghraib prison by US
soldiers. Shocking pictures of the abuse have been revealed. Both Jack Straw
and the PM are in the House for statements and I raise the issue again at FCO
questions on the 11th. Everything is going from bad to worse, bringing home
yet again the folly of going to war on a false premise.

Whenever possible I've been out with local party members campaigning
for Labour for the mayoral elections next month – so much easier this time
round with Ken Livingstone the official Labour candidate. I admire Ken and
think he's been an excellent mayor so it's no trouble to stop off at Lewisham
station where he is pressing the flesh. He's incredibly popular and it's a pleasure to be out on the streets with a positive Labour message.

Last year I spoke at a meeting of the Brockley Cross Action Group and
now they're asking for my assistance with the opening up of some 1,000 square
metres of wasteland around the station. This really would be worth having
and I'm keen to do whatever I can. They've started with an application to
the Living Spaces Trust for £25,000. I'll follow up on all the actions over the
next few months and TfL and LBL agree to meet. In the afternoon another
station meeting before going into the Commons. This time it's New Cross
Gate and a meeting with Sainsbury's to discuss potential redevelopment plans.

Saturday, we are boarding a train at Paddington for Cardiff. Millwall are playing Manchester United in the cup final – an incredible achievement. I'm an official guest and although no football fan, I feel really excited and proud of them for getting here. We get beaten 3–0 but it's a great day out.

Back in the constituency the next morning for election canvassing and then a reception for Millwall at the civic suite.

Last day in the office before the Whitsun recess. Frank and I are up early and off to the Royal College of Art for breakfast and to see their show. We rarely take advantage of these invitations as there's so much work to be done but we should – it refreshes the soul and it's wonderful to see such talent on display.

Whitsun recess. Frank and I have planned a really special five-day break in Venice. I'm glad to be able to think about something else. We arrive to find St Mark's Square underwater but nothing spoils our delight at being in this fabulous and truly romantic city.

I return to a poignant letter from George Francis. He writes to ask if I can help with recommending DCI Peter Newman and DC Peter Burns for an honour for the total support they have given the families over the past seven years. He goes on to say 'they instilled confidence in us and also in the wider black community. This enabled us to work with them and more importantly for us the families and the survivors to be able to have a total trust and confidence in them.' Remarkable. Of course I'll help.

Really good news: a letter from the Planning Inspectorate. The O2 appeal on Harding Place has been dismissed. A great success and the inspector refers to my representations – always pleasing.

10 June: An excellent result for Labour in London – Ken takes 55 per cent of the vote against Tory Steven Norris with 44 per cent. The European elections, however, are disastrous. Labour, already second to the Tories, loses six seats, the Tories eight and UKIP gains ten with a popular vote above the Lib Dems. The month rolls on with more select committee evidence sessions, visits to

local schools, an HIV support centre, Jobcentre Plus and various small media appearances as issues of interest are picked up sporadically.

A record attendance at my Deptford station roundtable. Progress at last. The architects give a presentation including a futuristic design for a new station building. Spacia reports issuing a Section 146 notice on the head lease tenant as he had failed to rectify the many breaches of the tenancy. Spacia regained the site and secured it over the weekend only to learn that the tenant had got an emergency injunction and had to be allowed back on. There is unlikely to be a court hearing until September and possibly no trial hearing until February. What a disaster. Spacia should have acted years ago. The only alternative will be to pay him to leave. We press on with reports from Southeastern who have now got a fully staffed ticket office and a new cleaning contract. LBL are providing real leadership and have employed a project manager to pull together all the strands. The carriage ramp will be a significant issue in any development and further heritage funds will be needed. All in all a very positive meeting and I just love the station design. Two months later, great news. Spacia agree terms to get vacant possession of their archways site. The council is willing to buy it, which will enable Spacia to pay off the tenant. Progress at last.

30 June: The PM is reporting on the NATO summit where the main topics were Iraq and Afghanistan. This gives me an opportunity to make the case for all departments of government paying attention to the needs of women in both countries in preparation for democratic elections and for more NATO troops to be sent to give protection to election officials, candidates and voters.

Earlier this year one of the women I met in Afghanistan came to the UK on an FCO-sponsored visit and somehow we foolishly agreed it would be great if we could showcase Afghan women's handicrafts in the House of Commons. Shukria brought with her some embroideries and I thought these, plus local jewellery, could be of interest. I've got permission for an exhibition in the Upper Waiting Hall in the Commons for a week. Now I'm in meltdown.

There's been no clarity on what Shukria will bring, big problems with her visa, endless discussions with the FCO and big logistics for Heidi and me as to how to display the materials. Two people rescue us at the eleventh hour. Matt Biggs, who volunteered for me some time ago (now running an exhibition business), and Rohina Sidiqi, whom I met when she used to work for the UN in Kabul. She has a sister, Rahela, who is resident here and has lots of Afghan cultural contacts. We pull together ideas, exhibits and a backdrop of my pictures from Afghanistan and prepare for the Afghan arrivals amid great trepidation.

The Afghan handicrafts exhibition all looks terrific and is much visited. What a relief.

Next day an important session of the Modernisation Select Committee. Pressure mounted by opponents of the hours has forced Peter Hain into agreeing to a review by the committee and we are taking evidence. George Howarth submits his EDM calling for the review, which now has 244 names. The forces of darkness in the Whips' Office are pushing this hard.

I'm up at DEFRA questions to press Elliot Morley on the coexistence and separation regime for GM and non-GM crops. The EU has set a legal limit of 0.9 per cent contamination. Clearly this level would ruin the purity of organic crops and we are currently fighting it hard. Elliot says the government is prepared to look at it in relation to organic but otherwise accepts the EU limit.

I have one very important letter to write before the recess. The New Cross fire families group wants to go for a judicial review of the coroner's decision. I write a letter in support referring to various remarks made by the judge himself in his summing up, the acceptance that people lied and others refused to speak and particularly the failure to fully explore all the evidence relating to Dawn Ruddock and Danny Higgins. I end with 'I consider the coroner's verdict was perverse and frankly inexplicable to those of us who had carefully followed the reinvestigation and the new inquest.'

Thursday morning, we fly to Dublin. My friend Leila's son, Michael, is getting married there at an amazing location. I've got a nice pink linen outfit

and matching hat and the wedding takes place in beautiful sunshine. Everything is just perfect and we enjoy the weekend enormously – so good to see
Leila and family so happy.

My caseworker, Ruth, has decided to move on and Heidi and I decided
not to try to recruit over the summer. Now we're calling on Fiona Roberts
who can do part-time casework to help out and Heidi thinks she can cover the
rest. Little did we know that this will prove to be a bad decision as the work
of the DEFRA select committee escalates with the pre-legislative scrutiny of
the Animal Welfare Bill and my work with the 'defend the hours' group
becomes more intense.


1 September: News comes in of a school siege at Beslan in North Ossetia in
Russia. Over 1,000 people, the majority of them school children, have been captured by armed Islamists demanding independence for Chechnya and Russian
withdrawal. On day three the school is stormed by Russian security forces using
tanks and other heavy weapons. At least 334 hostages, including 186 children,
are reported dead and many others injured or missing. What a terrible tragedy and I'm expecting to go to Russia within weeks. The IPU facilitates visits
between parliaments and I've not been there since the fall of the Soviet Union.

Satha Bessarami, an Iraqi woman, contacted me earlier this year and we've
met a number of times. Now, at her request, I'm holding a meeting for Iraqi
women who are interested in exploring how women could get involved in the
elections for the Transitional National Assembly. I give them the benefit of
my long experience of selection and election processes and the many hurdles
faced by woman candidates. It's an interesting meeting but my heart sinks
to think of the dangers and disappointments that undoubtedly lie ahead.

Then the House rises for the conference recess. Two days later we're all
at my caseworker Ruth's wedding – a delightfully informal affair. Next morning I'm on the flight to Moscow.

Following the tragic conclusion of the Beslan siege, inevitably, terrorism
is the backdrop to our first day of meetings hosted by Gennadiy Seleznyov

MP, vice co-chair of the Russian IPU. Although Duma members come from different political parties, everyone seems to be 'on message' – Chechnya is not an independence struggle, the West has double standards and as for Kyoto (climate change agreement), it would seriously weaken Russia's economy.

Our hosts are unanimous in believing that terrorism in Russia is part of a wider international conspiracy designed to fuel violence in the Caucasus, particularly in (Muslim) Ossetia and (Orthodox) Ingushetia. They are particularly sensitive to the criticisms made in the West over the handling of the Beslan crisis. They point out that Chechnya is part of the Russian Federation and Chechens in other parts of Russia do not support separation.

Parallels with Northern Ireland are all too obvious to us but any positive exchanges are crowded out by their anger that Akhmed Zakayev has been given political asylum in Britain. We explain that if sufficient proof were provided to our courts, he could be extradited but the Russian case fell apart when a man Zakayev was accused of murdering turned up alive in the court! Unconvinced, our hosts clearly believe that if Tony Blair really supported President Putin, he would immediately send Zakayev (and Boris Berezovsky) back to Russia. Although the accusation of 'double standards' probably still prevails, we hope our defence of an independent judiciary and our references to past US support for IRA activities might have given some insight into how democracy gets tested in the West.

Our conversations with Vladimir Vasilyev, the chair of the security committee, are refreshingly frank. He admits Russian special services and law enforcement organisations were not prepared for the spate of terrorist attacks Russia has recently experienced. Greater security is required on all forms of transport, particularly aircraft, and they are keen to work with UK experts. We have an interesting discussion on how to balance greater security with people's rights and how to tackle terrorists without oppressing whole ethnic groups. We are able to offer our experiences of the impact of terrorist outrages on our own Muslim populations. As for Chechnya itself, the government has promised additional funds and set up a commission to deal with restoration.

We get a different view when we meet Tanya Lokshina, a human rights activist. She gives a poignant account of the despair of the families of the disappeared and the sense of lawlessness and dereliction. She does not share the confidence voiced by MPs in the Chechen administration. She tells us the funds for reconstruction frequently go astray and that only a state of emergency and central rule could bring the transparency necessary to solve the Chechen problem.

Valery Draganov, chair of the economic committee, is obviously the face of new Russia. Passionately in favour of trade liberalisation, he is keen to dispel any impression that economic growth is slowing or that Russia is moving away from democracy. Our next meeting, with the environment committee, begins inauspiciously when their science advisor rejects entirely the international consensus on climate change. Equilibrium is restored when deputy chair Alexander Kosarikov states that the signing of the treaty is a political matter not a scientific one! Having heard that Russia aims to double GDP in a decade, we appreciate their concerns, but argue Russia could gain, particularly from the EU Emissions Trading System (EU ETS) arrangements. Mr Kosarikov says he expects ratification but Russia wants guarantees of help with modernising their energy sector. He urges the UK to make further investment.

Outside our meetings we are able to see the physical transformation of the city, the vibrant commercial centres, bustling crowds and horrendous traffic jams. The English language newspapers are packed with political debate, much of it critical of the government. We are told that the Russian press is just as diverse, though the electronic media toes the government line.

Our stay ends in St Petersburg and visits to the great palaces of the Russian tsars. I find myself reflecting on the vast accumulation of their wealth and power and the repression of the communist years that followed. It is easy to criticise but this is after all a very young democracy. A week after our return, the Kyoto Treaty is sent to the Duma for ratification (we claim no credit).

Back to London on Friday, Deptford Design Festival on Saturday and a surgery Monday morning, followed by a dash to party conference for a couple of days and a SERA fringe meeting on waste.

11 October: Back at Westminster. The pre-legislative scrutiny of the Animal Welfare Bill means the EFRA Select Committee is now meeting three times this week. People have no idea how much work MPs do in committees – they only notice empty seats in the Chamber.

On day one I've also got a meeting with Emily's List. Barbara Follett makes sure that the effort to support and finance the selection and training of women candidates is never off the agenda.

I'm also doing more work on climate change. This has been a passion of mine for years but work on GM has dominated my contributions to DEFRA questions and debates. The significance of Russia signing up to the Kyoto protocol means it can now come into force, increasing the pressure on the US, which has always opposed it. I get my first opportunity in the ballot for FCO orals on 12 October. Jack Straw is answering and I tell him of my recent discussions in the Duma and how controversial Kyoto is. I also ask him to pledge technical assistance to Russia as they requested and get a very positive response.

Geoff Hoon makes a statement on British troops in Iraq. The US has asked for some of our ground forces to move out of their assigned area and come under US command to strengthen their efforts in Baghdad and Fallujah. I point out that two-thirds of Iraqi civilians who die are killed by the coalition and ask if it is not time to review the conduct of the war rather than place British forces under US command. Geoff disagrees.

Claire Curtis-Thomas has obtained time for a Westminster Hall debate on the British Council's Africa programme. Claire also did an exchange with a Zambian MP so we will both get a chance to relate our experiences. Ever since my visit I've been collecting school books, pens and paper, rubbers and rulers and organising for space in a container to be sent to Zambia. The logistics are horrendous and not to be recommended but I want to do something practical as well as spread the word. However, this debate is a great opportunity to put on the record what life is really like in rural Africa. There's lots of interest too in my constituency. Many of my constituents have come from African countries and most send money back home to support extended families.

20 October: Protestors pack the public gallery at the council meeting to protest about new school proposals. Steve Bullock has decided to bring forward
the demolition of the Ladywell Leisure Centre and pool and build a new
school on that site. This is madness. The pool closure was planned for 2010
when the new Loampit Vale development would be underway, including a
new leisure centre to replace Ladywell. Now people are to be deprived of
their pool and will be waiting for a new school for five years after promises
were made. This is no longer a Telegraph Hill issue. It will unite the activists
there with Ladywell and Brockley. The Greens are on the case.

On Friday I make a visit to Lewisham hospital to discuss action on hos-
pital-acquired infections. The pensioners' action group DAGE is running a
campaign on it. I visit three wards and meet all those involved in infection
control. One thing I discover is that antibiotic-resistant bugs don't just occur
in hospitals. Two patients on the wards I visit were found to be infected when
they arrived. MRSA rates are increasing everywhere and the bacteria are
transmitted by both skin contact and from items such as bed linen and towels
etc. This is truly alarming. I've no doubt the less rigorous cleaning regimes
in hospitals as a result of privatisation and the outsourcing of laundry will
have contributed.

Clearly there are straightforward remedies but they are going to require a
lot of changes in procedure and a lot of staff time and effort, as well as money.
One immediate suggestion I have is to test everyone being admitted to the
hospital. I'm told this would not only be time-consuming but also very difficult to apply to people coming into A&E. I can accept that but I'm going
to take it up. (Mandatory screening for all NHS admissions was eventually
introduced between 2009 and 2011.)

A meeting on Convoys to explore both the culture and energy strategies being worked up by the developers, then back to the Commons for a
pre-arranged phone call to Rose Banda in Zambia. I just have to get the transfer
of goods organised. Rose tells me the British Council sent her a copy of the
speech I made last month. She's delighted with it and is having it translated

for the local people. Even more important is the aid they are now receiving. Next morning my good friend and minister Margaret Hodge is at the launch of Lewisham's Children Centre Programme. Despite all the foreign policy doom and gloom our domestic agenda is being delivered to the huge benefit of so many of my constituents.

Doreen Lawrence recently asked to see me about the difficulties she was experiencing over plans for the Stephen Lawrence Centre so I have convened a meeting with members of the St John's Society and the Stephen Lawrence Trust and their architects. The trust has been in negotiation for some years with St James Homes, Thames Water and Lewisham Council over a site for the techno centre they wish to establish in Stephen's memory. After the original site fell through for lack of money, they were offered another smaller site, which included a late Victorian disused Thames Water office building. The problem is that this site fronts onto Brookmill Road and its row of Victorian cottages within the St John's conservation area.

Initially the trust looked at converting the old building, but this isn't feasible so they commissioned a design for a new one. The local conservation society has reacted by applying for the old structure to be listed. I'm having to tread a very careful path allowing each side to present their case and encouraging them to listen to each other. I'm very supportive of the conservation area, which includes a lot of fine architecture, but I really want to see the trust achieve its objective and I know how incredibly hard it is to find suitable land. At least we get through the meeting in a civilised way.

The Modernisation Select Committee is finalising the sitting hours report. One of the things we've recommended and put into practice in earlier reports is modernising the language to help the lay reader. We are recommending keeping the changed hours adopted last year, plus starting Thursdays an hour earlier, reducing the minimum amount of time between standing committee sessions by half an hour and retaining September sittings. This year the latter is impossible as there is essential work to install a security screen between the Public Gallery and the Chamber. Given this means a long recess we propose allowing questions to be tabled for a second period in the summer. Our report complete, we turn again to the sitting hours and to the results of the questionnaire sent out by the Procedure Committee. They of course have to be independent, but I don't think their sympathies lie with us. Ominously they report that there is a small majority in favour of reverting to the previous hours on Tuesdays.

14 November: The annual remembrance service. It's a simple one in Deptford. We assemble at Lewisham College and walk solemnly to the war memorial. Different clerics come from the local churches but they are always radical in their approach, with a world view and prayers for peace that suits me very well. Interesting to see how local people just join in when they see us – all very informal and inclusive. Afterwards I go to a homeless project, a local evangelical church that offers a hearty Sunday lunch.

The *Evening Standard* runs a huge article as part of its 'Clean Up Our Stations' campaign. Very helpful to us. It carries a piece on Deptford station quoting a constituent as saying 'by Sunday it's like a war zone. The ticket machines never work – the help machines don't work and one has been stolen. For months there were no lights on the platform ... and we have to travel back from work at night.'

We're now canvassing and standing at street stalls most weekends. There's a lot of ground to make up and I go to branch meetings whenever I can to try to rally the troops. This weekend I'm also at the Afghan Saturday school, run by Dr Nassimi. These supplementary schools are brilliant, run by volunteers, many of whom were teachers.

1 December: A new parliamentary session means a new ballot for Private Members' Bills. I put in as usual. Very few people have ever had two Bills and even fewer got them through, so I'm being greedy, but I'd love to do another one. Heidi is rather pleased when I don't.

It's the party season and One World Action has a do at the Swedish embassy to celebrate its fifteenth anniversary and Sayes Court Community Centre invite me to the OAP Christmas lunch. I've got something on every evening of the week. A reception for Asquith Gibbes, one of our most prominent black community leaders, who's stepping down as chair of the Police Community Consultative Group, then on to Vani Fine Arts for a wonderful performance with young sitar players and dancers. Next day the official opening of the Crossways Sixth Form Centre and then I'm switching on the Christmas lights in Deptford. In between I'm opening an international conference in Portcullis House, followed by a British Council reception in the evening. I should be signing Christmas cards but as usual the piles are still waiting on my desk. After my surgery it's a Labour Party fundraiser at a local Indian restaurant. Saturday morning a street stall, then Millwall for the match and Sunday I'm reading at the St Paul's Christmas carol service.

I'm not sure I can keep this up for the next two weeks but there's little choice and I certainly have to do the CLP Christmas fundraiser and my own staff meal in the Adjournment. Letters of complaint about the decision on the new school and the leisure centre are pouring in.

17 December: After my surgery I catch a train to Shoreham by Sea – sadly, not a little break but a conference on Afghanistan organised by the Foreign Office at Wilton Park. It's such a privilege to be there and I have lots to say. I'm feeling very tired but it is a stimulating discussion and there is of course good food and wine in the evenings.

A battle to get the Christmas cards signed. Parliamentary business is always light at this time of year so I'm able to fit in a site visit at Brockley Cross and an NDC event at Besson Street Gardens and then relief – the House rises.

Six days later we're on a flight to Rome for a short New Year holiday. Frank's first visit so we do all the sights – can never tire of them. The weather is wonderful and on New Year's Day we are sitting outdoors in a café in T-shirts and turning our faces to the sun. Bliss.

## 2005

We go home to Aberdeen for five days and then back in time for a Sunday street stall and a return to the House on Monday for the Clean Neighbourhoods and Environment Bill. For once I'm going to speak in total support of a government Bill. Fighting environmental crime has always been a passion of mine and Lewisham Council has frequently complained of insufficient powers when we MPs have pressed them to tackle certain issues. Now I can relate what is going on locally, give the council recognition and support the government.

I say that the courts 'may not regard leaving piles of rubbish in plastic bags on the landings of communal blocks as a serious matter but it is soul destroying for residents. It is also hazardous as bags leak, break, stain walkways, create smells and physical hazards and attract vermin.' I give credit to Lewisham Council for securing two convictions for such offences with thirteen prosecutions pending but say how much they welcome the fixed-penalty notice provided for in this Bill. There's also a very welcome extension of powers for the searching, seizing and impounding of vehicles involved in fly-tipping – the defence of acting on an employer's instruction is to go.

I record that Lewisham Council over the past nine months has removed over 5,000 items of graffiti within six days of reporting, removed 538 untaxed vehicles and 1,165 abandoned vehicles. Despite the difficulties, thirty people have been prosecuted for abandoning vehicles and eighty-three people for fly-tipping and littering.

Some progress at Deptford station too. Spacia believe the head lessee will cooperate as he's keen to take the money and with his agreement the site is being fenced. The police attending the meeting report a real reduction in crime and all is much calmer, though there is still some drug-dealing at night. LBL have approved a project manager who is liaising with a specialist at National Rail. The first grant will provide for the site acquisition but then another £4 million is required for the station redevelopment. The timetable is ambitious – a developer is to be signed up by the middle of this year, much of the station is to be built off-site and then the old station is to be demolished in March 2006. Sounds too good to be true but a great start to the New Year.

The Hours Group we set up last year now meets urgently to work on the recommendations of the Modernisation Select Committee and possible amendments for when motions are tabled – so much at stake. I've collated all the results of the London canvass and it's not looking good for Tuesday evening. It's nominally a free vote (though whips are twisting arms), which means there's always a high rate of absenteeism. Last time thirty-one Labour MPs from London voted for earlier hours, thirteen against and ten were absent. Now I've got four switchers and one absentee from last time coming in to vote against us. With such a small margin, if London is not holding up then we've had it.

The debate and voting on the hours is scheduled for 26 January. We work feverishly to pull in every supporter we can and ensure that they commit to being present. I feel passionately about this; the last thing I want is to return to those terrible late nights, sitting around exhausted, trying to work while those who support the old hours are in the bars, the dining rooms or the smoking room. It's not about MPs' convenience or preferences, it's about efficiency, keeping sane and trying to have some semblance of a normal life.

I make a number of interventions during the debate and get to make my own speech. We've got an answer to all the things people say in opposition to the select committee's proposals, but the whips are exerting huge pressure on backbenchers. Several Tory backwoodsmen make outrageous speeches. Patrick Cormack regrets that, because of the new hours, 'The camaraderie that existed in this place for evening after evening in the smoking room and the dining room is a thing of the past.' He records with pride, 'Much to my wife's chagrin I invariably come to London on a Sunday, so that I can be in my office by half-past seven on a Monday morning.' What an argument and Monday hours have of course not changed.

We lose the Tuesday vote by sixty-seven. Despair, but we stay for more votes, which we win, though remarkably fourteen Tories vote against our report on 'Connecting Parliament with the Public'. We've improved a lot of procedures, made questions more topical, Parliament a little more accessible and understandable, and increased pre-legislative scrutiny, but we are still light years behind other Parliaments. For now, the whips have the upper hand. Our subsequent analysis will show that Labour MPs voted 163 to 162 to retain the existing hours. Labour ministers voted thirty-seven to twenty-four, Labour women sixty to twenty-four. The Tories came slightly towards us but their whips worked hard with the Labour whips to deliver a no vote. The Lib Dems demonstrated the biggest switch against us.

Really depressed at losing the Tuesday vote last night. What gets me is the way those of us who want more normal hours are portrayed as workshy. I've got a party branch AGM tonight, my charity Deptford First on Friday, a local councillors meeting Saturday, a street stall Sunday morning, a women's forum Sunday lunchtime and a safer neighbourhoods police/community launch Sunday evening, followed by a 10 a.m. meeting of the Brockley Common group on Monday morning. We will have to adopt different tactics if we want progress on select committee membership and House business.

February recess and I'm spending the weekend away. Ever since I led the IPU delegation to Russia I've been to meetings of the Russia APPG. Now the group and the Foreign Policy Centre are having a weekend at Ditchley Park and I've been invited.

For a busy politician there's nothing better than a weekend at Ditchley – a chance to think, listen and talk about serious issues in the company of experts in a delightful country house. The guest list is impressive: Russian politicians, journalists and academics joining UK counterparts. Our discussions range over issues of convergence and divergence between the two countries, political challenges, the media, priorities in the war on terror and international institutions. With hindsight, several opinions stand out. The war on terror cannot be won – both Bush and Putin are wrong. 'Ukraine is the playing field upon which the US and EU battle will play itself out'; 'the EU needs to remove elements of conflict; the Ukraine does not need to be a geo-strategic issue'. 'Britain and Russia share a common problem – how to bring Muslims into the mainstream of our societies.' A truly stimulating weekend and I really wish I could take more interest in Russia, but it's quite impossible with everything else I've got on.

Frank arrives back from Aberdeen in time for us to attend a performance by Random Dance at Laban. It's good for us to do something together and Frank takes a great interest in dance. Tomorrow will be the fifth Sunday out of the last six that I've worked, so Frank gets dragged along to a Labour branch fundraiser.

Monday afternoon I'm off to Helsinki with the Modernisation Select Committee. We've spent months on an inquiry into the scrutiny of European business. This is a really important subject but deathly dull. Very few MPs care about European legislation and the mechanisms for its scrutiny are, I'm sure, entirely unknown to the public, who are equally disinterested. It's hard going but the experts tell us it's better done in some other countries, which is why we're spending just two days at the Helsinki Parliament. We arrive after 11 p.m. and see nothing, but in the morning as we exit the hotel for our minibus I find I can hardly breathe. We're told it's -25°C. Whether that is true or not I've never experienced such cold but the sun is shining and it looks to be a fine city. Eight hours of talks follow. It's definitely a better model and it does catch our interest.

I've been invited to join a commission set up under the auspices of the Royal Society for the Arts (RSA) to look at drugs policy. This is an area that really interests me. Tony King, professor of government at Essex University, is chairing it. It'll be good to get my teeth into something new, even though I'm sure it will be a lot of work.

A letter from Kew Gardens in response to my phone call asking them if I could sponsor a tree in memory of Keith. For a substantial sum of money I can dedicate one of the great cedars on the Broad Walk. These young trees, now five metres high, were planted in 2000 to replace some very old ones brought down in the great storm of 1987. I can't think of any better way to honour Keith's memory. I complete the form for the dedication that will be entered into the commemorative register. 'In memory of my beloved husband,

Keith, and the golden years of our youth when we walked together in Kew Gardens'. It's a deeply emotional moment.

Two pressing issues. I'm negotiating all the arrangements for a local office on one hand and another visit to Afghanistan on the other. This is, I think, the greatest test of an MP's resilience – to keep all the routines going, all the committees and questions and voting while taking care not to mess up on something requiring a lot of attention. At least the office gets sorted. A developer I've worked with has a block of rundown offices in which we can rent a single large room with our budget. I will have two staff in the local office and Heidi will continue to work from Westminster.

10 March: The start of the debate on Lords amendments to the Prevention of Terrorism Bill. There's a hard whip to get this through before parliament ends for the general election. I find all these Bills depressing as I'm only too aware of the likelihood of miscarriages of justice. The controversy now is about control orders. In the event, we are up all night with the debate in the Commons adjourning at 8 a.m. and again later on Friday morning. A constitutional crisis is finally averted with a compromise but not until the Lords has clocked up its longest ever sitting at thirty hours.

This ludicrous situation demonstrates yet again the folly of long hours when the *Mail on Sunday* reports 'wild scenes took place as the thirty-hour debate on Thursday and Friday turned into a marathon drinking session involving Labour MPs and ministers'. I couldn't be more angry. I've got Saturday events and only Sunday before going to Afghanistan.

14 March: Teatime Monday and Ruth Turner, from Labour's National Executive Committee, and I are on the overnight flight to Islamabad from where we'll take the UN flight to Kabul. We are going as part of a programme financed by the Westminster Foundation for promoting democratic institutions and assisting in transitions. The Labour Party wants an assessment of emerging democratic parties and whether there might be a suitable party with which to work.

Islamabad airport is a turbulent, noisy and quite overwhelming place. Nonetheless, we find our way to the UN flight and board the plane. This is decidedly worse than the one from Dubai. A turbo-prop with light canvas and wire seats – it feels seriously unsafe. It's early morning and as we approach Kabul the cloud is thick and low. The pilot announces we may have to turn back – this is when I wish I'd never agreed to come again, but as we edge towards the perimeter of the high mountains surrounding the city the clouds lift sufficiently to make the rapid descent. The armoured car is there to collect us and we speed off to the embassy. It's now relocated to a fortified austere building and more Portakabins. We arrive and are given fifteen minutes to 'freshen up', then a security briefing before we meet with Rosalind Marsden, the ambassador. I really like her and now of course I'm glad we are here. Sadly the news is bad. They've been in lockdown for months – unable to move about because of the security situation. Our visit will be limited to going to other securely protected buildings.

Our first meeting is at the Friedrich Ebert Foundation, an impressive German foundation associated with the SPD and in Afghanistan to promote democracy and political education. We are meeting their young leaders group and have a stimulating and wide-ranging discussion. Then on to the National Democratic Institute. After a long briefing on their work we have two successive roundtables, each with three fledgling Afghan political parties. Our discussions would be so much more meaningful if we weren't aware of the dominance of Afghan politics by corrupt tribal individuals and warlords. But it's really important for us as Westerners to see the huge challenges faced by any Afghan who shares our concept of multi-party democracy and there is no doubt that technical advice is essential.

Eight hours of meetings, then a brief interlude before a dinner at the embassy with an international group of political commentators. It's a very different life from other embassies and I think it must be quite stifling here. I'm amused to see that I am to 'overnight in the VIP room' and Ruth in '2nd VIP room'.

The following morning, we are at the justice ministry before 9 a.m. for a discussion on representation of political parties and the conduct of elections. Then a very nice meeting with my friend Sima Samar, the chair of the Afghan Human Rights Commission. She is such an inspiration. Then a meeting with the UN Development Programme and a visit to a media and culture centre that offers support and training for journalists, followed by lunch with local journalists in a 'safe' restaurant.

In the afternoon I have my final session with the British Council and women candidates – a video link with London in which I talk about how local issues can be brought to Parliament and the special challenges encountered by women MPs. A meeting with the UN Deputy Special Representative for Afghanistan ends the day.

We leave early morning for the UN flight to Dubai. It's clear the formation of democratic parties is at an extremely early stage. They are small and almost all geographically and ethnically restricted. They all say they support national unity, democracy and women's rights but the development of policy is virtually non-existent.

Back in London, I'm chairing a meeting of the Brockley Common group. There's so much to be done. A topographic survey, searches by Network Rail and implications for the design – fencing, fundraising and then all the issues about maintenance and accountability for finance. There's a lot of support from the community and from the local Labour Party.

Having been a member of Laban's Development Council, I was invited to become a member of the main board some time ago. Now we have a merger underway with Trinity College of Music and it is a huge responsibility. There are endless problems and large amounts of paperwork to be digested, particularly on finance.

1 April: Our environment select committee report on climate change is published today. I think this is one of the most important we've done. The UK will hold the presidency of the EU and the G8 from July and the PM has

announced climate change will be one of the two priority issues. We call for tougher measures across all sectors to reduce UK greenhouse gases and recommend a minister for climate change or a select committee to work across government. We accuse the government of failing to get to grips with encouraging energy efficiency at household level and having no serious strategy to reduce emissions from transport. We stress the importance of increasing the uptake of simple measures such as insulation and low-energy lightbulbs as a means of reducing emissions and raising public awareness. After the general election, 412 MPs will sign an EDM calling for a Climate Change Bill to be introduced. A record number.

7 April: The start of a month-long campaign. Every morning and evening we leaflet a different rail station – we have eight and share Lewisham with Lewisham East. In the afternoon we leaflet parents at over twenty primary schools and in between it's canvassing and leafleting. People still invite me to events but I attend sparingly, giving priority to one-offs such as the sod-turning ceremony for the new St John's Medical Centre. Frank comes back from Aberdeen for a Saturday and Sunday night in the middle of the campaign but otherwise a relentless slog until polling day on 5 May. The Iraq War is a huge problem on the doorstep with some people saying they can't vote Labour even though they support me and know I voted against. They want to 'give Blair a bloody nose'.

The historic third term win wasn't in doubt but we lose forty-seven seats and the vote is the lowest of any majority government in British history. The Lib Dems are the main beneficiaries of the anti-Iraq vote, winning their most seats since 1923. The greatest tragedy is the defeat of Oona King by the obnoxious George Galloway who fought a single-issue campaign on Iraq in her predominantly Muslim constituency (Oona voted in favour of the war but subsequently changed her views).*

---

* In January 2011, Oona became a life peer as Baroness King of Bow.

Frank can't compare his results with 2001 because of the changed boundaries but he ends up with a majority of 7,000 in a four-way fight. My majority
is reduced and the Lib Dems overtake the Tories for second place. The Greens
stay in fourth place despite a massive effort locally.

6 May: Michael Howard resigns as Tory leader and will be replaced by David
Cameron – a bit of an unknown quantity.

Both Frank and I think it's time for a change. We are never going to get
ministerial posts so we concentrate on the back-bench opportunities. Select
committees have to re-form after an election and I've decided it's time to give
up the environment committee. I'm going to try for a place on the International Development Select Committee. Frank has been on the committee
for culture, media and sport throughout the last parliament. He has loved
doing this, particularly the work on the film industry and on dance. Now
he's looking for a bigger challenge and might go for chair of the Administration Committee. I'm also keen to come off the Modernisation Committee
and a number of us are considering putting our names forward for the Parliamentary Committee. Members of this committee represent backbenchers
in weekly meetings with the PM. If a number of like-minded people can get
elected, we might be able to pursue some of the measures we couldn't get
through the Modernisation Committee and try to ensure the Cabinet has
a better understanding of back-bench concerns. We might even be able to
wrest some of the power out of the hands of the whips. Ann Coffey, Martin
Salter and I begin to organise.

10 May: Back at the Commons. I've advertised for new staff and so I've got
hundreds of applications to read. After taking the oath I leave for Wilton
Park. The FCO has invited me to a conference called 'Afghanistan: Beyond
Bonn'. The idea is to look at the successes and failures of the Bonn process
and what lies beyond its final goal of this year's parliamentary elections.
Nine very senior Afghans are down to address us including Foreign Minister

Abdullah Abdullah, Women's Minister Massouda Jalal and Ahmad Hakim, the deputy director of the Afghan HRC, all of whom I've met before. One new acquaintance is the Minister for Rural Development. He has a fine record in aid and development and obtained degrees at York University. I'm really impressed by his understanding of the women's agenda and his quiet charm – very unlike most of the other Afghans in power. We have a terrific two days of discussion – lots of common ground and agreement on what needs to be done – but will it be? I particularly enjoy my conversations with Massouda who very much values the support of the international community.

At some point I will have to consider whether to keep the UK Women's Link with Afghan Women going. When we set it up the idea was to shadow the Bonn process, which is now coming to an end, but there's plenty to keep reporting on at the moment.

My mother was eighty-five last week, so I go straight from Wilton Park to South Gloucestershire on Saturday evening for a party on Sunday.

Monday, and I'm at the RSA Drugs Commission. We are going to spend quite a lot of time understanding current policies, practices and statistics. Tony King is going to be a challenging chairman and I can see we are going to have a great deal to read before each monthly meeting.

18 May: I make my first intervention of the new parliament in a debate on foreign affairs and defence. I raise Sima Samar's report on the lack of justice in Afghanistan and praise the courage of her and her team, travelling throughout the country to gather evidence of atrocities and lack of justice, despite receiving constant death threats. I praise the work of NGOs and remind the House that twenty-four NGO workers were killed last year and five already this year. I point to the fact that although 50,000 people have gone through the demobilisation process, 150,000 men continue to carry illegal arms and to operate illegally. I don't want to diminish the efforts made by the international community, including the UK, but I say, 'The challenges today outweigh the successes.' I reiterate the need for increased security for the coming election campaigns,

particularly for women and the fact that UNAMA (United Nations Assistance Mission in Afghanistan) says the budget to run elections is $50 million short. I explain the electoral system, which is likely to favour groups dependent on warlords and drug dealers, making women particularly disadvantaged. I point to the enthusiasm of Afghan women to stand for election and the fact that women's participation in the presidential election was 40 per cent.

As usual I put into the ballot for Private Members' Bills but I'm not successful and although I continue to try again every year for the next nine years I'll never be lucky again.

I get a round robin from Lord Joffe who has done lots of work on physician-assisted dying. He drafted a Bill that a special select committee of the Lords looked into and took evidence from around the world. It's a massive report but a subject I've always had an interest in so I write back saying I'll be happy to help if there's anything I can do.

I manage to get my staff interviews done and appointments made. I have Eleanor Hoyle as an admin assistant, though she does so much more, and Lucy Doig as senior caseworker and office manager. The greatest loss will be Heidi, who wants to move on. I've worked so closely with her for so long but I can't begrudge her the opportunity to progress her own career, especially when she's carried me through these past six months.

We get a week off for the summer half term and then it's back for a serious session. Nominations open for the Parliamentary Committee. Together with Angela Eagle and Kevan Jones, we all apply as the modernisers slate and get elected.

I've got huge demands in the constituency – always the case after an election when people suddenly think the MP can solve any problem. There's also a tendency to be invited to more events. This week I'm visiting two primary schools and opening new facilities – a product of the government's investment programme. On Saturday the refurbished Telegraph Hill Park is being opened, with Steve Bullock and me making speeches and cutting ribbons. It really is a splendid job and a lovely day all round. On Sunday the Lewisham

Art House, still going strong, has open studios and early evening there's a women's forum dinner at Ladywell Tandoori.

Good news from the council, who expect to be able to select four or five developers to make detailed tenders for the housing development around Deptford station. They will select a preferred developer and runner-up in the autumn with a view to the successful company taking vacant possession of the site next year.

Network Rail, however, are not making enough progress, so I'm asked to write to the chairman as the service agreement must be secured within two months. Yvonne Order, the Deptford traders representative, queries what is happening at the job centre, which is virtually opposite the station. Apparently the lease is running out and the owner of the site wants to develop it. Another headache for me.

All year the Make Poverty History campaign has been gaining momentum, with lobbies of Parliament and huge postbags from constituents. It's a remarkable coalition with three demands: Trade Justice, Drop the Debt, More and Better Aid. We are all wearing the white wristbands that signal our support and Gordon Brown has made clear the government's support. Today Gordon and Hilary Benn (Secretary of State for International Development) are providing a briefing on how the G8 will take it forward. This is potentially transforming and very popular with most of our constituents.

Saturday: It's up early and off to Norwich with Frank who has stayed in London. It's his elder son Frank's wedding to Paula. I really love weddings so I'm looking forward to it, though I'm very conscious of how Frank and his former wife Pat must be feeling. It proves to be a lovely relaxed day and good for Frank to see so many members of his family.

I make a major speech at an equalities conference at Church House on the likely impact of the subsuming of the Equal Opportunities and other commissions into the Equality and Human Rights Commission. Many of us had reservations about this initially, fearing it might disadvantage women and that it was simply a cost-saving measure, but now Labour women and the EOC are convinced this is the best way forward. I begin by recording the unequal position of women. Today women make up only 7 per cent of senior police officers, 7 per cent of the judiciary, 9 per cent of top business leaders, 20 per cent of MPs and 29 per cent of health authority chief executives. The extensive consultations around the new structure have resulted in demands for a Single Equalities Act and the DTI (the department in charge) has committed to carrying out a review to that end. I detail how the new legislation is drafted and how new duties on public authorities will boost opportunities for women. We have a radical agenda, largely due to Julie Mellor at the EOC and Patricia Hewitt while at the DTI.

The month ends with a welcome answer to a PQ I put down on recycling rates and doorstep collections. Both have significantly increased in the eighteen months since my waste Bill was enacted – but collection rates are still low so there's more to do.


6 July: We're all crowded around the TV screen in the Members' tearoom at lunchtime waiting for the announcement on the winning bid for the 2012 Olympics. Paris is the favourite. Silence, then he says it: 'awarded to the city of...' – pause – 'London'. A great cheer. That evening Jack Straw makes a statement in the House – a rare occasion when good feelings pervade the Chamber. Transitions, the contemporary dance company of Trinity Laban, were among the performers in Beijing this week. I ask Jack to congratulate them and to ensure that 'London's diverse arts community is fully engaged and involved in the preparation for the Games'. He responds positively on both counts.

The next day, I'm at home as I'm going to a local councillor's funeral at 2 p.m. and it's a one-line whip. As usual I have Radio 4 on for the news while I'm getting ready. Frank has left for Aberdeen. I'm stopped in my tracks; the Tube has been bombed. My first thought is Frank but no, he's not in the area. Then there's another attack on a Tube, and another. I phone my staff.

They are safely in the Commons, though shocked like everyone else. They mustn't move even though this has to be a terrorist attack and we know the Commons is a prime target.

Another attack, this time on a bus. The TV pictures are terrifying – a sense of panic being suppressed as everyone fears for the next attack and the next location. It has to be Al-Qaeda.

The PM flies back from the G8 in Gleneagles and Charles Clarke makes a short statement to the Commons. All Tube stations are closed and there are no bus services in central London

11 July: A statement in the Commons by the PM. Fifty-two people are dead, fifty-six in hospital, some with very serious injuries. The government believes the suicide bombings were the work of Islamist extremists. The PM confirms there will be new legislation introduced in the autumn. This is the worst terror attack ever in England and it will have serious repercussions for a long time to come.

My application to become a member of the Select Committee on International Development is successful and today it's confirmed on the Order Paper.

Frank has been appointed chair of the Administration Committee. It's a new committee, amalgamating several others that cover the parliamentary estate, catering and security. We're both delighted.

I'm interviewing for my new parliamentary assistant but thankfully not starting early as there's a 9.30 a.m. Westminster Hall debate I simply must attend. Frank Field has obtained it and says that the debate is a challenge to the euthanasia lobby's growing voice. He questions whether people should have the right to control the end of their lives. This gives me my first opportunity to intervene on this subject. I refer to what he has said and then add, 'Even the best palliative care available may not satisfy the person who believes that their time has come, and that they should be in a position to make that decision.' I argue for a choice and not to impose on others and refer to physician-assisted dying. The Lib Dem Evan Harris, who was a hospital doctor, makes a very powerful and thoughtful speech based on his own expertise and the discussions around Lord Joffe's Bill.

My interviews produce one excellent candidate, Susan Adams, to whom I offer the job.

The summer recess is upon us and I'm at an evening reception organised by the EOC and held at the Atrium at 4 Millbank where I meet so many of the women I work with on equality. Then the next evening it's the PLP women's group, held in the River Room of the Lord Chancellor's apartments. Then the House rises, leaving me with just a Friday surgery and a Labour Party barbecue on Saturday before going to Aberdeen. These visits enable me to make a bit of a contribution to Frank's life in Scotland, particularly dealing with the large garden, which I love and which is looking beautiful the moment I've finished weeding. Frank loves to cook and each summer we try to have at least one large barbecue party, having had a permanent barbecue pit created when I designed the garden.

6 August: Terrible news. Robin Cook has had a heart attack while on holiday with Gaynor in the Highlands. He's dead. I'm totally stunned. Robin was so full of life and so happy with Gaynor. It's just too awful to contemplate.

The following Friday I fly to Aberdeen so that we can drive down to Robin's funeral in Edinburgh. It's an impressive affair with a fine eulogy from Gordon Brown. Tony Blair is on holiday and doesn't attend. Robin's great friend the eccentric racing pundit John McCririck criticises the PM and I think he's right.

Afterwards at the reception someone tips red wine on the white linen suit I'm wearing – a second wardrobe accident at an Edinburgh funeral. As we leave we pay condolences to Gaynor, who is standing alone and looking extremely frail. All so very sad. I decide to stay in Aberdeen until my next surgery in ten days' time.

19 August: More sad news. Mo Mowlam has died. Not such a shock as Robin;

last time I saw her she looked so old and ill. What a tragic end to a life that held such promise, only partly fulfilled.

We send out our September newsletter to the UK Women's Link with Afghan Women, documenting what's been happening in the run-up to the elections and wishing all the women candidates luck for 18 September. It will be a very tense time. In the past six months three women have been killed in Baghlan province with notes left on their bodies warning women against working for NGOs. A female election worker was shot in an election office and a peasant woman executed by the Taliban, who accused her of being an American spy. The UK has committed £6.7 million to support these elections and is also providing funding and training for the parliament.

I fly up to Edinburgh. Sod's law, I'm having to sandwich today between a surgery last night and speaking at a Labour Party fringe meeting on Monday. Such a shame because Frank's sister Karen is getting married to her long-term partner Thomas. All good fun but a mad timetable.

17 October: I've convened a meeting at Goldsmiths with the warden's support to discuss the New Cross Road. The long months of frustration and disruptions over the road bridge and the long wait for the extension of the East London line have all added to the general sense that this road and its environs are the pits. Now I've managed to get Sainsbury's, Goldsmiths, the council, Southern Trains (who operate the station), Network Rail, British Land (the freeholder of the Sainsbury's site), the NDC and the police all in one room. Most have never met each other before yet each has a significant role.

The road is a real barrier to the communities on both sides and there's no direct access to Sainsbury's from the rail station. We explore a range of planning issues and each party's potential. Everyone agrees there is apathy among those who own properties along the road. The council has grants for improving shop fronts but they're not taken up. I point out they own some of them! Goldsmiths also owns five shops that are derelict and could serve both the local community and the students. The NDC has various investments going into the area, which are very welcome, but there are only five years left in their programme. Everyone wants more money to do things but I've no doubt it's drive and enthusiasm we need. Three bilateral meetings are agreed for outside the meeting, which is very positive and the station manager says he's happy to hold talks with anyone from the meeting to discuss strategy for improving the station and passenger facilities. This is a great start – the type of result that makes me feel it's worth being an MP!

On to the Commons for my first meeting of the Assisted Dying Group (which I go on to chair), and later a meeting for London MPs to discuss next year's elections with the PM at Downing Street.

25 October: I'm attending my first evidence session of the International Development Committee (IDC), hearing evidence on the G8 summit and whether promises made at Gleneagles will 'make poverty history'.

For weeks a group of us have been discussing the latest terrorism Bill. We are all much exercised by the government's proposals, which we are certain will create alienation, particularly in Muslim communities. We meet with Charles Clarke and also the police. Charles seems willing to seek compromise but the PM is putting real pressure on people to support the government, and the whips are applying maximum pressure. It all comes to a head on 9 November. The government wants the power to detain people for up to ninety days, arguing that the current fourteen days is inadequate. Charles makes his case, taking dozens of interventions from our group. I ask him if it is correct that 'people held under existing terrorism laws have been charged in all cases and that no one has been set free after being held for that period?' I make the point that, if more time is needed, why not twenty-eight days? Charles confirms my facts but cites Lord Carlisle's assessment that ninety days is appropriate.

After hours of debate, the vote is taken. Tremendous tension. The government is defeated. The 28-day amendment succeeds with a majority of thirty-three.

A meeting of the APPG Britain–Palestine where there's a speaker from the 'Open Bethlehem' campaign. This is such a poignant matter. They make such a compelling case for the international community to recognise the great religious significance of their city and the fact that the separation wall is such a huge deterrent to tourism. Even though I'm an atheist I feel like going there for Christmas myself. Instead I content myself with a question to Jack Straw at the next FCO orals. I invite Jack to protest to the Israelis, who have opened a new crossing at the site of Rachel's Tomb in Bethlehem. I point out it is 'deep inside Palestinian territory and there can be no justification for choking off its tourism industry'. I ask for support for the 'Open Bethlehem' initiative. Jack says he'll continue to make representations.

The weekend is spent in preparation for Monday's US visit by the International Development Committee. Lots of papers to digest and agendas to peruse, not to mention the choice of clothes, shoes and toiletries. The briefing papers take up half a wheelie bag by themselves. We leave the Commons midday on Monday and fly to Washington. We're away for the rest of the week.

We leave the hotel at 7.30 a.m. for breakfast and briefing at the deputy head of mission's residence, then on to the World Bank for the rest of the day. Back-to-back meetings with very senior people ending with the managing director of the bank and then a reception hosted by the director of the UK mission to the IMF. 'Heavy hors d'oeuvres will be served' – in other words, this is dinner!

A similar pattern for the next day and a half. Exhausting but incredibly interesting and learning a lot about how these international institutions work. Thursday we leave at lunchtime for New York by train. We go direct to the UN from the station for briefings by our UK Missions, finally checking into our hotel around 6 p.m. in time to change for dinner where we will have a discussion on post-conflict reconstruction and peace-building. I reflect wryly on the fact that the public see these trips as 'jollies' while the schedules are actually punishing. The only people working harder than us are the clerks and advisors who have to back us up, advise and record our discussions with a view to eventually pulling together the report of our inquiry. Both the World Bank and IMF are major players in international development.

Next day I've organised a meeting with Fatiha Serour who I know through my work in Afghanistan. She's now back in the States and I'm thrilled to see her again, albeit for such a short time. Six hours of meetings at the UN then into the minibus and off to JFK for the return flight.

Patricia Hewitt, now Secretary of State for Health, introduces the Health Bill. It provides a legally binding code of practice on healthcare-associated infections for any relevant NHS body and also the ground-breaking provision for banning smoking in enclosed public spaces and work places. This has been a passion of mine for decades and I've been part of the campaign in the Commons led by Kevin Barron. The only problem now is, under pressure from the trade, the government has exempted licensed premises, other than restaurants, from the provisions.

I welcome part two of the Bill and I reiterate our experience in Lewisham and the falling rates of MRSA. However, I declare aspects of part one of the Bill making bars and clubs exempt from the smoking ban to be unworkable. I have lots of statistics and examples to draw on to make my case. I quote the TUC, which compared 235 deaths at work due to accidents and the estimated 700 deaths of non-smokers from second-hand smoking. I say in the case of accidents 'we ask "could this accident have been prevented?" Then we ask "was the employer negligent?" It is my view that in the future any employer who exposes his or her employees to second-hand smoking will indeed be negligent.' I argue that those bars which offer minimal food now will give it up and become smoking bars, which will only exacerbate the problems we have with excessive drinking. The Bill passes without a vote but it will be heavily contested in committee.

I'm off for the weekend so that I can go to an event with Frank. We rarely accept freebies but this one is special. Chevron Texaco have invited us to Drum Castle for a light supper and a performance from young opera singers the company is sponsoring. Just a wonderful evening – how much I miss the musical life I used to have before entering Parliament.

Back on Sunday night and at our regular meeting with Lewisham Council next morning. I leave early to get to Robin Cook's memorial service at

St Margaret's in Westminster – a stirring occasion of great tributes to an exceptional politician. I'm in a taxi minutes after the service ends and on my way to Waterloo to catch the afternoon train to Brussels with the IDC. After a reception organised by the UK representative's office we are free to make our own dinner arrangements so I take the opportunity to see Glenys Kinnock MEP, who takes me to a restaurant serving incredible duck!

Next day, we do eight hours of meetings to include ambassadors to Brussels from a number of developing countries, UK officials and members of Peter Mandelson's Cabinet (he's now EU Trade Commissioner) and other senior people involved in development in three formal evidence sessions. Then we collect our luggage and get the train back to London at 7 p.m.

Last week we published our first report (on Aids) since I've been on the IDC and today's oral questions gives us a chance to put points to ministers. I draw Hilary Benn's attention to the report and the problem of people with Aids not being able to pay for drugs. I ask him to support UNAIDS* and the World Health Organization (WHO) 'in issuing an international policy statement on free access to treatment for Aids'.

Each member of the RSA drugs commission has to prepare a paper and make a presentation relating to the evidence we have taken and it's my turn. My pitch is that we need to see illegal drugs in context, in a spectrum of psychoactive substances. When we look at the health effects of tobacco and alcohol in society as a whole, they cause more harm and arguably cost more in health services than illegal drugs. Most of these substances, including prescribed pharmaceuticals, are used on the basis of 'managed use'. Accepting that illegal drugs cannot be eradicated, we need to look at policies with a holistic health approach rather than increasing punishment.

A last DEFRA orals and an opportunity to ask questions about the climate change summit. I congratulate our ministers on the part they played in getting a good outcome (the Kyoto parties consented to launch a process

---

*    The Joint United Nations Programme on HIV/Aids.

for agreeing greenhouse gas targets beyond 2012 and all parties to renew the framework convention). Given that China is building fifty coal power stations a year I suggest to the minister that one EU demonstration plant for clean coal technology is not enough. I ask if he has any plans for bilateral technology exchanges with China and if he will look to the Export Credits Guarantee department to support UK industry to that end. A positive reply.

My last major task in the constituency is to pack the boxes of goods for Zambia. A significant task but I want to make it fun and invite the local press. Eight students from Addey and Stanhope School volunteer to help and we get great pictures for the local papers. We have two and a half tons of goods and I've got a free flight. Then I'm packing presents and getting the house ready before we drive to pick up Mum. For the first time ever she is spending Christmas with us in London. This is such a treat being in our own home and I hope she'll enjoy it equally. We take her back six days later and we go to spend New Year's Eve in Paris with our friends, Lynda and Richard. A really special couple of days.

## 2006

The House returns. We've all had a good break. It's the only time of year that I close the office and it's really worth it for everyone.

My very first meeting is the Deptford station roundtable. I've been told in confidence that the architects and the council are no longer able to work together and are only speaking through their lawyers. This does not augur well. The positive news is that Railway Heritage has provided an extra £70,000 for viaduct arches work and promises double that next year for work on the ramp. Network Rail has responded to my letter and the council agreement will be signed this month. Govia, a French consortium that owns Southern Trains, has won the franchise for the train service from April and is expected to take over all prior commitments. I make a note to contact them. By Easter, the council will have chosen Cathedral as the developer for the station site and I will have my first meeting with them.

I go directly to Westminster. I want to speak in the debate on energy security. I've become much exercised by the government's change of attitude to nuclear power. My very first speech to a Labour conference was on opposition to nuclear energy. I never placed it on a par with nuclear weapons but I've always believed strongly that it is an energy source that should be phased out.

Alan Johnson, Secretary of State for Trade and Industry, opens the debate and gives a fair summary of where we are – North Sea oil and gas supplies declining, coal much reduced and ageing nuclear plants. Then he goes to the heart of the matter: 'whether we need a new generation of nuclear power stations, or whether we are content to see nuclear disappear from our energy mix' (the latter has been the assumption in previous energy White Papers). Immediately Alan does what all the pro-nuclear lobby casually do – he says 20 per cent of our *energy* comes from nuclear. This is just not true. The 20 per cent figure refers to electricity generation. I make an intervention telling him the correct figure is 7 per cent. He says he's grateful for the correction – is he heck!

I get to make my own speech and refer to the 2003 White Paper, which acknowledged that energy generation and use could not be separated from environmental consequences. Annual reports since then have shown real progress with the first straw-fired station in Cambridgeshire, the first commercially operational wave power station in Islay and the rapid development of wind turbines. What has changed? I ask. The Secretary of State has spoken of the decommissioning and the need to import gas. These were all recognised three years ago. All the issues now raised had solutions thought to be achievable without new nuclear build. I tackle the points raised in debate and point out that nuclear is neither clean nor carbon-free if a whole life cycle analysis is carried out from mining uranium through to decommissioning. It also produces highly toxic waste. I compare the primary energy sources: nuclear, 7 per cent; coal, 16 per cent; oil, 30 per cent; and gas, 40 per cent. Transport uses 35 per cent of energy supply, domestic heating 30 per cent and industry just 21 per cent. Few of us use electricity to heat our homes or power our cars.

I suggest the costs, the risks, the development and build time for new nuclear are out of proportion to any benefits. I also tackle the argument about relying on imports. We have a framework treaty with Norway guaranteed to meet 20 per cent of UK gas demand. I counter the claim that Algeria is an unreliable partner by pointing out that they have supplied energy to Europe for forty years without significant interruption. I applaud the many positive green technologies in the field and tell ministers nuclear is not the answer and that environmentally sustainable development needs to be at the heart of the energy review. I raise the issue at the next DEFRA orals, pressing the case for energy efficiency and asking the minister to feed this into the climate change and energy review so that it gets as 'much attention as whether electricity generation should be nuclear or not'. Elliot doesn't make any promises. Energy efficiency is always at the bottom of the agenda – no doubt No. 10 doesn't find it very sexy. I, and others, keep up the pressure over the coming months, arguing for the energy review to be integrated with the climate change review.

*The Times* publishes a big article from me headlined: 'Why nuclear energy produces hot air'. Very pleasing to be able to set out a comprehensive argument. I've decided to mount an exhibition on renewable technologies to boost the case I and my colleagues have been making. It will take a lot of effort, not least to get the Attlee Suite for a whole day. It will be sponsored by the Renewable Energy Association and PRASEG, The Associate Parliamentary Renewable and Sustainable Group.

19 January: I'm enjoying my time on the Drugs Commission. It's challenging intellectually and I'm learning a lot. Today I'm in the Chamber for Charles Clarke's statement on cannabis. He asked for a report from the Advisory Committee on Drugs and they have advised leaving the cannabis classification at C. We know he's been under pressure to reclassify to B so it's important I attend.

A very sensible statement. No reclassification and a wide-ranging approach to health, education and policing. I congratulate him and add that with more

than 9 million people admitting to taking the drug at some time, classification status is not the issue. I ask him to ensure a comprehensive programme
on healthy living and reduction and avoidance of all harms is made available
to primary school children where it is most necessary. Charles agrees. This is
good news. Let's hope he's still in post when we finish our study.

A meeting of the New Cross Road roundtable. Sixteen stakeholders
attend. TfL has plans to completely change the gyratory and one-way system. Potentially this will produce chaos and I doubt it will ease congestion,
but other road changes could produce a pleasanter environment for local
people. The NDC also has development plans that are going out for public
consultation (I'm opening the exhibition on Saturday). The council is proactive and has appointed consultants to do some master planning around New
Cross Gate station and the retail park. All Saints Church is working on a plan
to improve its community facility and the London Development Agency is
likely to finance the development of the old Laban building, adjacent to Goldsmiths, as a creative incubator business site. So, lots of positives but clearly
a need for coordination. The police report they have caught a burglar who was
committing half a dozen crimes a night on Telegraph Hill and CCTV is now
definitely going into the Goodwood Road area. The council has appointed
an excellent town centre manager and she's very keen to work with us.
A good morning's work.

This week the government is hosting a conference on Afghanistan so I've
got a lot of extra meetings, starting with an IDC meeting with Afghan ministers. I arrange meetings with women's groups and our UKWLAW for the
Afghan women MPs and my friend the Women's Minister and happily join
the formal reception at the FCO and take Massouda to dinner. The conference itself is important as it sets out to agree a compact between the Afghan
government and the international community with a view to 'consolidating
democratic institutions, curbing insecurity, controlling the illegal drug trade,
stimulating the economy, enforcing the law, providing basic services to the
Afghan people, and protecting their human rights'.

February recess and we're spending four days in Italy looking at property. After many years of staying with Gabriella we've decided to try to buy something modest for ourselves. On our last night we look online and see an apartment in a hamlet that is close by and very lovely. Gabriella tries to get the keys but it's impossible so we drive up there in the morning before going to the airport. It's beautiful. Even without seeing inside the flat we decide we have to have it.

25 February: Leaving for the overnight flight to Johannesburg with the IDC, arriving next morning for the onward flight to Lilongwe. We'll be away for twelve days with a tough schedule as we visit Malawi, Botswana and Mozambique. We will be looking particularly at how DfID is delivering its private sector development programme. Our meetings range from field trips to some of the poorest communities to meetings with all three Presidents. No amount of evidence-taking at home can compare with this.

In Malawi we visit a UN food distribution centre. It's all well organised but seeing the people standing in lines and children who are severely malnourished is heartbreaking. Even more so is a hospital visit where we learn of the horrors of child marriage and pregnancies that result in permanent internal damage even if mothers and their babies survive. We visit wards where people are dying of Aids and discuss the international support for treatment and drugs. Many of the nurses are of small stature and appear little more than teenagers themselves, despite the heavy burdens they bear. Most disturbingly we are told of the tiny numbers of medical staff in the country and the numbers who are attracted to the high wages and better conditions in the UK.

In Botswana we see better hospital conditions and provision for Aids treatment but it's clear that the mining industry, particularly diamonds, has its own contribution to make as miners live at the mine and see little of their families, resulting in prostitution and the spread of disease. Lots of interest in development and particularly for the private sector. A real contrast to the dire poverty of Malawi. Mozambique offers another contrast – rather than drought, their problems have been floods. A lot of discussion and interest in developing their utilities and excellent field visits to look at water and sanitation. Encouraging growth in the private sector from such a low base is hugely challenging and we have some tough questioning for DfID, World Bank officials and the mining interests in Botswana.

Before we left I made a plea for us to have one day off rather than working through the whole twelve days. An 'optional' trip has been arranged! I stand firm – I'm going nowhere. John Bercow and Quentin Davies do the same. John has mellowed so much since his neocon days and Quentin is always amusing, so to my shame I have a hugely enjoyable day in the company of two Tory men. I try not to be too jolly when my Labour colleagues return exhausted from their very disappointing day on the road.

Overnight from Johannesburg and straight to the Commons. It's Gregory Barker's Private Member's Bill on climate change so I have to be there. My heart sinks: Eric Forth is in the Chamber, which can only mean he intends to talk out the Bill and after five hours he's done just that. The Bill is dead. I drag myself to my surgery – thank goodness I've kept the weekend free.

The weeks roll on with all the usual local and parliamentary committees to attend. I keep up a stream of oral and written questions to DEFRA, DfID and the FCO and am glad of the occasional distraction. Today's is mega – Bill Clinton is in town and I'm going to hear him speak at the Smith Institute. What a performance. He's so charismatic and now of course hugely respected for his humanitarian work.

29 March: Tremendous pressure mounting for Blair to go. Ashok Kumar, normally a gentle soul, has stirred things up with an article in the *Northern Echo* calling for a smooth and rapid succession. Tony's abroad and John Prescott is chairing the Parliamentary Committee today, where I raise the issue. Confidences are usually kept but after the meeting the *Glasgow Herald* reports my comments and the *Daily Telegraph* reports that 'Mr Prescott left her with the clear impression that he would attempt to act as a go-between to ensure a "smooth transition"' Naturally I haven't spoken to either paper!

Easter recess is a mixture of Aberdeen, Mum's and loads of leafleting and campaigning for the May elections. We had expected to go to Italy to advance our purchase but our bid fell through – a huge disappointment. I've also got to proofread a chapter I've written for a book called *The Men Who Made Labour*, celebrating the centenary of Labour in Parliament. One of the first Labour MPs to be elected was my predecessor in Deptford. Charles Bowerman was elected in 1906, taking a seat from the Conservatives, who had held it continuously since 1885, when the seat was created. Bowerman would hold the seat for twenty-seven years.*

I get home after an early-evening canvass and see a message on the answerphone. I'm stopped in my tracks – it's the estate agent from Tuscany. He's just been instructed to sell a second property in the same hamlet. Are we interested before it goes to advertising tomorrow? What can we do? We have to have it. I phone Frank in Aberdeen. When we lost the first one I asked the agent to inform us if something else came up but he said that was the first in twenty-five years and he didn't expect another. The pictures are beautiful. We can't go so I phone Gabriella and ask them to visit. As usual they respond instantly: they will go tomorrow and report back. They say it's a good buy and that I'll love the garden. This is the chance of a lifetime. It seems like madness but we agree to buy it unseen. There will be no regrets.


4 May: Disastrous election results. The Greens take all three seats in Brockley and in Ladywell – a direct result of the mayor's decision on Ladywell Leisure Centre and the new school. It's obvious something is wrong when activists can get thousands of signatures on a petition against a local government decision. I couldn't even persuade Steve to write to them all – something we always do when petitioned. A lot of anger in the local party as good people are defeated.

After yesterday's disastrous results Blair reshuffles his Cabinet, an indication he's not intending to go soon. Charles Clarke is out and Jack Straw and

---

* I would eventually hold mine for just a year longer.

Geoff Hoon demoted. Margaret Beckett's unswerving loyalty to the leader lands her the most surprising promotion to Foreign Secretary. Newspapers full of bile again today. Jane Kennedy, a loyalist who resigned, accuses Blair of riding roughshod over ministers. Stephen Byers says, 'Tony has got a desire for a few more years to achieve…' Critics of Blair are quoted as saying he lives in 'a parallel universe'. It just goes on and on, giving huge succour to the Tories.

8 May: The FCO publishes the UK Action Plan for the implementation of UN Security Council Resolution 1325 on Women, Peace and Security. I decide to try to get an APPG together. We'll get a lot of support from an NGO already in existence and made up of ex-pats in peace-building and development. Over the next two months, we decide on an Associate Parliamentary Group rather than the usual APPG. This enables outsiders to be members and in this case, very importantly, civil servants from the MoD, FCO and DfID. There's an excellent turnout at our inaugural meeting, including five civil servants and lots of NGOs. Our speakers are Zarin Hainsworth from Gender Actions for Peace and Security, and Joan Link, head of conflict issues at the FCO. Both are experts in their field. I get elected to the chair.

Newspapers are again fanning the flames with reports of mudslinging, poisonous exchanges, internecine warfare, coups, threats and counter-threats. Gordon Brown on the *Marr Show* calls for an orderly transition of power. I decide I'm going to try to get called at tonight's PLP meeting.

6 p.m.: The room is utterly packed, so I'm forced to enter at the Cabinet end and stand. Blair addresses the meeting – terrible tension in the room. I get called and make an impassioned speech, praising both men's contributions but demanding the feuding should stop, regretting the damage being done and telling the two men directly that they have to come to an agreement. The majority of speakers argue for an orderly transition. After an hour of heated debate, we are left simply with a pledge that the successor will be given 'adequate time' to prepare for the next election.

Next day massive coverage of the 'private' PLP meeting. I'm quoted in the *Financial Times* and *The Times* – the latter recording my speech as greeted by cheers (which was actually true although I never spoke to a journalist!). I've no doubt last night was a watershed even though it's being denied.

The security situation in Afghanistan continues to worsen. Malalai Joya, a young radical feminist recently elected, has been attacked in the Parliament. She is now moving every night to a different safe house. Elected women councillors in Helmand have received death threats and the head of the women's affairs department in the province has narrowly escaped an assassination attempt. I raise these matters at FCO questions, remind the minister of our obligations under UN Resolution 1325 on women, peace and security and urge him to discuss the protection of elected women representatives with the Afghan government.

25 May: The final report of the Health Impact Assessment of SELCHP on local residents begun five years ago. As I expected they conclude that no effects on health can be ascertained. They do, however, point to obvious causes of ill health, such as air pollution from road-borne traffic. SELCHP contributes a small amount as a result of 200 lorry movements each day. They make a lot of sensible recommendations for small improvements but there's nothing that couldn't have been said before the work was undertaken.

Eric Forth, the scourge of Private Members' Bills, died last month, creating a by-election in Bromley and Chislehurst. Our candidate is a young woman called Rachel Reeves. I don't know her but I'm off to campaign in her by-election. (Sadly, Rachel will come fourth behind the Lib Dems and UKIP – represented by a man called Nigel Farage – but I think she'll go far.)

Off the whip to go to Wilton Park at the invitation of the FCO. A three-day conference on implementing UN Security Council Resolution 1325. This really is a breakthrough. A terrific programme and probably more women speakers than ever before at Wilton Park. The first session is led by Ellen Johnson Sirleaf, the President of Liberia. What an impressive woman. This is such a brilliant initiative by the government and I'm thrilled to spend time with old friends like Fatiha who has come from New York. The conference ends with an address from Mary Robinson, the former President of Ireland. We've got some serious allies in the FCO civil service.

Our 1325 Women, Peace and Security Group activities are now becoming well-known in the NGO community and we are being contacted by women from other conflict zones. The latest is Nepal. I'm very wary of spreading our efforts too thinly but the very universality of the resolution makes us feel obliged. There has been civil war in Nepal for a decade, with 14,000 lives lost and an economy wrecked. On 27 April, Maoist insurgents responded to a demand by the newly appointed Prime Minister and announced a three-month truce. A week later, the new Cabinet declared a ceasefire. Since then talks have been held with the international community, including Britain. I've been contacted by Lily Thapa who leads an organisation of widows. They have been demonstrating every day outside Parliament because not a single woman is included in the draft constitution committee. At the next FCO orals, Ian McCartney is answering questions on Nepal. I refer to the demonstrations and to 1325 and ask his officials in Kathmandu to meet Lily to 'see what assistance can be given to those women (widows), who are traditionally shunned in Nepal, and who are, after all, probably the most potent symbols of the conflict'. A really positive response, which includes an offer to meet with me to discuss the situation further.

19 June: Both Harriet and I are in this week's *The House* magazine; Harriet on equality and me on energy. Harriet's is a profile piece, which gives an impressive synopsis of her parliamentary life and ends with her making the point that there should always be a woman in Labour's leadership team, but, no, she's not going to say whether she will run until there's a vacancy.

An exciting interlude in a very busy week – I'm going to hear Al Gore speak on climate change.* He's always been a committed environmentalist

---

* Gore was awarded the Nobel Peace Prize for his work together with the IPCC in 2007.

and since he lost the presidential election to George Bush in 2000 he's devoted himself to promoting the slideshow that has become the basis of the film *An Inconvenient Truth*. He's an awkward speaker but his slides make up for it. A devastating warning to the world. It should be shown to every legislator – and every school child. The following week, David Miliband, DEFRA Secretary of State, makes a statement on climate change. It's excellent. I do so much work on this in our back-bench groups and with NGOs and SERA that it's great when the government is driving the agenda forward. In passing he refers to the corporate leaders group, which I know well, so I ask him if he'll meet with them to discuss their proposals for hydrogen storage and wave and tidal electricity generation. He compliments me on my 'distinguished record' and says the less developed technologies must be given a chance to develop. Other members of our climate change group also intervene. We have a champion here and feel greatly encouraged.

But all too quickly there's another less pleasing statement on the energy review from Alistair Darling. He does give a boost to renewables and energy efficiency but, as expected, promotes a new nuclear build. He says by 2020 the contribution of nuclear will be down to 6 per cent. The obvious question is what will new nuclear contribute by 2020? (I anticipate nothing.) Alistair dodges the question.

7–9 July: In Brussels for the weekend and chairing a meeting of MPs from the G8+5 countries at which we draft a statement on climate change for the G8. On my return I'm up at international development questions to draw it to the minister's attention and make a plea for the international financial institutions (the UK has a say in all of them) to increase investment in low carbon energy and to assist developing countries to adapt to climate change. A favourable response. I get another chance to press on clean energy the very next day when the Secretary of State makes a statement on his DfID White Paper.

It's a whole week since the conflict in Lebanon began and the PM has refused to condemn Israel for its utterly disproportionate response to Hezbollah. Feelings are running very high in the PLP. We have sharp exchanges at the Parliamentary Committee. For me this is the last straw – our declared objectives for peace in the Middle East are a complete scam. Constant speculation in the media is hugely damaging for us all but Blair brushes it off, saying he's just getting on with the job, 'which is what the public want'. I really can't bear to be in the same room as him.

I spend the morning at the graduation ceremony at Trinity for the music students. A lovely event but I have to rush away as soon as it's over. Margaret Beckett is opening a foreign affairs debate. She allows me an early intervention when she refers to Hezbollah. I agree with her that Hezbollah started the conflict but ask if she agrees that Israel's response – 300 Lebanese civilians dead, 1,000 injured (a third of them children) and half a million people displaced – is utterly disproportionate? Margaret expresses regret but declines to agree. I have no doubt this is on orders from No. 10.

It's that time of year again – Ladywell barbecue and then we're off to the civil partnership of friends Isobel and Eileen. Frank knew Isobel in Dundee. In London, she volunteered in my office and now works at the TUC. Next day it's the annual Brockley Garden Party, Hilary Benn's drinks party on Monday and the women's PLP on Tuesday. I've put in for the end-of-term adjournment debate on 25 July. These debates have no theme but it's a good opportunity to put a statement on the record.

I open with reference to last Friday's iconic front page of *The Independent*. On the left were the flags of 189 countries that support the UN call for a ceasefire in the Middle East, on the right a white space with three dots of colour – Israel, the US and the UK. I say, 'That is not where I want my country to be – isolated, tied to a US administration run by neocons and headed by a religious zealot.' I make a wide-ranging speech covering the Middle East and the 'special relationship'. I also take the opportunity to point to the contradictions between our work on the non-proliferation treaty and the recently announced proposal to renew Trident.

Leaving later that night I reflect on how much time I'm now spending on foreign affairs. Although always an interest of mine, it is the government's agenda that's driving it all. When I left home to go to university I thought British involvement in war was a thing of the past, but we seem to have been in conflict somewhere ever since I came to London.

Three whole weeks in Italy. So exciting. We are going to sign the contract on our property, which we won't get possession of until next Easter, so it's all a bit surreal. It would be really scary if we didn't have such good friends who know about property and Italian law. We are quite intoxicated at the thought of being the custodians of a tiny bit of historic Tuscany.

Much restored and back for the official opening of Brockley Common. A lovely sunny day, great atmosphere and sense of achievement. Harriet asks to see me. She wants me to be a part of the team preparing for her deputy leadership campaign. I'm very happy to agree. Mike Foster, the Hastings MP, will be the campaign manager.


7 September: All hell breaks loose in the media, led by Blair's outriders Milburn and Byers. Tony Blair announces this year's party conference will be his last. He will step down as Labour leader within the next twelve months. Tom Watson, one of the junior ministers who signed one of the 'secret' 'Blair must go' letters, resigns. Seven PPSs follow. Charles Clarke attacks Gordon.

This is all such a tragedy. Blair and Brown camps will be worse than ever – and for what? Gordon is the only possible successor and as I and others keep saying at our weekly meetings, the briefings and counter-briefings are causing huge damage. Harriet will definitely contest the deputy leadership.

Geoff Hoon calls for Blair to quit before next year's local elections. Much speculation about the deputy leadership. *The Independent* has Alan Johnson in the lead at three to one, and Harriet last at thirty-three to one.

Mike Foster and I meet with Harriet to go over our strategy for conference. We already have half a dozen key supporters – people Harriet has worked with over the years, who will be the backbone of the campaign – but we need to move quickly to sound out those most likely to be willing to declare their public support at the earliest possible stage. This is not easy when no contest or date is announced but it's vital to get pledges now as everyone else who might stand will be doing the same. Our most likely supporters outside the immediate circle of friends will be progressive women and MPs who voted with us on the hours.

At conference we will need to be targeting likely MPs, trade unionists and party delegates. The MPs are the priority – forty-five MP nominations are needed to get onto the ballot paper and there are likely to be up to half a dozen people wanting to stand. With no September sitting most MPs haven't been in the same place for months, so this is a crucial time.

In Manchester for the start of the conference and a meeting with Harriet to go over her diary. She's always had a high profile at party conference and has visited so many constituencies that lots of members know her from personal contact. We've drawn up lists and grids for all of us to record as we go and we will meet every day.

The House returns and we report back on Harriet's campaign. Lots of people vaguely sympathetic but not ready to commit. Some want to see who else comes forward, some want to know what their CLP position will be, others have local loyalties to other potential candidates. Very few people willing to commit at this stage but we have to doggedly work through the lists, gain as much intelligence as possible and record it. Recording, checking and rechecking will be critical to our progress. The work is piling up and all three of us will need volunteers from our offices to assist – they come forward enthusiastically. We will now meet every Tuesday and more often if needed.

A meeting of the Deptford station roundtable. Just when I thought our work might have been concluded we are faced with a major setback. When the contract with the architects who designed the elegant station for the council was discontinued a firm of specialist rail architects was brought in. I've been told that lots of amendments have had to be made for technical reasons and this morning we're to see the result. Absolute horror. This is not a technical adjustment, it's a total redesign. It looks as bad as that other blot on the landscape, the Sainsbury's petrol station fronting onto New Cross Road that everyone wants rid of. I say as much. Now, instead of winding up the group, we are going to have to go on and try to influence future developments.

17 October: After months of effort and a few dramas getting all the equipment through Portcullis House security, my renewable energy exhibition is in place. Major companies have come from all over Britain to exhibit. Fascinating stuff – from solar to wave energy, tidal stream turbines to biofuels, wind power, heat pumps and lots, lots more. The fuel cells and hydrogen technologies are fascinating – a field I haven't really looked at before. The innovation is spectacular. Perhaps my favourite is a small portable solar-powered refrigerator made for carrying vital vaccines in developing countries. So many market opportunities for British industry to pursue. I only wish the exhibition could stay for a week rather than a day. Lots of people come, including Gordon Brown. A triumph! But, after just a year in my office, Susan has secured a much better job for herself, leaving me to find a new employee – huge irritation.

David Blunkett has made a spiteful intervention in the deputy leadership campaign with an updated note in his memoirs and an interview in the *Evening Standard* that gets the headline 'We don't need a female deputy'.

A rare event. I'm called at PMQs. In breast cancer week we are always lobbied and I have a particularly pressing case. A constituent with breast cancer is paying for her own Herceptin as our primary care trust doesn't fund it. I refer to the postcode lottery for this and other cancer-related needs and ask the PM to ensure equal access for treatment.

Next day I'm speaking in the debate on DfID's White Paper. I praise Chapter 7 – 'Climate change poses the most serious threat to development and the Millennium Development Goals' – and refer to our visit to Malawi, where we saw food aid as a result of the drought, and Mozambique where we saw the effect of floods. But I go on to criticise the lack of a gender strategy. African women are the world's poorest people. They have the lowest life expectancy and the greatest disparity with men in access to education, literacy and income in the world. I recall that six years ago the UK led the international community in promoting Security Council Resolution 1325 on Women, Peace and Security. I tell the House I am astonished that a fifteen-page consultation document on conflict policy produced by DfID does not mention the word '*women*' once.

30 October: Nick Stern* published his report into the economics of climate change this morning and David Miliband is making a statement. He quotes from the conclusions: climate change 'could cause more human and financial suffering than the two world wars and the Great Depression put together'; the 'costs of inaction far outweigh the costs of action'; 'the window of opportunity to reverse the rise in emissions is narrowing'. I get a chance to raise a question about home heating grants but not before I've congratulated everybody and said that, if we embrace the Stern Report, 'history will see today was a turning point in the global treatment of climate change'.

Next day an important session of the IDC. We are undertaking an inquiry into the Occupied Territories and will make a field trip next week. This will be a complex and difficult inquiry. When Hamas won the Palestinian Council elections and took over the Palestinian Authority (PA) in January, it provoked a crisis within the international community. The EU, Russia, US and UN (the Quartet) set out the terms on which financial support could continue to be given to the PA. Hamas's refusal to accept them has led to the current humanitarian crisis. We need to understand whether DfID aid is being effectively delivered in the new circumstances. The Quartet has set up a temporary international funding mechanism, which is channelling funds through the office of the moderate President Abbas.

DfID's role in the Occupied Territories is unlike any it undertakes elsewhere. Arguably aid bolsters the status quo, removing Israeli responsibility for the people it occupies, and we have to question that. ·

---

\* Now Sir Nicholas.

6 November: After initial briefings we travel to Ramallah for discussions at the office of the President. We will spend all day discussing the economic, political and humanitarian situation. Over the next two and a half days we will travel around the West Bank, through innumerable checkpoints (there are 528) looking at security and development – plenty of the first, precious little of the second. Our visit to Hebron gets cancelled due to the threat of violent demonstrations in reaction to the killing of civilians by Israeli forces in Beit Hanoun.

The situation is so extreme I wonder how the UN, DfID and NGO workers can ever keep going, without hope of any improvement and the prospects for peace and the two-state solution ever receding. I feel this particularly when we meet Hanan Ashrawi, a woman politician I've always admired. Our final afternoon is spent in discussions with members of the Knesset, the PM's office, the Ministry of Defence and with Shimon Peres.

At the Israeli PM's office, we are told there is no humanitarian crisis in the Occupied Territories – just a decline in living standards.

The House returns for the Queen's Speech and Susan's replacement, Mike Smith, starts work. A very busy couple of days with induction for Mike and an IDC evidence session on HIV/Aids, Lewisham Race Equality Action AGM, a surgery, a health meeting, a Deptford First reception and the second half of an evening of Indian music and dancing.

Saturday morning, we drive to Norfolk for a relaxing weekend with our friends Margaret and Henry Hodge.

I get called on the last day of the Queen's Speech debate and take the opportunity to speak about the visit to Palestine – not the development aspects, which will be the focus of the report, but the politics. I speak again about the wall, international obligations and illegal settlements but I want to draw the House's attention to more recent developments.

> Earlier this year, the occupation took on an even more insidious dimen-
> sion when Israel stopped transferring to the Palestinian Authority

the revenues, around $60 million a month, it collects on behalf of the
Palestinians from trade. As a consequence, health workers, teachers,
police and others have gone unpaid for eight months. With no resolution in sight the health workers in Gaza stopped going to work this
month, resulting in every emergency room being closed.

I refer to the Prime Minister seeking to engage Syria and Iran in tackling
the problems of Iraq but say, 'It makes no sense to talk to the leaders of Syria
and Iran if we cannot talk to the democratically elected leadership of Hamas
in the Palestinian Authority.' I conclude that without justice for the Palestinians, Israel will never be secure and there will be no prospect for peace in
the wider region.

Menzies Campbell asks about the White Paper on Trident. Blair replies
it will be published before the end of the year. Broadsheets all respond with
articles and I get asked to do media. Very interesting article by Richard Nor-
ton-Taylor in *The Times* raising all sorts of questions such as: 'The government
has yet to explain who now would be deterred by Trident.' Exactly.

An important meeting of the 1325 APPG. Janet Benshoof from Harvard
Law School addresses the group on the importance of 1325 in transitional
states. She has been working on the training of judges for the War Crimes
Tribunal in Iraq. Civil servants report excellent progress on getting a UK
Action Plan on 1325 adopted by FCO, MoD and DfID. Lots of discussion and
input from NGOs and a marked increase in politicians' interest.

Spectacular results from the YouGov poll we commissioned. It tested
Harriet's appeal to the public against the other five people we now know
will stand for the deputy leadership. Harriet comes out top on all counts but
particularly important is her standing among swing voters and women voters. Since 2005, the Tories have made significant inroads into the women's
vote, opening up the gender gap Labour closed for the first time in 1997.
Twenty-nine per cent of swing voters said electing Harriet would make them
more likely to vote Labour (putting Harriet ten points up on Hilary Benn

in second place). Seventeen per cent of women said electing Harriet alongside Gordon Brown would make them more likely to vote Labour, while none of the other candidates got into double figures. This is a real boost so I draft a letter for Harriet to send to the whole of the PLP.

29 November: A fortieth anniversary party for Shelter. I just have to go.

4 December: The Trident White Paper is published and I get to spend the morning doing media before going in for the PM's statement. The Speaker calls me and I ask, 'Given the importance he [the PM] attaches to an independent nuclear weapons system for the UK, would he advise the twenty-three *non-nuclear* NATO states to acquire similar independent nuclear weapons? And if not, why not?' Of course he says no and goes on to cite the non-proliferation treaty as giving the right of the major nuclear powers to remain nuclear powers. This is just not true but will be repeated ad nauseum. The treaty actually requires the nuclear states to work towards nuclear disarmament.

Next day Gordon Brown is in Lewisham. Keen though I am for him to become Prime Minister, I reflect ruefully on the fact that he too supports the renewal of Trident (odd that two religious men should be prepared to annihilate millions of people and wreck the global environment in a nuclear holocaust).

Nine meetings today including the IDC as we run up to the Christmas recess. Importantly the modernisers group meets to discuss the possibility of going for re-election for the Parliamentary Committee. We've had a turbulent year, frequently putting a lot of pressure on the PM on behalf of the backbenchers. We're all keen to stay on and try to influence the transition. There's also quite a lot of activity around Trident, but most important is my regular meeting with Harriet and the team, which now includes Julie Morgan, the Cardiff MP.

We're running an 'open' list of those MPs willing to commit publicly and other private lists for canvassing. The open list has nine men and sixteen women and we now let them know who they all are. We've also recruited twenty-four other supporters: council leaders, trade unionists, peers, all of whom will have votes. Just one more name and we will have the fifty for our first press release.

19 December: I'm meeting Prince Charles and Camilla at the Deptford Churches Centre. They are supporting the efforts of the local food charity, which supplies food to the centre. Camilla accepts a gift – a canvas bag emblazoned with the words 'I'm an old bag from Deptford'! She's totally unfazed and poses for a photograph. More than I would do!

I draft a New Year greeting that will be emailed in the recess, thanking everyone and reinforcing the message – 'Please make your New Year's resolution to recruit one more MP for Harriet'. The office Christmas lunch at The Adjournment restaurant at Portcullis House, then we're all off for the holidays. The East London line has closed.

## 2007

January and we're up and running with all the regular commitments of the Drugs Commission, the APPGs, the Afghan Link and constituency roundtables. Harriet's preparations also need my attention and I'm standing again for the Parliamentary Committee.

Letters go out from Harriet to key contacts inviting them to an inaugural meeting to develop a BAME strategy. Harriet has an excellent track record and staunch support from the black community in her constituency so this should be a very important aspect of our campaign.

She's been assembling a PR team from among old friends in the trade over the past year, including Janice Muir and Scarlett McGwire. They've been joined by Joe Calouri, a volunteer, and together they've been working on a website.

29 January: We launch Harriet's campaign website. My endorsement reads: 'I'm backing Harriet because she's the best champion of women I know. She puts her philosophy into practice by supporting women throughout the party – she deserves to win.' I get involved in checking Harriet's position papers, biography etc. and chasing up endorsements and letting our committed fifty know their names will be put on the site. It will be really important to keep adding names and placing news of Harriet's and the campaign's activities. It will also be possible to make donations through the site. This is really important. As our treasurer Anita Gale tells us, we have no major backers and no trade union donations. Grim.

Chairing a New Cross roundtable with a big turnout again, including my former researcher, Heidi Alexander, now Deputy Mayor of Lewisham. Lots of developments, including getting funding for disabled access at New Cross Gate station. The closure of the East London line from NXG in connection with the southern extension is a major concern, with 1,300 students and staff from Goldsmiths responding to an online survey. The NDC master planners are in dialogue with all the stakeholders and have proposed two development plans to Sainsbury's. They are also accepting tenders for the NDC centre. Hyde Housing present their proposals for taking over the local council housing stock as the residents have chosen them to be the preferred bid. A great deal of discussion about every aspect of the issues raised and suggestions for amendments and greater integration of the many plans.

A debate on Iraq and the wider Middle East opened by Margaret Beckett with a staunch defence of government policy. Tory Malcolm Rifkind makes a very interesting speech with many acute observations. I particularly like 'What the Prime Minister and President Bush have been doing is trying to provide some new world paradigm, and all the real facts have to be forced within that artificial construct. That explains the mess that we have today.'

I get called after five hours. I quote Blair on the exercise of hard power: 'With Saddam consistently refusing to abide by UN Resolutions and with alarm at the proliferation of chemical, biological and nuclear weapons, Iraq was invaded,' I say.

> There was no analysis of what that exercise cost. There was no acknowl-
> edgement that Al-Qaeda had never been active before the invasion,
> no mention of the tens of thousands of Iraqis who have died in the
> sectarian violence we unleashed ... no mention of the millions who
> fled the country ... no mention of the fact the country's infrastruc-
> ture lies in ruins and the whole region faces destabilisation.

I refer to our history in the Middle East: we first occupied Basra in 1914, ruled Iraq in the 1920s and invaded a sovereign Iraq to establish a pro-British government in the 1940s. Our involvement in Iran followed a similar pattern. Our defence of international interests and regime change is nothing new. We should have learned the lesson that we cannot impose foreign solutions and that arming one dictatorship to fight another as we did with Iran and Iraq only increases oppression and bitterness.

The IDC report on Development Assistance and the Occupied Palestinian Territories is published. We lay out the facts. Seventy-five per cent of the Palestinian Authority's budget is being withheld by Israel. As a result, it is facing financial crisis; 51 per cent of Palestinians are food insecure and 66 per cent of families live below the poverty line. We explicitly question whether the withholding of funds from a democratically elected government in the conflict-affected territories is the most effective response to Hamas's refusal to accept the Quartet principles. We argue that increasing donor assistance is not the answer and list the Israeli actions on settlements, the barrier wall, checkpoints, permits etc. as militating against development. We acknowledge Israel's need for security and right to protect its citizens but question the proportionality of its actions. We suggest a first step to improving the situation would be the implementation of the Agreement on Access and Movement made in November 2005, and largely ignored by Israel. We conclude that the international community is in danger of preventing the creation of a viable Palestinian state.

We have several ongoing inquiries and it's impossible to do all the visits. Water and sanitation are particularly interesting and feature in the Millennium Development Goals. Our next African inquiry will look at progress towards the goal of halving the proportion of people without access to safe drinking water and adequate sanitation by 2015, together with DfID's organisational capacity for support to water and sanitation. I decide to go.

We leave in the afternoon and arrive in Addis Ababa around 4 a.m. Off to the hotel and a few hours' rest, then briefings from DfID and embassy staff in town and on to a reception and speeches at the ambassador's residence.

Ethiopia is desperately poor and ranked 170 out of 177 countries in the UN Human Development Report. Eighty-one per cent of the population live on less than $2 per day. An important meeting with the PM Meles Zenawi before we begin our field trips. For some years the UK government's preferred method of delivering aid has been through direct budget support to elected governments, which has the advantage of enabling them to develop and sustain their own programmes within an agreed poverty-reduction framework. Ethiopia had been a model of such cooperation until the violent aftermath of the 2005 elections when Zenawi put opposition leaders on trial. As a consequence, DfID withdrew all budget support and directed funds instead to subregional bodies and local NGOs, so this is a delicate meeting in which we reinforce the position of our government. Despite it all, the PM is able to outline the government's impressive poverty-reduction programme, which is not disputed. He acknowledges DfID support – the country's most important donor.

In Addis we see a biogas project with simple metal tanks set underground, with latrine waste fed into the digester to be broken down into methane gas, which is used for cooking and boiling water. The latrines represent huge progress as traditionally people have had to defecate in the open – hazardous enough in the countryside but lethal in cities. The project committee makes the facilities available to the poorest: about twenty households with an average of six children using half a dozen latrines and a communal kitchen with four gas burners.

On other days we drive a few hours from the capital and meet remarkable women leading local NGOs combining health education with sanitation projects run by WaterAid and funded by DfID. Another project is led by a village woman who has basic training as a health worker (a national programme). She and her committee have sourced a mountain spring to establish a water point, which they control, after finding that 50 per cent of disease is the result of dirty water and poor sanitation.

In Alaba, a drought-prone area, we see a project on a bigger scale set up by an Ethiopian NGO with assistance from WaterAid. Women tell us that before the bore-holes were drilled they had a 24km round trip to the river to collect water every day. While walking they faced abductions and rapes and often pregnant women gave birth prematurely. Once handed over, the project is controlled by a local committee that sets the tariffs and collects the money, and the government becomes responsible for maintaining contact with the community. This is exactly the kind of development we want to see. A truly humbling experience – I'll never waste water again or take my flush toilet for granted.

Our final meetings back in Addis include relevant ministers, water ministry officials, the EU, the World Bank, the Africa bank and Members of Parliament. Once again I reflect on how utterly invaluable these visits are in giving MPs an understanding of how taxpayers' money is spent and how extreme are the challenges of the Millennium Development Goals. Both Malcolm Bruce, our chair, and I take up the issues at the next DfID orals. I invite the Secretary of State to commend the health extension workers scheme as an example of how DfID can both support and encourage African governments to give priority with their own spending departments. Excellent response from Hilary. At the end of the month, I do another 'Reporting Africa' meeting in my constituency.

10 February: An evening at Laban with Frank. We are seeing a performance by the National Boys Youth Dance Platform. Ever since *Billy Elliot*, boys' interest in dance has grown and is positively promoted by Laban in our outreach programme.

A day off, then I'm packing again. I'm spending the recess in Washington. Adam Matthews, our GLOBE coordinator, has done a brilliant job since he was appointed. Not only has he made the UK GLOBE into a thriving organisation and got DEFRA to second a civil servant to assist us, but he's made a big impact in both the US and the EU. Now we are going to a G8+5 legislators dialogue on climate change.

Lots of papers to read on the lunchtime flight to Washington. It's an all-party delegation, including Lord Jay, a former ambassador and head of the Foreign Office who is now an active GLOBE member and a great asset to us. We arrive and get whisked off to our hotel. My room is an enormous suite, bigger than the ones I used to be given in the old days of the Soviet Union. It's boiling hot, trashy music is playing and the air is full of strong perfume – and we're here to tackle climate change! I turn down the heating and summon someone from reception to get the music disconnected permanently and ask if the perfume dispenser can be removed. It seems it may come with the air conditioning!

The conference is one of the best. Excellent contributions from US Senators McCain and Lieberman, who are unlikely heroes in the battle to get climate change taken remotely seriously in the US. Also inspiring to hear Barbara Boxer and John Kerry. Some very senior CEOs give accounts of developments in industry and their embrace of the climate agenda, including Richard Branson. Then there's the President of the World Bank, Paul Wolfowitz, and most importantly Nick Stern. We learn a lot and feel optimistic as we approve a statement with an analysis, action points and suggestions, which will go forward to the G8 participants meeting in Germany in June, and the Bali meeting of the UNFCCC (the United Nations Framework Convention on Climate Change) in November.

20 February: Fighting the jetlag, a catch-up with Mike Foster on the campaign. Requests are pouring in for Harriet to speak at local meetings and various organisations are setting up platforms for all the declared candidates. We're also seeing lots of emails and invitations being put out by other candidates. We continue working through our lists, recording every detail of the 350 MPs eligible to vote. We list 'declared', 'potential', 'probable', 'possible', 'won't say' and 'no' for first preference, supporting other candidate and second preferences. An enormous task, but the grid is filling up. More and more letters need drafting, especially to trade unionists, and Jim Sheridan MP joins the core team to assist.

The *Telegraph* publishes a YouGov poll on the deputy leadership contest. This time it's a poll of Labour Party and trade union members. We need to get an email out immediately to all our declared nominators. Harriet is number three of the six. We remind everyone of last November's poll showing she's the best electoral asset, point out that she's the preferred woman and in the top three. We don't want anyone backing out at this stage. Hilary is leading with Alan second.

8 March: International Women's Day and the launch of our report 'Drugs – Facing Facts, the RSA Commission on Illegal Drugs, Communities and Public Policy'. It's been a phenomenal amount of work but a brilliant result that I'm proud to be a part of. We have taken vast amounts of evidence and debated among ourselves (a diverse group from across the political spectrum) for two years. One of our central themes is the need to shift drugs policy away from the focus on crime reduction and the criminal justice system and onto a concern with drugs posing a much more varied and complex set of social problems. The Misuse of Drugs Act 1971 is no longer fit for purpose. We say it should be scrapped and replaced by a new Misuse of Substances Act that sets drugs in the wider context of substance misuse, alongside alcohol, tobacco and other psychoactive substances, and which is linked to an evidence-based index that makes clear the relative risks of harm from individual substances. It should also seek to focus punishment mainly on harmful

behaviours stemming from drug use rather than the simple possession of drugs. Personally, having heard all the evidence, I would have gone further and proposed the decriminalisation of all drugs as Portugal did six years ago.

Lots of media coverage – I just hope the government will pay attention.

9 March: The draft Climate Change Bill is published – the first in the world. It sets targets for 60 per cent $CO_2$ reduction by 2050 with an interim target of 26–32 per cent on 1990 levels by 2020. Good news too in the Budget – higher taxes on gas-guzzling cars and duty cut by 30 per cent for drivers of the cleanest.

14 March: A momentous day. This is the debate on the renewal of Trident. Everyone will want to speak – I'll die if I'm not called. Margaret Beckett opens with the government's case. William Hague responds. First up is Nigel Griffiths. Nigel has resigned from his post as Deputy Leader of the House and now explains why he cannot support the government. A thoughtful, principled speech. Jon Trickett moves the amendment opposing the government motion. He raises important points about the legality of the government's actions and Blair's Trident correspondence with Bush. Tory grandee Michael Ancram follows, setting out his (rather surprising) opposition to Trident renewal. Good to have such people on side.

This is such an important speech for me and the first time I've voted against the government since the Iraq War. I make my critique of the White Paper:

> It makes no real analysis of the US-led and nuclear-armed NATO alliance of which we are a part, nor of the new Europe in which we live. It is a mass of assertions with no attempt to examine how best to approach security in a world where climate change and competition for resources will be paramount.

I look at the three scenarios posed for threats that can only be countered by renewing Trident. We are told that a major nuclear power, presumably

Russia, may re-emerge to threaten us – but 'why should Russia specifically aim their nuclear weapons at Britain? Whatever the potential conflicts, does anyone believe nuclear weapons could be used to settle such conflicts?' Secondly, we are told that new states could acquire nuclear weapons and threaten us – Iran being most often cited. I ask why that country, embroiled in Middle Eastern politics with a nuclear-armed Pakistan on one side and a nuclear-armed Israel on the other, would target nuclear weapons, if it acquired them, at Britain? The third threat posed is countries sponsoring nuclear terrorism.

> Frankly this is the most preposterous assertion of nuclear deterrence. Do we really believe that the dirty bomb in the suitcase is going to have a visible country of origin label on it? It would be impossible immediately to identify a sponsoring state so as to justify nuclear retaliation … The threats we face are not UK-centric – they are global, and they require global solutions. International cooperation on climate change, world trade and technology transfer are vital if we are not to face climate catastrophe and a scramble for diminishing resources.

I conclude that I have not heard any argument showing how Trident would be used to our advantage but I know the consequences of using it: 'Thousands of innocent people would be vaporised, millions would die in agony and radiation would persist for generations … I have never been willing to be party to such a barbarous act and I will not support the government tonight.' The Tories vote with the government, who win by 409 to 161, but over eighty Labour MPs, including Frank and me, vote against.

We have been madly preparing all the slides from Ethiopia so I can do another 'Reporting Africa' meeting on Thursday. On Wednesday night a perfect treat: John Baily, Professor of Musicology, and his wife Veronica are performing Afghan music at Goldsmiths. I love the haunting sounds and my Afghan friends tell me Veronica's Farsi is perfect.

6 April: Such a happy day. We now own a little terraced house in a hamlet dating back 700 years. A cause for celebration. We take possession a few days later and sleep on the floor. Thankfully we've discovered an IKEA so we are able to order furniture and be back when the House returns in ten days.

Life is now dominated by preparations for the coming leadership contests. The pressure on Tony to go is relentless – partly because he has left us in this state of uncertainty for so long. We have to have everything in place for Harriet for the moment he resigns, but then we will be under even worse pressure ourselves for maybe months on end. At least the major commitment of the Drugs Commission is at an end but new issues are boiling up in the constituency. I've got lobbies from the Tamils about the situation in Sri Lanka (terrible); I've got lobbies from residents about the relocation of the travellers' site; and lobbies from refugee organisations about reductions in ESOL (English as a Second Language) classes. And GLOBE of course now has a major programme following success with the G8+5.

Frank has arranged a visit to Aberdeen for Harriet. It goes well with good press coverage and ends in our house, which I've cleared sufficiently to hold a large crowd. Everything looks lovely, we've got lots of food and drink and a roaring fire. Harriet speaks really well and gets a warm response.

We are expecting a Blair announcement any time now. We're still without the money we need. Huge amounts of literature will be required, plus renting an office, let alone financing all Harriet's travel etc. Fortunately, we have lots of willing and able young volunteers. The priority is literature. We've been operating on a simple flyer but now we have to have a campaign brochure. Don Brind, a former Labour Party press officer, has volunteered to help with the campaign. He'll be a much-needed safe pair of hands. We've got our forty-five nominators so we know we're in the race – just waiting for the starting pistol.

Don and I do a mock-up of a simple brochure and work out the various bits of script we need for Harriet and the photos that can illustrate the script. Pinning Harriet down is a real problem when she is run off her feet giving interviews and travelling to meetings all over the country.

The workload is now such that I'm doing more than Mike Foster as I'm on hand in London while he has to be in his marginal seat. Harriet asks me to become the campaign manager, with Mike as the agent overseeing all the technical compliance and the finances. While I see the sense of this I'm somewhat daunted at having the major strategic role in the campaign. My resilience is tested very quickly. I have to find a printer and make arrangements for the brochure to be produced. I end up cutting and pasting stuff myself. While I've done so much of this in the past my amateur techniques are not really what we need. I plough on with Don's help.

2 May: A government debate on Sri Lanka. Many of us have been pressing for this and writing to ministers about the 24-year violent civil war. Constituents expect the government to take a stand – at least on arms exports and on aid. Most MPs with sizeable Tamil communities are in the Chamber and we all rehearse the litany of horrors that have befallen the Tamils. I ask specifically about aid distribution as there are suspicions that aid is not getting through and constituents are regularly sending medical supplies to relatives. Gareth Thomas, the minister, gives a detailed account of DfID assistance but agrees some aid has been held back due to the renewed fighting (last year twenty-six aid workers were killed). A depressing debate.

3 May: We're sure the PM's announcement will be next week so a morning conference call between Mike, Harriet, Jim, Julie and myself. Monday is a bank holiday so we need everything in place in case it comes on Tuesday. We've got letters to go to all MPs as soon as the poll is announced enclosing a leaflet, letters to go out at the close of poll to all MPs who didn't nominate anyone and letters to all those who nominated someone else to ask for their second preferences. We are all on edge. We agree to meet at 8.30 a.m. on Tuesday morning when we work on Harriet's manifesto for the official launch of our campaign.

The Guardian does a special on all the candidates. I organise a meeting for all our nominators. We've taken a chance and Harriet has gone to Brussels to address MEPs today. Tomorrow a PR team meeting.

10 May: The official announcement – Blair will stand down on 27 June. Mike and I send an email to all our potential nominators, now sixty-strong. There will be a special PLP at 2 p.m. on Monday to give details of the conduct of the election followed by the opening of nominations at 2.30 p.m. We arrange a photo call immediately afterwards at Members' entrance. We ask everyone to attend the photo call first, then collect their nomination form, complete it, return it and then call us to let us know it's been delivered. This is now deadly serious. These nominations will appear on the party website (and ours of course) as they come in. Everyone will be watching to see how we're doing. We've opened an office and taken delivery of thousands of leaflets. We've got letters to go to all union general secretaries and all CLP secretaries asking both to distribute Harriet's campaign material. This is going to take over my life!

Our campaign launch goes really well and we get great photos of happy, enthusiastic people. We meet every day now. We are besieged by requests from all over the country, there are endless questionnaires to be answered and comment pieces to be drafted. Harriet will be travelling a lot and the PR team will be needed in support. Don and I will work on everything else in the evenings. We have policy positions on most things, but every so often a new angle pops up. We are constantly on our toes. New names are vital to create stories and today we release a web TV interview by Neil and Glenys Kinnock backing Harriet and Gordon. Neil reminds people of how well the two of them worked when Gordon was shadow Chancellor and Harriet was shadow Chief Secretary. Glenys says, 'It's unthinkable that the Labour Party should elect a deputy leader who wasn't a woman [and] that woman has to be Harriet'! Good publicity too about Alistair Darling backing Harriet.

Most of us have also nominated Gordon but his support is so overwhelming that no one can stand against him so there's no contest. Nonetheless, he is constantly campaigning and one of his visits is to Lewisham College, so I just have to be there for 9 a.m. this morning. I'm utterly desperate for time to finalise Harriet's brochure, which I have to get back to the printers. Mike has mailed all our nominators with a list of requests, from writing press releases to member and trade union canvassing.

Huge embarrassment following yesterday's meeting at Lewisham College. Gordon embraced me on meeting and went to kiss me on the cheek but missed! We are pictured in what looks like a 'brief encounter'. Secretly I think it's rather nice, but not quite what you expect from the PM!

In the Chamber for Martin Salter's Bill on MPs' 'remunerated employment', which I've sponsored. Martin quotes from our Modernisation Committee's report 'Connecting the Public and Parliament', which concluded: 'Too often the impression is given that the House of Commons is a private club run for the benefit of its members, where members of the public are tolerated only on sufferance.' Martin jokes the report might better be called 'Reconnecting MPs with Parliament' as a quarter of MPs are pursuing parallel careers as company directors, consultants or in the courts. He points out that seven Tory shadow Cabinet members have thirty-two directorships and consultancies between them. One MP has fourteen other jobs listed in the register of interests. The Bill to end second jobs gets a good airing but of course goes nowhere.

17 May: Nominations close. Alan Johnson leads with seventy-three. Harriet is second on sixty-five – perfectly placed. We've got mobile numbers for virtually all our supporting MPs and peers and one of our volunteers, Caitríona, has mastered the art of sending broadcast texts so we can get instant communication. We need it – everything is moving so fast. Don and I start work again going over all the policy material our office volunteers haven't been able to process. Then he's home for supper and I'm finishing the proofing of the brochure. Suddenly I'm overwhelmed with exhaustion and the heavy burden of responsibility. Frank is in Aberdeen. I'm sitting in the office at 10 p.m. staring at the walls. Slowly a tear runs down my face – I feel so alone.

The first official Labour Party hustings has been set for Sunday in Coventry. Thereafter hustings in Bristol, Bradford, Leicester, Glasgow, Newcastle, Cardiff, Oxford and finally London before final closure of ballots on 22 June. Now we have to slot in all the other meetings Harriet has agreed to do. The grid is a nightmare.

To the printers. The brochure is a weekend job and will be dispatched in bulk around the country. I feel a great sense of relief. Our letters go out to all the MPs who've nominated other candidates – each one tailor-made to include points from the other candidates' manifestos with which Harriet agrees. Second preferences are very likely to decide this contest so we are going to work extremely hard to get them.

I'm fretting because before I anticipated Harriet's campaign we had booked flights to Italy for the half-term holiday. I can't let Frank down now. I convince myself that I will be able to keep in touch. With Parliament not sitting there will not be the same intensity and I'll ensure every vital bit of the office programme is complete before I leave.

Our treasurer Anita reports that we have raised just over £19,000 and have more than spent it already. Other campaigns have got much more, as evidenced by the glossy brochures that are piling in.

Harriet is doing well in the hustings but I nag her to wear lipstick. She's naturally pale and in strong platform lights she can look insipid and less than forceful, so 'don't forget the lippy' is my constant mantra whenever she goes out.

Jon Cruddas is getting a lot of union backing and money. This leaves us with little hope as both Peter and Alan also have very strong union connections. Money is now an extremely pressing issue. The Folletts as always have been extremely generous, as have Harriet's closest friends, but we are going to have to go direct to people with money, and Mike has got Chris Bryant and Keith Vaz to assist.

Thousands of leaflets are leaving our Dartmouth Road office every day as teams of volunteers pack and dispatch. The brochures are pleasing, though

I say it myself, in lilac and red, though clearly more cheaply produced than those of other candidates. Mixed reports are coming back from the hustings. Harriet holds her own and sometimes comes out on top but this contest is far too close to call.

We are reaching as many members as we can through MPs, CLPs and union officials at regional level but we are missing tens of thousands of members who never go to meetings and won't be at the hustings. I think our only hope of winning is to get a letter direct to each and every one of them.

I contact the printers. They can print an A4 letter, stuff it and address for mail sort. Perfect logistics but the cost is £14,850 to print and £39,000 for postage. We just haven't got that kind of money and there is no hope of getting it. The more I think about it the more I am convinced we have to do it, but I'm sick with worry. I decide to discuss it with Harriet and Jack. I go to see them at home. We have a very sober discussion – this is a huge amount of money and a decision has to be taken quickly if the letter is to get through letter boxes at the same time as ballots arrive. Any later and it's a complete waste.

Harriet and Jack will raise the money. I start drafting. One side will be a letter from Harriet with the major policy points, on our letterhead with her lovely photo. The back will be pictures and messages from key endorsers. I'm desperate not to go to Italy and I know I'm going to have a wretched time. We leave nonetheless. We haven't got a computer but we'll buy a fax as soon as we arrive. The letter text is coming together and I'm busy cutting and pasting, moving things around until I'm satisfied. Then the fax stops working and nothing will drag it back into life. The hours are ticking by and there's no one we can call on for help. Then we remember the estate agent from whom we bought the house. He's got a large photocopier and fax. There's no alternative but to go and beg to use it. They're all terribly obliging. I've got Don at the other end setting it all up. He faxes, I read. Lots of changes needed. It's cold and pouring with rain but I go outside to talk to him on the mobile. The signal is poor and the ink begins to run. I am so miserable and fighting back a sense of panic at the potential recklessness of this exercise.

Backwards and forwards and eventually we agree the final version for the printer. The 'holiday' is ruined.

Back in London and everything is now running to plan. Our second You-Gov opinion poll is published. Harriet beats everyone else. Once again she is seen as the candidate most likely to persuade people to vote Labour, but also the person most in touch with family life and rated the most trustworthy. She's also far and away the most recognised – by 65 per cent of the population. Brilliant. Our broadcast texts are working overtime.

On *Newsnight*, when asked who he would support if he were not standing, Jon Cruddas says Harriet. An invaluable endorsement, interpreted as meaning 'give your second vote to Harriet'. Ballots are starting to arrive and to my huge relief the letter from Harriet arrives as well. Daily strategy and briefing meetings continue. It's now all about raising Harriet's game, giving feedback and preparing for media. She takes it all in her stride but the pressure is acute and she must be very tired. We all go along to the last hustings in Kennington. I'm now back to a few committee meetings, particularly of the IDC, which is doing an inquiry into Burma's refugees. I've also no choice but to cover a World Bank lunch, a Russian Finance Minister and the Iraqi Minister for Foreign Affairs.

Finally, the campaign is over. The various ballots close over the next two days. Harriet, Jack, Frank and I take an evening off at the Pimlico Tandoori as the waiting game begins.

Covering the constituency work has been really difficult and I've slightly overreached myself by planning a climate change day. But, with Mike's help, it goes really well. Lots of people have come and the talk and slideshow are a success. It's time for me to leave and I give Mike the keys to load the projector into my car. I pick up my handbag to say goodbye. Then someone asks for a photo. I put the bag down and turn around. Photo done, I turn back. My handbag has gone. Money and cards and house keys are bad enough, but also my phone was inside. It's got the numbers of loads of MPs and half the Cabinet. I have to cancel it immediately. How could this happen now? Frank, of course, is in Aberdeen but fortunately a neighbour has my house keys. A year later someone finds my bag in Brockley Cemetery and hands it in. The cash and phone are gone but the only card missing is my Tesco Clubcard!

I'm also forced to hold a Deptford station meeting. Predictably a funding gap has now opened up. I am utterly determined to get this station built and keep pressing and challenging all the stakeholders. If this gap isn't closed, Cathedral's planning application won't go in this autumn and then another year could easily be lost. It could be we will have to go to the Department of Transport, but whatever, we have to get more funding. This project is now in the balance. A major setback. Six months later we plug the gap – 41 per cent from government, 40 per cent from Lewisham Council and 19 per cent from Network Rail.

23 June: A hair appointment at 12 o'clock. I struggle to wake and to pack my bag – checking and rechecking. Hair looking good, I'm on the 3 p.m. train to Manchester. We're going to Ann Coffey's house. Ann has been a stalwart supporter, with reach in the north that none of the rest of us have. Now she's putting us up so we can talk in private. We spend the evening going over all the intelligence we have received. We could win but I can't bear to hope.

Harriet and I have to be at the conference hall at 12 p.m. in front of the stage to be briefed on procedure. Then backstage in the holding room at 1.30 p.m. where we will stay incommunicado until we enter the hall again after learning the result.

In the holding room, the tension is unbearable. It's difficult to know where to look let alone make conversation. I'm composing my face, preparing to cope with defeat. Peter Watt, General Secretary, comes in and says, 'We now have the result, congratulations Harriet Harman.' I experience the greatest instant rush of adrenaline in my whole life. What a triumph. We're absolutely thrilled and hug each other in a moment of pure joy. Then it's congratulations and commiserations and off to a private room to prepare the acceptance speech. Of course we have a draft but now it's all different.

We tweak it for real. We're desperate to tell Jack and Frank who are in the conference hall but no communication is allowed. We've even been told not to give any indication as we enter the hall – how hard it will be to stop grinning from ear to ear.

We all sit in the front row as the elaborate charts are rolled out showing the votes from the different parts of the electoral college. Gordon of course has been elected already so all the focus is on the deputy. Eventually the result is declared and Harriet goes to the platform. Gordon and Harriet raise their arms together to acknowledge the cheers. I fight back the tears. The pictures look wonderful on TV. Thereafter it's a whirl of media, loads of congratulations and posing for more pictures.

Next day, back in London and down to earth. I'm on a statutory instrument committee! Lots of catching up, then Harriet's thank-you party on Wednesday. A terrific evening and I get presented with the most expensive handbag ever. Lots of interest in Gordon's new appointments. Harriet has previously announced that she would not want to combine the deputy leadership with a departmental role – she becomes chair of the Labour Party, which is excellent news for the party but not a job I'd want.

I'm in my surgery on Friday when I see my phone has a call coming through. I step outside to hear: 'I have the Prime Minister for you.' I am completely taken aback. I've lived for so many years not receiving such a call that I've not even considered speaking to Gordon about a position. Now he's saying he would like me to join Hilary Benn at DEFRA. I thank him fulsomely and say I'd like to speak to Hilary before getting back to him. My mind is racing. I've got such strong ideas about the environment and it's a junior position so I need to know what kind of hierarchy Hilary will operate. A very helpful discussion with Hilary and a return call to Gordon and I'm the new Parliamentary Under-Secretary at DEFRA.

Chapter Eight

# GOVERNMENT AGAIN

3 o June: Two unexploded car bombs were discovered in London yesterday and now reports are coming in of a car exploding after being driven into Glasgow International Airport. Al-Qaeda is suspected.

A rapid reorganisation in the next few days. As a minister I'll have to give up all my APPGs, the Parliamentary Committee and the DfID select committee, though I'll still have all the constituency issues to deal with.

Meetings in the department with the Permanent Secretary Helen Ghosh and the media team, then it's sitting on the front bench for Hilary's statement on the flooding. The torrential rains last month have caused tremendous damage and weather forecasts for July are grim (it will prove to be the wettest on record). The department and Hilary are under great pressure. What a start to Gordon's premiership!

We sort out our portfolios at DEFRA. I'm delighted to have part of the climate change brief – adaptation, together with waste, which I love, and biodiversity. Other members are Phil Woolas with the major climate change brief, Jeff Rooker with farming and Jonathan Shaw with fisheries. I'm wary of civil servants piling anything and everything onto ministers so I insist on a pro-forma where everything for the red boxes will be listed and ranked from urgent down to noting and at this stage I want to see all letters that I will sign.

I'm preparing for my first debate as the minister. It's in Westminster Hall and entitled 'Global Warming' but the civil servants tell me the Member raising the debate wants to focus on adaptation.

I get excellent briefings and I like my private office staff led by Naomi. This is going to be a great job. Naomi as head of the office deals with the Secretary of State and major issues. Liz does waste, Jane climate change and David biodiversity. Then I get to meet my driver, Ken Brown.

Most ministers acknowledge their drivers become their closest confidantes. They are always with us, always expected to look out for us and keep our secrets, though we know they are great gossips. Karl, my driver when I was Minister for Women, was young, quiet and empathetic. Ken is older and much more in your face. I'm not sure how this will work.

I get briefed on forestry, which is a new field for me but very interesting, on DEFRA's work on biopolymers, which is relevant to waste, and on the forthcoming climate Bill.

Everything has now changed. It's summer party season. I never accepted the annual Livestock Commission's barbecue invitation, but now I have to go – as a DEFRA minister! The meat is terrific – pity Hilary is vegetarian.

For months I've been preparing for a celebration to mark my twenty years as an MP. Now it's a mad rush checking and rechecking. A wonderful event. A full theatre at Laban for an international evening showcasing performances by a host of local cultural organisations. A few embarrassing speeches in praise of my twenty years. Then it's a private supper for forty of my closest friends and family who have sustained me over the years. One small setback – Frank forgets his camera and my brother-in-law David finds his jammed after the first few shots! Too much pressure these past few weeks.

My first controversy. London Councils (Tory controlled) are putting a Bill to Parliament that includes a provision to charge 10p for a plastic bag. DEFRA is opposed and I get sent all the reasons why the supermarkets want

'carrots not sticks'. Frankly I think their analysis is a bit doubtful and personally I'd go with it, though probably 5p. Watch this space.

Tonight's box illustrates just how quickly new ministers have to get to
grips with the brief. It covers a spectrum from the environmental transformation fund to a statutory instrument on game regulation, carbon offsetting,
EU eco design directives and packaging policy and the Severn Barrage.

In my box, eighteen pages of press cuttings on fortnightly collection
schemes for household waste. DEFRA has been consulting local authorities
about incentive schemes. Eric Pickles, the shadow Environment Secretary,
is stirring it up – interesting to see the regional press where this is playing
very big, particularly in the north.


19 July: First oral questions. The Secretary of State's office assigns the questions on the Order Paper to the various members of our team. I'm to answer
on the impact of climate change on food security. Within this question are two
controversial issues – food imports to the UK and agricultural land used for
biofuels. I get briefed extensively on both. I'm confident of my knowledge of
climate change and of course IDC has given me an insight into development
and food insecurity in developing countries. Nonetheless, I'm just slightly
apprehensive but I hope I exude a confident air at the Dispatch Box.

Everyone knows that the House likes to test a new minister and women
are particularly vulnerable to taunts from the opposition. I'm determined no
one's going to undermine me today. I also intend to treat backbenchers with
respect and give proper answers rather than evade the difficult questions, as
I'm afraid some of my colleagues are prone to do.

I give my answers. I'm then questioned by the opposition shadow minister, then by my colleague Barry Sheerman, then by climate change denier
Christopher Chope and finally by Peter Ainsworth, the shadow Secretary of
State himself! This is a very good run for a first outing and I'm more confident by the minute. Peter Ainsworth welcomes me to my position, saying he
looks forward to my pronouncements on GMOs and nuclear power. I bat it

away with good humour – in the share-out of portfolios it was speedily agreed that I could cover neither of these.

A little later and I'm on another run, when Bob Russell asks about the promotion of local food production and criticises supermarkets for describing food as local when it isn't. He's followed by my close colleague David Drew, Tory Michael Jack and James Paice (another taunt) and finally Anthony Steen, who asks me about the Transition Town Totnes project. My last question and I don't know the answer. I say I'm not yet familiar with it but I soon will be. Next day a nice note from Anthony telling me my question time was a success and I'm popular on both sides of the House! Not a bad start. I'm so pleased to have this job.

I'm going to have to work hard at keeping in touch with my local and parliamentary offices while I spend most of my time at DEFRA and on ministerial duties. I'm very dependent on Lucy keeping all the casework going and Mike for the Westminster office. Eleanor is moving on and I can't blame her as her job will now be far less rewarding, but she's not going far – just to join Heidi in the Cabinet Office at Lewisham Council. I replace her with Abena Oppong-Asare (Abby).

I've now got a sense of direction for waste. The strategy document published by David Miliband earlier this year set out the major goals: halving the amount of waste to landfill by 2020; increasing recycling to 50 per cent; and cutting greenhouse gas emissions from waste by over 3 million tonnes $CO_2$ equivalent per year. We're also going for targeted action on paper, plastics, glass, wood, aluminium, textiles and food.

The biodiversity portfolio is more difficult. The civil servants are based in Bristol and much of the portfolio relates to international treaties with which I'm as yet unfamiliar, but I do get to have a meeting with a bishop about the menace of bats in churches and a delightful moth and bat evening event at the Commons, put on by my colleague Madeleine Moon and her husband, who is a conservation officer.

On public engagement our climate change officials have already made a brilliant start with an online personal calculator through which we can all judge our carbon footprint and steps by which to reduce it. Mine is fine on most things but flights are the exception and I'm sorry to say I'm off to Aberdeen to spend a much-needed weekend with Frank after spending so much time with Harriet.

The House rises today, which gives me a chance to catch up with constituency work before going on holiday. I told Hilary on arrival that we were booked to go away at the very start of the recess for three weeks. This is never popular with colleagues as we each have to cover as duty minister throughout the recess. My only defence is that I didn't expect to be a minister and I can't change things now. I have a major meeting in the constituency on Friday morning. I've brought together the Church Grove residents and council officers for a site visit and discussion of the proposed travellers' relocation. I am totally in support of the residents and press for the other potential sites to be adopted instead. Two more meetings and a surgery. A note from Lewisham Council on their meeting with various stakeholders on the New Cross Road. It's looking good. A new station and a pedestrian/cycle bridge over the railway and a bus interchange are being built into the plans.

On Saturday, Leila's daughter Susie is married. A beautiful sunny day and a lovely wedding. Amazed I've made it through the past few months. I finish my box and get it collected, then we're off to Italy.

August: A very enjoyable time putting our Italian house together and seeing friends. Margaret and Henry Hodge are staying nearby. We spend a lovely day with them.

A message from the office. Some cows have been found to have foot and mouth disease. After the last disastrous outbreak this is very bad news. More disease identified and then the suggestion that the virus has leaked from an animal health laboratory at Pirbright. Both Gordon and Hilary return from their holidays. I don't have to make an early return but I'm sorry for everyone else; we are all extremely tired.

I can work on boxes at home in the recess, and only go to DEFRA for occasional briefings and events. My first public engagement is our roadshow on climate change at Dartford's Bluewater. It's a great success. Shoppers are curious to know what it's all about and are soon persuaded to calculate their carbon footprint. We have Energy Saving Trust freebies and our own material to give away. People are surprised by the results. This is a great way to raise awareness and give people confidence that they can do more to save the planet with small steps of their own. Over the next few weeks we'll take the roadshow to Bristol, Nottingham and Manchester. Excellent publicity in local papers and on local radio stations.

28 August: I announce a new Biodiversity Action Plan with a list of priority species and habitats for conservation. Sadly, I have to add the common hedgehog and the house sparrow to the list of species under threat. There's a lifetime of work in this.

Back in earnest at DEFRA to progress a number of key issues: first a meeting of stakeholders on environmental regulations, and a meeting with Hilary on the truly controversial financial incentives for recycling.

I open a conference on sustainable clothing at Chatham House. I've had detailed briefings on the whole cycle from crop growing to dying, bleaching, manufacture, distribution and disposal. The latter is significant as most clothes end up in landfill. It's a fascinating field and I intend to do what I can to raise awareness and behaviour change. I'm learning how complex and wide the sustainability agenda is. Later in the day I meet with the Waste and Resources Programme (WRAP). Their new CEO, Liz Goodwin, is a real enthusiast and I'll enjoy working with her. They are opening up a new field on food waste. Having recycled my own food waste for years I'm really up for this – it's a scandal that we currently waste one third of the food we buy.

September: In Nottingham for a roadshow but also fascinating visits to experimental eco-homes and teaching facilities at the university, followed by a tour of the Boots factory and discussions about more sustainable transport, packaging and waste. There's such scope for industry in this field – virtually everything that's environmentally sustainable ends up saving them money.

What a week. A visit to London Fashion Show to see amazing clothing made from bamboo and hemp and loads of sustainable techniques, a *New Statesman* roundtable on carbon, the launch of a climate champions youth competition at Holland Park School and a meeting with Ken Livingstone on London waste issues. And in between I'm preparing for the fringe meetings I have to address at Labour Party conference. I do six fringe meetings, the women's reception, the gala dinner, *The Guardian* women's dinner and the Policy Commission seminar on sustainable communities. In the conference hall for the PM's speech, which is great, and for our session and Hilary's speech on Thursday.

14 September: Northern Rock has run into trouble. People are queuing round the block to get their money out.

Much talk of a snap election. Gordon is doing so well and we're ahead in the polls. I'm not sure. The public is notorious for punishing people who cause 'unnecessary' elections. I can see the argument for achieving legitimacy but I'm not backing it myself (I was wrong). Nonetheless, we arrange a local election strategy meeting.

I can't believe it. There's been an outbreak of blue tongue disease – Hilary will never have a holiday now. I'm also going to have to take on some of his commitments, notably a carbon-capture and storage meeting in Paris. This is an experimental technology that I think could be extremely important and about which I do know a little. However, I get several intense briefings and then off to Paris to deliver my speech and back again the same night.

8 October: The House returns and I've a packed diary of meetings and briefings. Four days ago there was a terrible incident in my constituency. A homecare worker, Magda Pniewska, was shot dead in John Williams Close. She was leaving work in the afternoon and got caught in the crossfire as two

young criminals settled a dispute. Everyone is totally shocked. I visit the care
home and talk to her colleagues and then convene an urgent meeting for
the local community, the local police and the specialist Met Trident team.
A reminder again of how precarious our lives are.

I'm making a keynote speech at an Environmental Services Association
(ESA) conference on anaerobic digestion. I think it's an extremely promising
technology and both DEFRA and DTI have shown interest in it over the past
year. It has great potential for dealing with biodegradable waste and sewage
sludge. It can also be used to produce biogas, and the digestate can be used as
a fertiliser. This is another issue I intend to pursue and the ESA are old allies
of mine since I did my recycling Bill.

All ministers are invited to a meeting to discuss bovine TB. After ten years
of research the Independent Group on Bovine TB published its report on 18
June when the government's chief scientific advisor was asked to review it.
Now we've got David King's advice.

We are trying to book in as many constituency meetings as possible on
Friday mornings, especially on surgery days when I never go to the department. Today I'm doing a New Cross Road roundtable. Sainsbury's' architects
give us a presentation. The plan incorporates the new station, green areas
and a public square, which will give New Cross Gate a sense of identity and
place. Best of all, the petrol station will be removed from the front of the site
and the new station entrance will be in the new square. All excellent news.

21 October: I'm attending a biodiversity event in Glasgow, hosted by the Scottish minister. It's an international conference and we are promoting the new
international agreement on protecting birds of prey in which DEFRA has
been very active. We're outdoors doing media with a bird handler showing a
golden eagle. Predictably the press ask me to take the bird on my arm. This
is a dangerous ploy but I forget all the advice about children and animals and
agree. I get the protective glove and the bird is on a chain but it weighs a ton.
I have to hold my arm steady but after a few minutes the weight is bearing

down on me and I move slightly. The great bird flaps its gigantic wings, hitting me in the face! Great pictures but a scary moment. The Scottish minister decides he must also get a photo but they all show him looking *very* nervous!

Back in the department and I'm doing lots of work on packaging. This is a major issue with green NGOs and in the EU. It's not good enough just to recycle; we need to reduce the waste in the first place. Lots of good work on minimisation and using recyclable materials. There's also an active APPG and I address their conference.

Oral questions. Alan Whitehead asks about diverting waste wood from landfill into the production of energy. This is a good question as it's a much neglected field. I answer that we want to encourage prevention and reuse first but we are working on the potential energy markets for waste wood. I get two follow-up questions, which I'm delighted to answer as yet again it illustrates the potential uses of waste.

A really nice evening out, even if I am on show. It's a dinner at Kew Gardens to celebrate their conservation work, which is global. I've always loved Kew Gardens and now, unknown to my fellow guests, I have Keith's memorial here.

A very important part of our developing waste strategy is tackling packaging waste, which the public rightly complain about. I address a major industry conference on the issue but find it goes unreported.

I've asked for a meeting with Hilary's head of office to complain that I'm not getting the press office back-up I think appropriate for major conferences like this one. We need so badly to push this agenda and get ourselves good publicity. Next day the press office say they didn't know about it. Well, this needs to change – I know only too well what happens to 'invisible' ministers.

11 November: At the local remembrance ceremony then home for lunch and off to Heathrow for a one-day attendance at the international biodiversity conference in Lisbon, which our biodiversity team is attending.

I'm now working very long hours. I work going home in the car and on into the evening, even after a 10 p.m. vote. Midnight is my deadline and I've insisted on not being picked up until 8.30 a.m. unless there's a real necessity. I'm now getting on well with Ken. Every morning he greets me with the latest attacks on Labour by the *Daily Mail*. He's a great enthusiast for their messages while insisting he's non-political. He does, however, prove a good absorber of all my tales of woe and exhaustion.

Hilary and Phil are very tied up in preparation for the Climate Change Bill. I'm often covering for them which results in a surprising weekend in Slovenia instead of Phil, which is both interesting and enjoyable.

14 November: Our Climate Change Bill launched and introduced in the House of Lords.

The pattern of my work is now set. Endless meetings discussing and making policy on all fronts. Meetings with industry, user groups, outside experts and NGOs. Regular ministers' meetings and press briefings and several public engagements – including speeches – every week. My greatest struggle is with the proposals for incentives to get more recycling at household level. Eric Pickles gets a story into the tabloids with monotonous frequency opposing the fortnightly black bin collections that allow local authorities to collect recyclates in between. Some people see me as getting a bad press constantly but I'm determined to stand up to him and get great support from Jean, the press officer who covers waste. Interestingly, Tory local authorities are on-side. The other contentious issue on plastic bags rumbles on and on. I think we'll have to introduce charging but the department is keen to give the supermarkets their chance to prove they can reduce through their own programmes.*

No. 10 is expressing concern about the constant media battle over bins. I ask for a meeting with Gordon and explain our huge dilemma. We really need to be able to continue to work on means of reducing the waste going to landfill, not least to comply with the landfill directive. We are looking at ways

---

* Charging will eventually be introduced in October 2015.

of rewarding recycling through a revenue-neutral scheme. He's persuaded for now but I'm on thin ice.

27 November: Peter Watt, the Labour Party's General Secretary, has resigned, taking full responsibility for a series of donations to the party that broke the rules on proxy donations. A bizarre situation whereby large sums of money were paid over in the names of other people. This terrified all of us who ran Harriet's campaign as we had scrupulously checked every donation. Sure enough, we received one in a false name. Harriet will pay the money back as soon as possible.

I'm doing my first late-night adjournment debate. These debates follow the end of government business, this one starting at 10.19 p.m. Desmond Swayne is raising the issue of Lymington harbour and the local mudflats. Naturally I've had to get substantial briefing on this but because the format is simply a speech from the backbencher and a reply from the minister, it's not too onerous. It's a very complicated situation in which commercial development is in conflict with the international biodiversity conventions. I explain everything in detail but I'm not sure it's much use to him.

Our last oral questions before the recess. I'm answering on the Competition Commission and the role of food producers in the grocery supply chain. Not very exciting. A few supplementaries and it's all over.

December rolls on with the same mix of departmental work with attendance at Christmas events squeezed in. One new strand is work on wildlife crime and I start a dialogue with Vernon Coaker in the Home Office to discuss the National Wildlife Crime Unit.

Hilary and Phil are in Bali for the UN climate change talks – tough going. As usual the US is obstructive but last-minute compromises have kept the agenda alive with prospects for agreement next year.

18 December: The House rises today but I'm still hard at work. I've called in Tower Hamlets Council to discuss their failure to make progress on recycling. It's a worthwhile meeting as they have had good warning and come prepared

to show how they are making improvements. I also sign off letters to another four under-performers including Lewisham. The latter is truly embarrassing. Being in the vanguard of authorities that went down the energy from waste road with SELCHP, the authority was slow to embrace recycling. I know they're now improving but nonetheless ministers can show no favours. Next morning my last DEFRA engagement – a Green TU leaders breakfast hosted by Frances O'Grady.*

20 December: A day at the office trying to clear as much box work as possible. Everyone else has tried to clear their desks so there's loads to do. Then it's drinks with Helen Ghosh and back to the constituency for the Afghan Eid celebrations at Goldsmiths College.

21–24 December: Duty minister but not disturbed!

## 2008

The Labour Party has sunk in the polls and we're all being asked to spend time campaigning in marginal seats. This is an added strain as Mike has to set up the arrangements, but ministerial work always takes priority and is unpredictable. I make an early start volunteering for a Saturday in Bristol to see a recycling furniture project and stay overnight at Mum's.

An appearance before the Environmental Audit Committee, which is doing an inquiry into environmental labelling. This is covered by EU legislation, which I've had to study hard. I'm impressed with the work going on in the EU – it takes years to research particular products and agree labelling regulations. There's a huge body of work on sustainable consumption and production for which I've acquired responsibility. It's complex but fascinating, requiring a continuous dialogue with scientists and manufacturers.

---

* Subsequently General Secretary of the TUC.

31 January: Our first orals of the New Year. Mark Lazarowicz has seen the Act on $CO_2$ display, which I have had erected in Portcullis House for MPs and staff to find out their carbon footprints. He asks for the public engagement programme to operate in Scotland. I then get a series of questions about low-energy lightbulbs and their disposal, with MPs suggesting a detrimental effect on health and a hazard from mercury if they are broken. On disposal, we do need to do more, but the questioner who slagged off his own council gets his facts wrong. I took the precaution of ringing up their enquiry point anonymously and got the correct information on disposal and the sites available!

In the constituency, several ongoing issues are really troubling. The council is determined to go ahead with the travellers' relocation to the utterly inappropriate Church Grove site and there's a big controversy over merging a popular primary school with poor results with the local academy. I find myself increasingly at loggerheads with the council and of course have less time now to be spending with councillors and officers. One very pleasing event, however, which is a credit to everyone involved, is the opening on 7 February of the Stephen Lawrence Centre in Brookmill Road. I'm so thrilled for Doreen and all the members of the trust. It's a very fine building and I'm proud to have it in my constituency.

My New Year's resolution was to think about the future. I'll definitely stand again at the next election, but I think that may be my last. I'd like to move to a different part of the borough for when I'm no longer in Parliament. I could do with a distraction so I decide to visit estate agents. I know where I'd like to live and it will probably take years to find an affordable property in the area.

I stop at the first estate agent's window. I can't believe it. There's a picture of a tiny coach house with a patio garden that is just about affordable. This isn't going to come up again any time soon. I swallow hard and make enquiries. I arrange to see it. This is total madness. I phone Frank in Aberdeen who can't believe what he's hearing. The estate agent is not impressed – my house is not on the market and it's obvious I've made no provision for a purchase (I haven't even got a solicitor). Over the next week I find a solicitor but then

I get a call to say the owner has accepted an offer from a no-chain buyer. I'm gutted but it's hardly surprising. Frank is very relieved.

6 February: Ian Gibson has a Westminster Hall debate on recycling. A great opportunity for me to set out the issues and what we're doing. Ian is an enthusiast so it's a pleasure to be there. With 100 million tonnes of waste being produced each year, there is enormous scope for recycling by business and industry as well as households. There's also a huge spectrum of local authority performance – the best sending just 7 per cent of their waste to landfill, the worst 93 per cent. I tackle the controversial 'alternate weekly collections' and point out that it's a misnomer – the councils with this policy collect *every* week – just different things. We are using the landfill tax escalator to push commerce and industry into more recycling, and are working with them on the difficult issue of recycling plastics. We're also working on metal waste streams and aluminium in particular, and with WRAP we've launched a programme tackling food waste. I demonstrate comprehensively the detailed work we're undertaking on the waste strategy including our latest consultation on batteries, having discovered every household is throwing away on average twenty-one portable batteries each year, with the loss of all the valuable raw materials they contain. Whatever else is going wrong around government, DEFRA is doing very valuable work that will need to continue for many years to come.

We're in Italy for the recess. Bitterly cold and the tiny electric fires in the house are utterly inadequate. Lots of log-burning in our main living space but lots of work to do anyway. We're just going shopping when Frank gets a phone call. His younger sister Annette has been rushed to hospital unconscious. Within the hour we learn that she is dead. Our return flight is not for two days, but Frank will go to Edinburgh as soon as we get back. This is such a shock – it's really difficult to take in.

Back in DEFRA, I'm seeing candidates for my new Private Secretary. I appoint Martin Meadows who proves to be an excellent choice. Next day it's back-to-back meetings until I get the sleeper to Edinburgh.

21 February: Annette's funeral. Frank gives a loving and emotional eulogy with the appropriate degree of light humour. It's a moving event. Incredibly sad for her young adult children. Annette was such a dynamic woman. At the start of the Iraq War, to everyone's horror, she took herself off to Baghdad with an international peace group. She was billeted with an Iraqi family close to a grain silo where they acted as human shields. We've often wondered since if her exposure to the lethal cocktails arising from the bombing had anything to do with her premature death.

26 February: A day out. I'm off to the Wildfowl and Wetlands Trust London Centre to coincide with my announcement on extra protection for a number of animals under threat, namely angel sharks, the Roman snail, two seahorse species and the water vole. The latter has of course iconic status, having been portrayed as 'Ratty' in *Wind in the Willows*. I'm given a water vole to handle. It's a delightful creature but it promptly nips me through my protective glove! Lots of publicity follows.

Amid all the misery of press torment on the 'bins', the *Daily Mail* has decided to launch a campaign against plastic bags. The editorial begins: 'Each year 13 billion "free" plastic bags are handed out. They are used for an average of 20 minutes. And they take up to 1,000 years to rot away.' They refer to the litter in streets, and countryside, and the devastating effect on wildlife: 'Seabirds, dolphins, turtles and puffins are strangled, suffocated, or starved by bags carried vast distances across the oceans.' How extraordinary and what a boost (I know they still hate us, really).

28 February: Another Westminster Hall debate. The Communities and Local Government Select Committee chaired by my colleague Phyllis Starkey has produced two reports that have provoked more press coverage on fortnightly black sack collections and our plans to allow incentive schemes to boost recycling. It gives me the chance to give the lie to the preposterous claims of a *Daily Express* journalist that we are going to impose charges that will cost

the average family £1,000 a year! The truth is the Climate Change Bill is going to allow for five pilot schemes to test models that we know work in other countries – basically those who recycle can get a reward and those who don't can be charged a very modest amount. From consultations, we know the public think this is fair and some local authorities are keen.

2 March: I've decided to start looking at properties again as I've got an easy day. My first call is the agent where I saw the coach house. When I walk in he says, 'You won't believe this but the property you were interested in has just come back on the market!' Now the owner has said: 'Sell it in a week or it's going for letting.' It's not been processed but I can bid if I want to. Of course my property isn't on the market so it's mission impossible. Nonetheless, I ring Frank and tell him what I want to do. 'It's your house,' he says! I go straight back to Ladywell and to an estate agent at the bottom of the road. Can he advertise my home immediately? No, he reminds me I have to have the Home Information Pack report that my government introduced! OK, I ask him, please book someone to come on Monday and meanwhile, if you have people looking for Edwardian semis (I knew he would have), please send them round for an informal chat. Three couples arrive next day. Within the week I have everything set up and advertised and my offer accepted for the coach house. I can't believe I'm doing this in the middle of such a heavy workload and having taken on a holiday home just a year ago. Poor Frank. He's always loved space and the present house is spacious, beautifully decorated, furnished with antiques and stuffed full of all our pictures, books and ornaments. What am I doing?

Next week there are two more debates for which I have to prepare. The first is one in Jonathan Shaw's brief on bovine TB. Jonathan can't be there so it's down to me. Fortunately, Hilary has involved all of us in looking at this extremely contentious subject. Personally, I accept the view of the Independent Scientific Group on cattle TB, that culling badgers is unlikely to make a significant effect but of course people raise the Chief Scientist's contrary advice. For now there's no decision so nothing new

to say. The debate is dominated by Tory MPs representing farming interests. There's no doubt the disease has had devastating effects on cattle and
farmers alike, and I'm happy to give what comfort I can on compensation
and research into vaccines.

The Act on $CO_2$ roadshows and all my minor media coverage are generating a lot of interest from outside organisations. Now we're experimenting
with web chats – not ideal for me as I have really poor computer skills.

In Cambridge for another excellent roadshow. I spend a lot of time with
the civil servants who run this programme. As a lifelong campaigner I'm able
to have positive input and I know they like working with a committed minister. We're launching a new Act on $CO_2$ advertising campaign that directs
people to the carbon calculator measuring carbon footprints and offering
ways of saving money and reducing $CO_2$ emissions. There's also an advice
line offering tailored advice run by the Energy Saving Trust and funded by
DEFRA. The emphasis is now on saving money first and $CO_2$ second, given
the rising costs of energy.

5 March: Monday morning's regular liaison meeting with the council. This
meeting remains a priority and gives me the opportunity to raise ongoing
issues, which includes the local area health reorganisation that has been
exercising us for the past year. It's a subject on which we are all united –
Lewisham Hospital cannot be downgraded in the way the document 'Picture
of Health' appears to envisage. I'm also fighting a post office closure on New
Cross Road and campaigning in Lewisham Central ward over the weekend.
Boundary changes brought this ward into my constituency, adding 10,000
residents with whom I've not had much contact. Thankfully, the CLP is now
running really well and people are out campaigning with greater frequency.
To supplement what I can do I'm now sending out surveys on topics of concern such as drugs and post office usage, with very useful results.

A quick visit and speech to the national conference of the WI on sustainable consumption, then it's back to Westminster for a climate change

debate initiated by Andrew Tyrie, one of the climate sceptics who criticises every aspect of the IPCC analysis and attempts to rubbish the Stern Report. He's got lots of his mates in the Chamber and the debate becomes, as Greg Barker, my Tory opposite number, says, a 'sceptic fest'. Greg does an excellent job of demolishing their arguments and making the case for mitigation. This gives me the chance to concentrate on adaptation. With higher temperatures, heavier rainfall, drought and other severe weather patterns, we need an adaptation strategy that involves all departments of government.

I tell the House of our climate impacts programme that provides information and tools for organisations to use to help them adapt to climate change. We are also working with the Met Office on projections that can be drilled down to 25km grid squares over land regions and river catchments. Wildlife is already feeling the effects, with birds moving north as southern habitats fail them. We've introduced climate change adaptation into the new local government performance framework and are taking powers to request reports and action plans from public bodies and statutory undertakers, such as water companies. I end by referring to our responsibilities to the poorest of the world, drawing on what I had seen at a recent Oxfam exhibition. There I met a Bangladeshi woman who had moved and rebuilt her home five times due to increases in flooding, and who is now supported by DfID-funded Oxfam projects.

12 March: Alistair's first Budget. It's cautious and downgrades growth but has lots of good things for the environment, poorer families and child benefit. He believes Britain is well placed to withstand the financial turmoil going on in the US, where the banking system is in deep trouble.

13 March: Oral questions and I'm pressed on the Chancellor's announcement in the Budget that we will take powers in the Climate Change Act to require certain retailers to charge for single-use carrier bags. Tories see it as a tax. Clearly it isn't but I am reluctant to increase retailers' profits. I refer

to the good example set by M&S who have voluntarily introduced a charge, with the money raised going to environmental causes. Several more questions on waste, including construction waste, where I'm doing lots of new and interesting work with a surprisingly receptive industry.

I spend Easter in the attic bedroom. It contains all the things that I brought from the house when Keith died and masses of my books, and archive papers from decades of campaigning. I am going to have to dispose of virtually everything. It's a horrendous weekend. Everything possible will go to Lewisham and Goldsmiths and to charity. It's a heartbreaking task as I relive so much of my college life with Keith and the horror of his death. I find myself in tears frequently. I'm consoled by thinking that ultimately someone would have to do this task and better that I do it, even if prematurely. A harrowing four days.

Back in the Commons for an important debate on plastics. People are much exercised about plastics going to China for recycling. While I agree it would be better not to export it, the Chinese ships that bring manufactures to the UK would otherwise return empty. Big efforts are being made to develop domestic markets and I'm able to give a lot of examples of our work with WRAP and the private sector, including the opening of the first UK plant to recycle PET (the most common form of plastic used in food and drink containers).

A major speaking engagement at the Environment Agency's spring conference where I present our work on adaptation, which is advancing on all fronts. Our only problem is the cuts we have to make as Alistair tries to reduce public expenditure.

The Climate Change Bill has completed its Lords stages so we need to prepare for the debate in the Commons. I've three debates this week. Metals recycling, packaging waste and then an end-of-day adjournment debate on Basildon golf course! The latter are the bane of every minister's life. They use up lots of officials' time and require a lot of briefing. The issue here is the owner of the site has put in a planning application to take 120,000m$^2$ of landfill waste to 'improve' the golf course. This is truly bizarre. It's possible this is a scam and I can tell Angela Smith that we are going to introduce a mandatory system of site waste management plans, but too late for Basildon, I fear. Next is a government topical debate on supermarkets. They are such major players in our society and their roles in the economy, agriculture, waste and $CO_2$ emissions are worthy of discussion. I announce that we are introducing the Carbon Reduction Commitment in the Climate Change Bill which will create a domestic cap and trade emissions scheme covering many enterprises including supermarkets. Lots of issues raised and good media coverage follows.

The month ends with a weekend of campaigning. Ken Livingstone is still very popular in Lewisham and if it just depended on us and the other inner London boroughs he would certainly be re-elected, but Boris Johnson has had an excellent campaign. I've met quite a lot of Labour supporters on the estates who always vote for me but admit they're going to vote for Boris. When I ask why, they say 'he makes me laugh'.

1 May: Ken loses to Boris and the BNP take an assembly seat. Sickening. Len Duvall, our Assembly member, is easily re-elected. Detailed analysis later shows that Ken did indeed win handsomely in Lewisham and Greenwich.

A supermarket forum on plastic bags. Hilary is chairing in an attempt to keep them onside and get more progress. There's no agreement among them since they are all in competition. I've calculated that on the rate of reduction we're getting with the voluntary agreements, it would take twelve years to eradicate the single-use plastic bag and that's just too long. A more promising initiative is Recycle on the Go. The idea is to increase the recovery of recyclable materials away from home. There's so much eating and drinking 'on the go' these days that we have to encourage the provision of proper recycling facilities in public spaces. We've got the backing of major companies such as Coca Cola, and I do a photo-op in Hyde Park. Good publicity.

Really good news. After ten days of talks in Dublin a new convention prohibiting the use, production and stockpiling of cluster munitions has been agreed. This is such a breakthrough and we can be proud of the part the UK has played in it.

Occasionally, I get out on a visit. Today I'm in Exeter looking at butterfly conservation and other projects. We visit some wetlands. Despite giving my foot size, the wellies provided are much too big and as I'm literally bogged down I pull my foot up only to free it from the wellie and plunge ignominiously into the mud. Thank goodness no one takes a photograph!

Barbara Follett and I go to Val Price's funeral in Swindon. A sad occasion attended by lots of women activists. Val did so much to support other women, particularly aspiring Labour candidates and was very much a fixture of our lives at party conferences.

The second reading of our flagship Climate Change Bill – our big day. The plan is for Hilary to open and Phil Woolas to close, but Hilary is taken ill unexpectedly. So Phil opens the debate and I close. Fortunately, I know the subject backwards. It's an excellent debate with a great deal of common ground. MPs from all parties know that we are making history here. We have been under pressure to raise the target of 60 per cent reduction in emissions by 2050 to 80 per cent. We know that the science has moved on since the target was set some years ago, and Nick Stern (now in the Lords) has advised going to 80 per cent, but we're holding the line for now. The Tories have taken this up and also annual targets, which by contrast are of course a complete nonsense. The few climate deniers on the Tory side press their case. In my wind-up speech I'm able to dispense thanks and praise for contributions liberally across the parties, answer a raft of questions, and conclude: 'It is clear that the UK has a fine record of leadership internationally on the enormously challenging issue that we have been discussing. The Bill provides the essential framework for ensuring that our response at home is commensurate with the challenge.' Five Tories, including Peter Lilley, Christopher Chope and Andrew Tyrie, vote against. Sorry for Hilary, but thrilled to have had my say today.

At the next oral PQs and I'm tackled again on charges for rubbish. The tabloid press hysteria continues to worry MPs, though it's largely sport for the Tories. I put the record straight once again – it is not a tax, it's revenue-neutral – it's an incentive scheme. Any charge would be around £50 a year and only impact on those who recycle least, and of course we're only looking for five pilot projects!

Several members tackle me on low-energy diode (LED) technology and David Taylor raises nanoimprint lithography. Most MPs quite reasonably don't know what they're talking about but fortunately I'm briefed and we're doing things.

24 June: The first committee session of the Climate Change Bill. Phil Woolas and I will be in committee Tuesdays and Thursdays, mornings and afternoons, for several weeks. Standing committees entail an incredible amount of preparatory work for ministers and a lot of speaking and concentration during the actual sessions.

We start at 10.30 a.m. with Frank Cook in the chair. He has an important announcement. Our committee has been chosen for an experiment. Committee members are allowed to have laptops (we were advised in advance). Few laptops have appeared! Phil and I will need to be on our toes – not least because there's a lot of expertise on our own side. Amendments are constantly tabled by the opposition (that's their job), so briefing has to be done every day and officials are working around the clock. It's a far more complicated business than the public could ever imagine. The Bill team is superb – extremely able civil servants who keep their cool and cope with the pressure of little notice of what will be up for debate and in what order.

Whatever the pressures of the Bill, I still need to keep up with constituency engagements on a Friday. Today I'm meeting a local developer, then it's the Deptford First tea party, which we hold at Lewisham College's Deptford campus, and finally a campaigners' meeting at Joe Perry's house, where he provides supper. Joe is the absolute anchor of our constituency party and real progress has been made in our organisation and campaigning due to his leadership.

29 June: An absolutely horrific murder in Sterling Gardens in my constituency. Two bodies have been found by firefighters attending a blaze at one of the flats. This is a quiet, private estate built not so long ago, from which I rarely get casework.

As information is released over the next few days, we will learn that the bodies are of two young men, masters' degree students from France who were in the UK on a three-month DNA research project at Imperial College. I am really distressed that such a thing could have happened in my constituency and to students from my old college. The news gets worse and worse. They were tortured and then stabbed over 100 times. This is quite beyond belief and I cannot imagine the effect on their families. I decide not to go to the estate. It is crawling with police and media and I don't want to make a nuisance of myself and say something vacuous. There are no relatives to whom I can express condolences, so I'll wait.

Next day, I go to Sterling Gardens and talk to local people and to the police. The small block containing the flat is cordoned off so residents have had to leave for the time being. Everyone is deeply shocked. I offer any help and leave details. Eleven days later, Nigel Farmer is charged with the murder of the French students. Another man, Dano Sonnex, is arrested. He lives in Peckham but his parents live in New Cross. He too is charged with murder.

Another week dominated by the Climate Change Bill, where I'm dealing with all the amendments on adaptation, which go on for days. Finally, on Thursday afternoon we get onto the five pilot schemes for waste charging. Predictably a difficult debate, but the measure goes through.

We reach the part of the Bill dealing with plastic bags, which will provoke the Tories. I begin with the amendments that confer the power to make regulations to charge for single-use carrier bags. This doesn't mean we have decided to charge, simply that we want the power. The 13 billion single-use bags distributed each year are estimated to be responsible for almost 790,000 tonnes of $CO_2$ equivalent, which is why the measure is in this Bill. I also remind members that 40 per cent of emissions are due to the action of individuals, making behaviour change imperative. We debate the issue for nearly two hours and then it's agreed. After ten sittings, we are out of committee. What a relief, but also a sense of achievement.

It's the sixtieth anniversary of the NHS – one of Labour's greatest achievements. It forms the basis of my latest constituency consultation. I've also organised a meeting for all my local GPs to discuss care provision.

I've bought a new car! My very first. I've always had second-hand cars, a couple of which came from my sister Susan. My last purchase was a second-hand deluxe version Mondeo that is now on its last legs and won't make the journey to Italy, so I'm taking a loan and buying a small BMW. I've been driving for thirty-five years so I think I can justify the extravagance.

I've employed Jessica Maloney, who used to work for Michael Foster in Hastings, to replace Mike, who's moving on, and they're having a short handover period. Jessica's previous experience makes this straightforward, which is really helpful as I've been so preoccupied with the Bill.

Frank and I go to Ditchley Park for their fiftieth anniversary lecture given by Martin Rees, president of the Royal Society. A splendid occasion. The man is an absolute inspiration and the lunch is excellent. We take the option of staying overnight so that we can have just a little quality time together. Next morning, we take an early train to ensure I'm back in time to make a speech at the official opening of the Pincott Place People's Park.

Phil and I do a high-level stakeholder meeting on anaerobic digestion (AD). There's a great deal of interest and it has a very important contribution to make to our waste and climate strategies. At its full potential, anaerobic digestion could produce enough electricity to power 2 million homes and, importantly, it keeps organic waste out of landfill. I've visited a plant in Ludlow, part of DEFRA's £30 million New Technologies Demonstrator Programme. Seventy per cent of the local residents have got involved in the partnership by providing food waste to supply the plant. AD is even being discussed on *The Archers*.

I chair a meeting I've convened for the local community about the Sterling Gardens murders. A local resident has tipped off the press. I ask the meeting and put it to the vote – the meeting decides to exclude them. There's a lot of anger and tension. People are afraid. Even though Sonnex and Farmer are in custody, the community feels at risk. Several people tell of previous burglaries on the estate, including one only a week before in the block where the students were murdered. None of these burglaries have been properly addressed by the police. So many issues are raised and the police are really under pressure. They agree to increase reassurance measures and regular newsletters. The local neighbourhood officers are very responsive and there are lots of suggestions about how to improve security.

One shocking revelation is that the freeholders' management company has refused to change the locks on the main door to the murder block. I undertake to get on to them immediately. Such insensitivity is very hard to understand in a case like this. Most residents are at work all day and some come home after dark. People are very distressed at the massive publicity and horror that has been brought to their estate, and I feel particularly sorry for those who have to constantly pass the flat where such unimaginable crimes occurred. Four months later, I organise a follow-up with residents. The meeting is much more positive. Fulsome briefings and the local panel and neighbourhood police have got a much closer relationship with residents. As a consequence, a residents' association is to be set up and I offer to give support.

Parliament's last day and I catch an evening flight to Glasgow. I'm spending all day tomorrow assisting with last-minute canvassing for the parliamentary by-election. We have an excellent candidate in Margaret Curran. There's not much joy on the estates I've been sent to canvass. We lose to the SNP. The economic downturn continues to haunt us and there is worse news from the US, where the government has stepped in to prop up their two largest mortgage lenders, covering $5 trillion worth of house loans.

Another bout of hysteria in the tabloids. The *Daily Express* has a full front-page headline: 'Pay every time your dustbin is emptied'. The whole article is a pack of lies. They also accuse me personally of embarrassing the PM and at the same time record the fact that not a single council has come forward to carry out a pilot scheme. This is actually an embarrassment to *me* but the simple truth is, it was Tory council leaders who had called for the measures. They were ready to pilot them, but Eric Pickles, the shadow Environment Secretary, issued a ban on their taking part. I'm named again in the *Express* editorial as an eco-zealot (well that's probably true, unlike the rest of it).

Meanwhile, I've concluded my house sale and purchase. Our antique furniture, collected so lovingly, won't fit into the tiny coach house, so it all goes to auction where it realises pennies. We will leave beds and bits of modern furniture to the family moving in. I do feel sad at leaving the house and our nice neighbours, and very apprehensive at Frank's ability to cope with our much-reduced space. Then disaster strikes. I'd arranged for Kazia, who has been working for me for years, to clean the house from top to bottom as we move out, but she has had an accident and broken her arm. I'm panic-stricken and confide in Ken as usual. He assures me he'll sort it and comes back within the hour to say that his wife Sue will come and do the necessary. I'm reluctant to accept as it seems such an imposition, but she comes over and does a wonderful job. Subsequently, Kazia decides that she doesn't want to follow us to the new place and Sue volunteers to replace her. I couldn't want for anyone better and soon come to rely on her to look after the house long-term.

Summer is a quiet time apart from trying to get the new house into shape. I launch our climate change adaptation website – a really important tool for the many authorities and institutions that need to build adaptation into their polices and plans. I also announce new protections under the Habitats Directive for three now rare species – a pool frog (only found in Norfolk), a snail and a moth.

Time to take stock of my three roundtables. All is going to plan but I'm worried that the credit crunch and worsening economic prospects will cause Sainsbury's to pull back from their development in which we've invested so much hope. At Deptford, the railway carriage is a huge success – it's become a local landmark, and Rebecca Molina, who is now running it as a café, is a breath of fresh air and has a great eye for design.

At last we get to go to Italy, driving my new car. We'll take two days travelling out and two back and a couple of weeks in between. A wonderful opportunity to recharge the batteries and pay some attention to house and garden.

Back for the official opening of the Waldron Health Centre. Very well-attended, good speeches from us all, and very nice pictures of the ribbon-cutting. A great example of Labour's investment in the health service.

17 September: More grim news. Following a run on HBOS shares, the bank is to be taken over by Lloyds TSB.

Labour Party conference in Manchester and I'm meeting numerous green groups and doing a few fringes and seminars on my briefs. But the most important event is Gordon's speech. Sarah comes up to the podium and introduces her husband. It works! Gordon's speech is a success. He speaks more easily than usual, with personal examples from his life and references to his values. He offers fairness, stability and reassurance in challenging times. His jibe at Cameron, 'no time for novices', drives home the message. Let's hope he's done enough.

29 September: Government takes control of Bradford & Bingley's £50 billion mortgages and loans. Where will this end?

The autumn reshuffle. Gordon is to create a new department – bringing together energy and some DEFRA functions including climate change. He asks me what I want to do. Much as I've loved DEFRA, I'm thrilled to accept the new post available in the Department of Energy and Climate Change. Environmentalists such as myself have always argued for these policy areas to be brought together. Ed Miliband will be Secretary of State and although I don't know him, Harriet rates him as he once worked for her before going to the Treasury. So much to do, and decisions to make. Where will the new department be housed and will my private office staff transfer with me? I do hope so. We sort out the portfolios. Ed asks for an inaugural meeting to bring together all the staff who will make up DECC, so that the ministerial team can address them and take questions. I think this is rather a daunting prospect.

My portfolio will cover: delivering a low carbon economy and ensuring secure and affordable energy, with a focus on energy customers; taking forward the government's fuel poverty policy; energy savings (in the residential sector); carbon reduction commitments; behaviour change and the Act on $CO_2$ campaign (I specifically asked for that); climate change agreements; and supporting the SoS on international climate change and in promoting national debate in the run-up to the UN climate change conference in Copenhagen. I'm absolutely thrilled. This is the best job I could ever have.

Ed and I spend lots of time with officials working on our climate change strategy. I will be in charge of the remaining stages of the Climate Change Bill, and we need to make some crucial decisions about amendments, not least moving from 60 per cent reductions to 80 per cent by 2050.

The economic news is worsening. The collapse of the Icelandic banks has left local authorities and charities with up to £1 billion losses and the government is to rescue RBS, Lloyds TSB and HBOS in a £37 billion package.

My first outing as a DECC minister. Siobhain McDonagh has an adjournment debate on a constituency case. One of her constituents got into arrears with Scottish Power and ended up being cut off. The family has had no hot water, heating or cooked food for over four months and the company is attempting to get them to pay £500 for a new meter when of course they couldn't even afford the regular bills. The case illustrates so much of what is wrong with the regulation of energy prices. I assure her that ministers in DECC will be energetically pursuing the issues raised.

19 October: The Chancellor, Alistair Darling, announces a plan to pour billions into public works in an attempt to get us out of the worst of the economic downturn.

We debate the remaining stages of the Climate Change Bill. This is the stage where governments introduce new clauses and amendments that we want to add to the Bill after the committee stage. I begin with new measures on emissions from aviation and shipping. We have led the argument on this topic in the EU and there is now legislation to include the emissions in the EU emissions trading scheme, but we need action in the UK as well. I put forward a package of new rules, which should see the Independent Climate Change Committee, being set up in the Bill, bring forward proposals for including these emissions by 2012. A long technical debate follows, with members on all sides heavily engaged and me jumping up to speak with some frequency. After three hours of examination and skirmishes with the climate sceptics, I respond to the debate and the new measures are agreed without a vote.

My second raft of amendments will enable us to introduce the new Community Energy Savings Programme (CESP). It builds on our experience of CERT (Carbon Emissions Reduction Scheme) whereby energy suppliers must offer schemes to individual households that reduce their energy bills. The new CESP will be community-focused with delivery house by house and street by street. I also announce that we will table measures on feed-in tariffs before third reading in the Lords on 5 November (details still not finalised). I then have the difficult task of taking on some of my own colleagues who have supported a new (Tory) clause introducing a specific cap for emissions per unit of output from the power sector. They see this as a means of preventing any new coal-fired power stations from being built without carbon capture and storage (CCS). But the mechanism makes no sense as the power sector is covered by the EU emissions trading scheme and is capped anyway. Our position is to support CCS with our £1 billion competition, and to insist on any new coal-fired stations being built CCS-ready. A long and more acrimonious debate ends at 9 p.m. The government clauses are agreed without a vote, the Tory amendment defeated by a majority of seventy-eight, and a Lib Dem clause defeated by a majority of 218.

There are lots more technical amendments, including the crucial change from 60 per cent reduction to 80 per cent by 2050. Then everything is agreed. Ed opens the third (final) reading of the Bill at twenty to ten, and says, 'It will make us the first economy in the world to enshrine in law binding climate change targets – 80 per cent by 2050. They provide a scale of ambition that will enable us to play our part, with authority, in seeking a global agreement in Copenhagen at the end of next year.' Then a final vote: three Tories, Chope, Lilley and Tyrie, vote against. It's all over, and I couldn't be more proud.

No office building was available for a new department and so we are currently squatting in 1 Whitehall Place with our 1,000 civil servants mainly lodged in their parent departments. Ed's informal approach to things is a great advantage. There are some Secretaries of State who, I think, just couldn't tolerate our conditions, but he is driving the agenda and we're all up for it. I've just about forgiven him for his introduction at the all-staff meeting called to introduce us. To my great embarrassment he referred to me as his childhood heroine! I suppose the chair of CND would have been a popular figure in the Miliband household, but since I'm feeling at my most dynamic ever, I'm not keen for people to hark back to the past.

A weekend in Aberdeen – a reward for a very tough few weeks – but everdutiful Frank and I put in a day at the Glenrothes by-election supporting Lindsay Roy, who goes on to win. It's a tremendous boost for Gordon who threw everything into it, despite all the predictions we would lose.

4 November: Barack Obama easily wins the US presidential election against John McCain and his appalling running mate Sarah Palin. I'd supported Hillary in the primaries, but it really is thrilling to see a black man elected to the White House. I just hope no one assassinates him.

First DECC oral questions and I've got a heavy cold. David Chaytor asks about the 2020 EU climate change and renewable energy target ahead of the Poznan UN climate conference – are we fully supportive? I'm able to reassure him: we are and are resisting calls from other EU states to dilute the package in the light of the economic situation. We actually believe investment in renewables is a way out of recession. I'm then asked about linking vehicle excise duty to vehicle emissions – clearly a good idea, but a decision for the Chancellor in a few weeks' time.

I'm dealing with government amendments made in the Lords to the Climate Change Bill. We've had advice about the drafting from counsel and also from Lord Turner, the chair of our shadow Independent Climate Change Committee. As a consequence, we made some technical amendments on the aviation and shipping emissions that I now have to introduce into the Commons. Then onto further amendments strengthening the regime on domestic effort and overseas credits. Half an hour later and all the Lords amendments are agreed – my very last word on the Bill.

Various stakeholder events on climate change and media follow. I also give evidence to the select committee on emissions from shipping, meet the Energy Saving Trust and have my first fuel poverty stakeholders meeting. The latter is really tough. Huge dissatisfaction with the way the Warm Front programme is being run. I can see I've inherited a poisoned chalice here. I discover that the *Daily Mirror* has been raising issues for some time and is now claiming that 25 per cent of those households in receipt of Warm Front measures have complained, but the complaints have been 'covered up to avoid penalty charges'. This is going to require a major investigation.

3 December: The State Opening of Parliament and a lunchtime reception in the Speaker's rooms attended by the Queen.

I'm gradually working through plans to improve the new house, beginning with double-glazing. Because of the nature of the building, they're all being individually made with wood frames at very considerable cost. I'm also replacing all the radiators – more efficient and vertical so as to give us more wall space. The house is in a state of continuous chaos!

A meeting with the Peruvian Environment Minister. With a long coastline, high mountains and dense forests, Peru has a very real interest in climate change and their position on the UN talks is important to us.

Mid-December: Ed and I are in Poznan, Poland, for the UN climate change talks. These are a precursor to the conference in Copenhagen in a year's time. We discuss a second commitment period for Kyoto, Carbon Capture and Storage, the adaptation fund and, most importantly, a commitment of those present to submit their national reduction targets and measures for 2020 to the UN by mid-February. Our delegation plays a pivotal role in keeping the process on track for Copenhagen. I hold talks with a number of developing countries and we pledge £100 million for forestry projects.

Back in the office we're interviewing candidates for my private office and I appoint Summer Nisar, who will prove to be a great support. Then a briefing on Warm Front, our grant programme for energy efficiency measures. Not only do I find that very large numbers of complaints have come to officials (when at the DTI), but there are masses of outstanding letters that were never dealt with by my predecessor. An absolute minefield.

18 December: The House rises for the Christmas recess and it's time for a festive meal with my long-suffering parliamentary staff. Relief all round that a real break is coming up after one last surgery tomorrow.

## 2009

18 January: Ed is on *The World at One* defending our position on Heathrow. We've been on this ever since DECC was created. I've made my feelings clear from the start – the expansion of Heathrow will be hugely detrimental in terms of air quality and noise and inconsistent with our efforts to curb $CO_2$ emissions. Ed has negotiated hard in Cabinet, making clear that we oppose unconstrained aviation expansion. The outcome is a compromise that can be defended, to my utter relief given my commitment on climate change and my constituents' opposition. Only about half the slots sought are being allowed and very strict air quality and noise limits. On $CO_2$ we are getting the Committee on Climate Change to advise on strict, enforceable limits that will see

the UK carbon emissions from aviation back to current levels by 2050. We've also led the successful argument for including aviation emissions in the EU emissions trading scheme. But still an unpopular decision with many back-benchers. The Tories promise to cancel it.

I'm appearing before the DEFRA Select Committee to give evidence on energy efficiency and fuel poverty. Given the nightmare of Warm Front, I'm apprehensive.

DECC orals. I get tackled on the landfill directive and potential fines but I'm able to point to the £10 million spent on anaerobic digestion and the £2 billion of PFI (Public Finance Initiative) credits for waste infrastructure on energy efficiency. I point to the Thames Gateway eco region, the decent homes programme that has made 1 million homes more energy efficient and our zero-carbon homes agenda set for 2016. Several more questions follow as the Tories try to 'out-green' us. My opposite number recites Tory promises to offer all homeowners a £6,500 entitlement to energy efficiency measures. We've costed the programme at £150 billion – it'll never happen.

I then get a run of six questions from both sides of the House on fuel poverty. We are really vulnerable here. The energy companies are guilty of unfair pricing and Ofgem has failed to tackle them. Ed has read the riot act but they're a thick-skinned lot who've been allowed to get away with things for far too long. Clearly our perspective is different from that of the DTI, who dealt with them in the past. But we are running to keep up and people are suffering.

January: We wake to the news that the UK is officially in recession. Deeply depressing. We are being dragged into the pit by a global financial crisis that is not of our making but inevitably the public will blame us. It's strange to be part of a government that has to deal with a crisis a day when we at DECC are constantly scanning a horizon, decades ahead. Not only am I convinced of the importance of tackling climate change, I also believe that low carbon growth will be essential to our economic recovery.

I've agreed to do a pre-record for *The One Show* on fuel poverty. We're under so much pressure that I think it's best to explain what we're doing. I take it all on the chin, sympathise with all those who've encountered problems with Warm Front and point to the many other people who have found the scheme excellent, but they raise questions about invoices and overcharging, implying fraud. This is terrible and I demand to see officials immediately.

I've got to the bottom of the invoices issue. To my utter relief it's not fraud but invisible though legitimate VAT calculations. Eaga, the company who deliver, are entirely to blame. I instruct officials to get a grip. I brief Ed and arrange to give something to the *Daily Mirror* (who've been running highly critical stories). I can get some changes made but a proper overhaul will require secondary legislation. We will have to have it and have it in time to make changes ahead of next winter. The *Daily Mirror* headline 'A win on the Warm Front', and they claim credit for the overhaul. I don't mind as I get extensive quotes listing everything I'm doing including my aim to raise the grant level.

A lovely brave and generous note from Henry Hodge. Not long after we had seen him on holiday looking fit and swimming every day last year he became unwell and was eventually diagnosed with leukaemia. Now he's had a bone marrow transplant. I'm so glad he's survived it and hope he can recover.

Despite all the dramas of DECC, life goes on elsewhere. I'm making progress on the house, with plans drawn up to extend the downstairs front wall by one metre. This will enable us to create a shower room where the old damp walk-in cupboard is now. Not sure how I'm going to cope with all this work and do my job, but not the sort of thing I can put off for years. A local builder, John, is giving me lots of support. But in no time he is accosted by one of our neighbours accusing him of illegally removing trees! He is quite upset. I've designed a small patio and raised beds in the very small area in front of the house. This entailed removing six horrible leylandii. As we're in a conservation area I know permission has to be sought for native trees, but not these garden freaks. I explain in my letter and give assurances that the fence that blew down will also be replaced when the garden is finished.

I'm particularly keen not to cause offence as we were targeted within months of arrival. The whole side wall of the house was covered in graffiti, which looked as though it had a personal content.

Every day all ministers receive up to 100 pages of photocopied press cuttings. This enables us to see how our policies and the wider issues are being reported. Occasionally we ourselves are the news but this one is rather unexpected. A columnist in the *Yorkshire Post* has written a piece relating the new TV series on Margaret Thatcher to women in Parliament today. She is savage in her criticisms but then says, 'There are some honourable exceptions such as Joan Ruddock who has always stuck to her principles and Theresa May, bless her, with her shoe habit and leather jackets!' Can I be pleased? Well, just a little. Good thing is Lindsay Duncan, who is the star of the TV programme, is quoted as saying she loathed Thatcher and everything she stood for.

Our public engagement work is developing apace. We launch our People Power campaign in Birmingham. It's part of a three-city challenge where a group of residents become climate champions. It's going really well – individuals can save up to £300 a year by changing behaviour in the simplest ways, turning off lights and standbys, installing draught excluders and long-life lightbulbs. I visit a household that has followed all the advice and made a big reduction. Lots of excellent local publicity and hopefully lots of people contacting our Act on $CO_2$ advice line as a result.

My only debate in February is initiated by Barry Gardiner on peak oil, for which I need quite a lot of briefing, but it goes well. Which is more than can be said for the correspondence unit. Of the 1,143 letters, from ten days ago, 543 still remain, most, of course, falling to my brief. Because the unit has been instructed to process the most out of date first, another 200 have fallen beyond the deadline for answer and another 300 are now approaching it. One reason is that I keep sending them back. The correspondence unit work on standard paragraphs of information when composing a reply. One letter has ten paras, eight of which I have to delete as irrelevant or inaccurate. I am tearing my hair out. Ed and Moira (Permanent Secretary) have got to take action. Meanwhile, the Tories are having a field day on fuel poverty, alleging we don't understand the plight of families. Sheer hypocrisy on their part – they plan to cut DECC if they get into power. I understand only too well, but the real villain is the escalating cost of fuel and I can't increase the grant without secondary legislation. Meanwhile I fume daily and stay up till midnight signing letters.

An urgent meeting with the CEO and chair of TFL. Last November, the Department of Transport delivered a body blow to the East London line extension, doubting whether it could be built and saying our Surrey Canal Road station was axed. Since then I've been lobbying everyone and this is my last hope. The Department of Transport offers £7 million but the station cost is £12 million. I know if we don't get the station footprint into the plans at this stage it could never happen. I make a plea for passive provision in the plans. I'll have to stay on this case.

26 February: RBS reports the biggest loss in British corporate history. This is really scary.

Up at DECC questions dealing with a whole run on energy-efficient lighting starting with LEDs. I remember precisely my first demonstration of LEDs when I was at DEFRA. A manufacturer showed me what looked like a jewel case of diamonds – amazingly bright lights from pinprick sources. I'm happy to assure Members that we're working to stimulate development and take-up, and have included them for enhanced capital allowances. Always exciting to find new technologies that are environmentally sustainable.

An amazing email. Rafael Herrera, a friend from Venezuela and colleague of my late husband Keith, has written to me having read of my ministerial appointment. He's now living in Spain. I'm so pleased to hear from him as we were all great friends in the '70s.

12 March: Keith would have been seventy today.

A meeting with the Borough Commander. For the past five years I've been dealing with a case of cyber harassment. It recently came to a head when it looked as though the perpetrator was coming to the UK (from Jamaica) to launch an exhibition of his photographs at a local gallery. This man has made consistent threats to kill my constituent and rape his daughter. Although the identity of the perpetrator is known, authorities there cannot take action and they do not think it's serious enough for Interpol. I've got assurances from the Home Office that he will be intercepted if he arrives here, and eventually the gallery agree not to show the photographs (women posing with guns). I need to be sure there's nothing more we can do. I also ask for an update on the Sterling Gardens murders. The trial will begin on 21 April and we'll have a meeting with senior police officers just before it starts.

Last day before the Easter recess and I have an important meeting with a minister from Indonesia. There are huge issues to explore that cross all my DEFRA and DECC briefs. Deforestation and unsustainable palm oil cultivation are greatly adding to carbon emissions and loss of biodiversity. Many countries such as Indonesia, desperately pursuing growth to support their rapidly growing populations, need real help if they are not to add to climate change.

I've set aside recess time to tackle the huge backlog of Warm Front letters. My foolish pledge on *The One Show* to answer all complaints personally has seen the department deluged. Following my confrontation with him, the CEO of Eaga cancelled our next meeting and is now off work sick. I don't wish him ill but frankly he's got a lot to answer for.

The PM is travelling the world in the run-up to the G20 on 2 April. He has really come into his own since the financial crisis took hold. He's arguing for a global agreement akin to Bretton Woods, which shaped the post-war economic structure of the world. The G20 agrees a $1 trillion injection of funds to help stabilise the global economy and keep protectionism at bay. Gordon is riding high and I'm delighted for him.

Drinks with my private office staff. They chose the venue – it's a swanky place in Trafalgar Square with expensive drinks. Fun though.

Easter Saturday: Damian McBride, one of Gordon's closest advisors, has been forced to quit over his exchange with the blogger Derek Draper who used to work for Peter Mandelson. They've been making a series of scurrilous sex allegations against the Tories. It's shocking stuff and the thing that disgusts me most about politics and particularly the spin doctors and hangers on who inhabit the offices of the most senior figures in government. I am utterly sickened by it. Clearly it reflects badly on Gordon, just at a time when he personally was doing so well and we'd risen slightly in the polls against a resurgent Tory Party. I hate these people.

Over the recess, I've done huge amounts of work on Warm Front and I've now got a big submission on the contractual issues that are dogging us with Eaga. Consultants have been engaged and I get their report. I'm furious their brief did not include reference to the detailed complaints submitted over the past year by MPs. I spend hours going through it and send back my own complaints and detailed questions. I really want to fire someone!

I'm in Prague for an informal meeting of the EU Environment Council. This is the beginning of an intensive round of meetings preparing for the Copenhagen summit. My mission is to try to get movement from other EU countries on sources of finance and governance. We need the EU as a whole to have a progressive position. We know the US and China will be on the back foot. Several countries express positive views in private but then don't repeat them in the main forums, so we end without a consensus. Nevertheless, I have very useful bilaterals with France, Germany and Poland. The latter have been much exercised about burden-sharing as they push ahead with new industrial development and more intensive agriculture.

Back-to-back Friday constituency meetings as usual, beginning this week with Network Rail. They've chopped down trees all along the trackside, causing massive distress. They don't seem to realise in urban areas trees give some protection to nearby homes and also provide wildlife corridors. I appreciate the 'leaves on the line' argument, but there are better ways of doing this. Very good news on Lewisham Hospital. We have succeeded – Alan Johnson,

Secretary of State for Health, has accepted the recommendation to retain our 24-hour A&E.

19 April: J. G. Ballard has died. I'm reminded of how I failed to thank him when he sent me a copy of *Empire of the Sun* back in my CND days and how I didn't read it until many years later. I wish I'd been more appreciative.

In Syracuse for the G8 meeting. It's a beautiful place but cold and wet for our late evening arrival. Stupidly, travelling only with hand luggage as usual, I've nothing warm to put on. We are not allowed out of the hotel until our personal bodyguards have assembled! We've been told the area around the venue has been cleared of residents and there is tight security and no parking. Despite the latter, the street outside is full of cars – presumably the bodyguards. We are escorted the short distance to the freezing historic castle for the opening ceremony. We wait rather too long for the Italian minister, Stefania Prestigiacomo. She's one of the beautiful women appointed by Berlusconi who are all supposed to be air heads (she wasn't). While I have a distinctly blue pallor, she is glowing – my mood is darkening by the moment. Three days of difficult discussions that somewhat lack direction but I get on well with the German minister, Sigmar Gabriel, who is a good ally in a meeting where the North Americans are not out to settle for our agenda.

On our last night we're invited to a splendid dinner, accompanied by our bodyguards as usual. We leave rather late, intent on walking home without a fuss. Bodyguard appears from nowhere – completely drunk and vowing to protect us all the way home. I learn later that he tried to pick up one of my civil servants! So much for Italian security.

First day in my new fifth-floor office. Lots of furniture-moving but at least we can settle now and it'll be much easier to hold significant meetings in my own room after months in open plan. It's a bank holiday weekend and a one-liner on Thursday so I take the opportunity of a much-needed weekend in Aberdeen with Frank (plus red boxes, which I've insisted on being retired in favour of black canvas briefcases, which are a fraction of the weight). Back on Sunday and another box delivered two hours later.

Some people returning to the UK from Mexico have been found to be suffering from the new flu strain HINI, a form of swine flu. This could be serious as a lot of people have died. The FCO has advised against all but essential journeys to Mexico. COBRA is convened.

A thoroughly unpleasant piece in the *Daily Mail*. I rarely get targeted but these poisonous men are invariably sexist. They've taken to referring to my age and the latest piece suggests I should be retired because of my low level of workload, judged by the *Mail*'s record of my public engagements. This is infuriating. Women MPs are dogged by misogyny and sexism. Not only do I know that I don't look my age, I've never had more energy and regularly work eighty hours a week. The problem with working on such cutting-edge policy and ground-breaking developments is that they are far too serious and long term for the parasites who make a living out of gossip and scandal.

I'm planning a quiet constituency day, with a staff meeting, a surgery and just one visit to a local gallery, when all hell breaks loose. The *Telegraph* has obtained an unredacted copy of all MPs' expenses that were supposed to be published in July. Today they're making accusations against Gordon, Tony Blair, John Prescott, Hazel Blears, Alistair Darling, Peter Mandelson, David Miliband and Jack Straw. Really shocking. Some of it is really bad but other stuff is clearly innocent but looks odd, like Gordon's claim for his cleaner and Alistair's designation of his second home. More serious is Hazel's failure to pay Capital Gains Tax and Tony's claim for roof repairs submitted two days before he stood down. I manage a weak smile at John Prescott's alleged £300 claim for fitting mock Tudor beams to his constituency home and replacing two toilet seats. Apparently they'll publish new lists every day. It's leading the national news now and I feel utterly sick. Everyone is going to be buying the *Telegraph* tomorrow.

Sure enough, a huge number of new allegations against a long list of ministers, former ministers and backbenchers. I can't believe it. Elliot Morley and David Chaytor have both been found to have made fraudulent claims not picked up by the fees office. I've always had the greatest respect for both of them and cannot believe they could do such a thing. Others have made stupid claims entirely legitimately. Poor Phil Woolas has been fingered for something that is completely unjustified. MPs who have second homes in their constituencies can claim for certain household items. These frequently appear on a supermarket bill that contains other personal items. As is normal practice, he claimed only for the legitimate items but the *Telegraph*, seeing the whole bill attached to the claim, accuse him of claiming for the personal items that were for his wife and child. Phil quite rightly threatens to sue. Who knows who will be next.

Every night I switch on the radio beside the bed for the midnight news. We lie there in apprehension – which of our colleagues will be accused? Given the mistakes the *Telegraph* has made, what if it's one of us? It's so utterly sickening. If I were not doing the DECC job I'd really want to leave Parliament altogether.

Then it's the Tories' turn – David Cameron has claimed for having wisteria cleared from his chimney. A whole raft of Tory grandees are accused, plus ten members of their front bench. Several large sums of money are involved and it's all made slightly worse by the fact these people are known to be rich and have grand houses. Two cases will become notorious. Douglas Hogg is reported to have claimed for the cleaning of his moat and Sir Peter Viggers for the construction of a duck house. Long after the event it will emerge that neither of these 'claims' was ever paid, but the myth will persist. Half a dozen Lib Dems follow including rather weak accusations against Nick Clegg and Chris Huhne.

An appalling week. Resignations, sackings, deselections, public apologies, repayments and retirement announcements will follow. Frank and I have nothing to answer for and no illegitimate claims, but I know we are now all under suspicion. The public will never trust us again.

Somehow I have to get back to serious work despite the fact that Parliament is in a frenzy about the expenses. I appear before a European Scrutiny Committee on climate change. I don't suppose anyone is really interested.

Then I'm attending a meeting of COBRA on behalf of DECC. The very large room has the feel of a bunker, though it's not underground. The first case of person-to-person transmission of swine flu in the UK was recently recorded so we are no longer dealing with infected passengers from Mexico. I'll be taking my turn at these meetings over the next few months with officials providing continuity of briefings. At the meeting we receive extensive briefings from the Health Protection Agency and video-conferencing facilities ensure that the devolved nations participate, particularly important as the first people infected are in Scotland. Decisions are taken on immediate measures, such as school closures if a pupil is infected.

I'm slightly worried about Frank, who flies to Aberdeen and back every week in the company of the global workforce from the oil industry. I keep nagging him to wash his hands!

20 May: An email from the *Independent on Sunday* saying they intend to do their own investigations into claims over the past four years. They demand full details of my claims, ask if I believe they are reasonable, if I think I represent good value for money for the taxpayers, if I can justify every claim and if, in the light of current concerns, I now consider any claims questionable. Who the hell do these people think they are?

I receive a letter from the director of resources listing all the changes to the rules relating to allowances. None applies to any of Frank's and my claims, but the tightened procedures undoubtedly would have prevented most of the excessive claims that led to the scandal.

A short respite during the Whitsun recess when I get to grips with the extension and shower room. Although we're only gaining a metre there will be major disruption when the wall comes out. We've also decided to have stone floors laid throughout as I can't stand fitted carpets. Not sure how I'm going to manage it all. Reshuffle expected next week and Euro-elections on 4 June.

Officials have arranged a major conference of stakeholders, which I'm addressing on the subject of our Carbon Reduction Commitment. It's vital that all the major institutions that meet the criteria understand the scheme and how they can meet their mandatory obligations to reduce their carbon emissions. There's been a long consultation and lots of information available from civil servants but I need a twenty-minute presentation to cover it and then an hour of questions. It may seem like trouble but they all know they'll save money in the long term and the Carbon Trust is an excellent source of technical help.

DECC orals. Ed is on paternity leave following the birth of his son, so Mike and I are answering all the questions. The Tories are on the attack with what they think are clever points on energy efficiency and energy security, but I'm entirely confident of my ground now and I know our policies are working. Greg Barker is trying to make an amusing contribution and ends up listing all the government's programmes – quite an advertisement.

Peter Lilley peddles his usual climate sceptic line, suggesting we are committing £400 billion of taxpayers' money on the basis of incorrect science. Typical scaremongering. The figure is an estimate for a forty-year period. Another attack from a Eurosceptic suggests European legislation is adding £200 a year to household fuel bills. Total nonsense. The voice of the *Daily Express* in Parliament.

A good question time. I really am amazed at myself. It's only taken me a lifetime to gain the confidence I now have and over twenty years to feel in command of the Chamber.


3 June: Hazel Blears has quit the Cabinet. No doubt she expected to be dropped in the reshuffle, but to do this on the eve of elections is just unbelievable.

The Euro election results are disastrous. UKIP overtakes us in the popular vote to come second to the Tories. Two BNP candidates are elected. How appalling for Britain to be represented by people holding such obnoxious views. Labour far outstrips all other parties in Greenwich and Lewisham on a 30 per cent turnout. Everyone demoralised.

Another terrible blow for Gordon. As the polls close, James Purnell tells the media he is quitting the Cabinet and calling on Gordon to stand aside for the election of a new leader. Several ministers rush on to TV to declare their loyalty to Gordon, including, surprisingly, Caroline Flint, who is best friends with Hazel. But, later, less than twenty-four hours after swanning out to defend Gordon, Caroline releases a letter of resignation saying he had used her as 'female window dressing'. An extraordinary act of treachery from someone who has been given every opportunity. The letter suggests she expected to be offered a Cabinet post. Particularly ironic as she has projected a glamorous image for herself.

A slightly daunting event. I'm speaking at the Cheltenham Science Festival on climate change. I'm sort of looking forward to it and have done much of the speech preparation myself as I want to give it a philosophical campaigning flavour rather than the dry, awkward scripts that I get from the civil service. Summer and I take the train and it makes a pleasant change from the political turmoil of the moment.

A really busy week in prospect covering some of Mike's and Ed's commitments as well as my own. A good meeting with the National Farmers' Union (NFU). Farming contributes a lot to greenhouse gases, due to the use of fertilisers and the rearing of methane-producing cattle.

Reshuffle over, Mike O'Brien moves on and I get promoted to Minister of State. David Kidney joins the team as Under-Secretary. Our portfolios have yet to be reorganised but I'll now take some of the energy policy that Mike was doing. First up is a debate on the energy regulator Ofgem and company tariffs. Charles Hendry, the Tory shadow minister, in his welcome pays me a fine compliment saying he has found working with me in my previous role extremely productive and congenial. I appreciate this as in making policy for the long term the more political consensus we can find the better. A COBRA meeting follows. The modelling of the transmission of the virus is frightening.* We may need to treat huge numbers of people, with children

---

* Using data from nineteen countries, a study published in 2013 will show that 24 per cent of people, including half of all schoolchildren, were infected in the swine flu pandemic of 2009.

and young people most susceptible. At present, stocks of Tamiflu anti-viral drugs could treat 50 per cent of the population.

Ian Gibson has resigned as a result of the expenses scandal, which means a by-election in Norwich North.

The World Health Organization declares swine flu an official pandemic.

18 June: DEFRA's local climate predictions are launched today and we were expecting headline news, but no, it's MPs' expenses yet again. I've been awake since Frank left at 5.30 a.m. as usual for his Aberdeen flight, so I'm not in the best of moods when the builders arrive. The plumber and the bricklayer are both demanding more money up front for materials, which means I need to speak to the bank manager and I can't possibly do it today. The wall is up and the small flat roof on. I've arranged to get the materials for a green roof and have just taken delivery of over 200 sedum plants, which I now have to plant. We've also got to go and order everything for the shower room within the week. Frankly, I'm totally exhausted before the day begins. Then Ken arrives and the workmen stop work and chat to him. Today I'm doing the moaning and insist I don't want to hear a word of what Ken's read in the *Daily Mail*.

I respond to a complex debate in Westminster Hall on personal carbon budgets, but it's a bad day. I just want to get home but when I get back to DECC the box isn't ready. I'm now fuming. In the car eventually and on the way home when I get a text from Harriet about the Norwich by-election. Before I can respond, another text arrives. Henry Hodge is dead. I'm just stunned. The day evaporates into a void. My heart goes out to Margaret.

For months I've been working as one of Martin Salter's team on the election for a new Speaker – my job to canvass ministers. (Michael Martin announced his resignation after his poor handling of the expenses crisis.) Our candidate is Tory John Bercow. This is the strangest turn of events given that John was the scourge of Labour when he entered the Commons in 1997. But I got to know and like him when we were on the select committee together and, most importantly, he is a great moderniser. He's also mellowed, partly due no doubt to the influence of his wife Sally, who is very committed to the Labour Party. We've raised the reform agenda with all the candidates and there is no doubt this election will determine whether we have a Speaker who runs with that agenda or one who stands in the way.

We assemble at 2.30 p.m. to hear the candidates' speeches, beginning with Margaret Beckett. John Bercow's speech is extraordinarily good. He excels with his usual wit but delivers the ideas and moderniser's agenda.

The results of the first ballot are declared and John is in the lead. The results of the second ballot are declared just before 7 p.m. Finally, the third ballot between Sir George Young and John is declared at 8.30 p.m. John has 322 votes; Sir George 271. Our group leads the applause. John makes an emotional acceptance speech and we clap again. A bright spot at a very dark time for Parliament.

I get home to find the house is now totally dysfunctional. Floors up every-where and furniture banked to the sides. No dining room table and chairs accessible. I order a take-away curry, eat it on the laundry box I've pulled into the bedroom, and then get to my papers. What an idiot I am – poor Frank is glad to be in Aberdeen.

The Parliamentary Standards Bill is published. It will be rushed through Parliament to establish a new body to administer pay and expenses (IPSA) and a Parliamentary Commissioner to probe alleged breaches of the rules.

Up at 6 a.m. for an EU Environment Council in Luxembourg. Our mis-sion is always the same and I have my first one-to-one with Danish Minister Connie Hedegaard who is pivotal in the climate negotiations.

It's the launch of Road to Copenhagen (R2C).* Up at 5.30 a.m. and into DECC to do regional radio interviews. They go OK but the headlines are all about the death of Michael Jackson in the US yesterday. How could we be so unlucky!

---

* So called because the United Nations Climate Change Conference will be held there in December

We launch our campaign at London Zoo in glorious sunshine. Our R2C team of civil servants have worked incredibly hard, as have Ed and I. We have a very large document, beautifully designed, together with materials for public distribution and a website up and running. We've gone over every draft and materials design and I'm incredibly proud of the result.

Gordon at his best – a brilliant speech and gives me a name check. The Foreign Office have climate change specialists in all our relevant embassies and our audience of stakeholders this morning includes ambassadors and representatives from many countries. I talk to climate specialists from the US, Italy, Germany and Japan. We set out why an international climate change agreement is vital to the world. We argue that the deal must be ambitious – limiting temperature increase to 2°C, making sure that, after peaking, emissions start to reduce by 2020, to reach half this level by 2050. It must be effective with strong monitoring, reporting and verification. Money must flow to where it can make most difference through carbon markets and it must be fair, creating support for the poorest countries to mitigate and adapt to climate change.

I think we all feel part of an historic mission. I certainly do. Lots of very favourable reactions including from our greatest critics, the NGOs. Afterwards Martin Rees, the president of the Royal Society, comes across and introduces me to people, saying, 'We have a lot in common – old CNDers!' Such a lovely man. I can't linger – just grab a few canapés and I'm in the car with boxes of papers to get through en route to my afternoon surgery.

29 June: I work in DECC until it's time to leave for Henry Hodge's memorial service. So incredibly sad. Hundreds and hundreds of people. Henry was so well loved and had touched so many lives in the law and politics. As Frank and I enter into the large lobby we see Tony Blair standing alone and looking much older. We greet him and pass on to embrace Margaret. Moving tributes and a slideshow illuminating Henry's life and the family. Their obvious recorded happiness makes it even more poignant. The moment it's over I have to rush away. I'm on the 7 p.m. flight to Copenhagen.

Next morning, we leave Copenhagen en route for Greenland and an informal ministerial meeting at the invitation of the Danes who will be hosting the UN conference. I'm so looking forward to seeing the Arctic and participating in a manageable-size meeting over several days. We fly into an airport where we have to change to a smaller plane. There's just a landing strip and a large hut where we go to wait. The wait becomes a nightmare. The weather has closed in and we can't fly. We are so many people travelling there's not enough food or even seats to sit in. After some hours we turn to alcohol. I'm really apprehensive; small planes are bad enough but bad weather over the Arctic and I'm really feeling low. I'm also travelling with Jan, our lead official, without the comfort of my private office staff. Jan constantly travels the world. She is undoubtedly more robust than I am and I just can't be feeling sorry for myself. Eventually they say the weather is lifting and we must take off before the light goes. As we take off the plane banks steeply and I'm not the only one with a sharp intake of breath. We land in Ilulissat. It's an amazing place. Essentially all rock so every building, including the hotel, looks like an elaborate log cabin. Most striking of all is that these wooden buildings are painted in the most vibrant colours but they don't look garish because of the white and grey landscape – lacking trees, plants and flowers. Needless to say it's rather cold.

A warm welcome from Connie. Around thirty countries are represented – developed and developing. China hasn't turned up – apparently due to the Danish PM meeting the Dalai Lama, or maybe not.

Over the next few days Jan and I make some useful alliances and I promote the UK position, particularly Gordon's climate finance initiative, which is very well received. The different strands emerge as obstacles to an agreement. Emerging economies such as India believe they should have the right to further industrialise and the West should bear the burdens of its historic legacy. Vulnerable countries believe they have a right to exist and not disappear under rising sea levels. The US insists on developing countries making legal commitments. Despite Obama's embrace of climate change and his willingness to work with the international community, the fact that they still have not signed the Kyoto protocol greatly weakens their position with developing countries. Brazil and Mexico take a progressive stance, offering their own mitigation plans but demanding more from developed countries. Sweden and Norway are good allies and South Africa very challenging. Gordon's finance initiative – to commit $100 billion by 2020 to support adaptation in developing countries – has galvanised debate and will greatly assist progress towards Copenhagen.

While we all know a great deal about climate change, few of us have ever been in this part of the world. We get a technical briefing on the state of the Arctic and an option to fly over the ice flows in a helicopter. I have consistently refused to fly in the North Sea with Frank to visit an oil rig and fortunately it never came into my brief. Now I'm in a terrible dilemma. I really want to go. I'm speaking to the chief South African negotiator, a big, white, rugby-playing type who tells me he's not going. When I ask why he relates a horrific story of surviving a helicopter crash – never to get in one again.

I decide I'll admit my fears, go along, and see if I can do it and if not I'll just have to wait for them to return. I make it. The scenes are breathtaking and I wouldn't have missed it for anything. Totally unexpected is the fact that the icebergs have brilliant turquoise crevices where light is fractured by water. It's so utterly beautiful. Then a great avalanche of ice cascades into the sea to join the massive ice flows drifting below. And I remember, this is why we are here – to see for ourselves the effects of climate change on the polar icecaps. Back at the hotel, one of the staff tells me how they can now see new landscapes where once they only saw a wall of ice.

All too soon it's the farewell dinner after a short trip on an icebreaker and the obligatory group photograph. We dine on roast leg of reindeer and eat blackberries with liquorice and rosemary. I should love to come back.

I return to an urgent briefing from Lewisham Hospital. The first London death from swine flu happened there last week. The man was only nineteen, but, like the other fatalities so far in the UK, he had severe underlying health problems. The latest estimate is 85,000 people infected; twenty-nine fatalities, including more people without known underlying conditions. The speed of spread is increasing dramatically with cases all over the country. Containment is no longer a viable strategy and cases will simply be treated as they arise. Public information is stepped up with warnings not to self-medicate (apparently fake drugs are on the market) and to get medical advice over the phone rather than approach a surgery or A&E when symptoms arise. It's all looking pretty scary and brings home to me yet again how vulnerable globalisation has made us all. I'm fanatically washing my hands at every opportunity and avoiding being near anybody who looks like they might sneeze! Some people are wearing face masks but official advice is don't.

Oral PQs. Some good opportunities but attacks on wind farms and green energy obligations increasing fuel bills. I'm robust in my response – we can't have low energy bills and high fossil fuel use – the planet is being destroyed and we have to make a change. I reiterate that we have programmes to assist the poorest. A good run on questions about skills investment and a low carbon economy.

In the evening I'm doing a public meeting on the Deptford job centre, which is threatened with closure. Sixty people attend and they have 3,000 names on a petition. While I keep all the parties talking to each other there has to be a long-term solution, and finding premises is one of them, but for now we have to keep it functioning on the high street. I get through the meeting but there are a lot of disgruntled people. I arrange to see the Job Centre Plus director and arrange another meeting for three weeks later in Portcullis House. I bring together the heads of the various arms of Job Centre Plus, the developers, the DWP property people and the PCS Union in an attempt to push them into a strategy for keeping a job centre in Deptford. Walking through treacle, but the best I can do.

The government's low carbon transition plan is published. This is a collaboration across departments and heralds a truly revolutionary change in our economy, through energy, business and industry to building and land use.

All essential to the climate change agenda. Ed opens a short debate on the 'Road to Copenhagen', setting out our priorities and expectations. It's upbeat and reflects his most recent experience of the Major Economics Forum, where both the US and China demonstrated a positive attitude.

24 July: Out of the house at 6.30 a.m. and onto the Glasgow train. One of the policy areas I've acquired in my portfolio post reshuffle is CCS. I've always had an interest in this and now I'm off to see a demonstration plant run by Doosan Babcock, in Renfrew. Carbon capture and storage can be applied to both coal and gas plants and has the potential to allow coal, in particular, to continue to be used in the UK while carbon targets are met into the future. The existence of depleted oil wells around our coast makes $CO_2$ storage a feasible proposition. Even more importantly, it could be the solution to curbing $CO_2$ from China and India's massive coal-burning industries. The only downside is the massive cost of the technology at this stage, which is why we have invited companies to bid for £1 billion of government funding to develop an operational plan. A fascinating visit and at the end of the day I take the train on to Aberdeen for a proper recess weekend. No box and no meetings.

August: A week to clear the desks – most importantly the creative concept for our autumn Act on $CO_2$ campaign. We know the public get the message about saving energy and saving money but it's harder to get the dots joined up between individual actions and global climate change. After a lot of effort I'm really pleased with the result, which takes the form of a bedtime story about strange weather, what the scientists said, and what the grown-ups decide to do to protect their children. It ticks all the boxes and will direct people, at the end, to the helpline.

I sign off the last 100 email letters that followed from my fatal appearance on *The One Show*. Officials think we should be on the road every day of the recess visiting projects, but I have insisted on just one this week – the Energy Saving Trust's advice centre in Thornton Heath. Very interesting to see exactly how the advisors respond to the phone calls. They have computer programmes and scripts to work from and most of it is reasonably well done but I can easily see where there is room for improvement.

A press cutting of an amazing poll in my box. A survey of 18,500 people in nineteen countries on climate change. A majority worldwide want climate change to be a top priority including in China and India (only 44 per cent in the US). Only four countries consider that their government is focused on climate change: Germany, Britain, China and Indonesia. In Britain, 58 per cent credit the government with making climate change a priority, but 89 per cent believe the government could do more. Food for thought.

6 August: I'm introducing *The Age of Stupid* at a showing at Laban. The screening is to be done with a generator powered by people pedalling bikes fixed to the floor. I'm asked to join in, but only for the photo call, thank goodness. Never a cyclist, my thighs are not up to furious pedalling for long stretches. The film is quite disturbing – set in a devastated 2055, it features Pete Postlethwaite as a lonely archivist looking back on footage from 2008 and asking why we didn't stop climate change when we had the chance. A timely warning.

Summer Nisar and I take the overnight flight to South Korea. Summer dutifully carries decaf coffee, a strategy first adopted by Liz when she found I couldn't live without it.

We are tested for swine flu on arrival in Seoul for the Global Environment Forum. It's afternoon and we are immediately caught up in a vast traffic jam. The city is ultra-modern with impressive new skyscrapers everywhere. We arrive at our hotel where the sound of the traffic is replaced by the loudest cicadas I've ever heard. The hotel is glass and glitzy.

South Korea is an important player in the international climate talks. As a country with a constantly growing economy it can be an exemplar in using modern technology to restrict $CO_2$ increases as it grows. They are very positive in their approach and I am here to share our knowledge of green growth and the economics of climate change developed by Nick Stern. We're even distributing our excellent climate change brochure, translated into Korean. I meet a number of senior ministers, participate in the roundtables, attend a dinner with business leaders to discuss low carbon growth and UK–Korean cooperation and give a lecture at the university. The latter provides a real insight into Korean society. Eighty per cent of young people are now graduating – this must surely be the highest in the world. But the social cost is considerable. I get to talk to one young woman who tells me confidentially that parents work all hours to support their children's education and after school each day the children go to private tutors for several hours of additional lessons. Fear of failure is acute – I can identify with that.

We complete a gruelling schedule and then Summer and I are invited by the UK ambassador to a restaurant with him and his family. He knows our schedule but we end up with less than half an hour at the hotel to 'freshen up' and get back to the lobby. I make it amid much cursing but Summer doesn't appear. This is unprecedented in my experience and the ambassador cannot contain his irritation. I don't know whether to be embarrassed or amused. Then she appears and off we go. It immediately becomes apparent why we are leaving so early for dinner. It will take us more than an hour to reach the restaurant. When we get there we are offered beer. My turn to put my foot down. I insist on wine as I definitely need to relax.

Return from Seoul in the evening. Repack and leave early morning next day for Pisa. Utter relief despite the jetlag. Two weeks, three days. Not enough and I'm sleeping a lot but so good to be in our lovely house. I want to reorganise the front garden but fortunately it's too hot to plant. Good to get together with Gabriella and Franco again. We also meet our immediate neighbours, Italians Cristina and Antonio, Anita and Pietro, and Brits Margaret, Reg Huzzey and Toni, all of whom rescue us from various difficulties. On subsequent visits we will add Graziella and Bob to the circle of friends.

Back from holiday and my turn to be duty minister for the next few weeks. With the House not sitting I can do paperwork in the daytimes and not have to stay up working until midnight each night. Constituency matters also get some attention. We've stepped up the campaign on the Surrey Canal Road station. I persuaded TFL to recost their proposals and they've brought it down to nearer £10 million. I've got confirmation from Andrew Adonis, the new Secretary of State for Transport, that the £7 million is still available, so the case for building the station in a later phase of the work is strengthened. But, five months later, when I go to see him, Andrew is less than helpful, suggesting it can be dealt with after the election. Only the intervention of developer Mushtaq Malik of the Renewal Group will save the project. He, Lewisham Council and TFL meet Department of Transport officials and they agree to review their business case – he says my intervention has 'ruffled the feathers' of the officials and they are now on their mettle. Obviously worth getting angry occasionally.

We also leaflet local residents and get a large return from people saying they would use the station – the majority every day.

Just as I'm making progress on one front, another challenge opens up. TFL announce they are withdrawing the replacement bus service they promised to provide while the East London line was closed. I fire off a letter.

Brockley Common is coming on at last with a handrail fixed to the long ramp up to the station, allowing it to be opened to the public. Immediate positive comments from mums with buggies. Then its improving the soil on the bank and preparing for planting of what is now quite a large area, and hopefully an official opening next spring.

I keep a watching brief on the job centre – three alternative sites have been visited. In line with my policy of keeping constituents in touch with my ministerial work, I send out 9,000 letters marking the 'Countdown to Copenhagen'.

A meeting with the Secretary of State for the Environment from Argentina. Ed and I are now built into the FCO diaries for visiting ministers. It's incredibly interesting to get the different perspectives. As always, my task is to focus on the key elements of a possible agreement.

With just three months to go, a major stocktaking on the prospects for Copenhagen. We agree that the US is the key to unlocking the deal but their legislation has been derailed by delays over healthcare and they are unlikely to be ready for December. The Chinese are sounding positive and may be willing to announce ambitious domestic action. The new Environment Minister in India is more cooperative than his predecessor and developing countries, encouraged by the finance initiative, are unlikely to want to stand in the way of a deal. It's all so doable yet the prospects of success are clearly hanging in the balance.

One issue closer to home is the move within the EU from 20 per cent reduction in $CO_2$ by 2020 to 30 per cent. This remains unresolved, the only commitment so far being to make the move in the context of an ambitious deal. Truly a chicken and egg.

In Rome, at the start of my tour of European capitals. The Italians are not in the vanguard on this issue but need to be encouraged. Given the depth of the recession, we try the low carbon growth agenda. A mixed reaction from the business and industry leaders I address. No clear focus from the government, but we press our agenda.

16 September: US Senator John Kerry announces he's to submit a Bill to tackle climate change within two weeks, in a bid to get it passed in time for the Copenhagen summit.

At the UN pre-Copenhagen summit, which Gordon is attending, China's President Hu Jintao announces determined action on carbon emissions. The Institute of Economic Affairs says China could become a leader in the field if it meets its five-year plan targets by 2020, but others are not convinced.

President Obama says the US *will* back a global deal on emissions. At DECC, we are completely fired up. I'm dealing urgently with so much of the technical stuff we're putting in place for delivering all aspects of our domestic programmes, such as the CRC and CESP, and still getting to grips with EU ETS work while fending off innumerable requests for visits and speeches.

Gordon, still at the summit in New York, is forced to deny he is going blind and will step down on health grounds. Charles Clarke, our former Home Secretary, has made the suggestion, calling yet again for Gordon to resign. This is a repeat of Charles's performance last year, once again on the eve of party conference. This can only have one consequence – a Tory government next May.

I've got four fringe meetings at party conference and a plenary on 'Green Futures'. After all the traumas of recent months, the conference goes well and there's a lot of positive feeling. The truth is we are not a party divided on policy and we are clearly united against a Tory government. If only Gordon and the Cabinet could get it together we would still be in with a chance.

My only consolation is the bigger picture. Everyone at DECC is on a mission. With our world-beating Climate Change Act, our exceeding our Kyoto commitments, the Stern Report and Gordon's finance initiative, we are riding high in the world. The other thing I wish others could know is the way we're frequently greeted in European capitals with reference to the financial crisis – 'Thank goodness for your Gordon Brown – he saved us.'

A meeting with the Ecuadorian ambassador. The Ecuadorian rainforest is one of the most biodiverse places on the planet. For years the government has allowed drilling for oil in the region, resulting in deforestation, for road building and construction. Now they are taking soundings on whether the international community would pay them to keep the oil in the ground. It makes good sense to me as deforestation is a major threat to all of us as it greatly adds to climate change. We should look at their plan, though I can immediately foresee the difficulties in reaching such a deal. I subsequently agree to meet with the leaders of the campaign who are seeking charitable funds as well as government support. I receive a beautiful book of stunning pictures from the Yasuni, but with everything else going on I fear we can't give this much attention.*

3 October: DECC is one year old today. Impossible to believe the amount of cutting-edge policy we've worked through and delivered in this time. It's a great tribute to Ed that he could inject such dynamism into a new department. It has not been an easy ride for our Permanent Secretary Moira Wallace either – 1,000 civil servants from two completely different cultures, DTI and DEFRA, previously often at loggerheads and with different pay structures, HR policies and different IT systems. An amazing experience.

5 October: I'm visiting Detroit at the invitation of the Midwestern Governors Association (MGA). Michigan has the highest unemployment in the US and Detroit itself 28 per cent, but the Midwest has seven of the top swing senators. Our objective is to influence key stakeholders who have the ear of those senators whose votes will be critical for the passage of effective US climate legislation.

I meet with DTE Energy, a major utility with 80 per cent of its energy production in coal, with General Motors, which has suffered enormous losses due to the recession, and with the president of the United Automobile Workers (UAW).

DTE are prepared to support the proposed 'cap and trade' legislation provided there is more support for CCS. General Motors have seen the writing on the wall and are rapidly diversifying into smaller vehicles, more efficient engines and the electric 'Chevrolet Volt'. (A tour of the new facility and an impressive spin in a full prototype.) They see their future based on reduced oil dependency and low carbon markets. I lobby them to bring the production of their European model to the UK and emphasise our

---

* The project did get off the ground but in 2013 the President scrapped the scheme saying only $13 million of the $3.6 billion target had been reached. A year later drilling licences were granted, with oil production scheduled for 2016.

low carbon growth strategy. Both General Motors and UAW support 'cap and trade'.

The centrepiece of my visit is addressing the Midwestern governors and the business leaders, think tanks, NGOs and media assembled for their conference. I expound on our low carbon transmission programme and laying the foundation for a sustainable recovery while reducing emissions. The message is well received by people who are looking for a way out of recession and support from their own government. Several governors and CEOs are enthusiastic in their responses and encourage us to keep up the pressure on Washington.

All in all, a really satisfactory couple of days – much to my surprise.

I sign off our press release ahead of tomorrow's first screening of the new climate change information ads. This is critical stuff – three-quarters of people say they would act to change their lifestyle if they knew climate change would affect their children. I'm really pleased with the new ads of the bedtime story – TV, the national press, digital, billboards in November and cinema in December. I really feel we're making a difference. A hectic European tour follows.

The Eastern European countries, with their lower GDP, are much exercised by burden-sharing within the EU. I'm in Budapest meeting the Environment and Finance Ministers and their chief climate negotiators to emphasise that lack of detail or internal burden-sharing cannot be allowed to jeopardise Copenhagen. The EU must lead and be prepared to go to 30 per cent by 2020. It's amazing how much work can be done in a single day when the ground is so well prepared by our embassy and DECC staff.

Next, it's Madrid for meetings with Spanish ministers and negotiators. The Climate Minister, Teresa Ribera, is very impressive, and we have a detailed exchange about all Spain's concerns and positions. Overall, Spain is a key partner, sharing most of our perspectives on burden-sharing, the US and the difficulties with Poland.

Back at DECC and the latest assessment of developed country positions. The US, Canada, Russia and Ukraine are well below what is needed, but

Japan is offering 25 per cent, Australia 24 per cent and Norway a massive 40 per cent below 1990 levels by 2020 (the UK has legislated for 34 per cent).

Meanwhile, I'm busy working on our heat and energy strategy with which we want to be able to offer whole house retrofits. More urgent is the feed-in tariffs. Our mandatory consultation closed last week and we are committed to having FITS* in place by next April. Setting the levels of tariff required for different technologies and different sizes of installations is a complex task, so huge amounts of work ahead.

A more mundane submission – the correspondence monitoring report. Just thirty-nine over the fifteen-day deadline and 182 waiting. An improvement at last, all down to Rachel Reeves, who we put on the case – not her only talent. She is a great cake-maker and brings her offerings to the office to cheer us up.

27 October: *Channel 4 News* has a feature on the prospects for Copenhagen, presenting a pessimistic view and commenting on the 7 per cent US offer. Ed is on with a careful path to tread. We have to keep encouraging the US even though we are also dismayed. As Ed says, Bush planned for emissions to carry on rising up to 2025 and would never have entered the talks. Obama has changed all that. John Kerry has suggested a deal could be done even without legislation so we have got to remain optimistic.

Swine flu is hitting the headlines again with rapidly rising numbers of new cases. This week there are 78,000 new cases, up nearly 58 per cent on last week, and half a million have been infected. The only consolation is that death rates are low compared to some countries, currently 137. A mass immunisation programme is under way.

Another internal review of where we are on negotiations. Still in the balance. As an agreement becomes more likely, so the risks come into sharper focus and some are growing. All very confidential stuff. Different analyses are coming in from other countries on the position of the US and China.

---

* Feed-In Tarrif Scheme.

There's a lot of comparing who said what to whom and frustration at some stupid comments being made, such as the EU spokesman who said, 'Kyoto is dead.' One of the areas on which we agree to do more work is forestry, which could have an important bearing on the attitudes of developing countries.

I spend the weekend in Barcelona at another international UN preparatory meeting for Copenhagen. It's now becoming rather routine – I know who our allies are and who I need to lobby – but there is one new special contact: the Vice-President of the Maldives. He speaks so movingly of his country's fate – literally disappearing beneath rising sea levels. One thing is certain: we have to remain optimistic and lobby harder than ever. The doom-mongers can only create defeat.

Then a meeting to discuss our Energy Bill, which will be announced in the Queen's Speech. I also make a keynote speech at the British Insurers' climate change conference. They are an important constituency and recognise the potential for worldwide claims in runaway climate change.

November: DECC orals. The Act on $CO_2$ ads are currently being screened and we're receiving lots of criticism from people who are essentially climate change deniers. I'm delighted they're getting noticed and written about, so I'm not surprised when Peter Lilley challenges me on the subject. Lots more questions on low carbon and international climate change and then we are on to our climate change debate. Ed opens with reference to those he has met over the past year – from the northern desert of China to the Amazon forest of Brazil – and the realities of climate change. He continues with the science – atmospheric concentration of greenhouse gases at their highest for 650,000 years. In the UK nine of the ten warmest years on record occurred in the past fifteen. For the first time in recorded history the north-west passage of the Arctic was ice-free and open to shipping. Ed covers all the territory and takes lots of supportive interventions.

With the exception of climate sceptic Peter Lilley, it's a truly harmonious debate with good cross-party consensus as to what we need from Copenhagen and lots of good wishes. It just falls to me to answer the many questions raised and comment on other contributions. I end by saying:

> No one should be surprised if at times frustration leads to pessimism when more than 100 nations sit down to grapple with more than 200 pages of negotiating text. However, few doubt that this is a deal the world must have. I know, because I have had the privilege of going to Greenland and seeing for myself the melting sea ice. I know because I have met Ursula from the disappearing Carteret Islands who said: 'For leaders, it is a lifestyle choice, for us it is life or death.' I know because last week I heard the urgent plea from the Maldives. We need a deal to save the land, lives and livelihoods of millions of people in the developing world and we need a deal because climate change affects us too, with a cost to our economy, our environment, and our security. However, climate change is not just a message of threats and potential disaster … It is also a positive message – a call to a global transition to a low carbon economy. It is a call to a world in which unprecedented cooperation will have to come about, to a world in which technologies are shared for mutual benefit and resources are properly conserved, and to a world that respects nature and provides us all with a safer, cleaner and greener place to live and work.

I leave on a high.

A really lovely event in the constituency. After years of work, Steve Bullock and I are unveiling the new mosaic at Brockley station. It's extremely well done and enhances the approach to the ramp. I hope the spring planting scheme can pick up on the pleasing colour palette.

14 November: To Jakarta with Liz Kitchen. Indonesia will be an important player in Copenhagen. Prior to leaving I've been meeting with UK-based companies and discussing sustainable palm oil. Unbeknown to most of us,

palm oil is used in food, cosmetics, biofuels, animal feed, pharmaceuticals and industry. As a consequence of this ubiquitous global use, 'Sustainable Palm Oil' was set up in 2004 to try to address problems and develop sustainability criteria. Part of our contribution at Copenhagen will be to look at the whole question of how to help developing countries conserve their forests.

We travel very comfortably overnight on Malaysian Airways to Kuala Lumpur, then on to Jakarta and a long wait for a flight to Pekanbaru, capital of Riau province on Sumatra. This is where we'll see the palm oil plantations and meet local companies.

Nothing could compare with seeing this at first hand. We meet with environmental activists who take us to see areas of deforestation and illegal logging. It is quite shocking. Blackened tree stumps sit in waterlogged ground as far as the eye can see. We hear of the complexity of land ownership, of corrupt locals and criminals. National laws are quite explicit in their protection but there is immense difficulty in policing vast territories of dense forest where few people live. We see also the plantations where monoculture adversely affects wildlife and soil becomes depleted. The challenge is enormous but we get to talk to responsible companies who understand the issues and are working with the national authorities. Indonesia needs the palm oil industry so compromises have to be found together with sustainable growth.

Back in Jakarta I have meetings with the ministers of energy, finance, forestry planning and foreign affairs. There are obvious tensions between ministers and our strategy is to support the conservationists and to persuade those who grant licences that international finance could be available to help them on a more sustainable path. Gordon's finance initiative is once again the key to building trust. Reforestation, tackling forest fires and illegal logging are all essential to helping Indonesia stem the rise in $CO_2$ emissions. The governor of Jakarta and I do a photo call in the city centre and unveil 'Jakarta's Copenhagen Countdown' billboards with lots of fanfare and balloons. I also meet with companies that are certificated by the Round Table in Sustainable Palm Oil. I'm learning so much and realise how little developed countries understand these issues or care at all about the environmental devastation our consumer greed has brought about. Our hectic schedule has been very well organised, providing access to all the people who can make a difference. I'd love to be able to stay longer and Liz pledges to go back. The woman Trade Minister persuades us we should visit a store with a display of Indonesian handicrafts. It's amazing. Lots of beautiful things I'm longing to buy but we have to rush and they don't have my size (I feel like a giant) so I end up with a simple black plate and a gift of a fine silk scarf from the minister.

Back overnight, landing at 5.30 a.m. It's a one-line whip, which means I can go home for a rest, tackle an urgent box in the afternoon and then go to a very special Trinity Laban evening, 'Harmony of the spheres' at the Greenwich Planetarium. Sublime.

Everyone else is working so hard in the constituency in preparation for a general election. They've stuffed 9,000 envelopes in the past few weeks and have regular canvassing sessions. I've managed to do a short series of coffee mornings in community centres and this Saturday it's Telegraph Hill. I'm canvassed by a group of young skateboarders who want to be able to practise locally. I agree to support them (little realising this will entail years of work and controversy!).

25 November: I've insisted no appointments. I'm working on the desk and then taking a long break to get my hair straightened. I'm sure I'll have no time to look after my appearance in Copenhagen so it's a necessary precaution!

Another new experience: I'm doing 'warm-up calls' to ministers attending the Commonwealth Heads of Government meeting starting tomorrow. Singapore, Malaysia, Tanzania and New Zealand are on my list – officials brief.

This evening a reception at No. 10 on the 'Future of our forests – Copenhagen and beyond'. We are making a concerted effort on this front, which has also been given a boost by a Prince of Wales' initiative. Then a meeting with the BMA to discuss the medical effects of climate change and later a meeting with a Mongolian minister.

The Copenhagen talks open for a week of negotiations between officials. Ministers will attend next week and heads of state at the end if necessary. Gordon has said he will definitely go to secure a deal.

Today is the second reading of our Energy Bill. Ed explains one of the central purposes of the Bill – to provide for a levy for clean coal technology. At £9.5 billion over twenty years it will be the largest investment in Carbon Capture and storage in the world. We will also provide for three additional projects alongside the current CCS competition. The Bill also introduces more regulation by Ofgem and mandatory money-off tariffs for vulnerable households.

Lots of challenges from Tory members with their front bench going on as usual about power cuts. I'm in a combative mood and dispatch the answers to question rapidly. Last appearance in the Chamber this year!

The next day, a sad reunion at the funeral of Ron Dick. Ron was our first director of Shelter in Scotland. In the '70s I introduced him to my Iranian friend Shahla. They later married but I hadn't see either of them in years. Now it's just Shahla and her sister and brother-in-law who moved to the UK and whom I last saw forty years ago in Tehran. Lots of Shelter colleagues as well. Doug Smith, who was a close friend and colleague of Ron at Shelter, gives a fine eulogy. I promise to reconnect with Shahla.

I manage to get to my GC for once and report on my many activities. There's trouble on Milton Court so I'm off there in the morning and then a surgery.

A huge feature on me in the *South Wales Argus*. Quite extraordinary. Obviously written by a rabid climate denier with a subtitle 'A leftie for all seasons', it's headed 'Whatever happened to the big freeze?' The references are unbelievable – he says I would have 'made a wholesome snack for any marauding polar bear in 1974, it's a credit to Pontypoolians that they ceded Ms Ruddock to the electoral embrace of Lewisham Deptford where they are much pottier'; 'she's a member of the National Secular Society – a front organisation for atheists and a swivel-eyed carbonista'. Who is this crazy person and how could he be so angry? Strangely, his picture editor hasn't gone along with the theme – printing quite the best picture of me I've seen in a long time!

12 December: Brockley Christmas Fair, then turn on the Christmas lights in Deptford, then home to pack – Copenhagen on Monday.

The United Nations Framework Convention on Climate Change was signed at the Rio Earth Summit in 1992 and came into force in 1994. One hundred and ninety-six countries have ratified the convention, which sets an overall framework for intergovernmental efforts to tackle climate change. In 1997, an additional protocol to the UNFCCC was adopted in Kyoto, Japan, and was championed by the Labour government. It set binding targets for reducing greenhouse gas emissions for thirty-seven industrialised countries and the EU and entered into force in 2005. It was signed by 190 countries but not by the US. Developing countries were not included in emissions reduction, so increasingly big emitters such as China were not covered. In Bali in 2007 the Bali Action plan was adopted with a view to bringing the US into Kyoto and getting a second commitment period from those already signed up (the first commitment will expire in 2012).

14 December: Arrive to a bitterly cold Copenhagen and on to our hotel. We've been warned about the chaos of registration so our paths have been smoothed. Nonetheless, even the VIP queue at the Bella Centre is daunting in the biting wind. Non-VIPs have queued for as much as five hours. Apparently more than 40,000 people have turned up. First priority is the UK Delegation Coordination meeting, a daily occurrence to enable us to share intelligence and coordinate our efforts. We, like all other delegations, have been allocated 'offices' in a vast warehouse structure. It is so cold we have to keep coats, gloves, and scarves on indoors – not quite the jamboree the press predicted for us.

There are two tracks to negotiations. Under Kyoto, developed countries are committed to move to a second commitment period, but the US has said it won't ratify and Japan also appears unwilling. Under the UNFCCC all countries are obliged to discuss long-term cooperation to strengthen the convention.

Two texts are circulating and mitigation offers are on the table but nothing yet that could be the prelude to a treaty.

Already the conference has been suspended several times because of disagreements, the most serious of which is the demand to limit climate change to a 1.5°C rise rather than 2°C.* This was raised by Tuvalu and supported by other small island states. The science tells them that above a 1.5°C increase they will all lose significant territory to rising sea levels. Realistically this conference will struggle to commit to achieving 2°C. How awful to have to accept that some whole island communities will have to abandon their land and homes entirely.

My first public engagement is a meeting organised by Indonesia and addressed by the EU representative who has sharp words for those not stepping up to the plate.

15 December: A twelve-hour official programme starting at 7.30 and an evening stand-by to cover for Ed if needed post 7.30 p.m. My task every day, apart from all the UK delegation meetings and briefings, is to hold talks with individual ministers or if necessary groups of ministers to forward the progressive agenda within the EU and our support for developing countries. I'll also do the early-morning media such as *News 24* and again cover anything for Ed. Today I'm live on Sky, then talking to ministers and officials from the Maldives, Finland, Indonesia, New Zealand and any others depending on what's happening. We are also holding a session to brief UK parliamentarians attending the conference and I've a working lunch with EU ministers.

Over the next two days I meet with counterparts from South Korea, Netherlands, France, Sweden, Germany, Poland and Ireland. Our aim is to try to convince our colleagues that the EU should commit to raising our offer

---

* The 2015 global temperature rise was recorded already as 1°C above pre-industrial levels.

from 20 per cent to 30 per cent. We have good allies but my task is to encourage vocal support from Sweden, Belgium and the Netherlands, to strengthen resolve with Germany, France, Slovenia and Estonia and clarify our case for the EU moving to 30 per cent with Poland and Italy. We are convinced this is necessary to get a better offer from the US and to satisfy developing countries. I have good arguments to put – the cost of moving to 30 per cent is now about the same as 20 per cent because of the recession, the risks to EU competitiveness are limited and can be addressed through the free allocation of carbon allowances to exposed sectors, and a 30 per cent target would reduce uncertainty for firms and investors about the price of low carbon emissions.

It's really hard going. The UK team, DECC and FCO, PM, ministers and civil servants are throwing everything we have at this process. We are so obviously in the vanguard and have a very clear vision.

While all this is going on our negotiators are also attending plenary sessions and Ed and Gordon (who has arrived ahead of other heads of state) are spending a lot of time with the major powers and with others on climate finance.

There is immense media interest and NGO pressure, but the conference itself is totally bogged down. Initial chairing of the plenaries by the Danes has been utterly chaotic and still well below what we would expect for such a conference.

Some progress with the arrival of Hillary Clinton, who has signalled the US *will* take part in Gordon's global finance initiative, but by Thursday evening there is no overall deal in sight. We push our case at EU Coordination but EC President José Manuel Barroso opposes. Personally I also think a coalition of those willing to move to a second commitment period for Kyoto could make an impact but Japan's objections have been allowed to crush that possibility.

At my frequent TV interviews, I can only keep holding out hope as the media gloom and doom spreads. We absolutely cannot give up, nor can we tell people much of what we are doing for fear of upsetting those we are trying to push. Rows break out, rumours fly – it's like being on the edge of a volcano. The intensity of our effort and the long hours have left us all exhausted and tomorrow was supposed to be our last day. China's position is now very confusing, occupying, as it does, a place alongside the G77 of developing countries while being a major economy and major emitter.

17 December: Everything is now hanging on whether world leaders can prise open the deadlock that has been reached. Thirty leaders agree to meet after the Royal Banquet – Gordon among them. Chinese President Wen refuses to participate and India's President is delayed. Both countries send their officials to the meeting in a complete breach of protocol. This is where all the action is now and those of us who are not players congregate close to the meeting rooms, keeping ourselves going with snacks and drinks and hanging on every text to find out what is happening. The hours pass and there's no progress. Ed later reports that substantive negotiations did not begin until 3 a.m. on Friday morning.

Obama flies in and we all rush to see him in the flesh. We don't doubt that he wants to be helpful but of course like all US Presidents he has to get consent from Congress and it's not forthcoming. Nonetheless, we are willing him to pull something out of the bag. He joins the leaders' meeting for an update, and then addresses the plenary. A nice speech but no new offer and everyone knows that what's on the table is not enough.

News is out that Obama has postponed his departure and will make a statement before leaving. He holds negotiations with China, Brazil and India. Finally, he meets with Gordon, Sarkozy, Merkel and other European leaders.

Meanwhile, many of those who have spent the past years travelling the world and negotiating on behalf of their countries are in a state of frenzy or despair. The vast majority of politicians are furious that meetings are going on behind their backs.

Obama announces an 'unprecedented breakthrough'. The agreement is between the US, China, India, Brazil and South Africa. Few details are available as they are still being negotiated with several other countries. Once a text has been finalised it will be put to a reconvened plenary for adoption. It's now midnight.

19 December: A text has been hammered out and Ed says we've done everything we can. The Copenhagen Accord will call on participating countries to pledge specific actions that they will undertake to mitigate greenhouse gas emissions. Developed countries should provide quantified, economy-wide emission targets for 2020; developing countries nationally appropriate mitigation actions; and the least developed countries and small island states voluntary actions, on the basis of financial support.

This is a first but falls short of the specific targets we have sought. We are all utterly exhausted and there is a huge sense of anti-climax. Some people need to stay for the plenary – the rest of us can go to our hotel. As soon as we get there the message comes that there is mayhem at the plenary. The chair cannot cope and several countries, including Sudan, Venezuela and Bolivia, are objecting to the adoption of the Accord. Hysteria reigns as the Venezuelan representative holds up a bloody hand and Sudan likens the process to the Holocaust. Ed returns to the convention hall and makes a critical intervention, calling for an adjournment. The chair is rescued. A group led by the UK, the US and Australia work out a compromise strategy to put to the conference. On resumption of the plenary the delegates agree to *note* the Copenhagen Accord. Pathetic it may be but by this mechanism the global agreement is rescued from outright rejection. We've kept the show on the road.

The team gathers for a farewell drink and on to Copenhagen Airport. Such bright lights, such good cheer – I can't believe it's Christmas! I drag myself into the Christmas shop and buy some beautiful glass tree decorations and the luscious Danish chocolates my mother loves. I'll sleep on the plane.

21 December: Back to DECC for a couple of hours on the desk, then a whole department event to welcome us back from Copenhagen. It really is Christmas. Time to stop and travel for a few days with my family.

26 December: Our colleague David Taylor has collapsed and died. He was an exceptional campaigner and had already said he was standing down at

the election due to pressure of work. It's a warning to us all. Workload and the vilification of MPs over expenses are taking their toll.

## 2010

5 January: House returns and I'm in charge of the Energy Bill going into committee this morning. Rachel, our Bill manager, has done an excellent job of preparation but it's still a daunting prospect. We're also having an unusual procedure, whereby we take oral evidence in the Bill sessions – again, something we've not done before. We agree a timetable. We'll sit for two sessions on Tuesdays until 7 p.m. and two sessions on Thursday until 5 p.m. finishing on 21 January. A total of sixty-six hours.

We begin with witnesses from E.ON, Scottish Power and the Grid to answer questions on CCS. A Tory asks how feasible our competition is for a project to be up and running by 2014. Scottish Power answer positively – they've already got a pilot at Longannet. E.ON are co-owners of the rig and say they are considering up to seven projects in Europe – a positive start to the day.

Next, questions are asked on the social tariffs we have written into the Bill. The witnesses agree with our putting the tariffs on to a statutory footing (it took a lot of negotiation!). Finally, questions on our amended remit for Ofgem and lots of technical points, another series of witnesses for a further hour and then we break for lunch.

The committee meets again for more witnesses and questions but I'm in the Chamber for the Copenhagen statement, leaving David Kidney to sit through the session.

Ed opens by expressing our disappointment that Copenhagen did not establish a clear timetable for a legal treaty and we do not yet have the commitments to the cuts in emissions we were looking for. However, he emphasises the fact that the forty-nine developed and developing countries that signed the Copenhagen Accord account for more than 80 per cent of global emissions. Furthermore, the 2°C limit was endorsed and all leading developing countries agreed to lodge specific commitments on tackling emissions in the Accord by 31 January. Significantly all countries have signed up to the comprehensive monitoring, reporting and verification process and commitments have been made on finance.

Predictably, Greg Barker, leading the Tories' response, has dropped the Tories' supportive pre-Copenhagen stance and now makes a series of petty and partisan remarks about Gordon. Others ask serious questions and of course we're at one with them on the massive task that lies ahead if we are to get where we need to be.

Back to the committee and the evidence session continues until 7 p.m. A total of 196 questions asked and answered today – quite a useful process at the start of a standing committee.

Rachel and her team, David and I are all working flat-out on the Bill. We work so late that Rachel decides she can't get home and back again for the morning start. The Bill session will be especially onerous as the committee will be questioning Rachel herself and two other officials plus David and me.

6 January: Geoff Hoon and Patricia Hewitt have attempted to stage a coup against Gordon. Total madness. No way could a public initiative of this kind succeed in doing anything except bring vitriol on themselves. If the Cabinet had a successor in mind and wanted to get rid of Gordon they would have had to be united and done it behind closed doors.

We're in the Chamber for oral questions before our Bill session. I'm asked about energy costs for off-grid households. This is of particular concern. Oil and liquid gas prices are very high and no one has a real answer except to better insulate the homes, which in itself is problematic as rural houses are often older and without cavity walls. Can't give much comfort there but I am looking for solutions, which could be air source heat pumps. Then a series of questions on the outcomes of Copenhagen, where I stress the positives and our commitment to follow through both with our own emission reductions through our low carbon transition plan and in our foreign affairs work and financing.

Then I'm first up for questioning in the Bill committee. Initially very straightforward, explaining the contents of the Bill – the levy for funding CCS and the social tariffs – but then it gets very technical and I'm grateful for the officials who can explain how a contract for difference would work in relation to the carbon price. Forty-nine more questions and answers before we're done. A truly exhausting session – I think they got their money's worth.

In between Bill sessions and preparations we are now doing huge amounts of work on the aftermath of Copenhagen. Our detailed analysis throws up a whole programme of potential work we need to agree – from working with the UN and Mexico (who will chair the next meeting) on improving the bureaucracy and preparations, to a major diplomatic effort with key countries to get their commitments added to the Accord by the end of the month. Our lead officials are to be deployed in the field again immediately. The PM and Ed and I will all take on further tasks in building support for the Accord, setting out a view on the eventual form of a legal agreement and developing proposals to address the legal and institutional weaknesses Copenhagen exposed.

There's also the small problem of a general election coming down the tracks. Fortunately, the CLP have decided to employ a part-time organiser, Matt Simms, who has just joined us. This will take the pressure off Jessica, who is also my agent, and off me. Telephone canvass sessions are starting. The terrible weather that started before Christmas is getting worse and it's impossible to go house to house.

On Friday, Matt Simms, Jessica and I sit down to plan the election campaign.

11 January: Monday's PLP and people rally round Gordon. Harriet, Douglas Alexander and Peter Mandelson give presentations on the approach to the election. Lots of appeals for unity.

Amid all the pressure and turmoil, we've managed to get the house finished, and Frank and I have decided to get married. Given our crazy schedules, we decide on a September wedding. Hopefully if we let everyone know the date soon, it will work. Having spent so much on the house we'll need a really tight budget so a local registry office will have to do. I phone Lewisham, but when I visit the registry office, I find it's gloomy and has a strange smell – more like a funeral parlour. I ring Greenwich and they send me a glossy brochure of all the wonderful historic houses it's possible to be married in locally. I make an appointment to visit Woolwich Town Hall.

After several weeks of going line by line through the energy Bill clauses, we are out of committee. Opposition parties argued for a widening of social tariffs, introducing CCS for gas in addition to coal and setting a floor price for carbon in relation to carbon trading. We voted against and now have our Bill out of committee on schedule.

A major submission in my box on a document for our post-Copenhagen strategy. There is so much to be done, both in countering those now attacking the science and in challenging the defeatist attitude of many of the green NGOs and commentators. Even more importantly we need to maintain our global leadership and work with those who want the plans to go forward.

We are in a battle with the EU about the target to be entered into the Copenhagen Accord. With a domestic target of 34 per cent reductions ourselves, we argue that the EU as a whole should enter 30 per cent. It's a battle we will lose as other countries such as Poland want only 20 per cent. Our allies are France, Denmark and the Netherlands, but in the end, the compromise will be 20 per cent guaranteed and up to 30 per cent conditional on others. I'm meeting El Salvador's Environment Minister in the afternoon and we share our thoughts. He makes the point that lots of the smaller vulnerable countries like his own were effectively excluded by the power brokers. I can sympathise and we'll need to learn from this.

A very odd engagement. The press department has persuaded me to do an interview with an Italian comedian who has turned to environmental campaigning and tackling climate change. I'm not at all sure this is a good use of my time but I have to concede getting our message across in Italy has to be worthwhile. His name is Beppe Grillo. It's a provocative but serious interview and subsequently we are sent a DVD. A couple of years later I rediscover the DVD and realise this is the leader of the new Five Star Movement, which has just taken a quarter of the votes in the Italian general election!

An email from Pam Isherwood to say the National Portrait Gallery has put together a collection of twenty examples of the portrait work of Format Photographers that she was part of in the '80s and '90s and a photograph of me is included. It will go into the national collection and they have made 1,000 postcards as well! A lunchtime visit to see my CND picture. Big surprise! It's been used for the poster advertising the exhibition and is framed and attached to the railings outside the gallery! What fun.

We are under intense pressure on the energy Bill. Report stage will be next month and an amendment is going to be tabled by Alan Simpson and opposition frontbenchers on an emissions performance standard. This goes back to the 2008 Energy Act when a similar clause was tabled by the Tories.

Its purpose is to curb coal-fired power stations, but it cuts across our CCS plans and the EU carbon trading scheme. We're fearful the Bill will be jeopardised and the CCS programme lost. Rapid research into who on our side might support. Ed and I will have to talk to people and there'll be a hard whip on this. Emily Thornberry, our excellent team PPS, will be a great help.

Meanwhile, a very constructive meeting with a Japanese Foreign Minister on post-Copenhagen. Japan has submitted a 25 per cent reduction to the Copenhagen Accord and expressed their disappointment at the EU position. I agree of course and get commended for the UK efforts. He will go on to the AU meeting in Ethiopia and build on work Gordon has done recently with Commonwealth countries. So good to talk to allies who want to keep Copenhagen alive. Much cheered up. It's a one-line whip so I collect my boxes and head off in time to pay the marriage fee for our wedding, scheduled for 18 September. I also manage to attend a Trinity Laban board meeting – something I've not done for a very long time.

I organise a meeting with WWF, Greenpeace and FOE to explain our attitude to the Emissions Performance Standard. After lunch it's a Convoys Wharf meeting in my parliamentary office, then tea and cakes with Liz as sadly she's leaving my private office to go back to policy. I'll really miss her decisive views and sharp personality. Then it's surgery time.

Busy in the constituency at the weekend, gearing up for the election. Matt is able to get branches organised and Darren, Mike and Stella, our council candidates in Lewisham Central, are working incredibly hard, giving me the cover I need.

A meeting with Ed and the whole team on handling the energy Bill. We'll draft a new clause on decarbonisation reports, which will add greater transparency, and I'll send a letter to all Labour MPs advising of our policy and why they shouldn't vote for the new clause on an EPS.

5 February: Alan Simpson tables his EPS clause.

On Sunday, a great turnout for canvassing thanks to the leadership of Joe Dromey and Vicky Foxcroft, our joint campaign coordinators. It's such a relief to have a solid party machine in the constituency. Then it's back to the desk to work on the Energy Bill. I approve a draft letter to all Labour MPs on the EPS. Both the CBI and the TUC have already written pointing out the EPS could mean no investment in new coal, thus making CCS impossible in the UK. It could also apply to gas and could affect gas investment as well.

One hundred and eight countries have signed up to the Copenhagen Accord, with seventy-one submitting mitigation actions/commitments on emissions.

I take a morning flight to Aberdeen. It's half-term recess. Frank and I need some quiet time to agree the lists of guests for our wedding. Haven't booked a venue yet but we plan on sending out sixty 'hold the date' letters. It's so good to be planning, but a bit surreal given how much is going on.

The next day I decide I'll take a break and go to the shops. Aberdeen has a number of boutiques and I reckon they will have the sort of clothes that would be suitable for a September wedding. I'm not intending to buy – just to look. Fatal last thoughts. One shop has a range of suitable dresses and jackets but none in the cream I think I need. I find one that's exactly right in style but I don't think I could wear the colour – it's a light silvery grey silk – just about the colour of my skin at this time of the year. Against my better judgement I'm persuaded to try it on and fall in love. It's very close fitting and I've put weight on over the past few months of much sitting, eating and drinking. Then a further negative – I'll never get a hat to match. But the assistant goes to her store cupboard and produces a fabulous creation with a luxurious black trim. The whole outfit is way beyond what I meant to pay but I just have to have it. Amazing – it's February and I have my wedding outfit.

Back to earth on Monday. I've got to ring round all our dissenting MPs who've signed the new clause. I try to put wedding thoughts out of my mind.

24 February: Report stage and we've done all we can to ensure the Bill's passage, but will it be enough? A very tense time. We begin at 2 o'clock with our new clause, with which Alan Simpson's is grouped. After three and a half hours of debate, the government's new clause is accepted. We come to the vote on the EPS. Twenty-seven Labour MPs rebel and we win by just eight votes. Huge relief – I'm totally drained. Everything else goes through and we're on to third reading at 6.30 p.m.

Ed opens and bestows fulsome praise on me for my 'fantastic' job on the Bill and proceeds to list its merits. At 7 p.m., it's all over. Because of the short time left in this Parliament, a truncated procedure has been made with the Lords for the passage of Bills where agreement can be reached between the parties. Our Bill will go to the Lords for just one day.

Next day, we're up at orals. Not sure how I've managed to prepare for this. I'm so tired I have difficulty getting up let alone being at the Dispatch Box at 10.30 a.m. First question is on feed-in tariffs and how those who were early adopters are now at a disadvantage. Unfortunately, that's the case, but we are about incentivising a new generation. I get asked a couple of questions on climate science then it's on to boiler scrappage, the CRC and oil-fired power stations. Tom Brake can't resist pursuing the EPS and suggests the industry needs a stronger signal. I give a robust response – we have the most radical and most environmentally demanding coal policy in the world.

March begins with a round of ministerial engagements, including another enjoyable one at Earls Court Ecobuild where I meet Kevin McCloud. Summer subsequently tells me I displayed distinctly coquettish behaviour – oh dear!

Our document, 'Beyond Copenhagen', is looking good and ready to launch. Over the past few months there's been a concerted attempt to undermine the science and set the debate back. Much though I fear we cannot win the coming general election, it's so important to secure the UK's radical programme on international climate change. We set out the progress we believe is being made with the Copenhagen Accord – more than seventy countries have now registered targets or actions to limit their greenhouse gas emissions. We give a robust defence of the science and the economic case for low carbon and how to deliver action in the UK, EU and globally. We set out how we can contribute to unblocking negotiations, strengthening the international process and moving towards a legally binding agreement.

To Paris for an overnight stay and an all-day meeting on forestry. The UK has a good story to tell and we want to encourage others to match our partnerships in support of projects in developing countries. We are entertained to a grand dinner in the Élysée Palace when Summer, sitting all of four tables away, rushes up and almost snatches the fork from my hand. She's read the French menu and realised I was about to eat crab, to which I am allergic!

President Sarkozy opens the conference with a rousing speech designed to lift post-Copenhagen spirits, and avoiding rich/poor clichés in favour of building progressive partnerships and not being held back by the EU. A positive meeting moving us on from Copenhagen to new partnerships on Reducing Emissions from Deforestation and Forest Degradation (REDD), and looking forward to the next major conference led by Mexico. Germany, Spain, Slovenia and Finland come forward to join the rest of us who pledged $3.5 billion fast start for REDD at Copenhagen. I confirm the UK's $450 million contribution, describe our current support in Indonesia and Congo and urge rainforest countries to come forward with more information on their needs. Important discussions on monitoring and verification follow. A better visit than the last time we were here when we felt the need to escape to get a steak and red wine, which was somewhat desperate for a vegetarian like Liz.

15 March: News comes through of the death of Ashok Kumar. This is such a shock. Everyone liked Ashok, who was a quiet, unassuming person devoted to his constituency. He had been put under a lot of pressure, unjustifiably, over expenses claims and people are suggesting this could have contributed to his premature death.

The women's section has agreed to organise leafleting outside all our twenty-six primary schools, so I'm in Lewisham Central for my first early-morning stint – never at my best but the reception we get is very good. Next day the same routine before going to DECC, then preparing and delivering two speeches; one on fuel poverty, the other on climate change.

A phone call to my German counterpart re. the Copenhagen Accord, and a follow-up meeting with UK companies dealing in palm oil. After seeing what can happen in Indonesia, I regard this work as really important but I think there's little I can do now to take it forward.

23 March: Second reading of the Energy Bill in the House of Lords. Then drinks with the Energy Bill team. They were just wonderful – twenty-one people altogether but Rachel was outstanding.

A photo shoot for the *Sunday Times Style Magazine* – flattered to be asked. I put on my very best suit – the Armani I bought as two separates in a sale in Milan some years ago. They insist on doing full make-up on top of what I have done, but there's nowhere to go so I sit in Westminster Hall being gawped at by all and sundry! Then a whole reel of photographs standing on the steps. When it comes out, everything is fine until I get to the insert piece on 'my stuff'. Nothing wrong with the references to my lipstick (I always wear it) or the Jo Malone body cream (which I always ask for at Christmas), but then they refer to the silver cuff I always wear – they've sourced one themselves and it cost £495. I'm really upset. In that one sentence the whole feature is ruined. My cuff was bought for me by Frank in Italy and cost £40. I'm mortified to think how constituents would view my spending so much money on a piece of jewellery. My only consolation is maybe not many of them buy the *Sunday Times*.

A very busy constituency Friday to make up for all the ones I've missed. A New Cross roundtable, an East London line visit, and a follow-up with residents on Milton Court and a surgery at the Ackroyd Centre. I've insisted on no more weekend boxes – all the papers are now being cleared on the desk mid-week. Lots of canvassing on Saturday but Sunday I just can't get up – I'm taking the morning off. I do a bit of tidying and take a long bath, then load two or three days' worth of dishes into the machine and make the bed (total neglect when Frank is away). Nearly late for the afternoon canvass. Pretty dismal, not many people at home – or at least answering the door. When it's finished I leap into the car, pick Frank up from the station and drive to the garden centre to buy plants that will bloom in the garden for our September wedding!

April: It's only five months to the wedding and I'm really worried about how to get everything organised with an election next month and a tremendous rush to finalise everything we can at DECC. My friend Pat has someone who organises all her social events at home and I've decided to seek her help. Sarah is surprisingly affordable and it's an enormous relief to get some back-up. My visit to Woolwich Town Hall was a revelation. As I approached, the street was gridlocked, with a massive building opposite under construction – not a good omen. But then I went through the doors into a glorious great Victorian hall, beautifully decorated and displaying dazzling antique chandeliers. A perfect wedding venue. The ceremony room was equally delightful and our chosen date available. The next major decision is the venue for the meal. Apart from the expense, none of the venues seem as potentially attractive as being at home. Our little coach house is attached to a great Victorian villa and we have a communal garden perfect for a marquee. I pluck up the courage and raise it at a residents' meeting, knowing it will be contentious.

I give every assurance about not damaging the lawn or restricting people's access, having public liability insurance etc. One very strong objection, but eventually it is agreed. Now I'm needing Sarah to recommend a company that hires marquees and a caterer to do the food. We'll bring all the wine when we return from Italy in August.

Oral questions – our last before the election. I'm asked about progress on climate change with India and China. I can answer on China, which has submitted proposals on reducing its emissions. I say nothing about India because there's nothing positive to say. With an election round the corner, questions are more partisan than usual – Henry Bellingham objects to on-shore wind but I have to tell him it must be part of the mix; even though we are world leaders in off-shore wind technology, we have to bear in mind it is very much more expensive than on shore. Charles Hendry then asks me to admit I've done too little on wave and tidal power – 'as the tide finally goes out on the government and we wave them goodbye'. I point out it is not an immediately viable technology but we have promoted its development and provided £60 million for a wave-hub in the south-west. Alan Beith tackles me on energy efficiency in solid-wall rural houses, and Barry Sheerman does a follow-up. I point out that in January I announced all four gas networks would link up in a scheme to connect more rural homes to the grid – 20,000 new connections are expected, enabling people to switch from oil and liquid gas. We've also got 5,600 homes treated with solid-wall insulation under CERT. I remind members of our increased standards under building regulations that apply to retrofit as well as new build, which we plan to be carbon neutral by 2016. And that's it. My very last question time.

8 April: Amendments made to the Energy Bill in the Lords are back with us this afternoon. I propose that the House accepts the Lords' amendments, Charles Hendry begins with a tribute to my 'courtesy, thoughtfulness and constructive approach' and goes on to ask a lot of questions and list many of the things he would have wanted to see in the Bill. Phil Willis responds

for the Lib Dems with a few more questions and points ending: 'I hope that when an incoming government returns to this matter, they will treat it with the same compassion and sense of importance that the minister has shown and we can move on to the next stage as quickly as possible.'

I compliment each of them by return and answer the questions. My speech ends with reference to DECC, set up less than two years ago, 'It has been a whirlwind of a department, which has enabled the country to begin that absolute change in the way we generate and use our energy, and at the same time tackle the threat of dangerous climate change.'

The amendments are agreed. It will be my last appearance in the Chamber as the Minister for Energy and Climate Change. Royal Assent is granted and parliament ends for the general election.

Ministers remain in office until a new government is formed following the general election. Of course there's no legislation or questions or announcements to be made but the machinery has to be kept ticking over. Our parliamentary offices have to be vacated and those who are leaving have to remove everything from the estate. I and my office simply decamp to New Cross, happy to have secure premises and a paid election coordinator. The campaign takes over the bulk of the office (the party pays the whole rent for the month) leaving Lucy in a corner continuing to do casework, which inevitably increases at election time.

It's great to be able to focus on the campaign. Ever since Matt joined us we've been writing and producing really good materials and have lots of people out campaigning. Now it's the rush to get the election address sorted and all the complex technicalities of running a general election.

15 April: The first leaders' debate and we're all glued to the TV screen. Nick Clegg, the Lib Dem leader, gets mega exposure for the first time and comes out on top. Gordon is far less suited to this kind of performance and we fear our solid record of achievement will be overshadowed by this beauty contest. There's also the perpetual charge that the economic crisis is Labour's

fault, when of course it was made in the US and became global. Our election themes of aspiration not austerity, securing growth rather than choking it off, protecting frontline services rather than putting them under the knife and cutting the deficit fairly, rather than cutting taxes for the few, are substantial and real. But will people hear us?

22 April: The second debate. Gordon has upped his game but the polling still puts Cameron and Clegg as joint winners. Cleggmania has erupted. He's being seen as a serious player and there's growing talk of a hung Parliament.

A week later and my sole invitation to do a debate on climate change. As I arrive at the studio, news is coming in of a major gaff by Gordon. Apparently he left his lapel mike on and referred to a pensioner who had given him a hard time over immigration as 'just a sort of bigoted woman'. I'm completely unsighted and we go on air as I desperately try to read the messages coming in on my mobile phone. The climate change discussion is completely derailed. I defend Gordon as a human being, say it was wrong and that I (now) understand that he's apologised. What a total disaster. We've all been there – the campaign trail is totally exhausting, people eat you up and letting off steam in private is the only way to keep sane. But for a Prime Minister there is no private, even if you don't have a microphone attached.

The last leaders' debate and we're all gathered in a local pub to watch our man. After yesterday's fiasco with Gillian Duffy we are extremely apprehensive. At the beginning of the debate Gordon refers to it – 'There's a lot to this job, as you saw yesterday, I don't get all of it right.' He looks contrite and I'm relieved. It goes well enough but the debates have not been to our advantage.

Our vote is holding up well, though the campaign in the country is less than brilliant. The Lib Dems are on a roll. Heidi is under more pressure in Lewisham East where the Lib Dems have been the challengers for some time, but she's done so much work and had a fantastic campaign. I'm confident she'll win, as will Jim in Lewisham West.

6 May: Election day and the usual scramble to get out the vote and for me to visit all our committee rooms and polling stations. Turnout proves higher than usual, taking council officials by surprise. When eventually I go home to clean up and change for the count, I reflect on the possibility that this might be my last election. I haven't told anyone but I've been thinking it.

The count and all home and dry. The Lib Dems have taken some votes from me but I still end up with 53 per cent of the vote and a majority one short of 12,500. Heidi, in her first election, has returned a majority similar to Bridget's last time, keeping the Lib Dems at bay. Frank is safely re-elected in Aberdeen North.

Up most of the night watching results. Margaret Hodge wins a magnificent victory in Barking over Nick Griffin, the BNP leader. For years she has fought the BNP as they took council seats and exploited the fears of local people at the rapid demographic change in that part of London. Margaret is typically bullish. In her election speech she says, 'The message of Barking to the BNP is clear, get out and stay out. You are not wanted here and your vile politics have no place in British democracy.' She has doubled her majority – an incredible achievement. So proud to be her friend.

Charles Clarke and Jacqui Smith lose their seats. The Greens win their first seat in Brighton. Gisela Stuart hangs on but five junior ministers, including Ann Keen, lose their seats.

7 May: Apparently the Queen has ordered a cooling-off period, saying no party leader should approach the palace before 1 p.m. The Lib Dem surge hasn't been maintained and losses come in. Nonetheless, Clegg looks like the king-maker – Gordon arrives back at Downing Street. He's still PM and seventy seats have yet to be counted. More of my ministerial colleagues lose their seats including, sadly, David Kidney, Mike O'Brien and Vera Baird, but great news that Glenda Jackson has clung on with just forty-two votes and Karen Buck, who has been such a steadfast colleague on modernisation, is also back.

What's going on? None of us knows. The Tories have won, no doubt about that, but they've not got a majority. Everyone is talking of coalition. I can't believe the Lib Dems would want to prop up a Tory government but then Nick Clegg won't work with Gordon. Everyone is on edge. I am willing us to return to government in a coalition. There's so much to do now that the recovery is just beginning to show.

8 May: Gordon is said to have offered the Lib Dems a referendum on electoral reform in a bid to form a coalition. Clegg is meeting his MPs. Reports come in that Gordon is still carrying on his role, making phone calls to other European leaders about the Euro crisis following the Greek bail-out.

Poignant pictures of the three party leaders standing side by side at the Cenotaph marking VE Day. Lib Dem negotiating team to meet Tories tomorrow. Conservatives say discussions are unlikely to conclude before Monday.

10 May: More negotiations, then late afternoon Gordon announces he will step down as Labour leader in September. This prompts Lib Dem/Labour talks.

My mother is ninety today – we'll go to celebrate next weekend.

11 May: More and more talks behind closed doors, then Gordon announces he is resigning and an hour later Cameron is at No. 10. The next day the coalition with the Lib Dems takes shape.

12 May: David Miliband announces he will stand for leader. Two days later, to most people's surprise, Ed also announces he will stand. Others follow. I had expected to be supporting David but strangely he's never asked for my support and now Ed's running I will definitely back him. I admire the way he ran DECC. Also I think David is fully formed and won't be likely to develop a new approach for 2015, but Ed should be able to grow into the job – so much will have changed in five years.

19 May: I take the oath. All ex-ministers who've returned to Parliament automatically retain their portfolios, so I'm now the shadow minister and Charles and I have swapped places. It's just awful looking across from the opposition benches and knowing – unlike many colleagues – how wretched life can be when you no longer hold the reins of power. I'm sorry too for our party, all the people who worked so hard and now have to gear up to electing a new leader. Harriet hasn't entered the race and will continue as deputy leader and as leader of the opposition in Gordon's place until the new leader is elected. I'm helping Ed's campaign as much as I can. I'm so familiar with the process of gathering names and canvassing but don't want a leading role this time round – I've got too many domestic matters to attend to.

June: Loads of planning still to do for 18 September. Nagging Frank to buy a new suit, which he keeps putting off. I've done two separate invitations – to closest family and friends to the ceremony and an additional twenty people to the reception and lunch. We've chosen a delicious range of canapés and a chicken or salmon main course for the lunch. I'm now able to spend time in the garden, ensuring it will be looking lovely in time. My friend Sabire is doing the flowers for the tables, my bouquet and the buttonholes – the colours are lilac and silver. Mum is providing the wedding cake, not handmade any longer, but a traditional iced fruit cake nonetheless. I'm so looking forward to the wedding and hoping against hope that the sun will shine.

To Ditchley Park for the climate change conference I was invited to when still a minister. It's an odd situation, I have more experience than many of the participants yet I'm no longer able to take forward any of our programmes. The theme is 'Can the multilateral system handle climate change?', so I have a lot to say.

One of the few benefits of being out of office is time to focus on the constituency. Having been told of the rental agreement to keep the job centre open before the election, I've now been told the deal was never sealed. I manage to get called at DWP questions and tackle Iain Duncan Smith. I tell him that last week the government announced the job centre, serving 2,500 of my constituents, would close – 'will he meet me to discuss? Or is this how the coalition works to protect the poorest and most vulnerable from its savage cuts?' He agrees to meet me! Ten days later I put to him the case for keeping a job centre in Deptford. We have a lot of people with poor education and skills and disabilities, and most walk to the centre and respond well to the Job Centre Plus programmes. He says he will provide money to keep a full service in Deptford if suitable premises can be found.

15 June: A letter from the Cabinet office enclosing an order telling me that I have been appointed a member of 'Her Majesty's Most Honourable Privy Council'. I will have to go to a Privy Council meeting, kiss the royal hand and thereafter be ready to attend in the event of 'the death of the Sovereign'. (Only government members attend the regular meetings.) I am now the Rt Hon. Joan Ruddock. I'm really pleased.

I've tabled a question to the new Transport Minister Theresa Villiers about the Surrey Canal Road station and whether the value for money evaluation has been completed. I ask if she will meet me. She agrees. Two ministers in one week! This won't last. Simon Hughes and I meet with Theresa Villiers about the station. We have a strong case but she's going to be implementing a cuts agenda and there's nothing in it for her. Perfectly polite meeting but officials hardly animated.

A government debate on energy efficiency led by Greg Barker. He begins by repeating Cameron's pledge to be 'the greenest government ever'. If only we could believe him. Greg makes the kind of remark for which he will become known: how many lightbulbs does it take to change a Labour government – the answer: 262 million. I jump up and point out that when the low-energy bulbs were more expensive and people were resistant to change, getting them free into people's homes was an effective thing to do. He ends by saying the coalition will build on our work. I reprise our work and emphasise all we did on housing and with local authorities on energy efficiency and question whether this will disappear under the draconian cuts just announced to council budgets. Greg intervenes several times. I can see how keen he is to prove he can do better but they'll never manage it with the cuts programme they've started. Ed has appointed Emily Thornberry, who was our PPS, as the new shadow in place of David Kidney. I'm really pleased for Emily and she makes her debut in the wind-ups.

DECC orals and I ask about renewable energy. The Tory manifesto said 15 per cent by 2020, the Lib Dem 40 per cent. Who won? The Tories.

Frank and I are at Woolwich Town Hall to finalise the arrangements for the wedding. I'm excited; Frank is laid back. In the evening, there's a leadership hustings with Ed in Greenwich.

26 July: A meeting of Ed's parliamentary supporters to agree our strategy over the summer and the House rises for the recess. We're off to Italy for our longest stay ever. I haven't been this free of responsibilities for years but the deep exhaustion we both feel post-election takes a while to lift.

Back in the constituency for a packed surgery. I'm keeping constituency engagements to the minimum but we have a leaving meal for Matt Simms, who was such a strength in the election campaign. An enjoyable event at Brockley station. The planting has been done extremely well and it looks marvellous. This has been such a good initiative and ultimately there will be a fully accessible station, a joy to use. Job well done.

6 September: The House returns. Whole rafts of new legislation are being brought forward, none of which will be of benefit to my constituents.

I've told Ed I'll not be standing for the shadow Cabinet and don't wish to continue in a shadow post. If he's the leader, he will need to get new people into position and then move them on if they don't make the grade. Also I really feel I've done it all. I had three shadow portfolios over our previous ten years in opposition and I really don't want to do any more. Secretly I've made up my mind that should the coalition fall in the next eighteen months, I will offer myself for re-election, but if it goes beyond 2012, then I won't stand again.

16 September: The wedding is just two days away but, as shadow minister, I have to be in the Commons for DECC orals. The coalition is in a mess on the renewable heat incentive that we were developing prior to leaving office. This morning the SoS said he was strongly committed to the renewable heat incentive but yesterday in evidence to a select committee he said he had simply forgotten about it when drawing up the coalition agreement. This makes for a good last question to Greg and in my supplementary I tell him we had convinced the Treasury that it made sense for investment and jobs and ask if he will fight for the same (knowing he will get strong opposition). He pledges to do so and that is my farewell to the Dispatch Box. When we come back after the recess I'll be back on the back benches for good.

17 September: The wedding marquee arrives and is erected on site with a wooden floor, large side windows and satin drapes inside, but – horror of horrors – the chandeliers are gold-coloured! They were supposed to be black to complement the silver everywhere else. I'm throwing a wobbly but the company agrees to go and source the correct lights and have them changed by morning.

When we fixed our wedding date we had no idea the Pope would be visiting London – but he is and my poor family spend hours trying to get through the London traffic to their hotel in south London. The evening meal we planned to have together is cancelled and we simply speak by phone. Disappointing but not enough to spoil my anticipation of tomorrow's event.

18 September: Up early and trying to stay calm. Sue's daughter, who's a hairdresser, comes to do my hair. Thank goodness I hadn't planned to go up to town. Sabire arrives with lovely lilac decorations and lilac roses, as requested, for the bouquet. Sister Susan, David and my mum arrive when I'm dressing.

Neither has a hat, which disappoints, given my magnificent creation. I managed to lose the weight I promised myself (Frank had me on a strict exercise regime in Italy) and the dress goes on easily. Nice cars arrive on time. Sarah is here to supervise and Chloe has the food.

We arrive at Woolwich Town Hall to find the ceremony in front of ours is running late. We are given a very nice side room to wait but then our guests start arriving so we're all chatting nervously to each other – not quite what we expected. Harriet arrives following an audience with the Pope! Eventually Frank and I are taken to the ante room and our guests to the ceremony room. Finally, we are walking down the aisle together. Everything looks lovely and the ceremony is just perfect. We leave to one of our shared favourite opera pieces, 'Soave sia il Vento' from Mozart's *Cosi fan Tutte*.

We pose for photographs on the splendid staircase of the town hall. I've frantically texted Sarah to explain the delay. All our additional guests are going to be at our house before we arrive. Thank goodness Sarah is there to play host and the canapés and wine can be served. When we do arrive everyone is already in the party mood and we get a great cheer.

Lunch is excellent. I do the welcome, telling everyone that I never thought Frank would ask me to marry him and – in truth – he never did. He replies in kind. Later Harriet makes a lovely speech and finally Neil Kinnock, who has everybody in stitches. A truly fabulous day and we are extremely happy.

Next day we fly to Rome where we're having a real holiday in a good hotel, eating out and seeing the sights – and of course waiting with bated breath for the results of the leadership contest. Walking back to our hotel, phones in hands, the call comes. Ed has won. I literally jump up and down in the street.

## Chapter Nine

# BACK BENCHES AGAIN

6 October: Back to London and my new, relaxed regime. I've agreed to speak at the Tadley CAB jubilee celebrations. Now that it's upon me I wonder what I'm doing and have to wrack my brains to think up a narrative that will work for them. But then I remember how difficult it is to find people to do these things and the fact that people are quite interested in asking questions about politicians' lives. So a short personal speech with recollections of my own time at the CAB, nearly getting sacked and then going on to Parliament will work. I suddenly feel as though I've re-joined the human race!

Next day I visit Second Wave, an exemplary youth project in the constituency led by Ann Considine. They have developed a really good partnership with the police, which is vital in an area where crime is high and there's always gang potential. Most of the users are black and building a relationship between them and the police, particularly over policies such as stop and search, is invaluable. They also do a lot of drama and workshops, which enable young people to gain confidence and speak for themselves.

On Friday I'm back at the Commons to host a visit from Prendergast School. I'm glad to be able to return to doing these sessions as the children always ask lots of questions – sometimes a little too frank, like 'How much do you earn?' I always answer directly but now I guess they think I'm very rich (though parents in some of my more prosperous wards will be earning much more than I do). I'm not asked if I cheat on my expenses.

11 October: The House returns and an opportunity to congratulate Ed in person. Next day, 6.30 p.m., at the Privy Council. I've been practising the kneeling and have chosen my clothes carefully. The skirt cannot be too fitting. I have a horrible vision of it splitting as I kneel – so I can't wear my best suit. I choose a matching black skirt and jacket and a crisp white blouse. When I get there I find the woman in charge of us dressed almost identically. I blot my lipstick repeatedly – I must be sure there's nothing to transfer in the kiss (no, remember, 'brush'). I know it's all very simple but it's quite a small room and such an odd thing to do that I'm quite uncomfortable. The Queen is wearing a light-turquoise chiffon dress and diamonds and as always I'm struck by how small she is. I try to look relaxed as I walk forward. I manage not to stumble and get up and down as gracefully as possible and then join the short line of other privy councillors. We all remain standing while the Queen addresses us on matters she wishes to raise. We listen dutifully, then a few exchanges and it's all over.

My priority this month is recruiting new staff. Abby left for a job at the GLA in August and I've had temporary cover over the summer. Lucy has a new job starting in December so I'm able to advertise two jobs, one for a caseworker, the other an office manager. Jessica and I will end up trawling through nearly 400 applications.

I'll now table every week for PMQs. As hundreds of MPs do the same, the chances of getting called are slim and just as slim if you jump up and down in the Chamber. But two days back, I'm in luck. I ask Cameron why his government is closing the only job centre in my constituency when I have high unemployment. He doesn't answer, just blames the Labour government and praises the new work programme – no mention of my job centre.

I get to grips with the New Cross Road roundtable. The road gyratory removal has gone well and the East London line is running, Goldsmiths' new building has opened on time and the disability access will go ahead at New Cross Gate. But, ominously, Sainsbury's say their plans are on hold due to the decline in the market. Lewisham Council are also in difficulty, having to make cuts, but they've done the promised environmental work around Fordham Park and Margaret McMillan Park, greatly improving pedestrian and cycle routes. Besson Street Gardens will also be improved and Deptford Green School will be rebuilt. Good news, but Sainsbury's are crucial to the master plan, so not brilliant. The NDC is winding down and the flagship NDC centre is still not on the starting blocks.

Very sad news – Ray Ashley has died. Ray and his wife Cathy have been my supporters ever since the selection in 1986. Ray was a lovely man and a fine silversmith. While Cathy was always the activist, I know Ray was a real support to her and he will be a great loss. I'll go to his funeral on the 22nd.

The deadline for compliance with the provisions of the recycling Bill I got through parliament in 2003 is rapidly approaching, so I ask for a progress report. I'm told 94 per cent of households were receiving the service on the latest figures. Not bad, but a typical Tory response to my second question on what he will do to ensure compliance – he says that local councils are responsible to their local customers on how they comply with the legislation. Actually, no – it's a government responsibility.

19 October: David Cameron is making a statement on the Strategic Defence and Security Review. To my amazement he announces that a third of DfID's budget is to be reallocated to conflict prevention. This is a disaster. I've always argued for more conflict prevention but it's for the military and the FCO to train people in these policies. The priority of DfID is in helping countries achieve the millennium development goals, so I intervene. A typically arrogant answer. He recommends a book he's read on broken states! This is so disappointing given how DfID has been working and their focus on women and children, the greatest victims of conflict.

In the afternoon I'm in the Chamber again to speak on the Parliamentary Voting Systems and Constituencies Bill. The government wants to reduce the number of constituencies by equalising them on the basis of numbers of registered voters. Potentially this destroys communities and takes no account of the gross under-registration of voters in certain (mostly Labour) areas. The Electoral Commission have found that, among 17–24-year-olds, 56 per cent are not registered, neither are 49 per cent of public-sector tenants, nor 31 per cent of ethnic minority British residents. Furthermore, it also found highest concentrations of under-registration in metropolitan areas and where there were high levels of deprivation. A fair description of my constituency. I speak passionately about the rights of people to be represented even if they are not registered and also on behalf of those who do not qualify for registration. I refer to poor people who are never at home because they have two or three jobs and work all hours and people who contribute in other ways but have poor English. We have to recognise real people – registered or not – we need to recognise their existence and value them; surely 'we are not suggesting that only voters count'? But it all falls on deaf ears – the Tories just want to break up constituencies like mine.

The very next day I'm up again at George Osborne's spending review. He is axing the Education Maintenance Allowance. This has been a Labour flagship in my constituency, enabling young people from the poorest homes to provide for their needs – from equipment to travel – while remaining in post-sixteen education. His answer is that he's raising the school leaving age and will be looking for more targeted support. What a cop-out. This will be a real blow in Lewisham where thousands of families have been helped.

The debate on the spending review and I'm up again making a speech on housing benefits. The Tories and the tabloids have been going hysterical about some extreme cases where housing benefit has been paid on large expensive properties in central and west London. Of course that shouldn't happen but they are a tiny minority that could be sorted. Instead the 'reforms' will be hitting my very poor constituents for whom I have to speak. The average wage in London is around £26,500 p.a. and the mean house price in sales last year £240,000. Ministers have spoken of claims for luxury accommodation but in my constituency the biggest payments are for large families often living in squalid conditions. More than half of the recipients of housing benefit in Lewisham are in work. Where will they find the money? An extra £11 a week for a one-bedroom property and £34 for a three-bedroomed. Ministers say rents will fall – I say they will not. So many young professionals cannot get mortgages that they take up any slack in the rental market. I end: 'This is a catastrophe in the making – for my people in Lewisham, for London as a whole … I remember when people slept in cardboard boxes on the South Bank. This government is planning to bring back those conditions.'

I've been approached by a young black woman who wants to be an intern in my office. There is no budget to pay for such a position and I explain this, saying she can have a couple of weeks, which we do for school children anyway. Toyin has left school and is working for a year part-time and desperate to get into university. She is convinced that she stands little chance and begs me to take her. I really don't want to because I can't pay, but in the end we all agree that if it could really make the difference she believes, we must let her come.

David Willetts is making a statement on higher education funding and student finance. This has great implications for both Trinity Laban and for Goldsmiths. I'm now back attending board meetings at TL and they are much exercised about what they are hearing. Willetts proposes £6,000 for fees, £9,000 in exceptional cases. In a bland sentence towards the end he says, 'The bulk of universities' money will not come through the block grant, but instead will follow the choice of students.' Gareth Thomas, our shadow minister, immediately exposes the truth – 'this means an 80 per cent cut in the undergraduate teaching budget'. I ask Willetts if he has made any analysis of his proposals on world-renowned institutions, such as the music and dance conservatoire Trinity Laban in my constituency. I ask because I know that conservatoires have a special form of teaching grant based on the need for one-to-one teaching. The minister hasn't a clue – 'I am not aware of the specific funding point the Rt Hon. Lady has in mind.' This answer will be a real shock to conservatoires and drama schools everywhere.

4 November: A by-election in Ladywell. Jessica and I take the day off to canvass and I take the last flight to Aberdeen as we're hosting a party the very next day. Carl Handley wins the by-election. He'll be a good councillor.

All day in frantic activity, tidying house and garden, cleaning glasses and plates and preparing food. Frank's invited his Aberdeen friends, party members and neighbours to a fireworks party and belated celebration of our wedding. The weather is fine. We cook loads of sausages, baked potatoes and add dips, bread and cheese and set a roaring fire. The garden looks wonderful after my recent efforts, making up for years of neglect. It's got a lot of structure that works in winter and at night. We've also got lights at the base of the walls to the derelict part of the steading and at the water feature, which we switch on. Lots of people bring fireworks, which make a splendid display. It was impossible to invite all these people to the wedding and it's great to have a party in the house, which I've seen far too little of in the last few years.

Back in London and I'm interviewing for my new staff. Lucy supervises the tests we give and Jessica and I do the interviews together. I appoint Nicky Sowemimo as my caseworker and Vicky Flippance as my office manager. Jessica is staying. Vicky goes off immediately to IPSA training. The new online system is a nightmare and the IPSA staff are quite unable to cope. I deem her a safe pair of hands – I don't want to touch it myself.

I'm now able to meet people who want to discuss a whole host of issues, attend APPGs such as Afghanistan and Palestine and even receptions – one for climate week, one for the Woodland Trust, and one at the British Museum with Frank. Life has changed quite dramatically. The best thing is the ease with which I now approach the daily work of the Commons. At long last I feel I can go into the Chamber, listen to any debate or question time, and get up if so minded, confident in my ability to make a contribution.

Some people have done this from day one, though sometimes their confidence has been more apparent than the quality of their contribution.

The weeks are becoming quite routine, with lots of time in the Chamber, constituency events, and follow-through on issues with written questions. There's just one breaking major controversy, which is a Lewisham Council decision to close five libraries, two of which are in my constituency. They've been persuaded to consult in an attempt to find community or non-profit solutions. The most vulnerable is New Cross, where there is low patronage and a deprived community unlikely to be able to meet the challenge. A very unusual evening out for us – the jazz singer Norma Winstone is receiving a TL award at the Blackheath Concert Halls. A great evening in contrast to the Trinity Laban board meeting dominated by concerns about fees and cuts in funding. If the special grant were to end the conservatoire couldn't exist.

Michael Gove is presenting the government's White Paper on education. It's a disaster for my constituents. He speaks a lot about poverty so I challenge him on the fact that no matter how much money is in the schools budget, it's the family budget that matters when the £30 a week education maintenance budget is cut. He replies, 'I am a great fan of the Rt Hon. lady!' and goes on to evade the question with talk of pupil premiums.

29 November: The Autumn Statement and more bad news.

In the evening we have a farewell dinner for Lucy. She's carried a tremendous weight of responsibility over the years, taking all the pressure of other people's problems, day-in, day-out. Caseworkers are the unsung heroines of MPs' offices.

I'm beginning to think it might be worth looking again at the sitting hours. I've been impressed by the new Tory women, several of whom are real go-getters and I'm sure they have little patience with the old-fashioned ways of the House. I mention it to Ann Coffey and she agrees. I can't resist. I ask the library to produce lists of the MPs who voted for our Monday-to-Wednesday proposals in 2002 who are still in the House today; those who voted for the Thursday proposals who are in the House today, and those who voted to reverse the earlier Tuesday in 2005 who are also still with us.

6 December: We've got an opposition day debate on the unfair distribution and impact of arts and local authority funding. Heidi, who is already making her mark in the House, is going to make a major speech with reference to Lewisham, so it's my intention simply to make interventions. Eric Pickles, the Tory bully boy who is Secretary of State for Local Government, responds to Caroline Flint's opening remarks. As usual his sentences are loaded with sarcasm and rudeness. He goes on about all the measures that councils could take to reduce their expenditure. I tell him that Lewisham has done all the things he has mentioned and made efficiency savings of £40 million over five years. Now they've been forced to cut another £16 million, costing 300 jobs. Quick as a flash he responds saying they've got nearly £60 million in reserves and it's their own decision. Someone protests and then, looking my way, he says, 'It might not be for the Rt Hon. Lady – I know she lives a champagne lifestyle – but £60 million is a lot of money.' I'm flabbergasted. No one has ever accused me of that.

Heidi is called and tells the House of the violent protests at Lewisham Town Hall last week as the cuts were announced. The £16 million is just the tip of the iceberg – they expect to have to cut £77 million in the next four years. She lets me intervene on the SoS's point about the reserves. I say she knows, as I do and he does, that the majority of the reserves is for capital funding. The general fund is only 2.5 per cent of total budget and wouldn't it be irresponsible to spend emergency reserves? Heidi does us proud, drawing on all her experience as the deputy mayor of the borough. Just before the frontbenchers are due to conclude the debate and the House is full, I get up on a point of order. I tell the Speaker I've been in the House long enough to take the rough and tumble of debates, but the Secretary of State's remark, of a 'champagne lifestyle', I found really offensive and rude. I ask the Speaker to advise whether I might expect that remark to be withdrawn.

John Bercow makes one of his delightful statements. First, he refers to 'good temper and moderation', second, to his privilege of serving with me on the international development select committee travelling around the world ('I cannot recall her consuming champagne at any stage'). Third, he says it is his distinct recollection that the 'Rt Hon. Lady is a modest person with very little to be modest about'. I can hardly stop myself from grinning as I fix my eyes on a squirming Eric Pickles. Afterwards, Alison Seabeck, who was sitting directly in front of me, says she thinks maybe he meant her as the tabloids had been having a pop at her partner's (my neighbour Nick Raynsford) external earnings! Alison, I think, is even more of a modest person, so Pickles got his comeuppance.

A one-line whip allows me to attend the Trinity Laban music degree ceremony in the magnificent chapel at the old Royal Naval College. In the evening, by contrast, a delicious meal served in the Deptford railway carriage as a guest of developers Cathedral, who are working with us on Deptford station.

It's DEFRA questions and I get called to ask the hapless Richard Benyon again about councils' compliance on recycling – this time he's briefed and gallantly refers to my expertise and says it's an absolute priority! Well, that's a result.

In the evening a very enjoyable CLP social – Christmas really is upon us.

Sunday: The All Saints' carol service, which I always look forward to. It so reminds me of how Christmas used to feel when I was a child. Perhaps Christmas itself is always a disappointment to grown-ups. I'm reminded of all those Christmas cards I have yet to sign – priority for next week.


13 December: Eric Pickles makes a statement on local government finance. I'm determined to keep up the pressure on behalf of my constituents. I tell him he speaks of fair and sustainable proposals but he must be using a different dictionary from the one on my bookshelf. Forty per cent of Lewisham's budget is spent on elderly and children's care, which means draconian cuts in everything else. 'Will he not admit that his real agenda is shrinking the state and shifting the blame?'

Insolent as always, he accuses me of making my reputation 'by shroud waving' in the Chamber and tells me I should be addressing the needs of the people of Lewisham, who will continue to receive a high level of support from the central state. I'm really pissed off but happily the day ends with a carol concert in the Speaker's rooms – truly uplifting.

I draft a letter on sitting hours with a brief history and pointing to one significant change since 2005. IPSA has discontinued payments for a second home for outer London MPs, so forty-seven now have to make their way home late at night. We believe it might be a good time to reconsider Tuesday sittings. Also there is still a small number of MPs who cannot get home on Thursday nights, so a slightly earlier start and finish that day might be appropriate. Ann agrees the letter, which goes in both our names – very important – a northerner as well as a Londoner. We enclose a form for tickbox responses. We mail all past supporters and all the 2010 intake.

A morning meeting with John Miller at Lewisham Council to review progress (or lack of it) on the Convoys development. Then into the Commons in time for PMQs. I'm now such a regular attender that my chances of being called have increased, even though I never get drawn out of the ballot. In answer to an earlier question, Cameron referred to unemployment, so I point out that unemployment in his constituency is 1.5 per cent but in mine it is 7.3 per cent, yet Witney has a full Job Centre Plus service while he has decided to close mine. I ask him to review the situation. He replies he is more than happy to look at the distribution of job centres ... but 'we put a lot more money into deprived areas in our country'. Why do I bother? This man is just an empty vessel.

My first opportunity to get called in DECC questions. The new Secretary of State is a Lib Dem, Chris Huhne. He's continued our policies, so for once I'm congratulating someone in the government. I ask him if he agrees that individual European countries could commit to a second Kyoto commitment and that the EU could raise its emission reduction target to 30 per cent at very little extra cost. Chris entirely agrees and says that is the government position and that there is some progress as Spain has just committed to 30 per cent.

A really pleasant end to the week – a concert by St Paul's Sinfonia – so long since I've been able to go.

All year I've had real problems with my shoulder and now I can hardly raise my arm. It's been X-rayed but today it's an MRI scan before I go to the office. I'm so in need of some relief. I see a consultant at the Queen Elizabeth in the New Year and he recommends an operation. This is going to be a real drag. I won't be able to drive for six weeks and I'll also have to have lots of physio. I ask to be transferred to St Thomas'. At least that will cut down the time I have to spend travelling.

A routine couple of days at the office and then the House rises for the Christmas holiday. Our usual stay with my mother, so much more relaxed this year. Then Pat and David's for my birthday and New Year in Aberdeen. Great.

## 2011

Following the stabbing of our colleague, Stephen Timms, all MPs have been advised to hold surgeries in secure places where staff are on duty. This means I'm giving up all but two of my venues. The Ackroyd fought hard to keep us and even put in a volunteer to stay after the manager left at the end of the day. We're so sorry to leave them. John always had a cup of tea and a biscuit ready for us when we arrived in the afternoon. Now it'll be Albany and Leemore only.

An email from local activist Sue Lawes who is involved in a campaign against betting shops. She reminds me there are already seven betting shops in Deptford High Street and three more around the corner in Evelyn Street, the most recent casualty being the John Evelyn pub, only a couple of months after the same bookmaker took over the Deptford Arms. I'm going to have to do something about it. More reports come in of drug-dealing, drinking and antisocial behaviour that appear to be associated with the betting shops.

Eric Illsley, who was charged with three counts of false accounting for his expenses shortly after last year's election, has pleaded guilty. In May, Elliot Morley will also plead guilty and be imprisoned. David Chaytor, who, like Elliot, stood down last year, suffers a similar fate. Both David and Elliot were friends and I'm incredibly sad and still shocked by what they did.

Unusually I'm in the Chamber for a Treasury Bill. The government is proposing a national insurance holiday for business start-ups, but London is excluded. This makes no sense so I intervene. In deprived communities like mine, with higher unemployment and where people have few resources, they struggle to set up a business. In London, business births are higher by 12.6 per cent but deaths are also higher, so there's no reason to exclude us.

I've received a letter from Cameron's office following our exchanges on the job centre telling me that the cost of keeping Deptford open is 'prohibitive'. This just cannot be true so I table a series of written questions on surface area and costs per square metre of each job centre in each London borough. I'm absolutely right. The bigger Lewisham job centre at Rushey Green is just over 2,000m², Brixton over 4,000 m², and Bromley 5,464 m². When I get the reply on cost I am furious. Exactly as I thought: the cost in Deptford is £352 per m², around the average for London; the cost in Bromley £531 per m², and Ealing £577 per m². They simply lie. I write again to the PM to ask how and why the decision was taken not to renew the lease on the Deptford job centre building.

We've won the Oldham and Saddleworth by-election and Debbie Abrahams will be joining us. She looks to be a promising MP. After my surgery at the Albany I join the special tribute to the New Cross Fire families. It's the thirtieth anniversary and sadly there seems nothing more we can do except remember.

An opposition day debate on the education maintenance allowance gives me the chance to raise the hundreds of students at Lewisham College, mostly from ethnic minorities, in receipt of EMA. I suggest it would be invidious for the Principal to have to select just 10 per cent of them to receive the government's revised payments scheme and second-year students are to be cut off entirely. Gove tells me he visited the Knights Academy in Lewisham and they would like to see changes! These Tories haven't the slightest idea what poverty is. Next month, I get another chance to raise EMA at education questions. This time a better response. I ask John Hayes to guarantee no student will be forced to discontinue their second year because of lack of financial assistance. He gives me that assurance and says he will take account of representations made by me and others on this point.

Andy Coulson, the former editor of News International and now David Cameron's director of communications, has resigned over the allegations of phone-tapping when he was in charge. Looks like a story that's going to run and run.

The AGM of the Albany Theatre. I've had a long-standing relationship with the theatre and it's ups and downs over the years. Gavin Barlow is making a great success of his job as CEO and for the first time they are showing a surplus this year. Tuesday evening, I go to a St Paul's Sinfonia concert and then the Holocaust memorial day at the Catford Synagogue on Saturday. We have a very small Jewish community in Lewisham and I've had little contact with them, but I'm glad to be able to attend this solemn ceremony and reflect on the terrible history.

I am now heavily involved in the Save Lewisham Libraries campaigns. Several councillors are also very prominent and working with the council leadership to try to save the five libraries on the closure list. My bottom line is that the buildings should remain in public ownership and hopefully not-for-profit solutions can be found. I make a visit to the Pepys Resource Centre to discuss Darren Taylor's work in creating and running this facility. He's making a bid to Lewisham Council to run four of the five libraries they have up for closure. I'm very impressed by what he has done but a bit concerned at the breadth of his ambition.

A Westminster Hall debate on decent homes where I raise the issue of Lewisham Homes, the arm's length management organisation in my constituency, which had been promised £153 million by Labour if they reached two-star rating. They did so last July but have now been told the money has been withdrawn. This is so infuriating for the tenants who have seen the improvements on other estates and who now will be left without the new kitchens, bathrooms and windows that similar council homes enjoy. Throughout our time in office we systematically improved millions of the 2 billion homes left in disrepair by the previous Tory government. It's tragic to see such a reduction in the programme today.

We are receiving unprecedented numbers of emails on the Tories' proposed sell-off of large amounts of our national forests. People are rightly outraged, even in an inner-city community like mine. On 2 February, Mary Creagh, our shadow Secretary of State for DEFRA, opens an opposition day debate opposing the sell-off of the forests. The campaign in the country is growing apace and Mary has been doing a great job. James Gray, one of the real old fogies of the Tory Party, asks her if she thinks the 'Woodland Trust and the National Trust will or will not be able to compete in the free market to purchase important forests'. Extraordinary. Mary slaps him down, telling the House the National Trust has come out this morning saying the government's plans are no way to manage the forest and the Woodland Trust has a big petition on their website saying 'Save our Forests'. As she rightly says, 'They are not going to pay their members' subscriptions to the Treasury to buy something we already own.' I raise the Capital Woodlands project, which cares for biodiversity in urban areas of London. More than 300 of my constituents have contacted me. Labour members pile into the debate and Tory SoS Caroline Spelman is out of her depth. The government defeats our motion though three Tories vote with us – a sign of unease in the constituencies of forest members.

In January, I mailed a questionnaire to hundreds of backbenchers on the sitting hours. A huge undertaking but a truly worthwhile legacy if we win. The current chair of the procedure committee is Greg Knight, who was a Tory whip and not a fan of modernisation. Now, Caroline Lucas has a debate in Westminster Hall on parliamentary reforms. I want to keep my powder dry so I simply make interventions suggesting starting Tuesdays three hours earlier – it worked before – and taking Private Members' Bills afterwards. To my surprise, our Labour shadow leader of the House, Hilary Benn, agrees with me – he'll definitely be taken to task by the whips, who are fundamentally opposed to mid-week Private Members' Bills. Dinosaurs out in force of course, but a useful way of spotting allies. Lots of responses to our questionnaire are coming back and being collated.

We're debating youth unemployment. The coalition has cancelled our Future Jobs fund that would have created 200,000 jobs for young people. In my constituency the government-funded specialist agency dealing with unemployed young people 'Opening Doors' is to be closed, alongside cuts to the Connexions Service. I make the point that this will surely result in more unemployment. No joy from the minister.

Later on I meet with the developers, Renewal, who own the land around Millwall. We discuss their plans, which are being submitted to Lewisham Council, and the government's refusal last year to fund the Surrey Canal Road station. Renewal is prepared to put money in themselves so it may be worth my while taking it up again.

1 March: The back-bench Business Committee has granted me a debate on the future of the Forestry Commission. When I applied, the government was still planning to sell off up to 100 per cent of our public forest estates. Now there's to be a review. Poor Caroline Spelman; the PM revealed the policy the day before she had to make her humiliating climb-down. A huge success for Mary and the public campaign. It also happens to be the tenth U-turn of the coalition government but undoubtedly the highest public profile. I tell the House I only hope that the half a million people who rose up in protest over forests will do so again to defeat another Secretary of State and his plans to reorganise the NHS.

When we were in office, we commissioned an independent review that took nearly a year and went to the Forestry Commission just as we left office.

I quote its main findings, which are entirely at odds with what the government propose. The Tories are extremely agitated and I think we have them on the run and their review won't allow them to return to the original agenda. Nonetheless, the 25 per cent reduction in the commission's budget will still mean the loss of hundreds of jobs and the skills that are needed to maintain healthy forests.

We now have responses from 183 people on the sitting hours: 159 in favour of one or more options for change, virtually all in favour of changing the Tuesday start from 2.30 p.m. to 11.30 a.m. Canvassers, allocated by region, will approach those who haven't responded. This will be very time-consuming as we have mailed over 500 MPs to date. We email everyone again, separately by party, telling them the results so far and informing them of the further canvass. I also need to carefully brief 2010 entry MPs who are canvassing as they know nothing of the past and can easily be fobbed off with 'it won't work'. We know it did. A week later I organise the first meeting of the new sitting hours campaign. A select group of us look at the returns and share intelligence about which members of other parties we might ask to work with us.

At transport questions, the Secretary of State responds to one of his colleagues saying, 'Any scheme that levers in private money to reduce the cost to the taxpayer is likely to have an advantage in future competition [for government funds].' I leap to my feet. I tell the Secretary of State that Lewisham Council and developers Renewal are putting money into the Surrey Canal Road station. I ask for government support. To my surprise he says he is happy to consider it and raise my points with the Mayor of London.

8 March: International Women's Day. This used to be the purview of Labour women but this year Tory women are organising Women's Day events at the Commons. Mary Macleod is the leading light. I'm going to work with her on modernisation but feel a bit guilty as she defeated Ann Keen in Brentford and Isleworth. Two photo calls and two meetings. Two days later, Eleanor Laing, a Tory backbencher, is leading a debate on women and the UN Agency –

UN Women, headed by the former President of Chile, Michelle Bachelet. Eleanor makes a robust speech. I refer to the situation here and abroad and how the international conventions of equality apply. Already we have evidence of the government's policy disproportionately affecting women. The Women's Budget Group, an independent group of academics, has examined the coalition budget and found 'an immense reduction in the standard of living and financial independence of millions of women' and a return to the 'male breadwinner, dependent female model of family life'. I then turn to what is happening in the Arab Spring. Women appear to have had enormous success but I warn that, as I saw in Afghanistan, all too soon the usual male patterns emerge. In Egypt, the eight legal experts appointed by the military to review the constitution don't include a single woman. I have been speaking to women activists in Cairo in the past few days so I praise their efforts, outline their aims and their appeal to the international community for solidarity and support. I end by referring to the renowned international writer, Nawal El Saadawi, who I was privileged to meet in the '80s and to whom I've just spoken again. She has inspired generations of Egyptian women, been banned, and imprisoned. Today she is still fighting and was one of the organisers of the 8 March demonstrations in Cairo.

Two separate sessions to talk to Tory MPs who were identified as strong supporters of changing the hours. A core group of half a dozen Tories will be essential if we are to plan a campaign with real prospects of success. All looks promising and Elizabeth Truss, another Tory woman who was in business, can't see why we shouldn't work nine to five – she's just raring to go!

Over several days we get statements and debates on foreign affairs, mainly focused on Libya and the Middle East. William Hague and I have a good exchange on women's involvement.

Cameron comes to the House to explain the UK mission in Libya as part of an international operation to protect the people of Benghazi in their uprising against the Gaddafi regime. Ed makes a thoughtful and questioning response but gives support to the UN-sanctioned action. There is no question this time of legality. The request has come from the Arab League and there is a UN resolution. I vote with the government. There are just thirteen votes against.

After Cameron promised no top-down reorganisation of the health service before the election, he has now given Andrew Lansley a free hand and everything is up for grabs. I've held meetings with all the stakeholders in my constituency and the vast majority are totally opposed. Labour calls a debate and John Healey, our shadow minister, sums it up when he says, 'Only one in four of the public back giving profit-making companies free access to the NHS, two-thirds of doctors think the reorganisation will lead to worse not better patient services.' I intervene on Lansley to express my GPs' views but it is water off a duck's back. There's a great deal of anger in the constituency and a march is organised for 26 March.

We assemble at the Lewisham Clock Tower with the NHS SOS banners to travel to central London for the 'March for the Alternative – jobs, growth and justice'. People are angry that a party that didn't win a majority should be following such an ideological right-wing agenda. Unlike after the 1992 defeat, party activists are not in despair; rather, people are up for a fight.

Jos Bell, who is heavily involved in the NHS SOS campaign, is providing us with lots of information on the health service. One particular issue is the problem of midwives. David Cameron promised 3,000 before the election, so I raise the issue at health questions and invite the Secretary of State to tackle this rather than his reckless reorganisations. Lansley is under a lot of pressure and we intend to keep it up. Sure enough, a 'pause' is announced by the government in the progress of the Health and Social Care Bill to allow them to 'listen, reflect and improve' the proposals. Round one to us. A week later, 96 per cent of delegates at the Royal College of Nursing Conference back a motion of no-confidence in the Health Secretary.

A landmark day for me. It's bitterly cold and the ground is solid but I turn the 'first sod' (they pre-prepared it!) at the new Deptford railway station. I can hardly believe we've got started at last. Some other good news.

The council have turned down Betfred's application to take over the former Halifax building on Deptford High Street.

Then the House rises for Easter and we are off to Italy for ten days, mainly spent overhauling the garden and pruning shrubs. Frank has taken to buying paperbacks for me to read and generally it's a good choice – contemporary women authors picked out from the *Guardian* reviews. He meanwhile reads endlessly about films (his passion) in between the detective novels he's often reading for the second time. My only problem is once I start a good book I find it very hard to stop so I read very quickly and forget it just as quickly. Back to do a surgery and then we divide the Easter days between visits to my mum and Aberdeen.

First day back and the Foreign Secretary is updating the House on developments in the Middle East and North Africa. The Gaddafi regime is continuing to kill its own people. The international community has agreed that the regime has lost all legitimacy, and that the national transitional council should be offered further support and that the UN Special Envoy should take forward an inclusive political process. The military situation is dire, with very heavy action in several cities. I'm concerned about the use of cluster ammunition and depleted uranium weapons (used by the coalition in Iraq). I ask Hague whether depleted uranium weapons have been, or will be, used in this conflict. (Depleted uranium weapons leave a lasting legacy affecting civilians long after the conflict is over.) Hague says he would be very surprised if such weapons were being used, and: 'I think I can give her the reassurance she seeks.' An odd reply.

27 April: Another all-party meeting on the hours. We're getting through the mammoth task of canvassing hundreds of MPs. We get organisers for all the Labour Party regions and for shadow ministers. Matthew Hancock, Mary Macleod, Karen Brady and Elizabeth Truss are organising the Tories; Jo Swinson and Tessa Munt the Lib Dems. I send out another email to MPs on behalf of Ann Coffey and myself thanking those who responded to the

hours questionnaires, and referring to the personal canvassing still going on. Now we are asking if people would support moving Private Members' Bills to Tuesday evenings if they were to finish earlier. I attach a pro forma giving two options.

In Lewisham, real progress on the libraries. Ian Mills has organised an amazing campaign in Blackheath to convert the existing Age Exchange into a library alongside its current functions. It requires huge financial investment but he's obviously up for the challenge. Other libraries are to be run by Darren Taylor, including Crofton Park, but no solution has been found for the New Cross library. The campaign to save New Cross has been focused on getting the council to change its view and protesting when it doesn't. What we need is a group who can do something practical but, while Blackheath is one of the richer wards in Lewisham, New Cross has people with few resources and no money. Then, to my surprise, two women, Gill Hart and Kathy Dunbar, come forward. They strike me as much more reliable than the leading lights of the local campaign and have a very practical approach. The challenge is daunting but I hope we might be able to take things forward. After months and months of difficult discussions and negotiations the library finally opens and is run by volunteers a few days a week. The problems have been immense, beginning with who actually owned the building, then the problems of disrepair, then the issue of the books that had been removed. The local group led by Gill and Kathy do not have charitable status but will operate under the umbrella of another local charity. Lewisham Council have agreed a licence and for it to be rent-free initially, though money has to be raised for all the running costs. Telegraph Hill councillors Joan Millbank and Paul Bell have been very supportive and I think it's going to work.

Although there are no local elections in London this year, there is the referendum on the Alternative Vote system for parliamentary elections. It's been a terrible campaign. Confusion, bad temper and, in the case of the 'no' campaign, a total lie about the cost of introducing AV. I'm in the 'yes' camp. But Cameron has decided to throw everything into the 'no' campaign and there are some notable Labour figures supporting him. Much as I would love to think we will achieve a majority Labour government in the future, I believe all the trends are in the wrong direction. Progressive governments can be delivered by coalition and we need to be protected from future right-wing majority Tory ones. (We will go on to lose the AV referendum by two to one.) Only in six areas of London, Oxford, Cambridge, Edinburgh Central and Glasgow Kelvin did the 'yes' vote poll over 50 per cent. In my constituency the vote was split 50:50. This is a really bad outcome but Scotland is a disaster. Under a voting system that was supposed to guarantee permanent coalition, the SNP have taken twenty-two constituencies from Labour and formed a majority government. Iain Gray, the Scottish Labour leader, resigns immediately. Everyone is stunned – it's bound to have repercussions for West-minster. In England, the position is quite different, with a great success for the party and for Ed. We've taken 857 council seats from other parties.

Heidi has a Westminster Hall debate on English as a second language. The coalition are changing the rules and linking learning English to 'active benefits'. The problem with this is that refugee and asylum-seeking women who have children are not required to sign for active benefits but are perfectly entitled to claim what are now termed 'inactive benefits'. This is hugely dam-aging and discriminatory for women who are generally bringing up children alone. I know how difficult it is for women without English to access services and it's not uncommon for a primary school child to accompany his or her mother to a GP to explain the woman's symptoms and the doctor's advice. In my speech, I relate a meeting I had with Somali mothers where we found seventeen children and young people not attending school. Their mothers had no idea how to get them into school as they couldn't speak English. The children had had no schooling in Somalia and the mothers came to me for help as so many of the boys were turning to crime. This is such a short-sighted policy, saving the government pennies. Women are critical to family life and integration into the host community, yet stupid barriers are being erected by a myopic government.

I am participating in a debate called by Jeremy Corbyn. Jeremy has campaigned long and hard on housing. He, along with Karen Buck, Oona King and others, myself included, frequently warned the Blair government that we were not doing enough to provide new, affordable housing in London. The new starts we did make in our later years now look likely to be the last in the line.

Today I'm making a wide-ranging speech on behalf of my constituents, over 900 of whom are in temporary accommodation with 16,000 on the waiting list for social housing. The coalition changes to housing benefit, the draconian cuts and the plans to raise housing association rents to 80 per cent of market value will force people into arrears and evictions. Increasing rents already put decent private lettings beyond the reach of so many of my constituents, some of whom earn as little as £10,000 a year. House purchase is not an option and if rents go to 80 per cent market value, a household will need an income of £35,500 for a one-bed flat and £83,700 for a four-bed, yet the average median wage in Lewisham is £26,500. Lewisham Council housing re-lets dropped by 30 per cent this year. If re-lets continue to drop along with new build decreasing as a result of reduced grants, the available supply will be dramatically reduced. I urge the government to look again at the practicalities – it is not that Londoners cannot earn their own living and pay their way – they can – but they must have access to social housing.

I go to my long-time hairdressers, Michaeljohn, and then to the House car park to pick up the car and drive to my mother's with Frank. On Saturday we are all going to Cardiff for the wedding of Ben, my sister's elder son. He and Tracey have been together for some years and now have a daughter, Annie, and her older step-sister, Abi. The wedding venue is nicely decorated. Everyone looks their best, including Susan in a fine hat. A very enjoyable day.

We've heard from the Boundary Review. Five constituencies are to go from London and it's calculated from the electoral register that Lewisham will only have 2.2 constituencies. There will be major changes in seats and probably many new constituencies crossing borough boundaries and splitting existing communities. It's not looking good. Extensive consultations ensue between the party HQ and all the constituencies involved. We submit our proposals and, in October, the Boundary Commission reports again. They have created a Deptford and Greenwich constituency, which means we keep Evelyn, New Cross, Telegraph Hill, Brockley and Ladywell, acquire Blackheath from Lewisham East (Heidi), Greenwich and Blackheath Westcombe from Greenwich and Woolwich (Nick Raynsford); lose Lewisham Central (which we've just acquired) to a new seat in Heidi's area, and Crofton Park to a new seat, which would be in Jim Dowd's area. There will be uproar in Greenwich at the idea of splitting their historic town centre down the middle. We consult again and alternative proposals are put to the Boundary Commission. These proposals are a compromise for everyone but better than the Boundary Commission's. A huge amount of time, energy and expense will go into this exercise, which will eventually be abandoned in January 2013 when the Lib Dems and Tories fail to agree on Lord's reform – an essential part of this deal.

An early-morning meeting at Lewisham Hospital and then a tour. There are always funding issues and loads of pressures but the CEO, Tim Higginson, is always calm and focused. Now they're facing their biggest cuts ever – 7.2 per cent. They've done everything they can to cut their £220 million budget but still need to find £3 million. They are asking the government for more time. In the intensive care unit for premature babies I talk to parents who can't praise the hospital enough. I also look in on the state-of-the-art Birthing Centre where 700 babies have been born over the past year.

On Tuesday I'm visiting the job centre. We've lost the battle over provision in Deptford and all I can do is try to ensure my constituents get properly looked after at Rushey Green, where the majority will have to go. I'm assured by the manager that they have one of the best rates of getting people into employment, but I later learn that Deptford had the best of all. No tracking is in place to monitor what happens to people from Deptford but I've asked for further information and will be monitoring the unemployment levels.

I now regularly attend DECC questions and debates and get my first opportunity to make a couple of interventions on Chris Huhne, who's moving

the second reading of the Energy Bill. I'm still convinced their Green Deal*
for household energy efficiency measures is not going to work, and my own
experience of talking to the banks suggests they're not interested. However,
he's convinced it will go ahead.

A week later, Chris Huhne is up again. Our ground-breaking Climate
Change Act put in place an independent Committee on Climate Change with
responsibility for advising government on the limit on emissions required in
each four-year period out to 2050. The fourth carbon budget for the years
2023–27 has to be agreed by next month and Chris Huhne is reporting that
the government has accepted the committee's advice. This is good news but I
tackle him on renewables where there are few signs of the government making
real progress. The problem for him is that so many of the Tory backbenchers
are opposed to renewable energy measures. After the statement it's the Localism Bill and I'm on the list to speak.

David Lammy has tabled an amendment to the Bill on betting shops,
which I am supporting. In an effort to head off our amendment, Greg Clark,
the Planning Minister, says that he will be undertaking a review of 'change
of use' and will look at our concerns. We make our speeches nonetheless. It's
such a clear-cut issue he could easily accept an amendment now.

I describe the situation on Deptford High Street – I'm reading from
local campaigner Sue Lawes's briefing – at 'No. 14 we have Better Betting, at
Nos. 34–40 we have William Hill, at No. 44 we have the Money Shops for
payday loans, at Nos. 49–50 we have Ladbrokes, at No. 55 Paddy Power,
at No. 60 we have Fish Bros, pawnbrokers, at No. 70 we have Coral and at
No. 72 H&T Pawnbrokers'. I stress that this is an area of great deprivation
and 700 local people have signed a petition calling for a change in the law.

The Tory Philip Davies gets up to attack us saying 'betting shops go where
there is a demand for them', completely ignoring the exploitative aspects of

---

* It never really got off the ground and is cancelled by the incoming Tory Secretary of State
in 2015.

betting facilities where people are poor and often desperate. Our amendment is defeated when the Tories and Lib Dems vote it down.

A statement on Trident, which is profoundly depressing, by the Defence Secretary, Liam Fox. The government have made the decision to take Trident renewal to the next stage. They have approved what is called 'initial gate', investment that will allow submarines to deliver the nuclear capability well into the 2060s. What a thought – another fifty years of Cold War mentality.

I ask the only question I think worth asking, 'Given the phenomenal cost of this weapons system and given that we will commit future generations to it … I believe people have the right to understand whether it can be used. Will the Secretary of State tell the House what are the circumstances in which Trident would be used?' Liam Fox replies that the whole point is the uncertainty and 'we would hope that such weapons would never be used'. But that *is* the point – when and how? What if there *were* – why is that *never* discussed?

The House is rising for the Whitsun recess so I allow myself a rare treat and visit the Chelsea Flower Show. I absolutely love the show. If I were twenty years younger, I might embark on a second career as a garden designer. I've designed three gardens of my own.

President Obama is on a state visit to Britain and the next day he addresses both Houses of Parliament in Westminster Hall. I'm a real fan of both Obamas and there's no doubt Michelle is a great role model for young black women as she proves with aspiring school girls in north London. Great to see Obama in the flesh. I'm sitting at the end of a row and am decidedly disappointed when he leaves by the other aisle, shaking hands as he goes. I'm not normally a groupie but he really is charismatic.

A routine week of briefings and meetings follows, including one with the team working on a major construction project to introduce new tunnels and sewers that will go under my constituency – the Thames Tideway Project. Following objections to their chosen site in Greenwich, they tell me they are now looking at a site adjacent to St Paul's, Deptford, to erect a venting shaft.

I've accepted an invitation to visit the Evelina Children's Hospital at St Thomas', which isn't in my constituency but treats some very sick children from all over south-east London. A moving and inspiring experience. I talk to the organ transplant team in the children's kidney unit. Such wonderful work and dedicated people. I also talk to some parents and children about the transformation in their lives when a child is taken off dialysis and given a life-saving transplant. I've always believed my organs should be donated but I'm ashamed to say that I've never signed up. I promise to do so. I'm contacted later with a request to table an EDM for organ transplant week, which I am very happy to do, calling on the government to tackle organ donation and transplantation during the reform of the NHS. In addition to saving and transforming lives, it's estimated £500 million a year could be saved by a tripling of deceased organ donation.

Ever since the election, which added an extra ward of 10,000 electors to my constituency, we have been inundated with casework. All the remaining advice agencies are in a similar position and we are dependent on a small number of lawyers who take civil legal aid cases. Now the government proposes to remove legal aid from areas of law that will directly affect our constituents. Ken Clarke comes to the House to make a statement and I tackle him on this point. His reply is nonsensical: 'The taxpayers' money cannot be used to give access to justice to large numbers of people in large areas of law where the ordinary citizen on an ordinary income would not think they could afford to embark on it.' I usually rate Ken Clarke but this is awful – it really will be a denial of justice.

Once again the poor are paying the price for a Tory-led coalition, and more and more work will fall on MPs' caseworkers. This is a constant topic of conversation among inner-city MPs in the tea room. A number of colleagues have successfully applied to IPSA for additional funds to employ more staff. I decide to make an application myself based on the additional 10,000 electors. To my and Nicky's great relief it is agreed and we put out an ad.

14 June: Jamie Reed, our shadow minister, has forced Caroline Spelman to come to the House to answer an urgent question on the waste review. He notes

that it has signally failed to introduce the weekly collections that were the obsession of Eric Pickles, the Communities Secretary, and the subject of pre-election promises. Jamie quotes the ridiculous Pickles: 'It's a basic right for every English man and woman ... to put the remnants of their chicken tikka masala into their bin without having to wait a fortnight for it to be collected.' I tell Caroline I suspect she eats rather less tikka masala than the Communities Secretary and ask her if she doesn't think the remains would be better in a food waste collection than a black sack.

A statement by Andrew Lansley follows on the outcome of the NHS Future Forum that deliberated during the 'pause' on the Health and Social Care Bill. He has been forced to take back the responsibility for the NHS that he sought to divest himself of under the Bill. I tell him that I remember the time when people died on waiting lists and that Labour targets transformed that. I ask him if he will make a specific promise about waiting lists under his jurisdiction? He says, 'We will not let waiting lists rise.'

A good run on oral questions over the next few weeks. I table for several ministries on a regular basis but only occasionally come out in the shuffle. But now I'm on for DEFRA, DECC and BIS. The first two are on my old hobby horses of waste and insulation but the latter is on higher education. I've been pursuing the issues of funding for conservatoires through written questions as well but there is still huge concern at Trinity Laban as to how government financing will be structured in the future. I've got a technical question for David Willetts and a reply that indicates he is now addressing the issue. This is not only crucial to Trinity Laban but all the other conservatoires and drama schools across the country that train so many of the people who enrich our national culture.

1 July: Deptford First tea party. We're holding it at Besson Street gardens – a lovely venue, much improved for community use by NDC money. A perfect day and a very good turnout. Everyone is assembled in the gardens for me to say my customary few words. I take out my phone to turn it to silent and

it rings. It's my sister. My mother has had an accident and they are all at the hospital. I establish that she's alive and say I'll ring back as soon as I can. Heart thudding, I go on, make my speech and apologise for the fact that I have to leave. I get into my car, fortunately parked nearby, and drive to Bristol. My mother looks terrible and has eighteen stitches in her face and head. I stay the weekend until I'm sure she's going to recover.

5 July: The anniversary of the founding of the NHS. The Lewisham SOS NHS petition now has over 3,000 signatures, so Heidi, Jim, Jos and Barbara, campaign organisers, myself and others assemble for a photo at the DOH and then hand it in for the Secretary of State.

All hell has broken out over the *News of the World* phone-hacking scandal, which has rumbled on since Coulson resigned. On Monday, *The Guardian* reported that the voicemail of the murdered schoolgirl Milly Dowler was hacked by the *News of the World*, where Rebekah Brooks (a personal friend of Cameron) was editor. This is so sickening I can hardly believe it. The *News of the World* always was a ghastly newspaper but this is quite depraved. There's no escape for Cameron. He has to come to the House to condemn their actions.

Furious exchanges at PMQs when Ed opens a broadside on Cameron on the hacking of the phones of the 7/7 victims, the parents of murdered schoolgirls Holly Wells and Jessica Chapman, and that of Milly Dowler. He calls for a full independent inquiry.

Several exchanges later, Ed raises the question of the Rupert Murdoch bid to buy BSkyB, a deal that Labour has consistently said should be referred to the Competition Commission. Cameron defends his government's actions robustly, saying all the proper processes have been followed. In Ed's final question, he tells Cameron he must 'accept that he made a catastrophic judgement in bringing Andy Coulson into the heart of the Downing Street machine'. Uproar in the Chamber.

Cameron announces he will set up an inquiry under Judge Leveson. Ed makes an appropriate response.

Next day, News International announce the closure of the *News of the World*.

Andy Coulson and Clive Goodman are arrested and charged. Other arrests follow and, on 15 July, Rebekah Brooks resigns as CEO of News International. Two days later she will be arrested and Sir Paul Stephenson, the Met Commissioner, also resigns. Now, with Murdoch's reputation in the gutter, Jeremy Hunt is under extreme pressure to block the deal. Hacked Off, the new pressure group calling for an inquiry, has gained a very effective spokesperson in the actor Hugh Grant, and 38 Degrees is spearheading an email campaign. We receive over 500 emails – Jeremy Hunt over 150,000.

On 13 July, Ed tables a motion calling for News Corporation to rescind its offer for BSkyB. In an astonishing move, the Tories and Lib Dems announce they will support it. I've never known a U-turn like this in twenty-four years in the Commons. Just before the debate is due to begin, News Corporation withdraw their bid. High drama indeed.

We're working hard on the hours and receive a boost when first Mumsnet and then the Hansard Society publish research on the attitudes of MPs to their work and family life. Today I'm meeting the Hansard Society and tomorrow Mumsnet with Elizabeth Truss and Jo Swinson.

The Hansard Society survey of new MPs found that 56 per cent had taken a pay cut and 80 per cent were dissatisfied with IPSA. The average working week is sixty-nine hours plus travel, 63 per cent spent in Westminster and 37 per cent in the constituency. But constituency casework takes 28 per cent of their time, with 21 per cent constituency meetings and 21 per cent in the Chamber. The Hansard Society comments: 'They are largely satisfied by how Parliament works, but the hours, the division of time between Westminster and their constituency and the effects of IPSA's expenses system combine to make the maintenance of any semblance of family life a struggle for them.'

The Mumsnet survey finds over a quarter of MPs saying the stress of the job has made them consider quitting and nearly two-thirds say being an MP has had a negative impact on their family. Almost half want an end to late-night sittings. To cope with life in Parliament, MPs reported moving house, moving children's schools, relying on partners to give up work and even divorcing.

We send letters to campaign organisers on the sitting hours telling them we now have returns for all parties with a small majority for change. The Procedure Committee is expected to produce proposals for consideration in October so we will need to mobilise hard after we return from summer recess. We stress this will be the only opportunity in this parliament to make a change.

I present a Ten Minute Rule Bill on betting shops. The Bill requires the Secretary of State to create a new planning use class for betting shops, give power to local authorities to assess demand for premises in that use class and to place a cap on the number of betting shops in any one area. My speech coincides with the appearance of Rupert and James Murdoch before a select committee. Laurence Robertson, MP for Tewkesbury, opposes my Bill with a paean of praise for the betting industry, finally suggesting that my Bill 'represents a solution looking for a problem'. Some of the Tories seem to have no grasp of reality and unfortunately there's no come-back on a Ten Minute Rule Bill speech. He says he won't call a vote – no doubt the MPs attending the extraordinary hearing upstairs do not want to lose their front-row seats.

At the committee, Murdoch apologises but blames his staff. He gets a foam pie thrown in his face, causing the grilling to be suspended while the perpetrator is arrested.

Recess begins with my usual series of constituency meetings and catch-up, including the Mayor's Monday morning liaison meeting with the three MPs, and on this occasion with our health partners as well.

We hold a Deptford station meeting in the train carriage – an enjoyable sunny breakfast meeting – discussing some of the issues the Cathedral group has encountered with Lewisham council and the historic ramp. I'm also interviewing for my additional employee who will share casework with Nicky and provide some assistance to Vicky and Jessica. I appoint Matt Dix.

5 August: I get my hair and nails done for tomorrow. Heidi is marrying her long-term partner, Martin, who has been the most amazing support to her, while having a significant career himself. A delightful day. Heidi looks lovely, everyone's happy and the venue – the Victorian conservatory at the Horniman Museum – is perfect.

Off to the shuttle and the drive to Italy. We haven't booked ahead and have a bit of difficulty locating somewhere to stay. We're travelling through Switzerland and decide to stop in a small town as dusk is falling. We drive into the hotel car park when my phone rings. It's the Borough Commander from Lewisham, Jeremy Burton.

Yesterday, there'd been very serious rioting in Tottenham sparked by protests following the shooting of a black man, Mark Duggan, by police the previous day. Apparently since we left there've been copycat actions all over London and they've spread to Brixton, Croydon and now Lewisham. Youths have been attacking the police, blocking the high street and setting fire to cars. Jeremy says he believes they have the situation under control – the shopping centre closed early as rumours of trouble reached Lewisham. So far no loss of life but a very dangerous situation. He'll keep me updated – I explain where I am.

Frank and I order some food and review the situation. Nothing we can do this moment. I text Heidi. She has just arrived in New York for the start of their honeymoon. An hour later we're told that everything is under control, though shops have been looted and property destroyed.

Next day, we have to make a decision on what to do. I get a police update and talk to my staff. The situation in Lewisham is calm, if shocked, this morning. Mayor Steve Bullock tells me that by the time the council workmen arrived to clean up, ordinary people had been there before them clearing the streets around shops and homes. Losses are considerable. There's lots of CCTV footage of looters walking out of high street shops with valuables and things like trainers. It's not all youths either; there are pictures of elderly people and women with buggies stealing what they could.

Poor Heidi. She's been up all night and now says she should go back. I really don't think she should consider it, but then we find that her shop front office has been broken into and looted. She has to return for the sake of her staff if nothing else.

Sure enough, Parliament is to be recalled for Thursday. I have to make a tough decision. We can complete our journey, arrive in Pisa this evening and try to get a flight. It makes no sense to drive back and back again and I'm not leaving Frank to drive all the way to Italy even if we could find a Swiss airport and a flight for me. Given that everything is under control in Lewisham and my office and staff are safe, I decide not to return. Of course, some people will expect to see my name in the line of speakers in the debate on Thursday but long experience teaches me that no backbencher will get more than five minutes and Heidi can speak for Lewisham. I feel so sorry for her – she and Martin have sacrificed a lot for her career but ruining a honeymoon is just too much. I keep in constant touch with my staff, the police and council. Thank goodness for the BlackBerry. Constituents are emailing and I ask Jessica to send the emails on to me so that I can answer them personally. Whenever I'm in the passenger seat, I'm permanently on the BlackBerry.

On holiday at last but hardly relaxed.

1 September: Back in the Commons. It's Matt's first day and he'll be accompanying me to my surgery tomorrow as Nicky is on leave. Toyin, our intern, is leaving, having successfully applied to Goldsmiths. It will be good to have four full-time members of staff for the first time and hopefully not have everyone working under intense pressure.

In the morning I have a meeting with the Lewisham town centre manager for a debrief on last month's riots and subsequent developments. When the centre closed early on 8 August it was their first live test of their evacuation procedures and they managed to get everyone out in eight minutes. Overall, I think the police did a good job and they are now going through 1,200 CCTV images. Eighty-three businesses suffered losses and 118 people have been arrested so far.

The report and third reading stages of the Health and Social Care Bill. The government have put forward hundreds of amendments with little time to debate them. They appear not to have listened at all and are bent on rushing everything through. The Lib Dems are appalling. They say in debate they want change but then vote down the line with the Tories. Our only hope now is the Lords. Hundreds of emails from constituents over the course of this Bill but I've nothing positive to tell them.

How unusual. I've been called in for pre-operative tests on a Saturday. I didn't realise hospitals did this but it's a good idea.

14 September: I give my evidence to the Procedure Committee. In the past eight months we have done an enormous amount of work, which I have turned into tables that give a clear picture of an appetite for change. We've surveyed 554 MPs and have a 70 per cent return. Forty-six per cent favour an 11.30 a.m. start on Tuesday instead of 2.30 p.m., 40.5 per cent a 10.30 start on Tuesday, Wednesday and Thursday, and 60.6 per cent are in favour of one or the other. We are *not* proposing to work fewer hours. I also indicate the range of opinion as a few people wanted much more radical changes than we proposed. All, however, wanted *more* control over their time and *more* predictability in the parliamentary timetable.

I point to the survey recording the exhaustion felt by many MPs. I argue for PMQs to be moved to Tuesdays on the back of a return to an 11.30 a.m. start and Fridays to be clearly designated a constituency day for all.

I caution against moving Private Members' Bills to a Wednesday as this would just add to the long hours culture. I also refer to the fact that the House worked perfectly well following the Cook reforms and would do so again. I answer a barrage of questions in which all the counter arguments I have heard a hundred times are put forward yet again. I stress the proposals are modest and designed to make MPs and Parliament more effective.

A back-bench business committee day and Tory Amber Rudd and Labour's Heidi Alexander have tabled a motion on the UK response to famine relief in the Horn of Africa. When the Secretary of State, Andrew Mitchell, speaks, he refers to women as the prime victims of famine and allows me to intervene to ask him to ensure that DfID continues the work we did, in recognising that women are the majority food producers in Africa, yet often have few rights and decision-making powers. I ask him to ensure that his department puts women at the heart of its policies. He replies with vigorous reassurance – I like Andrew, I think he has a genuine commitment to development.

The House rises later for the conference recess, and I go off for a very pleasant dinner with my former civil servants.

Jessica, Matt and most of my friends are off to party conference but I'm having a short break with Frank before going into hospital for my shoulder operation.

Two important constituency developments. The outline planning application for Convoys has been submitted by the developers and Lewisham Council has decided to resurrect the Church Grove site as a possible travellers' site, despite the fact that all the Thurston Road travellers have now been rehoused. Lots more protest meetings on the cards.

10 October: The House returns amid some extraordinary reports of the behaviour of the Secretary of State for Defence Liam Fox and a personal friend who he's taken with him on official trips. He is making a statement in the House. I get the chance to intervene to say that in my experience as a minister the Diary Secretary would record in the margins of visits where the minister intends to be. I ask if this was the case 'on the eighteen separate occasions on which the SoS met his friend on official visits'. A very confused reply. I think he'll be gone before the week is out!

Next day, off to Guy's Hospital for my operation. Once I've had it I'm told I have to exercise it immediately and I'm given a series of diagrams and a rubber strip. I am told to take the heavy painkillers before each exercise session. At home I start the regime. The pain is excruciating. As I exercise the tears stream down my face. There is nothing I can do. Of course, I can't sleep and the pain goes on and on. I have a week and a half at home and then do a surgery at the Albany, still in pain. A follow-up appointment on 24 October and then it's business as usual.

27 October: A Labour opposition day devoted to the health service, where I can refer to my recent experience of having asked my surgeon directly whether I should have the operation as there was a small risk of making things worse. I tell Lansley I was able to trust this man when he answered because he wasn't having to think about the competitiveness of his hospital or his department, nor whether the bed I was to occupy might be better filled with a private patient. Pointless though it is, I urge him to abandon the Bill. I make two more interventions, one on the competitiveness and the fact that the cap on private patients is to be removed, and tackle a Tory enthusiast with the fact that the PM had said prior to the election there would be no top-down reforms of the NHS.

I stay in the Chamber for the second debate of the day on environmental protection and green growth, when I remind people of the constant opposition we faced in government from Lib Dems and Tories who opposed wind farms in their constituencies. I challenge the minister on the millions the Secretary of State has offered councils to return to the weekly collections they had abandoned to boost recycling. I ask him to get the money diverted to waste-food collections, which my local authority would introduce if they had the money. He dodges the question.

31 October: A CPA request for me to take part in a discussion with visiting parliamentarians. Today it's a delegation of members of the South African Parliament's climate change committee. I leave promptly to get to the Chamber for local government questions to challenge Greg Clark yet again on why, given his championing of localism, local people don't have the right to say no to more betting shops. He says he's looking at it carefully and will have more to say. What does that mean?

Then comes an urgent question from Caroline Flint, who has forced the government to come to the House to explain the changes they have peremptorily introduced to feed-in tariffs without waiting for their own consultation to finish. It will have a devastating effect on the solar industry, which has been growing apace. By reducing the rate of return by 50 per cent, the government is undermining the viability of schemes such as the one I visited recently, where the housing charity Peabody installed solar on the roofs of tenanted small houses to great success, helping some of the poorest families to reduce their electricity bills. I ask what the implications are for them. A convoluted reply that ends: 'We simply cannot give an open cheque for unfettered deployment.' This is such a blow. We still have only 3 per cent of the solar deployed in Germany where its spectacular growth has been built on feed-in tariff.

I'm having a heavy day. The report stage of the Sentencing and Punishment of Offenders Bill is next and the debate is on civil legal aid services. I am much exercised on this subject because of the way it will impact on constituents who are going through an acrimonious divorce. The minister's reply is typically harsh – 'People should not rely on legal aid for carving up the family assets or settling contact issues.' The minister then gets into real difficulty explaining how legal aid will still be available in domestic violence cases. His Tory colleague and solicitor Helen Grant (a good woman) puts to him that 'uncertainty, especially at the beginning of court proceedings, will create even more hardship for the victim' and urges him to be more precise.

I follow through asking if he's made an estimate of the savings, given people who would have obtained legal aid in cases of violence who will now not do so. He replies this definition is not about saving money. I despair.

Many others intervene, urging the minister to understand that making the legal aid application conditional on the victim seeking an injunction or having already reported the crime to the police is to fail to understand that many victims believe such action will only increase their torment. Evidence should be accepted from other sources, which is what the aid agencies have pressed upon MPs. I quote from Gingerbread in my constituency and my own experience of constituents in violent relationships. Helen Goodman points out that the reality is, on average, women will experience twenty episodes of violence before they go to the police. But the minister is unmoved.

Theresa May makes a statement on gangs and youth violence. This is so hypocritical when youth services, which had been massively improved, are among the first things to go in local authority cuts. I ask her if she thinks there might be a connection between the fact that since she came to power the community safety and youth offending teams in Lewisham have been cut by 20 per cent and the number of victims of knife crime has gone up 40 per cent. She doesn't, of course.

2 November: We're on the third day of debating the Legal Aid, Sentencing and Punishment of Offenders Bill and I'm determined to speak. I describe the kinds of problems brought to me and my caseworkers and why some of the time we know legal assistance is required. There's the person who's been wrongly deprived of a benefit who may be sick or have complex needs. We can work out what might be possible but we cannot spend the hours necessary to assemble the paperwork for an appeal. Then there are the tenants unfairly deprived of housing benefit or the home owner in difficulty with mortgage repayments and those living in properties in great disrepair who cannot take action against their landlords. So many people who will be deprived of justice. Under the government's proposals a worker unfairly dismissed will only be eligible for legal aid if they can prove discrimination. Will people be told, in my multiracial community, 'Could you dress this up as discrimination so you can get legal aid?' I then turn to two specific cases where legal aid for immigration issues will no longer be available. My constituent's sister died in Africa and her young son was brought to the UK by a visitor. His aunt is looking after him and wants to adopt him, and Lewisham Social Services agrees. But the child has no legal status in the UK and the Home Office has refused to assist. They need legal aid. Another constituent was trafficked to the UK, repeatedly raped and gave birth to twins. She has been here for

twelve years, effectively living as a fugitive. Again she has no legal status and no paperwork. She needs legal aid. I appeal to the minister Jonathan Djanogly to think again. I look to the Tory front bench. He's sitting there laughing.

Bonfire night: We've been in our London home for three years and this seems a good time to invite our neighbours with whom we share our freehold and who we meet at occasional residents' association management meetings. We cook a variety of delicious sausages from a local butcher together with baked potatoes and lots of wine before going out to watch the local fireworks. Good cheer all round.

William Hague is updating the House on events in the Middle East and the declaration by the national transitional council that Libya is liberated. The situation in Syria, however, is deteriorating. He then turns to Israel and Palestine. He condemns Israel's eighth announcement in six months of more settlement building and the withholding of tax revenues from the Palestinian Authority. He refers to the latter's application to the UN for recognition as a state and tells the House that the government will abstain on the vote in the security council. Clearly the government doesn't want to cross the US, who have said they will use their veto. Hague goes out of his way to praise the Palestinian Authority and the leadership of Mahmoud Abbas and his Finance Minister Salam Fayyad but still says the government will abstain. For what it's worth, I tell him an abstention is as good as a no and suggest this will only encourage Hamas and undermine President Abbas. Hague does not agree.

Autumn recess and I'm really busy in the constituency with both new and old issues. There have been shootings on the Honor Oak estate, probably drug turf war related, which have caused a great deal of anger and fear. Years ago this was a troubled area for crime, but Labour investment improved so much of the housing and environment and the community centre became a real hub of activity. People don't want a return to the past so I chair a local residents meeting, organised by Cllr Joan Millbank, to address their concerns.

I also chair a public meeting for a local group called 'Don't Dump on Deptford'. They've set themselves up to oppose the Thames Water plans associated with the super sewer. Thames Water make a very unconvincing case.

Then I get to meet with Richard Rogers, who is working with Cathedral, the developers for the Deptford station land. He arrives on the back of a motorcycle – apparently a taxi scheme – previously unknown to yours truly, but he tells me it's the fastest way to get around town!

My high spot of the month is a meeting of local campaign group 'Deptford Is' at the Shipwright's Palace on Convoys. I'm thrilled by the presentation of plans by local boat builder Julian Kingston and his friends to build a replica seventeenth-century ship on the Convoys development. It's an amazing ambition and everyone is inspired by the vision and the honouring of the history of the site. Making this dream a reality is almost too difficult to contemplate, but we have to try.

Another CLP dinner to raise funds for next year's GLA and mayoral elections. Neil Kinnock is our guest speaker and all the food is being made by party members. The venue is unusual; it's held in the body of a church that is vast and gothic but quite atmospheric. It's a bitterly cold night and when I arrive it appears there is no heating. I'm correct; it's not just that it hasn't warmed up – it's not on. We run round to the vicar's house to be confronted with a notice on her front door that this is her day off and she cannot be contacted. We telephone but to no avail. No one can find any means of getting the central heating to work. It's just appalling. The hire wasn't cheap and people have turned out in smart clothes. I'm mortified when Neil arrives. The evening is ruined as far as I'm concerned, but he remains infinitely cheerful, begins his speech with amusing anecdotes about me and lifts the spirits as he lays into the coalition. We manage to make quite a lot of money but I have never been so cold at any function in all my life.

21 November: The House is returning this afternoon but Frank and I are up early. We've got an invitation to a private viewing of the Da Vinci exhibition at the National Gallery at 8.15 a.m. Despite my being so hopeless at getting up this really is worth it and such a privilege to see in a calm space.

Grant Shapps, the Minister for Housing, has come to announce the government's new strategy. It includes help with deposits for aspiring home-owners. He says that instead of a £40,000 deposit, people will only be required to find £10,000. I tell him that my constituents cannot raise £10,000 and ask him how long it will take for the 17,000-plus families on Lewisham's waiting list to secure affordable decent homes.

He expresses his sympathy and goes on to tell me that in London the deposit would be £60,000, but he hopes I'll welcome the fact that under his scheme deposits will come down to £15,000. These Tories just don't live in the real world.

Two opposition day debates give me an opportunity to raise constituency issues again – the lack of a job centre, with 1,000 young people now unemployed, and the change in the feed-in tariffs, which has decimated the Peabody Trust's forward investment plans. But nothing comes of it.

It's ten years since we invaded Afghanistan. I can't believe where the time has gone. I'll be at the APPG tomorrow for a discussion and reflection on where the country is going. The international community is meeting in Bonn next week and today I'm telling William Hague the views of Afghan women recently surveyed – two-thirds think their lives have improved but nine out of ten fear a return to Taliban-style government. I ask him to make clear in Bonn that women's rights must not be traded away in any future peace settlement. A positive reply: 'A sustainable peace in Afghanistan will not be achieved without the extensive and whole-hearted commitment of the women of Afghanistan.' Let's hope they get the chance.

The following day I'm up at DECC questions raising feed-in tariffs yet again. I tell Chris Huhne that, at Peabody, the four jobs and the eight apprenticeships are at risk and at Breyer, which supply their solar panels, 150 jobs are at risk. How can he square that with his claim to support a green economy? He replies that he's putting the solar industry on a sustainable basis for growth!

Little of interest in the House in these few weeks of December and very light whipping so I can attend lots of constituency meetings and events,

beginning with a Cockpit Arts exhibition and sales from their Deptford studios. This is such a joy and there is always something lovely to buy. I do have
some business to do, particularly a meeting with Aileen Buckton at Lewisham
Council, where I'm trying to get more resources for the New Cross library.

7 December: A very early start for a breakfast meeting at Lewisham College with the East London Chamber of Commerce, where I have to make a
short speech, then a catch-up with the Principal. All is not going well with
the merger of Lewisham and Southwark colleges and she asks me to contact
Simon Hughes. Southwark is a failing college so this is their only hope but it's
pretty complicated and I'm fearful it might bring down Lewisham College.

I go into the House but don't get called at DfID questions. Then I meet
the Lewisham Pensioners' Forum, who have come to the House to lobby us,
and leave mid-afternoon for a meeting with the mayor about the travellers'
site. Next morning, I call into the Calabash Centre to have a chat during their
Christmas lunch, then to the House for a vote and back to Brockley for the
CLP Christmas Social. Friday it's the degree ceremony at Laban and Sunday
evening will be the Christmas Carol Service at All Saints. In between we go
to Norwich for a Christmas meal with Frank's son and his family. By Monday
I'm knackered and I've got a dentist appointment first thing in the morning.

Jessica and Vicky have been attending sessions on Facebook, Google
and Twitter. MPs are being encouraged to embrace social media but I've
absolutely refused. I'm not at all sure it adds anything to MPs' accountability. People already contact me in their thousands and we are very accessible
through the surgeries and the meetings I attend. My observation is that on
Twitter most MPs' followers are from outside their constituency and either
they themselves spend far too much time tweeting or they hand it over to staff
to do it for them. I've just not got the time to waste and I don't have the same
desire for self-publicity that many of my colleagues do. I'm also thinking I
probably won't be standing again so it doesn't matter if people think I should
do it. A visit to the Samaritans for an update, a mince pie and a Christmas

message. Then my last surgery of the year. Saturday, a lovely evening with Sabire and Mustapha.

19 December: Can't believe it's Christmas week already. I post some last-minute cards as always and tie up loose ends. Wednesday morning a site visit at Convoys Wharf and that's it. All done for yet another year.

## 2012

Some months ago the Chief Whip asked to speak to me. I wracked my brains to remember some misdemeanour but, no, she was enquiring whether I would accept, if I were offered, a damehood! I couldn't have been more surprised. I said I was grateful and would get back to her. I'd never been a fan of the honours system myself and was often surprised by the names on the lists. Frank said to do whatever I wanted, but I needed to know he didn't disapprove. What would my friends think? Then I thought of wonderful women such as Judi Dench and Helen Mirren – I'd quite like to be in their club! Would I get a barrage of criticism from the peace movement radicals who still popped up from time to time? In the end I thought how thrilled my mother would be – and then what a feeble reason that was. Finally, I decided I did want to accept and take the consequences. I duly appear in the New Year Honours list.

10 January: Today I arrive in the Commons as 'Dame Joan'. Lots of congrat-ulations to add to the messages I got when the list was published. 'There's nothing like a Dame...' being received rather too often! Some people bow but it's all very good humoured – no snarls in sight. Lots of nice cards in the office. It's health questions and there's a brief on my desk that's come in over the recess on Group B streptococcus, which is one of the topics on the Order Paper. I hurry to the Chamber and stand when the question is reached. A bit of a thrill as John Bercow calls *Dame* – pause – Joan Ruddock.

Next day it's PMQs. I haven't been successful in the shuffle but I have a question in mind if John will call me. He calls the three men who have been knighted and just as we reach the end of time he calls me, emphasising 'Dame' once more. I ask my question about a woman of thirty-two who has lived alone for the past eight years and has been forced onto housing benefit because of redundancy. Her benefit has now been cut by 50 per cent to the shared accommodation rate. I ask the PM, which does he think most likely: 'that her landlord will reduce her rent by 50 per cent or that she will be made homeless?'

The PM replies sarcastically that he supposes he should congratulate me on my preferment but goes on to say that he profoundly disagrees with many of the things I have tried to do, 'mostly to disarm Britain one-sidedly'. He tries to continue in that vein but Harriet and Angela Eagle sitting on the front bench start up a chorus of 'answer the question'. As Simon Hoggart says in his sketch the next day, the combined sisterhood 'alarmed him enough to force him to give her a proper response'. Possibly a first?

Anne Begg opens a debate on parliamentary representation arising from the Speaker's Conference. She points out that, despite progress, the House still has only 22 per cent female members and 4 per cent ethnic minority members. Furthermore, the proportion of people with disabilities (Anne herself uses a wheelchair), who are gay, bisexual or transgender falls far short of the make-up in society.

Tory Adam Afriyie argues against positive action, believing that rapid progress is being made – two black Tory MPs in 2005, twelve now. I point out to him that the Fawcett Society has calculated that for women at present rates it will take fourteen parliaments, nearly seventy years, to get equality. I relate some of my own experiences and quote experts but also argue for parliament to continue to reform itself in the hours, the calendar and procedures. The good thing is all three party leaders have committed themselves to increasing diversity – so maybe more progress next time.

I do a tour of the Olympic park on a rather grey morning. It looks really impressive and everything is going to schedule. I'm not going to apply for tickets but I'd like to see it when it's finished.

I get back in time to go to the Chamber for a general debate on high streets obtained by a Tory MP. It gives me the chance to put on the record that my Ten Minute Rule Bill is on the list for this Friday and ministers could let it through and provide the means to end the proliferation of betting shops. Of course they won't.

I spend Tuesday in Westminster. My Bill is too far down the Order Paper to be reached but I need to be there. First up is a Bill on daylight saving introduced by Tory Rebecca Harris. Her colleague, Christopher Chope, has been the scourge of Private Members' Bills ever since Eric Forth died. Now he tables hundreds of amendments. The proceedings begin at 9.30 a.m. and end at 2.30 p.m. Rebecca gets to speak for a few minutes at 11.15 and Chope, aided and abetted by a few other obnoxious colleagues, is on his feet for virtually all five hours. He calls a couple of votes that reveal there are 124 MPs present and voting against him and a dozen followers. Total farce. When my Bill is called the government whip shouts 'object' and that's that. A wasted day.

Chris Huhne has been caught out over the feed-in tariffs. The high court has ruled against DECC for making changes when a consultation had not been concluded. I rub his nose in it at DECC questions and ask him to apologise to those whose plans have been ruined and whose jobs have been lost. He doesn't, but says lessons have been learned.

1 February: Every Bill that comes before the House brings measures that are damaging to my constituents. Today it's the Welfare Bill and the minister is speaking on the benefit cap. The focus is always on people who don't work and how it is wrong for them to get more money than people in work. I tell him I can agree, but people have no choice. The acute housing shortage means landlords charge higher and higher rents. If people can't get housing benefit they will become homeless. He counters with, why should people on £35,000 pay for those who are not working? I point out to him that half my

housing benefit claimants are *in* work. He then says he's not aware that it is paid to families on £35,000. I can't do the sums immediately but yes it is – a couple with two children and a rent of £250 a week will receive housing benefit. Extraordinary he doesn't know his own legislation. Tory members say people should move, but where to? Surrounding boroughs are just the same and Croydon is looking to move its homeless families to the north of England.

2 February: Chris Huhne resigns, charged with perverting the course of justice over a 2003 speeding case where he got his wife (Vicky Pryce) to say she was driving. What a waste of talent. He's replaced by Ed Davey.

Friday, and I'm in the constituency as usual. I visit one of the studios on the Faircharm Estate, Creekside. They're all under threat from their landlord, Workspace, who want to redevelop the site into smaller units from which they can make more money. 'Based Upon' makes huge pieces of art from metal. I am amazed at the beautiful objects I'm shown. They make bespoke pieces, mainly for corporations and rich people, and export a great deal. Their craftspeople come mainly from Goldsmiths. There's only one piece I don't like – huge blue metal wall sheets – commissioned for Putin's office! I do so hope the company won't have to leave. I'm supporting the tenants, together with the council, who want to retain these amazing industrial work spaces in Deptford.

Polly Toynbee has an excellent article in *The Guardian* on health so I decide to dash into health orals. I begin to ask the minister if she's seen the article by the respected journalist Polly Toynbee (David Cameron referred to her as such). Tories fall about laughing and keep it up in the way they love, but I can't be put off and the Speaker intervenes. The article tells of a waiting list clerk who has resigned after seventeen years because she has been asked to adopt a range of devious methods to make sure that people coming up to the eighteen-week targets are taken off lists. The minister confirms she hasn't seen the article and says when she was in opposition she saw admin staff forced to do things they didn't want to do in order to tick boxes! Does that make it OK then?

An opposition day debate. Andy Burnham is demanding that the Health Secretary publish the national risk register so that we are able to see what the experts consider are the risks of the massive reorganisation that is being undertaken. In London, the Strategic Health Authority has published their risk register on the transition. It makes extremely disturbing reading. There are eighteen risk areas and I quote several. On the abolition of the primary care trusts next year, it says the results 'may be poor both in securing the best health outcomes for London's population and in maximising value for money'. On patient safety and clinical quality, it says the consequence 'could be poor or unsafe care for patients, and loss of public confidence in healthcare in London'. I acknowledge that the point of a risk register is to enable mitigation measures to be proposed but even after this is done, half the original red risk areas are still red and in all areas the risks after mitigation are still amber.

I point out that £21,000 has been spent in London already, reorganising the Primary Care Trusts (PCTs) and the number of patients waiting more than eighteen weeks has gone up by 73 per cent. I conclude by saying we now face rising waiting lists, a fragmented service, a focus on finance, profit and private patients and poorer outcomes for those who cannot pay or refuse to use private health insurance.

A week later a debate on the Water Industry (Financial Assistance) Bill. This is a perfect opportunity for me to put our objections to the Thames Water plans for Deptford. Caroline Spelman explains that in London, waste water containing untreated sewage overflows into the Thames between fifty and sixty times a year, which is why the super sewer is necessary. I agree with her but set out the case against venting it in Deptford. Even as I make the case I am struck by how strong it is and the fact that Thames Water have simply retreated from their preferred site Borthwick Wharf Greenwich in the face of middle-class pressure and turned to dump on a deprived community instead.

The Deptford site selected is a triangle of open space bounded by three streets, one of which is Church Street, a major dual carriageway that goes through the heart of the Crossfield housing estate. This small green is an oasis in a concrete jungle and provides an outdoor escape for the primary school adjacent to it. Thames Water proposes four years' work onsite with a permanent legacy of four main ventilation columns at six metres high with associated controls and maintenance requirements. Reasons given for choosing the site – over Borthwick Wharf – include relatively good access and fewer potential effects on residents, visitors and business amenity. Yet Borthwick Wharf is on the river, enabling materials to be brought to site and spoil removed easily by barge. No traffic impact assessment is provided and no data on the number of households and businesses affected at either site. In Deptford, the impact on the 260 children at St Joseph's Primary School is both direct and severe, as it is on the adjacent Grade I-listed St Paul's Church, the most significant historic building in Deptford. Closing the two north-bound lanes of the dual carriageway is a prescription for chaos and danger. As for the school, both indoor and outdoor activity will be impacted over a period equivalent to the majority of a child's school life.

Planning consents have already been granted for thousands of new homes close to the chosen site, adding to traffic congestion and air pollution. The planned work will put the Crossfield amenity green out of action for years. Already 1,300 people have signed a petition opposing the plans.

I leave the debate feeling really angry. On any objective criteria Thames Water's case doesn't stand up. I wish I had the resources and time to investigate this – I wouldn't be surprised if it wasn't about some planned millionaires' riverside development on the wharf.

A terrific morning at the official opening of the Deptford Lounge. Lots of primary school children in fancy dress, performing for us. It's amazing to see small black, white and Asian children rhythmically drumming away with confidence and obvious pleasure.

After the ceremony I'm meeting up with a delegation of visiting Vietnamese

MPs. This is another request from the IPU, who try to send visitors to nearby constituencies. They are fascinated by the high street shops, which include Vietnamese supermarkets, overflowing with fresh vegetables and every Vietnamese packaged product imaginable. They go in for a chat. Then I'm about to pass by an old-fashioned shop with a vast quantity of bric-à-brac when one of the MPs asks to go in. It's long and narrow with the shopkeeper sitting right at the back. The visitor wants to know if the old man has knitting wool. He does. Unopened boxes of big balls of soft wool in a few pastel colours. I'm completely taken aback when the MP buys the lot! Apparently his wife is a keen knitter and this wool is hard to find and expensive in Vietnam. I just hope she likes the colours!

An opposition day on jobs and growth in a low carbon economy. Caroline Flint opens and documents the great progress made under our Labour government. 'When we left office the UK was ranked third in the world for green business ... on this government's watch the UK has fallen ... to thirteenth.' The fact is we did begin the transformation of our economy to low carbon, we did double renewable energy (from a very low base) and did become a world leader in offshore wind. I content myself with interventions.

Frank has got a terrible welfare case that just has to be highlighted. For the first time in a year of applying, I'm on the Order Paper for PMQs, so I decide I'll take it up. The mother is a single parent with a daughter with cerebral palsy whose mobility allowance has been cut off despite her inability to walk to school and take care of herself. Knowing Cameron lost his son to cerebral palsy I wonder if I should say muscular dystrophy instead, but I can't really do that in case I subsequently need to give details.

This case so demonstrates the injustice of the Cameron reforms, and I'm so angry at him for targeting people with disabilities when he has had such a personal experience. I ask if 'he is proud of the decision to remove all disability benefits from a ten-year-old child who can hardly walk and who cannot toilet herself because she has cerebral palsy? Is he truly proud?'

Immediate barracking from the Tories and shouts of withdraw.

He replies he is not cutting the money that is going to disability benefits. Some of my colleagues shout 'answer the question', to which he replies that he knows how long it takes to fill out the form and the government are going to have a proper medical test so that disabled people can get the help they need more quickly.

I guess some people will think I made this up as I didn't refer to 'my constituent'. Quite a bit of abuse on social media but this is the harsh reality of what the government is doing and Cameron is responsible. I write to him presenting the facts in full, albeit without naming the family, who Frank is supporting through an appeal. Forty per cent of these appeals are successful, restoring benefits after many months of trauma and hardship. So it proves with Frank's case. I'm uncomfortable with having raised it, but it's nothing to compare with what so many people with disabilities are going through.

Another day without government business so we get another opposition day on health. I recently tabled a written question asking for details of waiting lists for private patients. I was told that ministers had no information, so I ask how 'NHS patients can believe their waiting times are consistent with their need for treatment when there are no figures to indicate what happens in the private sector'. No answer is forthcoming. Obviously there *are* no waiting lists, and given it's mainly the same surgeons operating, it stands to reason removing the cap on private patients can only lengthen the lists for NHS patients. The whole thing is so depressing.

More 'Drop the Bill' petitions to be handed in at the DoH. The local newspapers are always willing to print a picture of this health campaign and Jos and co. keep up the interest. Next day, Andy Burnham obtains an emergency debate on whether the House should defer consideration of the Bill until after disclosure of the NHS transitional risk register. Excellent speeches from everyone on our side. David Anderson speaks passionately, accusing the government of contempt for democracy, having promised no reorganisation, contempt for the House in starting to abolish the primary care trusts before the legislation is agreed, and contempt for all the people who work in the NHS. He lists those who oppose the Bill – The British Medical Association, the Royal College of Nursing, the Royal College of Midwives, the Royal College of Radiologists, the Royal College of Physiotherapists, the Royal College of Paediatricians, Child Health and the Faculty of Public Health. He castigates the Lib Dems, prompting other colleagues to quote Simon Hughes's angry tweet: 'Lib Dems have accomplished almost nothing on the NHS Bill'. I add my two pennies' worth on the London risk register. The interminable coalition speeches go on until the vote, when all the Tories and Lib Dems vote against our motion.

21 March: Budget day. The House is in uproar as George Osborne delivers an extraordinary Budget that reduces the top rate of tax for the very rich but imposes a raft of new taxes, quickly dubbed the 'granny tax', the 'pasty tax' and the 'church tax', not forgetting the 'caravan tax'. Five million pensioners will pay an extra £3.3 billion in income tax over the next four years as the age-related allowance is phased out. Ed makes an excellent response, challenging members of the Cabinet to put up their hands if they will benefit from the decrease in the top rate of tax. The ridicule that follows Osborne's other taxes results in the reversal of both the pasty tax and caravan tax two months later. I stay in for the debate.

Stephen Williams is lauding the Lib Dems' success in getting the general tax threshold raised. I can't resist intervening to say that he voted to reduce the income of the average family with children by £530 from the beginning of next month, and there is nothing in the Budget to compensate for that. He repeats his mantra about the threshold, oblivious that the effect is much less than the cuts and that the poorest workers are already *below* the threshold. The hypocrisy of these Lib Dems knows no bounds.

I'm now able to do more work in the constituency. This Friday it's a school visit, a surgery and canvassing. Vicky and Joe organise very efficient sessions in our target wards, which I join whenever possible. Turnouts are good and we have more activists than ever. On Sunday we canvass in Lewisham and Harriet Harman joins us, prompting an even greater turnout. After the session we all retire to the Talbot for lunch before going out again in Brockley.

I've had the oddest email from a constituent. She and her partner booked tickets for the Olympics last year. Subsequently she found herself pregnant and contacted LOCOG* to say she expected to have a few-weeks-old baby at the time of the event. The reply was so extraordinary that I tabled a question for today's DCMS questions. I relate the story: 'She was told to purchase an extra seat for the baby, but that the seat could not be guaranteed to be next to the parents.' Gales of laughter. I go on to tell the minister if 'airlines allow babes in arms at 35,000ft, surely it is possible in a stadium.' I ask him to intervene and he wisely responds, 'I will not even attempt to defend that one', and promises to sort it.

Less amusing is a lot of correspondence from carers and families about the bed linen laundry service and incontinence pads for the elderly and sick at home. These are being restricted and very poor families and lone pensioners are just unable to fund these purchases. I raise the issue at the next health questions and the minister agrees to make enquiries.

A Convoys meeting and a huge breakthrough. After my meeting with Edmund Ho, the London property director, it was agreed that Hutchinson Whampoa would organise a proper consultation onsite to hear peoples' views. It soon became clear that they would want to present *their* ideas to the community but I've argued forcefully that they need to listen first. We've now got an amazing programme agreed. Hutchison Whampoa will erect a marquee and toilets and provide food for a lunch. Exhibitions and tours of the site will be available in the morning, and after lunch Edmund Ho and I will make short introductions followed by the new master planner Terry Farrell. Then William Richards, Roo Angel and Bob Bagley, Julian Kingston and youth group Second Wave will give presentations on their visions for the development. I'll get to make the closing remarks. Locals turn out in force alongside the stakeholders we've

---

\* The London Organising Committee of the Olympic and Paralympic Games

invited. Amazingly, the sun shines on us. We really feel we've done ourselves proud. Terry Farrell responds positively. I think we might be getting somewhere.

On Saturday I'm at the official opening of the Telegraph Hill skateboard park. This has been the result of a marathon of meetings and protests and negotiations but now it's very well constructed at the top of the park, providing an amazing facility and lots of happy families and young people. I *don't* have a go!

In the evening it's the opera at Blackheath Halls. Now that we live nearer we attend a few events at the Halls, including my going to the Friends AGM. Given that we've reached the second year of the coalition, I've made up my mind not to stand again and I'm quietly ticking off those things I might be able to do more of once out of Westminster.

For years I have been involved with Dignity in Dying and have supported the cause of assisted dying. I've also chaired the APPG and we have sought to gauge support for a Private Member's Bill. As part of our strategy, Tory MP Richard Ottaway has secured a back-bench debate. Richard moves the motion to welcome the DPP's policy for prosecutions in respect of cases of encouraging or assisting suicide. As agreed with Richard, I have tabled an amendment, which I will move later. He begins by saying it is forty years since the subject was debated on a substantive motion. Under English common law, suicide was a criminal offence and some of those who attempted suicide were prosecuted – in 1953, thirty-three people were sent to prison. In 1961, suicide was decriminalised but it became an offence to assist a suicide – a unique case of a criminal offence of being an accessory to a non-criminal act. It carries a sentence of up to fourteen years in prison. The DPP was given discretion but no one knew how it was exercised. In 2008, Debbie Purdy, suffering from multiple sclerosis, asked the High Court to rule whether her husband would be prosecuted if he accompanied her to Dignitas to end her life. The Law Lords instructed the DPP to make clear the factors he would take into account when reaching a decision on whether or not to prosecute. Factors against prosecution include the fact that the person who committed suicide was of sound mind prior to the act, the assistance was only minor and the suicide was reported to the police. Richard is now seeking to get this recognised by Parliament.

The problem with the DPP's guidance is that it could be superseded by a new DPP. Keir Starmer is a liberal appointed by a Labour government but he could easily be replaced by a hardliner on these issues. I and Dignity in Dying are keen to see the guidance put into statute. My amendment simply 'invites the government to consult as to whether to put the guidance on a statutory basis'. I argue that placing the policy in statute would signal in the strongest possible way that Parliament agrees that those who maliciously or irresponsibly encourage suicide should be prosecuted, but it is not normally in the public interest to prosecute an otherwise law-abiding citizen who helps a loved one to die on compassionate grounds.

People make passionate speeches for and against but it's fairly predictable, until my Labour colleague Paul Blomfield gets to his feet. He relates how his father took his life at the age of eighty-seven last year, when suffering from terminal lung cancer. Paul says,

> I am sure that what drove him to end his life when he did was the fear that if he did not act while he could he would lose the opportunity to act at all. If the law had made it possible, he could, and I am sure he would, have shared his plans. He would have been able to say goodbye and die with his family around him and not alone in a carbon-monoxide-filled garage. He ... deserved better.

Later in the debate, Heidi is called. She quotes an open letter from Geraldine McClelland, who died at Dignitas. She wrote: 'I am not sad that I will die today. I am angry that, because of the cowardice of our politicians, I can't die in the country I was born in, in my own home ... If you feel anything when you read this letter, then please turn it into a fight to change the law...'

The debate lasts for five hours. The strength of opposition is such that the group of us supporting my amendment decide it is best not to press it to the vote. Richard has the last word as the mover of the original motion, saying, 'In the twenty-four years I have been an MP, I have witnessed many dramatic debates, but this has been probably the most remarkable in which I have taken part.' The House agrees Richard's motion. We are all drained by the experience and I fear, despite the support of over 80 per cent of the public, assisted dying itself will never get through the Commons.

I'm canvassing for the mayoral selections with just a few meetings, including the important launch of Lewisham Creative Industries. We have so many talented artists of every kind in Deptford, now with our own Deptford X, Brockley Open Studios, Brockley Max, APT, the Art House, activities around the Train Carriage, Cockpit Arts, Midi Music, Goldsmiths College and of course Trinity Laban. There's also a growing digital industry and lots of young people with ideas. It makes a lot of sense for Lewisham Council to invest in generating employment in this field.

16 April: I table an EDM congratulating Aung San Suu Kyi and her party on their success in Burma's (Myanmar) election. Campaigning for the first time since her long years of house arrest, her party has won forty-three of the forty-five seats they contested (forty-eight were vacant). Aung San Suu Kyi herself has been elected – what a triumph.

I've had a meeting with the Speaker, who has always supported the Burma campaign. Cameron has invited Aung San Suu Kyi to visit Britain and we agree it would be great if she could be invited to address Parliament. The only problem is that invitations normally go to heads of state. We agree I'll give it a go at business questions on Thursday. I ask the Leader of the House if he is able to make a statement about her visit: 'Perhaps he might agree with me that an invitation to address both Houses of Parliament in Westminster Hall would be a fitting tribute to her and a great honour to us all.'

Sir George says he thinks such an invitation is above his pay grade but will make sure it goes to the relevant authorities in view of her record on human rights. Now it's up to John.

Shocking news has been coming in from Iraq and I go to FCO questions to raise it. I ask if the government is aware that at least sixty-five executions, including women, took place in January, and that the Iraqi criminal justice system largely depends on confessions routinely extracted by torture? 'Surely that is a legacy that shames us all.' A reasonable answer from Alistair Burt, who says the government will continue to work to oppose the death penalty and continue to work for the improvement of justice in Iraq.

Three-line running whips every day, so I attend lots of meetings of interest groups in the Commons but I do get let out to go to a very special memorial service for Stephen Lawrence. It's nineteen years since his murder. In January this year, two of the four white youths, named the day after the murder, were sentenced to life. Their trial was made possible by the lifting of the double jeopardy rules.

I'll spend today and the next two days canvassing for the mayoral and GLA elections. Lots of support and it's going well for us, though Ken's campaign hasn't been as good as we'd hoped. On election day I'm just having a conversation with a local police officer about witnesses to a stabbing when my phone rings. I can see it's my friend Mirella, the director of dance at Laban. Very unusual for her to ring and not text so I take the call. Marion North is dead. I'm so so sorry. She was a towering figure in contemporary dance, transforming dance training in the UK, fighting to establish academic status and public funding for students. She leaves Deptford with a magnificent legacy and will be replaced by Anthony Bowne, who proves a very worthy successor.

I think about my long association with Marion as I finally leave polling day to take the last flight to Aberdeen. Frank and I are having a two-day break before returning on Saturday evening to pack for a Parliamentary visit to Palestine.

Sadly, the election proved that Ken was less popular than the Labour Party and Boris more popular than the Tories.

I draft a letter to all my party members for Jessica to send out with my report to the 10 May GC, which I will miss. While expressing our disappointment at

Ken losing, I tell members it was a very good night for the party. Len Duvall, our GLA candidate, got an extra 12,000 votes and we gained four seats in the Assembly. I believe this is testimony to the fightback we've made. Despite media hostility, Ed has stood by his principles and been right on the economy, the squeezed middle, responsible capitalism and taking on Murdoch. I tell them we must aim to make this a one-term Tory government.

Frank and I join our colleagues John Denham and Ian Lucas together with Kate and Duncan from Caabu (Council for Arab–British Understanding) and Palestine APPG for our flight to Tel Aviv. We arrive in the afternoon and get driven to our hotel in East Jerusalem for our first briefing with the British Consul General.

Over the next few days we will do many of the things I have done and seen before, with the exception of Gaza, which is still under siege and which we cannot visit. Much though I wanted to come and much though I love this part of the world, I am profoundly depressed. The UN briefing paints a tragic picture of the constant clashes between Palestinians, Israeli settlers and the Israeli security forces. Palestinian protests at the closure of gates in the infamous wall, denying them access to their agricultural land, and against the constant expansion of settlements on their land, have resulted in 651 people injured in the first four months of this year and three people killed by the Israeli forces. Settler violence against Palestinian property continues with more than 2,000 olive trees vandalised. Demolition of Palestinian homes by the Israeli authorities also continues apace, with 209 this year, displacing 418 people. In Gaza, the situation is worse – twenty-nine Palestinians killed by Israeli forces and an average of ten people injured every week. Some 1.6 million Gazans are dependent on a single power plant and Israeli restrictions on fuel to Gaza mean power cuts of twelve hours a day. The ongoing blockade affects even the most basic commodities being brought into the strip – pasta, tomato puree and artificial sweeteners are banned and cooking gas is heavily restricted. Eighty per cent of the population now rely on UN aid.

It is so shocking to receive these briefings from people on the ground who are not politicians but international, neutral civil servants. No one disputes

Israel's right to demand security for itself or to take action against those who fire rockets from Gaza into Israeli territory, but this collective punishment, the illegal wall and the lack of justice for all Palestinians is an absolute outrage.

We meet with the Palestinian Prime Minister and other key players. Fatah is a secular party and a member of the Socialist International. They point out that the Palestinian Authority has done all that the international community asked of it. They hope that perhaps the Arab Spring will lead to more democratisation in the Middle East, which could in turn affect US attitudes. At present they say there is no coherent position in the Quartet. Any initiative by the Quartet that annoys Israel is vetoed by the US. We are told that Hamas accepts the two-state solution and has started arresting and imprisoning those firing rockets into Israel. We go on to visit Hebron and meet with the governor. He explains the restrictions faced by the indigenous Palestinian population, then we go to see for ourselves. There are over 100 road blocks and checkpoints manned by heavily armed soldiers. The heart of the city is like a fortress. We have to go through turnstiles to approach the centre, then we see the main street with its abandoned homes and shops. Beit Hadassah, a settlers' compound, is 100 metres from Palestinian homes. As a consequence, most of the main street is literally cut off to Palestinians, who are not allowed to walk there. As elsewhere, the adjacent roads are for set-tlers' cars only. It's the worst thing I've seen outside Gaza. The atmosphere is terribly intimidating and it's not difficult to understand why youths would throw stones in protest.

Then we head to Ramallah to meet Saeb Erekat, the long-time head of negotiations for the PLO, who is still the recognised interlocutor for the Pal-estinians. He negotiated the Oslo Accord with Israel in 1995. I never cease to be amazed by the fortitude of Palestinian politicians. Which one of us could live a lifetime of such oppression and still be willing to keep trying?

Israel itself is a democracy subject to the rule of law and under the Geneva Convention Israel has responsibility for the Palestinians. Currently, 4,800 Pal-estinians are in Israeli jails, including twenty-seven Palestinian MPs, most of whom are being held without charge. A third of the prisoners are currently on hunger strike in a mass protest that began on 17 April. Ever since the Israeli occupation of Palestine began in 1967, Palestinians have been charged under military law and tried in military courts.

We have a meeting with Defence for Children International (DCI) who recently published the testimonies of 300 children. Arrangements have been made for us to visit Ofer military court. Outside high railings and the guarded entrance there are impoverished Palestinian families waiting in the hope of seeing their children. There is also a group of well-dressed women who we discover are Israeli human rights observers. They explain they can do nothing but they come to bear witness each day to the injustice of their state. What a remarkable thing to do and no doubt courageous too.

We are let in through the railings and barbed wire and sit in the simple court room. Armed soldiers and court officials mill about, as do families with children – everything seemingly quite chaotic. The first prisoners are called in – all children, handcuffed together and their legs shackled. They immediately look around the room, finding relatives and trying to communicate with them. People call out. The judge, a woman, seems totally disinterested and hardly looks up. It's clear nobody has any respect for the proceedings. People move about holding discussions while the boys gesticulate to their families. It's explained to us that at their trials deals are done rather than evidence produced.

We see the trial of one sixteen-year-old boy. Like many young Palestinian people, he is malnourished and looks much younger than his years. He's very nervous. He's accused of stone-throwing, car damage and making two petrol bombs. The judge asks if the accusations are true. He looks utterly bewildered and looks to his family for help. People shout out but his lawyer is doing a deal and tells him to say yes. The boy had already served four months – he gets a further twenty.

Increasingly, Palestinians on the West Bank are organising peaceful protests against a variety of Israeli actions. We visit one such community where they protest against being denied access to their agricultural land near the settlement of Karmei Tzur every Saturday.

I have a long conversation with Hamda, whose husband is a member of the committee that organises the protests. She tells me her son Yusuf was arrested when he was twelve for throwing stones. He was sent to prison and has been jailed three times since. On the last occasion, soldiers came to the house at 1.30 a.m., surrounded it and banged on the door. They had their faces masked. When let in they seized Yusuf, tied his hands behind his back, made him lie face down and then hit and kicked him. As he screamed, Hamda went to him only to be knocked back by a rifle butt, which fractured her rib. Yusuf was blindfolded and the family forced back indoors, when the departing soldiers threw tear-gas canisters into the house.

Hamda is certain her family is being targeted because of the peaceful protests. Another son, aged sixteen, has been in prison for the past three weeks awaiting trial for stone-throwing. When we leave the house, we have to walk through a group of heavily armed Israeli soldiers.

Hamda's story is typical of those documented by DCI. Following these terrifying night raids, children are taken to police stations often on the illegal settlements where they are questioned and then transferred to the Israeli interrogation centre, which may include further ill-treatment. Once interrogation is complete, the majority remain in pre-trial detention. Children are frequently questioned alone. Most children will eventually plead guilty. The conviction rate is over 99 per cent. Whatever the guilt or not of these children, Israel is in breach of its international obligations on justice. When I ask Hamda what she thinks of the future, she says, 'There *is* no future for my sons.'

Back from Palestine. A surgery and then a completely free weekend. We need it.

It's the foreign affairs day of the Queen's Speech debate and the perfect opportunity for me to speak about the Palestinian visit. Yesterday the huge strike of prisoners ended as the result of Egyptian diplomacy. The Israelis have made concessions, the most important of which is to discontinue the practice of automatically renewing the terms of those prisoners who are held without charge or trial. I ask the government to monitor this promise and redouble their efforts to get peace talks started again.

DECC questions and Greg Barker is expounding the benefits of the Tory plans for a Green Deal. I ask him what's happened to the 30,000 people who applied to Warm Front last year but got nothing despite an underspend in the Budget. Greg is now much more partisan and under pressure so he angrily attacks me about the level of complaints when we were in government. Of course I can't come back to say I fixed the problem and raised the grant levels. Very frustrating. A week later, he has to come to the House to explain the result of rerunning the consultation on the feed-in tariffs. Luciana Berger, our shadow minister, delivers a scathing response, including the fact that it has cost the department £80,000 in legal fees. I remind Greg that when we were in government he always wanted to go further and faster but he's fallen at the first hurdle. I then ask him about social housing and feed-in tariffs because I know this is still a problem. He says it's all OK and of course better than when we were in office – depressing really.

There's a sense that the Procedure Committee is dragging its feet on the Sitting Hours and Parliamentary Calendar inquiry they've been undertaking, so I decide to tackle the Leader of the House at business questions. I ask him if he knows when they might report and if he will ensure that when they do there will be a full debate with amendable motions. He responds – hopefully before the summer recess and structured so that members' preferences can be identified.

Protocol dictates that after asking a question a Member remains seated at least until the next question is asked and answered, so I get to hear Bob Russell on IPSA. Their website reveals that, on 30 January and 8 March, no members attended the board meetings. Apparently, they were available on the telephone and they are paid £400 a day. Of course, there's nothing any of us can do about it. They draw money at public expense while making life more and more difficult for us to do our jobs. The organisation now costs three times as much as the old Fees Office.

On Friday morning I meet a delegation of MPs from Pakistan and Afghanistan who want to discuss options and support for women in Parliament. Then Frank and I are off to France for the weekend. I try not to do weekend foreign travel now I'm no longer a minister but this is special. Mirella and her partner David have invited us to visit them at their French home. We are greatly looking forward to it, but have just heard that their house is uninhabitable due to delayed building work and we're all in a B&B. In the event, the B&B is the special home of some close friends and we all have an immensely enjoyable weekend of simple pleasures in the French countryside, with lots of delicious food and wine. Wonderful to be so relaxed for once.

Off to south Gloucestershire to collect my mother. She's coming to stay in London overnight in preparation for the presentation of my DBE. I've been eating carefully for the past month to ensure I can still get into my wedding outfit, which being a dress and jacket is eminently suitable for the Palace. The wedding hat, however, is far too flamboyant so I commissioned one from a hat-maker in Greenwich market. She's done a lovely job so I'm feeling really pleased. I persuade my mum to wear a fascinator that goes with her black-and-white outfit. My sister wasn't able to come so my friend Pat makes up the party. She's wearing a blue outfit and a hat with exotic plumes. We're all being a bit girly.

As soon as we're inside I'm taken aside and led into the preparation room. There are just a few of us assembled – apparently those receiving the highest honours. I am asked if I'd like a drink – I could do with a stiff one, but it's only water. Then I'm told that I will be the first person to be presented. My heart sinks – what if I do something wrong? I concentrate very hard on all the instructions – when to walk out, when to pause, when to walk again, when to curtsy and how to walk away and where to go afterwards. Prince Charles is presenting, which is a relief as he'll be much easier to talk to. I get hooks placed on my jacket so that the Prince can pin on the medal and the brooch that accompanies it. As we leave the room to walk the long corridors to the function room, I realise the tip has come off one of my heels. I start gingerly walking without pressing that heel down too hard but then realise I'll look like an idiot so I'll have to get on with it – thank goodness it's carpet and not parquet.

I'm standing in the wings at the head of a long queue. The music stops, announcements begin, and I walk. A tense moment but I get there and stand before Prince Charles, who gallantly addresses me by my first name, saying he's particularly pleased to be doing my award. We exchange a few words about the environment. He fiddles with the fixings and then I step back and bob and I'm on my way. In the corridor I'm unhooked and the heavy objects are placed in a box. Then the down side – I join the audience to sit through the presentations of a very large number of other people.

We were invited in advance to sign up and pay for a DVD of the event and unknown to us the clever organisers ensure that each family group is identified and filmed in addition to the person being presented. I'm so glad I did because we get a lovely record of the day with all four of us looking like cats who've got the cream.

I've arranged a very special lunch in a private dining room of a local restaurant. All my closest lifelong friends are there, plus Mirella and David and Keith's cousin Janet and her husband Adrian and, of course, Mum and Frank. We have a very long lunch and end up singing. A truly happy day.

I'm speaking at Goldsmiths for the launch of their Confucius Institute. This is a very prestigious occasion with a large Chinese delegation. Confucius Institutes are dedicated to promoting Chinese culture and language – their equivalent of the British Council. It's the first Confucius Institute in the world dedicated to dance and performance. After the speeches we're treated to a magnificent series of performances from dance, theatre and music. Goldsmiths will now have two Mandarin teachers from China and an exchange of performers between the two countries. A real coup.

The government, in pursuit of their goal of getting immigration down from the 'hundreds of thousands to the tens of thousands', are introducing new immigration rules. Some things we would all support – rooting out sham marriages and ensuring that migrants acquire English. However, I can think of several categories of immigration where the new rules might be adversely applied. I frequently have people in my surgery who have left children behind in the Caribbean or Africa while working here. Often the grandparents who have cared for the children become ill or die and it's imperative the children, now often teenagers, re-join their parents. The new rules set a minimum income that families must have before they can bring a partner with or without children into the UK: £18,000 for a partner, £22,400 for a partner and one child, and £2,400 for each further child. I ask if this will apply to children needing to join parents here. I also ask about another common occurrence – people who want to bring into the UK a very elderly parent who can no longer survive alone abroad. 'Will these people have to pass the English language test before they can be granted a visa?' Theresa May says the minimum income levels will apply to bringing children into the UK, but doesn't comment on the language point, so I write to her for clarification. Over the next few years the minimum income of £18,000 will cause huge hardship in my constituency when women and men weep because they don't earn quite enough, despite being in full-time work, and they cannot get any more hours. People from black families are used to such humiliation, but white people trying to bring future spouses from North America are absolutely outraged.

On Thursday I go to Terry Farrell's office to look at progress on the master plan for Convoys. This team definitely appears to have understood the brief and the need to honour the heritage. I come away hopeful.

Several more constituency events in the week, including Vietnamese Refugee Day and a wonderfully imaginative children's exhibition at the Art House. The art teacher who is based at Myatt Garden School is obviously quite exceptional in the projects and guidance she has given to her primary school pupils. I'd be happy to have quite a few of the exhibits in my own home.

One of the hazards of being a very available MP is that constituents believe that you can trump any authority in the land and solve their problems.

Sometimes this is the case but rarely if the courts are involved. In this internet age, an MP can easily be accused of not helping someone and vilified when in fact the constituent is obsessively refusing to accept something the MP knows has gone through every possible appeal. After so many years of dealing successfully with mentally ill and potentially violent constituents (thanks to my CAB training), I've now acquired a serious male cyber stalker and a hugely problematic woman who has visited my surgery and now harasses my staff on a daily basis.

In the latest development, the female constituent has told a local councillor that she intends to put an axe through my head. Meanwhile, I learn that the man is also potentially dangerous and I have to call in the police and House authorities. I can see that this is likely to be an increasing problem for MPs.

21 June: The Speaker has succeeded in getting agreement for Aung San Suu Kyi to address both Parliaments in Westminster Hall. She is the first non-head of state and first woman apart from the Queen. I'm absolutely thrilled and even more so because I'm invited to the reception for her that will follow.

She makes a passionate plea for Britain and the world beyond to reach out to help Burma at 'the moment of our greatest need'. We give her a rare standing ovation. Afterwards, I get held up and arrive late in the Speaker's House to find that she has retired next door to a private room for tea. The Speaker's secretary ushers me in and there she is, almost alone. I'm asked to sit beside her and take tea. I take her tiny hand and greet her. I'm incredibly moved and feel tears pricking the back of my eyelids. She smiles her enigmatic smile and we chat about all the challenges ahead. One of the most precious moments of my political life.

On Thursday, a very special treat. Harriet has asked me to join her at Wimbledon. She's been invited by the Lawn Tennis Association. I've never been and no longer watch much tennis but this is a must. We're invited to lunch and sit with a few other guests including the singer Tony Bennett. Really interesting guy – rather left-leaning, I think. Then it's the royal box on centre court where we're in the front row! No royals, though Pippa Middleton is seated behind us. We see first Serena Williams and then Andy Murray win their matches and the sun shines all afternoon. Enjoyed myself much more than I was expecting.

The Procedure Committee publishes its report on the sitting hours and the chairman, Greg Knight, invites me to a meeting. We have a helpful discussion in which he explains how the options are likely to be presented. I'm really hopeful my evidence to the committee and all the pressure from us modernisers will pay off. My absolute priority is getting the members mobilised for the votes on the hours. The media are up to their tricks again, ably abetted by some of the backwoodsmen. I quickly draft a memo to go to all our supporters on frequently asked questions, dispelling the myths that we are wanting fewer hours or a four-day week. I advise against asserting that the hours are more family friendly as all families are different but they are *people* friendly, giving the choice on how to spend our evenings. We go over and over the records – we canvass every declared supporter. We warn people that the procedures will be complex and the votes could take hours. There will need to be commitment. The Procedure Committee have recommended the status quo for Monday, Tuesday and Wednesday, so there could be votes on status quo as well as amendments. My office manager Vicky is a star – keeping meticulous records on paper in orderly files.

All the real work is now entering returns from the canvassers. I add some additional canvassers to make sure we can get to everyone before the debate is scheduled. We also work out a team of people who will always stand next to the entrances to division lobbies to point out which way we are voting on each amendment. It will be a military-style operation. (We don't expect any formal whipping.) I write some online pieces based on the evidence we have from the surveys. Interestingly, there's only a small difference between the views of MPs with family in London and those whose families are in their constituency.

9 July: The very last meeting of the Hours Group to plan our strategy for the debate on Wednesday. It's too close to call. We will need to keep reminding

people of the procedure, to look to us for direction to the right lobby and to stay for every single vote – potentially two hours of continuous voting.

The great debate. There are eight motions on the Order Paper and pages of standing orders that would change in line with motions passed. Greg Knight, the chair of the Procedure Committee, begins. He makes a very fair speech, factual and to the point, though he's interrupted every few paragraphs. He explains each motion in turn, including the one on the earlier Tuesday, which I will propose. He gets through in remarkably good time and the Speaker calls me next. This is an important occasion for me. I begin with a little history of the House when I entered: 'Forty per cent of our sittings lasted until midnight and beyond and we were here five days a week. We had no computers, no mobile phones, no email and very little time for constituency work.' Lib Dem Bob Russell shouts 'Utopia!', to which I reply that 'indeed, there were members who boasted about how infrequently they visited their constituencies. A few could recall the days when a brass band and the station master greeted such an arrival!'

I refer to the Procedure Committee and Hansard Society research on MPs' working patterns, seventy hours a week, few holidays and the universally negative effect on personal and family life. I set out the case for starting earlier and take sixteen interventions, the most hostile of which are from Jack Straw and Kevin Brennan on my own side, who want to keep the status quo. This is one occasion when I feel I have an answer for everything – I've spent so much time on it. A sweet moment when the feisty Tory Anna Soubry jumps up to say the Rt Hon. Lady 'has completely won me over to her arguments, which she has made so powerfully'. The only setback is on moving Private Members' Bills from Friday – Greg Knight tells the House his committee will undertake an inquiry into Private Members' Bills next. This is clearly an attempt to head off a vote. Anyway, I end by urging people to vote for an earlier start on Tuesday, Wednesday and Thursday and for moving Private Members' Bills from Friday. I say it's a small change and a small gain but it is an opportunity that will not come to this Parliament again.

The first motion on keeping Monday hours goes through without a vote, then the big one. Frantic marshalling of our supporters as people rush into the Commons from their offices – eight minutes to get through the division lobbies, a total of fifteen including counting. This is critical. We have to defeat the status quo vote before we can vote on my amendment. Explaining procedure in advance to the team who are advising people where to vote has been crucial.

The motion to keep the status quo on Tuesdays is defeated by fifteen votes. Much cheering but we beg people to calm down and listen. My motion for the earlier Tuesday hours is next. The Speaker has to read at length the standing order changes. Then the vote. We win by thirty-four. This is the culmination of years of work for me personally and a dedicated group of modernisers, including Ann Coffey, who's been there throughout. The earlier Thursdays vote is easily won and will enable all MPs to travel to their constituencies that night.

I've consulted with the team and we decide to put the motion to move Private Members' Bills to Tuesday to the vote. We lose by just thirteen. Given the pressure from the whips on this and Greg's statement, it is a remarkable result and more than our canvassing had indicated. The only disappointment in an otherwise thrilling afternoon. Lots of warm congratulations from all sides of the House and a big smile from our modernising Speaker.

Great article by Polly Toynbee in *The Guardian*. I love Polly's writing. She's such a wise woman and not just when she's saying things I agree with. But today I most definitely agree with her and more importantly I think she's being objective. She refers to this week's PMQs.

> Red faced and undignified, Cameron was reduced to pathetic school-boy insults: 'We're for the workers, they're for the shirkers!' Miliband – cool, assured, with better jokes and more agile barbs – was undisputed master of the scene. Some 10 per cent ahead in the polls, Labour is united, focused on the chaos unfolding before its eyes. George Osborne's budget fiasco is still regurgitating, as one Cameron policy disaster after another unravels.

It is astonishing how our fortunes have changed in two years. Ed, as I predicted, has grown into the job. I'm so pleased for him and hopeful that we will indeed be a one-term opposition. Polly's article ends, 'A solid third of the electorate always vote Tory, the rest are to be won by the party with the most imaginative plan for reviving an economy pole-axed by Cameron's ideological austerity.'

Who then would have believed that party would be the SNP?

The House rises for the summer recess. A week of constituency visits and a long lunch with my staff in a local tapas restaurant – we so rarely get time all together away from the pressures of the office.

23 July: An early-morning event at Laban. The Olympic torch is setting off on the final leg of its journey to the Olympic Stadium. It's great to be associated with this and to showcase our wonderful Laban building. Pride, too, in the fact that the torch was designed by a Brockley resident. In the evening the CLP has organised a dinner in a local restaurant to celebrate my twenty-five years in Parliament. Harriet is our chief guest and we make speeches of mutual admiration.

A morning flight to Aberdeen where I watch the amazing opening ceremony of the Olympic Games. Danny Boyle has provided a spectacle far surpassing anything I thought possible. I only wish we were in government and sharing the limelight. On Sunday we drive to London in Frank's car in readiness for our Italian holiday. We're taking Frank's grandchildren, Jessica and Lewis, with us for a week, so I think we will be pretty busy.

1 August: My last constituency appointment before our holiday. I talk to Tim Higginson about the neighbouring South London Healthcare Trust (SLHT). The trust runs three neighbouring hospitals, including the Queen Elizabeth at Greenwich, and is bankrupt. Andrew Lansley has put in a Special Administrator to run the trust. This is very unsettling for Lewisham but it is a completely separate trust and we are holding our own financially, so hopefully we don't have to worry. Famous last thoughts.

11 September: An opposition day debating universal credit. This obsession of Iain Duncan Smith has gone badly wrong at every turn. There are so many questions unanswered. I raise the fact that it appears every employer in the country will have to question HMRC on the circumstances of every employee on a monthly basis and sometimes weekly instead of annually. Surely an added burden to struggling businesses?

Little of interest in this short September sitting, but Heidi and I are up at DCLG (Department for Communities and Local Government) questions to tackle Eric Pickles. He has changed the rules on section 106 agreements, the mechanism by which Lewisham has been able to gain some social housing from private developers. He wants to boost private house-building on brownfield sites but release developers from the obligation to provide a percentage of social housing if it affects their profitability. I tell him this is an insult to my constituents, 18,500 of whom are on the council's waiting list and cannot afford to buy any of the new homes. Pickles gives no ground and the House breaks up for the conference recess.

Frank and I are not going to the party conference – we've seen it all before and don't need to do fringe meetings. Our summer holiday with the grandchildren was great fun but exhausting so we're going back to Italy for a week's rest before spending the rest of the recess working in our respective constituencies.

Still in recess so I'm able to go to the Trinity Laban board meeting. David Lipsey, a Labour peer, has been appointed to chair the board in place of Sir Bob Scott. A major problem has arisen over US funding of students coming to the UK. They have cut us off because we don't have our own degree-awarding powers (we intend to apply). This is a common problem for conservatoires but will have a serious impact as we always recruit in the US. I propose we contact the American embassy and David agrees. When we get the meeting a month later, the Americans agree to reverse the decision.

Frank and I go to Corby for the day to support Andy Sawford, who is fighting a by-election caused by the resignation of Tory Louise Mensch, who only arrived in 2010. There's another one in Cardiff today due to

Alun Michael leaving to contest for the Police Commissioner's job, and another in Manchester where Tony Lloyd resigned for the same reason. We hold both Labour seats and Andy wins in Corby against a stiff UKIP challenge. An excellent result for the party. Next month we'll win another three by-elections in previously Labour-held seats. The fightback continues and we are all in good spirits.

The first Tuesday with the new sitting hours. Lots of cheery greetings as we finish business at 7 p.m.

The multipurpose Waldron Health Centre in New Cross has opened a drop-in café for mothers with new babies and I'm invited to launch it. So many of the mothers tell me how isolated they have been with no family around them, how difficult they've found breast feeding and what a lifeline the Waldron is in bringing them all together. Great pics with the toddlers and new babies. In the evening I've a meeting with Network Rail, Lewisham Council and some local residents to find out what's going on with the Thameslink works at St John's station. The overnight work is causing absolute misery for those nearby. We subsequently arrange a community-wide meeting. Lewisham Council is very supportive and trying hard to enforce the licence agreements, but Network Rail are a law unto themselves. Matt from my office is going to be my link in this campaign and Vicky Foxcroft, who's the local councillor, will take the lead.

19 October: I'm at Malcolm Wicks's memorial service. He died last month while we were in Italy. He was such a good man, a witty speaker and very popular. The huge minster is packed and there are many fine eulogies, including from the presiding cleric who acknowledges that Malcolm was not a religious man.

A sad letter when I get back. Maureen, one of my workers at the Reading CAB, has written to tell me that Jackie Griffiths, my deputy who trained all the volunteers, has died. They are getting together to remember her. I'll not be able to go but later on accept an invitation from Jan David, who was also a volunteer, asking me to speak at their AGM. I go and meet again with the irrepressible

Cherry Church and other volunteers and stay over with Jan and husband How-ell, whose wonderful Welsh accent and anecdotes have us in gales of laughter.

Caroline Spelman, DEFRA Secretary of State, was reshuffled out last month and now we have Owen Paterson – not an obvious environmental champion. He's in trouble already as a disease of ash trees has been found affecting trees in East Anglia. I tell him he should have banned the import of ash seedlings the minute the disease was found in nurseries. I ask for an assurance that the forestry commission has all the resources it needs to deal with the outbreak. He replies I'm being pretty unfair as 'the minute we heard about it we launched a consultation'. People laugh and shout 'look at the evidence'. He says, 'Tomorrow evening I will look at the evidence.' Not his finest hour.

Four days later, Mary Creagh, our excellent shadow Environment Sec-retary, secures an urgent question bringing the minister back to the House to answer further questions. Apparently he has announced a ban on imports and restrictions while on a visit to Staffordshire instead of in the House! Mary points out that experts fear it is the biggest threat to British trees since Dutch elm disease. Mary asks why action wasn't taken in February when the disease was found in a nursery in Buckinghamshire. An internal forestry commis-sion document had warned that 'the government cuts (25 per cent) would leave them with no capacity to deal with the costs of disease'. Seven regional offices have been closed and 250 staff cut.

Current information indicates that the pathogen is airborne and could have reached East Anglia from the Continent. I ask the minister if he has con-tacted the Danish authorities, who have a decade of experience in this field and if he will publish the research that indicates spores could have reached the UK from the Continent. He answers neither question but says there was an international problem identifying the pathogen. Some 100,000 trees have already been destroyed.

Those who lost the vote on the hours are putting it about that the new hours are only an experiment and another vote could be organised before the next election. I'm certain this could not be the case but I go into business questions. Andrew Lansley was such a disaster at health that he's been demoted to Leader of the House, where he's distinctly unhappy. I ask him to quash the ugly rumours that the new hours are a mere experiment and to confirm there are no plans to review the earlier hours. He simply says the House was invited to make a decision and a decision was made. Not helpful.

Matthew Kershaw, the Trust Special Administrator (TSA), holds a briefing session at the House for south London MPs to outline the issues at the South London Healthcare Trust, his powers and the fact that he will publish his draft recommendations on Monday. To our astonishment, Lewisham Hospital has been brought into his considerations. MPs will meet again on Monday, and on Wednesday we will have an urgent meeting with the CEO of Lewisham Hospital.

3 November: We're having dinner with our new friends, Esther and Julius. One of the bonuses of our move has been getting to know and socialise with new friends – not quite what you expect later in life.

We devour the details of the TSA proposals. They are outrageous and we'll be questioning Jeremy Hunt at the first opportunity. Meanwhile, the Lewisham NHS SOS campaign has turned its focus to 'Save Lewisham Hospital' (SLH) and organised a meeting. Hundreds of people turn up, necessitating the use of two overflow venues. Huge anger and determination to fight the plans, which include closure of the A&E and downgrading of the maternity service.

A Deptford station roundtable and we're getting to the end of the process. Most of the new station has been built behind the old one, so the public have been accessing it since April, while the old buildings have been systematically demolished. It's due to be signed off soon once all the snagging problems are resolved. I'm thrilled to see the new station but what will really make a difference is the redevelopment around it. Once Cathedral creates the public space and the listed ramp is restored, it's going to be wonderful. Sad thing is, because it's moving in such extended phases, there'll be no ribbon to cut and I was looking forward to that after a decade's work.

A consultation meeting to hear presentations on behalf of the TSA and the plans for Lewisham Hospital. The panel is totally inadequate and failing to answer many of the questions put. There are signs of the hard left wanting to take over the campaign, which must be resisted at all costs – the non-party nature of the Lewisham NHS SOS campaign is what has given it its strength. Even though the chair, Dr Louise Irving, has stood against Labour in the past, we all support her.

24 November: The first demonstration in support of Lewisham Hospital. It's estimated as many as 15,000 people turn out in pouring rain. Staff and supporters join hands around the hospital while others gather in Ladywell Fields for a rally. I've agreed to speak but I have visions of being transported to hospital myself as I approach the stage, wet and cold. There is a single-rung metal ladder that has to be climbed – it's running with water. I've no head for heights at the best of times but this is really scary. I make it on to the platform just hoping there won't be a fault with the electrics, which of course are also sodden. I pick up the mic and do my best rally speak. A good response but in truth we all just want to go home.

Heidi started an online petition as soon as the news broke and now everyone is using it.

Health questions. I ask Jeremy Hunt, now Health Secretary, how it is possible to close a full A&E service at Lewisham Hospital – which currently sees 115,000 people a year – and transfer 30 per cent of the department's work to the community, given a cash-strapped NHS and a local authority suffering from deep cuts. He evades the question, saying there's a consultation finishing on 13 December. He will receive the results in January and then take his decision. My colleague, Clive Efford, reminds him that the Tory manifesto 2010 said, 'We will stop forced closures of A&E and maternity wards.'

Next day, Jim Dowd has an adjournment debate on the hospital. He puts on record one of the things that we have discovered, which wasn't immediately apparent: £12 million was spent only two years ago on refurbishing the A&E

and maternity services but now, not only are they proposed for closure, there's a plan to sell off two-thirds of the whole hospital site. This just beggars belief. Anna Soubry, the minister answering, doesn't make any effort to deal with Lewisham Hospital but explains the procedure of the TSA and the problems with the SLHT. She then draws attention to the fact that the Secretary of State, in making his decision, must have regard to the four tests for NHS service change – support from GP commissioners, the strength of public and patient engagement, clarity on the clinical evidence base, and support for patient choice. These words will come back to haunt them as Jim, Heidi and I constantly refer to the tests in future campaigning.

Cameron makes a statement on the Leveson Inquiry. Predictably, he praises Leveson and agrees with his principles but has concerns and doubts, so he's inviting cross-party talks. He allows me to intervene. I tell him he is splitting the House and that it 'would be a dereliction of our duty if we did not establish the legal framework recommended by Lord Leveson'.

Ed responds, accepting all of Leveson's proposals and puts us on the moral high ground, where, I think, the public would expect us to be.

5 December: The Autumn Statement. Everything we set in train for a low carbon economy is being undermined by the Tories. The independent Committee on Climate Change has recommended a decarbonisation target for 2030, which has the support of 1,500 leading UK companies, but the government is opposed. I ask Osborne why and point out that investment in renewable energy has fallen by a half since the government came to power. I ask him if he doesn't think we should invest in green jobs. He lists a whole lot of other things and says they will adopt a target – but after 2016!

An opposition day debate on health and of course I've put in to speak. I begin by saying that in opposition the Prime Minister had spoken passionately about retaining local services and named Lewisham Hospital as one of the twenty-four hospitals he would personally defend – I say today he has that opportunity. I quote the four tests and say not one of them is met. I refer to the TSA and how, when he couldn't find the savings from SLHT, he grabbed a successful, solvent and highly regarded hospital and proposed to destroy it, including selling off its land – a proposal *not even mentioned* in the consultation document. As I list the closing of the A&E, the closure of the intensive care unit, the coronary care unit, and the acute medical and elderly care unit, I can hardly believe it myself. If the proposals were to go ahead, three-quarters of a million people would be dependent on the single A&E in Greenwich.

The TSA consultation ends. We've all worked hard on our submissions. The consultants at the A&E department and the chief executive have been able to brief us on the complexities of the case. The more we know about it, the more we realise how insane and extreme these proposals are.

The SLH campaign has organised a vigil at the hospital this evening, which I join and address. All written questions to ministers are answered by reference to the responsibilities of the TSA and the consultation. They won't be able to say that for much longer.

Dinner with my former civil servants. I just love meeting up with them – they are such good fun. I get a bit of gossip but no state secrets. A further treat when we spend an evening with another new friend, Francesca, who has joined the Trinity Laban board and taken a particular interest in Blackheath Halls. She's arranged a soiree in her lovely home in support of young opera singers at Trinity Laban.

14 December: I'm at Goldsmiths in the morning and Trinity Laban at lunchtime for the dance degree ceremony. I hurry home to organise for the evening. I've invited my party officers to tell them in confidence that I've decided I will definitely not contest the next general election.

The last days of session and I'm on the Order Paper for DCLG and raise the relentless increase in statutory homelessness. I remind the minister that his own Secretary of State warned the PM it would increase by tens of thousands as a result of government policies. The minister says they're dealing with homelessness at its roots – obviously to precious little effect.

Then it's the second reading of the Energy Bill. I press my case again on the decarbonisation targets. Governments normally accept the recommendations of the Committee on Climate Change and they believe the decarbonisation target for 2030 is vital to meeting the overall trajectory of the Climate Change Act 2005 reductions. I add to my standard question the fact that apparently Cameron endorsed this position two years ago. This time Ed Davey sounds more positive, saying he is very sympathetic to the argument. I bet officials at DECC are working hard on him.

Two quiet days in the office, getting an iPad set up, finishing last-minute correspondence, checking we haven't forgotten anyone from the Christmas card list and writing my newspaper column for the New Year.

## 2013

8 January: The Speaker has granted me an urgent question. I ask the Secretary of State for Health if he will make a statement on the Trust Special Administrator report into the South London Healthcare NHS Trust and the NHS in south-east London.

Jeremy Hunt replies: 'I have today published the report ... I am under a statutory duty to make a decision by 1 February...' He takes us through the process of consultation, of meetings undertaken, documents distributed and responses received – 8,200. He repeats the four tests that have to be met and concludes that in appointing the TSA the government's priority 'was to ensure that patients continue to receive high-quality, sustainable NHS services'.

I reply:

> Neither I nor my Hon. friends the Members for Lewisham East or Lewisham West and Penge are opposed to change or to greater efficiencies, but we are opposed to the destruction of Lewisham Hospital, which is a solvent, well-regarded trust that meets all its performance and financial standards.

There is a fundamental question at stake. My Rt Hon. friend who was the Secretary of State [Andy Burnham] has made it clear that the powers associated with the failure regime under which the TSA acts were *not* intended to be used to encompass the services of other hospitals. Yet, in order to tackle the huge deficit sustained by SLHT, the TSA proposes to close Lewisham Hospital's accident and emergency services, including the acclaimed children's A&E, to end all medical and surgical emergency care and to demolish maternity services. He then proposes to sell off half the hospital's land. That cannot be justified. Each year around 120,000 people use Lewisham A&E, more than 30,000 children use the children's A&E and more than 4,000 babies are born in the hospital. There is no current capacity at any of the other hospitals in the area to provide for these patients. These proposals amount to a major reconfiguration by the back door.

I ask him if he believes a reconfiguration of services in south-east London is necessary and tell him if he does then it has to have 'relevant consideration for patient safety and healthcare standards and meet his four tests. These proposals do none of that and must be rejected.'

Hunt replies that he understands the concerns and that he's taken legal advice on the 'powers' and will take further advice. *So will we!*

Other colleagues pile into him and he agrees to meet everyone concerned.

An uneventful afternoon follows, but my mind is on tomorrow night's meeting of my constituency party and the announcement I intend to make. My monthly report has already been distributed but contains no mention of it. I draft a letter that will go to the whole membership on Friday.

10 January: I can think of nothing else all day. I know I'm making the right decision but after more than twenty-five years it's a momentous one to take. I arrive at the well-attended meeting. The officers have kept my secret and the meeting proceeds as normal, including my report and an account of

the hospital campaign. Jos and Barbara outline the plans for a mass demonstration on 26 January and then it's time for me.

My heart is thumping as I say that I have come to tell them, in advance of the wider membership and Ed, that I don't intend to stand at the general election in 2015. I'm giving long notice to enable the party to make a considered selection and the new candidate time to make him or herself (preferably the latter) known to the electorate. I thank people for their support both past and present and assure the meeting that I intend to play no part in the selection process and will endorse no candidate.

Ripples around the room as some people are surprised, some really sorry and others with minds working overtime on getting their person into the seat. Kind words are said. I know it's important for all to have their say, so chair Joe Perry invites everyone else to stay while I get up and take my leave.

As I step into a frosty New Cross Road, I feel a sudden chill and a sense that my whole existence is about to unravel. The threads that have bound me to Parliament, to my local party, to my office staff and to my constituents will all loosen and fall away. For a moment, I feel very alone.

Then a wave of euphoria sweeps over me. I look at the bright lights in the street and realise I have a whole new life ahead of me. And a book to write.

# POSTSCRIPT

Little did I know when I announced I wouldn't stand again that two of my most challenging constituency issues still lay ahead. I didn't abandon any of the causes I'd followed all my political life, such as women's rights, justice for Palestine and the abolition of nuclear weapons. Nor did I neglect to raise constituency issues or to do my surgeries, but two issues would dominate: Lewisham Hospital and Convoys Wharf.

Within days of my urgent question on Lewisham Hospital, Heidi obtained a Westminster Hall debate and in the weeks and months that followed Heidi, Jim, and I kept up a barrage of written and oral questions. The broadcasting of BBC's *Question Time* from Goldsmiths College on 10 January gave us an unexpected boost. A general question to the panel on the NHS gave Cathy Ashley the chance to raise Lewisham Hospital. Thereafter the programme was dominated by the issue, bringing the local campaign to the attention of the national media.

By the end of January 2013, with snow still on the ground, 25,000 people demonstrated in support of the hospital. We all got to speak as usual but there were other important voices that drew more media attention. Nick Ferrari, the writer and broadcaster, had a personal story to tell – his son's life had been saved by none other than Dr John O'Donoghue and the A&E team at Lewisham. John himself was already a leading light in the campaign. We handed in a petition of 50,000 names, including over 400 GPs.

When Jeremy Hunt made his decision on the TSA report, he backed away from closure, offering instead a downgraded A&E, which arguably might have been less safe given all the other closure plans, which remained intact. Hunt went on to say that he had asked Sir Bruce Keogh, the NHS medical director, to review the recommendations before his final decision was made. He then made the astonishing assertion that it was Keogh's view that higher clinical standards arising from the proposals 'could save up to 100 lives a year'. I pursued this point relentlessly only to find eventually that Keogh had never said this in reference to Lewisham Hospital – it had been extrapolated from Keogh's research designed for a different purpose.

We dug deeper and deeper into the decision. Local campaigners videoed how difficult it was for a sick person to travel by public transport from parts of Lewisham to Queen Elizabeth in Greenwich, ridiculing claims in the TSA report that it would be two or three minutes longer. Jessica had fun with the TFL journey planner demonstrating journeys from randomly chosen addresses. We knew we were winning all the arguments but only the courts could stop the process.

Lewisham Council, in its general duty towards the well-being of its citizens and its concern about the knock-on effects into its social care provisions, decided to take advice on the possibility of a legal challenge. The SLH campaign also decided to go to court. Applications were made to the High Court for judicial review and three days set aside for the hearing in July. On the day, several hundred people demonstrated with banners and flags outside the High Court. So many people wanted to get in that the judge delayed proceedings for half an hour while court officials found more chairs. It was a nail-biting time. I was particularly gratified to find that my questions to Jeremy Hunt and the Prime Minister were quite central to the case put by the barrister and extensively quoted. At the conclusion of the hearing, Judge Silber said he hoped to make a decision by the end of the month. By now the campaign was constantly in the headlines. Bruce Keogh, who had agreed to meet the Lewisham MPs, cancelled and never agreed another date.

Mr Justice Silber arrived to deliver his verdict on 31 July. The summer recess was already under way and I was nervously checking my phone, outside Poggibonsi railway station in Italy. With utter joy I heard the result – Jeremy Hunt had acted illegally. As Jos Bell wrote later, 'As he [the Judge] spoke, for a split second the world stood still – then he allowed a burst of spontaneous applause, which brought a smile to his face.'

Jeremy Hunt appealed and we had to wait another three months for the result.

The decision of the High Court was upheld. It had been an incredible rollercoaster ride for everyone involved. Unprecedented in my political career for the breadth and size of the campaign, for its vigour and focus and staying power. Even Judge Silber remarked that those who attended his court had been a credit to the campaign and their cause.

In the days before the judgement came, the government slipped a new clause on hospital closures into legislation going through the Lords. It would become the new battleground for hospital campaigners everywhere.

Following my decision to step down, the local party held a meeting to discuss whether or not to volunteer for an all-women shortlist and I was invited to attend. It was my dearest wish to be followed by another woman and I knew there was a lot of support. I didn't intend to play much of a part until a woman supporter of mine prompted me by saying, 'Perhaps, as we've had a woman, we should consider a man.' I couldn't help but retort: 'Before me, *every* candidate was a man.' An all-women shortlist was agreed and a few months later Vicky Foxcroft became Labour's prospective parliamentary candidate for the 2015 general election.

Since the beginning of 2013, Lewisham Council had been diligently working through all the responses to the consultation on Convoys Wharf, following their receipt of the outline planning application. In early autumn they indicated to Hutchison Whampoa that they expected to make a decision by the following February. The developers weren't satisfied and requested the Mayor of London, Boris Johnson, to take over the application. This was a highly unusual move but Boris accepted their request. John Miller and his team, despite the insult, offered to share their expertise and the concerns that had prompted the delay with the GLA.

We ended 2013 with the premature death of my first agent, Jim Stevenson, whom I remembered with affection. Margaret Thatcher also died earlier that year. I couldn't mourn her, but she was an absolutely remarkable woman.

Nelson Mandela's death on 5 December was not unexpected but it represented the passing of an era for so many of us who had been active in anti-apartheid. Following tributes in the House, I paid my own at a local civic ceremony:

> I joined the Anti-Apartheid Movement as a student. It was a movement particularly well understood by multicultural London where, despite the universal right to vote, racial discrimination was rife and there were no laws to prevent it. For the radical youth of my generation the causes were inseparable, justice at home and abroad ... I quote the final lines of Mandela's speech at the Rivonia Trial:
>
> 'I have cherished the ideal of a democratic and free society in which all persons live together in harmony and with equal opportunities. It is an ideal which I hope to live for and to achieve. But if needs be, it is an ideal for which I am prepared to die.'
>
> He wasn't sentenced to death but spent a total of twenty-seven years in prison. In 2001, I visited Robben Island and Mandela's former cell. It was a chilling experience. I could not conceive of anyone surviving such confinement.
>
> [...] Along with thousands of others I demonstrated for years outside South Africa House. When I became an MP, Mandela was still a prisoner, but things were changing. After his release he came to London

to thank anti-apartheid activists and spoke at a private meeting of Labour MPs. It was utterly thrilling to be in the presence of such an inspirational and iconic figure.

I was but a foot soldier in the movement, but like millions throughout the world, my life was touched by the magic that was Mandela. He set the greatest standard of integrity and courage in public office and taught us all the power of diplomacy and reconciliation.

My top priority for 2014 had to be Convoys Wharf. My greatest fear when the application was handed to the GLA for determination was that the GLA officers would rush it through to meet the developers' demands and fail to take account of all the painstaking preparation and submissions made by local people, especially the project leaders of Sayes Court Garden and Build the Lenox. But, our initial meetings with the planners and Sir Edward Lister, Deputy Mayor in charge of planning, went well, and we agreed further meetings involving the developers. In the meantime, I decided to bring the matter to the attention of the House and applied for an adjournment debate on the heritage aspects of the site. For me this was a very important opportunity to put into the parliamentary record an account of the unique heritage at stake and the great potential of the development for the whole of London.

I began by describing Henry VIII establishing the dockyards in 1513 and the *Golden Hind*, Sir Francis Drake's ship, being moored there in 1581. I went on to document John Evelyn, the great diarist and horticulturist in Sayes Court in 1653, and Samuel Pepys taking charge of Charles II's great ship-building programme in 1667. I referred to the house built in 1708 by Master Shipwright Joseph Allin, which remains intact today and is owned by William Richards and Chris Mazeika.

I document the changes that occurred over the years from when Tsar Peter the Great rented Evelyn's house and wrecked it, to the scandalous demolition of the Tudor store house in 1952, when 20,000 Tudor bricks were disposed of, to 1979, when the site, now known as Convoys Wharf, was sold by the Ministry of Defence to News International.

I take the minister through the history of my thirteen-year involvement and the details of the archaeology that require listing. I continue:

> As developers' plans have come forward, so too have local aspirations. We want to create a destination that both honours the past and creates a vision of the future that embraces the robust and dynamic community that is Deptford ... The Sayes Court project, developed by Roo Angel and Bob Bagley and their architect David Kohn, seeks to create a new garden and a centre for urban horticulture...

I point out that, 'though Hutchison Whampoa have embraced the project ... their planned new buildings will obliterate much of the original garden site and isolate the proposed centre'.

Then I turn to building a replica of the *Lenox*. 'The *Lenox* would be built using modern techniques and enable apprentices to be trained in modern transferable skills. Once again, Hutchison Whampoa have recognised the support for the project, but failed to place it appropriately in its plans.'

Finally, I draw a picture of how we see our projects adding to the development overall:

> The development would be approached through the extensive Sayes Court Garden, leading to the horticultural centre and the Olympia building with its myriad of activities. It would be a place of which everyone in Deptford could be proud, a place that would sit alongside the world heritage sites that are Greenwich, the *Cutty Sark* and the National Maritime Museum ... It would be not just for the people of Deptford ... but for London ... Once again Deptford and its dockyards could become a jewel in London's crown.

When it came, the meeting with the whole of the Hutchison Whampoa team, the project leaders, myself, Lewisham planners, English Heritage and others, was a turning point. We got agreement to continue exploring the issues with the developers, by now more positive about accommodating both projects on site, though still not quite in the ways we sought.

Following the consultation, the Mayor held a hearing at the GLA – a tense affair. The Mayor's officers set out the technical details of the application, and Sir Steve Bullock on behalf of Lewisham Council then had five minutes to respond. I was asked to speak for the Sayes Court Garden and Build the Lenox. I said,

> Years of research and expertise have gone into designing these projects. Those who lead them and those who advise have looked at all the options. Today's presentations set out what is still required to make them a reality ... Without Sayes Court Garden and the *Lenox*, Mr Mayor, you would be looking to approve a riverside development that would obscure the great heritage of this site for ever. Instead we are offering not dusty, static museums, but living enterprises that honour the past but look to the future ... This is an extraordinary opportunity to create a unique destination, new to London, but steeped in our magnificent history. We appeal to you to support us in realising that legacy.

Boris granted consent to the developers but made two stipulations for the section 106 agreement: 1. GLA officers to work with LBL and the developer to look at space in Sayes Court Garden Park and around the development to come up with a secure and deliverable Sayes Court Garden Project; and 2. A feasibility study for the *Lenox* to be concluded asap to produce clear options and the agreement of the developer to contribute to the most feasible option.

The negotiations on the Convoys 106 agreement dragged on for many months. Eventually the Sayes Court Garden project was agreed to everyone's satisfaction by changing the layout within the development and not encroaching on the public park. We involved English Heritage and wrote again to Boris Johnson as yet another deadline passed and an extension was agreed.

I began to fear that having suffered a further year's delay so unexpectedly at the hands of the GLA, the developers might decide to sell and we'd be back to square one. At the point when I ceased to be an MP, the project was mired in huge controversy over the terms of the feasibility project, but as a patron of Build the Lenox (together with Dan Snow), I continued to be copied into the volumes of emails that flowed between the Lenox team and the GLA. I could only admire the fortitude of David Graham from the Lenox team and Graham Clements of the GLA and wonder that they were still on speaking terms one year and nine months after the Mayor said the study should be completed asap.

The consultants' feasibility study was finally published on 15 December 2015 after many months of hard negotiations from initial terms of reference to amendments to the draft. The ship will be built on the safeguarded wharf. Now we just have to raise the millions necessary to build it – I'm sure we will.

Other projects did not reach such positive conclusions. Despite our making a good case to the Planning Inspectorate where we felt we had been heard, the government gave the go-ahead to Thames Water's super sewer project in September 2013. Two months later I met with the project's CEO. At the outset I emphasised the outrage we all felt that our arguments had not prevailed. He acknowledged that we had valid concerns and gave a series of undertakings, which I hope will be honoured when the works start this year. The Sainsbury's development, put on hold during the recession, sank without trace, though other small improvements took hold in New Cross Road.

As for Deptford station, it was eventually finished in 2013, and the Cathedral development surrounding it had its topping-out ceremony in March 2015.

Life outside policies began to take a new shape. I took Frank to his favourite city, New York, for a very special birthday treat and I realised one of my ambitions when Frank and I went on a tour of Vietnam and Cambodia. The magnificent temple ruins of Angkor Wat were everything I had imagined. We also had a great few days in Edinburgh when Frank's best friend Will married his long-term partner Marion. At home, I became the chair of the local Friends of Blackheath Halls and also accepted engagements for pleasure, such as the

British Library's 'Sisterhood: Greenham in Common'. I met again some of the activists of the time and our excellent former CND press officer, Alison Whyte. The chair remarked of the panel, 'One is a Doctor of Philosophy, one a professor, one a baroness, and one a dame.' Not bad for Greenham women!

Life in Parliament was inevitably overshadowed by the relentlessly bad news from around the world as the Arab Spring vanished into brutal civil wars, Syria disintegrated, and the so-called Islamic State began its murderous rampage.

For me, one hopeful international development was a global initiative to abolish nuclear weapons. In December 2014, I was invited to attend a conference organised by the Austrian government on the Humanitarian Impact of Nuclear Weapons. It was attended by 157 countries, together with the UN, the International Red Cross, the Red Crescent and hundreds of people from civil society. It was an extraordinary experience to hear ministers and officials from around the world expressing a common view and effectively criticising the nuclear weapons states for continuing to threaten the planet. The conference concluded that there was no national or international capacity that could adequately respond to the human suffering and humanitarian harm that would result from a nuclear weapon explosion in a populated area.

Following the conference, Austria called on all states to work with it to identify and pursue effective measures to fill the legal gap for the prohibition and elimination of nuclear weapons. This is an initiative that will not be much heard of in nuclear weapons states such as Britain, whose governments will do everything to frustrate it. But, for the majority of countries in the world, these weapons are a perpetual threat as they remain on hair-trigger readiness to eradicate vast areas of our planet. Despite their individual love affairs with nuclear weapons, it would be to the advantage of all nuclear weapons states if the weapons were declared illegal in the way biological and chemical weapons are.

My interest in the Labour Party's fortunes didn't waver because I wasn't standing again. I was in Scotland for the referendum and pronounced Glasgow lost to us after just one afternoon canvassing outside a shopping centre. In Aberdeen we fared better, with sixty per cent of the electorate voting against independence. For a while we thought this guaranteed that Frank's successor, Richard, would be elected to Westminster the following May.

As our national fortunes rose and fell throughout the years, I always believed we were likely to win the 2015 general election, or at least lead a coalition. I can still hear the chimes of Big Ben and the 10 o'clock news announcement 'Exit polls predict … a Tory majority' and the chill silence that fell over the assembled activists in Deptford.

Results in London bucked the trend. Vicky and all my neighbouring MPs had hugely increased majorities. Most satisfying of all, Labour's Neil Coyle, whom we'd all supported, took Bermondsey and Southwark from Simon Hughes.

Then, as 2015 drew to a close, the UN Climate Change Conference took place in Paris, and I despaired at the thought of the UK government's fall from grace in that global arena. In less than a year, the Tories had removed support for new onshore wind farms, axed our plans to make all new homes zero carbon, killed off their own 'Green Deal' for homes, removed subsidies for larger solar farms, ditched our £1 billion CCS project and removed tax incentives for cleaner cars.

As the talks progressed I relived every moment of Copenhagen in 2009. I had always believed the Copenhagen Accord could be built upon and lead to further progress. In Paris, the strands were still in place – Nick Stern's economics of climate change and Gordon Brown's climate fund – same amount, same time frame. Making the agreement work will take years of endeavour but I can only marvel at the successful outcome and be thankful. Nothing could be more important.

My final months in Parliament were spent trying to close down an operation that had lasted for twenty-eight years. I had tremendous support from Jessica, Vicky, Nicky and Matt, with all but Matt, who moved to Bristol, staying to the very end, despite my encouragement to look for other jobs. Inevitably we scrambled to shred hundreds of case files and move masses of paperwork to New Cross when Parliament closed prior to the election. Our very last task in Portcullis was to prepare my farewell. Sir George Young had proposed that the final debate in the Commons should be devoted to valedictory speeches. Indulgent it certainly was, but I applied and looked forward to an orderly final day. It was not to be. The previous evening, Peter Francis, a former undercover police officer, revealed that he had seen secret files on ten MPs during the eleven years he had worked for Special Branch. I was named as one of the MPs.

So, on my very last day, there I was with Peter Hain, Harriet Harman, Jack Straw (yes, Jack Straw, former Home Secretary), Jeremy Corbyn and Diane Abbott, protesting at the outrage, asking, as I did, who authorised the surveillance and on what grounds it was authorised.

We also demanded that our cases should be looked into by Lord Pitchford's inquiry, already announced into undercover policing in the wake of a series of scandals. But the drama didn't end there. William Hague, now leader of the House, brought a last-minute motion to change the rules regarding the election of the Speaker. No one had any doubt about the reason – the Tory establishment hated John Bercow and the PM's fingers were all over the move. As William Hague was also leaving the Commons, this was a particularly sad way for him to exit. In the event, the Lib Dems deserted the coalition, a few Tories voted with us and the government was defeated by twenty-six votes.

And so the valedictory speeches began: Sir George Young, followed by Gordon Brown and Charles Hendry, and then the Speaker calls me.

> This place has shaped my life for the past twenty-eight years but before that I remember my late father Ken and my mother Eileen, who instilled in me my values, and my late husband Keith, who introduced me to socialism and was a great support for thirty years.
>
> I hope that I have remained true to those values. First and foremost, I have been a *woman* Member of Parliament who did not want to play the boys' games – probably to my detriment at times. I am proud to

have been the first full-time Minister for Women, even though my efforts got me sacked a year later.

I have had many opportunities as a backbencher, particularly in Private Members' Bills. My first was a Bill to tackle fly-tipping. My second was to place a duty on local authorities to introduce doorstep recycling. Both passed. I always hoped to win a third place in the ballot so that I could introduce a Bill to permit assisted dying, in which I believe passionately.

Another privilege has been membership of select committees, beginning with the Committee on Televising of Proceedings of the House, in which I had the distinction of proposing the hanging lights we now have today, as none were there before. From the moment I arrived I wanted change. I got my first opportunity on Robin Cook's Modernisation of the House of Commons Committee, which brought in many of our changes in procedure. It led to my Hon. Friend, the Member for Stockport [Ann Coffey] and me organising the first successful campaign to change the House's sitting hours. When those changes were partially reversed, we organised again in 2010. With much help we achieved the more sensible timetable we have today. I also greatly enjoyed my time on the Environment, Food and Rural Affairs Committee and later the International Development Committee, when you, Mr Speaker, were also a member.

Inevitably, there were bad times. Rejection from government was one of them, but by far the worst was the Iraq War. Despite the horrors of Saddam Hussein's regime, I did not believe that he possessed weapons of mass destruction, and I could not support an illegal war that I knew would have repercussions for a generation.

As I leave, I reflect on some of the great issues that remain unresolved, most notably the outdated notion of nuclear deterrence, when the real threats to our security are cyber-warfare, terrorism and climate change. Nuclear weapons have no utility; they cannot be used to defend or gain territory, and their financial cost is an obscenity. I only hope that the new initiative for a global ban on nuclear weapons, spearheaded by Austria and now signed by over fifty states, will succeed.

Another great regret is to see the plight of yet another generation of Palestinians. I cannot believe that the international community has tolerated such oppression for so long.

By contrast, my greatest joy came late in my career when my Rt Hon. Friend for Kirkcaldy and Cowdenbeath [Mr Brown] gave me the job of Climate Change Minister under the inspired leadership of my Rt Hon. Friend the Member for Doncaster [Mr Miliband]. I am proud of the many achievements of our Labour governments – our equalities legislation, the minimum wage, and our investment in public services – but so much has been undermined by coalition policies.

Let me end with friendship, which makes life tolerable in this place. My first new friend, my Hon. Friend the Member for Stoke-on-Trent North [Joan Walley] has become chair of the Environmental Audit Committee, and my Rt Hon. Friend the Member for Barking [Margaret Hodge] the most notable chair of the Public Accounts Committee. In 1986, my Rt Hon. Friend the Member for Camberwell and Peckham [Ms Harman] wrote me a note saying 'Joan, Deptford is wide open – go for it.' She has done more for women's equality than anyone else and I am proud to have managed her successful campaign for the deputy leadership.

I also value the friendship of the irrepressible Member for Lewisham West [Jim Dowd] and my Hon. Friend the Member for Lewisham East [Heidi Alexander], who has already made her mark in this her first parliament. I am also grateful for all the hard work of my constituency party, my constituents and the many staff who have worked for me over the years. Last but not least, there is my dearest parliamentary friend and now husband, Frank Doran, with whom I have shared the rollercoaster life of two MPs with constituencies 500 miles apart.

Mr Speaker, it has been a privilege to serve in a House over which you preside as a truly modernising Speaker. I wish you, all the Officers and staff of the House and all those who continue to serve, a fond farewell.

Well, what of my life so far? Someone once said to be happy you need four things: somewhere to live, someone to love, something to do and something to look forward to. Apart from the darkest times, too personal to record, I have had, and still have, all four.

As for my career, well, it wasn't really a career at all, it was just what I did. Best of all, I was never bored.

# ACKNOWLEDGEMENTS

I am grateful to all those who have been part of my life and find themselves between these pages and to those not here who nonetheless played a part. But I particularly want to thank my husband Frank, without whose constant support this memoir could never have been written.

I wrote by hand, necessitating the employment of two wonderful women, Vicky Flippance and Sandra Den Hertog, who typed a number of versions of the manuscript.

I am also grateful to Boni Sones who got me started, to Jessica Maloney for support and help with research and the many staff who sustained me during my twenty-eight years in the House, particularly Heidi Alexander, who eventually joined me as an MP.

I hope in writing my story I have also been able to highlight the contributions of those women who inspired me, particularly Harriet Harman.

Finally, I am grateful to Iain Dale of Biteback for agreeing to publish me and to my editors Olivia Beattie and Victoria Godden for their patience, light touch and real encouragement. Also to Vicky Gilder and Sam Jones, who have efficiently organised the book's promotion.

# INDEX